1:4 250 000 map pages

Calais

	Dublin	**Dublin ▶ Göteborg = 477 km**
548		
726	346	**Edinburgh**
575	1123	1301	**Frankfurt**
1342	477	176	1067	**Göteborg**
760	477	1486	485	582	**Hamburg**

000 = ———

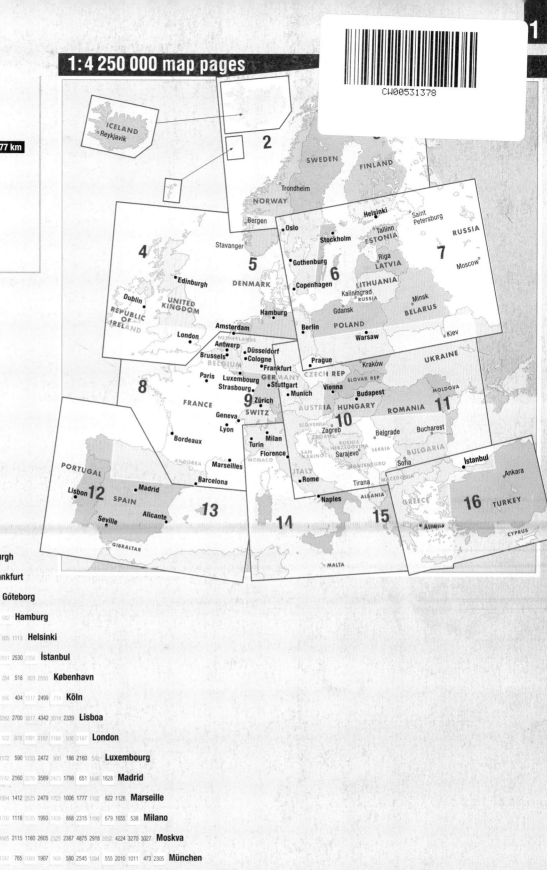

Amsterdam

2945	**Athina**
1505	3192	**Barcelona**
1484	3742	2803	**Bergen**
650	2412	1863	1309	**Berlin**
197	2895	1308	1586	764	**Bruxelles**
2245	1219	2644	3037	1707	2181	**Bucuresti**
1420	1530	1999	2212	882	1358	852	**Budapest**
367	3100	1269	1783	956	215	2398	1573	**Calais**
533	3630	1817	270	1504	763	3021	2196	548	**Dublin**
1093	3826	1995	176	1696	941	3124	2299	726	346	**Edinburgh**
441	2499	1313	1508	550	383	1804	979	575	1123	1301	**Frankfurt**
1029	3080	2362	819	668	1145	1734	1510	1342	477	176	1067	**Göteborg**
447	2719	1780	1023	286	563	2014	1189	760	477	1486	485	582	**Hamburg**
1560	2539	2338	1063	475	1239	1834	1009	1431	1318	1236	1598	505	1113	**Helsinki**
2756	1145	2990	3653	2223	2706	690	1341	2911	3537	3657	2314	2891	2530	2350	**İstanbul**
965	2782	2090	1103	370	1081	2077	1252	1278	752	479	795	284	518	803	2593	**København**
256	2684	1376	1427	566	198	1983	1158	390	938	1116	180	986	404	1517	2499	714	**Köln**
2331	4460	1268	3723	2869	3141	3917	3222	2069	2617	2795	2400	3282	2700	3817	4342	3014	2339	**Lisboa**
480	3200	1387	458	1074	333	2591	1766	118	430	608	693	122	878	1991	3107	1188	508	2187	**London**
406	2661	1190	1613	749	209	2052	1227	424	972	1150	240	1172	590	1703	2472	900	186	2160	542	**Luxembourg**
1790	3809	617	3163	2364	1600	3262	2622	1528	1634	2254	1930	2742	2160	3276	3589	2473	1651	1646	1628	**Madrid**
1210	2683	509	2435	1541	1030	2154	1505	1063	1588	1789	1023	1994	1412	2525	2479	1722	1006	1777	1182	822	1126	**Marseille**
1085	2182	1038	2141	1060	890	1668	992	1072	1620	1798	683	1700	1118	1535	1993	1468	868	2315	1190	679	1655	538	**Milano**
2457	2930	3655	2223	1821	2585	1761	2099	2800	3348	3526	2312	1665	2115	1160	2605	2325	2387	4875	2918	2852	4224	3270	3027	**Moskva**
839	2106	1340	1788	594	789	1497	672	994	1524	1720	398	1347	765	1069	1907	969	580	2545	1094	555	2010	1011	473	2305	**München**
1347	3372	2680	503	960	1463	2642	1842	1660	773	729	1385	316	900	697	3089	590	1304	3604	1778	1490	3063	2312	2018	1823	1559	**Oslo**
510	2917	988	1922	1051	320	2307	1482	281	829	1007	591	1481	899	2012	2727	1209	495	1821	399	351	1280	782	857	2903	810	1799	**Paris**
950	2067	1750	1675	345	888	1352	537	1097	1635	1816	512	1013	652	770	1878	715	690	2870	1205	753	2329	1399	853	1853	388	1305	1061	**Praha**
1691	1140	1385	2706	1502	1520	1904	1263	1678	2226	2404	1289	2265	1683	1977	2237	1993	1474	2653	1796	1285	2002	876	606	3362	918	2583	1389	1309	**Roma**
2347	4223	1031	3736	2894	2150	3709	3010	2078	2626	2804	2344	3295	2713	3826	4034	3023	2318	401	2196	2178	550	1540	2078	4774	2371	3613	1830	2781	2446	**Sevilla**
2206	828	2453	3103	1673	2156	391	790	2361	2891	3087	1764	2341	1980	1800	550	2043	1949	3706	2461	1922	3037	1929	1443	2252	1367	2632	2177	1328	1687	3484	**Sofiya**
1393	3418	2726	1063	1006	1509	2713	1888	1673	2254	1069	1431	505	946	167	3185	590	1350	3650	1824	1536	3109	2358	2064	1228	1600	530	1845	1351	2629	3659	2679	**Stockholm**
1256	2128	2366	1909	606	1350	1473	648	1542	2110	2268	1136	1274	886	361	1989	956	1152	3480	1660	1345	2960	2015	1469	1245	996	1506	1677	616	1853	3397	1439	1612	**Warszawa**
1168	1772	1856	1970	640	1114	1067	242	1308	1954	2034	731	1308	947	1088	1583	1010	916	3100	1524	993	2473	1353	818	2137	430	1600	1240	295	1126	2876	1033	1646	727	**Wien**
816	2426	1030	1938	863	619	1810	985	804	1352	1530	464	1497	915	2164	2323	1433	589	2296	922	410	1647	699	292	2552	303	1615	592	691	898	2061	1173	1861	1307	743	**Zürich**

km

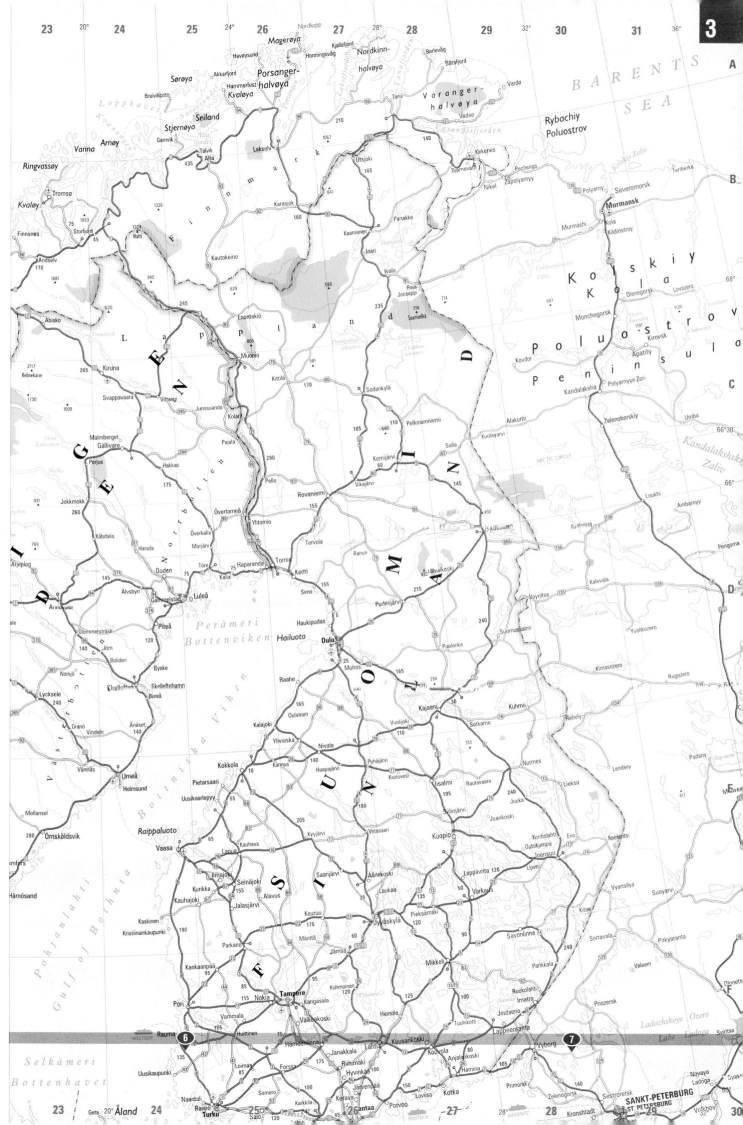

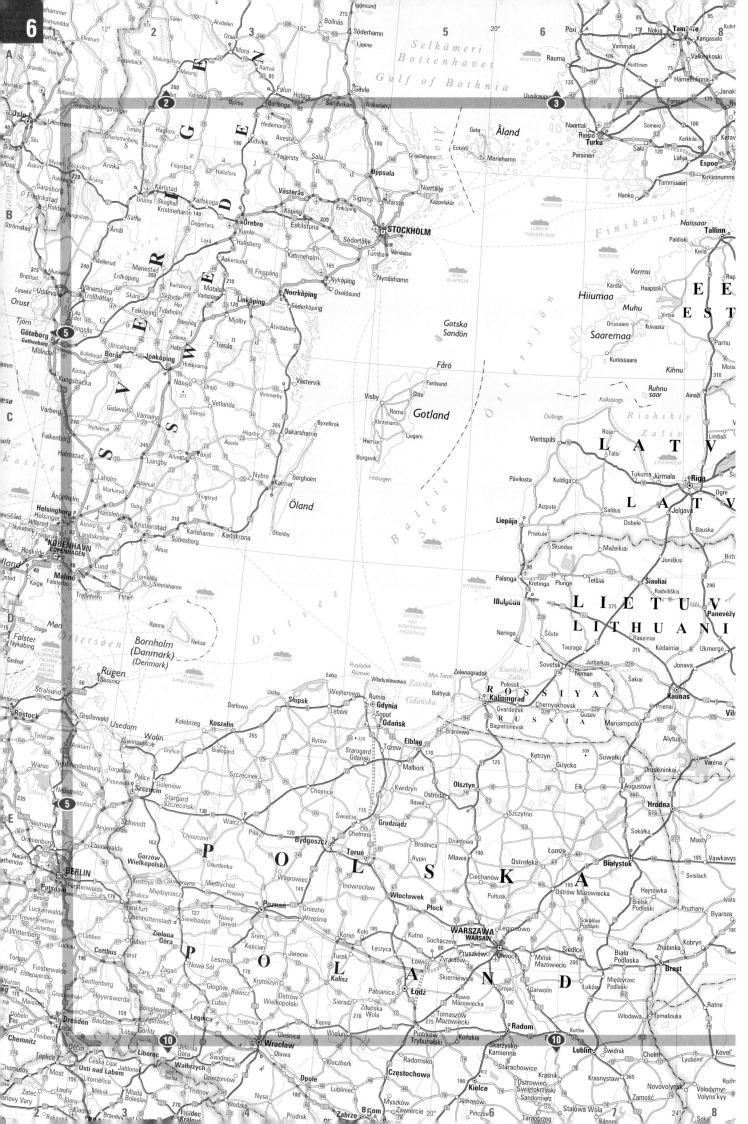

Map labels

ROSSIYA
RUSSIA
Valdayskaya vozvyshennost
ESTONIA
STI ONIA
IJA
IA
A
BELARUS

Scale
0   40   80   120   160   200 km

Major cities
Helsinki, Vantaa, Porvoo, Lahti, Kouvola, Kotka, Lappeenranta, Imatra, Mikkeli, Heinola, Kuusankoski, Anjalankoski, Hamina, Loviisa, Järvenpää, Hyvinkää

SANKT-PETERBURG / ST. PETERSBURG, Kronshtadt, Sosnovyy Bor, Petrodvorets, Pushkin, Kolpino, Gatchina, Tosno, Vyborg, Primorsk, Zelenogorsk, Sestroretsk, Ust Luga, Volosovo, Kingisepp, Narva, Sillamäe, Kohtla-Järve, Jõhvi, Kunda, Rakvere, Tapa, Paide, Põltsamaa, Viljandi, Tartu

Novaya Ladoga, Syasstroy, Volkhov, Tikhvin, Pikalevo, Babayevo, Kaduy, Cherepovets, Seksna, Chebsara, Shugozero, Lodeinoye Pole, Svirstsa, Olonets, Voznesenye, Podporozhye, Annenskiy Most, Megra, Belozersk, Kirillov, Vytegra

Priozersk, Valaam, Pitkyaranta, Ladozhskoye Ozero / Lake Ladoga

Novgorod, Luga, Plyusa, Strugi Krasnye, Shimsk, Soltsy, Staraya Russa, Dno, Porkhov, Pskov, Ostrov, Pechory, Võru, Valga, Valka, Alūksne, Gulbene, Balvi, Pytalovo, Novorzhev, Opochka, Loknya, Toropets, Velikiye Luki, Nevel, Idritsa, Sebezh, Novosokolniki, Pustoshka

Chudovo, Malaya Vishera, Okulovka, Borovichi, Lyuban, Kirishi, Boksitogorsk, Nebolchy, Khvoynaya, Lyubytino, Pestovo, Lesnoye, Ustyuzhna, Vesyegonsk, Krasnyy Kholm, Sonkovo, Bezhetsk, Uglich, Volga, Rybinsk, Rybinskoye Vdkhr.

Krettsy, Valday, Bologoye, Vyshniy Volochek, Ostashkov, Torzhok, Likhoslavl, Tver, Kashin, Kalyazin, Kimry, Goritsy, Dubna, Konakovo, Redkino, Vysokovsk, Klin, Solnechnogorsk, Dmitrov, Sergiyev Posad, Krasnozavodsk, Pushkino

Demyansk, Lychkova, Parfino, Pola, Kholm, Kuvshinovo, Selizharovo, Peno, Andreapol, Staritsa, Rzhev, Zubtsov, Volokolamsk, Zelenograd, Mytishchi, MOSKVA / Moscow, Lyubertsy, Elekt, Podolsk, Odintsovo

Nelidovo, Olenino, Zapadnaya Dvina, Bely, Sychevka, Tupik, Gagarin, Borodino, Mozhaysk, Naro-Fominsk, Borovsk, Klimovsk, Mikhnevo, Obninsk, Serpukhov, Tarussa, Yesnogorsk

Velizh, Surazh, Haradok, Vitsyebsk / Vitebsk, Beshenkovichi, Lyozna, Rudnya, Demidov, Dukhovshchina, Yartsevo, Safonovo, Vyazma, Dorogobuzh, Yelnya, Smolensk, Krasnyy, Pochinok, Mosalsk, Meshchovsk, Spas-Demensk, Kaluga, Kondrovo, Yukhnov, Aleksin, Tula

Polatsk, Navapolatsk, Vyerkhnyadzvinsk, Druya, Braslaw, Daugavpils, Kräslava, Zarasai, Utena, Vidzy, Pastavy, Hlybokaye, Lyepyel, Senno, Orsha, Talachyn, Shklow, Horki, Mstsislaw, Krychaw, Mahilyow, Bykhaw, Slawharad, Cherykaw, Klimovichi, Kastsyukovichy, Roslavl, Kirov, Lyudinovo, Dyatkovo, Zhukovka, Seltso, Fokino, Bryansk, Karachev, Orel

Minsk, Dzyarzhynsk, Maladzyechna, Vileyka, Smarhon, Barysaw, Zhodzina, Krupki, Cherven, Hrodzyanka, Asipovichy, Babruysk, Ragachow, Zhlobin, Bykhaw

Vilnius, Ashmyany, Valozhyn, Lida, Navahrudak, Dzyatlava, Slonim, Baranavichy, Lyakhavichy, Klyetsk, Nyasvizh, Stowbtsy, Slutsk, Hantsavichy, Salihorsk, Glusk, Svyetlahorsk, Homyel / Gomel, Rechytsa, Dobrush

Pinsk, Luninyets, Dragichyn, Ivanava, Tsyelyakhany, Davyd Haradok, Stolin, Dubrovytsya, Sarny, Staryy Chartoriysk, Kivertsi, Lutsk, Rivne, Zdolbuniv, Kostopil, Korets, Novohrad-Volynskyy, Korosten, Malyn, Radomyshl

Mazyr, Pyetrikaw, Kalinkavichy, Khoyniki, Yelsk, Ovruch, Olevsk, Belokorovichi, Chornobyl, Vasilevichi, Loyew, Horodnya, Chernihiv, Nizhyn, Oster, Kozelets, Nosivka, Ichnya, Borzna, Bakhmach, Konotop, Buryn, Bilopillya, Sumy, Romny, Pryluky, Lokhvitsa, Lebedyn, Okhtyrka, Trostyanets, Bohodukhiv, Kharkiv

Surazh, Mglin, Pochep, Trubchevsk, Unecha, Starodub, Klintsy, Novozybkov, Shchors, Novhorod-Siverskyy, Shostka, Hlukhiv, Krolevets, Koryukovka, Seredyna-Buda, Sevsk, Lokot, Komarichi, Dmitrovsk-Orlovskiy, Zheleznogorsk, Dmitriyev Lgovskiy, Lgov, Rylsk, Korenevo, Sudzha, Oboyan, Belgorod

Kromy, Maloarkhangelsk, Fatezh, Kolpny, Shchigry, Kursk, Grayvoron, Oktyabrskiy

Kovrov, Mtsensk, Bolkhov, Belev, Plavsk, Shchekino, Kosaya Gora, Suvorov, Odoyevo, Chekalin, Kozelsk, Sukhinichi, Zhizdra, Kletnya, Navlya, Verkhovye, Novosil, Mtsensk

Suomenlahti / Gulf of Finland, Ozero Ilmen, Ozero Chudskoye, Ozero Pskovskoye, Voru Jarv, Lubanas Ezers

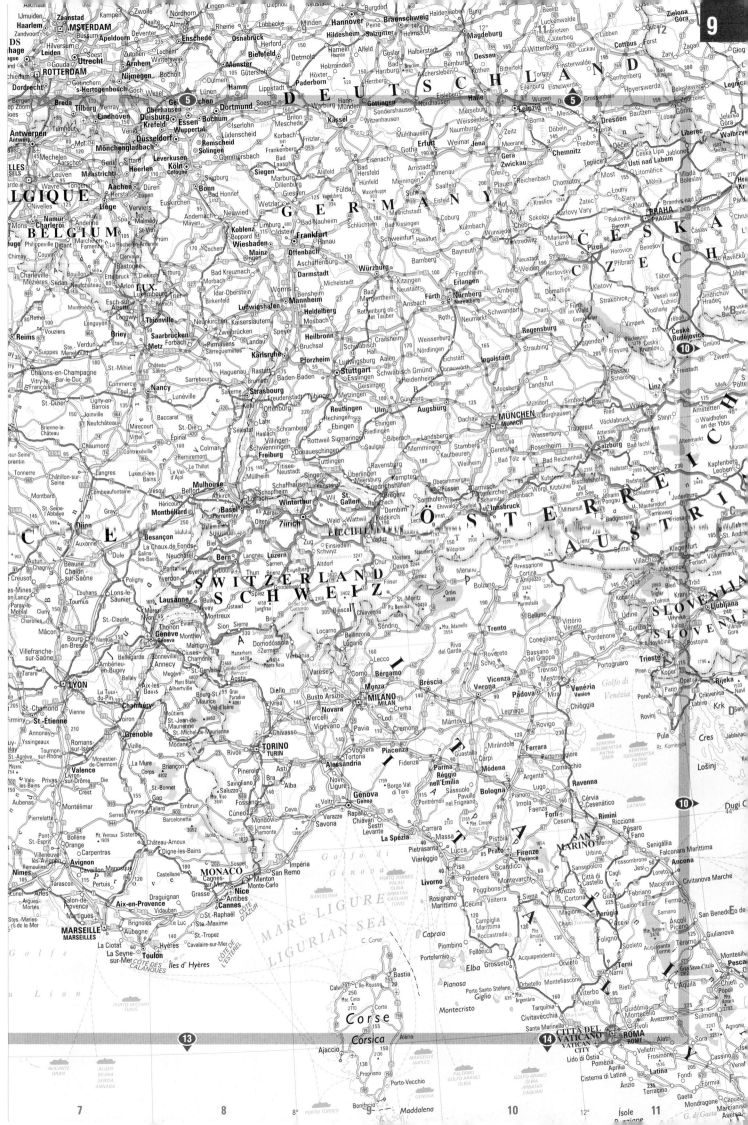

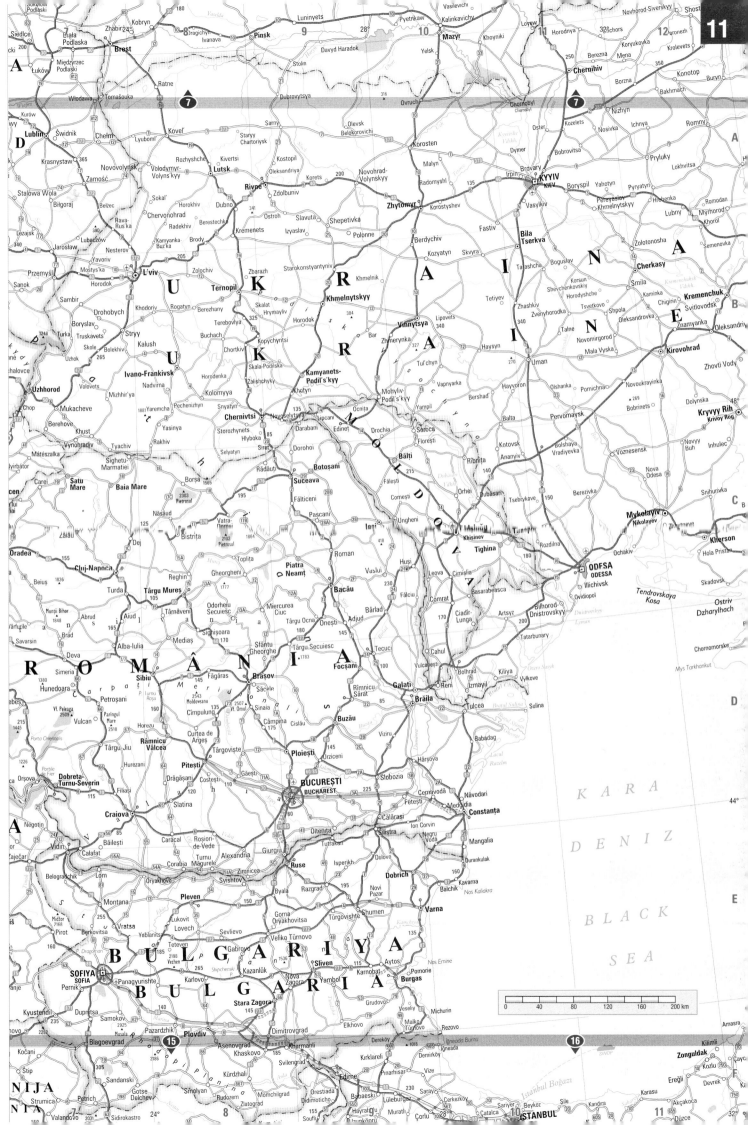

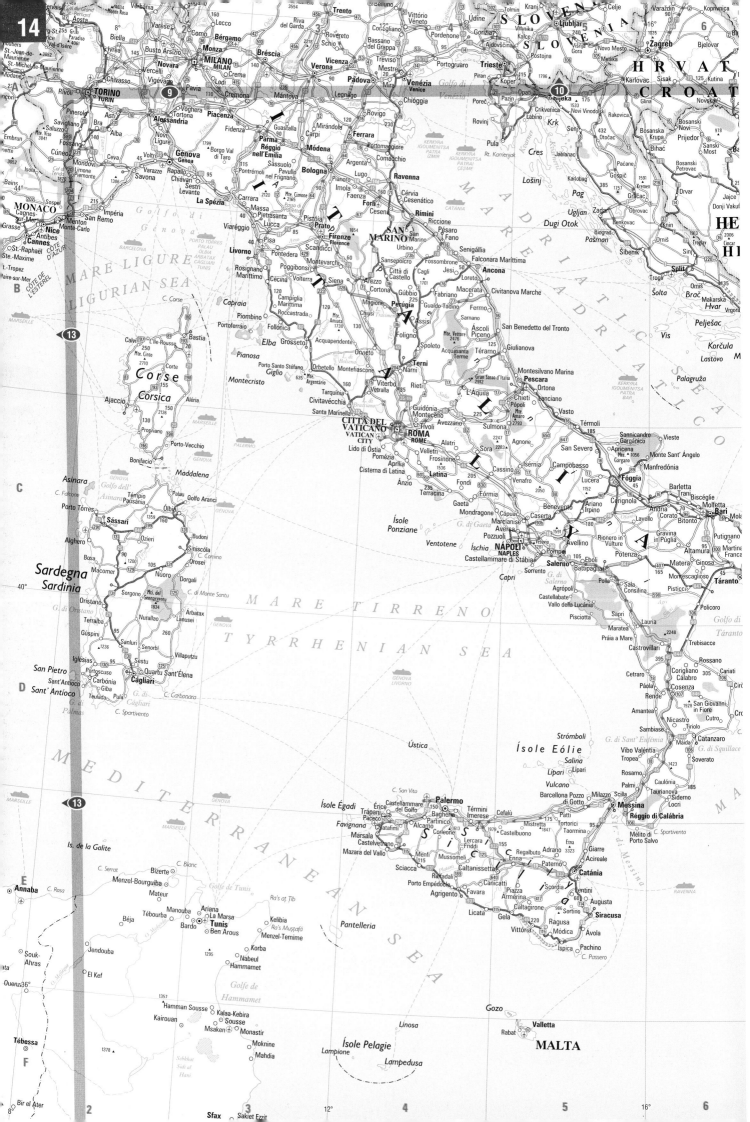

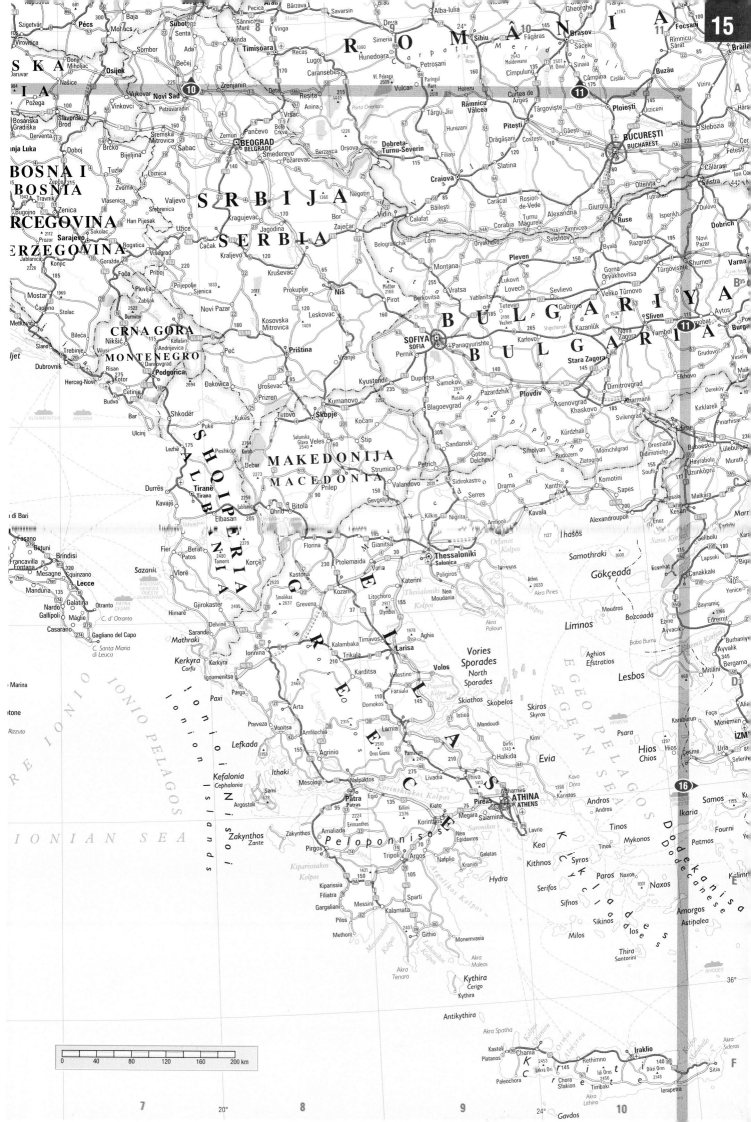

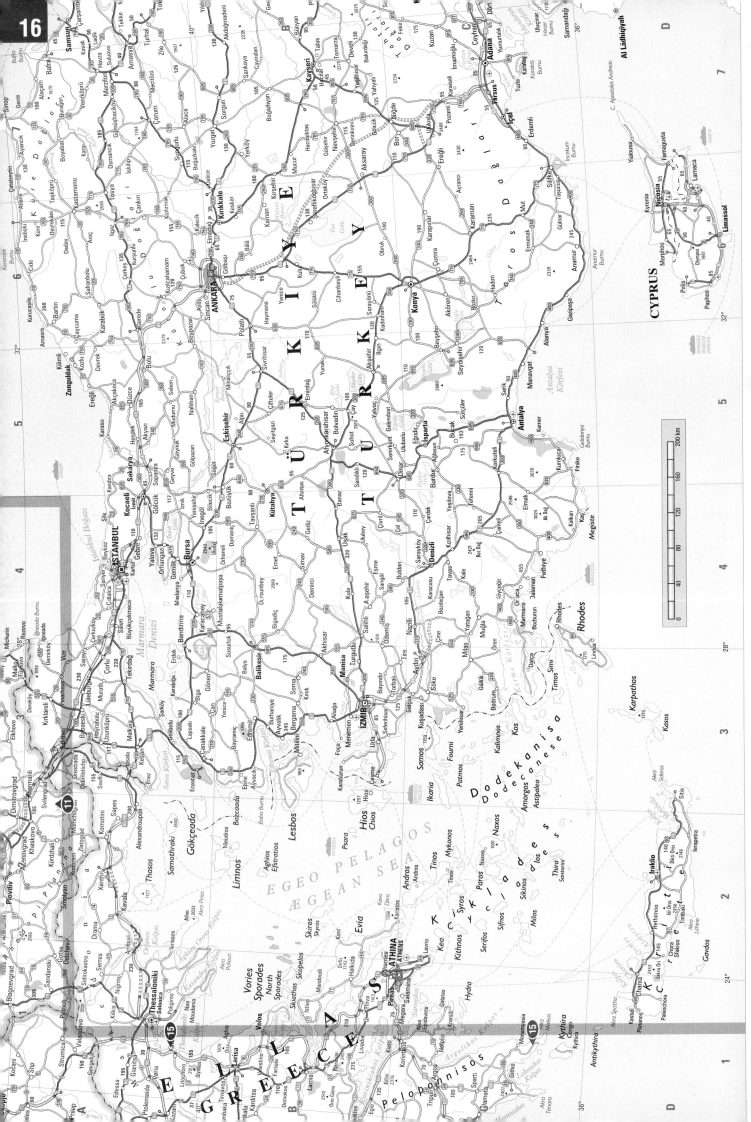

Key to road map pages

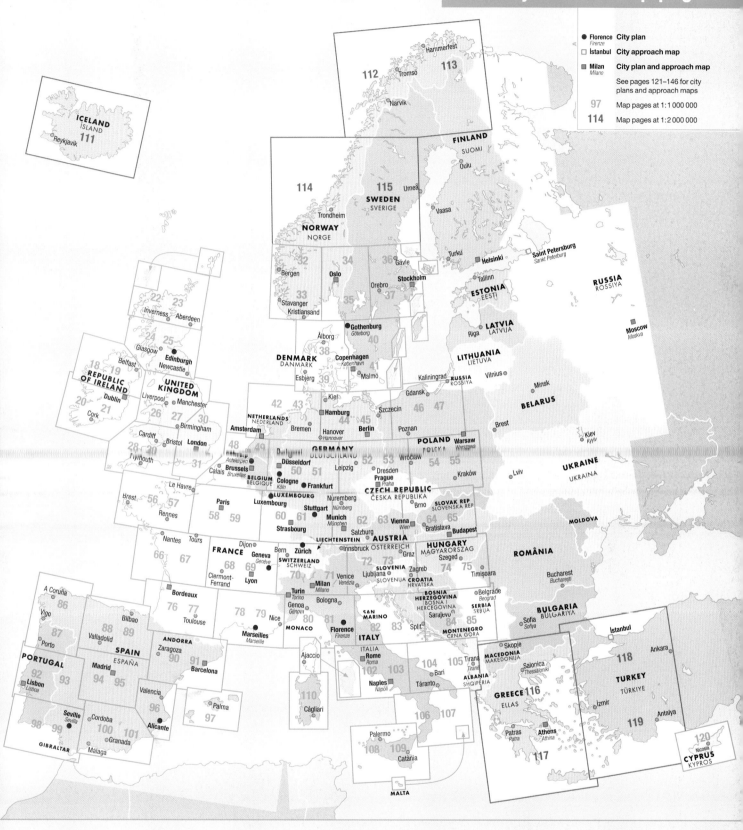

● Florence *Firenze* **City plan**

□ İstanbul **City approach map**

■ Milan *Milano* **City plan and approach map**

See pages 121–146 for city plans and approach maps

97 Map pages at 1:1 000 000

114 Map pages at 1:2 000 000

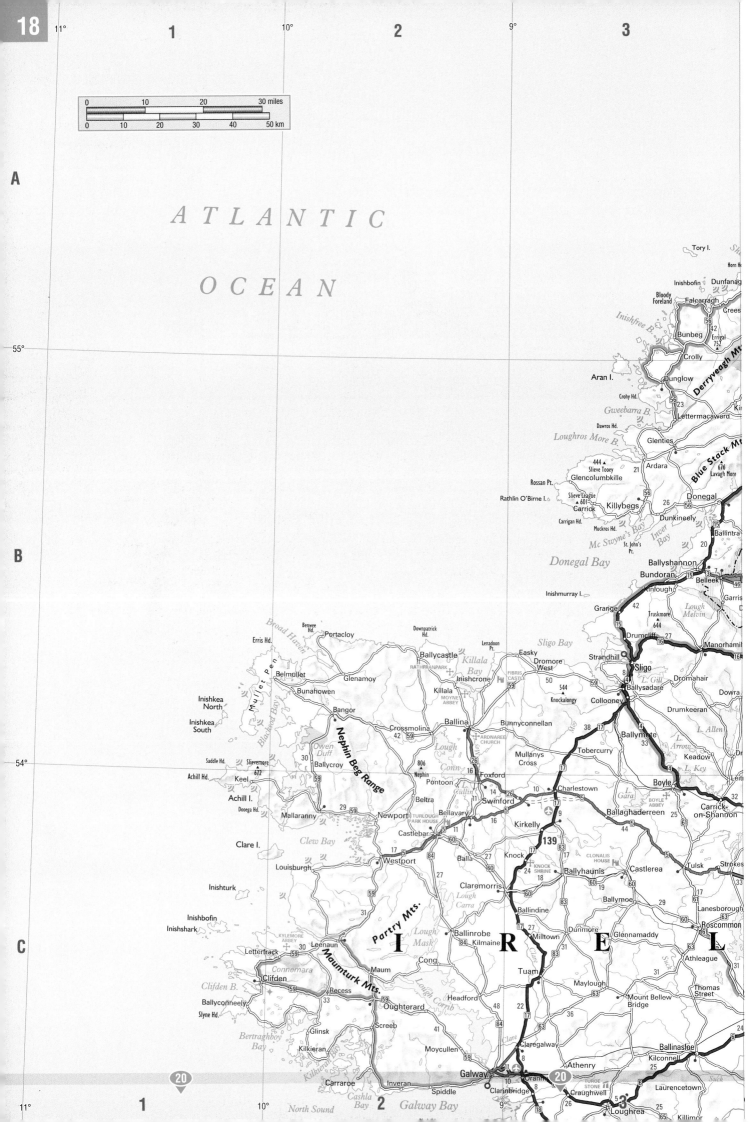

A

ATLANTIC

OCEAN

B

C

0   10   20   30 miles
0   10   20   30   40   50 km

55°

54°

11°

Tory I.

Horn H

Inishbofin   Dunfanag
Bloody
Foreland   Falcarragh
Crees
Inishfree B.   Bunbeg   56
42
Errigal 752
Aran I.   Crolly
Dunglow   Derryveagh Mts
Crohy Hd.   56   23
Gweebarra B.   Lettermacaward   Ki
Dawros Hd.
Loughros More B.   Glenties   Blue Stack Mt
444   Ardara   676
Slieve Tooey   21   Lavagh More
Rossan Pt.   Glencolumbkille
Rathlin O'Birne I.   Slieve League
601   Donegal
Carrick   56   26
Carrigan Hd.   Killybegs   Dunkineely   15
Muckros Hd.   Ballintra
Mc Swyne's Bay   St. John's
Pt.   Inver   20
Donegal Bay   Bay
Ballyshannon   Ballysh
Bundoran   15   3   7
Inishmurray I.   Belleek   46
Kinlough   Garris
Lough
Grange   42   Melvin
Truskmore   Garris
644
Drumcliff   16
Sligo Bay   15   Manorhamil
Lenadoon   Easky   Strandhill   Sligo   16
Pt.   Dromore   L. Gill   Dromahair
Ballycastle   West   Ballysadare
Killala   RATHFRANPARK   Inishcrone   FIBRIS   50   Collooney   Dowra
Bay   CASTLE   59   Knockalongy   Drumkeeran
MOYNE   544
ABBEY   Ballymote   L. Allen
Crossmolina   Ballina   Bunnyconnellan   38   17   33   Keadow
42   59   ARDNAREE   L. Arrow
CHURCH   Mullanys   Tobercurry   L. Key   L
Owen   Lough   Cross   17   Boyle   Leit
Duff   Conn   806   Charlestown   L.   BOYLE
Slievemore   Nephin   Foxford   10   Gara   ABBEY   Carrick-
672   L.   14   26   17   5   Ballaghaderreen   25   on-Shannon
Keel   Ballycroy   Cullin   Swinford   44
Achill Hd.   Pontoon   9   61
Achill I.   29   59   Beltra   Kirkelly   139   83   CLONALIS   Tulsk   Strokes
Dooega Hd.   Bellavary   Knock   HOUSE   Castlerea   33
Mallaranny   Newport   TURLOUGH   16   KNOCK   24   Ballyhaunis   17
PARK HOUSE   5   SHRINE   18   19   60   Roscommon
Castlebar   11   60   Balla   27   60   Ballymoe   29   Lanesborough
Clew Bay   17   5   Claremorris   83   17   17
Louisburgh   Westport   84   27   Ballindine   60   Dunmore   Glennamaddy   63   Athleague   31
Lough   Ballinrobe   84   Kilmaine   31   Milltown   Maylough   Mount Bellew
Carra   I   R   Cong   83   Tuam   Bridge   Thomas
Partry Mts.   Lough   Ballinrobe   22   E   L   Street
KYLEMORE   30   Leenaun   Mask   Kilmaine   Headford   17   48   Moylough   24
ABBEY   59   Connemara   Maum   Cong   84   63   36   Ballinasloe
Letterfrack   Maumturk Mts.   Clare I.   Kilconnell
Clifden   Recess   59   Oughterard   Claregalway   Athenry   25
Clifden B.   33   Screeb   41   Moycullen   8   Laurencetown
Ballyconneely   Glinsk   59   17   Galway   Oranmore   TUROE   Craughwell
Slyne Hd.   Kilkieran   Carraroe   Inveran   Spiddle   Clarinbridge   8   STONE   Loughrea
Bertraghboy   North Sound   Galway Bay   9°   18   65   Killim
Bay   Kilkieran Bay   Cashla   2   Craughwell

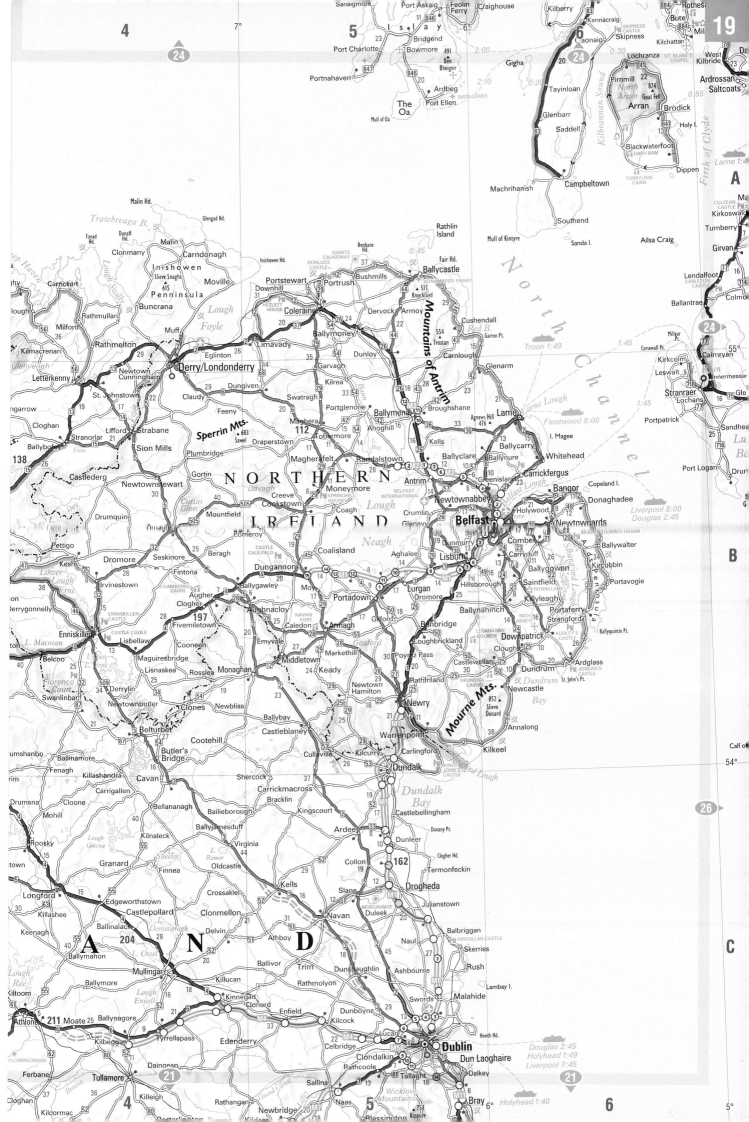

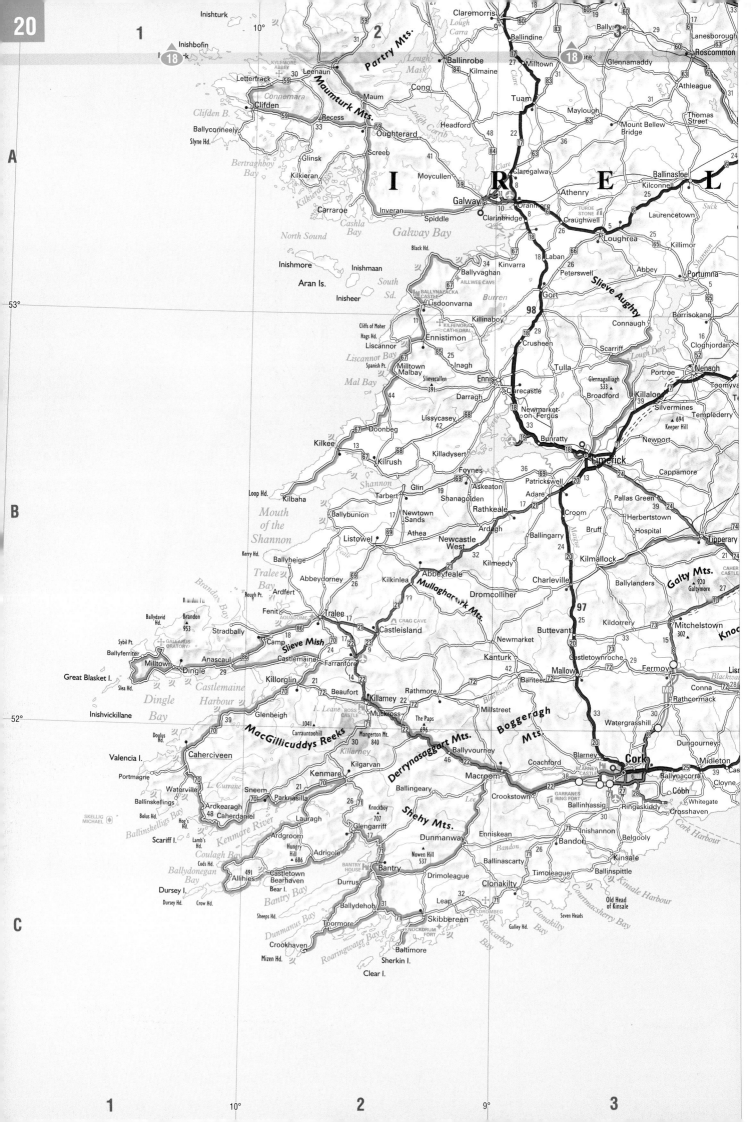

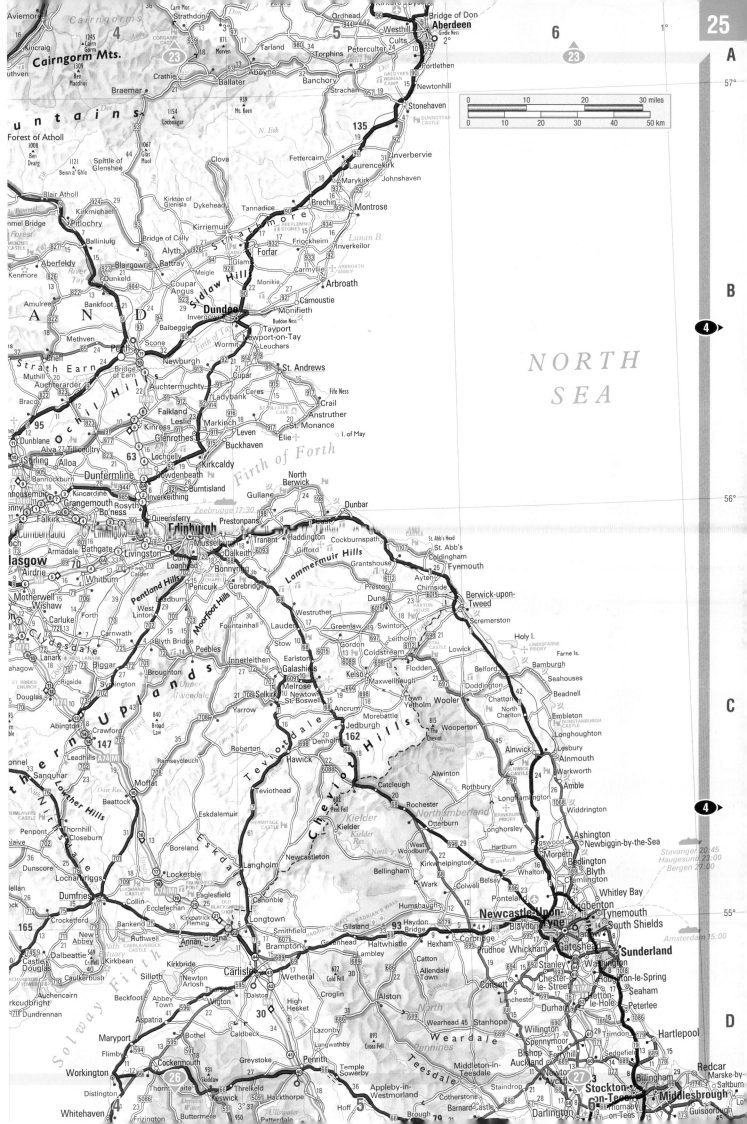

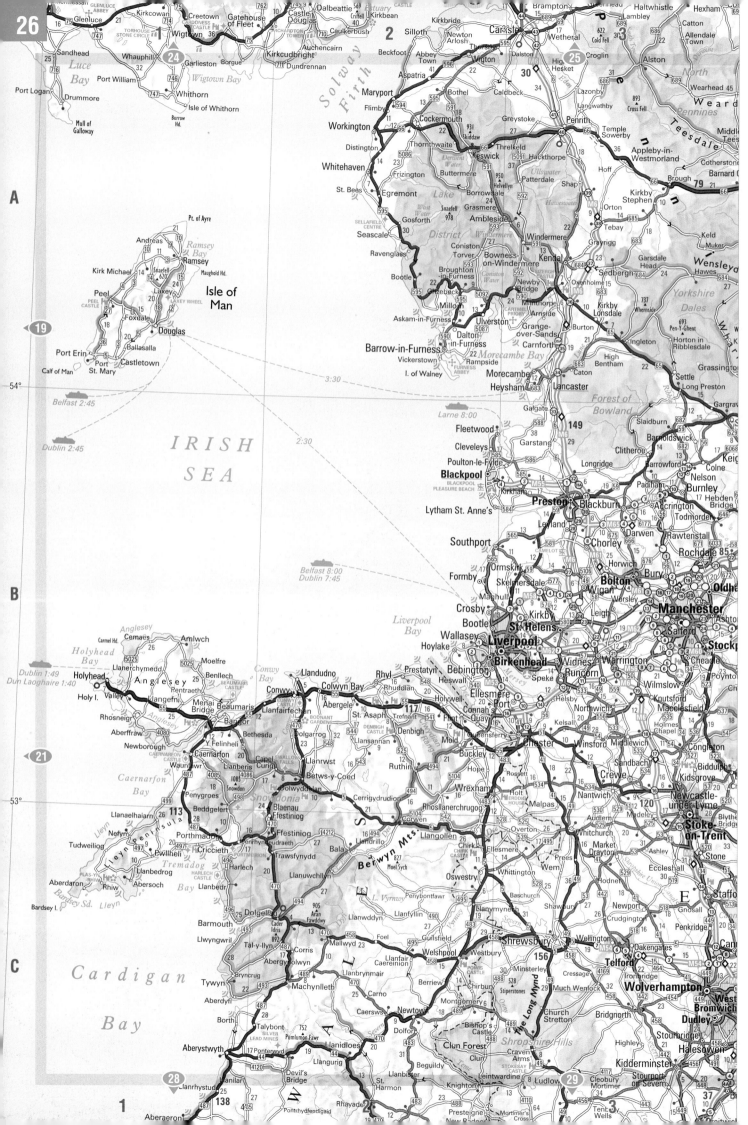

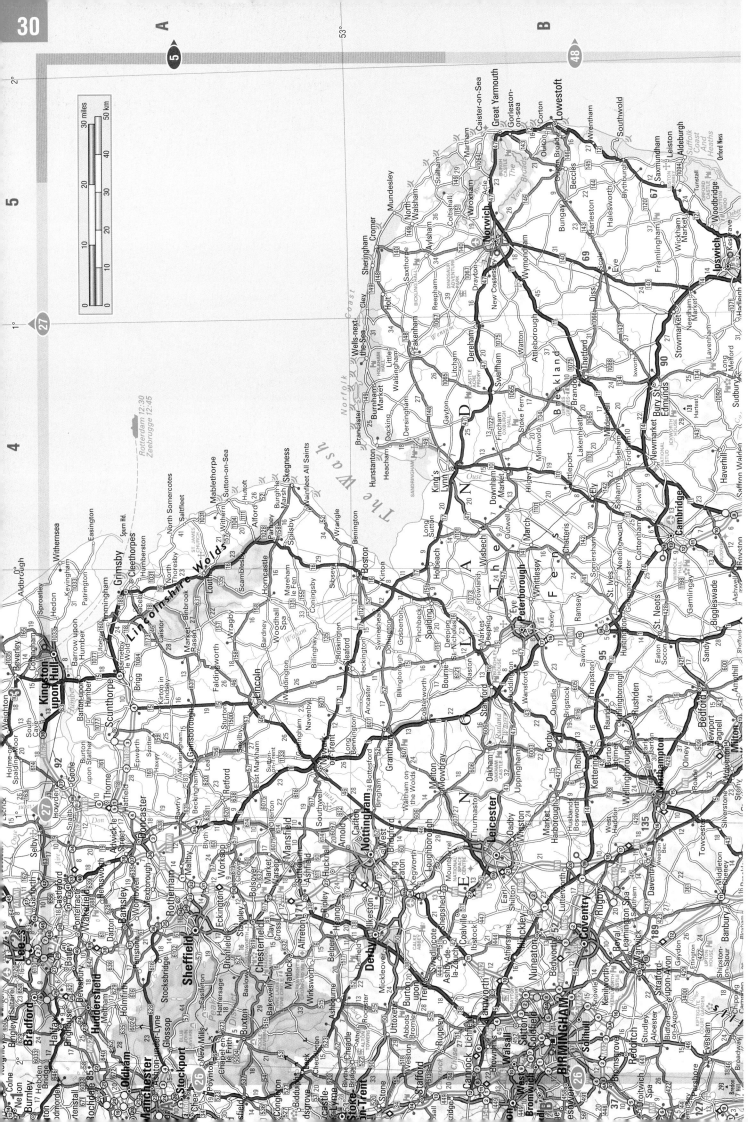

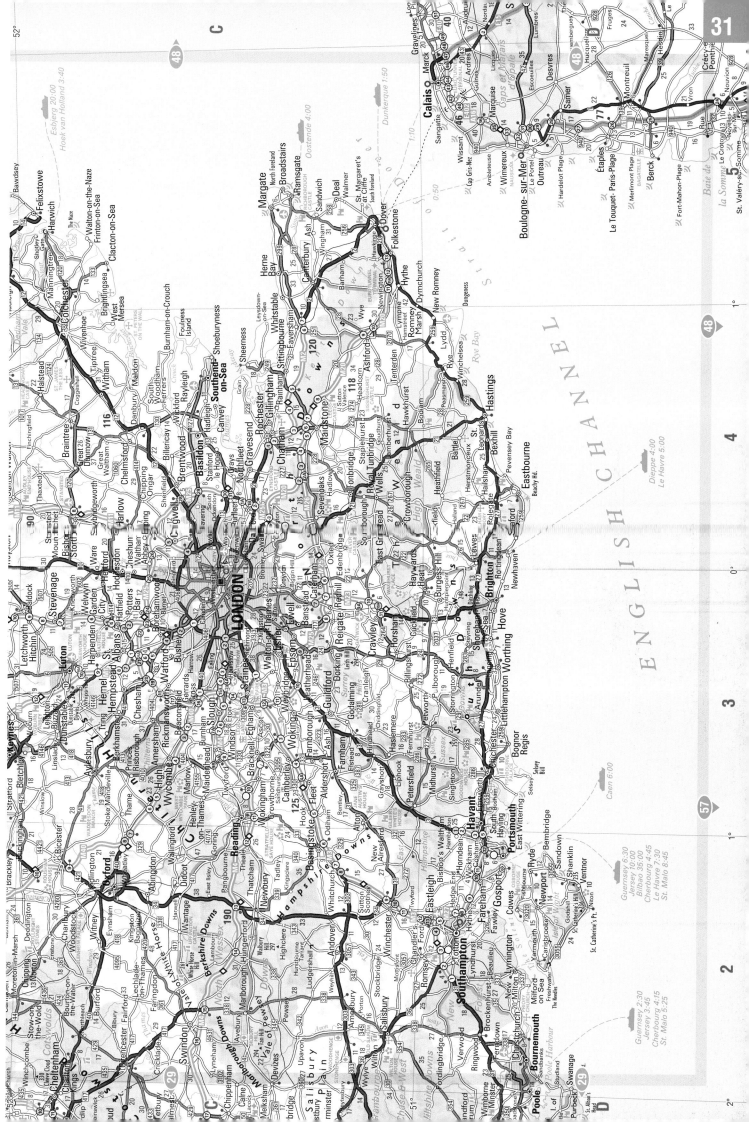

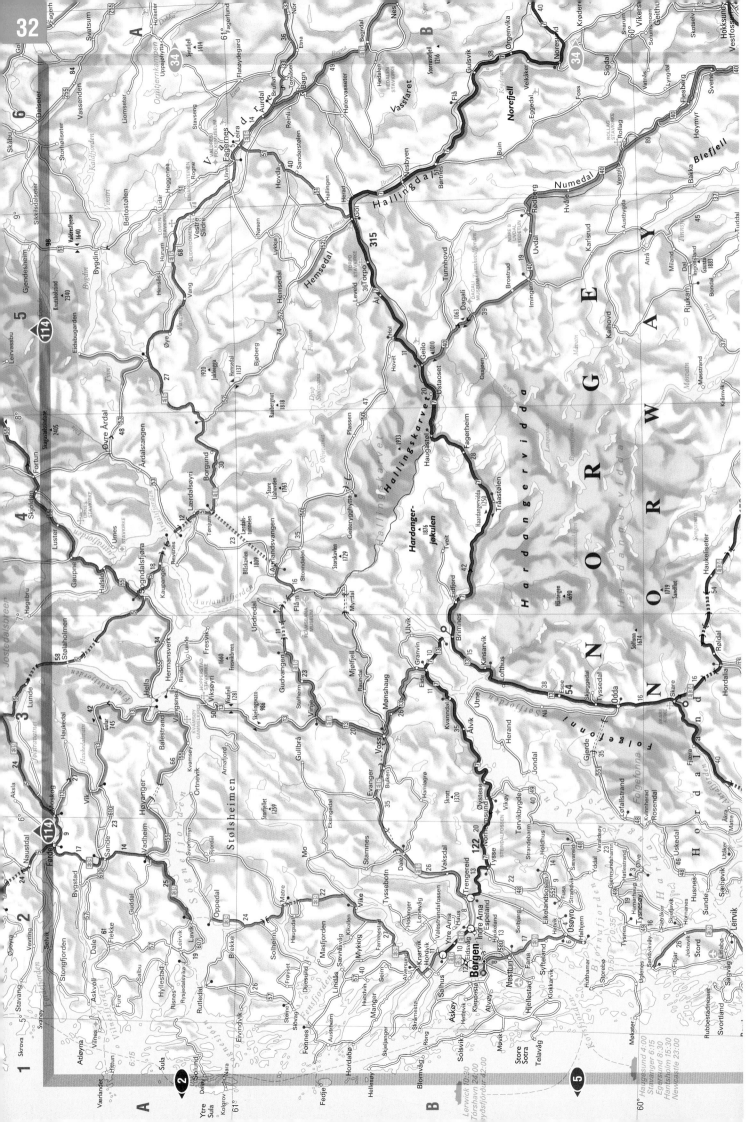

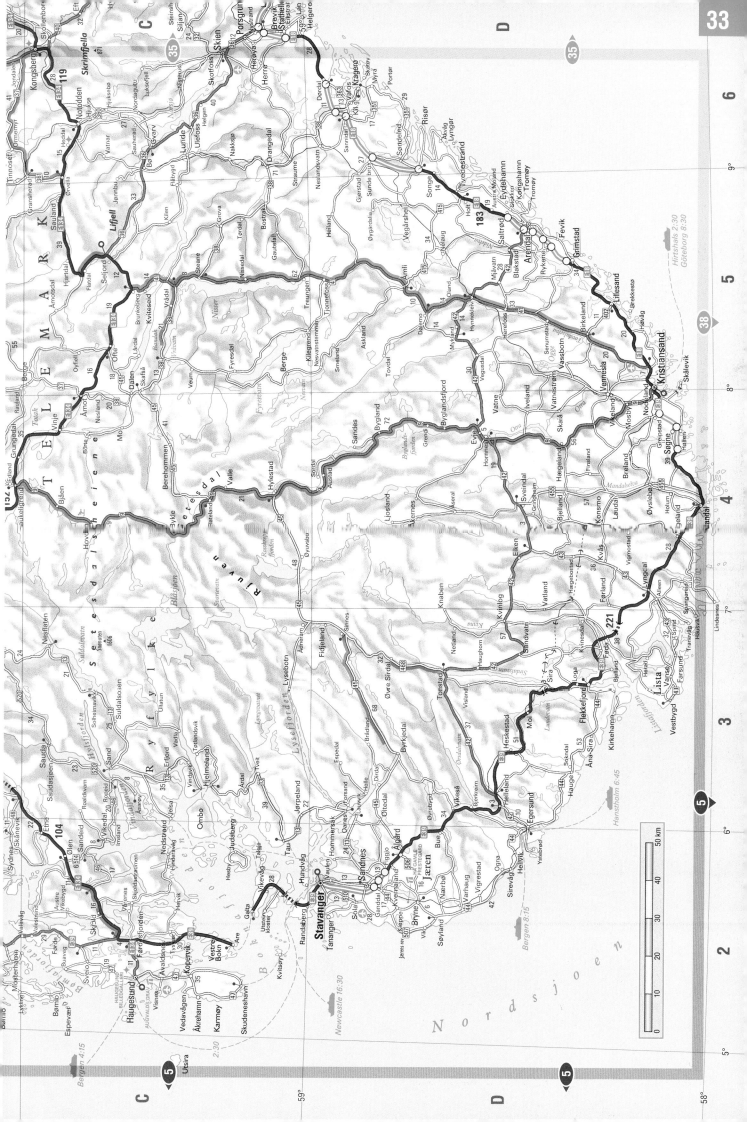

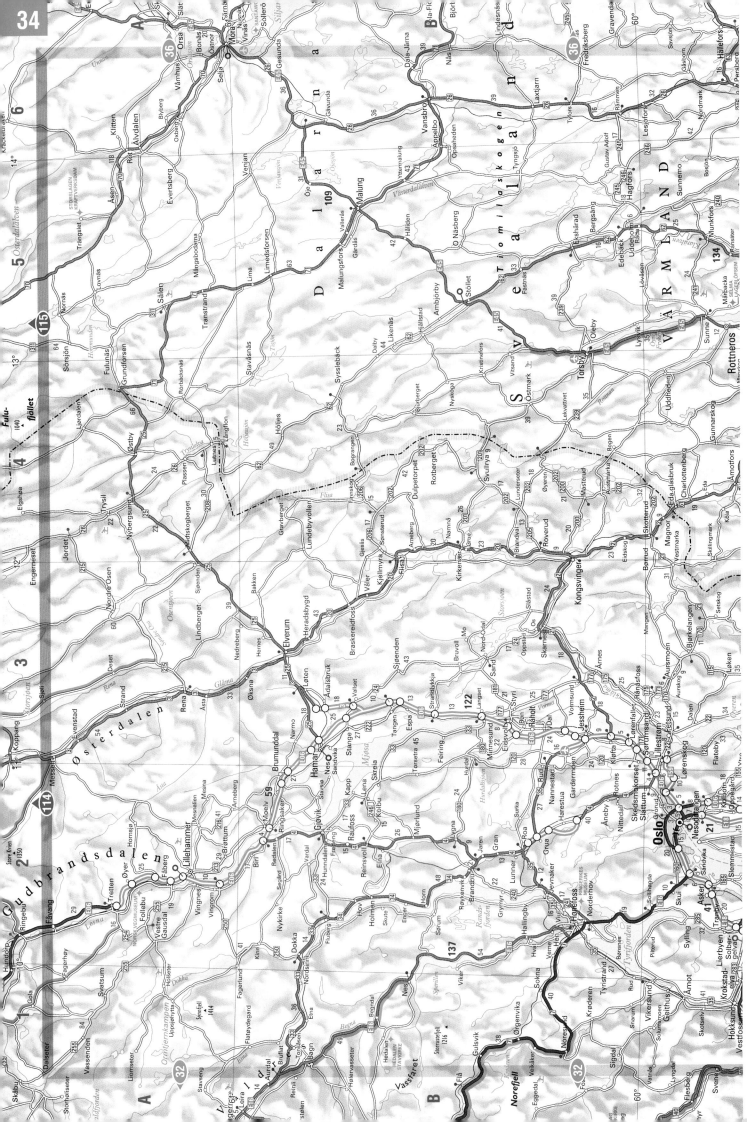

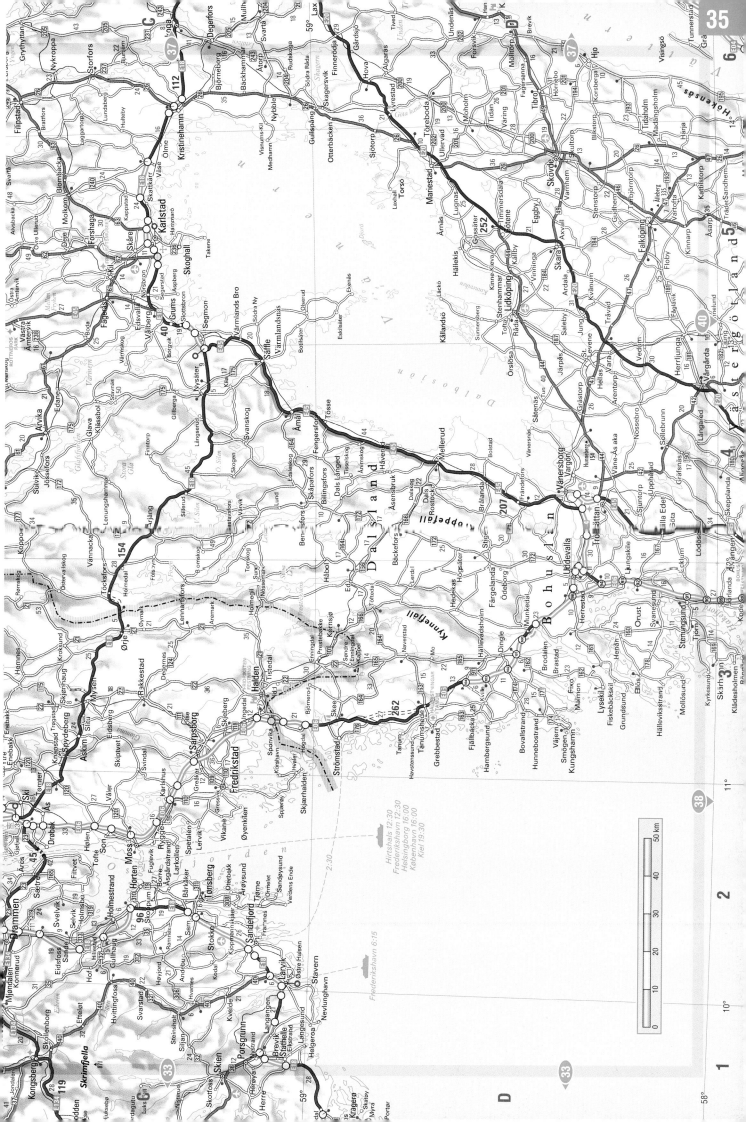

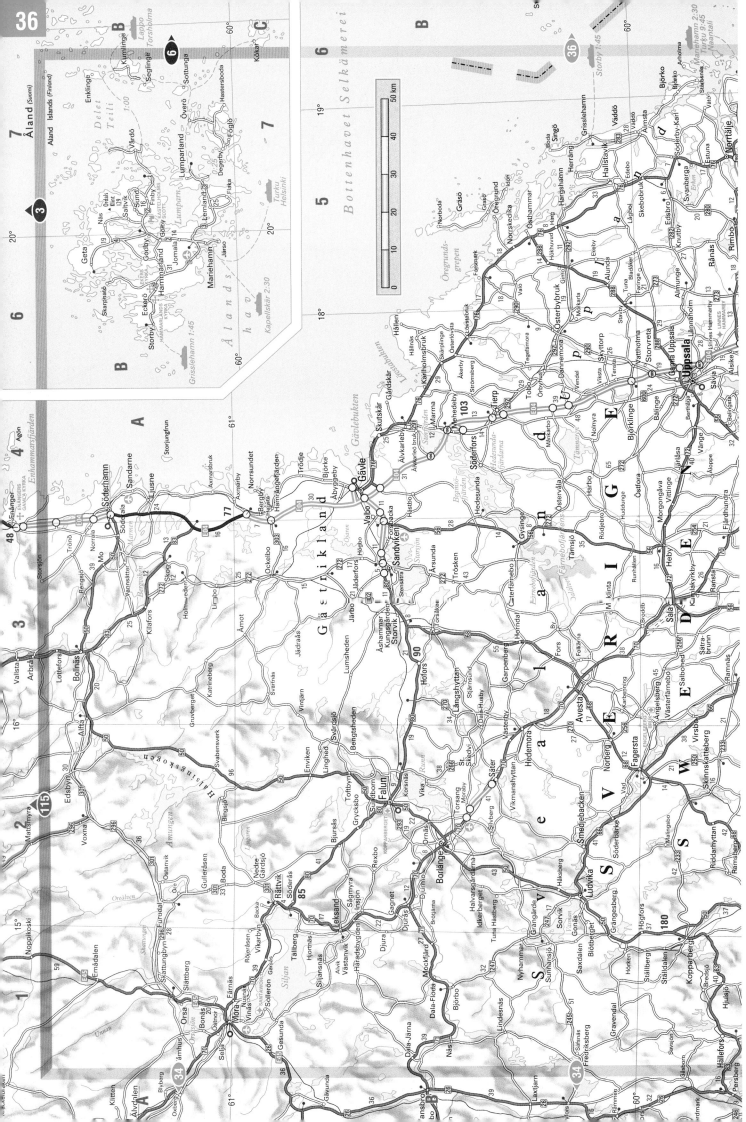

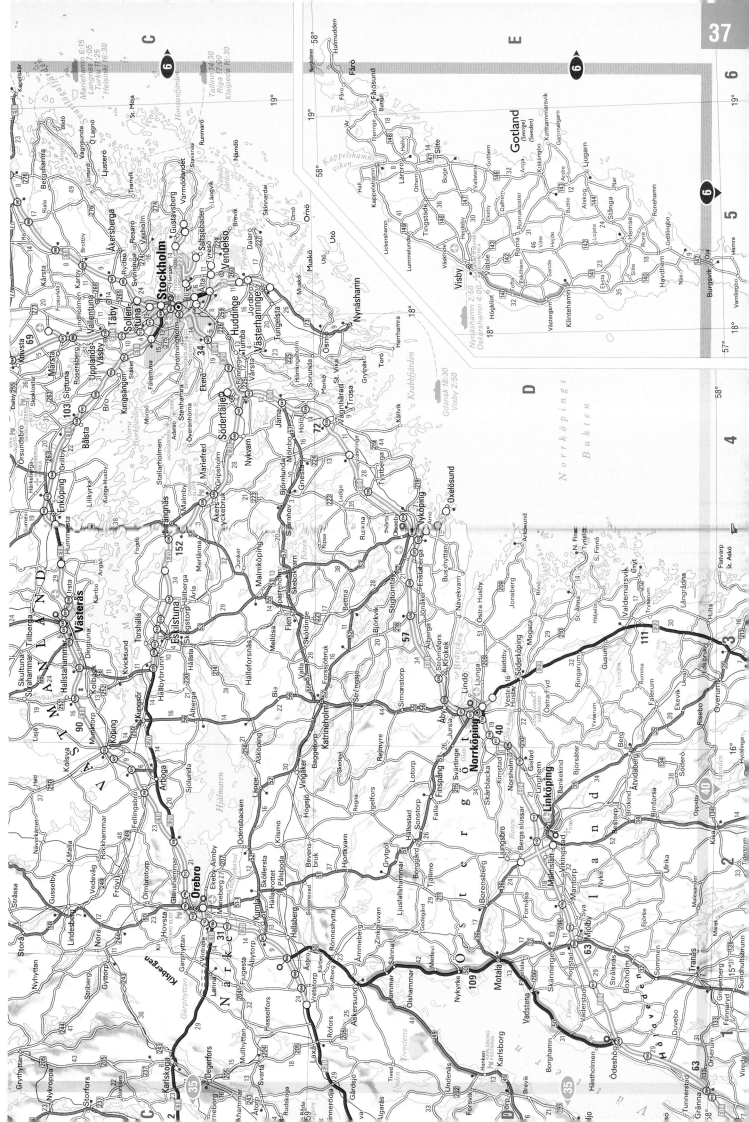

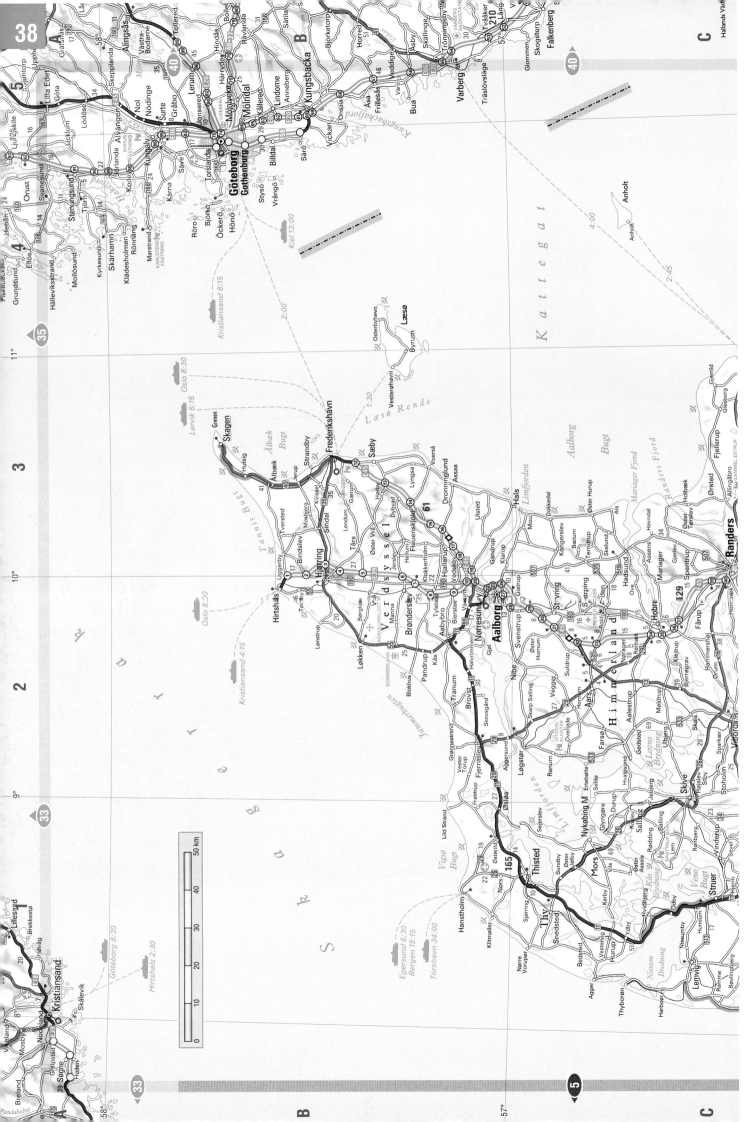

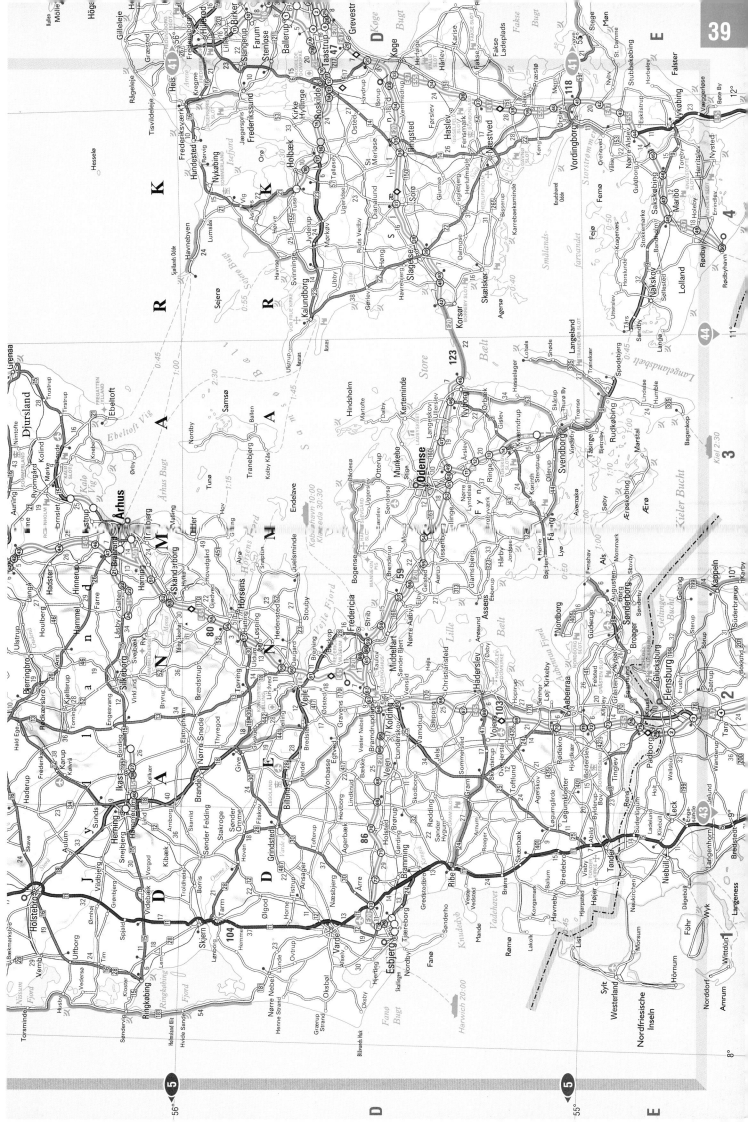

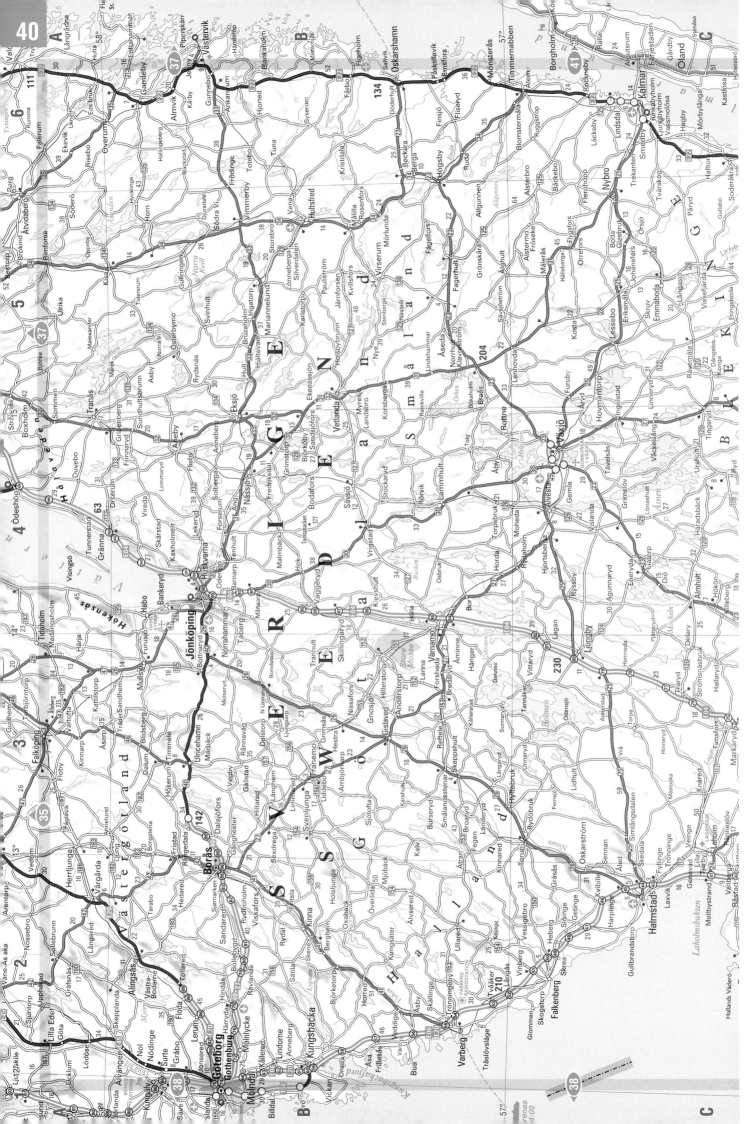

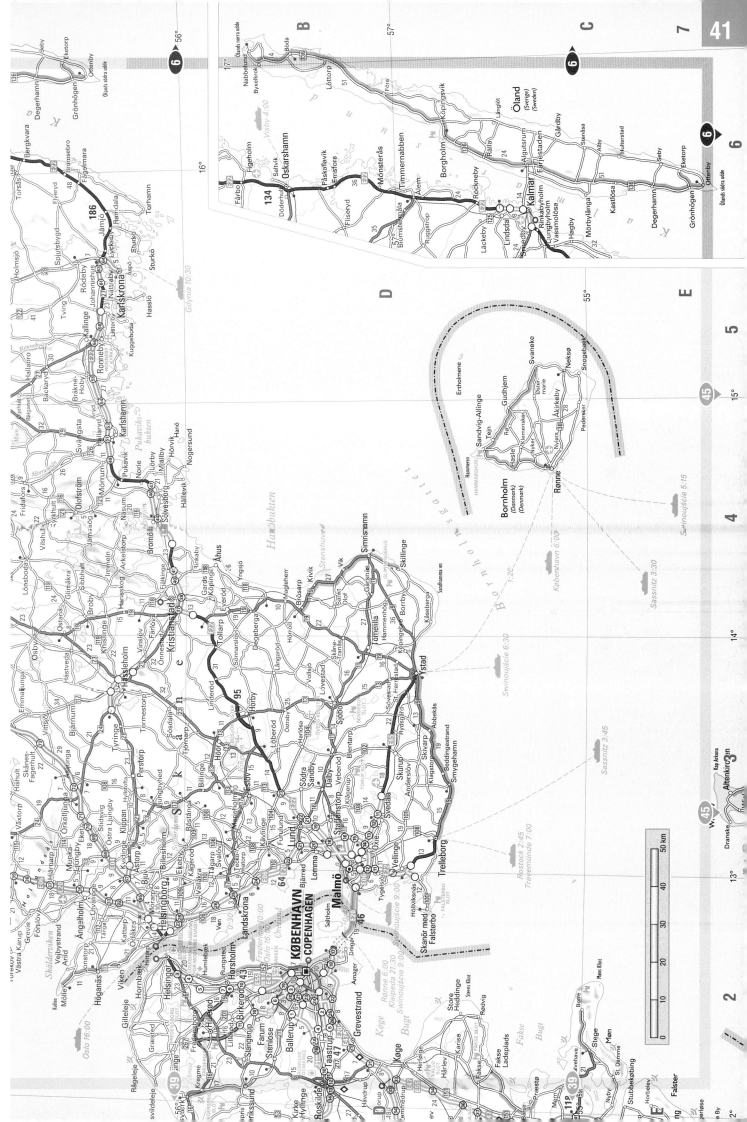

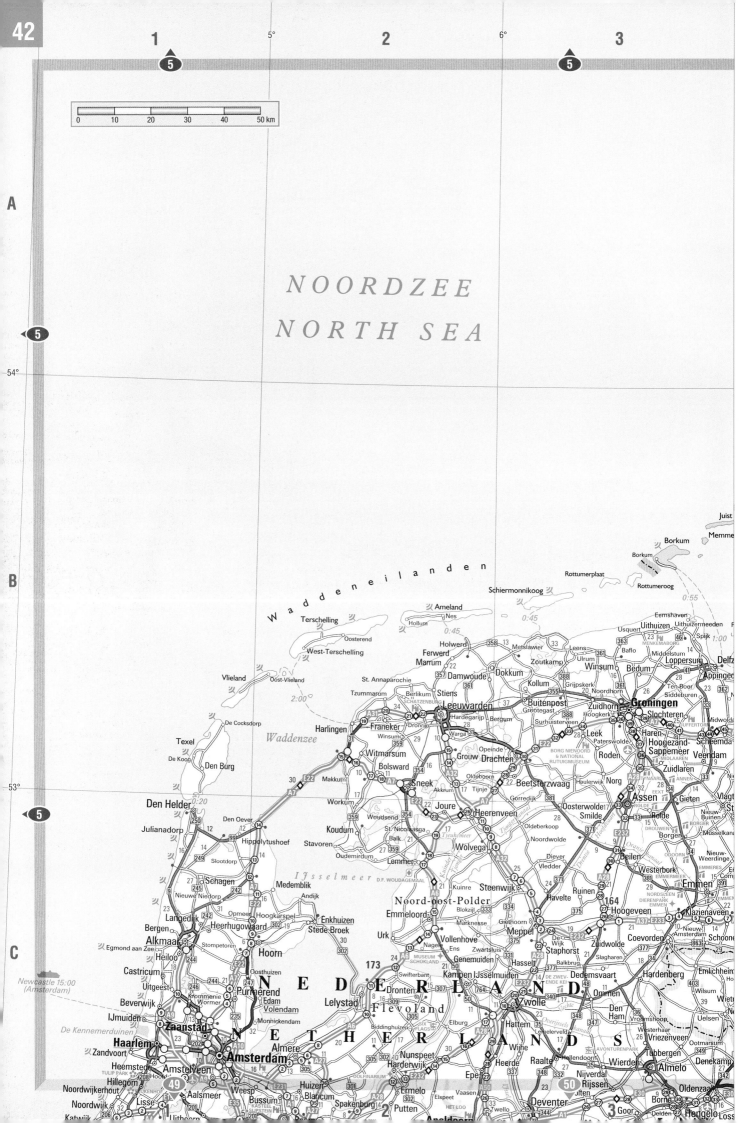

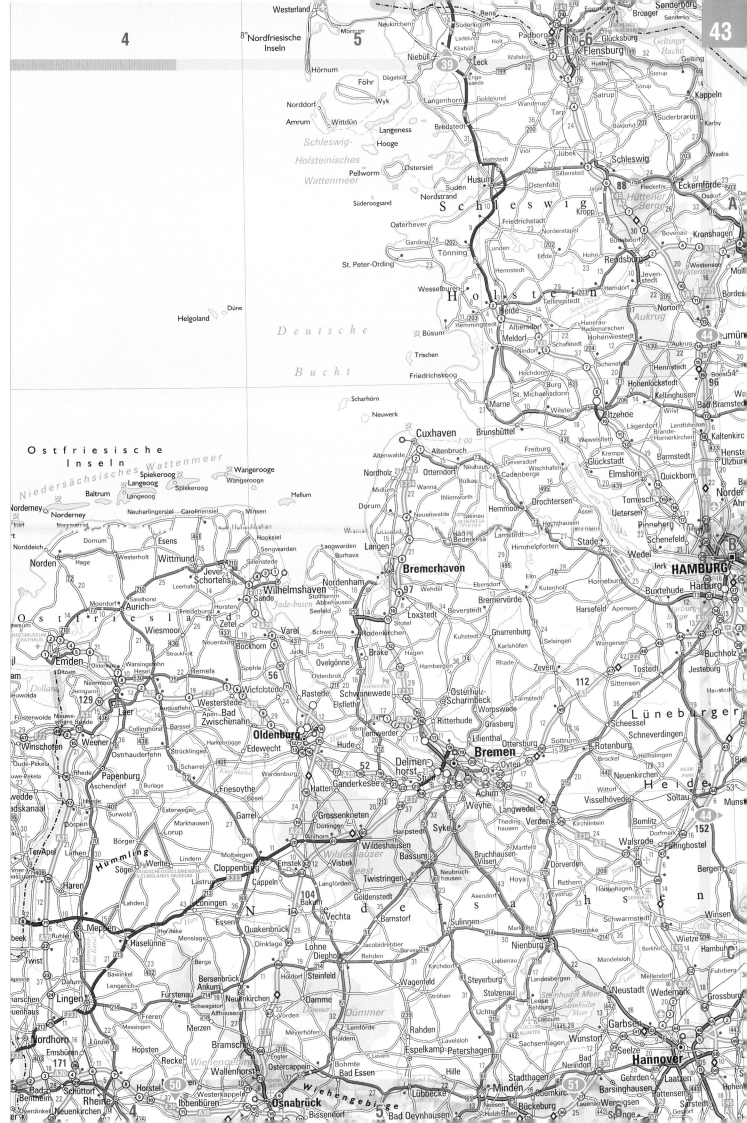

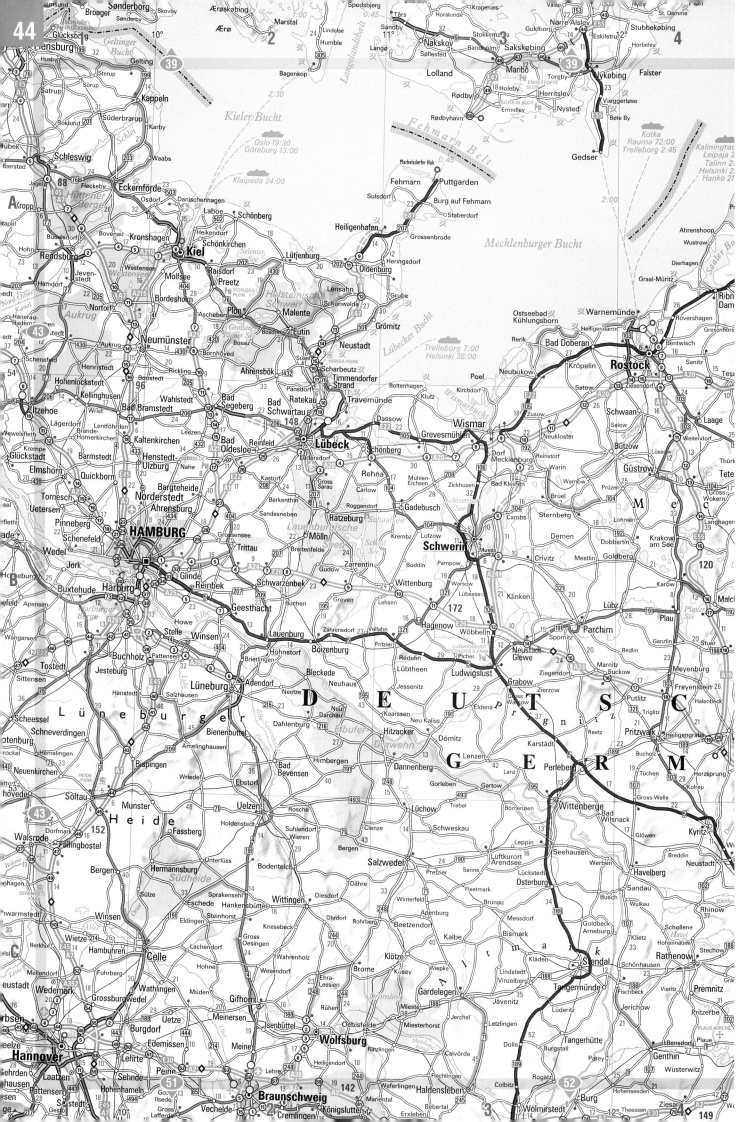

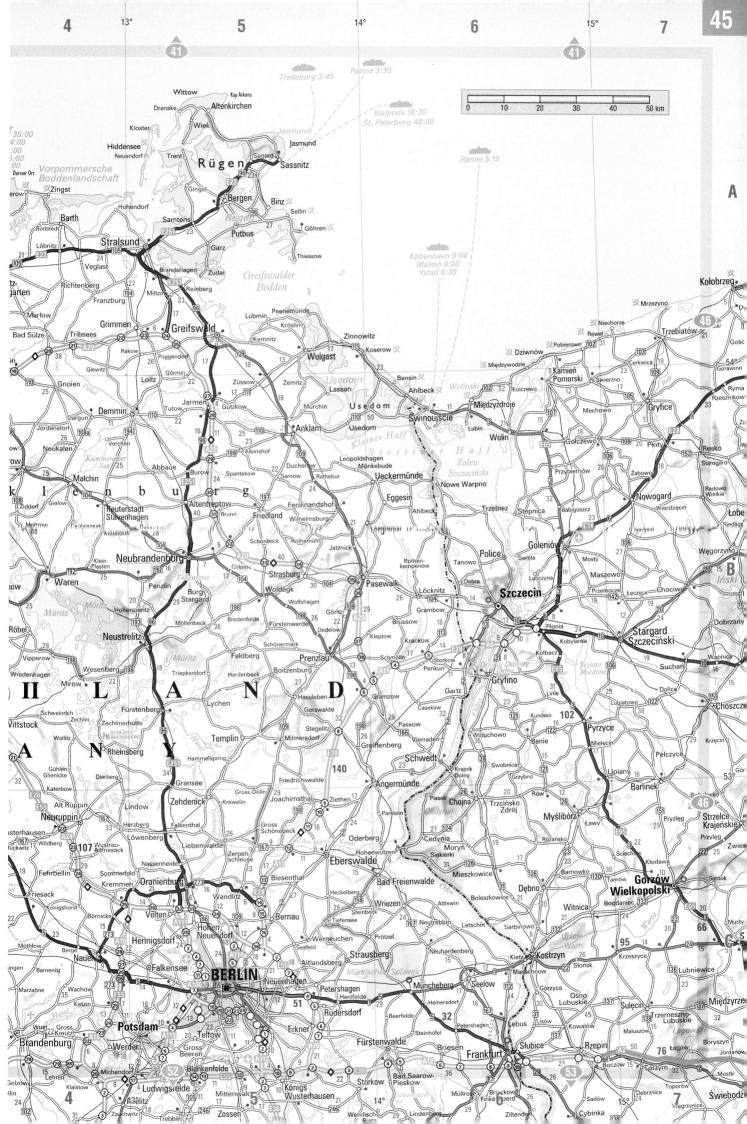

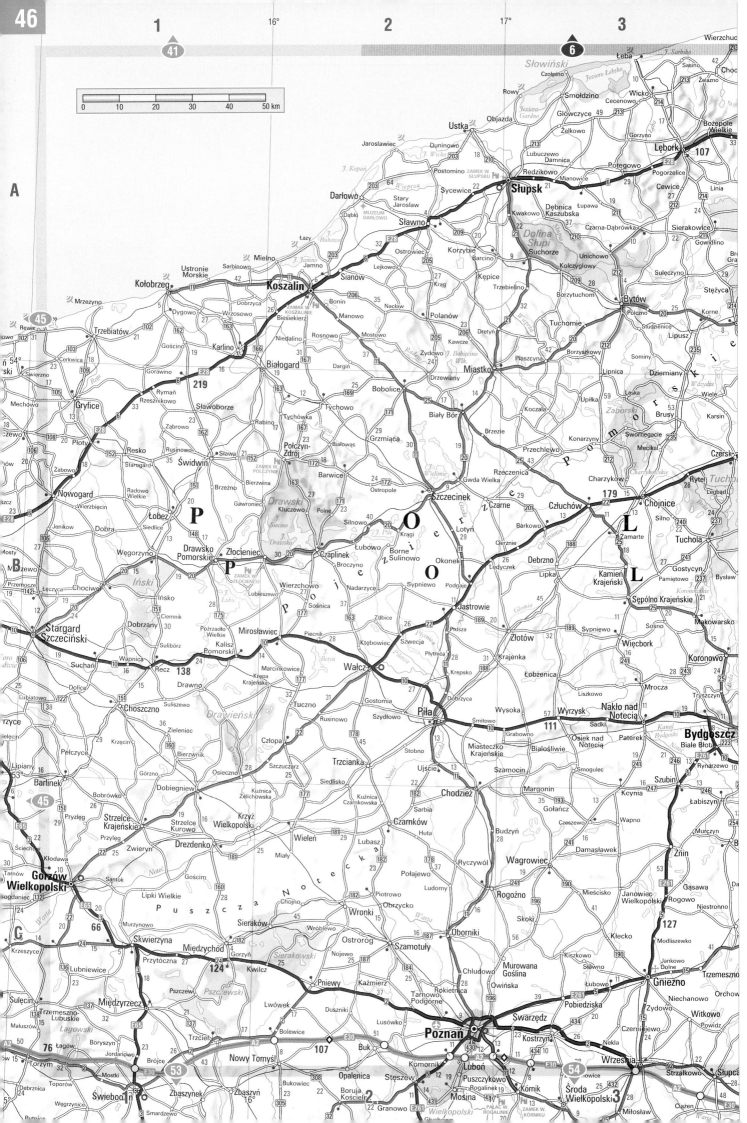

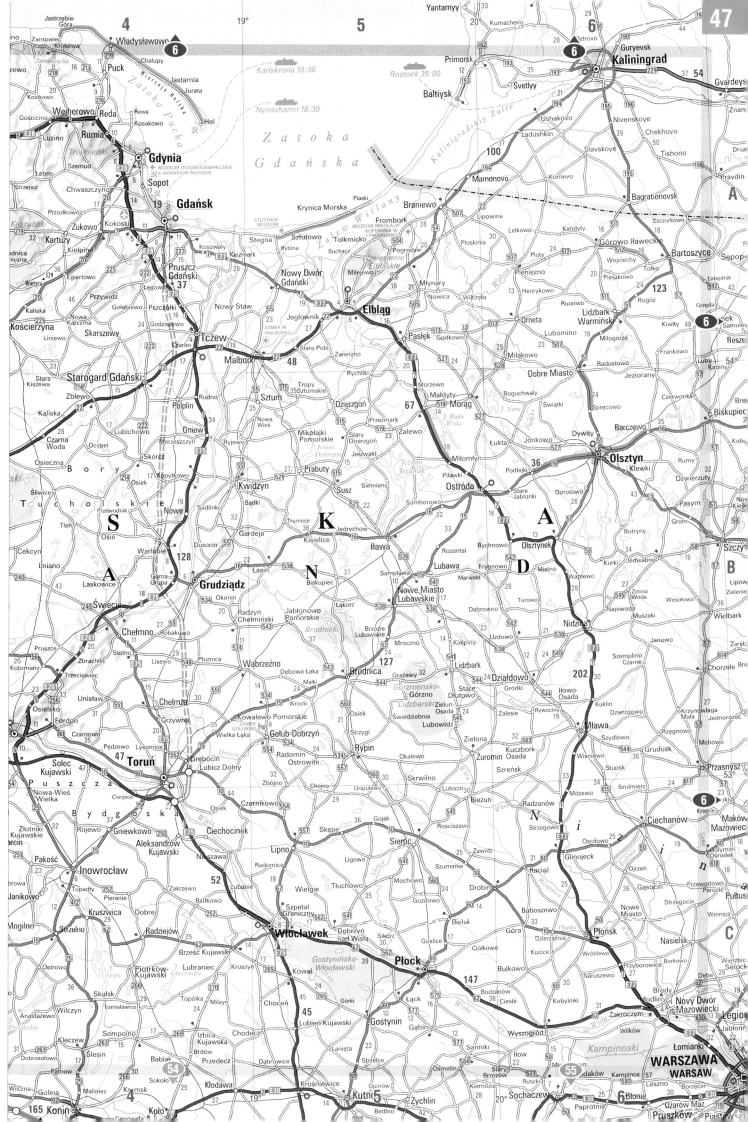

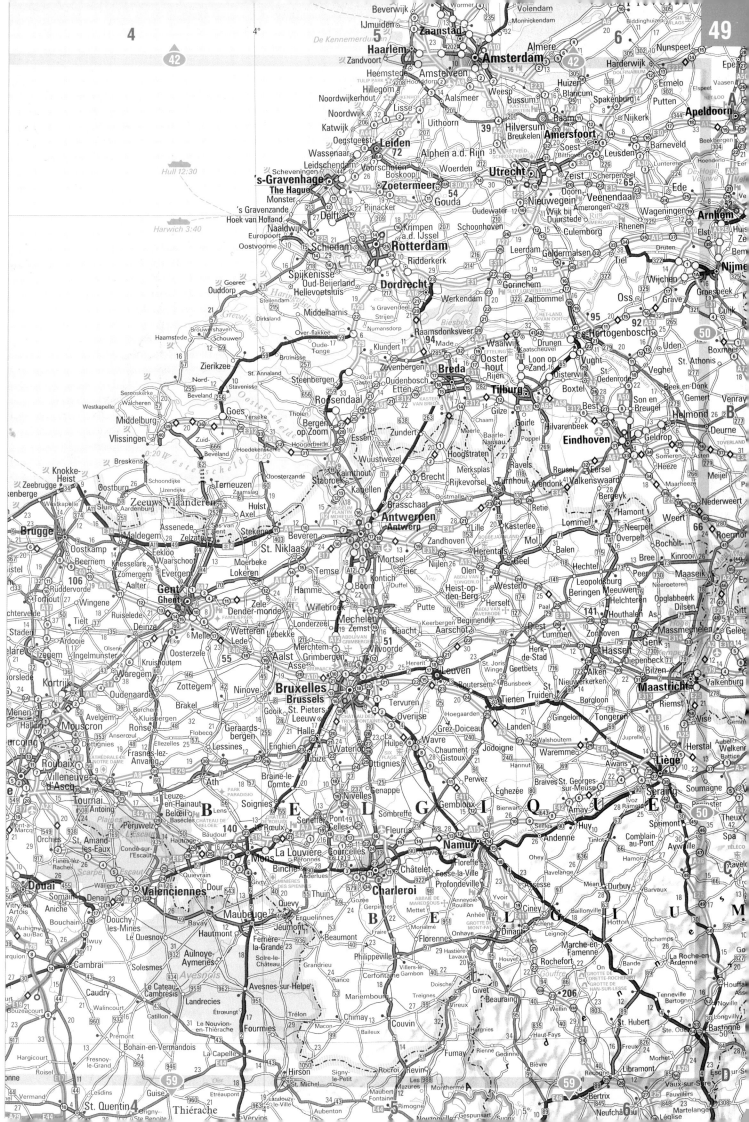

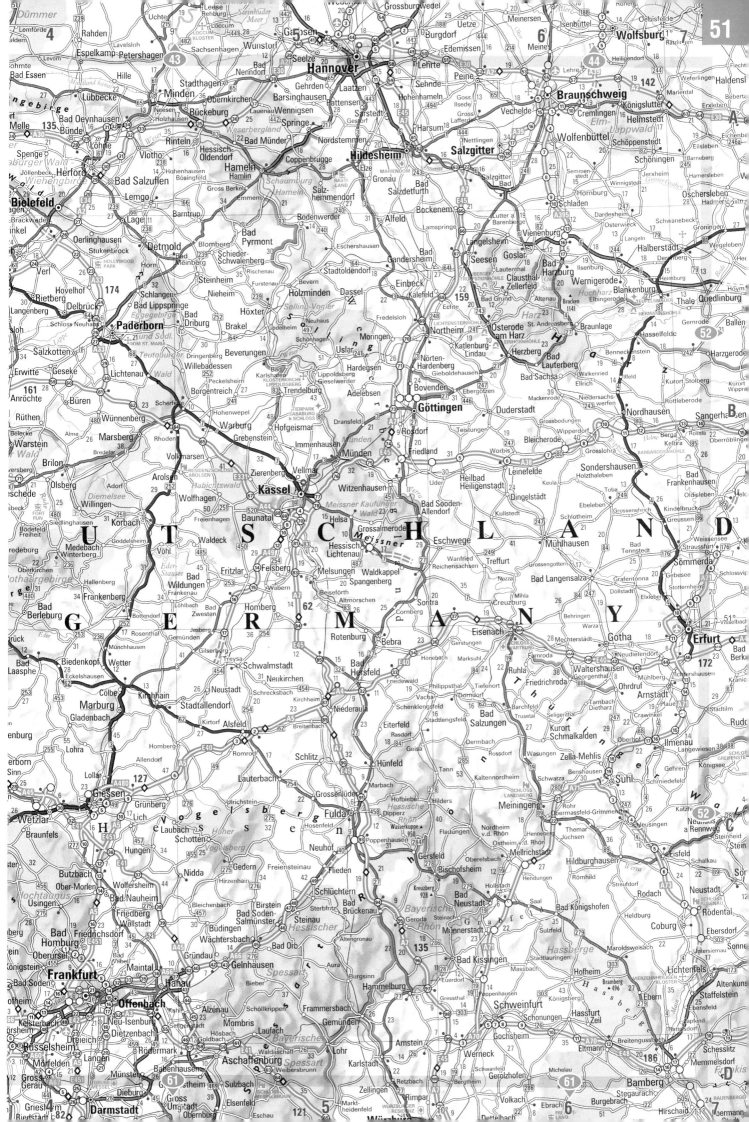

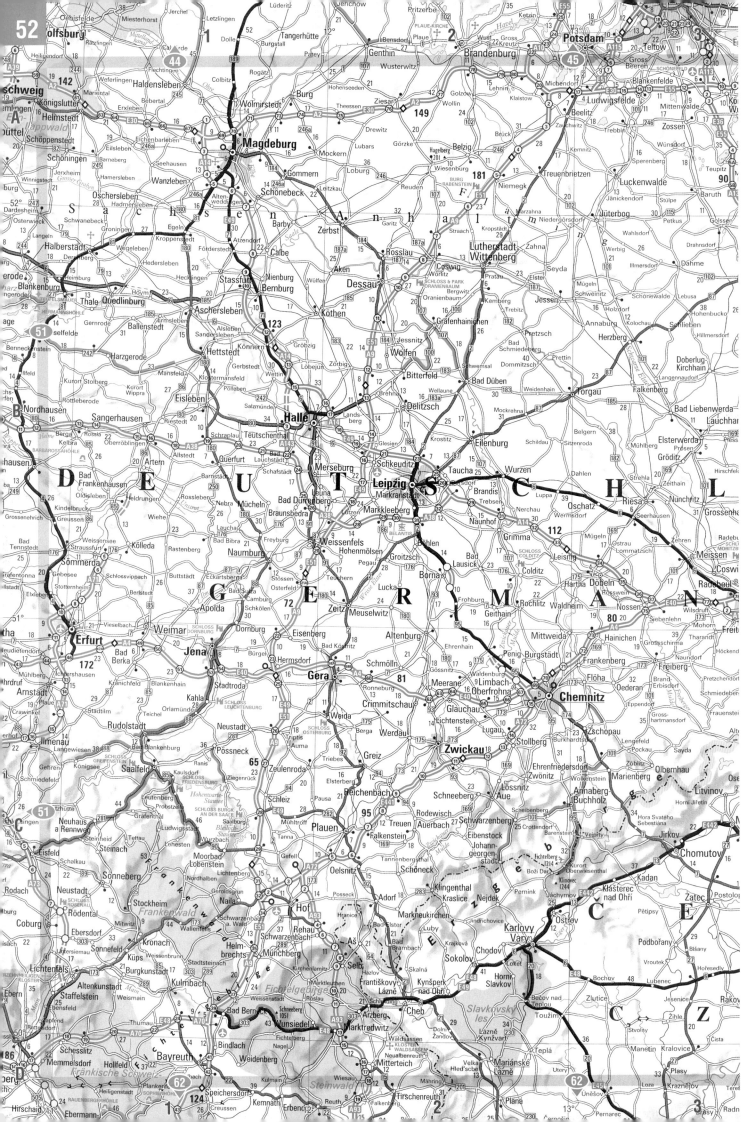

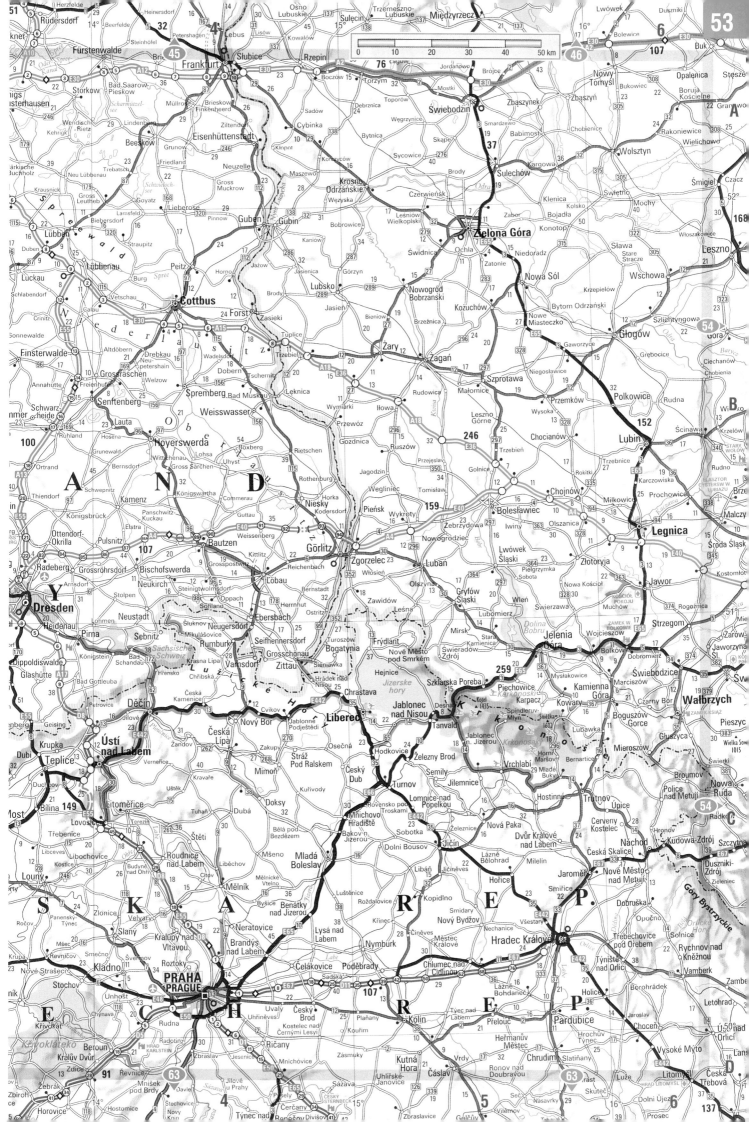

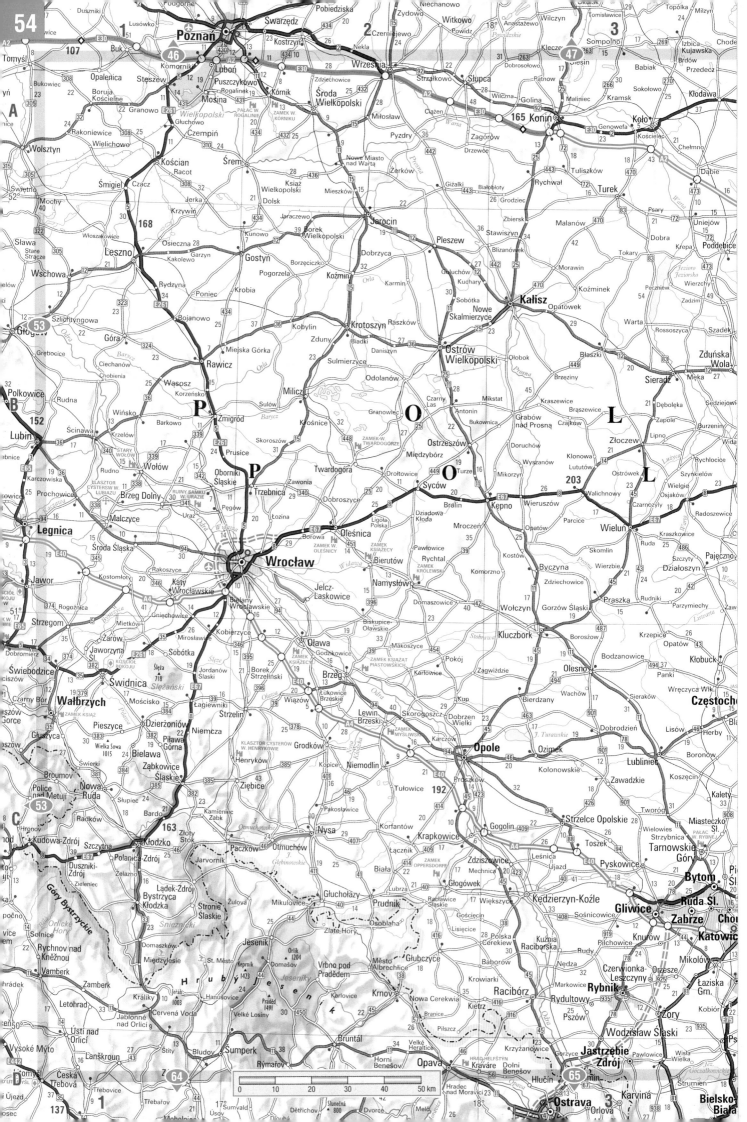

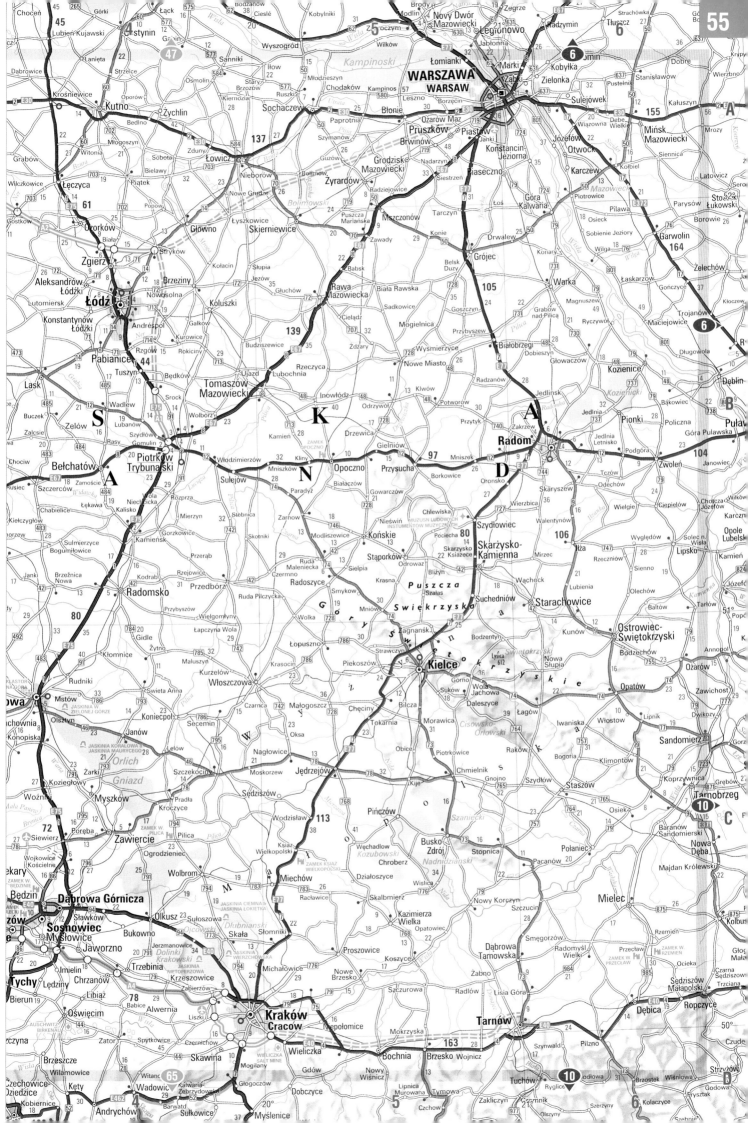

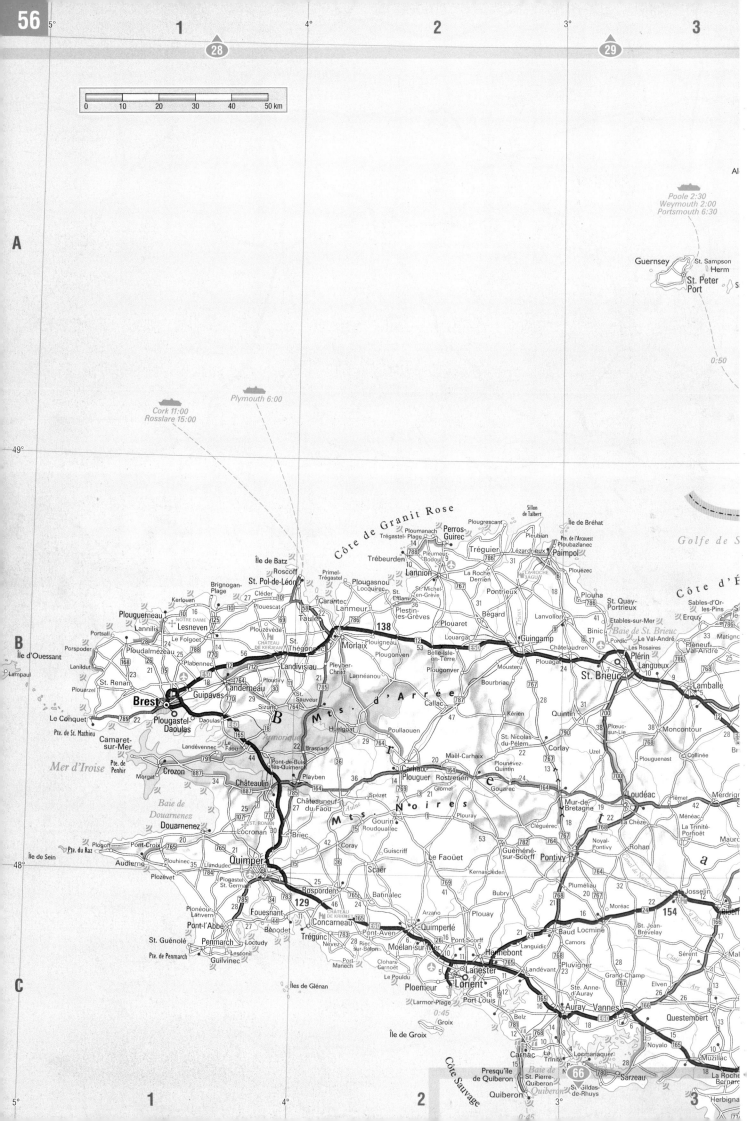

5°   1   4°   2   3°   3

28   29

0   10   20   30   40   50 km

Poole 2:30
Weymouth 2:00
Portsmouth 6:30

A

Guernsey   St. Sampson
Herm
St. Peter
Port   St.

0:50

Plymouth 6:00

Cork 11:00
Rosslare 15:00

49°

0:50

Côte de Granit Rose
Plougrescant   Sillon
de Talbert
Ploumanach-   Île de Bréhat
Plage   Perros-
Trégastel-   Guirec
Plage   Pleubian   Pte. de l'Arcouest   Golfe de S
14   Pleumeur-   Tréguier   Ploubazlanec
Île de Batz   Bodou   786   Lézardrieux   Paimpol
Roscoff   St.   31   Plouézec   6
Primel-   Trébeurden   Michel-   785   LA ROCHE
Brignogan-   St. Pol-de-Léon   Trégastel   Plougasnou   en-Grève   JAGU
Plage   Carantec   Locquirec   788   Plo-   788   Plouha   Côte d'É
Kerlouan   Cléder   58   Lanmeur   St.   36   Pontrieux   Louet   18   786   St. Quay-   Sables-d'Or-
Plouguerneau   Plouescat   22   Taulé   Plestin-   Effiam   Bégard   Lanvollon   Portrieux   les-Pins
10   16   69   les-Grèves   10   786   9   Binic   Etables-sur-Mer   Erquy
Lannilis   125   Plouzévédé   786   Plouaret   31   Guingamp   6   17   786
Lesneven   Plouédern   138   Belle-Isle-   E50   Châtelaudren   Pordic   Le Val-André   Pléneuf-   Matign
Portsall   14   Le Folgoet   St.   Morlaix   53   en-Terre   Mousteru   Plouagat   24   St. Brieuc   Val-André   768
Île d'Ouessant   Lannilis   788   770   Thégonnec   Plouigneau   Belle-Isle-   Bourbriac   Plérin   768   768
Porspoder   26   Plabennec   712   Landivisiau   Plougonven   Plounérin   St. Nicolas   Langueux   Lamballe
Ploudalmézeau   25   23   21   15   Ploudiry   11   Pleyber-   Lannéanou   du-Pélem   767   10   9   Quintin   31
Lanildut   168   St. Renan   764   Landerneau   30   Christ   785   Bourbriac   790   Corlay   Moncontour   28
Lampaul   22   789   Guipavas   770   29   Sizun   764   d'Arrée   Mts.   Callac   47   Ploeuc-   38   767   Plouguenast   Colliée   Br
Le Conquet   Brest   Plougastel   E60   Landévennec   44   Pont-de-Buis   36   Huelgoat   Poullaouen   Maël-Carhaix   sur-Lie   768   768   28
Plouzel   22   Daoulas   165   lès-Quimerch   Brasparts   29   764   20   Plounévez-   767   13   Uzel   Loudéac   Mérdrig
Pte. de St. Mathieu   Le Faou   791   Playben   36   Carhaix   Quintin   700   Piémet   42
Camaret-   Armorique   Quimerch   785   Châteauneuf-   14   Plouguer   Rostrenen   164   Mur-de-   19
sur-Mer   Landévennec   Châteaulin   du-Faou   Spézet   769   21   Gouarec   Bretagne   La Chèze   La Trinité-
Mer d'Iroise   Pte. de   887   887   164   27   Aune   Noires   Glomel   1064   Cléguérec   18   22   Porhoët   Mauro
Penhir   Morgat   34   St. Ronan   770   Gourin   Mts.   53   Guémené-   782   764   767   Rohan   Ménéac
Crozon   Briec   15   Roudouallec   Pontivy   Noyal-   Josselin
Baie de   107   Locronan   42   Scaër   Guiscriff   Le Faouët   sur-Scorff   Pivy   Pontivy   768   20   22   154
Douarnenez   Plogoff   25   Pont-Croix   765   21   Coray   769   Kernascléden   Bubry   767   Moréac   St. Jean-   166
Pte. du Raz   765   Quimper   15   Scaër   41   Arzano   Plouay   165   Locminé   Brévelay   17
Île de Sein   Audierne   Plouhinec   35   Llandudec   Rosporden   765   Bannalec   769   Landévant   24   Camors   Sérent   Mal
48°   Plozévet   784   129   46   24   Quimperlé   Pont-Scorff   23   Pluvigner   Grand-Champ   Elven
Plonéour-   785   Fouesnant   Concarneau   E60   Baud   765   Ste. Anne-   767   26   Questember
Lanvern   Pont-l'Abbé   44   165   Pont-Aven   Hennebont   d'Auray   Auray   Vannes
St. Guénolé   Penmarch   Bénodet   Trégunc   783   Moëlan-sur-Mer   Languidic   Landévant   166   13
Guilvinec   Loctudy   Nevez   Riec-   Clohars-   Lanester   11   Belz   768   14   6   Noyalo   165
Pte. de Penmarch   Lesconil   sur-Belon   Carnoët   Lorient   12   768   10   Muzillac
Port   Le Pouldu   Ploemeur   Port Louis   Larmor-Plage   Carnac   28   La Roche
Îles de Glénan   Manech   Groix   Locmariaquer   Bernar
C   Île de Groix   0:45   Presqu'île   66   780   Sarzeau   Herbigna
de Quiberon   St. Pierre-   St. Gildas-
Côte Sauvage   Quiberon   Quiberon   de-Rhuys
0:45

5°   1   4°   2   3°   3

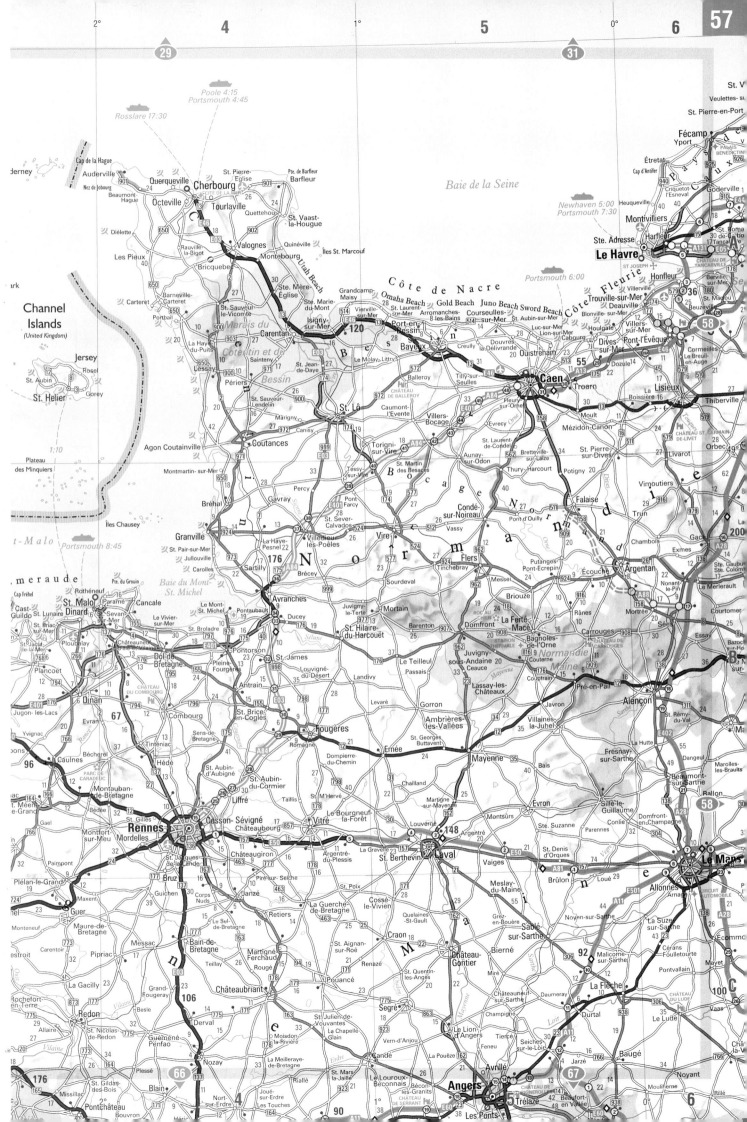

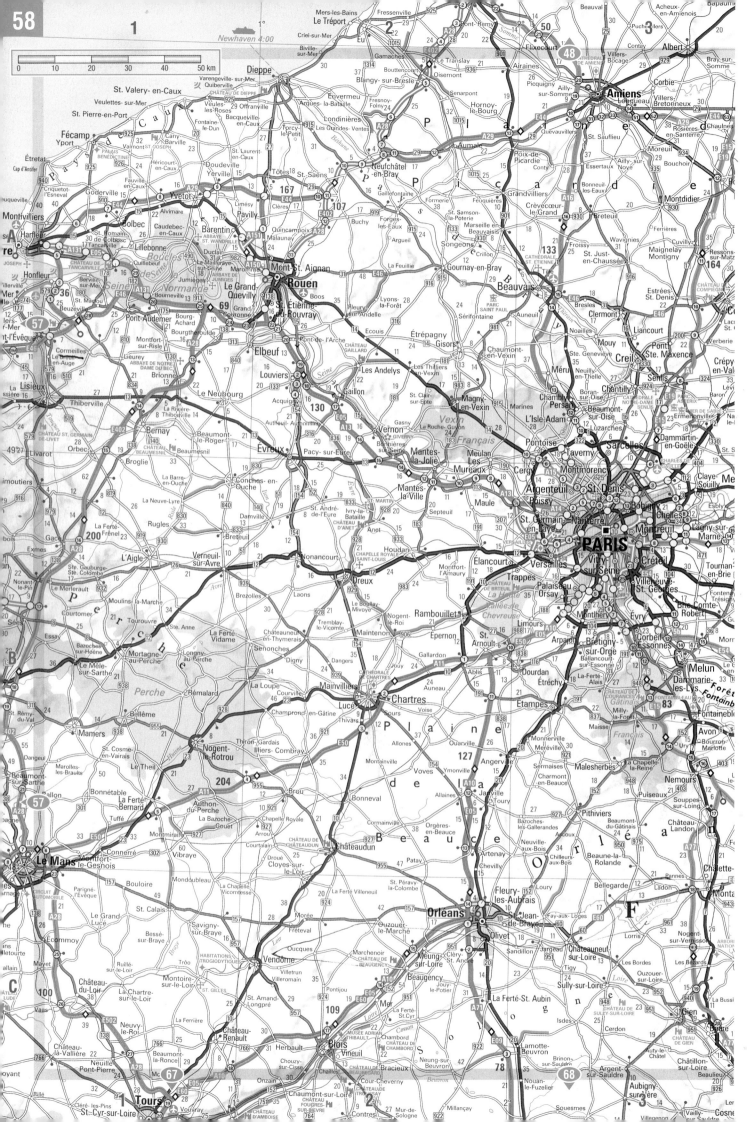

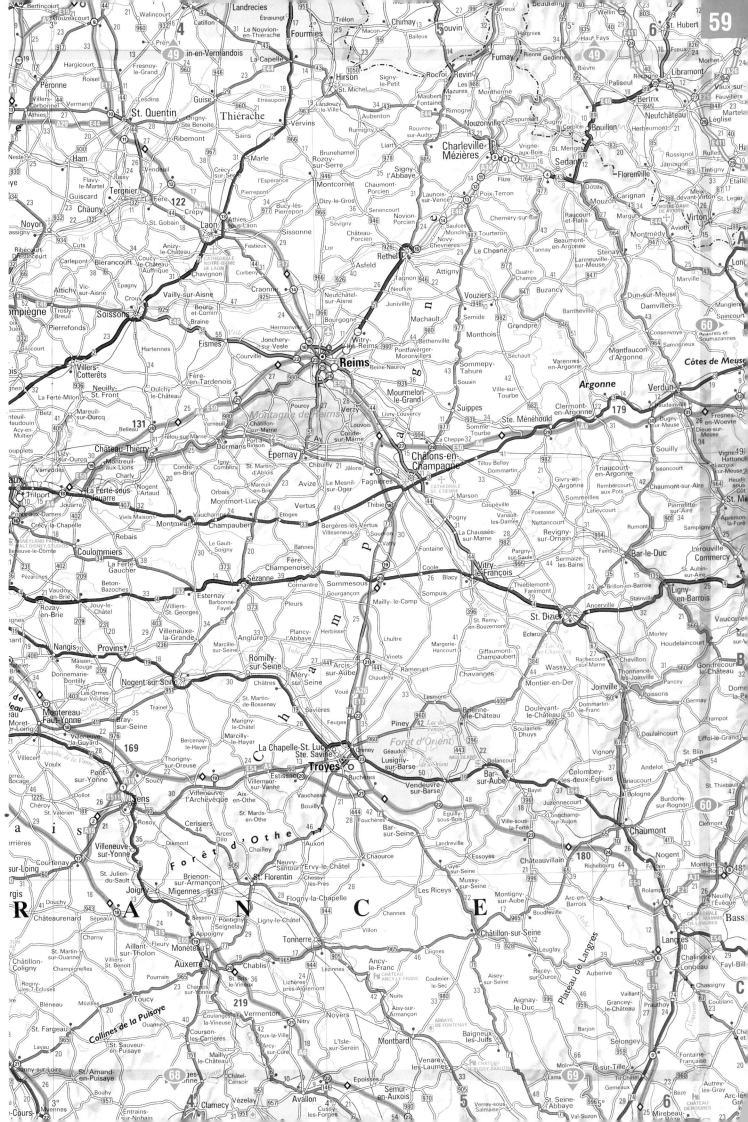

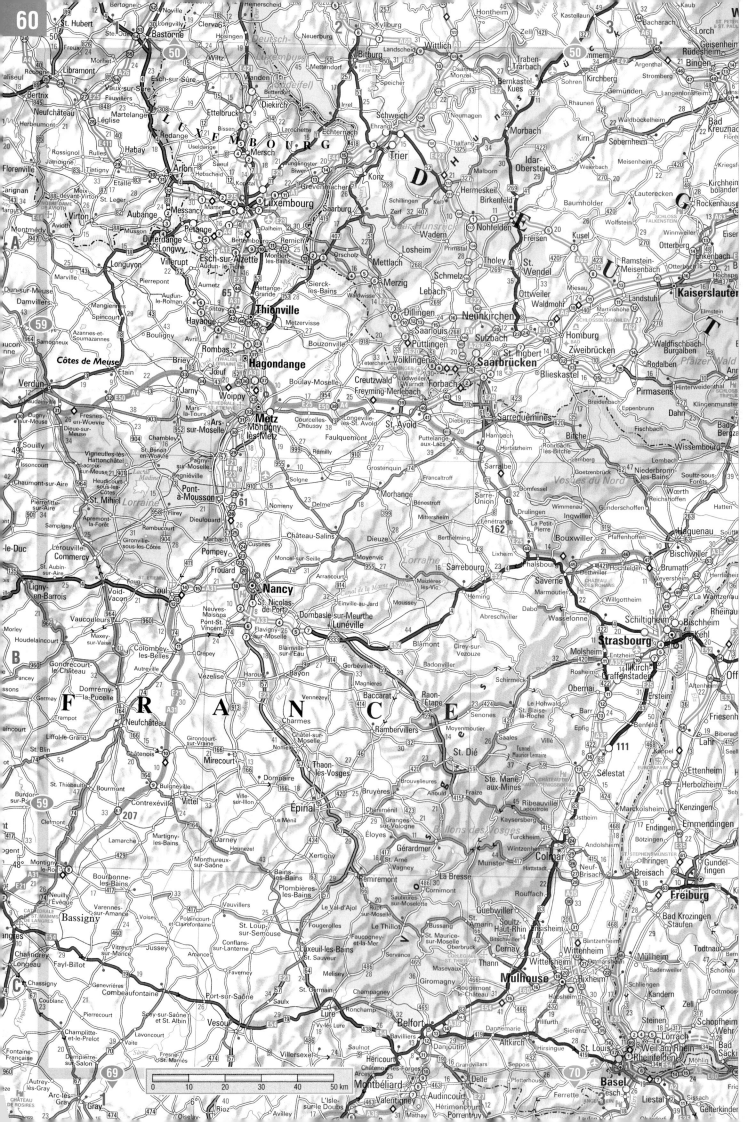

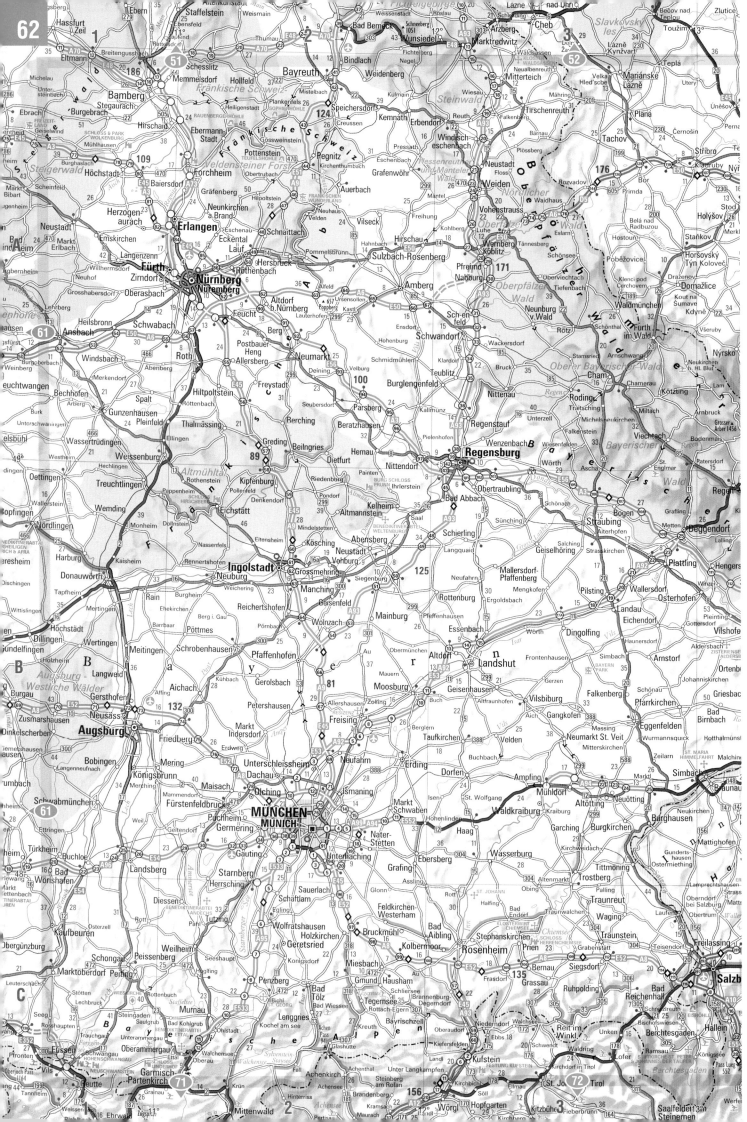

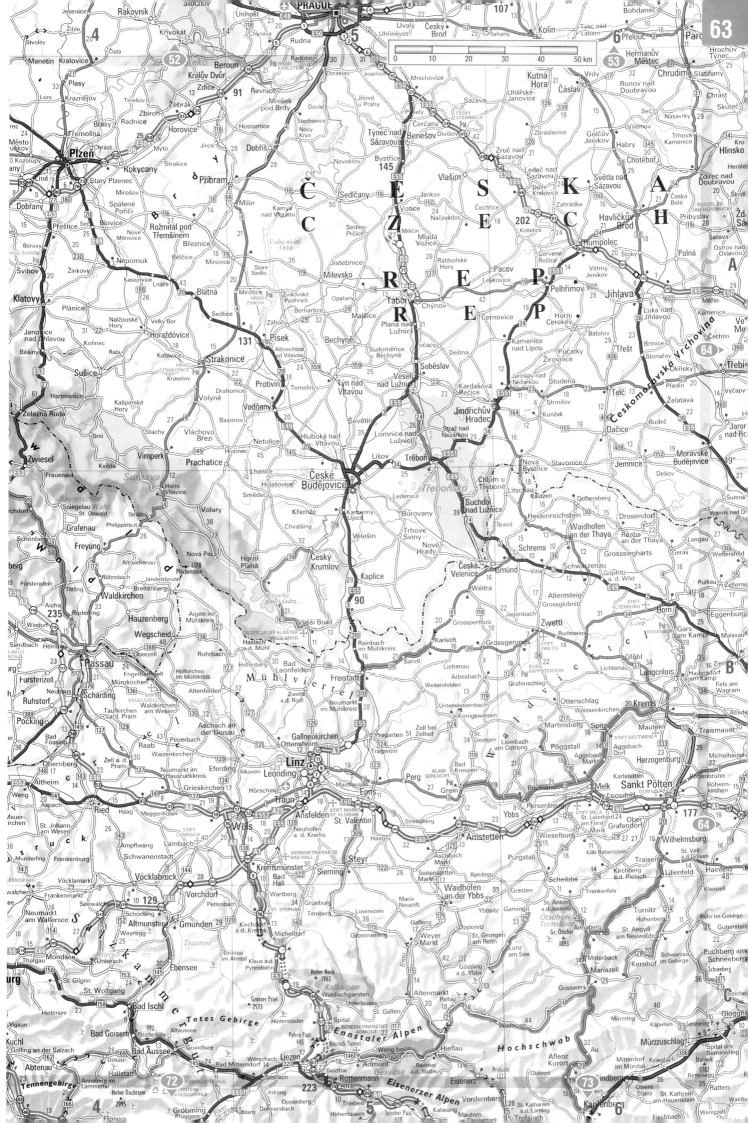

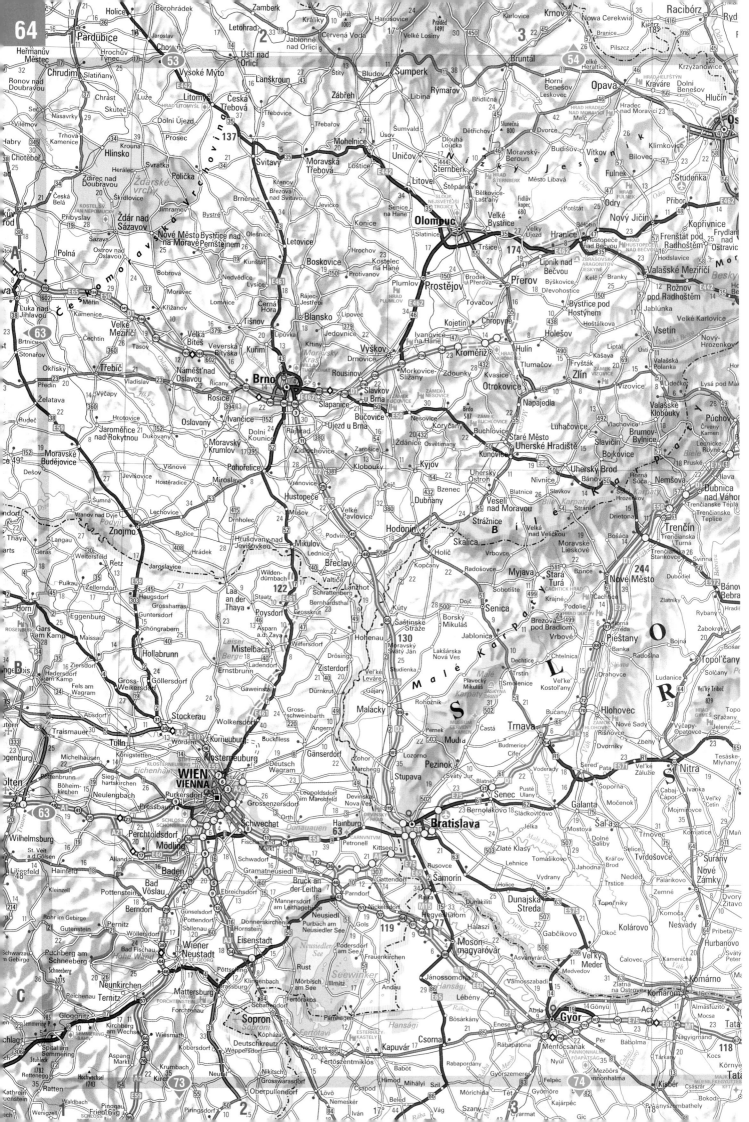

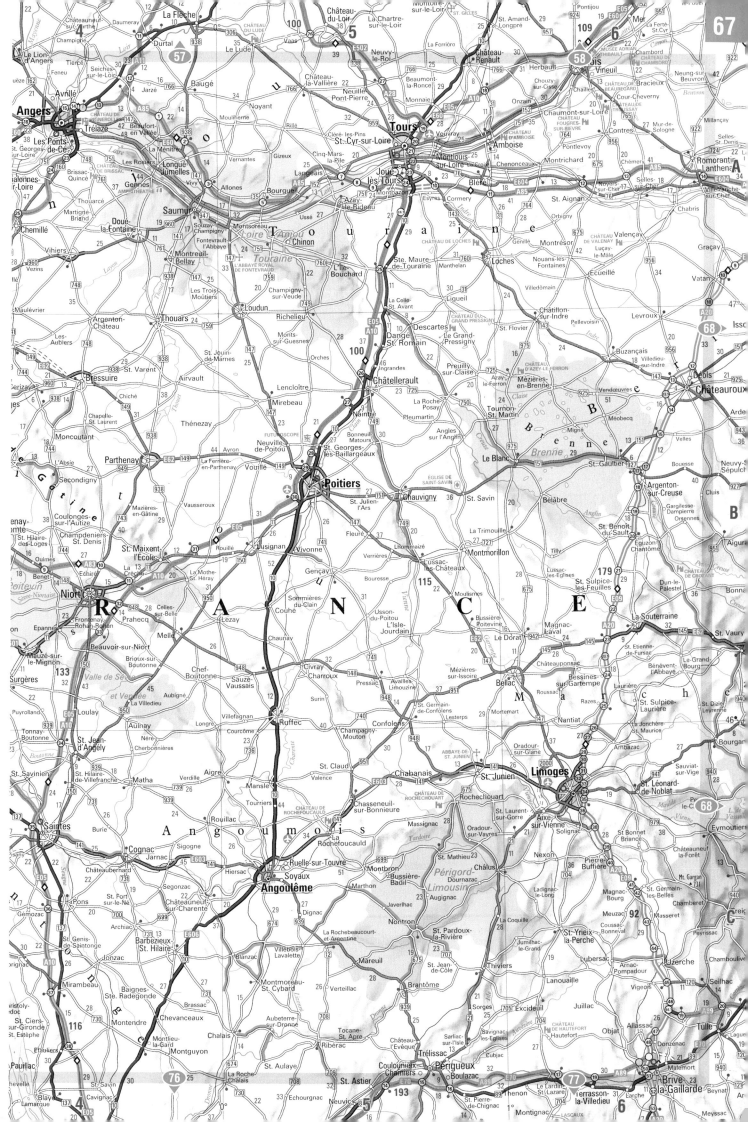

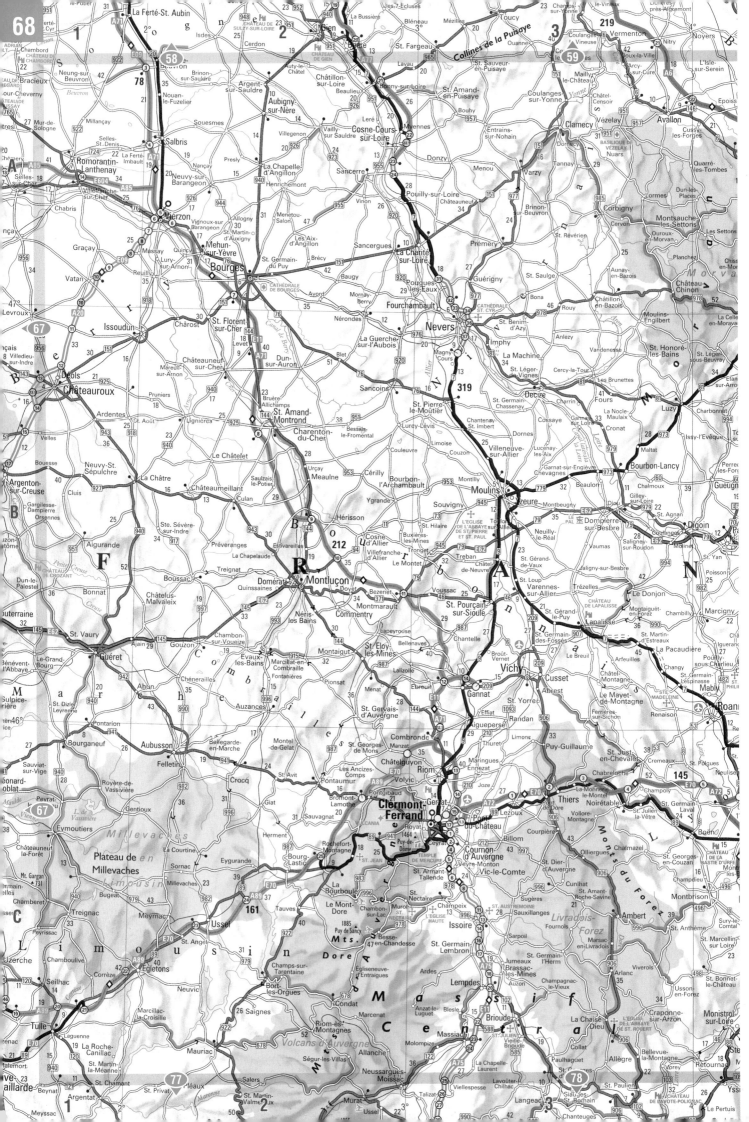

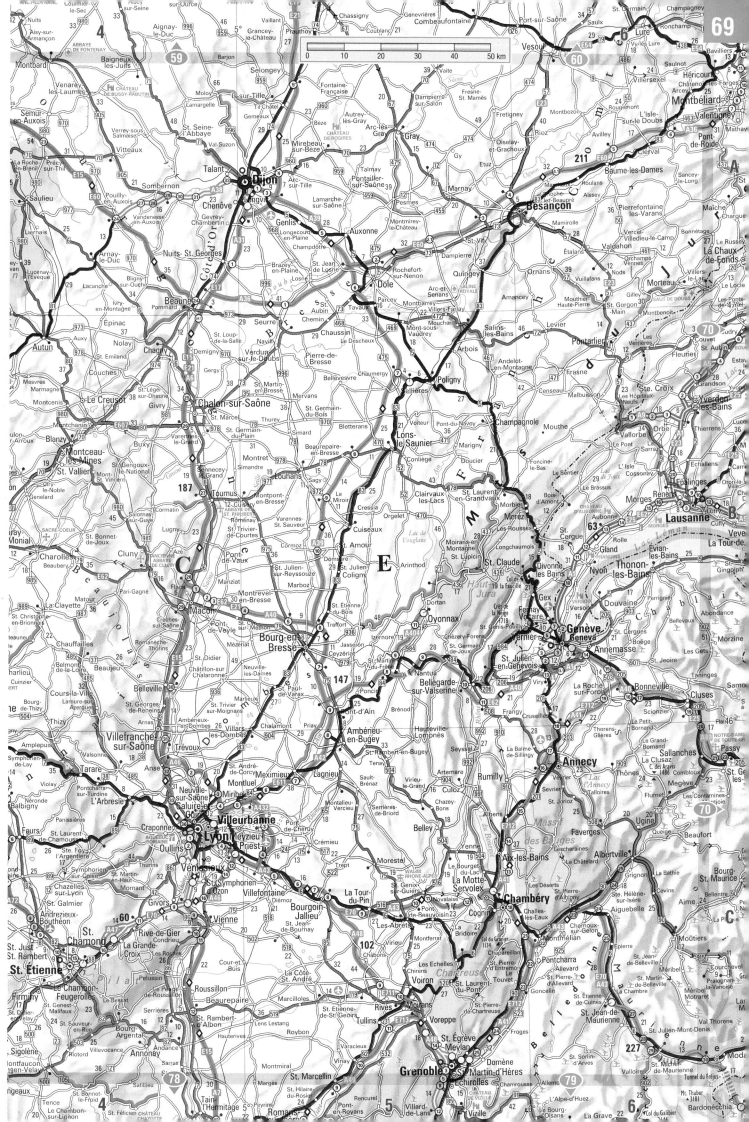

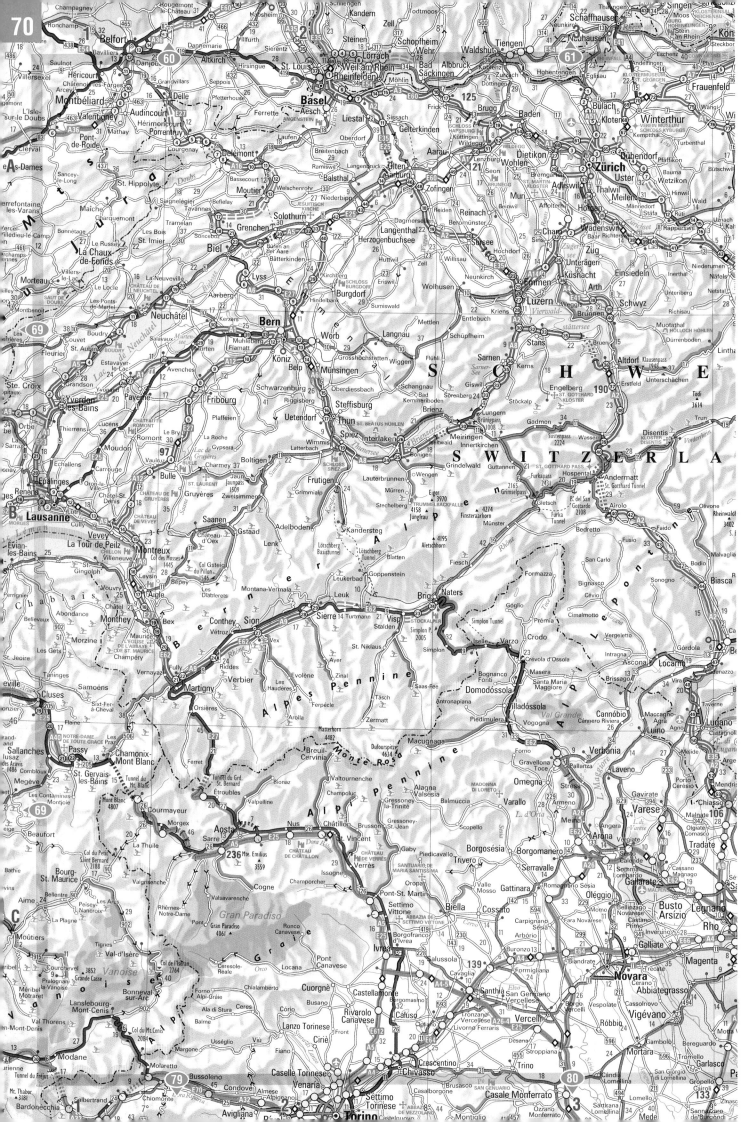

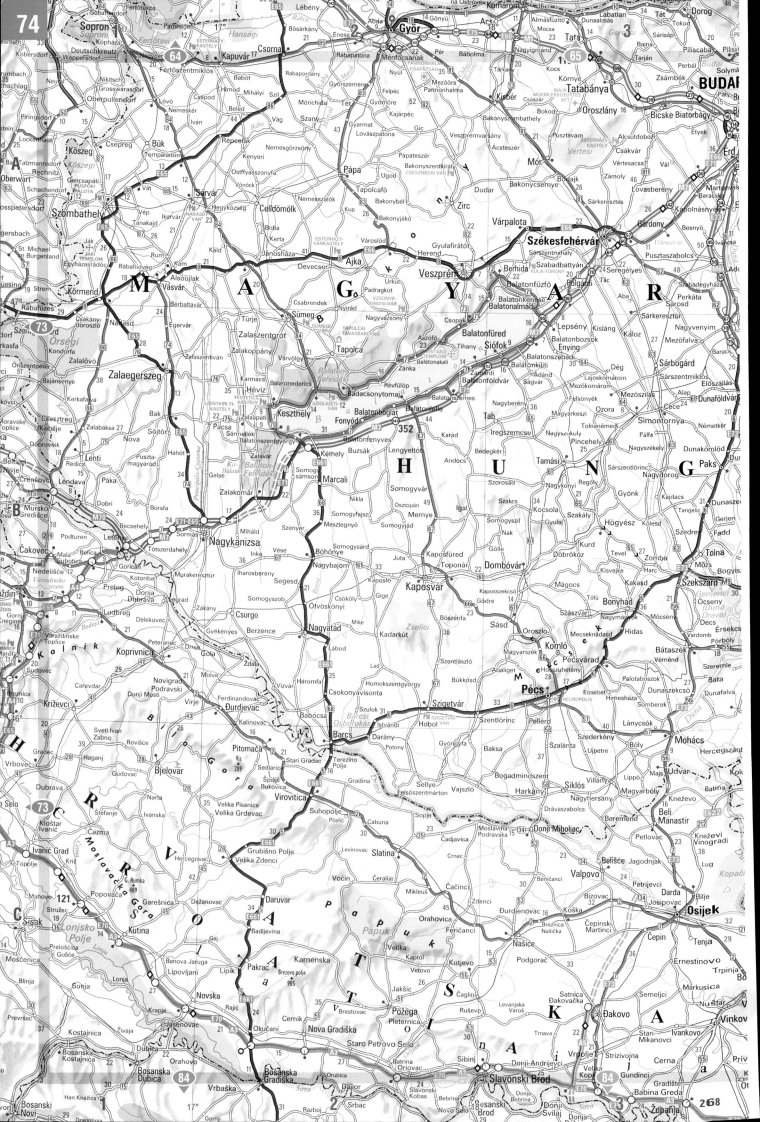

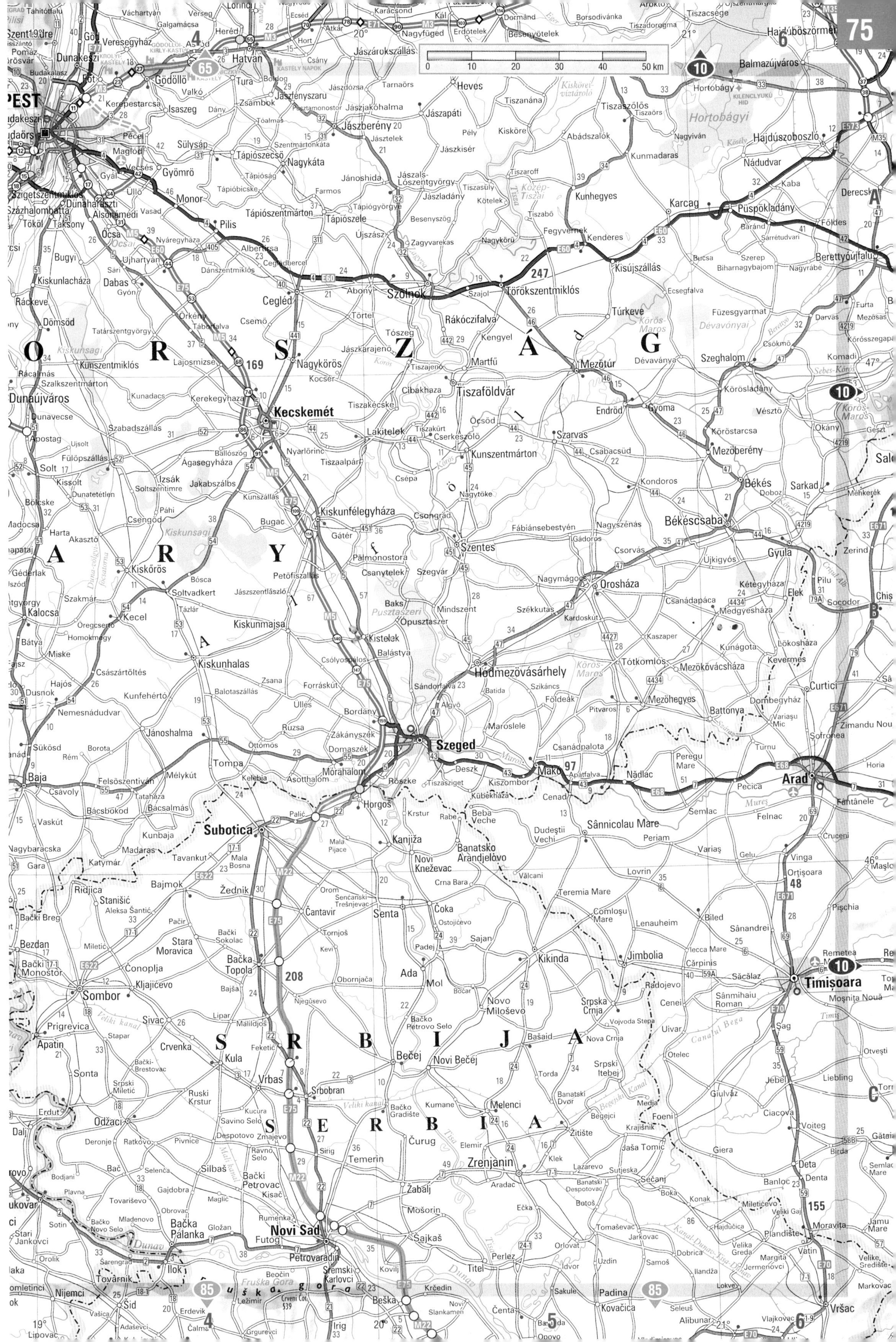

O R S Z Á G

A R Y

S R B I J A

S E R B I A

PEST
Budakalász
Dunakeszi
Göd
Szentendre
Veresegyház
Váchartyán
Galgamácsa
Heréd
Hatvan
Gödöllő
Kerepestarcsa
Isaszeg
Dány
Zsámbok
Tura
Boldog
Valkó
Jászfényszaru
Jászberény
Nagykáta
Tápiószecső
Szentmártonkáta
Tápiószele
Tápiószentmárton
Újszász
Zagyvarekas
Szolnok
Abony
Cegléd
Törtel
Tószeg
Jászkarajenő
Kocsér
Nagykőrös
Lajosmizse
Kecskemét
Nyárlőrinc
Tiszaalpár
Lakitelek
Tiszakécske
Cibakháza
Tiszaföldvár
Martfű
Mezőtúr
Túrkeve
Kisújszállás
Karcag
Kunhegyes
Kenderes
Fegyvernek
Törökszentmiklós
Rákóczifalva
Szajol

Budaörs
Szigetszentmiklós
Dunaharaszti
Alsónémedi
Gyál
Vecsés
Üllő
Monor
Pilis
Ócsa
Nyáregyháza
Albertirsa
Ceglédbercel
Dabas
Gyón
Örkény
Táborfalva
Csemő
Nagykáta

Dunaújváros
Dunavecse
Apostag
Szabadszállás
Kunszentmiklós
Szalkszentmárton
Solt
Fülöpszállás
Soltszentimre
Izsák
Ágasegyháza
Ballószög
Kunszállás
Kiskunfélegyháza
Csongrád
Szentes
Szegvár
Mindszent
Hódmezővásárhely
Orosháza
Nagymágocs
Székkutas
Tótkomlós
Mezőhegyes
Battonya
Mezőkovácsháza
Csanádpalota
Makó
Szeged
Deszk
Kiszombor
Röszke
Mórahalom
Ásotthalom
Horgos
Subotica
Palić
Kanjiža
Senta
Ada
Mol
Bečej
Novi Bečej
Kikinda
Zrenjanin
Novi Sad
Petrovaradin

Kalocsa
Kecel
Kiskőrös
Soltvadkert
Kiskunmajsa
Kiskunhalas
Jánoshalma
Tompa
Baja
Mélykút
Bácsalmás
Madaras
Sombor
Apatin
Odžaci
Kula
Vrbas
Srbobran
Bačka Palanka
Bačka Topola
Bajmok

Hortobágy
Balmazújváros
Nádudvar
Hajdúszoboszló
Püspökladány
Kaba
Berettyóújfalu
Derecske
Komádi
Szeghalom
Gyoma
Endrőd
Szarvas
Kunszentmárton
Csabacsüd
Kondoros
Békés
Mezőberény
Békéscsaba
Gyula
Elek
Sarkad
Mezőkovácsháza
Kevermes
Arad
Pecica
Nădlac
Sânnicolau Mare
Periam
Jimbolia
Timişoara
Biled
Sânandrei

Hortobágyi

Dunav
Tisza
Duna
Körös
Maros
Mureş
Canalul Bega
Veliki kanal

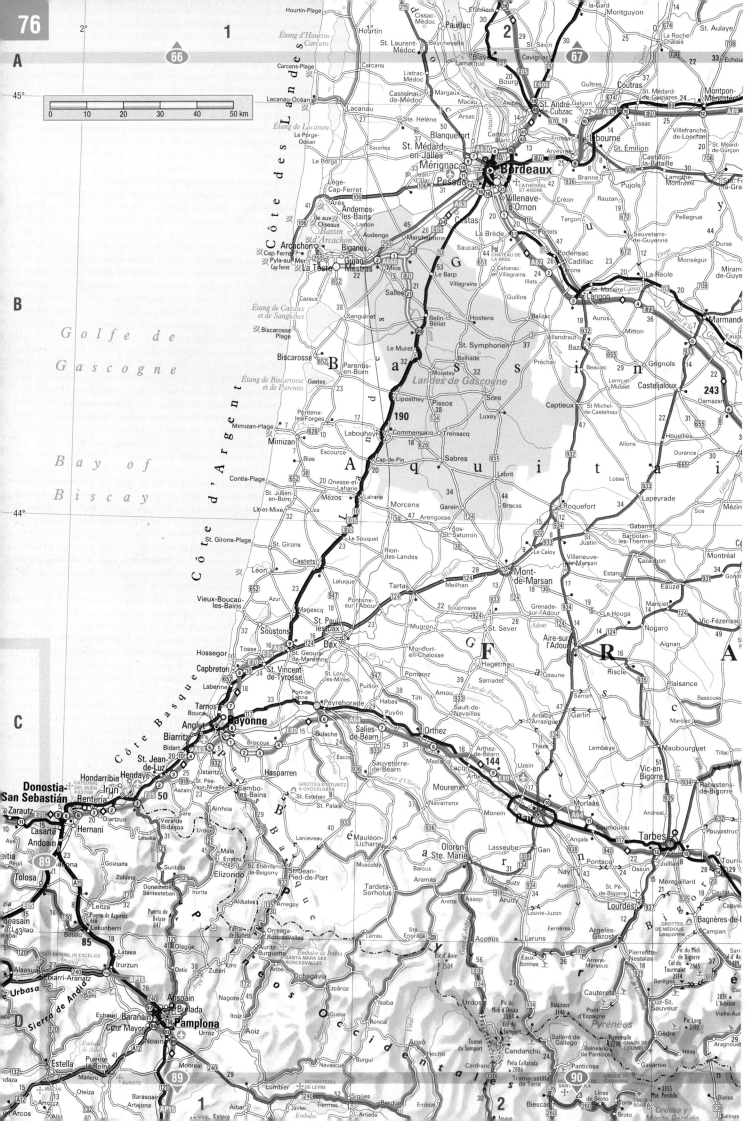

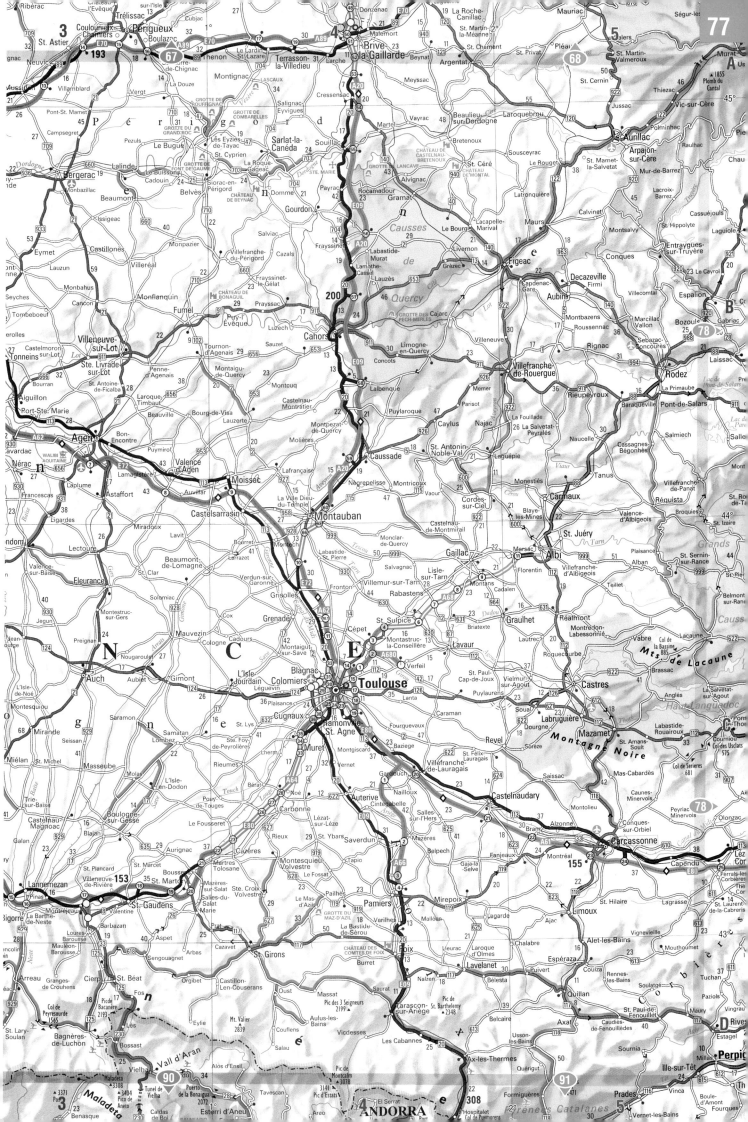

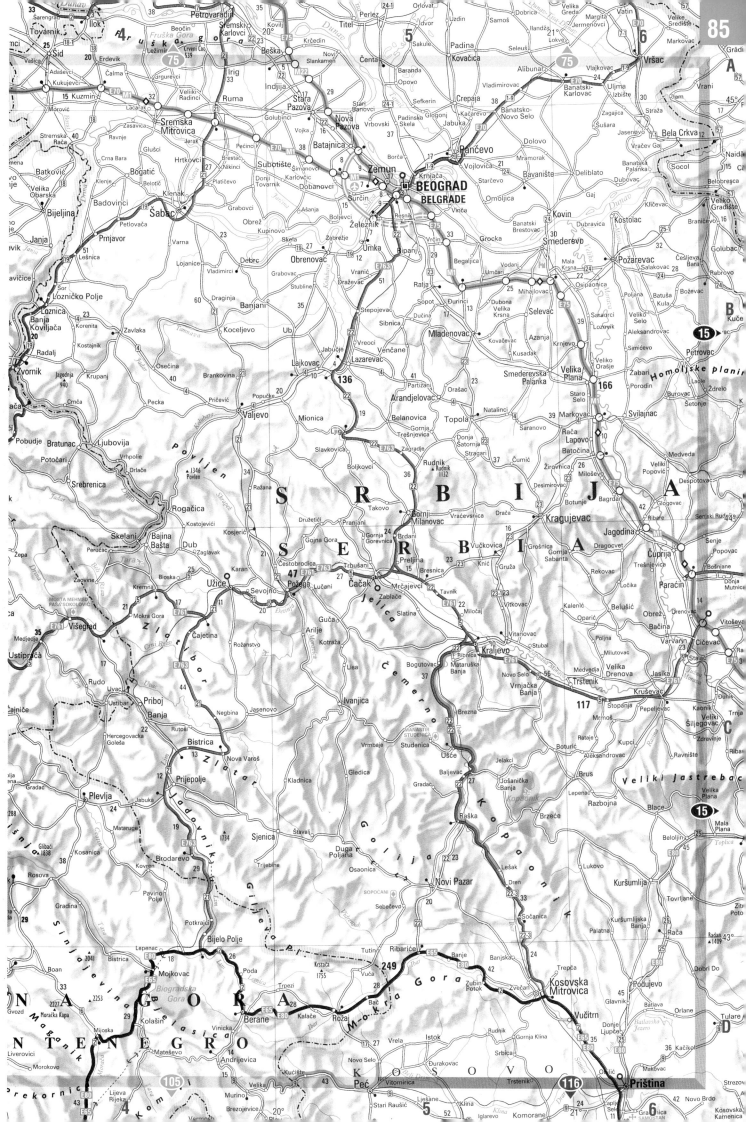

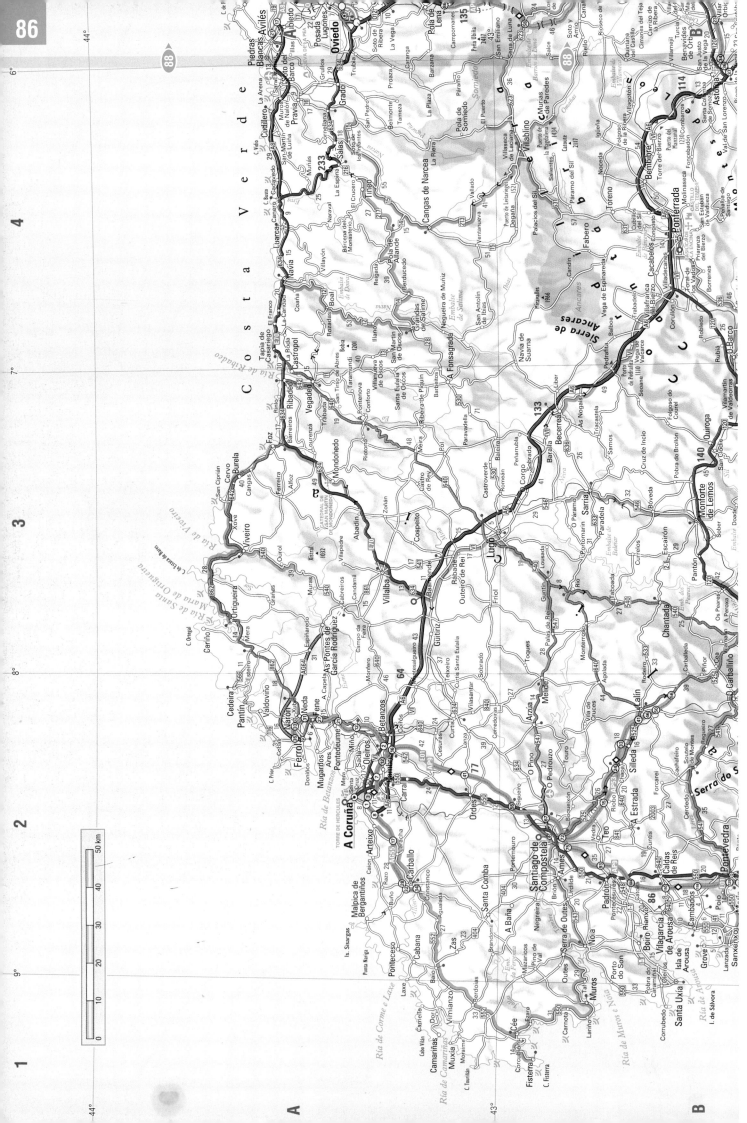

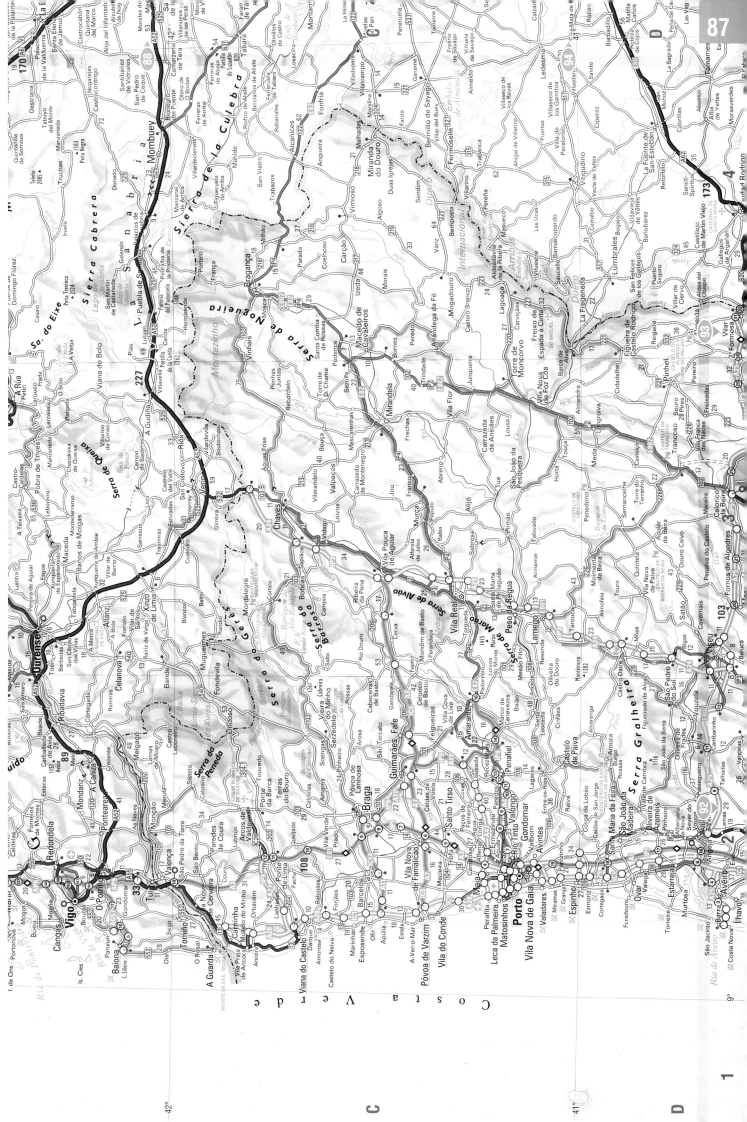

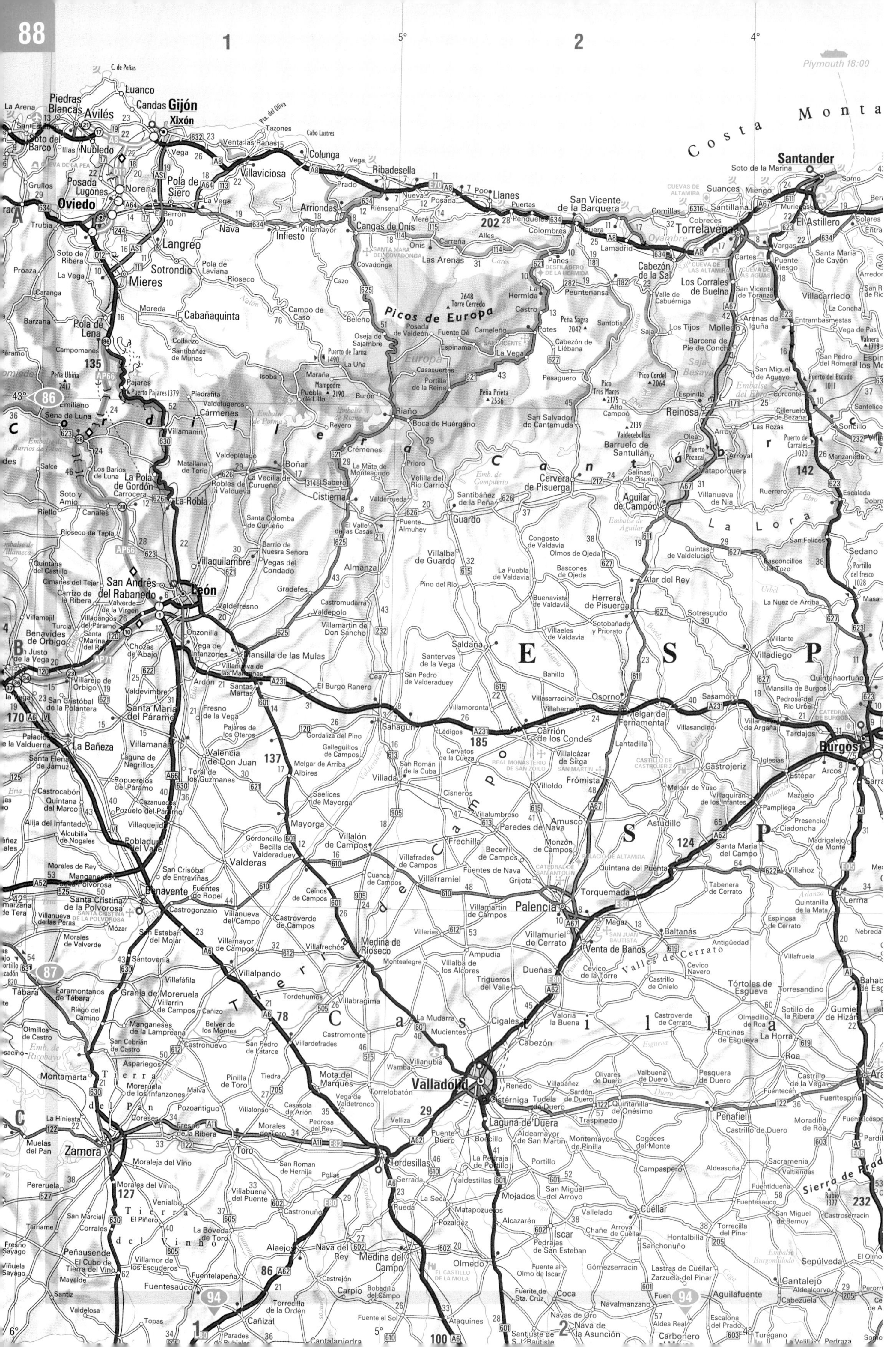

1 5° 2 4°

Plymouth 18:00

Costa Monta

C. de Peñas
La Arena
Piedras Blancas
Luanco Candás **Gijón**
Avilés **Xixón**
Santander
Soto de la Marina
Soto del Barco Illas Nubledo Vega Venta-las-Ranas Tazones Cabo Lastres Suances Miengo
Posada Lugones Noreña Pola de Siero Villaviciosa Colunga Ribadesella Comillas Santillana El Astillero
Oviedo La Vega Nava Arriondas Prado Llanes San Vicente de la Barquera Torrelavega Solares
Langreo El Berrón Infiesto Villamayor Cangas de Onís Posada Puertas Penduelas Colombres Cabezón de la Sal Los Corrales de Buelna Villacarriedo
Sotrondio Pola de Laviana Rioseco Cazo Covadonga Las Arenas Carreña Onís Alles Panés Peuntenansa Valle de Cabuérniga Arenas de Iguña
Mieres Moreda Cabañaquinta Campo de Caso Beleño **Picos de Europa** Castro La Hermida Saja Los Tijos Molledo Vega de Pas
Pola de Lena Collanzo Santibáñez de Murias Oseja de Sajambre Fuente Dé Peña Sagra Cabezón de Liébana Barcena de Pie de Concha San Miguel de Aguayo Puerto del Escudo
135 Campomanes Torre Cerredo 2648 Posada de Valdeón Potes 2042 La Vega Reinosa Corconte
Peña Ubiña 2417 Pajares Puerto Pajares 1379 Piedrafita Maraña Mampodre Espinama Pico Cordel 2064 Embalse del Ebro
86 Emiliano Sena de Luna Cármenes Valdelugueros Puebla de Lillo Burón Riaño San Salvador de Cantamuda **142**
Villamanín Embalse de Porma Reyero Boca de Huérgano Barruelo de Santullán Aguilar de Campóo **La Lora**
Matallana de Torío Boñar Crémenes Prioro Cervera de Pisuerga Salinas de Pisuerga Ruerrero
La Pola de Gordón La Vecilla de Curueño Sabero La Mata de Monteagudo Velilla del Río Carrió Santibáñez de la Peña Villanueva de Nia Sedano
La Robla Cistierna Valderrueda Guardo Alar del Rey Quintas de Valdelucio La Nuez de Arriba
Santa Colomba de Curueño El Valle de las Casas Puente Almuhey La Puebla de Valdavia Herrera de Pisuerga Masa
Villaquilambre Barrio de Nuesra Señora Almanza Villalba de Guardo Olmos de Ojeda Sotresgudo
Gradefes Castromudarra Pino del Río Bascones de Ojeda **E S P**
León Valdefresno Valdepolo Villamartín de Don Sancho Saldaña Buenavista de Valdavia Villadiego
San Andrés del Rabanedo Onzonilla Villamoronta Villaeles de Valdavia Quintanaortuño
Valverde de la Virgen Vega de Infanzones Cea Santervas de la Vega Sotobañado y Priorato Mansilla de Burgos **Burgos**
Chozas de Abajo Mansilla de las Mulas San Pedro de Valderaduey Bahíllo Osorno Sasamón Pedrosa del Río Urbel
Ardón Santas Martas El Burgo Ranero Villasarracino Villaherreros Melgar de Fernamental Villasandino Tardajos
Valdevimbre Fresno de la Vega Gordaliza del Pino Villamoronta Carrión de los Condes Arcos
Pajares de los Oteros Sahagún Lédigos **185** Lantadilla Castrojeriz Estépar
170 La Bañeza Valencia de Don Juan Melgar de Arriba **137** Cervatos de la Cueza Villalcázar de Sirga Frómista Melgar de Yuso
Toral de los Guzmanes Albires San Román de la Cuba Villada Villoldo Villanueva de los Infantes
Laguna de Negrillos Saelices de Mayorga Cisneros Villalumbroso Amusco Astudillo Santa María del Campo
Pozuelo del Páramo Mayorga Villalón de Campos Frechilla Paredes de Nava Monzón de Campos **124** Villahoz
Pobladura del Valle Gordoncillo Becilla de Valderaduey Becerril de Campos Quintana del Puente Tabanera de Cerrato Lerma
Valderas Villafrades de Campos Fuentes de Nava Grijota Torquemada Espinosa de Cerrato
Benavente Fuentes de Ropel Cuenca de Campos Villarramiel **Palencia** Magaz Baltanás Antigüedad
Castrogonzalo Villanueva del Campo Castroverde de Campos Villalón Villerías Villamuriel de Cerrato Venta de Baños Valles de Cerrato Villafruela
San Esteban del Molar Villamayor de Campos Villafrechós Medina de Rioseco Ampudia Dueñas Cevico Navero Villafuerte
Villafáfila Villalpando Tordehumos Montealegre Villalba de los Alcores Trigueros del Valle Cevico de la Torre Castrillo de Onielo Nebreda
87 Granja de Moreruela Tierra de Campos Villabrágima La Mudarra Cabezón Valoria la Buena Tórtoles de Esgueva Torresandino
Villarrín de Campos Belver de los Montes Castromonte Mucientes Olmedillo de Roa Gumiel de Hizán
Manganeses de la Lampreana San Pedro de Latarce Villardefrades Villanubla Encinas de Esgueva La Horra
Montamarta Aspariegos Tiedra Mota del Marqués Wamba Olivares de Duero Roa
Moreruela de los Infanzones Malva **Valladolid** Renedo Villabáñez Valbuena de Duero Castrillo de la Vega Fuentespina
Coreses Fresno de la Ribera Pedrosa del Rey Torrelobatón Cigales Tudela de Duero Quintanilla de Onésimo Peñafiel
La Hiniesta Morales de Toro Toro **29** Cistérniga Traspinedo Cogeces del Monte Moradillo de Roa
Zamora Venialbo Vega de Valdetronco Velliza Laguna de Duera Aldeamayor de San Martín Campaspero Aldeasoña
Muelas del Pan Villabuena del Puente Morales de Toro **Tordesillas** Puente Duero Bocigas Montemayor de Pililla Sacramenia Fuentidueña
El Piñero San Román de Hernija Rueda La Seca San Miguel del Arroyo Cuéllar Sierra de Prad
127 Venialbo Villalonso Pollos Mojados Vallelado Cantalejo
Morales del Vino La Bóveda de Toro Castronuño La Pedraja de Portillo Portillo Cogeces del Monte Fuentesaúco
San Marcial El Piñero Alaejos Nava del Rey Medina del Campo Íscar Chañe de Cuéllar Sanchonuño Hontalbilla Lastras de Cuéllar
Peñausende El Cubo de Tierra del Vino **86** Olmedo Fuente el Olmo de Íscar Zarzuela del Pinar
Mayalde Villamor de los Escuderos Bobadilla del Campo Coca Navas de Oro Navalmanzano Aguilafuente Cabezuela
Fuentesaúco Carpio Fuente de Sta. Cruz **94** Escalona del Prado Turégano
94 Torrecilla de la Orden Cantalpino Fuente el Sol Nava de la Asunción Aldea Real Carbonero
1 Cañizal **100** Ataquines Coca Sepúlveda

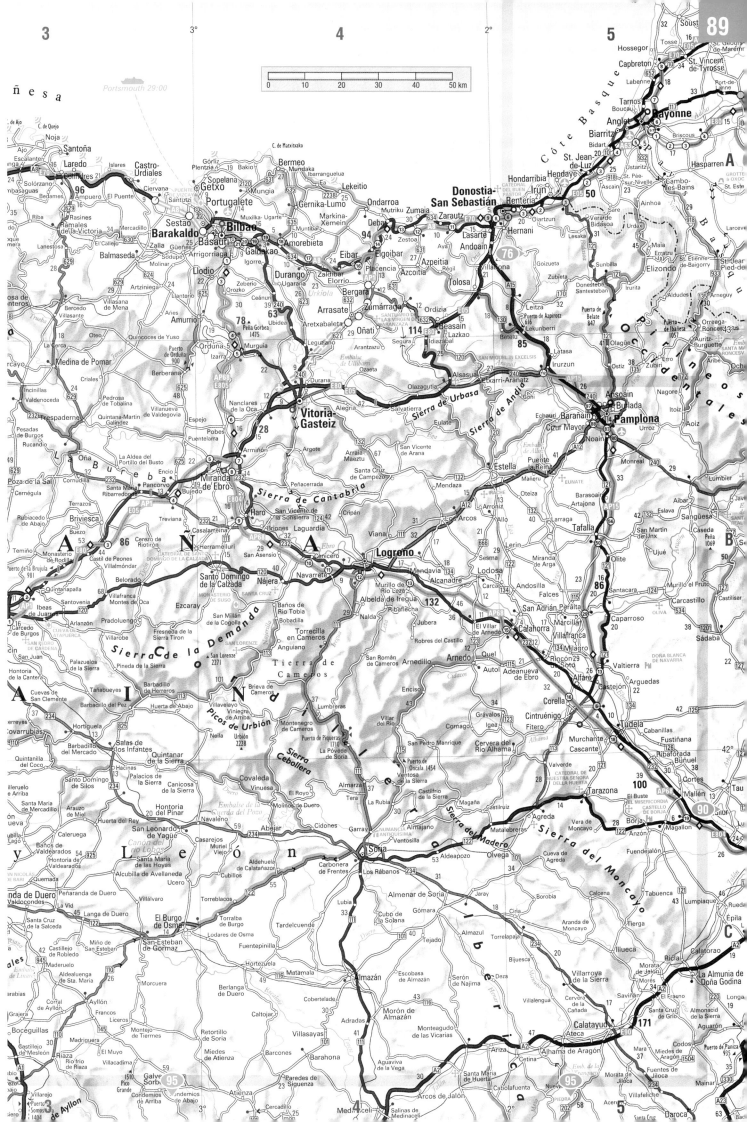

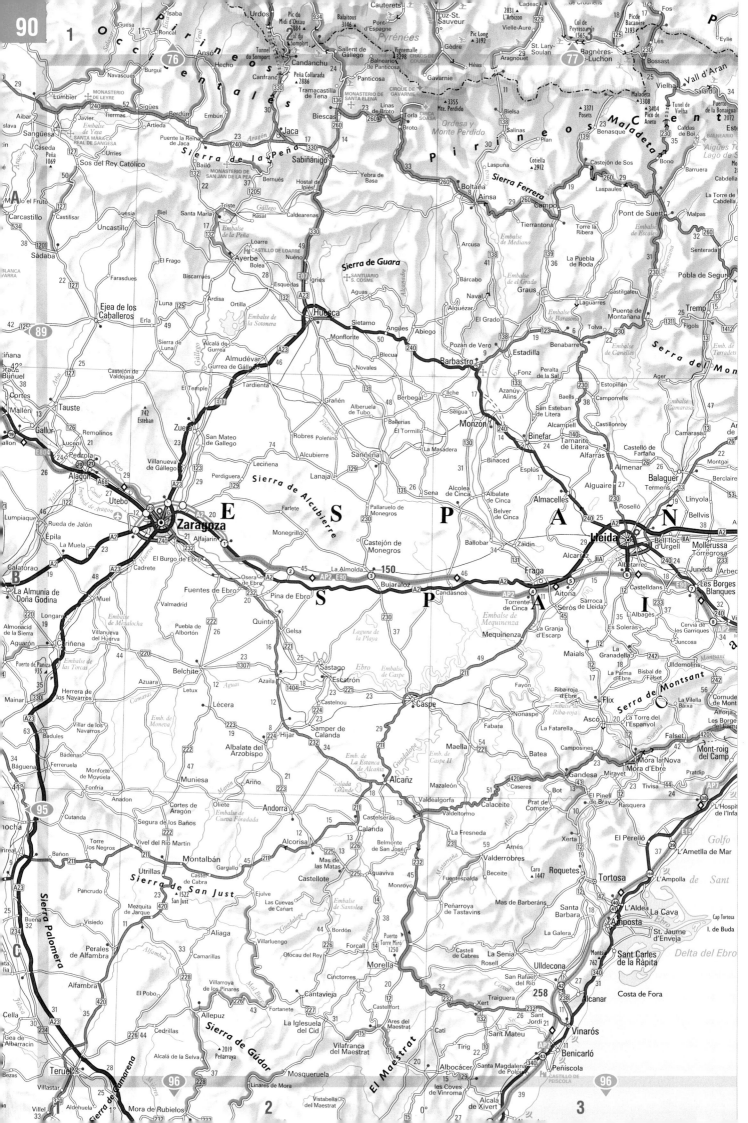

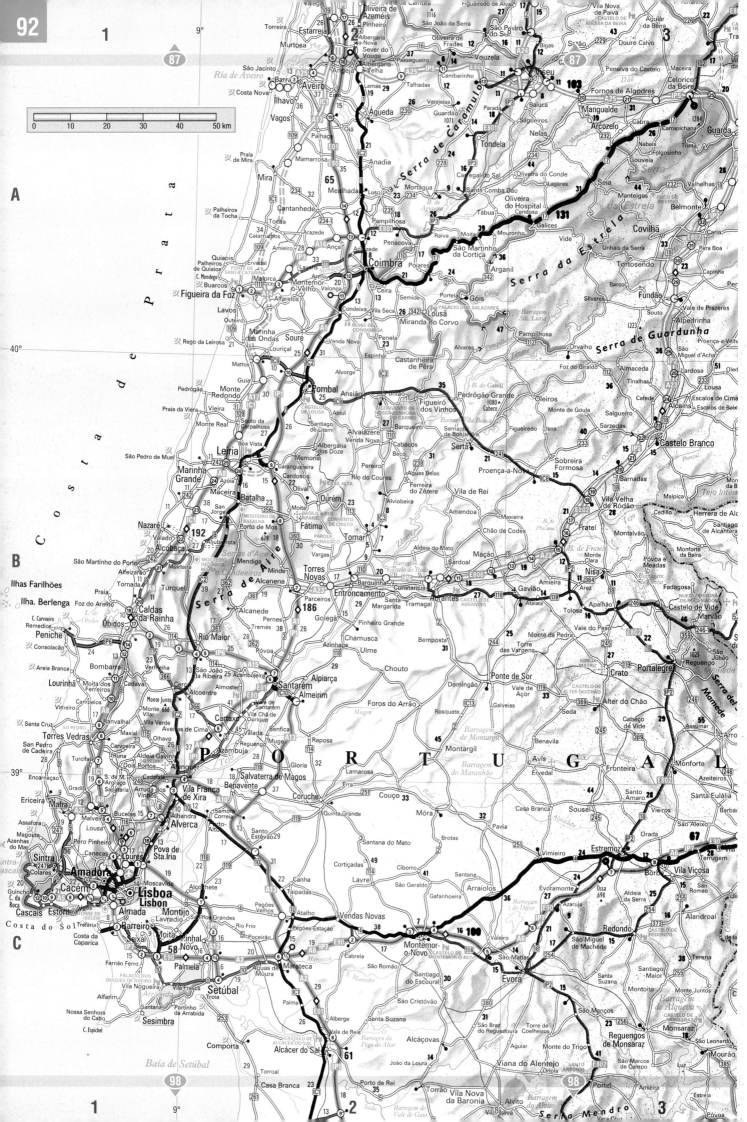

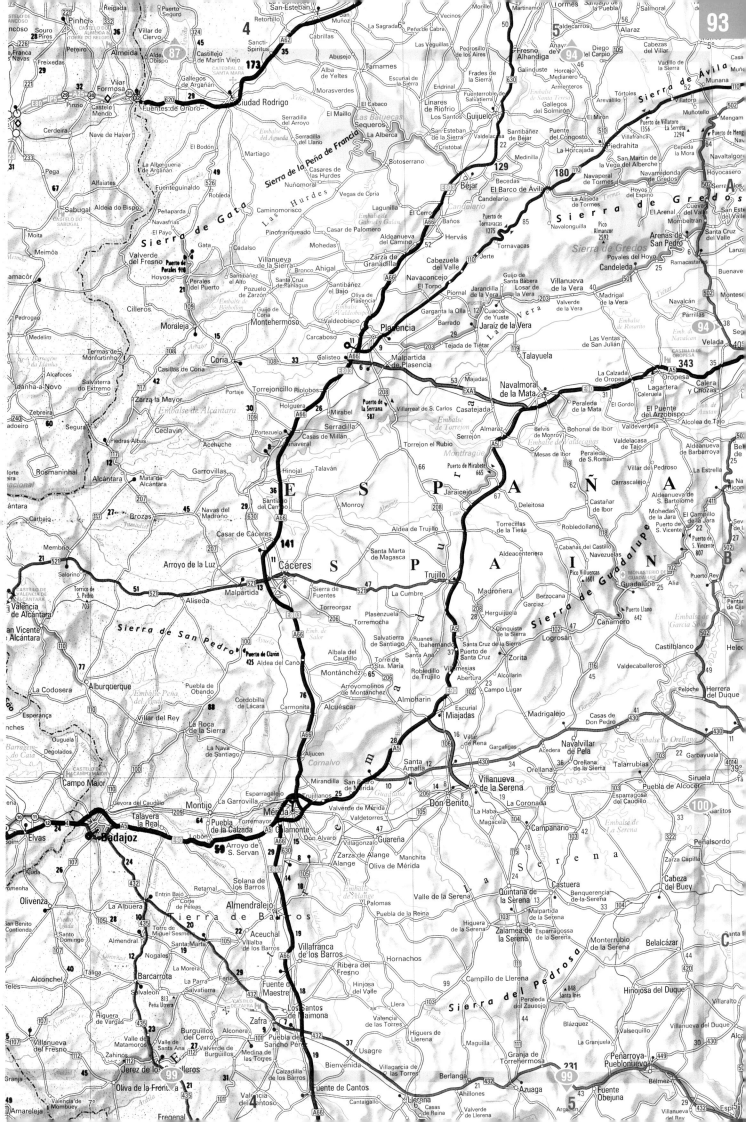

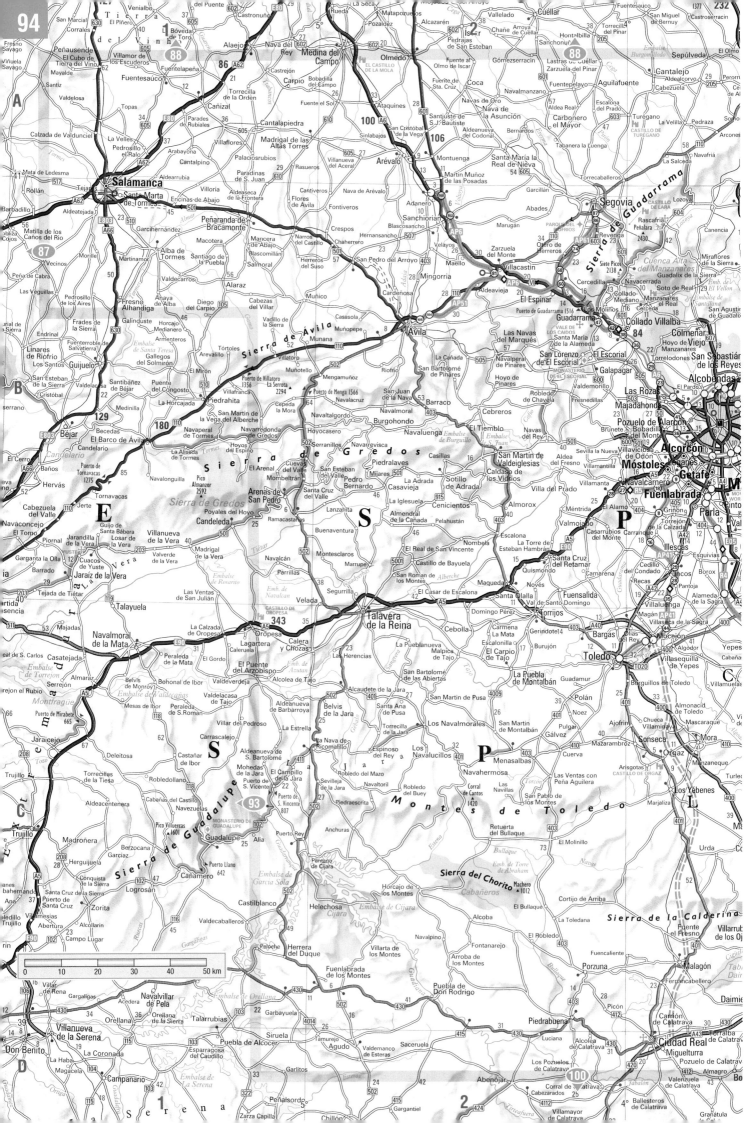

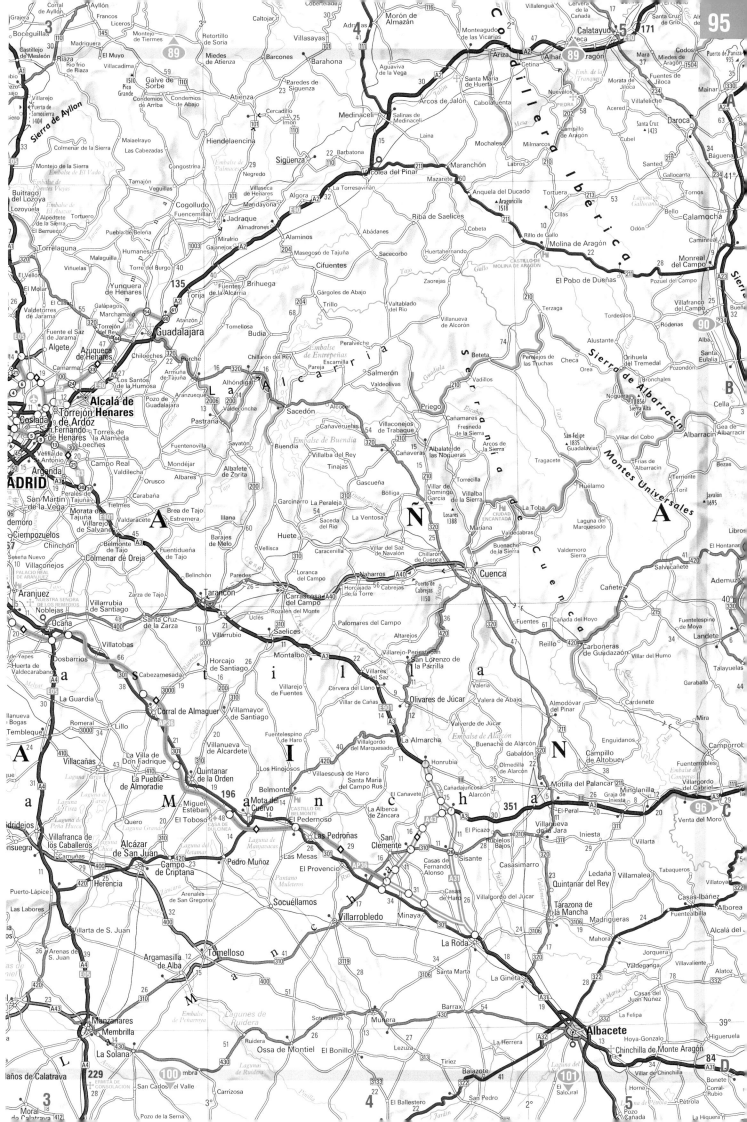

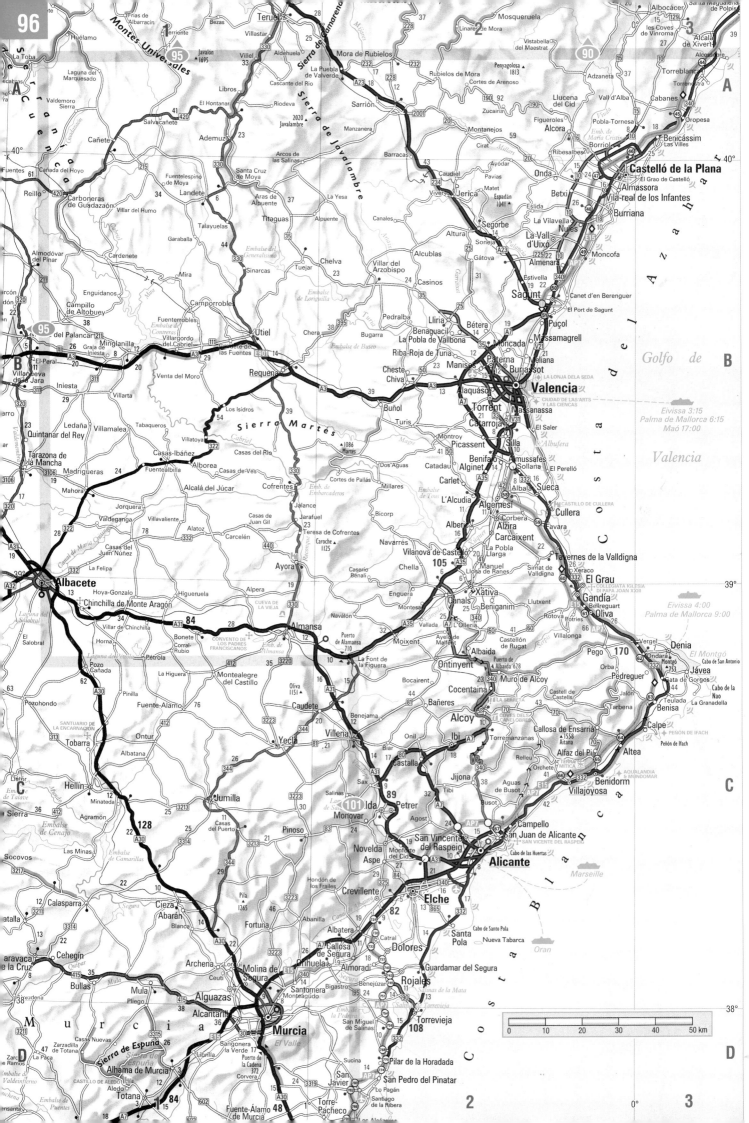

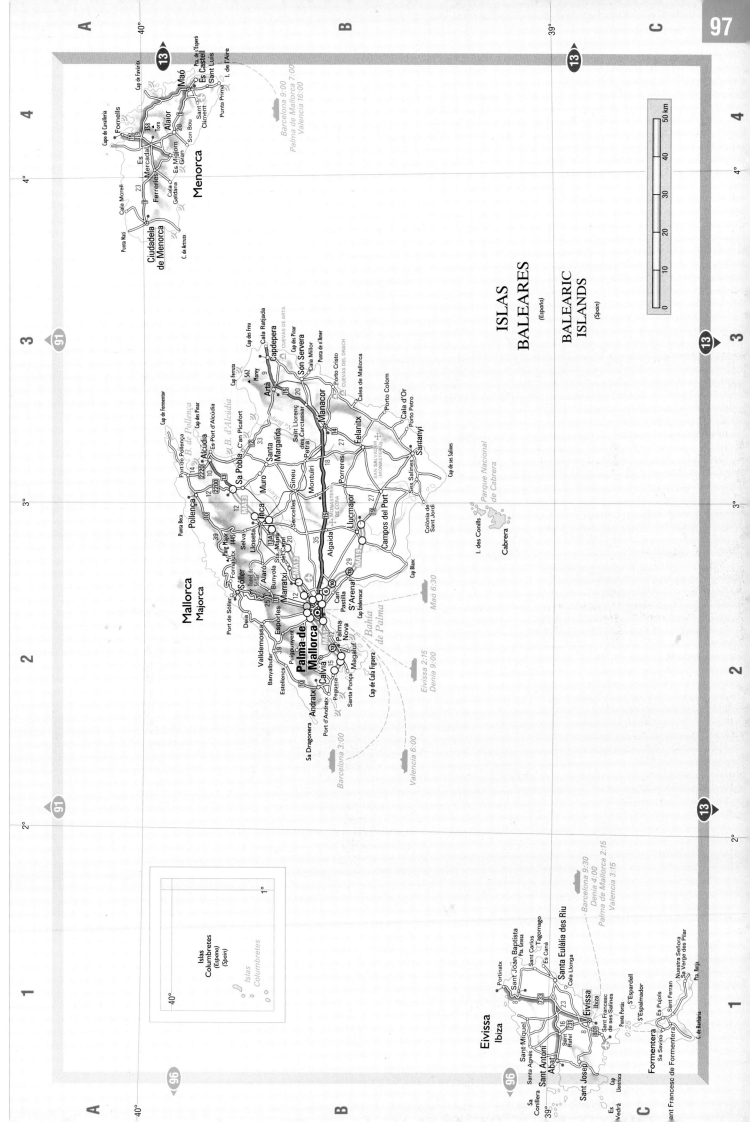

Menorca

Ciudadela de Menorca

Maó
Es Castell
Sant Luis

Fornells
Cap de Cavalleria
Es Mercadal
Alaior
Es Ferreries
Cala Morell
Punta Nati
C. de Artrux

Barcelona 9:00
Palma de Mallorca 7:00
Valencia 16:00

Mallorca
Majorca

Pollença
Alcúdia
Sa Pobla
Inca
Sóller
Palma de Mallorca
Manacor
Artà
Capdepera
Son Servera
Felanitx
Santanyí
Campos del Port
Llucmajor
Algaida
S'Arenal

Cap de Formentor
B. de Pollença
B. d'Alcúdia
Port de Pollença
Port d'Alcúdia
Cala Ratjada
Cap des Freu
Cala Millor
Porto Cristo
CUEVAS DEL DRACH
Cala d'Or
Porto Colom
Porto Petro
Colònia de Sant Jordi
Cap de ses Salines

Bahía de Palma
Andratx
Port d'Andratx
Calvià
Peguera
Magaluf
Cap de Cala Figuera
Cap Enderrocat
Cap Blanc

Valldemossa
Deià
Port de Sóller
Banyalbufar
Estellencs
Puigpunyent

Maó 6:30
Eivissa 2:15
Denia 9:00
Barcelona 3:00
Valencia 6:00

Sa Dragonera

ISLAS BALEARES *(España)*
BALEARIC ISLANDS *(Spain)*

Parque Nacional de Cabrera
I. des Conills
Cabrera

SAN SALVADOR (MONASTERIO)
MONASTERIO DE CURA
Montuïri
Porreres
Ses Salines
Santa Margalida
Muro
Sencelles
Sineu
Santa Maria del Camí
Alaró
Bunyola
Marratxí
Lloseta
Selva

Eivissa
Ibiza

Sant Antoni Abat
Sant Josep
Sant Miquel
Santa Agnès
Sant Rafel
Eivissa
Sant Francesc de ses Salines
Sant Carles
Santa Eulàlia des Riu
Sant Joan Baptista
Portinatx
Cala Llonga
Es Canà
Tagomago
Pta. Grossa
Es Pujols
S'Espardell
S'Espalmador
Punta Portàs
Cap Llentrisca
Es Vedrà
Sa Conillera

Barcelona 9:30
Denia 4:00
Palma de Mallorca 2:15
Valencia 3:15

Formentera
Sa Savina
Sant Francesc de Formentera
Sant Ferran
Nuestra Señora
Sa Verge des Pilar
C. de Barbària
Pta. Roja

Islas Columbretes *(España)* *(Spain)*
Islas Columbretes

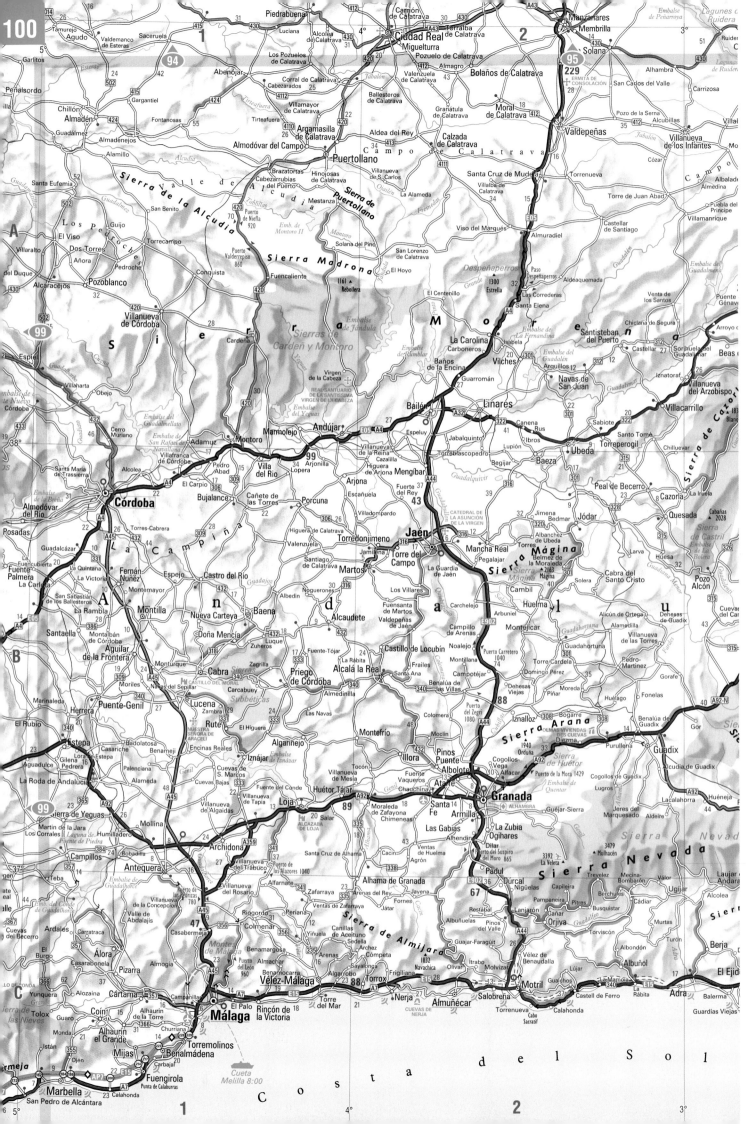

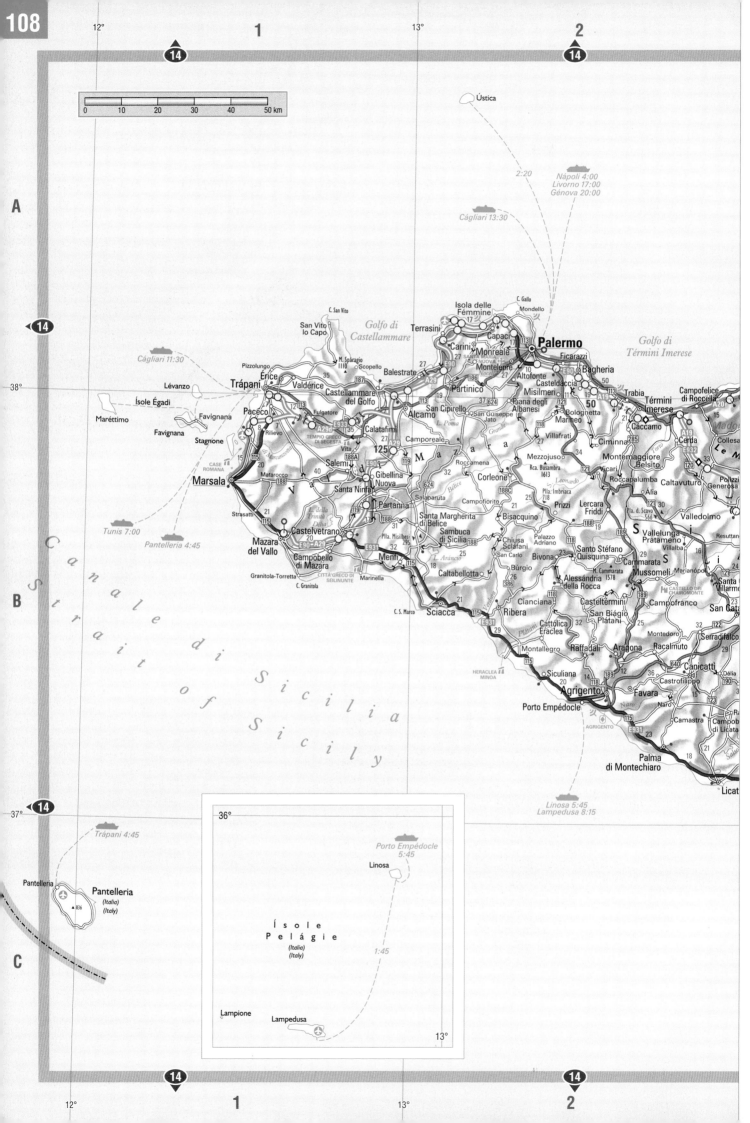

12°   1   13°   2

14   14

A

0 10 20 30 40 50 km

Ústica

2:20

Nápoli 4:00
Livorno 17:00
Génova 20:00

Cágliari 13:30

14

Cágliari 11:30

38°

C. San Vito

Golfo di
Castellammare

Terrasini

Isola delle
Fémmine
17

C. Gallo
Mondello

Palermo

Golfo di
Términi Imerese

San Vito
lo Capo

M. Spáragio
1110
Scopello

Carini Monreale
17
113

Ficarazzi

Pizzolungo
Érice
Valdérice

Capaci

E90 Bagheria
Altofonte 50
Casteldáccia
Misilmeri Trabia
121
Bolognetta 50
Marineo
A19
Caccamo

Campofelice
di Roccella
A20
15

Términi
Imerese

Trápani
Castellammare
del Golfo
Balestrate
27
187
113

Alcamo
San Cipirello
San Guiseppe
Jato
37 624
Piana degli
Albanesi
118

Ciminna
Cerda
285
E932
Collesa

Paceco
Rilievo
7
Fulgatore
20
12 113
A29
E933

Calatafimi
35
Camporeale
125
188A
29
119
Vita
M

Villafrati
27
Mezzojuso
Rca. Busambra
1613
34
Montemaggiore
Belsito
Vicari
Roccapalumba
Ália
121
120
Polizzi
Generosa
Le M
33

Ísole Égadi
Lévanzo

Favignana
Favignana

Stagnone

CASE
ROMANA
15
115

Salemi
40
Gibellina
Nuova
Santa Ninfa
Partanna
119
188A
17

Corleone
Roccamena
32
188C
Pila. Imbríaca
718
Prizzi
Lercara
Friddi
188
19
Caltavuturo
Valledolmo
30
189
121
Pila. d. Scavo
566
S Vallelunga
Pratameno
Villalba
16
Resuttan

Maréttimo

Matarocco
188
40
V
a
L. della
Trinità
Délia
624

Salaparuta
Bélice
Campofiorito
25
Bisacquino
Chiusa
Sclafani
San Carlo
Palazzo
Adriano
118
Bivona
23
Santo Stéfano
Quisquina
24
M. Cammarata
1578
Alessándria
della Rocca
386
Cianciana
Castelterminí

Strasatti
21
115
Castelvetrano
20
E90 A29

Santa Margherita
di Belice
Sambuca
di Sicília
188
Burgio
S Mussomeli
29
Marianopoli
Santa
Villarmo
122
San Cata
CASTELLO DEL
CHIAROMONTE
189
Campofranco
Serradifalco
29

Mazara
del Vallo
Campobello
di Mazara
Menfi
115
18
E931
32
Caltabellotta

Granitola-Torretta
CITTÀ GRECO DI
SEILINUNTE
26
Marinella
25
L. Arància

C. Granitola
C. S. Marco
21

Ribera
Platani
San Biágio
Plátani
25
Montedoro
32
Racalmuto
640
Canicatti
Délia
190
24

B

Tunis 7:00
Pantelleria 4:45

Sciacca
115
E931
29
Cáttolica
Eráclea
Raffadali
Aragona
123
Ri

HERACLEA
MINOA

Montallegro
115
Siculiana
20
189
118
12
36
Favara
Castrofilippo

Agrigento
AGRIGENTO
115
Porto Empédocle
Naro
E931
23
Camastra
Campob
di Lícata

Linosa 5:45
Lampedusa 8:15

Palma
di Montechiaro
18
21

Licat

37°

14

36°

Porto Empédocle
5:45

Linosa

Trápani 4:45

Pantelleria

Pantelleria
(Italia)
(Italy)
▲836

Ísole
Pelágie
(Italia)
(Italy)

1:45

Lampione Lampedusa

13°

C

Canale di Sicilia *Strait of Sicily*

14   14

12°   1   13°   2

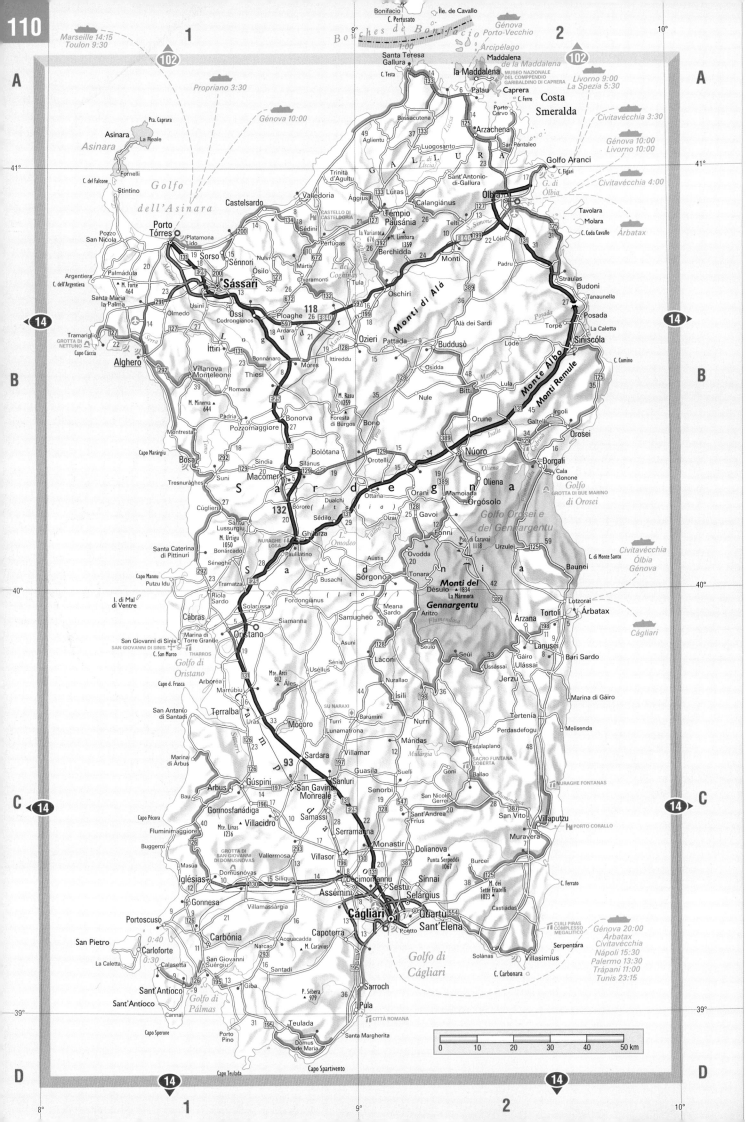

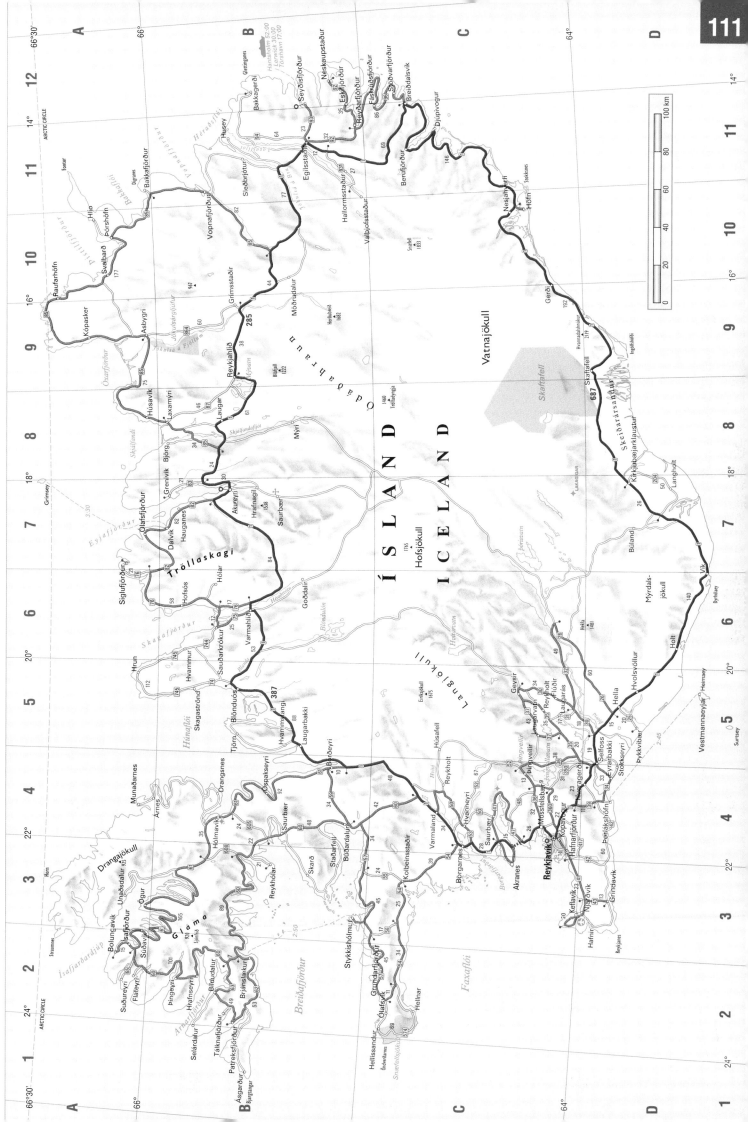

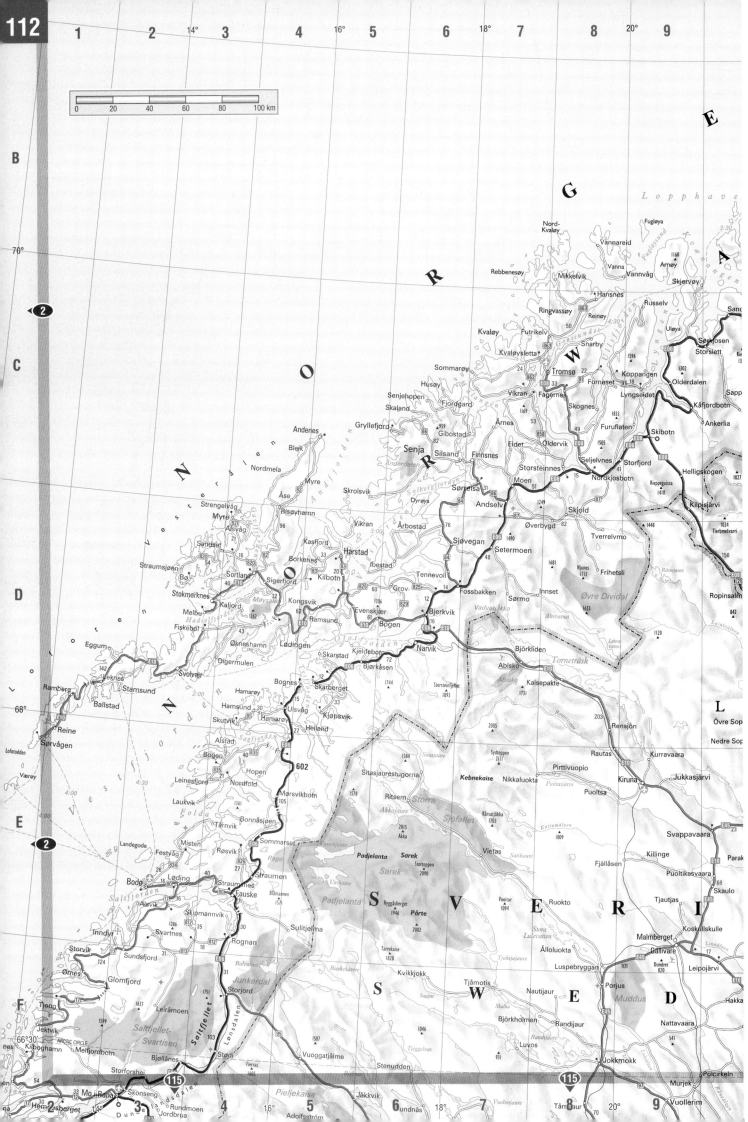

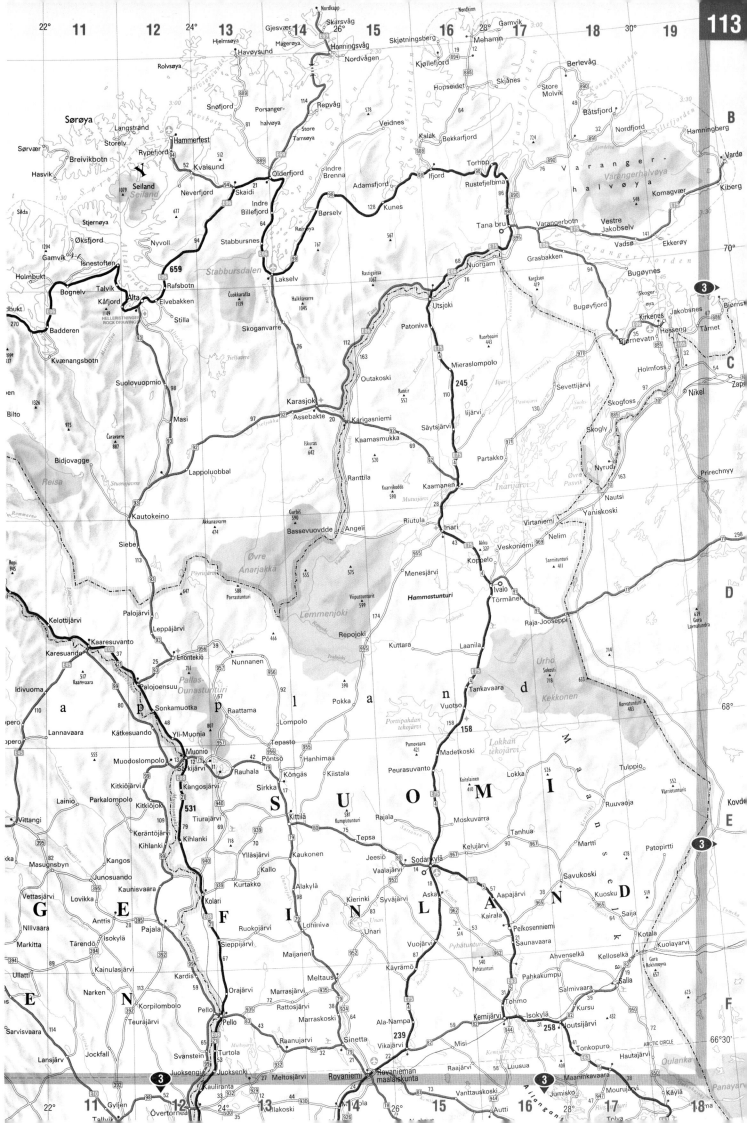

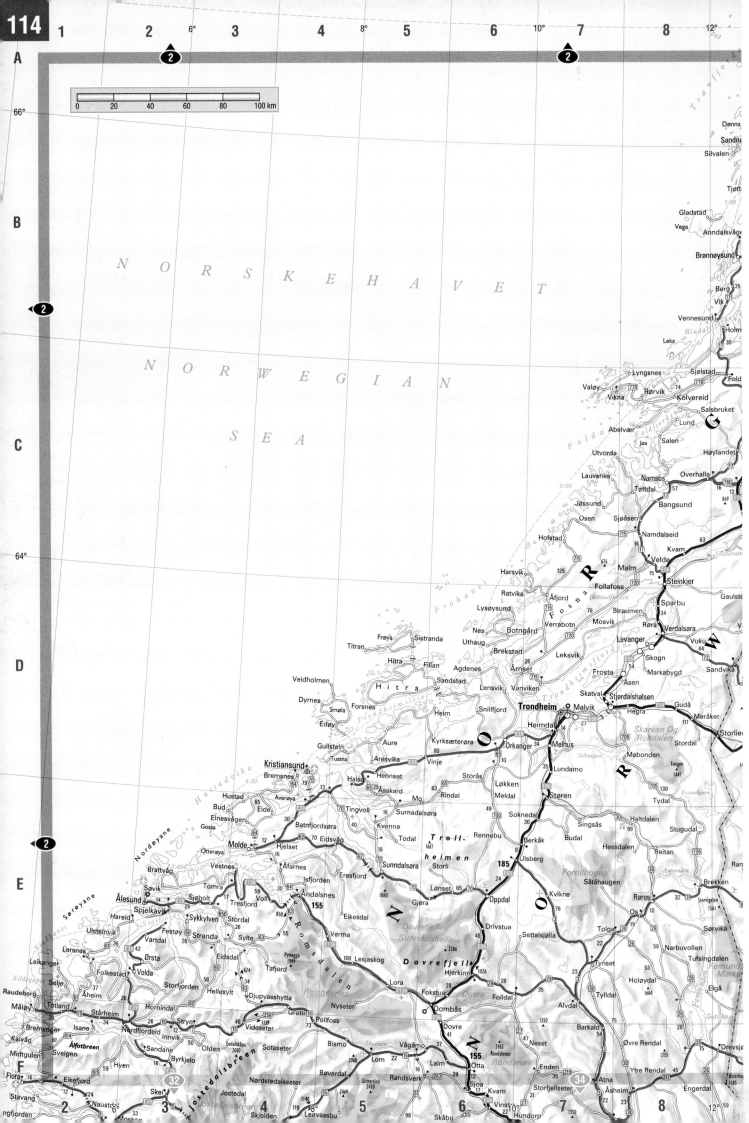

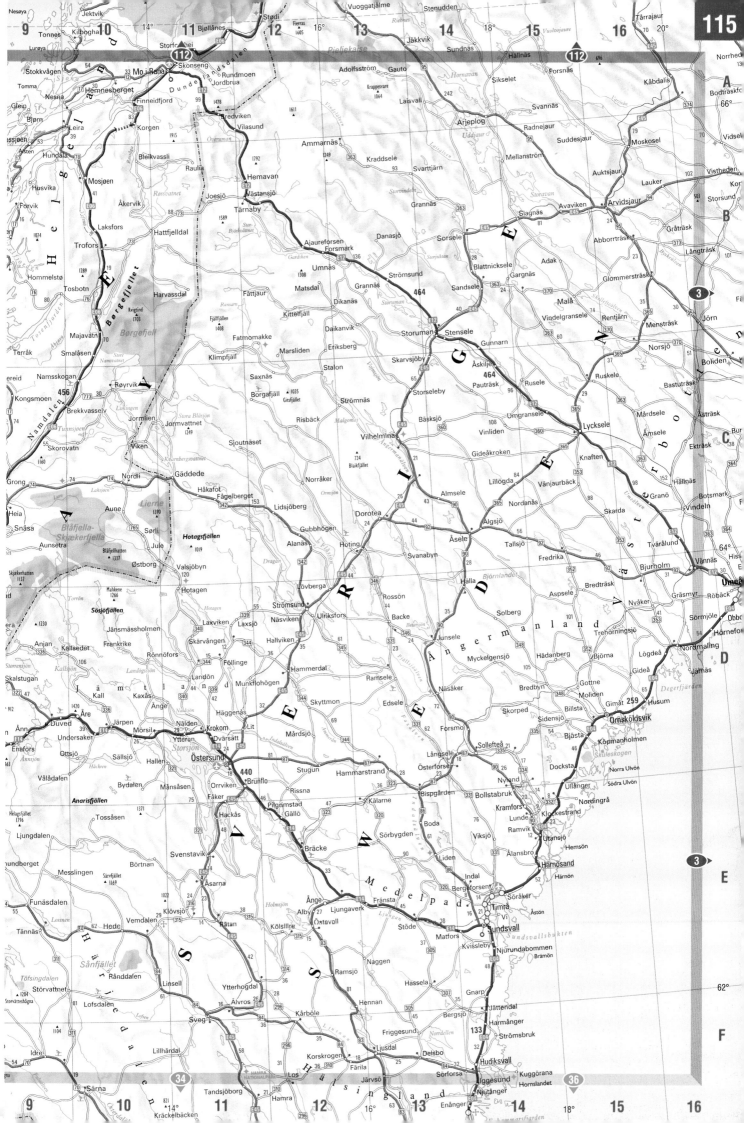

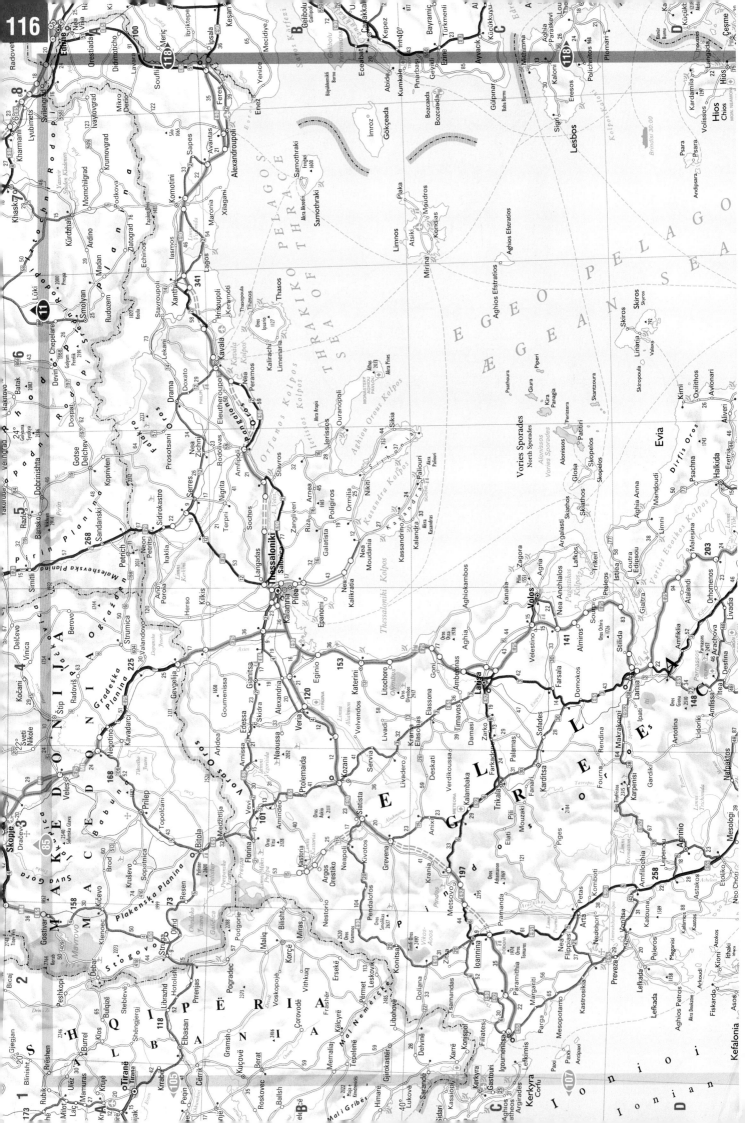

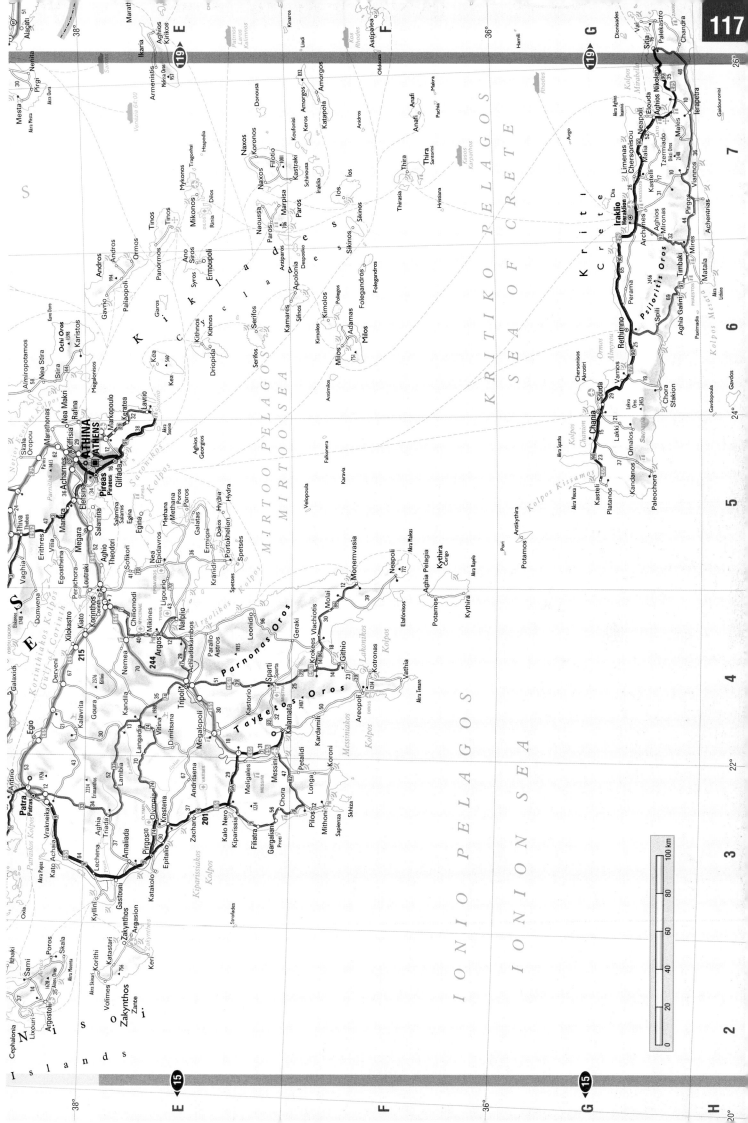

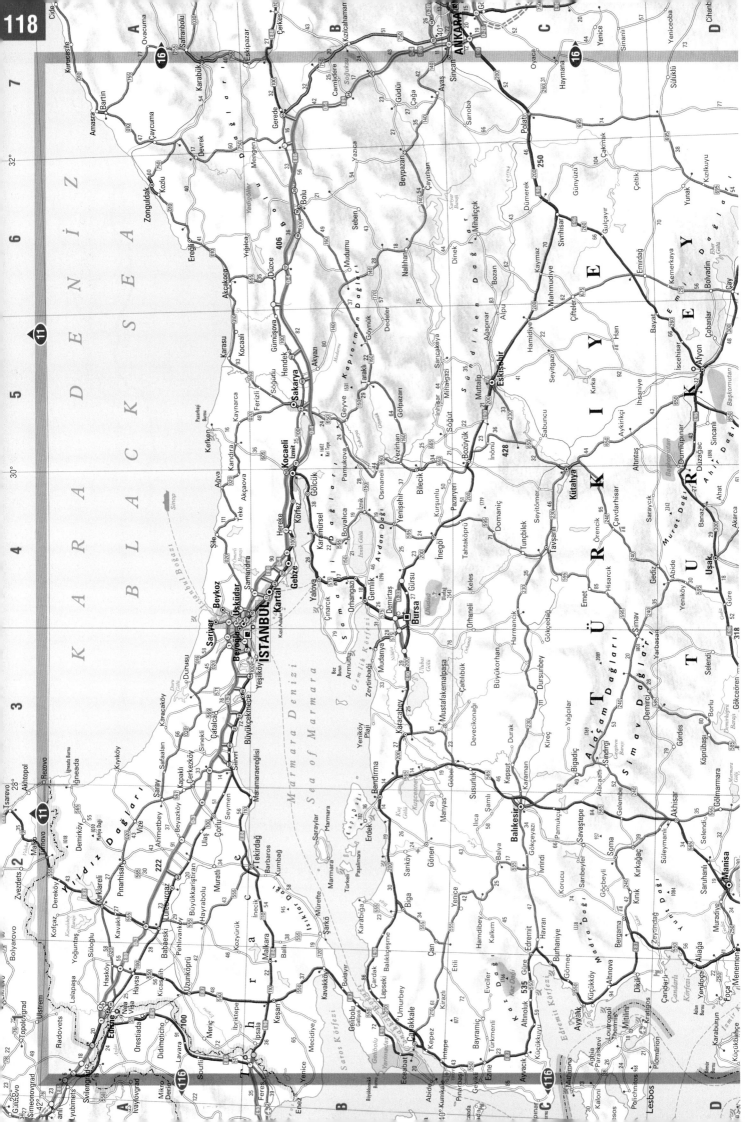

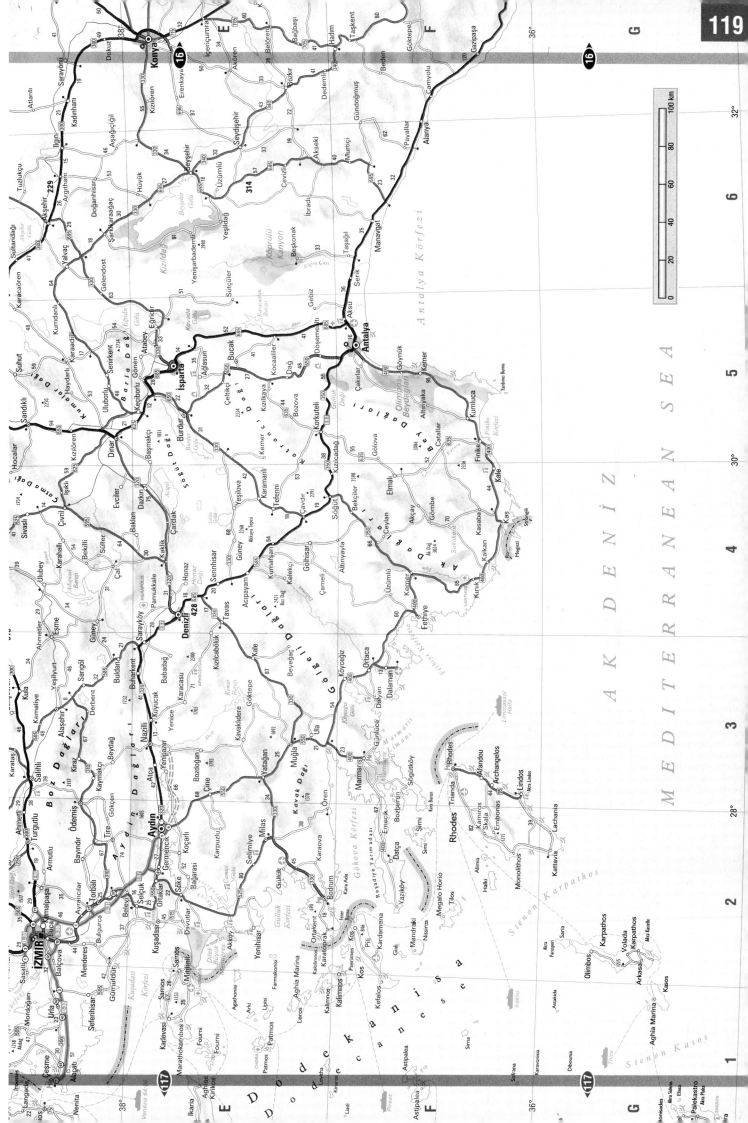

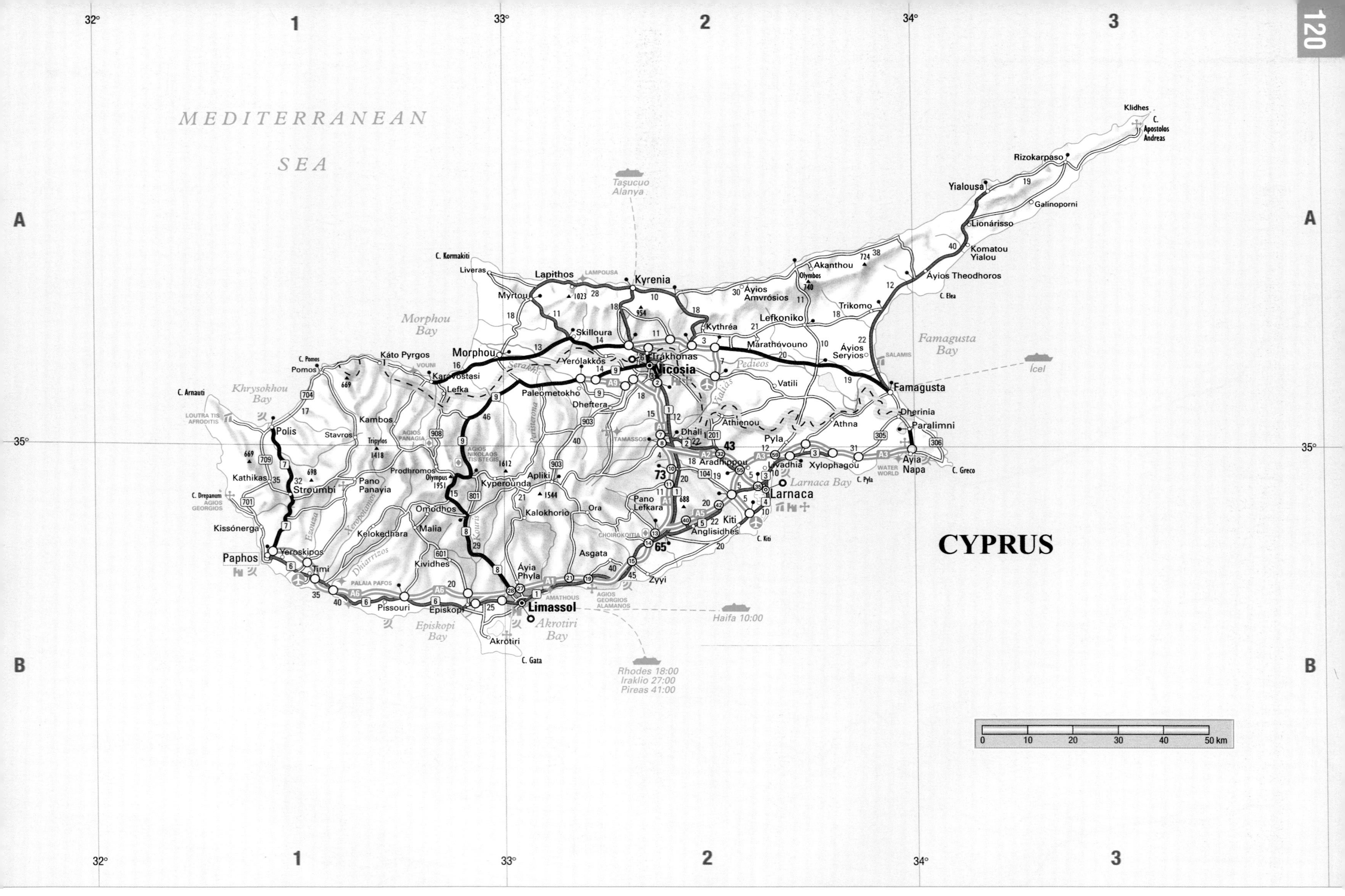

CYPRUS

MEDITERRANEAN SEA

Khrysokhou Bay
Morphou Bay
Tașucuo Alanya

Nicosia
Famagusta
Larnaca
Limassol
Paphos
Kyrenia
Morphou
Lapithos
Polis

Klidhes
C. Apóstolos Andréas
Rizokarpaso
Galinoporni
Lionárisso
Yialousa
Komatou Yialou
Ávios Theodhoros
C. Elea
Akanthou
Trikomo
Ávios Servios
Olympos
Ávios Amvrósios
Lefkóniko
Kythréa
Marathóvouno
Vatili
Athna
Dhrinia
Paralimni
Ávia Napa
C. Gréco
C. Pyla
WATER WORLD
Pyla
Athienou
Xylophagou
Ávadhia
Kiti
C. Kiti
Anglisidhes
Pano Lefkara
Zyyi
Kalavassos
Pano
Kalokhorio
Asgata
Ágios Geórgios Alamanos
Ávios Nikólaos
Akrotíri
Akrotiri Bay
C. Gata
Ávia Phyla
Amathous
Kyperounda
Kakopetria
Apliki
Palekhori
Ora
Kivides
Episkopi
Episkopi Bay
Pissouri
Kelokedhára
Avia Marina
Timi
Yeroskipos
Kissónerga
Kathikas
Stroumbi
Pano Panayia
Prodhromos
Omodhos
Malia
Dheftera
Dhali
Yerolákkos
Skilloura
Órmidhia
Myrtou
Liveras
C. Kormakiti
Káto Pyrgos
Lefka
Karavostasi
Palemetokho
Pomos
C. Pomos
Stavros
Kambos
Tripylos
Kámbos
LOUTRA TIS APHRODITIS
C. Arnauti
AGIOS GEÓRGIOS
C. Drepanum
PALAIA PAFOS
Ávios Seryios
Lefkonikó
Pedieos
Pyla
Athienou

Larnaca Bay
Famagusta Bay
Icel

Haifa 10:00
Rhodes 18:00
Iráklio 27:00
Pireas 41:00

50 km
40
30
20
10
0

City plans • Plans de villes
Stadtpläne • Piante di città

Motorway	Autoroute	Autobahn	Autostrada
Major through route	Route principale majeur	Hauptstrecke	Strada di grande comunicazione
Through route	Route principale	Schnellstrasse	Strada d'importanza regionale
Secondary road	Route secondaire	Nebenstrasse	Strada d'interesse locale
Dual carriageway	Chaussées séparées	Zweispurig Schnellstrasse	Strada a carreggiate doppie
Other road	Autre route	Nebenstrecke	Altra strada
Tunnel	Tunnel	Tunnel	Galleria stradale
Limited access / pedestrian road	Rue réglementée / rue piétonne	Beschränkter Zugang / Fussgängerzone	Strada pedonale / a accesso limitato
One-way street	Sens unique	Einbahnstrasse	Senso unico
Parking	Parc de stationnement	Parkplatz	Parcheggio
Motorway number	A7 Numéro d'autoroute	Autobahnnummer	A7 Numero di autostrada
National road number	447 Numéro de route nationale	Nationalstrassen-nummer	447 Numero di strada nazionale
European road number	E45 Numéro de route européenne	Europäische Strassennummer	E45 Numero di strada europea
Destination	GENT Destination	Ziel	GENT Destinazione
Car ferry	Bac passant les autos	Autofähre	Traghetto automobili
Railway	Chemin de fer	Eisenbahn	Ferrovia
Rail/bus station	Gare / gare routière	Bahnhof / Busstation	Stazione ferrovia / pullman
Underground, metro station	Station de métro	U-Bahnstation	Metropolitano
Cable car	Téléférique	Drahtseilbahn	Funivia
Abbey, cathedral	Abbaye, cathédrale	Abtei, Kloster, Kathedrale	Abbazia, duomo
Church of interest	Église intéressante	Interessante Kirche	Chiesa da vedere
Synagogue	Synagogue	Synagoge	Sinagoga
Hospital	Hôpital	Krankenhaus	Ospedale
Police station	Police	Polizeiwache	Polizia
Post office	Bureau de poste	Postamt	Ufficio postale
Tourist information	Office de tourisme	Informationsbüro	Ufficio informazioni turistiche
Place of interest	Theatre Autre curiosité	Sonstige Sehenswürdigkeit	Theatre Luogo da vedere

Athina Athens

0 km 1

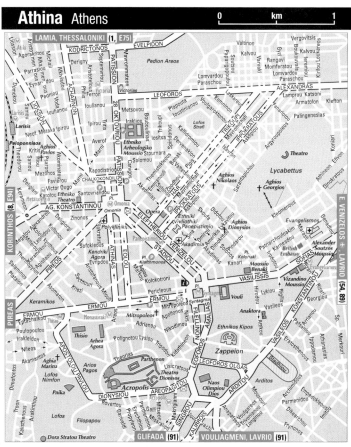

Amsterdam

0 km 2

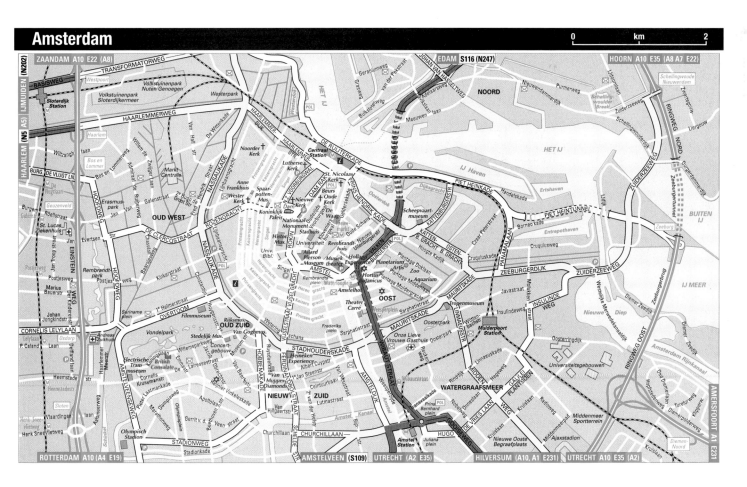

Berlin

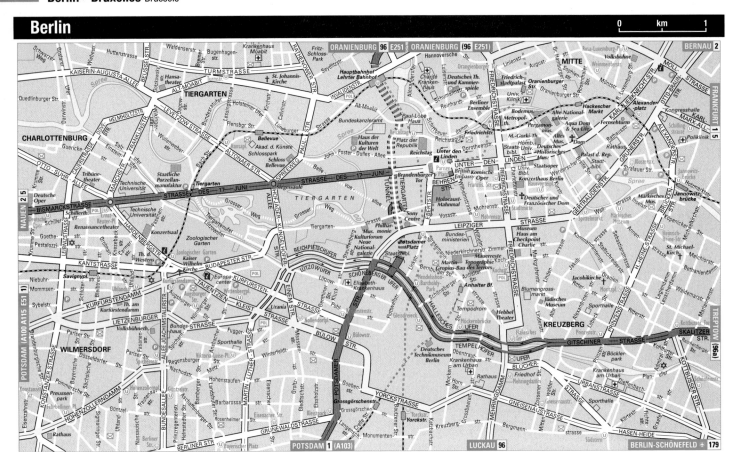

Bruxelles Brussels

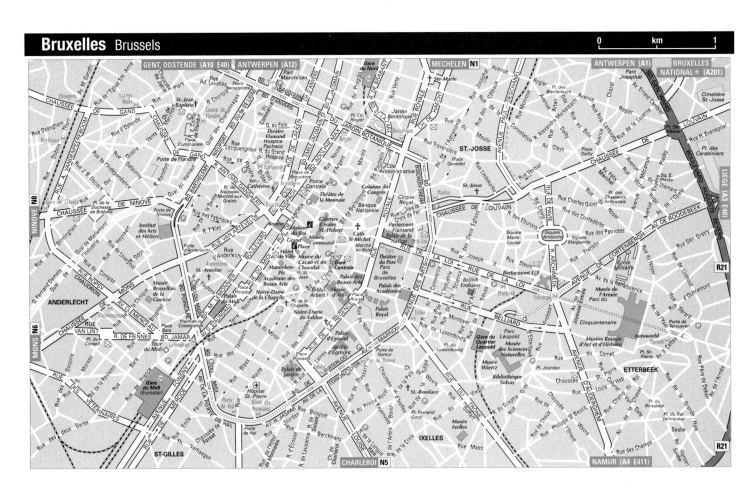

Budapest

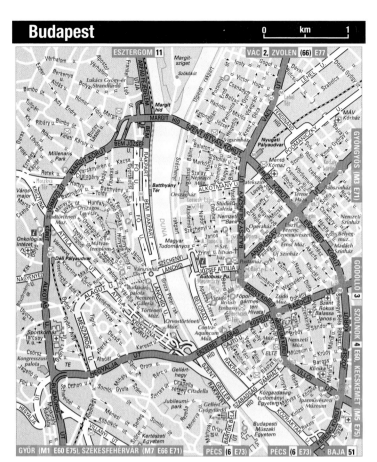

Dublin

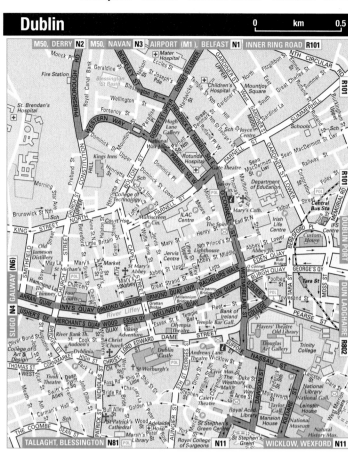

Genève Geneva

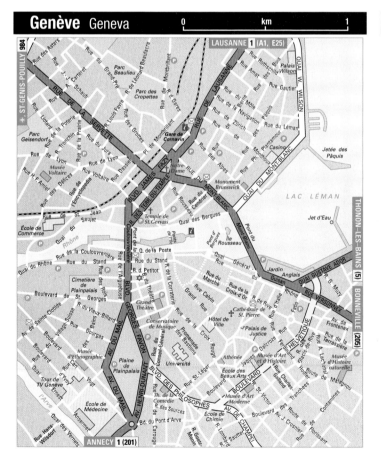

Helsinki

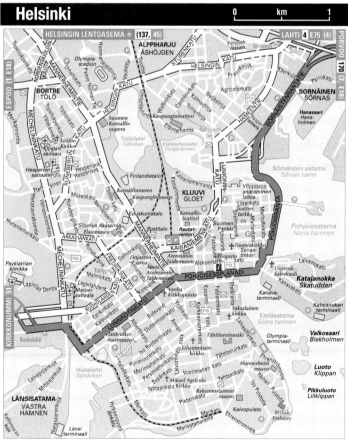

For **Copenhagen** see page 124

København Copenhagen

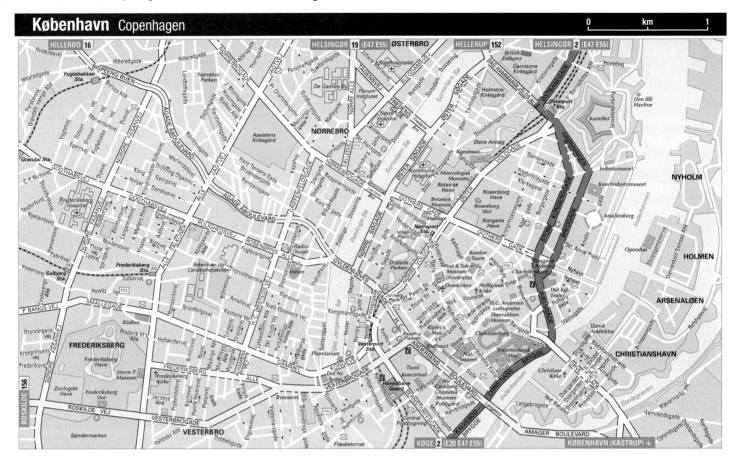

Lisboa Lisbon

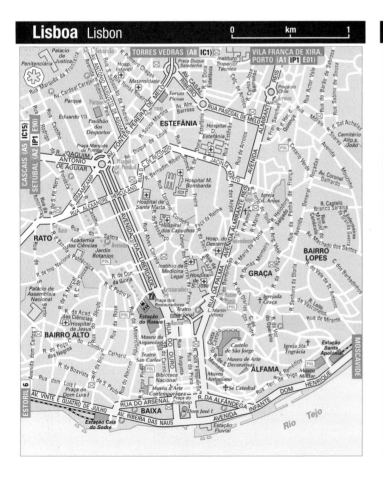

Luxembourg

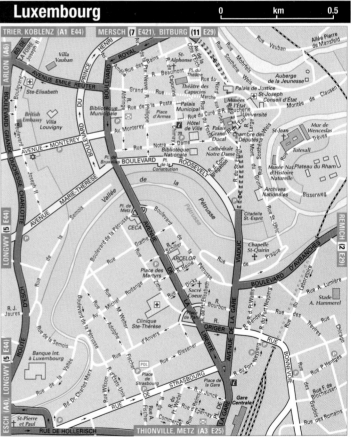

London

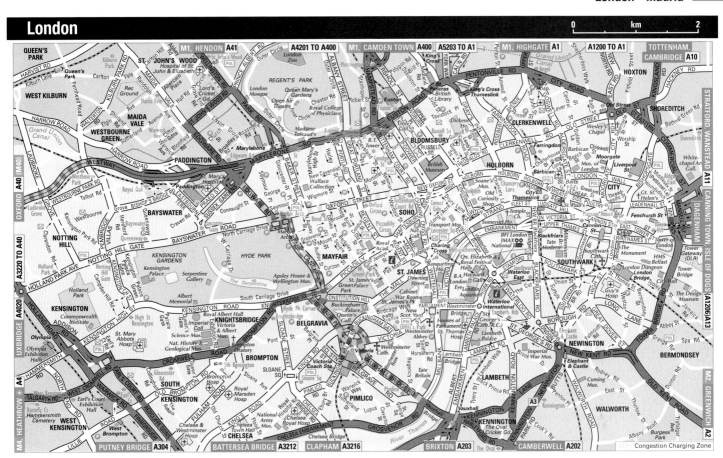

Madrid

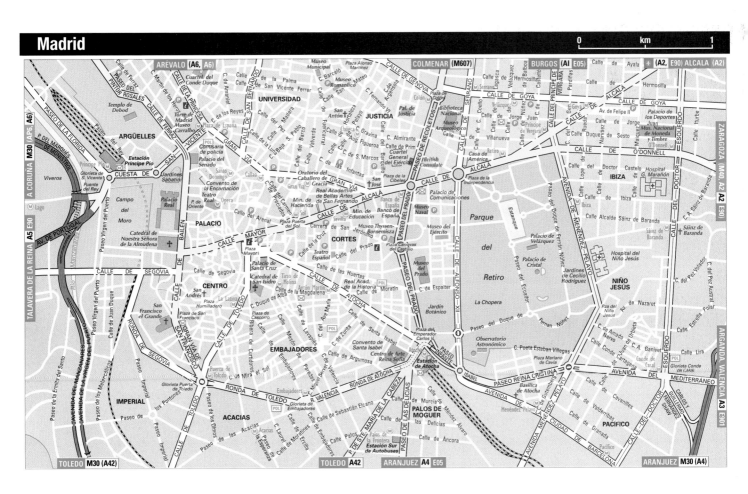

Oslo

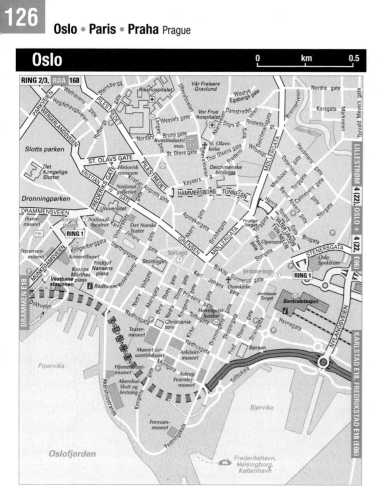

Praha Prague

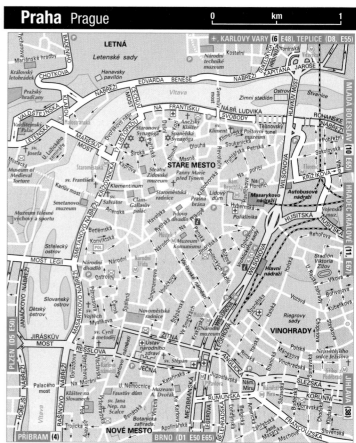

Paris

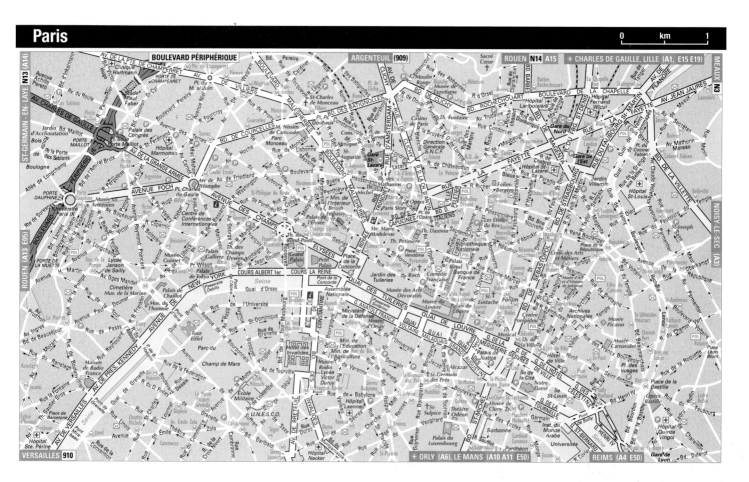

Roma Rome

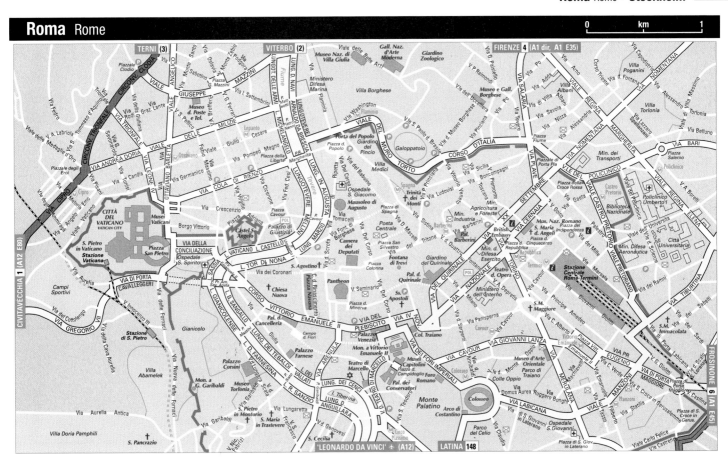

Stockholm

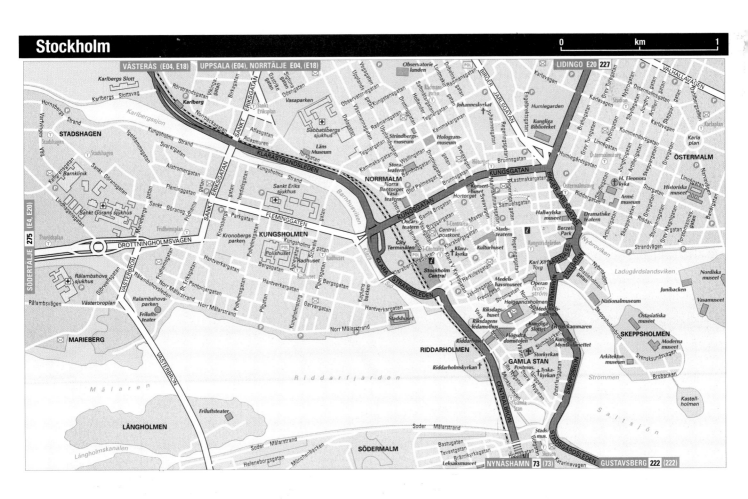

Strasbourg

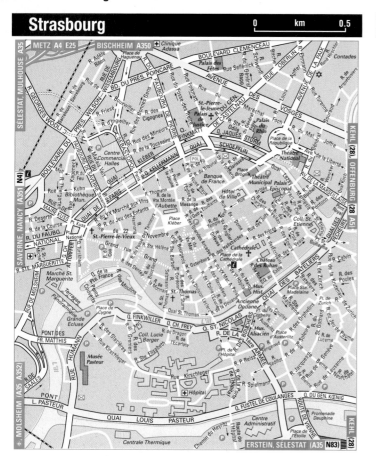

Warszawa Warsaw

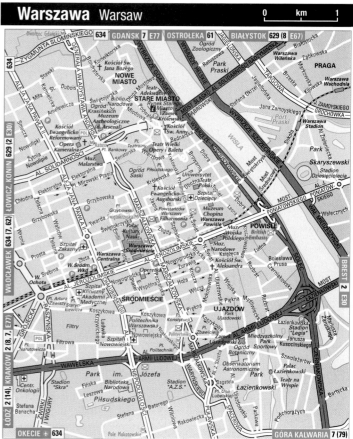

Wien Vienna

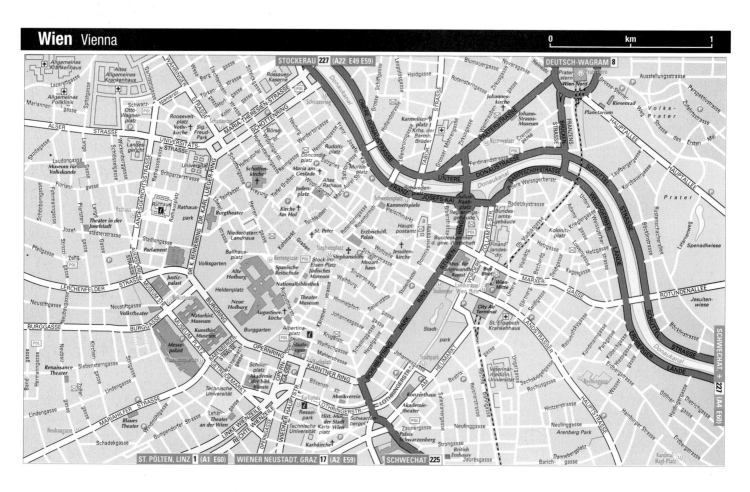

GB	F	D		I
Austria	Autriche	A	Österreich	Austria
Albania	Albanie	AL	Albanien	Albania
Andorra	Andorre	AND	Andorra	Andorra
Belgium	Belgique	B	Belgien	Belgio
Bulgaria	Bulgarie	BG	Bulgarien	Bulgaria
Bosnia-Hercegovina	Bosnie-Herzegovine	BIH	Bosnien-Herzogowina	Bosnia-Herzogovina
Belarus	Belarus	BY	Weissrussland	Bielorussia
Montenegro	Monténégro	CG	Montenegro	Montenegro
Switzerland	Suisse	CH	Schweiz	Svizzera
Cyprus	Chypre	CY	Zypern	Cipro
Czech Republic	République Tchèque	CZ	Tschechische Republik	Repubblica Ceca
Germany	Allemagne	D	Deutschland	Germania
Denmark	Danemark	DK	Dänemark	Danimarca
Spain	Espagne	E	Spanien	Spagna
Estonia	Estonie	EST	Estland	Estonia
France	France	F	Frankreich	Francia
Finland	Finlande	FIN	Finnland	Finlandia
Liechtenstein	Liechtenstein	FL	Liechtenstein	Liechtenstein
Faeroe Islands	Îles Féroé	FO	Färöer-Inseln	Isole Faroe
United Kingdom	Royaume Uni	GB	Grossbritannien und Nordirland	Regno Unito
Gibraltar	Gibraltar	GBZ	Gibraltar	Gibilterra
Greece	Grèce	GR	Griechenland	Grecia
Hungary	Hongrie	H	Ungarn	Ungheria
Croatia	Croatie	HR	Kroatien	Croazia
Italy	Italie	I	Italien	Italia
Ireland	Irlande	IRL	Irland	Irlanda
Iceland	Islande	IS	Island	Islanda
Luxembourg	Luxembourg	L	Luxemburg	Lussemburgo
Lithuania	Lituanie	LT	Litauen	Lituania
Latvia	Lettonie	LV	Lettland	Lettonia
Malta	Malte	M	Malta	Malta
Monaco	Monaco	MC	Monaco	Monaco
Moldova	Moldavie	MD	Moldawien	Moldavia
Macedonia	Macédoine	MK	Makedonien	Macedonia
Norway	Norvège	N	Norwegen	Norvegia
Netherlands	Pays-Bas	NL	Niederlande	Paesi Bassi
Portugal	Portugal	P	Portugal	Portogallo
Poland	Pologne	PL	Polen	Polonia
Romania	Roumanie	RO	Rumanien	Romania
San Marino	Saint-Marin	RSM	San Marino	San Marino
Russia	Russie	RUS	Russland	Russia
Sweden	Suède	S	Schweden	Svezia
Slovak Republic	République Slovaque	SK	Slowak Republik	Repubblica Slovacca
Slovenia	Slovénie	SLO	Slowenien	Slovenia
Serbia	Serbie	SRB	Serbien	Serbia
Turkey	Turquie	TR	Türkei	Turchia
Ukraine	Ukraine	UA	Ukraine	Ucraina

A

Alfena P 87 C2
Alferce P 98 B2
Alfhausen D 43 C4
Alfonsine I 81 B6
Alford, *Aberdeenshire* GB 23 D6
Alford, *Lincolnshire* GB 27 B6
Alforja E 90 B3
Alfoz E 86 A3
Alfreton GB 27 B4
Alfta S 36 A3
Alfundão P 98 A2
Algaida E 97 B2
Algar E 99 C5
Älgarås S 35 D6
Ålgård N 33 D2
Algarinejo E 100 B1
Algarrobo E 100 C1
Algatocin E 99 C5
Algeciras E 99 C5
Algemesí E 96 B2
Algés P 92 C1
Algete E 95 B3
Alghero I 110 B1
Älghult S 40 B5
Alginet E 96 B2
Algodonales E 99 C5
Algodor E 94 C3
Algodor P 98 B3
Algora E 95 B4
Algoso P 87 C4
Algoz P 98 B2
Älgsjö S 115 C14
Alguaire E 90 B3
Alguazas E 101 A4
Algutsrum S 41 C6
Algyö H 75 B5
Alhama de Almería E 101 C3
Alhama de Aragón E 89 C5
Alhama de Granada E 100 C2
Alhama de Murcia E 101 B4
Alhambra E 100 A2
Alhandra P 92 C1
Alhaurin de la Torre E 100 C1
Alhaurin el Grande E 100 C1
Alhendin E 100 B2
Alhóndiga E 95 B4
Ali Terme I 109 A4
Alia E 93 B5
Ália I 108 B2
Aliaga E 90 C2
Aliağa TR 118 D1
Alibunar SRB 85 A5
Alicante E 96 C2
Alicún de Ortega E 100 B2
Alife I 103 B7
Alija del Infantado E 88 B1
Alijó P 87 C3
Alimena I 109 B3
Alingsås S 40 B2
Alinyà E 91 A4
Aliseda E 93 B4
Aliveri GR 116 D6
Alixan F 79 B4
Aljaraque E 99 B3
Aljezur P 98 B2
Aljorra E 101 B4
Aljubarrota P 92 B2
Aljucen E 93 B4
Aljustrel P 98 B2
Alken B 49 C6
Alkmaar NL 42 C1
Alkoven A 63 B5
Allaines F 58 B2
Allaire F 57 C3
Allanche F 68 C2
Alland A 64 B2
Allariz E 87 B3
Allassac F 67 C6
Allauch F 79 C4
Alleen N 33 D4
Allègre F 68 C3
Allemont F 69 C6
Allendale Town GB 25 D5
Allendorf D 51 C4
Allentsteig A 63 B6
Allepuz E 90 C2
Allersberg D 62 A2
Allershausen D 62 B2
Alles E 88 A2
Allevard F 69 C6
Allgunnen S 40 B5
Allihies IRL 20 C1
Allingåbro DK 38 C3
Allmannsdorf D 61 C5
Allo E 89 B4
Alloa GB 25 B4
Allogny F 68 A2
Ålloluokta S 112 E8
Allones, *Eure et Loire* F 58 B2
Allones, *Maine-et-Loire* F 67 A5
Allonnes F 57 C6
Allons F 76 B2
Allos F 79 B5
Allstedt D 52 B1
Alltwalis GB 28 B3
Allumiere I 102 A4
Almaceda P 92 B3
Almacelles E 90 B3
Almachar E 100 C1
Almada P 92 C1
Almadén E 100 A1
Almadén de la Plata E 99 B4
Almadenejos E 100 A1
Almadrones E 95 B4
Almagro E 100 A2
Almajano E 89 C4
Almansa E 96 C1
Almansil P 98 B2
Almanza E 88 B1
Almaraz E 93 B5
Almargen E 99 C5
Almarza E 89 C4
Almásfüzitő H 64 C4
Almassora E 96 B2
Almazán E 89 C4
Almazul E 89 C4
Alme D 51 B4
Almedina E 100 A3
Almedinilla E 100 B1
Almeida E 87 C4
Almeida P 93 A4
Almeirim P 92 B2
Almelo NL 42 C3
Almenar E 90 B3
Almenar de Soria E 89 C4
Almenara E 96 B2
Almendra P 87 D3
Almendral E 93 C4
Almendral de la Cañada E 94 B2
Almendralejo E 93 C4
Almenno San Bartolomeo I 71 C4
Almere NL 42 C2
Almería E 101 C3
Almerimar E 101 C3
Almese I 70 C2
Almexial P 98 B3
Älmhult S 40 C4
Almiropotamos GR 117 D6
Almiros GR 116 C4
Almodôvar P 98 B2
Almodóvar del Campo E 100 A1
Almodóvar del Pinar E 95 C5
Almodóvar del Río E 99 B5
Almofala P 87 D3
Almogia E 100 C1
Almoharin E 93 B4
Almonacid de la Sierra E 89 C5
Almonacid de Toledo E 94 C3
Almonaster la Real E 99 B4
Almondsbury GB 29 B5
Almonte E 99 B4
Almoradí E 101 A5
Almoraima E 99 C5
Almorox E 94 B2
Almoster P 92 B2
Almsele S 115 C14
Älmsta S 36 C5
Almudena E 101 A4
Almudévar E 90 A2
Almuñécar E 100 C2
Almunge S 36 C5
Almuradiel E 100 A2
Almussafes E 96 B2
Almvik S 40 B6
Alness GB 23 D4
Alnmouth GB 25 C6
Alnwick GB 25 C6
Åloppe S 36 C4
Álora E 100 C1
Alos d'Ensil E 91 A4
Alosno E 99 B3
Alozaina E 100 C1
Alpbach A 72 A1
Alpedrete de la Sierra E 95 B3
Alpedrinha P 92 A3
Alpen D 50 B2
Alpera E 96 C1
Alphen aan de Rijn NL 49 A5
Alpiarça P 92 B2
Alpignano I 70 C2
Alpirsbach D 61 B4
Alpu TR 118 C5
Alpuente E 96 B1
Alqueva P 98 A3
Alquézar E 90 A3
Als DK 38 C3
Alsasua E 89 B4
Alsdorf D 50 C2
Alselv DK 39 D1
Alsfeld D 51 C5
Alsike S 36 C4
Alskog S 37 E5
Alsleben D 52 B1
Alsónémedi H 75 A4
Alsótold H 65 C5
Alsóújlak H 74 A1
Alstad N 112 E4
Alstätte D 50 A2
Alsterbro S 40 C5
Alstermo S 40 C5
Alston GB 25 D5
Alsvåg N 112 D4
Alsvik N 112 E3
Alt Ruppin D 45 C4
Alta N 113 C12
Älta S 37 C5
Altamura I 104 C2
Altarejos E 95 C4
Altaussee A 63 C4
Altavilla Irpina I 103 B7
Altavilla Silentina I 103 C8
Altdöbern D 53 B4
Altdorf CH 70 B3
Altdorf D 62 B3
Altdorf bei Nürnberg D 62 A2
Alte P 98 B2
Altea E 96 C2
Altedo I 81 B5
Alten-weddingen D 52 A1
Altena D 50 B3
Altenau D 51 B6
Altenberg D 53 C3
Altenberge D 50 A3
Altenbruch D 43 B5
Altenburg D 52 C2
Altenfelden A 63 B4
Altengronau D 51 C5
Altenheim D 60 B3
Altenhundem D 50 B4
Altenkirchen, *Mecklenburg-Vorpommern* D 45 A5
Altenkirchen, *Radom* D 50 C3
Altenkunstadt D 52 C1
Altenmarkt A 63 C5
Altenmarkt D 62 B3
Altenmarkt im Pongall A 72 A3
Altensteig D 61 B4
Altentreptow D 45 B5
Altenwalde D 43 B5
Alter do Chão P 92 B3
Altfraunhofen D 62 B3
Altheim A 63 B4
Altheim D 61 A5
Althofen A 73 B4
Altınoluk TR 118 C1
Altınova TR 118 C1
Altıntaş TR 118 C5
Altınyaka TR 119 F5
Altınyayla TR 119 E4
Altkirch F 60 C3
Altlandsberg D 45 C5
Altlewin D 45 C6
Altmannstein D 62 B2
Altmorschen D 51 B5
Altmunster A 63 C4
Altnaharra GB 23 C4
Alto Campoó E 88 A2
Altofonte I 108 A2
Altomonte I 106 B3
Alton, *Hampshire* GB 31 C3
Alton, *Staffordshire* GB 27 C4
Altopáscio I 81 C4
Altötting D 62 B3
Altreichenau D 63 B4
Altshausen D 61 C5
Altstätten CH 71 A4
Altura E 96 B2
Altusried D 61 C6
Alūksne LV 7 C9
Alunda S 36 B5
Alustante E 95 B5
Alva GB 25 B4
Alvaiázere P 92 B2
Alvalade P 98 B2
Älvängen S 38 B5
Alvarenga P 87 D2
Alvares P 92 A2
Alvdal N 114 E7
Älvdalen S 34 A6
Alverca P 92 C1
Alversund N 32 B2
Alvesta S 40 C4
Alvignac F 77 B4
Alvignano I 103 B7
Ålvik N 32 B3
Alvik S 36 B1
Alvimare F 58 A1
Alviobeira P 92 B2
Alvito P 98 A3
Älvkarleby S 36 B4
Älvkarleö bruk S 36 B4
Alvor P 98 B2
Alvorge P 92 B2
Alvøy N 32 B2
Älvros S 115 E11
Alvsbacka S 35 C5
Älvsbyn S 3 D24
Älvsered S 40 B2
Alwernia PL 55 C4
Alwinton GB 25 C5
Alyth GB 25 B4
Alytus LT 6 D8
Alzénau D 51 C5
Alzey D 61 A4
Alzira E 96 B2
Alzonne F 77 C5
Amadora P 92 C1
Åmål S 35 C4
Amalfi I 103 C7
Amaliada GR 117 E3
Amance F 60 C2
Amancey F 69 A6
Amándola I 82 D2
Amantea I 106 B3
Amarante P 87 C2
Amareleja P 98 A3
Amares P 87 C2
Amaseno I 103 B6
Amasra TR 118 A7
Amasya TR 16 A8
Amatrice I 103 A6
Amay B 49 C6
Ambarnyy RUS 3 D30
Ambazac F 67 C6
Ambelonas GR 116 C4
Amberg D 62 A2
Ambérieu-en-Bugey F 69 C5
Ambérieux-en-Dombes F 69 B4
Ambert F 68 C3
Ambés F 76 A2
Ambjörby S 34 B5
Ambjörnarp S 40 B3
Amble GB 25 C6
Ambleside GB 26 A3
Ambleteuse F 48 C2
Amboise F 67 A5
Ambrières-les-Vallées F 57 B5
Amden CH 71 A4
Amel B 50 C2
Amélia I 102 A5
Amélie-les-Bains-Palalda F 91 A5
Amelinghausen D 44 B2
Amendoa P 92 B2
Amendoeira P 98 B3
Améndola I 104 B1
Amendolara I 106 B3
Amer E 91 A5
Amerongen NL 49 A6
Amersfoort NL 49 A6
Amersham GB 31 C3
Ames E 86 B2
Amesbury GB 29 B6
Amfiklia GR 116 D4
Amfilochia GR 116 D3
Amfipoli GR 116 B5
Amfissa GR 116 D4
Amièira, *Évora* P 98 A3
Amieira, *Portalegre* P 92 B3
Amieiro P 92 A2
Amiens F 58 A3
Amindeo GR 116 B3
Åminne S 40 B3
Åmli N 33 D5
Amlwch GB 26 B1
Ammanford GB 28 B4
Ammarnäs S 115 B13
Åmmeberg S 37 D1
Amorbach D 61 A5
Amorebieta E 89 A4
Amorgos GR 117 F7
Amorosa P 87 C2
Amorosi I 103 B7
Åmot, *Buskerud* N 34 C1
Åmot, *Telemark* N 33 C4
Åmot S 36 B3
Amotfors S 34 C4
Åmotsdal N 33 C5
Amou F 76 C2
Ampezzo I 72 B2
Ampfing D 62 B3
Ampflwang A 63 B4
Amplepuis F 69 C4
Amposta E 90 C3
Ampthill GB 30 B3
Ampudia E 88 C2
Ampuero E 89 A3
Amriswil CH 71 A4
Åmsele S 115 C16
Amstelveen NL 49 A5
Amsterdam NL 42 C1
Amstetten A 63 B5
Amtzell D 61 C5
Amulree GB 25 B4
Amurrio E 89 A4
Amusco E 88 B2
An t-Ob GB 22 D1
Åna-Sira N 33 D3
Anacapri I 103 C7
Anadia P 92 A2
Anadon E 90 C1
Anafi GR 117 F7
Anagni I 102 B6
Anamur TR 16 C6
Ananyiv UA 11 C10
Anascaul IRL 20 B1
Ånäset S 3 D24
Anastażewo PL 47 C4
Anaya de Alba E 94 B1
Ança P 92 A2
Ancaster GB 27 C5
Ancede P 87 C2
Ancenis F 66 A3
Ancerville F 59 B6
Anchuras E 94 C2
Ancona I 82 C2
Ancora P 87 C2
Ancrum GB 25 C5
Ancy-le-Franc F 59 C5
Andalo I 71 B5
Åndalsnes N 114 E4
Andance F 69 C4
Andau A 64 C3
Andebu N 35 C2
Andeer CH 71 B4
Andelfingen CH 61 C4
Andelot F 59 B6
Andelot-en-Montagne F 69 B5
Andenes N 112 C5
Andenne B 49 C6
Anderlues B 49 C5
Andermatt CH 70 B3
Andernach D 50 C3
Andernos-les-Bains F 76 B1
Anderslöv S 41 D3
Anderstorp S 40 B3
Andijk NL 42 C2
Andoain E 89 A4
Andocs H 74 B2
Andolsheim F 60 B3
Andorra E 90 C2
Andorra La Vella AND 91 A4
Andosilla E 89 B5
Andover GB 31 C2
Andratx E 97 B2
Andreapol RUS 7 C12
Andreas GB 26 A1
Andréspol PL 55 B4
Andrest F 76 C3
Andretta I 103 C8
Andrezieux-Bouthéon F 69 C4
Ándria I 104 B2
Andrijevica CG 85 D4
Andritsena GR 117 E3
Andros GR 117 E6
Andrychów PL 65 A5
Andselv N 112 C7
Andújar E 100 A1
Anduze F 78 B2
Aneby N 34 B2
Aneby S 40 B4
Añes E 89 A3
Anet F 58 B2
Anfo I 71 C5
Ang S 40 B4
Anga S 37 E5
Angaïs F 76 C2
Änge, *Jämtland* S 115 D11
Ånge, *Västernorrland* S 115 E12
Angeja P 92 A2
Ängelholm S 41 C2
Angeli FIN 113 D14
Ängelsberg S 36 C3
Anger A 73 A5
Angera I 70 C3
Angermünde D 45 B6
Angern A 64 B2
Angers F 67 A4
Angerville F 58 B3
Anghiari I 82 C1
Angle GB 28 B2
Anglès E 91 B5
Anglés, *Tarn* F 77 C5
Angles, *Vendée* F 66 B3
Angles sur l'Anglin F 67 B5
Anglesola E 91 B4
Anglet F 76 C1
Anglisidhes CY 120 B2
Anglure F 59 B4
Angoulême F 67 C5
Angoulins F 66 B3
Angsö S 37 C3
Angueira P 87 C4
Angües E 90 A2
Anguiano E 89 B4
Anguillara Sabazia I 102 A5
Anguillara Véneta I 72 C1
Anhée B 49 C5
Anholt DK 38 C4
Aniane F 78 C2
Aniche F 49 C4
Ånimskog S 35 D4
Anina RO 10 D6
Anixi GR 116 C3
Anizy-le-Château F 59 A4
Anjalankoski FIN 3 F27
Anjan S 115 D9
Ankara TR 118 C7
Ankaran SLO 72 C3
Ankarsrum S 40 B6
Ankerlia N 112 C9
Anklam D 45 B5
Ankum D 43 C4
Anlauftal A 72 A3
Anlezy F 68 B3
Ånn S 115 D9
Annaberg A 63 C6
Annaberg-Buchholz D 52 C3
Annaberg im Lammertal A 72 A3
Annaburg D 52 B3
Annahütte D 53 B3
Annalong GB 19 B6
Annan GB 25 D4
Anndalsvågen N 115 B9
Anneberg, *Halland* S 38 B5
Anneberg, *Jönköping* S 40 B4
Annecy F 69 C6
Annelund S 40 B3
Annemasse F 69 B6
Annenskiy Most RUS 7 A14
Annerstad S 40 C3
Annestown IRL 21 B4
Annevoie-Rouillon B 49 C5
Annonay F 69 C4
Annot F 79 C5
Annweiler D 60 A3
Ano Poroia GR 116 A5
Ano Siros GR 117 E6
Añora E 100 A1
Anould F 60 B2
Anquela del Ducado E 95 B4
Anröchte D 51 B4
Ans DK 39 C2
Ansager DK 39 D1
Ansbach D 62 A1
Anse F 69 C4
Anserœul B 49 C4
Ansfelden A 63 B5
Ansião P 92 B2
Ansó E 76 D2
Ansoain E 76 D1
Anstruther GB 25 B5
Antalya TR 119 F5
Antas E 101 B4
Antegnate I 71 C4
Antequera E 100 B1
Anterselva di Mezzo I 72 B2
Antibes F 79 C6
Antigüedad E 88 C2
Antillo I 109 B4
Antirio GR 117 D3
Antoing B 49 C4
Antonin PL 54 B2
Antrain F 57 B4
Antrim GB 19 B5
Antrodoco I 102 A6
Antronapiana I 70 B3
Anttis S 113 E11
Antuzede P 92 A2
Antwerp = Antwerpen B 49 B5
Antwerpen = Antwerp B 49 B5
Anversa d'Abruzzi I 103 B6
Anvin F 48 C3
Anzat-le-Luguet F 68 C3
Anzi I 104 C1
Ánzio I 102 B5
Anzola d'Emilia I 81 B5
Anzón E 89 C5
Aoiz E 76 D1
Aosta I 70 C2
Apalhão P 92 B3
Apátfalva H 75 B5
Apatin SRB 75 C4
Apatity RUS 3 C30
Apc H 65 C5
Apécchio I 82 C1
Apeldoorn NL 50 A1
Apen D 43 B4
Apenburg D 44 C3
Apensen D 43 B6
Apiro I 82 C2
Apliki CY 120 B2
Apolda D 52 B1
Apolonia GR 117 F6
Apostag H 75 B3
Äppelbo S 34 B6
Appennino I 82 D2
Appenzell CH 71 A4
Appiano I 71 B6
Appingedam NL 42 B3
Appleby-in-Westmorland GB 26 A3
Applecross GB 22 D3
Appledore GB 28 B3
Appoigny F 59 C4
Apremont-la-Forêt F 60 B1
Aprica I 71 B5
Apricena I 103 B8
Aprigliano I 106 B3
Aprilia I 102 B5
Apt F 79 C4
Apúlia P 87 C2
Aquiléia I 72 C3
Aquilónia I 103 C8
Aquino I 103 B6
Ar S 37 E5
Arabayona E 94 A1
Arabba I 72 B1
Araç TR 16 A6
Aracena E 99 B4
Arachova GR 116 D4
Arad RO 75 B6
Aradac SRB 75 C5
Aradhippou CY 120 B2
Aragnouet F 76 D3
Aragona I 108 B2
Aramits F 76 C2
Aramon F 78 C3
Aranda de Duero E 88 C3
Aranda de Moncayo E 89 C5
Arandjelovac SRB 85 B5
Aranjuez E 95 B3
Arantzazu E 89 B4
Aranzueque E 95 B3
Aras de Alpuente E 96 B1
Arauzo de Miel E 89 C3
Arazede P 92 A2
Arbas F 77 D3
Árbatax I 110 C2
Arbeca E 90 B3
Arberg D 62 A1
Arbesbach A 63 B5
Arboga S 37 C2
Arbois F 69 B5
Arbon CH 71 A4
Arboréa I 110 C1
Arbório I 70 C3
Årbostad N 112 D6
Arbrå S 36 A3
Arbroath GB 25 B5
Arbùcies E 91 B5
Arbuniel E 100 B2
Arbus I 110 C1
Arc-en-Barrois F 59 C5
Arc-et-Senans F 69 A5
Arc-lès-Gray F 69 A5
Arc-sur-Tille F 69 A5
Arcachon F 76 B1
Arce I 103 B6
Arcen NL 50 B2
Arces-Dilo F 59 B4
Arcévia I 82 C1
Arcey F 70 A1
Archanes GR 117 G7
Archangelos GR 119 F3
Archena E 101 A4
Archez E 100 C2
Archiac F 67 C4
Archidona E 100 B1
Archiestown GB 23 D5
Archivel E 101 A4
Arcidosso I 81 D5
Arcille I 81 D5
Arcis-sur-Aube F 59 B5
Arco I 71 C5
Arcones E 94 A3
Arcos E 88 B3
Arcos de Jalón E 95 A4
Arcos de la Frontera E 99 C5
Arcos de la Sierra E 95 B4
Arcos de las Salinas E 96 B1
Arcos de Valdevez P 87 C2
Arcozelo P 92 A3
Arcusa E 90 A3
Arcy-sur-Cure F 59 C4
Ardagh IRL 20 B2
Årdal N 33 C3
Ardala S 35 D5
Ardales E 100 C1
Årdalstangen N 32 A4
Ardara I 110 B1
Ardara IRL 18 B3
Ardarroch GB 22 D3
Ardbeg GB 24 C1
Ardcharnich GB 22 D3
Ardchyle GB 24 B3
Ardee IRL 19 C5
Arden DK 38 C2
Ardentes F 68 B1
Ardenza I 81 C4
Ardersier GB 23 D4
Ardes F 68 C3
Ardessie GB 22 D3
Ardez CH 71 B5
Ardfert IRL 20 B2
Ardgay GB 23 D4
Ardglass GB 19 B6
Ardgroom IRL 20 C2
Ardhasig GB 22 D2
Ardino BG 116 A7
Ardisa E 90 A2
Ardkearagh IRL 20 C1
Ardlui GB 24 B3
Ardlussa GB 24 B2
Ardón E 88 B1
Ardooie B 49 C4
Ardore I 106 C3
Ardre S 37 E5
Ardres F 48 C2
Ardrishaig GB 24 B2
Ardrossan GB 24 C3
Are N 33 C2
Åre S 115 D10
Areia Branca P 92 B1
Aremark N 35 C3
Arenales de San Gregorio E 95 C3
Arenas E 100 C1
Arenas de Iguña E 88 A2
Arenas de San Juan E 95 C3
Arenas de San Pedro E 94 B1
Arenas del Rey E 100 C2
Arendal N 33 D5
Arendonk B 49 B6
Arengosse F 76 B2
Arentorp S 35 D4
Arenys de Mar E 91 B5
Arenys de Munt E 91 B5
Arenzano I 80 B2
Areo E 91 A4
Areopoli GR 117 F4
Ares E 86 A2
Arès F 76 B1
Ares del Maestrat E 90 C2
Aresvika N 114 D5
Arette F 76 C2
Aretxabaleta E 89 A4
Arevalillo E 93 A5
Arévalo E 94 A2
Arez P 92 B3
Arezzo I 81 C5
Arfeuilles F 68 B3
Argalasti GR 116 C5
Argallón E 99 A5
Argamasilla de Alba E 95 C3
Argamasilla de Calatrava E 100 A1
Arganda E 95 B3
Arganil P 92 A2
Argasion GR 117 E2
Argegno I 71 C4
Argelès-Gazost F 76 C2
Argelès-sur-Mer F 91 A6
Argent-sur-Sauldre F 68 A2
Argenta I 81 B5
Argentan F 57 B5
Argentat F 77 A4
Argentera I 79 B5
Argenteuil F 58 B3
Argenthal D 50 D3
Argentiera I 110 B1
Argenton-Château F 67 B4
Argenton-sur-Creuse F 67 B6
Argentona E 91 B5
Argentré F 57 B5
Argentré-du-Plessis F 57 B4
Argirades GR 116 C1
Argıthanı TR 119 D6
Argos GR 117 E4
Argos Orestiko GR 116 B3
Argostoli GR 117 D2
Argote E 89 B4
Arguedas E 89 B5
Argueil F 58 A2
Arholma S 36 C6
Århus DK 39 C3
Ariano Irpino I 103 B8
Ariano nel Polésine I 82 B1
Aribe E 76 D1
Aridea GR 116 B4
Arienzo I 103 B7
Arild S 41 C2
Arileod GB 24 B1
Arilje SRB 85 C5
Arinagour GB 24 B1
Ariño E 90 B2
Arinthod F 69 B5
Arisaig GB 24 B2
Arisgotas E 94 C3
Aritzo I 110 C2
Ariza E 89 C4
Årjäng S 35 C4
Arjeplog S 115 A14
Arjona E 100 B1
Arjonilla E 100 B1
Arkasa GR 119 G2
Arkelstorp S 41 C4
Arklow IRL 21 B5
Arkösund S 37 D3
Ärla S 37 C3
Arlanc F 68 C3
Arlanzón E 89 B3
Arlebosc F 78 A3
Arlena di Castro I 102 A4
Arles F 78 C3
Arles-sur-Tech F 91 A5
Arló H 65 B6
Arlon B 60 A1
Armação de Pera P 98 B2
Armadale, *Highland* GB 22 D3
Armadale, *West Lothian* GB 25 C4
Armagh GB 19 B5
Armamar P 87 C3
Armenistis GR 117 E8
Armeno I 70 C3
Armenteros E 93 A5
Armentières F 48 C3
Armilla E 100 B2
Armiñón E 89 B4
Armoy GB 19 A5
Armuña de Tajuña E 95 B3
Armutlu, *Bursa* TR 118 B3
Armutlu, *İzmır* TR 119 D2
Arnac-Pompadour F 67 C6
Arnafjord N 32 A3
Arnage F 57 C6
Arnas F 69 B4
Årnäs S 35 D5
Arnay-le-Duc F 69 A4
Arnborg DK 39 C2
Arnbruck D 62 A3
Arnea GR 116 B5
Arneberg, *Hedmark* N 34 A2
Arneberg, *Hedmark* N 34 B4
Arneburg D 44 C4
Arnedillo E 89 B4
Arnedo E 89 B4
Arneguy F 76 C1
Arnés E 90 C3
Árnes IS 111 A4
Årnes, *Akershus* N 34 B3
Årnes, *Troms* N 112 C7
Arnfels A 73 B5
Arnhem NL 50 B1
Arnissa GR 116 B3
Arno S 37 D4
Arnold GB 27 B4
Arnoldstein A 72 B3
Arnsberg D 50 B4
Arnschwang D 62 A3
Arnsdorf D 53 B3
Årnset N 114 D6
Arnside GB 26 A3
Arnstadt D 51 C6
Arnstein D 51 D5
Arnstorf D 62 B3
Arnum DK 39 D1
Aroche E 99 B4
Arolla CH 70 B2
Arolsen D 51 B5
Arona I 70 C3
Åros N 35 C2
Arosa CH 71 B4
Arosa P 87 C2
Årøsund DK 39 D2
Arouca P 87 D2
Årøysund N 35 C2
Arpajon F 58 B3
Arpajon-sur-Cère F 77 B5
Arpino I 103 B6
Arquata del Tronto I 82 D2
Arques F 48 C3
Arques-la-Bataille F 58 A2
Arquillos E 100 A2
Arraia-Maeztu E 89 B4
Arraiolos P 92 C2
Arrancourt F 60 B2
Arras F 48 C3
Arrasate E 89 A4
Årre DK 39 D1
Arreau F 77 D3
Arredondo E 89 A3
Arrens-Marsous F 76 D2
Arriate E 99 C5
Arrifana P 98 B2
Arrigorriaga E 89 A4
Arriondas E 88 A1
Arroba de los Montes E 94 C2
Arrochar GB 24 B3
Arromanches-les-Bains F 57 A5
Arronches P 92 B3
Arroniz E 89 B4
Arrou F 58 B2
Arroya E 88 B2

Arroya de Cuéllar E 88 C2
Arroyal E 88 B2
Arroyo de la Luz E 93 B4
Arroyo de San Servan E 93 C4
Arroyo del Ojanco E 100 A3
Arroyomolinos de León E 99 A4
Arroyomolinos de Montánchez E 93 B4
Arruda dos Vinhos P 92 C1
Års DK 38 C2
Ars-en-Ré F 66 B3
Ars-sur-Moselle F 60 A2
Arsac F 76 B2
Arsiè I 72 C1
Arsiero I 71 C6
Årslev DK 39 D3
Arsoli I 102 A6
Årsunda S 36 B3
Artà E 97 B3
Arta GR 116 C3
Artajona E 89 B5
Artegna I 72 B3
Arteixo E 86 A2
Artemare F 69 C5
Arten I 72 B1
Artena I 102 B5
Artenay F 58 B2
Artern D 52 B1
Artés E 91 B4
Artesa de Segre E 91 B4
Arth CH 70 A3
Arthez-de-Béarn F 76 C2
Arthon-en-Retz F 66 A3
Arthurstown IRL 21 B5
Artieda E 90 A2
Artix F 76 C2
Artotina GR 116 D4
Artsyz UA 11 C10
Artziniega E 89 A3
Arudy F 76 C2
Arundel GB 31 D3
Årup DK 39 D3
Arveyres F 76 B2
Arvidsjaur S 115 B16
Arvieux F 79 B5
Arvika S 35 C4
Åryd, *Blekinge* S 41 C5
Åryd, *Kronoberg* S 40 C4
Arzachena I 110 A2
Arzacq-Arraziguet F 76 C2
Árzana I 110 C2
Arzano F 56 C2
Aržano HR 84 C1
Arzberg D 52 C2
Arzignano I 71 C6
Arzila P 92 A2
Arzl im Pitztal A 71 A5
Arzúa E 86 B2
As B 49 B6
Aš CZ 52 C2
Ås N 35 C2
As Neves E 87 B2
As Nogais E 86 B3
As Pontes de García Rodríguez E 86 A3
Aså DK 38 B3
Åsa S 40 B2
Aşağıçiğil TR 119 D6
Ašanja SRB 85 B5
Åsarna S 115 E11
Åsarøy N 33 C3
Åsarp S 40 A3
Asasp F 76 C2
Åsbro S 37 C2
Åsby, *Halland* S 40 B2
Åsby, *Östergötland* S 40 B5
Asbygri IS 111 A9
Ascain F 76 C1
Ascea I 106 A2
Ascha D 62 A3
Aschach an der Donau A 63 B5
Aschaffenburg D 51 D5
Aschbach Markt A 63 B5
Ascheberg, *Nordrhein-Westfalen* D 50 B3
Ascheberg, *Schleswig-Holstein* D 44 A2
Aschendorf D 43 B4
Aschersleben D 52 B1
Asciano I 81 C5
Ascó E 90 B3
Asco F 102 A2
Áscoli Piceno I 82 D2
Áscoli Satriano I 104 B1
Ascona CH 70 B3
Ascot GB 31 C3
Ascoux F 58 B3
Åse N 112 C4
Åseda S 40 B5
Åsele S 115 C14
Åsen N 114 D8
Åsen S 34 A5
Asendorf D 43 C6
Asenovgrad BG 11 E8
Åsensbruk S 35 D4
Åseral N 33 D4
Asfeld F 59 A5
Ásgarður IS 111 B1
Åsgårdstrand N 35 C2
Asgate CY 120 B2
Ash, *Kent* GB 31 C4
Ash, *Surrey* GB 31 C3
Åshammar S 36 B3
Ashbourne GB 27 B4
Ashbourne IRL 21 A5
Ashburton GB 28 C4
Ashby-de-la-Zouch GB 27 C4
Ashchurch GB 29 B5
Asheim N 114 F8
Ashford GB 31 C4
Ashington GB 25 C6
Ashley GB 26 C3
Ashmyany BY 7 D8
Ashton Under Lyne GB 26 B3
Ashwell GB 30 B3
Asiago I 71 C6
Asipovichy BY 7 E10
Aska FIN 113 E15
Askam-in-Furness GB 26 A2
Askeaton IRL 20 B3
Asker N 34 C2
Askersund S 37 D1
Åskilje S 115 C14
Askim N 35 C3
Askland N 33 D5
Asköping S 37 C3
Askvoll N 32 A2
Åsljunga S 41 C3
Asnæs DK 39 D4
Ásola I 71 C5
Asolo I 72 C1
Asos GR 116 D2
Asotthalom H 75 B4
Aspach A 63 B4
Aspang Markt A 64 C2
Aspariegos E 88 C1
Asparn an der Zaya A 64 B2
Aspatria GB 26 A2
Aspberg S 35 C5
Aspe E 101 A5
Aspet F 77 C3
Äspö S 41 C5
Aspres-sur-Buëch F 79 B4
Aspsele S 115 D15
Assafora P 92 C1
Asse B 49 C5
Assebakte N 113 C14
Assel D 43 B6
Asselborn L 50 C1
Assémini I 110 C1
Assen NL 42 C3
Assenede B 49 B4
Assens, *Aarhus Amt.* DK 38 C3
Assens, *Fyns Amt.* DK 39 D2
Assesse B 49 C6
Assisi I 82 C1
Åsskard N 114 D5
Assling D 62 C3
Asso I 71 C4
Asson F 76 C2
Ássoro I 109 B3
Assumar P 92 B3
Åsta N 34 A3
Astaffort F 77 B3
Astakos GR 116 D3
Asten NL 50 B1
Asti I 80 B2
Astipalea GR 119 F1
Astorga E 86 B4
Åstorp S 41 C2
Åsträsk S 115 C16
Astudillo E 88 B2
Asuni I 110 C1
Asványráró H 64 C3
Aszód H 65 C5
Aszófö H 74 B2
Atabey TR 119 E5
Atalaia P 92 B3
Atalandi GR 116 D4
Atalho P 92 C2
Átány H 65 C6
Atanzón E 95 B3
Ataquines E 94 A2
Atarfe E 100 B2
Atça TR 119 E3
Ateca E 89 C5
Atella I 104 C1
Atessa I 103 A7
Ath B 49 C4
Athboy IRL 19 C5
Athea IRL 20 B2
Athenry IRL 20 A3
Athens = Athina GR 117 E5
Atherstone GB 27 C4
Athienou CY 120 A2
Athies F 59 A3
Athies-sous-Laon F 59 A4
Athina = Athens GR 117 E5
Athleague IRL 20 A3
Athlone IRL 21 A4
Athna CY 120 A2
Athy IRL 21 B5
Atienza E 95 A4
Atina I 103 B6
Atkár H 65 C5
Atlantı TR 119 D7
Atna N 114 F7
Åtorp S 35 C6
Atrå N 32 C5
Ätran S 40 B2
Atri I 103 A6
Atripalda I 103 C7
Atsiki GR 116 C7
Attendorn D 50 B3
Attichy F 59 A4
Attigliano I 102 A5
Attigny F 59 A5
Attleborough GB 30 B5
Åtvidaberg S 37 D2
Atzendorf D 52 B1
Au, *Steiermark* A 63 C6
Au, *Vorarlberg* A 71 A4
Au, *Bayern* D 62 B2
Au, *Bayern* D 62 C2
Aub D 61 A6
Aubagne F 79 C4
Aubange B 60 A1
Aubel B 50 C1
Aubenas F 78 B3
Aubenton F 59 A5
Auberive F 59 C6
Aubeterre-sur-Dronne F 67 C5
Aubiet F 77 C3
Aubigné F 67 B4
Aubigny F 66 B3
Aubigny-au-Bac F 49 C4
Aubigny-en-Artois F 48 C3
Aubigny-sur-Nère F 68 A2
Aubin F 77 B5
Aubonne CH 69 B6
Aubrac F 78 B1
Aubusson F 68 C2
Auch F 77 C3
Auchencairn GB 25 D4
Auchinleck GB 24 C3
Auchterarder GB 25 B4
Auchtermuchty GB 25 B4
Auchtertyre GB 22 D3
Auchy-au-Bois F 48 C3
Audenge F 76 B1
Auderville F 57 A4
Audierne F 56 B1
Audincourt F 70 A1
Audlem GB 26 C3
Audruicq F 48 C3
Audun-le-Roman F 60 A1
Audun-le-Tiche F 60 A1
Aue, *Nordrhein-Westfalen* D 50 B4
Aue, *Sachsen* D 52 C2
Auerbach, *Bayern* D 62 A2
Auerbach, *Sachsen* D 52 C2
Auffach A 72 A2
Augher GB 19 B4
Aughnacloy GB 19 B5
Aughrim IRL 21 B5
Augignac F 67 C5
Augsburg D 62 B1
Augusta I 109 B4
Augusten-borg DK 39 E2
Augustfehn D 43 B4
Augustów PL 6 E7
Aukrug D 44 A1
Auktsjaur S 115 B16
Auldearn GB 23 D5
Aulendorf D 61 C5
Auletta I 103 C8
Aulla I 81 B3
Aullène F 102 B2
Aulnay F 67 B4
Aulnoye-Aymeries F 49 C4
Ault F 48 C2
Aultbea GB 22 D3
Aulum DK 39 C1
Aulus-les-Bains F 77 D4
Auma D 52 C1
Aumale F 58 A2
Aumetz F 60 A1
Aumont-Aubrac F 78 B2
Aunay-en-Bazois F 68 A3
Aunay-sur-Odon F 57 A5
Aune N 115 C10
Auneau F 58 B2
Auneuil F 58 A2
Auning DK 39 C3
Aunsetra N 115 C9
Aups F 79 C5
Aura D 51 C5
Auray F 56 C3
Aurdal N 32 B6
Aure N 114 D5
Aurich D 43 B4
Aurignac F 77 C3
Aurillac F 77 B5
Auriol F 79 C4
Auritz-Burguette E 76 D1
Aurlandsvangen N 32 B4
Auronzo di Cadore I 72 B2
Auros F 76 B2
Auroux F 78 B2
Aurskog N 34 C3
Aursmoen N 34 C3
Ausónia I 103 B6
Ausservillgraton A 72 B2
Austad N 33 D4
Austbygda N 32 B5
Aústis I 110 B2
Austmarka N 34 B4
Austre Moland N 33 D5
Austre Vikebygd N 33 C2
Austrheim N 32 B1
Auterive F 77 C4
Autheuil-Authouillet F 58 A2
Authon F 79 B5
Authon-du-Perche F 58 B1
Autol E 89 B5
Autreville F 60 B1
Autrey-lès-Gray F 69 A5
Autun F 69 B4
Auty-le-Châtel F 58 C3
Auvelais B 49 C5
Auvillar F 77 B3
Auxerre F 59 C4
Auxi-le-Château F 48 C3
Auxon F 59 B4
Auxonne F 69 A5
Auxy F 69 B4
Auzances F 68 B2
Auzon F 68 C3
Availles-Limouzine F 67 B5
Avaldsnes N 33 C2
Avallon F 68 A3
Avantas GR 116 B7
Avaviken S 115 B15
Avebury GB 29 B6
Aveiras de Cima P 92 B2
Aveiro P 92 A2
Avelgem B 49 C4
Avellino I 103 C7
Avenches CH 70 B2
Aversa I 103 C7
Avesnes-le-Comte F 48 C3
Avesnes-sur-Helpe F 49 C4
Avesta S 36 B3
Avetrana I 105 C3
Avezzano I 103 A6
Avià E 91 A4
Aviano I 72 B2
Aviemore GB 23 D5
Avigliana I 80 A1
Avigliano I 104 C1
Avignon F 78 C3
Ávila E 94 B2
Avilés E 88 A1
Avilley F 69 A6
Avintes P 87 C2
Avinyo E 91 B4
Àvio I 71 C5
Avioth F 59 A6
Avis P 92 B3
Avize F 59 B5
Avlonari GR 116 D6
Ávola I 109 C4
Avon F 58 B3
Avonmouth GB 29 B5
Avord F 68 A2
Avranches F 57 B4
Avril F 60 A1
Avrillé F 67 A4
Avtovac BIH 84 C3
Awans B 49 C6
Ax-les-Thermes F 77 D4
Axams A 71 A6
Axat F 77 D5
Axbridge GB 29 B5
Axel NL 49 B4
Axmarby S 36 B4
Axmarsbruk S 36 A4
Axminster GB 29 C4
Axvall S 35 D5
Ay F 59 A5
Aya E 89 A4
Ayamonte E 98 B3
Ayancık TR 16 A7
Ayaş TR 118 B7
Aydın TR 119 E2
Ayelo de Malferit E 96 C2
Ayer CH 70 B2
Ayerbe E 90 A2
Ayette F 48 C3
Ayia Napa CY 120 B2
Áyia Phyla CY 120 B2
Áyios Amvrósios CY 120 A2
Áyios Seryios CY 120 A2
Áyios Theodhoros CY 120 A3
Aykirikçi TR 118 C5
Aylesbury GB 31 C3
Ayllón E 89 C3
Aylsham GB 30 B5
Ayna E 101 A3
Ayódar E 96 B2
Ayora E 96 B1
Ayr GB 24 C3
Ayrancı TR 16 C6
Ayrancılar TR 119 D2
Ayron F 67 B5
Aysgarth GB 27 A4
Ayton GB 25 C5
Aytos BG 11 E9
Ayvacık TR 118 C1
Ayvalık TR 118 C1
Aywaille B 49 C6
Azaila E 90 B2
Azambuja P 92 B2
Azambujeira P 92 B2
Azanja SRB 85 B5
Azannes-et-Soumazannes F 60 A1
Azanúy-Alins E 90 B3
Azaruja P 92 C3
Azay-le-Ferron F 67 B6
Azay-le-Rideau F 67 A5
Azcoitia E 89 A4
Azé F 69 B4
Azeiteiros P 92 B3
Azenhas do Mar P 92 C1
Azinhaga P 92 B2
Azinhal P 98 B3
Azinheira dos Bairros P 98 A2
Aznalcázar E 99 B4
Aznalcóllar E 99 B4
Azóia P 92 B2
Azpeitia E 89 A4
Azuaga E 99 A5
Azuara E 90 B2
Azuqueca de Henares E 95 B3
Azur F 76 C1
Azzano Décimo I 72 C2

B

Baad A 71 A5
Baamonde E 86 A3
Baar CH 70 A3
Baarle-Nassau B 49 B5
Baarn NL 49 A6
Babadag RO 11 D10
Babadağ TR 119 E3
Babaeski TR 118 A2
Babayevo RUS 7 B13
Babenhausen, *Bayern* D 61 B6
Babenhausen, *Hessen* D 51 D4
Babiak PL 54 A3
Babice PL 55 C4
Babigoszcz PL 45 B6
Babimost PL 53 A5
Babina Greda HR 84 A3
Babócsa H 74 B2
Bábolma H 64 C3
Baborów PL 54 C2
Baboszewo PL 47 C6
Babót H 64 C3
Babruysk BY 7 E10
Babsk PL 55 B5
Bač CG 85 D5
Bac GB 22 C2
Bač, *Vojvodina* SRB 75 C4
Bacares E 101 B3
Bacău RO 11 C9
Baccarat F 60 B2
Bacharach D 50 C3
Bačina SRB 85 C6
Backa S 36 B2
Bačka Palanka SRB 75 C4
Bačka Topola SRB 75 C4
Backaryd S 41 C5
Backe S 115 D13
Bäckebo S 40 C6
Bäckefors S 35 D4
Bäckhammar S 35 C6
Bački Breg SRB 75 C3
Bački-Brestovac SRB 75 C4
Bački Monoštor SRB 75 C3
Bački Petrovac SRB 75 C4
Bački Sokolac SRB 75 C4
Backnang D 61 B5
Bačko Gradište SRB 75 C5
Bačko Novo Selo SRB 75 C4
Bačko Petrovo Selo SRB 75 C5
Bácoli I 103 C7
Bacqueville-en-Caux F 58 A2
Bácsalmás H 75 B4
Bácsbokod H 75 B4
Bad Abbach D 62 B3
Bad Aibling D 62 C3
Bad Aussee A 63 C4
Bad Bederkesa D 43 B5
Bad Bentheim D 50 A3
Bad Bergzabern D 60 A3
Bad Berka D 52 C1
Bad Berleburg D 51 B4
Bad Berneck D 52 C1
Bad Bevensen D 44 B2
Bad Bibra D 52 B1
Bad Birnbach D 62 B4
Bad Blankenburg D 52 C1
Bad Bleiberg A 72 B3
Bad Brambach D 52 C2
Bad Bramstedt D 44 B1
Bad Breisig D 50 C3
Bad Brückenau D 51 C5
Bad Buchau D 61 B5
Bad Camberg D 50 C4
Bad Doberan D 44 A3
Bad Driburg D 51 B5
Bad Düben D 52 B2
Bad Dürkheim D 61 A4
Bad Dürrenberg D 52 B2
Bad Dürrheim D 61 B4
Bad Elster D 52 C2
Bad Ems D 50 C3
Bad Endorf D 62 C3
Bad Essen D 50 A4
Bad Fischau A 64 C2
Bad Frankenhausen D 52 B1
Bad Freienwalde D 45 C6
Bad Friedrichshall D 61 A5
Bad Füssing D 63 B4
Bad Gandersheim D 51 B6
Bad Gastein A 72 A3
Bad Gleichenberg A 73 B5
Bad Goisern A 63 C4
Bad Gottleuba D 53 C3
Bad Grund D 51 B6
Bad Hall A 63 B5
Bad Harzburg D 51 B6
Bad Herrenalb D 61 B4
Bad Hersfeld D 51 C5
Bad Hofgastein A 72 A3
Bad Homburg D 51 C4
Bad Honnef D 50 C3
Bad Hönningen D 50 C3
Bad Iburg D 50 A4
Bad Inner-laterns A 71 A4
Bad Ischl A 63 C4
Bad Karlshafen D 51 B5
Bad Kemmeriboden CH 70 B2
Bad Kissingen D 51 C6
Bad Kleinen D 44 B3
Bad Kohlgrub D 62 C2
Bad König D 61 A5
Bad Königshofen D 51 C6
Bad Köstritz D 52 C2
Bad Kreuzen A 63 B5
Bad Kreuznach D 60 A3
Bad Krozingen D 60 C3
Bad Laasphe D 51 C4
Bad Langensalza D 51 B6
Bad Lauchstädt D 52 B1
Bad Lausick D 52 B2
Bad Lauterberg D 51 B6
Bad Leonfelden A 63 B5
Bad Liebenwerda D 52 B3
Bad Liebenzell D 61 B4
Bad Lippspringe D 51 B4
Bad Meinberg D 51 B4
Bad Mergentheim D 61 A5
Bad Mitterndorf A 72 A3
Bad Münder D 51 A5
Bad Münstereifel D 50 C2
Bad Muskau D 53 B4
Bad Nauheim D 51 C4
Bad Nenndorf D 43 C6
Bad Neuenahr-Ahrweiler D 50 C3
Bad Neustadt D 51 C6
Bad Oeynhausen D 51 A4
Bad Oldesloe D 44 B2
Bad Orb D 51 C5
Bad Peterstal D 61 B4
Bad Pyrmont D 51 B5
Bad Radkersburg A 73 B5
Bad Ragaz CH 71 B4
Bad Rappenau D 61 A5
Bad Reichenhall D 62 C3
Bad Saarow-Pieskow D 53 A4
Bad Sachsa D 51 B6
Bad Säckingen D 70 A2
Bad Salzdetfurth D 51 A6
Bad Salzig D 50 C3
Bad Salzuflen D 51 A4
Bad Salzungen D 51 C6
Bad Sankt Leonhard A 73 B4
Bad Sassendorf D 50 B4
Bad Schandau D 53 C4
Bad Schmiedeberg D 52 B2
Bad Schönborn D 61 A4
Bad Schussenried D 61 B5
Bad Schwalbach D 50 C4
Bad Schwartau D 44 B2
Bad Segeberg D 44 B2
Bad Soden D 51 C4
Bad Soden-Salmünster D 51 C5
Bad Sooden-Allendorf D 51 B5
Bad Sulza D 52 B1
Bad Sülze D 45 A4
Bad Tatzmannsdorf A 73 A6
Bad Tennstedt D 51 B6
Bad Tölz D 62 C2
Bad Urach D 61 B5
Bad Vellach A 73 B4
Bad Vilbel D 51 C4
Bad Vöslau A 64 C2
Bad Waldsee D 61 C5
Bad Wiessee D 62 C2
Bad Wildungen D 51 B5
Bad Wilsnack D 44 C3
Bad Windsheim D 61 A6
Bad Wörishafen D 62 B1
Bad Wurzach D 61 C5
Bad Zwesten D 51 B5
Bad Zwischenahn D 43 B5
Badacsonytomaj H 74 B2
Badajoz E 93 C4
Badalona E 91 B5
Badalucco I 80 C1
Badderen N 113 C11
Baden A 64 B2
Baden CH 70 A3
Baden-Baden D 61 B4
Bádenas E 90 B1
Badenweiler D 60 C3
Baderna HR 72 C3
Badia Calavena I 71 C6
Badia Polésine I 81 A5
Badia Pratáglia I 81 C5
Badia Tedalda I 82 C1
Bądki PL 47 B4
Badkowo PL 47 C4
Badljevina HR 74 C2
Badolato I 106 C3
Badolatosa E 100 B1
Badonviller F 60 B2
Badovinci SRB 85 B4
Badules E 90 B1
Bække DK 39 D2
Bækmarksbro DK 39 C1
Baells E 90 B3
Bælum DK 38 C3
Baena E 100 B1
Baesweiler D 50 C2
Baeza E 100 B2
Baflo NL 42 B3
Bafra TR 16 A7
Baga E 91 A4
Bagaladi I 106 C2
Bağarasi TR 119 E2
Bagenkop DK 39 E3
Baggetorp S 37 C3
Bagh a Chaisteil GB 22 E1
Bagheria I 108 A2
Bagn N 32 B6
Bagnacavallo I 81 B5
Bagnáia I 102 A5
Bagnara Cálabra I 106 C2
Bagnasco I 80 B2
Bagnères-de-Bigorre F 76 C3
Bagnères-de-Luchon F 77 D3
Bagni del Másino I 71 B4
Bagni di Lucca I 81 B4
Bagni di Rabbi I 71 B5
Bagni di Tivoli I 102 B5
Bagno di Romagna I 81 C5
Bagnoles-de-l'Orne F 57 B5
Bagnoli dei Trigno I 103 B7
Bagnoli di Sopra I 72 C1
Bagnoli Irpino I 103 C8
Bagnolo Mella I 71 C5
Bagnols-en-Forêt F 79 C5
Bagnols-sur-Cèze F 78 B3
Bagnorégio I 102 A5
Bagolino I 71 C5
Bagrationovsk RUS 47 A6
Bagrdan SRB 85 B6
Báguena E 95 A5
Bahabón de Esgueva E 88 C3
Bahillo E 88 B2
Báia delle Zágare I 104 B2
Báia Domizia I 103 B6
Baia Mare RO 11 C7
Baiano I 103 C7
Baião P 87 C2
Baiersbronn D 61 B4
Baiersdorf D 62 A2
Baignes-Ste. Radegonde F 67 C4
Baigneux-les-Juifs F 59 C5
Baildon GB 27 B4
Bailén E 100 A2
Băilești RO 11 D7
Baileux B 49 C5
Bailieborough IRL 19 C5
Bailleul F 48 C3
Baillonville B 49 C6
Bailó E 90 A2
Bain-de-Bretagne F 57 C4
Bains F 78 A2
Bains-les-Bains F 60 B2
Bainton GB 27 B5
Baio E 86 A2
Baiona E 87 B2
Bais F 57 B5
Baiso I 81 B4
Baiuca P 92 A3
Baja H 75 B3
Bajánsenye H 73 B6
Bajina Bašta SRB 85 C4
Bajmok SRB 75 C4
Bajna H 65 C4
Bajovo Polje CG 84 C3
Bajram Curri AL 105 A6
Bajša SRB 75 C4
Bajzë AL 105 A5
Bak H 74 B1
Bakar HR 73 C4
Bakewell GB 27 B4
Bakhmach UA 7 F12
Bakio E 89 A4
Bakırdaği TR 16 B7
Bakka N 32 C6
Bakkafjörður IS 111 A11
Bakkagerði IS 111 B12
Bakken N 34 B3
Baklan TR 119 E4
Bakonybél H 74 A2
Bakonycsernye H 74 A3
Bakonyjákó H 74 A2
Bakonyszentkirály H 74 A2
Bakonyszombathely H 74 A2
Bakov nad Jizerou CZ 53 C4
Bąkowiec PL 55 B6
Baks H 75 B5
Baksa H 74 C3
Bakum D 43 C5
Bala GB 26 C2
Bâlâ TR 16 B6
Balaguer E 90 B3
Balassagyarmat H 65 B5
Balástya H 75 B5
Balatonakali H 74 B2
Balatonalmádi H 74 A3
Balatonboglár H 74 B2
Balatonbozsok H 74 B3
Balatonederics H 74 B2
Balatonfenyves H 74 B2
Balatonföldvár H 74 B2
Balatonfüred H 74 B2
Balatonfüzfö H 74 A3
Balatonkenese H 74 A3
Balatonkiliti H 74 B3
Balatonlelle H 74 B2
Balatonszabadi H 74 B3
Balatonszemes H 74 B2
Balatonszentgyörgy H 74 B2
Balazote E 101 A3
Balbeggie GB 25 B4
Balbigny F 69 C4
Balboa E 86 B4
Balbriggan IRL 19 C5
Balchik BG 11 E10
Balçova TR 119 D2
Baldock GB 31 C3
Bale HR 82 A2
Baleira E 86 A3
Baleizao P 98 A3
Balen B 49 B6
Balerma E 100 C3
Balestrand N 32 A3
Balestrate I 108 A2
Balfour GB 23 B6
Bälganet S 41 C5
Balıkesir TR 118 C2
Balıklıçeşme TR 118 B2
Bälinge S 36 C4
Balingen D 61 B4
Balingsta S 36 C4
Balintore GB 23 D5
Balizac F 76 B2
Baljevac SRB 85 C5
Balk NL 42 C2
Balkbrug NL 42 C3
Balla IRL 18 C2
Ballachulish GB 24 B2
Ballaghaderreen IRL 18 C3
Ballancourt-sur-Essonne F 58 B3
Ballantrae GB 24 C3
Ballao I 110 C2
Ballasalla GB 26 A1
Ballater GB 23 D5
Ballen DK 39 D3
Ballenstedt D 52 B1
Ballerias E 90 B2
Balleroy F 57 A5
Ballerup DK 41 D2
Ballesteros de Calatrava E 100 A2
Ballı TR 118 B2
Ballina IRL 18 B2
Ballinalack IRL 19 C4
Ballinamore IRL 19 B4
Ballinascarty IRL 20 C3
Ballinasloe IRL 20 A3
Ballindine IRL 18 C3
Balling DK 38 C1
Ballingarry, *Limerick* IRL 20 B3
Ballingarry, *Tipperary* IRL 21 B4
Ballingeary IRL 20 C2
Ballinhassig IRL 20 C3
Ballinluig GB 25 B4
Ballino I 71 C5
Ballinrobe IRL 18 C2
Ballinskellings IRL 20 C1
Ballinspittle IRL 20 C3
Ballintra IRL 18 B3
Ballivor IRL 21 A5
Ballobar E 90 B3
Ballon F 58 B1
Ballon IRL 21 B5
Ballószög H 75 B4
Ballsh AL 105 C5
Ballstad N 112 D2
Ballum DK 39 D1
Ballybay IRL 19 B5
Ballybofey IRL 19 B4
Ballybunion IRL 20 B2
Ballycanew IRL 21 B5
Ballycarry GB 19 B6
Ballycastle GB 19 A5
Ballycastle IRL 18 B2
Ballyclare GB 19 B6
Ballyconneely IRL 18 C1
Ballycotton IRL 20 C3
Ballycroy IRL 18 B2
Ballydehob IRL 20 C2
Ballyferriter IRL 20 B1
Ballygawley GB 19 B4
Ballygowan GB 19 B6
Ballyhaunis IRL 18 C3
Ballyheige IRL 20 B2
Ballyjamesduff IRL 19 C4
Ballylanders IRL 20 B3
Ballylynan IRL 21 B4
Ballymahon IRL 21 A4
Ballymena GB 19 B5
Ballymoe IRL 18 C3
Ballymoney GB 19 A5
Ballymore IRL 21 A4
Ballymote IRL 18 B3
Ballynacorra IRL 20 C3
Ballynagore IRL 21 A4
Ballynahinch GB 19 B6
Ballynure GB 19 B6
Ballyragget IRL 21 B4
Ballysadare IRL 18 B3
Ballyshannon IRL 18 B3
Ballyvaughan IRL 20 A2
Ballyvourney IRL 20 C2
Ballywalter GB 19 B6
Balmaclellan GB 24 C3
Balmaseda E 89 A3
Balme I 70 C2
Balmedie GB 23 D6
Balmuccia I 70 C3
Balna-paling GB 23 D4
Balneario de Panticosa E 76 D2
Balotaszállás H 75 B4
Balsa P 87 C3
Balsareny E 91 B4
Balsorano-Nuovo I 103 B6
Bålsta S 37 C4
Balsthal CH 70 A2
Balta UA 11 B10
Baltanás E 88 C2
Baltar E 87 C3
Baltasound GB 22 A8
Bălţi MD 11 C9
Baltimore IRL 20 C2
Baltinglass IRL 21 B5
Baltiysk RUS 47 A5
Baltów PL 55 B6

Balugães P 87 C2
Balve D 50 B3
Balvi LV 7 C9
Balvicar GB 24 B2
Balya TR 118 C2
Balzo I 82 D2
Bamberg D 62 A1
Bamburgh GB 25 C6
Banatska Palanka SRB 85 B6
Banatski Brestovac SRB 85 B5
Banatski Despotovac SRB 75 C5
Banatski Dvor SRB 75 C5
Banatski-Karlovac SRB 85 A6
Banatsko Arandjelovo SRB 75 B5
Banatsko-Novo Selo SRB 85 B5
Banaz TR 118 D4
Banbridge GB 19 B5
Banbury GB 30 B2
Banchory GB 23 D6
Bande B 49 C6
Bande E 87 B3
Bandholm DK 39 E4
Bandırma TR 118 B2
Bandol F 79 C4
Bandon IRL 20 C3
Bañeres E 96 C2
Banff GB 23 D6
Bangor F 66 A1
Bangor, *Down* GB 19 B6
Bangor, *Gwynedd* GB 26 B1
Bangor IRL 18 B2
Bangsund N 114 C8
Banie PL 45 B6
Banja SRB 85 C4
Banja Koviljača SRB 85 B4
Banja Luka BIH 84 B2
Banja Vručica BIH 84 B2
Banjaloka SLO 73 C4
Banjani SRB 85 B4
Banje SRB 85 D5
Banjska SRB 85 D5
Banka SK 64 B3
Bankekind S 37 D2
Bankend GB 25 C4
Bankeryd S 40 B4
Bankfoot GB 25 B4
Banloc RO 75 C6
Bannalec F 56 C2
Bannes F 59 B4
Bannockburn GB 25 B4
Bañobárez E 87 D4
Bañon E 90 C1
Banon F 79 B4
Baños E 93 A5
Baños de Gigonza E 99 C5
Baños de la Encina E 100 A2
Baños de Molgas E 87 B3
Baños de Rio Tobia E 89 B4
Baños de Valdearados E 89 C3
Bánov CZ 64 B3
Banova Jaruga HR 74 C1
Bánovce nad Bebravou SK 64 B4
Banovići BIH 84 B3
Banovići Selo BIH 84 B3
Bánréve H 65 B6
Bansin D 45 B6
Banská Belá SK 65 B4
Banská Bystrica SK 65 B5
Banská Štiavnica SK 65 B4
Banstead GB 31 C3
Banteer IRL 20 B3
Bantheville F 59 A6
Bantry IRL 20 C2
Bantzenheim F 60 C3
Banyalbufar E 97 B2
Banyoles E 91 A5
Banyuls-sur-Mer F 91 A6
Bapaume F 48 C3
Bar CG 105 A5
Bar UA 11 B9
Bar-le-Duc F 59 B6
Bar-sur-Aube F 59 B5
Bar-sur-Seine F 59 B5
Barabhas GB 22 C2
Barači BIH 84 B1
Baracs H 74 B3
Baracska H 74 A3
Barahona E 89 C4
Barajes de Melo E 95 B4
Barakaldo E 89 A4
Baralla E 86 B3
Barañain E 76 D1
Baranavichy BY 7 E9
Báránd H 75 A6
Baranda SRB 85 A5
Baranello I 103 B7
Baranów Sandomierski PL 55 C6
Baraqueville F 77 B5
Barasoain E 89 B5
Barbacena P 92 C3
Barbadás E 87 B3
Barbadillo E 94 B1
Barbadillo de Herreros E 89 B3
Barbadillo del Mercado E 89 B3
Barbadillo del Pez E 89 B3
Barban HR 82 A3
Barbarano Vicento I 71 C6
Barbariga HR 82 B2
Barbaros TR 118 B2
Barbastro E 90 A3
Barbate de Franco E 99 C5
Barbatona E 95 A4
Barbâtre F 66 B2
Barbazan F 77 C3
Barbeitos E 86 A3
Barbentane F 78 C3
Barberino di Mugello I 81 B5
Barbezieux-St. Hilaire F 67 C4
Barbonne-Fayel F 59 B4
Barbotan-les-Thermes F 76 C2
Barby D 52 B1
Barca de Alva P 87 C4
Bárcabo E 90 A3
Barcarrota E 93 C4
Barcellona-Pozzo di Gotto I 109 A4
Barcelona E 91 B5
Barcelonette F 79 B5
Barcelos P 87 C2
Barcena de Pie de Concha E 88 A2
Bárcena del Monasterio E 86 A4
Barchfeld D 51 C6
Barcin PL 46 C3
Barcino PL 46 A2
Bárcis I 72 B2
Barco P 92 A3
Barcones E 89 C4
Barcs H 74 C2
Barcus F 76 C2
Barczewo PL 47 B6
Bardejov SK 10 B6
Bårdesø DK 39 D3
Bardi I 81 B3
Bardney GB 27 B5
Bardo PL 54 C1
Bardolino I 71 C5
Bardonécchia I 79 A5
Bardoňovo SK 65 B4
Barèges F 76 D3
Barenstein D 52 C3
Barentin F 58 A1
Barenton F 57 B5
Barevo BIH 84 B2
Barfleur F 57 A4
Barga I 81 B4
Bargas E 94 C2
Barge I 79 B6
Bargemon F 79 C5
Barghe I 71 C5
Bargoed GB 29 B4
Bargrennan GB 24 C3
Bargteheide D 44 B2
Barham GB 31 C5
Bari I 104 B2
Bari Sardo I 110 C2
Barič Draga HR 83 B4
Barilović HR 73 C5
Barisciano I 103 A6
Barjac F 78 B3
Barjols F 79 C4
Barjon F 59 C5
Bårkåker N 35 C2
Barkald N 114 F7
Barkowo, *Dolnośląskie* PL 54 B1
Barkowo, *Pomorskie* PL 46 B3
Bârlad RO 11 C9
Barles F 79 B5
Barletta I 104 B2
Barlinek PL 45 C7
Barmouth GB 26 C1
Barmstedt D 43 B6
Barnard Castle GB 27 A4
Barnarp S 40 B4
Bärnau D 62 A3
Bärnbach A 73 A5
Barneberg D 52 A1
Barnenitz D 45 C4
Barnet GB 31 C3
Barnetby le Wold GB 27 B5
Barneveld NL 49 A6
Barneville-Carteret F 57 A4
Barnoldswick GB 26 B3
Barnowko PL 45 C6
Barnsley GB 27 B4
Barnstädt D 52 B1
Barnstaple GB 28 B3
Barnstorf D 43 C5
Barntrup D 51 B5
Baron F 58 A3
Baronissi I 103 C7
Barqueiro P 92 B2
Barquinha P 92 B2
Barr F 60 B3
Barr GB 24 C3
Barra P 92 A2
Barracas E 96 A2
Barraco E 94 B2
Barrado E 93 A5
Barrafranca I 109 B3
Barranco do Velho P 98 B3
Barrancos P 99 A4
Barrax E 95 C4
Barrbaar D 62 B1
Barre-des-Cevennes F 78 B2
Barreiro P 92 C1
Barreiros E 86 A3
Barrême F 79 C5
Barret-le-Bas F 79 B4
Barrhead GB 24 C3
Barrhill GB 24 C3
Barrio de Nuesra Señora E 88 B1
Barrow-in-Furness GB 26 A2
Barrow upon Humber GB 27 B5
Barrowford GB 26 B3
Barruecopardo E 87 C4
Barruelo de Santullán E 88 B2
Barruera E 90 A3
Barry GB 29 B4
Bårse DK 39 D4
Barsinghausen D 51 A5
Barssel D 43 B4
Barth D 45 A4
Bartholomä D 61 B5
Bartin TR 118 A7
Barton upon Humber GB 27 B5
Bartoszyce PL 47 A6
Barúmini I 110 C1
Baruth D 52 A3
Barvaux B 49 C6
Barver D 43 C5
Barwałd PL 65 A5
Barwice PL 46 B2
Barysaw BY 7 D10
Barzana E 88 A1
Bârzava RO 10 C6
Bárzio I 71 C4
Bas E 91 A5
Bašaid SRB 75 C5
Basaluzzo I 80 B2
Basarabeasca MD 11 C10
Basauri E 89 A4
Baschi I 82 D1
Baschurch GB 26 C3
Basconcillos del Tozo E 88 B3
Bascones de Ojeda E 88 B2
Basécles B 49 C4
Basel CH 70 A2
Basélice I 103 B7
Basildon GB 31 C4
Basingstoke GB 31 C2
Baška CZ 65 A4
Baška HR 83 B3
Baška Voda HR 84 C1
Bäsksjö S 115 C14
Baslow GB 27 B4
Başmakçı TR 119 E5
Basovizza I 72 C3
Bassacutena I 110 A2
Bassano del Grappa I 72 C1
Bassano Romano I 102 A5
Bassecourt CH 70 A2
Bassella E 91 A4
Bassevuovdde N 113 D14
Bassou F 59 C4
Bassoues F 76 C3
Bassum D 43 C5
Båstad S 40 C2
Bastardo I 82 D1
Bastelica F 102 A2
Bastelicaccia F 102 B1
Bastia F 102 A2
Bastia I 82 C1
Bastogne B 50 C1
Baston GB 30 B3
Bastuträsk S 115 C17
Bata H 74 B3
Batajnica SRB 85 B5
Batalha P 92 B2
Bátaszék H 74 B3
Batea E 90 B3
Batelov CZ 63 A6
Bath GB 29 B5
Bathgate GB 25 C4
Batida H 75 B5
Batignano I 81 D5
Batina HR 74 C3
Bátka SK 65 B6
Batković BIH 85 B4
Batlava SRB 85 D6
Batley GB 27 B4
Batnfjordsøra N 114 E4
Batočina SRB 85 B6
Bátonyterenye H 65 C5
Batrina HR 74 C2
Båtsfjord N 113 B18
Battaglia Terme I 72 C1
Bätterkinden CH 70 A2
Battice B 50 C1
Battipáglia I 103 C7
Battle GB 31 D4
Battonya H 75 B6
Batuša SRB 85 B6
Bátya H 75 B3
Bau I 110 C1
Baud F 56 C2
Baudour B 49 C4
Baugé F 67 A4
Baugy F 68 A2
Bauma CH 70 A3
Baume-les-Dames F 69 A6
Baumholder D 60 A3
Baunatal D 51 B5
Baunei I 110 B2
Bauska LV 6 C8
Bautzen D 53 B4
Bavanište SRB 85 B5
Bavay F 49 C4
Bavilliers F 60 C2
Bavorov CZ 63 A5
Bawdsey GB 31 B5
Bawinkel D 43 C4
Bawtry GB 27 B4
Bayat TR 118 D5
Bayel F 59 B5
Bayeux F 57 A5
Bayındır TR 119 D2
Bayon F 60 B2
Bayonne F 76 C1
Bayons F 79 B5
Bayramiç TR 118 C1
Bayreuth D 52 D1
Bayrischzell D 62 C3
Baza E 101 B3
Bazas F 76 B2
Baziege F 77 C4
Bazoches-les-Gallerandes F 58 B3
Bazoches-sur-Hoëne F 58 B1
Bazzano I 81 B5
Beaconsfield GB 31 C3
Beade E 87 B2
Beadnell GB 25 C6
Beaminster GB 29 C5
Bearsden GB 24 C3
Beas E 99 B4
Beas de Segura E 100 A3
Beasain E 89 A4
Beattock GB 25 C4
Beaubery F 69 B4
Beaucaire F 78 C3
Beaufort F 69 C6
Beaufort IRL 20 B2
Beaufort-en Vallée F 67 A4
Beaugency F 58 C2
Beaujeu, *Alpes-de-Haute-Provence* F 79 B5
Beaujeu, *Rhône* F 69 B4
Beaulac F 76 B2
Beaulieu F 68 A2
Beaulieu GB 31 D2
Beaulieu-sous-la-Roche F 66 B3
Beaulieu-sur-Dordogne F 77 B4
Beaulieu-sur-Mer F 80 C1
Beaulon F 68 B3
Beauly GB 23 D4
Beaumaris GB 26 B1
Beaumesnil F 58 A1
Beaumetz-lès-Loges F 48 C3
Beaumont B 49 C5
Beaumont F 77 B3
Beaumont-de-Lomagne F 77 C3
Beaumont-du-Gâtinais F 58 B3
Beaumont-en-Argonne F 59 A6
Beaumont-Hague F 57 A4
Beaumont-la-Ronce F 58 C1
Beaumont-le-Roger F 58 A1
Beaumont-sur-Oise F 58 A3
Beaumont-sur-Sarthe F 57 B6
Beaune F 69 A4
Beaune-la-Rolande F 58 B3
Beaupréau F 66 A4
Beauraing B 49 C5
Beaurepaire F 69 C5
Beaurepaire-en-Bresse F 69 B5
Beaurières F 79 B4
Beauvais F 58 A3
Beauval F 48 C3
Beauville F 77 B3
Beauvoir-sur-Mer F 66 B2
Beauvoir-sur-Niort F 67 B4
Beba Veche RO 75 B5
Bebertal D 52 A1
Bebington GB 26 B2
Bebra D 51 C5
Bebrina HR 84 A2
Beccles GB 30 B5
Becedas E 93 A5
Beceite E 90 C3
Bečej SRB 75 C5
Becerreá E 86 B3
Becerril de Campos E 88 B2
Bécherel F 57 B4
Bechhofen D 61 A6
Bechyně CZ 63 A5
Bečići CG 105 A4
Becilla de Valderaduey E 88 B1
Beckfoot GB 25 D4
Beckingham GB 27 B5
Beckum D 50 B4
Beco P 92 B2
Bécon-les-Granits F 66 A4
Bečov nad Teplou CZ 52 C2
Becsehely H 74 B1
Bedale GB 27 A4
Bedames E 89 A3
Bédar E 101 B4
Bédarieux F 78 C2
Bédarrides F 78 B3
Bedburg D 50 C2
Beddgelert GB 26 B1
Beddingestrand S 41 D3
Bédée F 57 B4
Bedegkér H 74 B3
Beden TR 119 F7
Bedford GB 30 B3
Będków PL 55 B4
Bedlington GB 25 C6
Bedlno PL 55 A4
Bedmar E 100 B2
Bédoin F 79 B4
Bedónia I 80 B3
Bedretto CH 70 B3
Bedsted DK 38 C1
Bedum NL 42 B3
Bedwas GB 29 B4
Bedworth GB 30 B2
Będzin PL 55 C4
Beek en Donk NL 49 B6
Beekbergen NL 50 A1
Beelen D 50 B4
Beelitz D 52 A2
Beer GB 29 C4
Beerfelde D 45 C6
Beerfelden D 61 A4
Beernem B 49 B4
Beeskow D 53 A4
Beetsterzwaag NL 42 B3
Beetzendorf D 44 C3
Beflelay CH 70 A2
Begaljica SRB 85 B5
Bégard F 56 B2
Begejci SRB 75 C5
Begijar E 100 B2
Begijnendijk B 49 B5
Begndal N 34 B1
Begues E 91 B4
Beguildy GB 26 C2
Begur E 91 B6
Beho B 50 C1
Behringen D 51 B6
Beilen NL 42 C3
Beilngries D 62 A2
Beine-Nauroy F 59 A5
Beinwil CH 70 A3
Beiseförth D 51 B5
Beith GB 24 C3
Beitostølen N 32 A5
Beiuş RO 11 C7
Beja P 98 A3
Béjar E 93 A5
Bekçiler TR 119 F4
Békés H 75 B6
Békéscsaba H 75 B6
Bekilli TR 119 D4
Bekkarfjord N 113 B16
Bela SK 65 A4
Bela Crkva SRB 85 B6
Belá nad Radbuzou CZ 62 A3
Bělá pod Bezdězem CZ 53 C4
Bélâbre F 67 B6
Belalcázar E 93 C5
Belanovica SRB 85 B5
Bélapátfalva H 65 B6
Belcaire F 77 D4
Bełchatów PL 55 B4
Belchite E 90 B2
Bělčice CZ 63 A4
Belcoo GB 19 B4
Belecke D 51 B4
Beled H 74 A2
Belej HR 83 B3
Beleño E 88 A1
Bélesta F 77 D4
Belev RUS 7 E14
Belevi TR 119 D2
Belfast GB 19 B6
Belford GB 25 C6
Belfort F 60 C2
Belgentier F 79 C4
Belgern D 52 B3
Belgioioso I 71 C4
Belgodère F 102 A2
Belgooly IRL 20 C3
Belgorod RUS 7 F14
Belgrade = Beograd SRB 85 B5
Belhade F 76 B2
Beli Manastir HR 74 C3
Belica HR 74 B1
Belin-Bèliet F 76 B2
Belinchón E 95 B3
Belišće HR 74 C3
Bělkovice-Lašťany CZ 64 A3
Bell-lloc d'Urgell E 90 B3
Bella I 104 C1
Bellac F 67 B6
Bellágio I 71 C4
Bellananagh IRL 19 C4
Bellano I 71 B4
Bellária I 82 B1
Bellavary IRL 18 C2
Belle-Isle-en-Terre F 56 B2
Belleau F 59 A4
Belleek GB 18 B3
Bellegarde, *Gard* F 78 C3
Bellegarde, *Loiret* F 58 C3
Bellegarde-en-Diois F 79 B4
Bellegarde-en-Marche F 68 C2
Bellegarde-sur-Valserine F 69 B5
Bellême F 58 B1
Bellenaves F 68 B3
Bellentre F 70 C1
Bellevaux F 69 B6
Bellevesvre F 69 B5
Belleville F 69 B4
Belleville-sur-Vie F 66 B3
Bellevue-la-Montagne F 68 C3
Belley F 69 C5
Bellheim D 61 A4
Bellinge DK 39 D3
Bellingham GB 25 C5
Bellinzago Novarese I 70 C3
Bellinzona CH 70 B4
Bello E 95 B5
Bellpuig d'Urgell E 91 B4
Bellreguart E 96 C2
Bellsbank GB 24 C3
Belltall E 91 B4
Belluno I 72 B2
Bellver de Cerdanya E 91 A4
Bellvis E 90 B3
Bélmez E 93 C5
Belmez de la Moraleda E 100 B2
Belmont GB 22 A8
Belmont-de-la-Loire F 69 B4
Belmont-sur-Rance F 78 C1
Belmonte, *Asturias* E 86 A4
Belmonte, *Cuenca* E 95 C4
Belmonte P 92 A3
Belmonte de San José E 90 C2
Belmonte de Tajo E 95 B3
Belmullet IRL 18 B2
Belobreşca RO 85 B6
Belœil B 49 C4
Belogradchik BG 11 E7
Belokorovichi UA 11 A10
Beloljin SRB 85 C6
Belorado E 89 B3
Belotič SRB 85 B4
Bělotín CZ 64 A3
Belozersk RUS 7 B14
Belp CH 70 B2
Belpasso I 109 B3
Belpech F 77 C4
Belper GB 27 B4
Belsay GB 25 C6
Belsh AL 105 C5
Belsk Duzy PL 55 B5
Beltinci SLO 73 B6
Beltra IRL 18 C2
Belturbet IRL 19 B4
Beluša SK 64 A4
Belušić SRB 85 C6
Belvedere Marittimo I 106 B2
Belver de Cinca E 90 B3
Belver de los Montes E 88 C1
Belvès F 77 B3
Belvezet F 78 B2
Belvis de la Jara E 94 C2
Belvis de Monroy E 93 B5
Belyy RUS 7 D12
Belz F 56 C2
Bełżec PL 11 A7
Belzig D 52 A2
Bembibre E 86 B4
Bembridge GB 31 D2
Bemmel NL 50 B1
Bemposta, *Bragança* P 87 C4
Bemposta, *Santarém* P 92 B2
Benabarre E 90 A3
Benacazón E 99 B4
Benaguacil E 96 B2
Benahadux E 101 C3
Benalmádena E 100 C1
Benalúa de Guadix E 100 B2
Benalúa de las Villas E 100 B2
Benalup E 99 C5
Benamargosa E 100 C1
Benamaurel E 101 B3
Benameji E 100 B1
Benamocarra E 100 C1
Benaocaz E 99 C5
Benaoján E 99 C5
Benarrabá E 99 C5
Benasque E 90 A3
Benátky nad Jizerou CZ 53 C4
Benavente E 88 B1
Benavente P 92 C2
Benavides de Órbigo E 88 B1
Benavila P 92 B3
Bendorf D 50 C3
Bene Vagienna I 80 B1
Benedikt SLO 73 B5
Benejama E 101 A5
Benejúzar E 101 A5
Benešov CZ 63 A5
Bénestroff F 60 B2
Benet F 67 B4
Bénévent-l'Abbaye F 67 B6
Benevento I 103 B7
Benfeld F 60 B3
Benfica P 92 B2
Bengtsfors S 35 C4
Bengtsheden S 36 B2
Beničanci HR 74 C3
Benicarló E 90 C3
Benicássim E 96 A3
Benidorm E 96 C2
Benifaió E 96 B2
Beniganim E 96 C2
Benington GB 27 B6
Benisa E 96 C3
Benkovac HR 83 B4
Benllech GB 26 B1
Benneckenstein D 51 B6
Bénodet F 56 C1
Benquerencia de la Serena E 93 C5
Bensafrim P 98 B2
Bensdorf D 44 C4
Benshausen D 51 C6
Bensheim D 61 A4
Bentley GB 31 C3
Bentwisch D 44 A4
Beočin SRB 75 C4
Beograd = Belgrade SRB 85 B5
Beragh GB 19 B4
Berane CG 85 D4
Beranga E 89 A3
Berat AL 105 C5
Bérat F 77 C4
Beratzhausen D 62 A2
Bérbaltavár H 74 A1
Berbegal E 90 B2
Berbenno di Valtellina I 71 B4
Berberana E 89 B3
Bercedo E 89 A3
Bercel H 65 C5
Bercenay-le-Hayer F 59 B4
Berceto I 81 B3
Berchem B 49 C4
Berchidda I 110 B2
Berching D 62 A2
Berchtesgaden D 62 C4
Bérchules E 100 C2
Bercianos de Aliste E 87 C4
Berck F 48 C2
Berclaire d'Urgell E 90 B3
Berdoias E 86 A1
Berducedo E 86 A4
Berdún E 90 A2
Berdychiv UA 11 B10
Bere Alston GB 28 C3
Bere Regis GB 29 C5
Bereguardo I 70 C4
Berehommen N 33 C4
Berehove UA 11 B7
Berek BIH 84 A2
Beremend H 74 C3
Berestechko UA 11 A8
Berettyóújfalu H 10 C6
Berezhany UA 11 B8
Berezivka UA 11 C11
Berezna UA 7 F11
Berg D 62 A2
Berg N 114 B9
Berg S 37 D3
Berg im Gau D 62 B2
Berga, *Sachsen-Anhalt* D 51 B7
Berga, *Thüringen* D 52 C2
Berga E 91 A4
Berga S 40 B6
Bergama TR 118 C2
Bérgamo I 71 C4
Bergara E 89 A4
Bergby S 36 B4
Berge, *Brandenburg* D 45 C4
Berge, *Niedersachsen* D 43 C4
Berge, *Telemark* N 33 C5
Berge, *Telemark* N 33 C5
Bergeforsen S 115 E14
Bergen, *Mecklenburg-Vorpommern* D 45 A5
Bergen, *Niedersachsen* D 44 C1
Bergen, *Niedersachsen* D 44 C2
Bergen N 32 B2
Bergen NL 42 C1
Bergen op Zoom NL 49 B5
Bergerac F 77 B3
Bergères-lès-Vertus F 59 B5
Bergeyk NL 49 B6
Berghausen D 61 B4
Bergheim D 50 C2
Berghem S 40 B2
Bergisch Gladbach D 50 C3
Bergkamen D 50 B3
Bergkvara S 41 C6
Berglern D 62 B2
Bergneustadt D 50 B3
Bergs slussar S 37 D2
Bergsäng S 34 B5
Bergshamra S 37 C5
Bergsjö S 115 F14
Bergtheim D 61 A6
Bergues F 48 C3
Bergum NL 42 B2
Bergün Bravuogn CH 71 B4
Bergwitz D 52 B2
Berhida H 74 A3
Beringel P 98 A3
Beringen B 49 B6
Berja E 100 C3
Berkåk N 114 E7
Berkeley GB 29 B5
Berkenthin D 44 B2
Berkhamsted GB 31 C3
Berkheim D 61 B6
Berkhof D 43 C6
Berkovići BIH 84 C3
Berkovitsa BG 11 E7
Berlanga E 99 A5
Berlanga de Duero E 89 C4
Berlevåg N 113 B18
Berlikum NL 42 B2
Berlin D 45 C5
Berlstedt D 52 B1
Bermeo E 89 A4
Bermillo de Sayago E 87 C4
Bern CH 70 B2
Bernalda I 104 C2
Bernardos E 94 A2
Bernartice, *Jihočeský* CZ 63 A5
Bernartice, *Vychodočeský* CZ 53 C5
Bernau, *Baden-Württemberg* D 61 C4
Bernau, *Bayern* D 62 C3
Bernau, *Brandenburg* D 45 C5
Bernaville F 48 C3
Bernay F 58 A1
Bernburg D 52 B1
Berndorf A 64 C2
Berne D 43 B5
Bernecebarati H 65 B4
Bernhardsthal A 64 B2
Bernkastel-Kues D 60 A3
Bernolakovo SK 64 B3
Bernsdorf D 53 B4
Bernstadt D 53 B4
Bernstein A 73 A6
Bernués E 90 A2
Beromünster CH 70 A3
Beroun CZ 53 D4
Berovo MK 116 A4
Berre-l'Etang F 79 C4
Berriedale GB 23 C5
Berriew GB 26 C2
Berrocal E 99 B4
Bersenbrück D 43 C4
Bershad' UA 11 B10
Berthåga S 36 C4
Berthelming F 60 B2
Bertincourt F 48 C3
Bertinoro I 82 B1
Bertogne B 49 C6
Bertrix B 59 A6
Berufjörður IS 111 C11
Berville-sur-Mer F 58 A1
Berwick-upon-Tweed GB 25 C5
Berzasca RO 10 D6
Berzence H 74 B2
Berzocana E 93 B5
Besalú E 91 A5
Besançon F 69 A6
Besenfeld D 61 B4
Besenyőtelek H 65 C6
Besenyszög H 75 A5
Beshenkovichi BY 7 D10
Besigheim D 61 B5
Běšiny CZ 63 A4
Beška SRB 75 C5
Beşkonak TR 119 E6
Besle F 57 C4
Besnyő H 74 A3
Bessais-le-Fromental F 68 B2
Bessan F 78 C2
Besse-en-Chandesse F 68 C2
Bessé-sur-Braye F 58 C1
Bessèges F 78 B3
Bessines-sur-Gartempe F 67 B6
Best NL 49 B6
Bestorp S 37 D2
Betanzos E 86 A2
Betelu E 76 C1
Bétera E 96 B2
Beteta E 95 B4
Béthenville F 59 A5
Bethesda GB 26 B1
Béthune F 48 C3
Beton-Bazoches F 59 B4
Bettembourg L 60 A2
Betterdorf L 60 A2
Bettna S 37 D3
Béttola I 80 B3
Bettona I 82 C1
Bettyhill GB 23 C4
Betws-y-Coed GB 26 B2
Betxi E 96 B2
Betz F 59 A3
Betzdorf D 50 C3
Beuil F 79 B5
Beulah GB 29 A4
Beuzeville F 58 A1
Bevagna I 82 D1
Bevens-bruk S 37 C2
Beveren B 49 B5
Beverley GB 27 B5
Bevern D 51 B5
Beverstedt D 43 B5
Beverungen D 51 B5
Beverwijk NL 42 C1
Bex CH 70 B2
Bexhill GB 31 D4
Beyazköy TR 118 A2
Beychevelle F 76 A2
Beydağ TR 119 D3
Beyeğaç TR 119 E3
Beykoz TR 118 A4
Beynat F 68 C1
Beyoğlu TR 118 A4
Beypazarı TR 118 B6
Beyşehir TR 119 E6
Bezas E 95 B5
Bezau A 71 A4
Bezdan SRB 75 C3
Bèze F 69 A5

Bezenet F 68 B2
Bezhetsk RUS 7 C14
Béziers F 78 C2
Bezzecca I 71 C5
Biadki PL 54 B2
Biała, *Łódzkie* PL 55 B4
Biała, *Opolskie* PL 54 C2
Biała Podlaska PL 6 E7
Biała Rawska PL 55 B5
Białaczów PL 55 B5
Biale Błota PL 46 B3
Białobłoty PL 54 A2
Białobrzegi PL 55 B5
Białogard PL 46 B1
Białośliwie PL 46 B3
Białowąs PL 46 B2
Biały Bór PL 46 B2
Białystok PL 6 E7
Biancavilla I 109 B3
Bianco I 106 C3
Biandrate I 70 C3
Biar E 101 A5
Biarritz F 76 C1
Bias F 76 B1
Biasca CH 70 B3
Biatorbágy H 74 A3
Bibbiena I 81 C5
Bibbona I 81 C4
Biberach, *Baden-Württemberg* D 61 B4
Biberach, *Baden-Württemberg* D 61 B5
Bibinje HR 83 B4
Bibione I 72 C3
Biblis D 61 A4
Bibury GB 29 B6
Biccari I 103 B8
Bicester GB 31 C2
Bichl D 62 C2
Bichlbach A 71 A5
Bicorp E 96 B2
Bicos P 98 B2
Bicske H 74 A3
Bidache F 76 C1
Bidart F 76 C1
Biddinghuizen NL 42 C2
Biddulph GB 26 B3
Bideford GB 28 B3
Bidford-on-Avon GB 29 A6
Bidjovagge N 113 C11
Bie S 37 C3
Bieber D 51 C5
Biebersdorf D 53 B3
Biedenkopf D 51 C4
Biel CH 70 A2
Biel E 90 A2
Bielany Wroclawskie PL 54 B1
Bielawa PL 54 C1
Bielawy PL 55 A4
Bielefeld D 51 A4
Biella I 70 C3
Bielsa E 90 A3
Bielsk PL 47 C5
Bielsk Podlaski PL 6 E7
Bielsko-Biała PL 65 A5
Bienenbuttel D 44 B2
Bieniow PL 53 B5
Bienservida E 101 A3
Bienvenida E 93 C4
Bierdzany PL 54 C3
Bierné F 57 C5
Biersted DK 38 B2
Bierun PL 55 C4
Bierutów PL 54 B2
Bierwart B 49 C6
Bierzwina PL 46 B1
Bierzwnik PL 46 B1
Biescas E 90 A2
Biesenthal D 45 C5
Biesiekierz PL 46 A2
Bietigheim-Bissingen D 61 B5
Bièvre B 49 D6
Bieżuń PL 47 C5
Biga TR 118 B2
Bigadiç TR 118 C3
Biganos F 76 B2
Bigas P 87 D3
Bigastro E 101 A5
Bigbury GB 28 C4
Biggar GB 25 C4
Biggin Hill GB 31 C4
Biggleswade GB 30 B3
Bignasco CH 70 B3
Biguglia F 102 A2
Bihać BIH 83 B4
Biharnagybajom H 75 A6
Bijela CG 105 A4
Bijeljani BIH 84 C3
Bijeljina BIH 85 B4
Bijelo Polje CG 85 C4
Bijuesca E 89 C5
Bila Tserkva UA 11 B11
Bilaj HR 83 B4
Bilbao E 89 A4
Bilcza PL 55 C5
Bildudalur IS 111 B2
Bileća BIH 84 D3
Bilecik TR 118 B4
Biled RO 75 C5
Biłgoraj PL 11 A7
Bilhorod-Dnistrovskyy UA 11 C11
Bílina CZ 53 C3
Bilisht AL 116 B2
Bilje HR 74 C3
Billdal S 38 B4
Billerbeck D 50 B3
Billericay GB 31 C4
Billesholm S 41 C2
Billingborough GB 30 B3
Billinge S 41 D3
Billingham GB 27 A4
Billinghay GB 27 B5
Billingsfors S 35 D4
Billingshurst GB 31 C3
Billom F 68 C3
Billsta S 115 D15
Billund DK 39 D2
Bilopillya UA 7 F13
Bilovec CZ 64 A4
Bilstein D 50 B4
Bilthoven NL 49 A6
Bilto N 112 C10
Bilzen B 49 C6
Bíňa SK 65 C4
Binaced E 90 B3
Binasco I 71 C4
Binbrook GB 27 B5
Binche B 49 C5
Bindlach D 52 D1
Bindslev DK 38 B3
Binefar E 90 B3
Bingen D 50 D3
Bingham GB 27 C5
Bingley GB 27 B4
Bingsjö S 36 A2
Binic F 56 B3
Binz D 45 A5
Bioče CG 105 A5
Biograd na Moru HR 83 C4
Bionaz I 70 C2
Bioska SRB 85 C4
Birda RO 75 C6
Birdlip GB 29 B5
Biri N 34 B2
Birkeland N 33 D5
Birkenfeld, *Baden-Württemberg* D 61 B4
Birkenfeld, *Rheinland-Pfalz* D 60 A3
Birkenhead GB 26 B2
Birkerød DK 41 D2
Birkfeld A 73 A5
Birkirkara M 107 C5
Birmingham GB 27 C4
Birr IRL 21 A4
Birresborn D 50 C2
Birstein D 51 C5
Biržai LT 6 C8
Birzebbugia M 107 C5
Bisáccia I 103 B8
Bisacquino I 108 B2
Bisbal de Falset E 90 B3
Biscarosse F 76 B1
Biscarosse Plage F 76 B1
Biscarrués E 90 A2
Biscéglie I 104 B2
Bischheim F 60 B3
Bischofsheim D 51 C5
Bischofshofen A 72 A3
Bischofswerda D 53 B4
Bischofswiesen D 62 C3
Bischofszell CH 71 A4
Bischwiller F 60 B3
Bisenti I 103 A6
Bishop Auckland GB 27 A4
Bishop's Castle GB 26 C3
Bishops Lydeard GB 29 B4
Bishop's Stortford GB 31 C4
Bishop's Waltham GB 31 D2
Bisignano I 106 B3
Bisingen D 61 B4
Biskupice-Oławskie PL 54 B2
Biskupiec PL 47 B5
Bismark D 44 C3
Bismo N 114 F5
Bispgården S 115 D13
Bispingen D 44 B1
Bissen L 60 A2
Bissendorf D 50 A4
Bisserup DK 39 D4
Bistango I 80 B2
Bistarac Donje BIH 84 B3
Bistrica BIH 84 B2
Bistrica CG 85 D4
Bistrica SRB 85 C4
Bistrica ob Sotli SLO 73 B5
Bistriţa RO 11 C8
Bisztynek PL 47 A6
Bitburg D 50 D2
Bitche F 60 A3
Bitetto I 104 B2
Bitola MK 116 A3
Bitonto I 104 B2
Bitschwiller F 60 C3
Bitterfeld D 52 B2
Bitti I 110 B2
Biville-sur-Mer F 48 D2
Bivona I 108 B2
Biwer L 60 A2
Bizeljsko SLO 73 B5
Bizovac HR 74 C3
Bjåen N 33 C4
Bjärnum S 41 C3
Bjärred S 41 D3
Bjästa S 115 D15
Bjelland, *Vest-Agder* N 33 D3
Bjelland, *Vest-Agder* N 33 D4
Bjelovar HR 74 C1
Bjerkreim N 33 D3
Bjerkvik N 112 D6
Bjerreby DK 39 E3
Bjerregrav DK 38 C2
Bjerringbro DK 39 C2
Bjøberg N 32 B5
Bjøllånes N 112 F3
Björbo S 36 B1
Bjordal N 32 A2
Björg IS 111 B8
Bjørkåsen N 112 D5
Björke, *Gävleborg* S 36 B4
Björke, *Östergötland* S 37 D2
Bjørkelangen N 34 C3
Björketorp S 40 B2
Björkholmen S 112 F8
Björkliden S 112 D7
Björklinge S 36 B4
Björko, *Stockholm* S 36 C6
Björkö, *Västra Götaland* S 38 B4
Björköby S 40 B4
Björkvik S 37 D3
Bjørn N 115 A9
Björna S 115 D15
Björneborg S 35 C6
Björnerod S 35 C3
Bjørnevatn N 113 C18
Björnlunda S 37 C4
Bjørnstad N 113 C19
Björsäter S 37 D3
Bjurberget S 34 B4
Bjurholm S 115 D16
Bjursås S 36 B2
Bjurtjärn S 35 C6
Bjuv S 41 C2
Blace SRB 85 C6
Blachownia PL 54 C3
Blackburn GB 26 B3
Blackpool GB 26 B2
Blackstad S 40 B6
Blackwater IRL 21 B5
Blackwaterfoot GB 24 C2
Blacy F 59 B5
Bladåker S 36 B5
Blaenau Ffestiniog GB 26 C2
Blaenavon GB 29 B4
Blaengarw GB 29 B4
Blagaj BIH 83 A5
Blagaj BIH 84 C2
Blagdon GB 29 B5
Blagnac F 77 C4
Blagoevgrad BG 11 E7
Blaichach D 61 C6
Blain F 66 A3
Blainville-sur-l'Eau F 60 B2
Blair Atholl GB 25 B4
Blairgowrie GB 25 B4
Blajan F 77 C3
Blakeney GB 29 B5
Blakstad N 33 D5
Blâmont F 60 B2
Blanca E 101 A4
Blancos E 87 C3
Blandford Forum GB 29 C5
Blanes E 91 B5
Blangy-sur-Bresle F 58 A2
Blankaholm S 40 B6
Blankenberge B 49 B4
Blankenburg D 51 B6
Blankenfelde D 45 C5
Blankenhain D 52 C1
Blankenheim D 50 C2
Blanquefort F 76 B2
Blansko CZ 64 A2
Blanzac F 67 C5
Blanzy F 69 B4
Blaricum NL 49 A6
Blarney IRL 20 C3
Blascomillán E 94 B1
Blascosancho E 94 B2
Błaszki PL 54 B3
Blatná CZ 63 A4
Blatné SK 64 B3
Blatnice CZ 64 B3
Blatnika BIH 84 B3
Blato HR 84 D1
Blato na Cetini HR 84 C1
Blatten CH 70 B2
Blattnicksele S 115 B14
Blatzheim D 50 C2
Blaubeuren D 61 B5
Blaufelden D 61 A5
Blaustein D 61 B5
Blaydon GB 25 D6
Blaye F 76 A2
Blaye-les-Mines F 77 B5
Blázquez E 93 C5
Bleckede D 44 B2
Blecua E 90 A2
Bled SLO 73 B4
Bleiburg A 73 B4
Bleichenbach D 51 C5
Bleicherode D 51 B6
Bleik N 112 C4
Bleikvassli N 115 B10
Bléneau F 59 C3
Blentarp S 41 D3
Blera I 102 A5
Blérancourt F 59 A4
Bléré F 67 A5
Blesle F 68 C3
Blessington IRL 21 A5
Blet F 68 B2
Bletchley GB 31 C3
Bletterans F 69 B5
Blidö S 37 C5
Blidsberg S 40 B3
Blieskastel D 60 A3
Bligny-sur-Ouche F 69 A4
Blikstorp S 35 D6
Blinisht AL 105 B6
Blinja HR 73 C6
Blizanówek PL 54 B3
Bliżyn PL 55 B5
Blois F 58 C2
Blokhus DK 38 B2
Blokzijl NL 42 C2
Blombacka S 35 C5
Blomberg D 51 B5
Blomskog S 35 C4
Blomstermåla S 40 C6
Blomvåg N 32 B1
Blönduós IS 111 B5
Błonie PL 55 A5
Blonville-sur-Mer F 57 A6
Blötberget S 36 B2
Blovice CZ 63 A4
Bloxham GB 31 B2
Blšany CZ 52 C3
Bludenz A 71 A4
Bludov CZ 64 A2
Blumberg D 61 C4
Blyberg S 34 A6
Blyth, *Northumberland* GB 25 C6
Blyth, *Nottinghamshire* GB 27 B4
Blyth Bridge GB 25 C4
Blythburgh GB 30 B5
Blythe Bridge GB 26 C3
Bø, *Nordland* N 112 D3
Bø, *Telemark* N 33 C6
Boa Vista P 92 B2
Boal E 86 A4
Boan CG 85 D4
Boario Terme I 71 C5
Boat of Garten GB 23 D5
Boba H 74 A2
Bobadilla, *Logroño* E 89 B4
Bobadilla, *Málaga* E 100 B1
Bobadilla del Campo E 94 A1
Bobadilla del Monte E 94 B3
Bóbbio I 80 B3
Bóbbio Pellice I 79 B6
Bobigny F 58 B3
Bobingen D 62 B1
Böblingen D 61 B5
Bobolice PL 46 B2
Boboras E 87 B2
Bobowa PL 65 A6
Bobrinets UA 11 B12
Bobrová CZ 64 A2
Bobrovitsa UA 11 A11
Bobrowice PL 53 B5
Bobrówko PL 46 C1
Boca de Huérgano E 88 B2
Bocairent E 96 C2
Bočar SRB 75 C5
Bocchigliero I 106 B3
Boceguillas E 89 C3
Bochnia PL 55 D5
Bocholt B 49 B6
Bocholt D 50 B2
Bochov CZ 52 C3
Bochum D 50 B3
Bockara S 40 B6
Bockenem D 51 A6
Bockfliess A 64 B2
Bockhorn D 43 B5
Bočna SLO 73 B4
Bocognano F 102 A2
Boconád H 65 C6
Boczów PL 45 C6
Boda, *Dalarna* S 36 A2
Böda, *Öland* S 41 B7
Boda, *Stockholm* S 36 B5
Boda, *Värmland* S 35 C5
Boda, *Västernorrland* S 115 E13
Boda Glasbruk S 40 C5
Bodafors S 40 B4
Bodajk H 74 A3
Boddam, *Aberdeenshire* GB 23 D7
Boddam, *Shetland* GB 22 B7
Boddin D 44 B3
Bödefeld-Freiheit D 51 B4
Boden S 3 D24
Bodenmais D 62 A4
Bodenteich D 44 C2
Bodenwerder D 51 B5
Bodiam GB 31 C4
Bodinnick GB 28 C3
Bodio CH 70 B3
Bodjani SRB 75 C4
Bodmin GB 28 C3
Bodø N 112 E3
Bodonal de la Sierra E 99 A4
Bodrum TR 119 E2
Bodstedt D 45 A4
Bodzanów PL 47 C6
Bodzanowice PL 54 C3
Bodzechów PL 55 C6
Bodzentyn PL 55 C5
Boecillo E 88 C2
Boëge F 69 B6
Boën F 68 C3
Bogács H 65 C6
Bogadmindszent H 74 C3
Bogajo E 87 D4
Bogarra E 101 A3
Bogarre E 100 B2
Bogatić SRB 85 B4
Bogatynia PL 53 C4
Boğazkale TR 16 A7
Boğazlıyan TR 16 B7
Bogdaniec PL 45 C7
Bogë AL 105 A5
Boge S 37 E5
Bogen D 62 B3
Bogen, *Nordland* N 112 D5
Bogen, *Nordland* N 112 E4
Bogen S 34 B4
Bogense DK 39 D3
Bogetići CG 84 D3
Bognanco Fonti I 70 B3
Bognelv N 113 B11
Bognes N 112 D5
Bogno CH 70 B4
Bognor Regis GB 31 D3
Bogoria PL 55 C6
Bograngen S 34 B4
Boguchwaly PL 47 B6
Bogumiłowice PL 55 B4
Boguslav UA 11 B11
Boguszów-Gorce PL 53 C6
Bogutovac SRB 85 C5
Bogyiszló H 74 B3
Bohain-en-Vermandois F 49 D4
Böheimkirchen A 64 B1
Bohinjska Bistrica SLO 72 B3
Böhlen D 52 B2
Böhmenkirch D 61 B5
Bohmte D 43 C5
Bohonal de Ibor E 93 B5
Böhönye H 74 B2
Bohumin CZ 65 A4
Boiro E 86 B2
Bois-d'Amont F 69 B6
Boisseron F 78 C3
Boitzenburg D 45 B5
Boixols E 91 A4
Boizenburg D 44 B2
Bojadła PL 53 B5
Bojano I 103 B7
Bojanowo PL 54 B1
Bøjden DK 39 D3
Bojkovice CZ 64 A3
Bojná SK 64 B4
Bojnice SK 65 B4
Boka SRB 75 C5
Böklund D 43 A6
Bokod H 74 A3
Böksholm S 40 B4
Boksitogorsk RUS 7 B12
Bol HR 83 C5
Bolaños de Calatrava E 100 A2
Bolayır TR 118 B1
Bolbec F 58 A1
Bölcske H 75 B3
Bolderslev DK 39 E2
Boldog H 65 C5
Boldva H 65 B6
Bolea E 90 A2
Bolekhiv UA 11 B7
Bolesławiec PL 53 B5
Boleszkowice PL 45 C6
Bolewice PL 46 C2
Bólgheri I 81 C4
Bolhrad UA 11 D10
Boliden S 3 D24
Bolimów PL 55 A5
Boliqueime P 98 B2
Boljevci SRB 85 B5
Boljkovci SRB 85 B5
Bolkhov RUS 7 E14
Bolków PL 53 C6
Bollebygd S 40 B2
Bollène F 78 B3
Bólliga E 95 B4
Bollnäs S 36 A3
Bollstabruk S 115 E14
Bollullos E 99 B4
Bollullos par del Condado E 99 B4
Bologna I 81 B5
Bologne F 59 B6
Bolognetta I 108 B2
Bolognola I 82 D2
Bologoye RUS 7 C13
Bolótana I 110 B1
Bolsena I 102 A4
Bolshaya Vradiyevka UA 11 C11
Bolsover GB 27 B4
Bolstad S 35 D4
Bolsward NL 42 B2
Boltaña E 90 A3
Boltenhagen D 44 B3
Boltigen CH 70 B2
Bolton GB 26 B3
Bolu TR 118 B6
Bolungavík IS 111 A2
Bolvadin TR 118 D6
Bóly H 74 C3
Bolzaneto I 80 B2
Bolzano I 71 B6
Bomba I 103 A7
Bombarral P 92 B1
Bömenzien D 44 C3
Bomlitz D 43 C6
Bømlo N 33 C2
Bøn N 34 B3
Bon-Encontre F 77 B3
Bona F 68 A3
Bonaduz CH 71 B4
Bonanza E 99 C4
Boñar E 88 B1
Bonarbridge GB 23 D4
Bonárcado I 110 B1
Bonares E 99 B4
Bonäs S 36 A1
Bonassola I 80 B3
Bonawe GB 24 B2
Bondal N 32 C5
Bondeno I 81 B5
Bondorf D 61 B4
Bondstorp S 40 B3
Bo'ness GB 25 B4
Bonete E 101 A4
Bonifacio F 102 B2
Bonigen CH 70 B2
Bonin PL 46 A2
Bonn D 50 C3
Bonnánaro I 110 B1
Bonnåsjøen N 112 E4
Bonnat F 68 B1
Bonndorf D 61 C4
Bonnétable F 58 B1
Bonnétage F 70 A1
Bonneuil-les-Eaux F 58 A3
Bonneuil-Matours F 67 B5
Bonneval F 58 B2
Bonneval-sur-Arc F 70 C2
Bonneville F 69 B6
Bonnières-sur-Seine F 58 A2
Bonnieux F 79 C4
Bönnigheim D 61 A5
Bonny-sur-Loire F 68 A2
Bonnyrigg GB 25 C4
Bono E 90 A3
Bono I 110 B2
Bonorva I 110 B1
Bønsnes N 34 B2
Bonyhád H 74 B3
Boom B 49 B5
Boos F 58 A2
Boostedt D 44 A2
Bootle, *Cumbria* GB 26 A2
Bootle, *Merseyside* GB 26 B2
Bopfingen D 61 B6
Boppard D 50 C3
Boqueixón E 86 B2
Bor CZ 62 A3
Bor S 40 B4
Bor SRB 11 D7
Bor TR 16 C7
Boran-sur-Oise F 58 A3
Borås S 40 B2
Borba P 92 C3
Borbona I 102 A6
Borča SRB 85 B5
Borci BIH 84 C3
Borculo NL 50 A2
Bordány H 75 B4
Bordeaux F 76 B2
Bordeira P 98 B2
Bordesholm D 44 A2
Borðeyri IS 111 B4
Bordighera I 80 C1
Bording DK 39 C2
Bordón E 90 C2
Bore I 81 B3
Borehamwood GB 31 C3
Borek Strzeliński PL 54 C2
Borek Wielkopolski PL 54 B2
Boreland GB 25 C4
Borello I 82 B1
Borensberg S 37 D2
Borgafjäll S 115 C12
Borgarnes IS 111 C4
Borgentreich D 51 B5
Börger D 43 C4
Borger NL 42 C3
Borggård S 37 D2
Borghamn S 37 D1
Borghetta di Vara I 81 B3
Borghetto d'Arróscia I 80 B1
Borghetto Santo Spirito I 80 B2
Borgholm S 41 C6
Borghorst D 50 A3
Bórgia I 106 C3
Borgloon B 49 C6
Børglum DK 38 B2
Borgo F 102 A2
Borgo a Mozzano I 81 C4
Borgo alla Collina I 81 C5
Borgo Pace I 82 C1
Borgo San Dalmazzo I 80 B1
Borgo San Lorenzo I 81 C5
Borgo Val di Taro I 81 B3
Borgo Valsugana I 71 B6
Borgo Vercelli I 70 C3
Borgoforte I 81 A4
Borgofranco d'Ivrea I 70 C2
Borgomanero I 70 C3
Borgomasino I 70 C2
Borgonovo Val Tidone I 80 A3
Borgorose I 102 A6
Borgosésia I 70 C3
Borgstena S 40 B3
Borgue GB 24 D3
Borgund N 32 A4
Borgvik S 35 C4
Borisovka RUS 7 F14
Borja E 89 C5
Bork D 50 B3
Borken D 50 B2
Borkenes N 112 D5
Børkop DK 39 D2
Borkowice PL 55 B5
Borkowo PL 47 C6
Borkum D 42 B3
Borlänge S 36 B2
Borlu TR 118 D3
Bormes-les-Mimosas F 79 C5
Bórmio I 71 B5
Bormujos E 99 B4
Borna D 52 B2
Borne NL 50 A2
Borne Sulinowo PL 46 B2
Bornes P 87 C3
Bornheim D 50 C2
Bornhöved D 44 A2
Börnicke D 45 C4
Bornos E 99 C5
Borobia E 89 C5
Borodino RUS 7 D13
Borohrádek CZ 53 C6
Boronów PL 54 C3
Bórore I 110 B1
Borosźow PL 54 C3
Borota H 75 B4
Boroughbridge GB 27 A4
Borovany CZ 63 B5
Borovichi RUS 7 B12
Borovnica SLO 73 C4
Borovo HR 75 C3
Borovsk RUS 7 D14
Borovy CZ 63 A4
Borowa PL 54 B2
Borowie PL 55 B6
Borox E 94 B3
Borrby S 41 D4
Borre DK 41 E2
Borre N 35 C2
Borredá E 91 A4
Borrenes E 86 B4
Borriol E 96 A2
Borris DK 39 D1
Borris IRL 21 B5
Borris-in-Ossory IRL 21 B4
Borrisokane IRL 20 B3
Borrisoleigh IRL 21 B4
Borrowdale GB 26 A2
Børrud N 34 C4
Borşa RO 11 C8
Borsdorf D 52 B2
Børselv N 113 B14
Borsfa H 74 B1
Borský Mikuláš SK 64 B3
Borsodivánka H 65 C6
Borsodnádasd H 65 B6
Bort-les-Orgues F 68 C2
Börte N 33 C4
Borth GB 26 C1
Börtnan S 115 E10
Børtnes N 32 B6
Boruja Kościelne PL 54 A1
Borup DK 39 D4
Boryslav UA 11 B7
Boryspil UA 11 A11
Boryszyn PL 46 C1
Borzęciczki PL 54 B2
Borzęcin PL 55 A5
Borzna UA 7 F12
Borzonasca I 80 B3
Borzyszkowy PL 46 A3
Borzytuchom PL 46 A3
Bosa I 110 B1
Bošáca SK 64 B3
Bosanci HR 73 C5
Bosanska Dubica BIH 74 C1
Bosanska Gradiška BIH 74 C2
Bosanska Kostajnica BIH 74 C1
Bosanska Krupa BIH 83 B5
Bosanski Brod BIH 84 A2
Bosanski Novi BIH 83 A5
Bosanski Petrovac BIH 83 B5
Bosanski Šamac BIH 84 A3
Bosansko Grahovo BIH 83 B5
Bošany SK 64 B4
Bösárkány H 64 C3
Bosau D 44 A2
Bósca H 75 B4
Boscastle GB 28 C3
Bosco I 80 B2
Bosco Chiesanuova I 71 C6
Bösdorf D 44 A2
Bösel D 43 B4
Bosham GB 31 D3
Bösingfeld D 51 A5
Bosjön S 34 C5
Boskoop NL 49 A5
Boskovice CZ 64 A2
Bošnjaci HR 84 A3
Bošnjane SRB 85 C6
Bossast E 77 D3
Bossolasco I 80 B2
Boštanj SLO 73 B5
Boston GB 27 C5
Bostrak N 33 C5
Böszénfa H 74 B2
Bot E 90 B3
Botajica BIH 84 B3
Bøte By DK 44 A3
Bothel GB 26 A2
Boticas P 87 C3
Botilsäter S 35 C5
Botngård N 114 D6
Botoš SRB 75 C5
Botoşani RO 11 C9
Botricello I 107 C3
Bottendorf D 51 B4
Bottesford GB 27 C5
Bottnaryd S 40 B3
Bottrop D 50 B2
Botunje SRB 85 B6
Boturić SRB 85 C5
Bötzingen D 60 B3
Bouaye F 66 A3
Bouça P 87 C3
Boucau F 76 C1
Bouchain F 49 C4
Bouchoir F 58 A3
Boudreville F 59 C5
Boudry CH 70 B1
Bouesse F 67 B6
Bouguenais F 66 A3
Bouhy F 68 A3
Bouillargues F 78 C3
Bouillon B 59 A6
Bouilly F 59 B4
Bouin F 66 B3
Boulay-Moselle F 60 A2
Boulazac F 67 C5
Boule-d'Amont F 91 A5
Bouligny F 60 A1
Boulogne-sur-Gesse F 77 C3
Boulogne-sur-Mer F 48 C2
Bouloire F 58 C1
Bouquemaison F 48 C3
Bourbon-Lancy F 68 B3
Bourbon-l'Archambault F 68 B3
Bourbonne-les-Bains F 60 C1
Bourbourg F 48 C3
Bourbriac F 56 B2
Bourcefranc-le-Chapus F 66 C3
Bourdeaux F 79 B4
Bouresse F 67 B5
Bourg F 76 A2
Bourg-Achard F 58 A1
Bourg-Argental F 69 C4
Bourg-de-Péage F 79 A4
Bourg-de-Thizy F 69 B4
Bourg-de-Visa F 77 B3
Bourg-en-Bresse F 69 B5
Bourg-et-Comin F 59 A4
Bourg-Lastic F 68 C2
Bourg-Madame F 91 A4
Bourg-St. Andéol F 78 B3
Bourg-St. Maurice F 70 C1
Bourganeuf F 68 C1
Bourges F 68 A2
Bourgneuf-en-Retz F 66 A3
Bourgogne F 59 A5
Bourgoin-Jallieu F 69 C5
Bourgtheroulde F 58 A1
Bourgueil F 67 A5
Bourmont F 60 B1
Bourne GB 30 B3
Bournemouth GB 29 C6
Bourneville F 58 A1
Bournezeau F 66 B3
Bourran F 77 B3
Bourret F 77 C4
Bourron-Marlotte F 58 B3
Bourton-on-The-Water GB 29 B6
Boussac F 68 B2
Boussens F 77 C3
Boutersem B 49 C5
Bouttencourt F 48 D2
Bouvières F 79 B4
Bouvron F 66 A3
Bouxwiller F 60 B3
Bouzas E 87 B2
Bouzonville F 60 A2
Bova I 106 D2
Bova Marina I 106 D2
Bovalino Marina I 106 C3
Bovallstrand S 35 D3
Bovec SLO 72 B3
Bóveda E 86 B3
Bóvegno I 71 C5
Bovenau D 44 A1
Bovenden D 51 B5
Bøverdal N 114 F5
Bóves I 80 B1
Bovey Tracey GB 28 C4
Bovino I 103 B8
Bøvlingbjerg DK 38 C1
Bovolenta I 72 C1
Bovolone I 71 C6
Bowes GB 27 A4
Bowmore GB 24 C1
Bowness-on-Windermere GB 26 A3
Box GB 29 B5
Boxberg, *Baden-Württemberg* D 61 A5
Boxberg, *Sachsen* D 53 B4
Boxholm S 37 D2
Boxmeer NL 50 B1
Boxtel NL 49 B6
Boyabat TR 16 A7
Boyalıca TR 118 B4
Boyle IRL 18 C3
Bozan TR 118 C6
Božava HR 83 B3
Bozburun TR 119 F3
Bozcaada TR 116 C8
Bozdoğan TR 119 E3
Božepole Wielkie PL 46 A3
Boževac SRB 85 B6
Boži Dar CZ 52 C2
Božice CZ 64 B2
Bozkır TR 119 E7
Bozouls F 78 B1
Bozova TR 119 E5
Bozüyük TR 118 C5
Bózzolo I 81 A4
Bra I 80 B1
Braås S 40 B5
Brabrand DK 39 C3
Bracadale GB 22 D3

Calatafimi I 108 B1
Calatayud E 89 C5
Calatorao E 89 C5
Calau D 53 B3
Calbe D 52 B1
Calcena E 89 C5
Calcinelli I 82 C1
Calco I 71 C4
Caldaro sulla strada del Vino I 71 B6
Caldarola I 82 C2
Caldas da Rainha P 92 B1
Caldas de Boì E 90 A3
Caldas de Malavella E 91 B5
Caldas de Reis E 86 B2
Caldas de San Jorge P 87 D2
Caldas de Vizela P 87 C2
Caldaso de los Vidrios E 94 B2
Caldbeck GB 26 A2
Caldearenas E 90 A2
Caldelas P 87 C2
Calders E 91 B4
Caldes de Montbui E 91 B5
Caldicot GB 29 B5
Caldirola I 80 B3
Caledon GB 19 B5
Calella, *Barcelona* E 91 B5
Calella, *Girona* E 91 B6
Calenzana F 102 A1
Calera de León E 99 A4
Calera y Chozas E 94 C2
Caleruega E 89 C3
Caleruela E 93 B5
Cales de Mallorca E 97 B3
Calestano I 81 B4
Calfsound GB 23 B6
Calgary GB 24 B1
Calimera I 105 C4
Calitri I 103 C8
Calizzano I 80 B2
Callac F 56 B2
Callan IRL 21 B4
Callander GB 24 B3
Callas F 79 C5
Calliano, *Piemonte* I 80 A2
Calliano, *Trentino Alto Adige* I 71 C6
Callington GB 28 C3
Callosa de Ensarriá E 96 C2
Callosa de Segura E 101 A5
Callús E 91 B4
Čalma SRB 85 A4
Calmbach D 61 B4
Calne GB 29 B6
Calolziocorte I 71 C4
Calonge E 91 B6
Čalovec SK 64 C3
Calpe E 96 C3
Caltabellotta I 108 B2
Caltagirone I 109 B3
Caltanissetta I 109 B3
Caltavuturo I 108 B2
Çaltılıbük TR 118 C3
Caltojar E 89 C4
Caluire-et-Cuire F 69 C4
Caluso I 70 C2
Calvello I 104 C1
Calvi F 102 A1
Calviá E 97 B2
Calvinet F 77 B5
Calvisson F 78 C3
Calvörde D 44 C3
Calw D 61 B4
Calzada de Calatrava E 100 A2
Calzada de Valdunciel E 94 A1
Calzadilla de los Barros E 93 C4
Cam GB 29 B5
Camaiore I 81 C4
Camarasa E 90 B3
Camarena E 94 B2
Camarès F 78 C1
Camaret-sur-Aigues F 78 B3
Camaret-sur-Mer F 56 B1
Camarillas E 90 C2
Camariñas E 86 A1
Camarma E 95 B3
Camarzana de Tera E 87 B4
Camas E 99 B4
Camastra I 108 B2
Cambados E 86 B2
Cambarinho P 92 A2
Camberley GB 31 C3
Cambil E 100 B2
Cambligeu F 48 C3
Cambo-les-Bains F 76 C1
Camborne GB 28 C2
Cambrai F 49 C4
Cambre E 86 A2
Cambridge GB 30 B4
Cambrils E 91 B4
Cambs D 44 B3
Camburg D 52 B1
Camden GB 31 C3
Cameleño E 88 A2
Camelford GB 28 C3
Çameli TR 119 E4
Camelle E 86 A1
Camerano I 82 C2
Camerino I 82 C2
Camerota I 106 A2
Camigliatello Silano I 106 B3
Caminha P 87 C2
Caminomorisco E 93 A4
Caminreal E 95 B5
Camisano Vicentino I 72 C1
Camlıdere TR 118 B7
Cammarata I 108 B2
Camogli I 80 B3
Camors F 56 C3
Camp IRL 20 B2
Campagna I 103 C8
Campagnano di Roma I 102 A5
Campagnático I 81 D5
Campan F 76 C3
Campana I 107 B3
Campanario E 93 C5
Campanillas E 100 C1
Campano E 99 C4
Campaspero E 88 C2
Campbeltown GB 24 C2
Campello E 96 C2
Campelos P 92 B1
Campi Bisénzio I 81 C5
Campi Salentina I 105 C4
Campico López E 101 B4
Campíglia Marittima I 81 C4
Campillo de Altobuey E 95 C5
Campillo de Aragón E 95 A5
Campillo de Arenas E 100 B2
Campillo de Llerena E 93 C5
Campillos E 100 B1
Câmpina RO 11 D8
Campli I 82 D2
Campo E 90 A3
Campo de Bacerros E 87 B3
Campo de Caso E 88 A1
Campo de Criptana E 95 C3
Campo Ligure I 80 B2
Campo Lugar E 93 B5
Campo Maior P 93 B3
Campo Molino I 79 B6
Campo Real E 95 B3
Campo Túres I 72 B1
Campobasso I 103 B7
Campobello di Licata I 108 B2
Campobello di Mazara I 108 B1
Campodársego I 72 C1
Campodolcino I 71 B4
Campofelice di Roccella I 108 B2
Campofiorito I 108 B2
Campofórmido I 72 B3
Campofranco I 108 B2
Campofrio E 99 B4
Campogalliano I 81 B4
Campolongo I 72 B2
Campomanes E 88 A1
Campomarino I 103 B8
Campomono F 102 B1
Camporeale I 108 B2
Camporeggiano I 82 C1
Camporrells E 90 B3
Camporrobles E 96 B1
Campos P 87 C3
Campos del Port E 97 B3
Camposa P 87 C2
Camposampiero I 72 C1
Camposanto I 81 B5
Camposines E 90 B3
Campotéjar E 100 B2
Campotosto I 103 A6
Camprodón E 91 A5
Campsegret F 77 B3
Camrose GB 28 B2
Camuñas E 95 C3
Çamyolu TR 119 F7
Çan TR 118 B2
Can Pastilla E 97 B2
C'an Picafort E 97 B3
Cana I 81 D5
Cañada del Hoyo E 95 C5
Cañada Rosal E 99 B5
Cañadajuncosa E 95 C4
Čanak HR 83 B4
Çanakkale TR 118 B1
Canal San Bovo I 72 B1
Canale I 80 B1
Canales, *Asturias* E 88 B1
Canales, *Castellón de la Plana* E 96 B2
Canals E 96 C2
Cañamares E 95 B4
Cañamero E 93 B5
Cañar E 100 C2
Cañete la Real E 99 C5
Cañaveral E 93 B4
Cañaveral de León E 99 A4
Cañaveras E 95 B4
Cañaveruelas E 95 B4
Canazei I 72 B1
Cancale F 57 B4
Cancellara I 104 C1
Cancello ed Arnone I 103 B7
Cancon F 77 B3
Canda E 87 B4
Candamil E 86 A3
Candanchu E 76 D2
Çandarlı TR 118 D1
Candas E 88 A1
Candasnos E 90 B3
Candé F 66 A3
Candela I 104 B1
Candelario E 93 A5
Candeleda E 93 A5
Cándia Lomellina I 70 C3
Candide Casamazzagno I 72 B2
Candin E 86 B4
Candosa P 92 A3
Canecas P 92 C1
Canelli I 80 B2
Canena E 100 A2
Canencia E 94 B3
Canero E 86 A4
Canet F 78 C2
Canet de Mar E 91 B5
Canet d'en Berenguer E 96 B2
Canet-Plage F 91 A6
Cañete E 95 B5
Cañete de las Torres E 100 B1
Canfranc E 76 D2
Cangas, *Lugo* E 86 A3
Cangas, *Pontevedra* E 87 B2
Cangas de Narcea E 86 A4
Cangas de Onís E 88 A1
Canha P 92 C2
Canhestros P 98 A2
Canicattì I 108 B2
Canicattini Bagni I 109 B4
Canicosa de la Sierra E 89 C3
Caniles E 101 B3
Canillas de Aceituno E 100 C1
Canino I 102 A4
Canisy F 57 A4
Cañizal E 94 A1
Cañizo E 88 C1
Canjáyar E 101 C3
Çankırı TR 16 A6
Cannai I 110 C1
Cannara I 82 C1
Cànnero Riviera I 70 B3
Cannes F 79 C6
Canneto, *Sicilia* I 106 C1
Canneto, *Toscana* I 81 C4
Canneto sull'Oglio I 71 C5
Cannich GB 22 D4
Cannóbio I 70 B3
Cannock GB 26 C3
Canonbie GB 25 C5
Canosa di Púglia I 104 B2
Cantalapiedra E 94 A1
Cantalejo E 94 A3
Cantalgallo E 99 A4
Cantalice I 102 A5
Cantalpino E 94 A1
Cantalupo in Sabina I 102 A5
Cantanhede P 92 A2
Cantavieja E 90 C2
Čantavir SRB 75 C4
Canterbury GB 31 C5
Cantiano I 82 C1
Cantillana E 99 B5
Cantiveros E 94 B2
Cantoria E 101 B3
Cantù I 71 C4
Canvey GB 31 C4
Cany-Barville F 58 A1
Canyet de Mar E 91 B5
Caol GB 24 B2
Cáorle I 72 C2
Caorso I 81 A3
Cap-de-Pin F 76 B2
Cap Ferret F 76 B1
Capáccio I 103 C8
Capaci I 108 A2
Capálbio I 102 A4
Capánnori I 81 C4
Caparde BIH 84 B3
Caparroso E 89 B5
Capbreton F 76 C1
Capdenac-Gare F 77 B5
Capdepera E 97 B3
Capel Curig GB 26 B2
Capellades E 91 B4
Capena I 102 A5
Capendu F 77 C5
Capestang F 78 C2
Capestrano I 103 A6
Capileira E 100 C2
Capinha P 92 A3
Ca'Pisani I 82 B1
Capistrello I 103 B6
Capizzi I 109 B3
Čaplje BIH 83 B5
Čapljina BIH 84 C2
Capo di Ponte I 71 B5
Caposile I 72 C2
Capoterra I 110 C1
Cappamore IRL 20 B3
Cappeln D 43 C5
Cappoquin IRL 21 B4
Capracotta I 103 B7
Capránica I 102 A5
Caprarola I 102 A5
Capretta I 82 D1
Capri I 103 C7
Capriati a Volturno I 103 B7
Caprino Veronese I 71 C5
Captieux F 76 B2
Cápua I 103 B7
Capurso I 104 B2
Capvern F 77 C3
Carabaña E 95 B3
Carabias E 88 C3
Caracal RO 11 D8
Caracenilla E 95 B4
Caráglio I 80 B1
Caraman F 77 C4
Caramánico Terme I 103 A7
Caranga E 86 A4
Caranguejeira P 92 B2
Caransebeş RO 11 D7
Carantec F 56 B2
Carapelle I 104 B1
Carasco I 80 B3
Carate Brianza I 71 C4
Caravaca de la Cruz E 101 A4
Caravággio I 71 C4
Carbajal E 100 C1
Carbajo E 93 B3
Carballeda E 86 B3
Carballeda de Avia E 87 B2
Carballo E 86 A2
Carbis Bay GB 28 C2
Carbon-Blanc F 76 B2
Carbonera de Frentes E 89 C4
Carboneras E 101 C4
Carboneras de Guadazaón E 95 C5
Carbonero el Mayor E 94 A2
Carboneros E 100 A2
Carbónia I 110 C1
Carbonin I 72 B2
Carbonne F 77 C4
Carbost, *Highland* GB 22 D2
Carbost, *Highland* GB 22 D2
Carcaboso E 93 A4
Carcabuey E 100 B1
Carcaixent E 96 B2
Carcans F 76 A1
Carcans-Plage F 76 A1
Carção P 87 C4
Carcar E 89 B5
Cárcare I 80 B2
Carcassonne F 77 C5
Carcastillo E 89 B5
Carcedo de Burgos E 89 B3
Carcelén E 96 B1
Carcès F 79 C5
Carchelejo E 100 B2
Çardak, *Çanakkale* TR 118 B1
Çardak, *Denizli* TR 119 E4
Cardedeu E 91 B5
Cardeña E 100 A1
Cardenete E 95 C5
Cardeñosa E 94 B2
Cardeto I 109 A4
Cardiff GB 29 B4
Cardigan GB 28 A3
Cardona E 91 B4
Cardosos P 92 B2
Carei RO 11 C7
Carentan F 57 A4
Carentoir F 57 C3
Careri I 106 C3
Carevdar HR 74 B1
Cargèse F 102 A1
Carhaix-Plouguer F 56 B2
Caria P 92 A3
Cariati I 107 B3
Carignan F 59 A6
Carignano I 80 B1
Cariñena E 90 B1
Carini I 108 A2
Cariño E 86 A3
Carínola I 103 B6
Carisbrooke GB 31 D2
Carlabhagh GB 22 C2
Carlepont F 59 A4
Carlet E 96 B2
Carlingford IRL 19 B5
Carlisle GB 25 D5
Carloforte I 110 C1
Carlópoli I 106 B3
Carlow D 44 B2
Carlow IRL 21 B5
Carlton GB 27 C4
Carluke GB 25 C4
Carmagnola I 80 B1
Carmarthen GB 28 B3
Carmaux F 77 B5
Carmena E 94 C2
Cármenes E 88 B1
Carmine I 80 B1
Carmona E 99 B5
Carmonita E 93 B4
Carmyllie GB 25 B5
Carnac F 56 C2
Carndonagh IRL 19 A4
Carnew IRL 21 B5
Carnforth GB 26 A3
Cárnia I 72 B3
Carnlough GB 19 B6
Carno GB 26 C2
Carnon Plage F 78 C2
Carnota E 86 B1
Carnoustie GB 25 B5
Carnwath GB 25 C4
Carolei I 106 B3
Carolinensiel D 43 B4
Carolles F 57 B4
Carona I 71 B4
Caronía I 109 A3
Carovigno I 104 C3
Carovilli I 103 B7
Carpaneto Piacentino I 81 B3
Carpegna I 82 C1
Carpenèdolo I 71 C5
Carpentras F 79 B4
Carpi I 81 B4
Carpignano Sésia I 70 C3
Carpineti I 81 B4
Carpineto Romano I 102 B6
Cărpiniş RO 75 C5
Carpino I 104 B1
Carpinone I 103 B7
Carpio E 94 A1
Carquefou F 66 A3
Carqueiranne F 79 C5
Carral E 86 A2
Carranque E 94 B3
Carrapichana P 92 A3
Carrara I 81 B4
Carraroe IRL 20 A2
Carrascalejo E 93 B5
Carrascosa del Campo E 95 B4
Carratraca E 100 C1
Carrazeda de Ansiães P 87 C3
Carrazedo de Montenegro P 87 C3
Carrbridge GB 23 D5
Carregal do Sal P 92 A2
Carreña E 88 A2
Carrick IRL 18 B3
Carrick-on-Shannon IRL 18 C3
Carrick-on-Suir IRL 21 B4
Carrickart IRL 19 A4
Carrickfergus GB 19 B6
Carrickmacross IRL 19 C5
Carrigallen IRL 19 C4
Carrión E 99 B4
Carrión de Calatrava E 94 C3
Carrión de los Condes E 88 B2
Carrizo de la Ribera E 88 B1
Carrizosa E 100 A3
Carro F 79 C4
Carrocera E 88 B1
Carros F 79 C6
Carrouge CH 70 B1
Carrouges F 57 B5
Carrù I 80 B1
Carry-le-Rouet F 79 C4
Carryduff GB 19 B6
Carsóli I 102 A6
Carsphairn GB 24 C3
Cartagena E 101 B5
Cártama E 100 C1
Cartaxo P 92 B2
Cartaya E 98 B3
Carteret F 57 A4
Cartes E 88 A2
Carúnchio I 103 B7
Carviçães P 87 C4
Carvin F 48 C3
Carvoeira P 92 B1
Carvoeiro P 98 B2
Casa Branca, *Portalegre* P 92 C3
Casa Branca, *Setúbal* P 98 A2
Casa Castalda I 82 C1
Casa l'Abate I 105 C4
Casabermeja E 100 C1
Casacalenda I 103 B7
Casaio E 87 B4
Casàl di Principe I 103 B7
Casalarreina E 89 B4
Casalbordino I 103 A7
Casalborgone I 70 C2
Casalbuono I 104 C1
Casalbuttano ed Uniti I 71 C4
Casale Monferrato I 70 C3
Casalécchio di Reno I 81 B5
Casalina I 82 D1
Casalmaggiore I 81 B4
Casalnuovo Monterotaro I 103 B8
Casaloldo I 71 C5
Casalpusterlengo I 71 C4
Casamássima I 104 C2
Casamicciola Terme I 103 C6
Casamozza F 102 A2
Casar de Cáceres E 93 B4
Casar de Palomero E 93 A4
Casarabonela E 100 C1
Casarano I 107 A5
Casarejos E 89 C3
Casares E 99 C5
Casares de las Hurdes E 93 A4
Casariche E 100 B1
Casarrubios del Monte E 94 B2
Casas de Don Pedro E 93 B5
Casas de Fernando Alonso E 95 C4
Casas de Haro E 95 C4
Casas de Juan Gil E 96 B1
Casas de Millán E 93 B4
Casas de Reina E 99 A5
Casas de Ves E 96 B1
Casas del Juan Núñez E 95 C5
Casas del Puerto E 101 A4
Casas del Rio E 96 B1
Casas-Ibáñez E 96 B1
Casas Nuevas E 101 B4
Casasimarro E 95 C4
Casasola E 94 B2
Casasola de Arión E 88 C1
Casasuertes E 88 A2
Casatejada E 93 B5
Casavieja E 94 B2
Casazza I 71 C4
Cascais P 92 C1
Cascante E 89 C5
Cascante del Rio E 96 A1
Cáscia I 82 D2
Casciana Terme I 81 C4
Cáscina I 81 C4
Cáseda E 89 B5
Casekow D 45 B6
Casella I 80 B3
Caselle Torinese I 70 C2
Casemurate I 82 B1
Casenove I 82 D1
Caseres E 90 B3
Caserio Benali E 96 B2
Caserta I 103 B7
Casével P 98 B2
Cashel IRL 21 B4
Casillas E 94 B2
Casillas de Coria E 93 B4
Casina I 81 B4
Casinos E 96 B2
Čáslav CZ 63 A6
Cásola Valsénio I 81 B5
Cásole d'Elsa I 81 C5
Cásoli I 103 A7
Casória I 103 C7
Caspe E 90 B2
Cassà de la Selva E 91 B5
Cassagnas F 78 B2
Cassagnes-Bégonhès F 77 B5
Cassano allo Iónio I 106 B3
Cassano d'Adda I 71 C4
Cassano delle Murge I 104 C2
Cassano Magnago I 70 C3
Cassano Spinola I 80 B2
Cassel F 48 C3
Cassíbile I 109 C4
Cassine I 80 B2
Cassino I 103 B6
Cassis F 79 C4
Cassolnovo I 70 C3
Cassuéjouls F 78 B1
Častá SK 64 B3
Castagnaro I 71 C6
Castagneto Carducci I 81 C4
Castagnola CH 70 B3
Castalla E 96 C2
Castañar de Ibor E 93 B5
Castanheira de Pêra P 92 A2
Cástano Primo I 70 C3
Castasegna CH 71 B4
Castéggio I 80 A3
Casteição P 87 D3
Castejón E 89 B5
Castejón de Monegros E 90 B2
Castejón de Sos E 90 A3
Castejón de Valdejasa E 90 B2
Castèl Baronia I 103 B8
Castel Bolognese I 81 B5
Castel d'Aiano I 81 B4
Castel d'Ario I 71 C5
Castel de Cabra E 90 C2
Castél del Monte I 103 A6
Castel del Piano I 81 D5
Castel di Iúdica I 109 B3
Castel di Rio I 81 B5
Castèl di Sangro I 103 B7
Castél di Tora I 102 A5
Castèl Frentano I 103 A7
Castel San Gimignano I 81 C5
Castèl San Giovanni I 80 A3
Castèl San Pietro Terme I 81 B5
Castél Sant'Elia I 102 A5
Castél Volturno I 103 B6
Castelbuono I 109 B3
Casteldáccia I 108 A2
Casteldelfino I 79 B6
Castelfidardo I 82 C2
Castelfiorentino I 81 C4
Castelforte I 103 B6
Castelfranco Emília I 81 B5
Castelfranco in Miscano I 103 B8
Castelfranco Véneto I 72 C1
Casteljaloux F 76 B3
Castell Arquato I 81 B3
Castell de Cabres E 90 C3
Castell de Castells E 96 C2
Castell de Ferro E 100 C2
Castellabate I 103 C7
Castellammare del Golfo I 108 A1
Castellammare di Stábia I 103 C7
Castellamonte I 70 C2
Castellana Grotte I 104 C3
Castellane F 79 C5
Castellaneta I 104 C2
Castellaneta Marina I 104 C2
Castellar E 100 A2
Castellar de la Frontera E 99 C5
Castellar de la Ribera E 91 A4
Castellar de Santiago E 100 A2
Castellar del Vallés E 91 B5
Castellarano I 81 B4
Castell'Azzara I 81 D5
Castellbell i Villar E 91 B4
Castelldans E 90 B3
Castelldefels E 91 B4
Castelleone I 71 C4
Castellet E 91 B4
Castelletto di Brenzone I 71 C5
Castellfollit de la Roca E 91 A5
Castellfollit de Riubregos E 91 B4
Castellfort E 90 C2
Castellina in Chianti I 81 C5
Castellina Marittima I 81 C4
Castelló de Farfaña E 90 B3
Castelló de la Plana E 96 B2
Castello d'Empùries E 91 A6
Castello di Fiemme I 71 B6
Castello Tesino I 72 B1
Castelloli E 91 B4
Castellón de Rugat E 96 C2
Castellote E 90 C2
Castellterçol E 91 B5
Castellúcchio I 71 C5
Castellúccio de'Sáuri I 103 B8
Castelluccio Inferiore I 106 B2
Castelmassa I 81 A5
Castelmáuro I 103 B7
Castelmoron-sur-Lot F 77 B3
Castelnau-de-Médoc F 76 A2
Castelnau-de-Montmirail F 77 C4
Castelnau-Magnoac F 77 C3
Castelnau-Montratier F 77 B4
Castelnaudary F 77 C4
Castelnou E 90 B2
Castelnovo ne'Monti I 81 B4
Castelnuovo Berardenga I 81 C5
Castelnuovo della Dáunia I 103 B8
Castelnuovo di Garfagnana I 81 B4
Castelnuovo di Val di Cécina I 81 C4
Castelnuovo Don Bosco I 80 A1
Castelnuovo Scrivia I 80 B2
Castelo Branco, *Bragança* P 87 C4
Castelo Branco, *Castelo Branco* P 92 B3
Castelo de Paiva P 87 C2
Castelo de Vide P 92 B3
Castelo do Neiva P 87 C2
Castelo Mendo P 93 A4
Castelraimondo I 82 C2
Castelsantángelo I 82 D2
Castelsaraceno I 106 A2
Castelsardo I 110 B1
Castelsarrasin F 77 B4
Castelserás E 90 C2
Casteltérmini I 108 B2
Castelvecchio Subéquo I 103 A6
Castelvetrano I 108 B1
Castenédolo I 71 C5
Castets F 76 C1
Castiádas I 110 C2
Castiglion Fibocchi I 81 C5
Castiglion Fiorentino I 81 C5
Castiglioncello I 81 C4
Castiglione I 102 A6
Castiglione Chiavarese I 80 B3
Castiglione d'Adda I 71 C4
Castiglione dei Pepoli I 81 B5
Castiglione del Lago I 81 C6
Castiglione della Pescáia I 81 D4
Castiglione delle Stiviere I 71 C5
Castiglione di Sicilia I 109 B4
Castiglione d'Órcia I 81 C5
Castiglione Messer Marino I 103 B7
Castiglione Messer Raimondo I 103 A6
Castil de Peones E 89 B3
Castilblanco E 94 C1
Castilblanco de los Arroyos E 99 B5
Castilfrío de la Sierra E 89 C4
Castilgaleu E 90 A3
Castilisar E 90 A1
Castilleja E 99 B4
Castillejar E 101 B3
Castillejo de Martin Viejo E 93 A4
Castillejo de Mesleón E 89 C3
Castillejo de Robledo E 89 C3
Castillo de Bayuela E 94 B2
Castillo de Locubín E 100 B2
Castillon-la-Bataille F 76 B2
Castillon-Len-Couserans F 77 D4
Castillonès F 77 B3
Castillonroy E 90 B3
Castilruiz E 89 C4
Castione CH 70 B4
Castions di Strada I 72 C3
Castirla F 102 A2
Castle Cary GB 29 B5
Castle Douglas GB 25 D4
Castlebar IRL 18 C2
Castlebellingham IRL 19 C5
Castleblaney IRL 19 B5
Castlebridge IRL 21 B5
Castlecomer IRL 21 B4
Castlederg GB 19 B4
Castledermot IRL 21 B5
Castleford GB 27 B4
Castleisland IRL 20 B2
Castlemaine IRL 20 B2
Castlemartyr IRL 20 C3
Castlepollard IRL 19 C4
Castlerea IRL 18 C3
Castleton GB 27 B4
Castletown, *Highland* GB 23 C5
Castletown, *Isle of Man* GB 26 A1
Castletown Bearhaven IRL 20 C2
Castletownroche IRL 20 B3
Castlewellan GB 19 B6
Casto I 71 C5
Castrejón E 88 C1
Castrelo del Valle E 87 C3
Castres F 77 C5
Castricum NL 42 C1
Castries F 78 C2
Castrignano del Capo I 107 B5
Castril E 101 B3
Castrillo de Duero E 88 C3
Castrillo de la Vega E 88 C3
Castrillo de Onielo E 88 C2
Castro E 88 A2
Castro I 107 A5
Castro-Caldelas E 87 B3
Castro Daire P 87 D3
Castro de Rey E 86 A3
Castro dei Volsci I 103 B6
Castro del Río E 100 B1
Castro Laboreiro P 87 B2
Castro Marim P 98 B3
Castro-Urdiales E 89 A3
Castro Verde P 98 B2
Castrocabón E 88 B1
Castrocaro Terme I 81 B5
Castrocontrigo E 87 B4
Castrofilippo I 108 B2
Castrogonzaio E 88 B1
Castrojeriz E 88 B2
Castromonte E 88 C1
Castromudarra E 88 B1
Castronuevo E 88 C1
Castronuño E 88 C1
Castropol E 86 A3
Castroreale I 109 A4
Castroserracin E 88 C3
Castroverde E 86 A3
Castroverde de Campos E 88 C1
Castroverde de Cerrato E 88 C2
Castrovillari I 106 B3
Castuera E 93 C5
Catadau E 96 B2
Cataéggio I 71 B4
Çatalca TR 118 A3
Catallar TR 119 F5
Çatalzeytin TR 16 A7

Catánia I 109 B4
Catanzaro I 106 C3
Catanzaro Marina I 106 C3
Catarroja E 96 B2
Catarruchos P 92 A2
Catcleugh GB 25 C5
Catenanuova I 109 B3
Caterham GB 31 C3
Cati E 90 C3
Čatići BIH 84 B3
Catignano I 103 A6
Catillon F 49 C4
Catoira E 86 B2
Caton GB 26 A3
Catral E 101 A5
Catterick GB 27 A4
Cattólica I 82 C1
Cattólica Eraclea I 108 B2
Catton GB 25 D5
Caudebec-en-Caux F 58 A1
Caudete E 101 A5
Caudete de las Fuentes E 96 B1
Caudiel E 96 B2
Caudiès-de-Fenouillèdes F 77 D5
Caudry F 49 C4
Caulkerbush GB 25 D4
Caulnes F 57 B3
Caulónia I 106 C3
Caumont-l'Evente F 57 A5
Caunes-Minervois F 77 C5
Cauro F 102 B1
Caussade F 77 B4
Causse-de-la-Selle F 78 C2
Cauterets F 76 D2
Cava de Tirreni I 103 C7
Cavaglia I 70 C3
Cavaillon F 79 C4
Cavalaire-sur-Mer F 79 C5
Cavaleiro P 98 B2
Cavalese I 71 B6
Cavallermaggiore I 80 B1
Cavallino I 72 C2
Cavan IRL 19 C4
Cavárzere I 72 C2
Çavdarhisar TR 118 C4
Çavdır TR 119 E4
Cavernais P 87 D3
Cavezzo I 81 B5
Cavignac F 76 A2
Čavle HR 73 C4
Cavo I 81 D4
Cavour I 80 B1
Cavtat HR 84 D3
Cawdor GB 23 D5
Çay TR 118 D6
Çaycuma TR 118 A7
Cayeux-sur-Mer F 48 C2
Cayiralan TR 16 B7
Çayırhan TR 118 B6
Caylus F 77 B4
Cayres F 78 B2
Cazalilla E 100 B2
Cazalla de la Sierra E 99 B5
Cazals F 77 B4
Cazanuecos E 88 B1
Cazaubon F 76 C2
Cazaux F 76 B1
Cazavet F 77 C4
Cazères F 77 C4
Cazin BIH 83 B4
Cazis CH 71 B4
Čazma HR 74 C1
Cazo E 88 A1
Cazorla E 100 B3
Cazouls-lès-Béziers F 78 C2
Cea, *León* E 88 B1
Cea, *Orense* E 86 B3
Ceánuri E 89 A4
Ceauce F 57 B5
Cebolla E 94 C2
Čebovce SK 65 B5
Cebreros E 94 B2
Čečava BIH 84 B2
Ceccano I 103 B6
Cece H 74 B3
Cecenowo PL 46 A3
Čechtice CZ 63 A6
Čechtín CZ 64 A1
Cécina I 81 C4
Ceclavín E 93 B4
Cedégolo I 71 B5
Cedeira E 86 A2
Cedillo E 92 B3
Cedillo del Condado E 94 B3
Cedrillas E 90 C2
Cedynia PL 45 C6
Cée E 86 B1
Cefalù I 109 A3
Céggia I 72 C2
Cegléd H 75 A4
Ceglédbercel H 75 A4
Céglie Messápica I 104 C3
Cehegín E 101 A4
Ceilhes-et-Rocozels F 78 C2
Ceinos de Campos E 88 B1
Ceira P 92 A2
Čejč CZ 64 B2
Cekcyn PL 47 B4
Cela BIH 83 B5
Čelákovice CZ 53 C4
Celano I 103 A6
Celanova E 87 B3
Celbridge IRL 21 A5
Čelebič BIH 83 C5
Celenza Valfortore I 103 B7
Čelić BIH 84 B3
Čelinac BIH 84 B2
Celje SLO 73 B5
Cella E 95 B5
Celldömölk H 74 A2
Celle D 44 C2
Celle Ligure I 80 B2
Celles B 49 C5
Celles-sur-Belle F 67 B4
Cellino San Marco I 105 C3
Celorico da Beira P 92 A3
Celorico de Basto P 87 C2
Çeltik TR 118 C6
Çeltikçi TR 119 E5
Cemaes GB 26 B1
Cembra I 71 B6
Čemerno BIH 84 C3
Cenad RO 75 B5
Cencenighe Agordino I 72 B1
Cenei RO 75 C5
Ceneselli I 81 A5
Cenicero E 89 B4
Cenicientos E 94 B2
Censeau F 69 B6
Čenta SRB 85 A5
Centallo I 80 B1
Centelles E 91 B5
Cento I 81 B5
Centúripe I 109 B3
Cepeda la Mora E 94 B1
Cépet F 77 C4
Čepin HR 74 C3
Čepinski Martinci HR 74 C3
Cepovan SLO 72 B3
Ceprano I 103 B6
Čeralije HR 74 C2
Cerami I 109 B3
Cerano I 70 C3
Cérans Foulletourte F 57 C6
Ceraso I 106 A2
Cerbaia I 81 C5
Cerbère F 91 A6
Cercadillo E 95 A4
Cercal, *Lisboa* P 92 B1
Cercal, *Setúbal* P 98 B2
Čerčany CZ 63 A5
Cerceda E 94 B3
Cercedilla E 94 B2
Cercemaggiore I 103 B7
Cercs E 91 A4
Cercy-la-Tour F 68 B3
Cerda I 108 B2
Cerdedo E 86 B2
Cerdeira P 93 A3
Cerdon F 58 C3
Cerea I 71 C6
Ceres GB 25 B5
Ceres I 70 C2
Cerese I 81 A4
Ceresole-Reale I 70 C2
Cereste F 79 C4
Céret F 91 A5
Cerezo de Abajo E 95 A3
Cerezo de Riotirón E 89 B3
Cerfontaine B 49 C5
Cergy F 58 A3
Cerignola I 104 B1
Cérilly F 68 B2
Cerisiers F 59 B4
Cerizay F 67 B4
Çerkeş TR 16 A6
Çerkezköy TR 118 A3
Cerkije SLO 73 B4
Cerknica SLO 73 C4
Cerkno SLO 72 B3
Cerkwica PL 45 A7
Çermë-Proshkë AL 105 B5
Černa HR 74 C3
Černá Hora CZ 64 A2
Cernavodă RO 11 D10
Cernay F 60 C3
Cerne Abbas GB 29 C5
Cernégula E 89 B3
Cernik HR 74 C2
Cernóbbio I 70 C4
Černošin CZ 62 A3
Cernovice CZ 63 A5
Cérons F 76 B2
Cerovlje HR 73 C4
Cerovo SK 65 B5
Cerqueto I 82 D1
Cerralbo E 87 D4
Cerreto d'Esi I 82 C1
Cerreto Sannita I 103 B7
Cerrigydrudion GB 26 B2
Cërrik AL 105 B5
Cerro Muriano E 100 A1
Certaldo I 81 C5
Certosa di Pésio I 80 B1
Cerva P 87 C3
Cervaro I 103 B6
Cervatos de la Cueza E 88 B2
Červena Řečice CZ 63 A6
Červená-Skala SK 65 B6
Červená Voda CZ 54 C1
Cerveny Kostelec CZ 53 C6
Cervera E 91 B4
Cervera de la Cañada E 89 C5
Cervera de Pisuerga E 88 B2
Cervera del Llano E 95 C4
Cervera del Río Alhama E 89 B5
Cervéteri I 102 B5
Cérvia I 82 B1
Cerviá de les Garriques E 90 B3
Cervignano del Friuli I 72 C3
Cervinara I 103 B7
Cervione F 102 A2
Cervo E 86 A3
Cervon F 68 A3
Cesana Torinese I 79 B5
Cesarica HR 83 B4
Cesarò I 109 B3
Cesena I 82 B1
Cesenático I 82 B1
Cēsis LV 7 C8
Česká Belá CZ 63 A6
Česká Kamenice CZ 53 C4
Česká Lípa CZ 53 C4
Česká Skalice CZ 53 C6
Česká Třebová CZ 64 A2
České Budějovice CZ 63 B5
České Velenice CZ 63 B5
Český Brod CZ 53 C4
Český Dub CZ 53 C4
Český Krumlov CZ 63 B5
Český Těšín CZ 65 A4
Češljeva Bara SRB 85 B6
Çeşme TR 119 D1
Cessenon F 78 C2
Cesson-Sévigné F 57 B4
Cestas F 76 B2
Čestobrodica SRB 85 C5
Cesuras E 86 A2
Cetin Grad HR 73 C5
Cetina E 89 C5
Cetinje CG 105 A4
Cetraro I 106 B2
Ceuta E 99 D5
Ceuti E 101 A4
Ceva I 80 B2
Cevico de la Torre E 88 C2
Cevico Navero E 88 C2
Cevins F 69 C6
Cévio CH 70 B3
Cevizli TR 119 E6
Čevo CG 105 A4
Cewice PL 46 A3
Ceyhan TR 16 C7
Ceylan TR 119 F4
Céyrat F 68 C3
Ceyzériat F 69 B5
Chaam NL 49 B5
Chabanais F 67 C5
Chabeuil F 79 B4
Chabielice PL 55 B4
Chablis F 59 C4
Châbons F 69 C5
Chabówka PL 65 A5
Chabreloche F 68 C3
Chabris F 67 A6
Chagford GB 28 C4
Chagny F 69 B4
Chagoda RUS 7 B13
Chaherrero E 94 B2
Chailland F 57 B5
Chaillé-les-Marais F 66 B3
Chailles F 67 A6
Chailley F 59 B4
Chalabre F 77 D5
Chalais F 67 C5
Chalamont F 69 C5
Châlette-sur-Loing F 58 B3
Chalindrey F 59 C6
Challacombe GB 28 B4
Challans F 66 B3
Challes-les-Eaux F 69 C5
Chalmazel F 68 C3
Chalmoux F 68 B3
Chalon-sur-Saône F 69 B4
Chalonnes-sur-Loire F 66 A4
Châlons-en-Champagne F 59 B5
Chalupy PL 47 A4
Châlus F 67 C5
Cham CH 70 A3
Cham D 62 A3
Chamberet F 68 C1
Chambéry F 69 C5
Chambilly F 68 B4
Chambley F 60 A1
Chambly F 58 A3
Chambois F 57 B6
Chambon-sur-Lac F 68 C2
Chambon-sur-Voueize F 68 B2
Chambord F 58 C2
Chamborigaud F 78 B2
Chamboulive F 68 C1
Chamerau D 62 A3
Chamonix-Mont Blanc F 70 C1
Chamoux-sur-Gelon F 69 C6
Champagnac-le-Vieux F 68 C3
Champagney F 60 C2
Champagnole F 69 B5
Champagny-Mouton F 67 B5
Champaubert F 59 B4
Champdeniers-St. Denis F 67 B4
Champdieu F 68 C4
Champdôtre F 69 A5
Champeix F 68 C3
Champéry CH 70 B1
Champigne F 57 C5
Champignelles F 59 C4
Champigny-sur-Veude F 67 A5
Champlitte-et-le-Prelot F 60 C1
Champoluc I 70 C2
Champoly F 68 C3
Champorcher I 70 C2
Champrond-en-Gâtine F 58 B2
Champs-sur-Tarentaine F 68 C2
Champs-sur-Yonne F 59 C4
Champtoceaux F 66 A3
Chamrousse F 69 C5
Chamusca P 92 B2
Chanac F 78 B2
Chanaleilles F 78 B2
Chandler's Ford GB 31 D2
Chandra GR 117 G8
Chandrexa de Queixa E 87 B3
Chañe E 88 C2
Changy F 68 B3
Chania GR 117 G6
Channes F 59 C5
Chantada E 86 B3
Chantelle F 68 B3
Chantenay-St. Imbert F 68 B3
Chanteuges F 78 A2
Chantilly F 58 A3
Chantonnay F 66 B3
Chão de Codes P 92 B2
Chaource F 59 B5
Chapa E 86 B2
Chapareillan F 69 C5
Chapel en le Frith GB 27 B4
Chapelle Royale F 58 B2
Chapelle-St. Laurent F 67 B4
Charbonnat F 68 B4
Chard GB 29 C5
Charenton-du-Cher F 68 B2
Charlbury GB 31 C2
Charleroi B 49 C5
Charlestown IRL 18 C3
Charlestown of Aberlour GB 23 D5
Charleville IRL 20 B3
Charleville-Mézières F 59 A5
Charlieu F 68 B4
Charlottenberg S 34 C4
Charlton Kings GB 29 B5
Charly F 59 B4
Charmes F 60 B2
Charmes-sur-Rhône F 78 B3
Charmey CH 70 B2
Charminster GB 29 C5
Charmont-en-Beauce F 58 B3
Charny F 59 C4
Charolles F 69 B4
Chârost F 68 B2
Charquemont F 70 A1
Charrin F 68 B3
Charroux F 67 B5
Chartres F 58 B2
Charzykow PL 46 B3
Chasseneuil-sur-Bonnieure F 67 C5
Chassigny F 59 C6
Château-Arnoux F 79 B5
Château-Chinon F 68 A3
Château-d'Oex CH 70 B2
Château-d'Olonne F 66 B3
Château-du-Loir F 58 C1
Château-Gontier F 57 C5
Château-la-Vallière F 67 A5
Château-Landon F 58 B3
Château-l'Evêque F 67 C5
Château-Porcien F 59 A5
Château-Renault F 58 C1
Château-Salins F 60 B2
Château-Thierry F 59 A4
Châteaubernard F 67 C4
Châteaubourg F 57 B4
Châteaubriant F 57 C4
Châteaudun F 58 B2
Châteaugiron F 57 B4
Châteaulin F 56 B1
Châteaumeillant F 68 B2
Châteauneuf, *Nièvre* F 68 A3
Châteauneuf, *Saône-et-Loire* F 69 B4
Châteauneuf-de-Randon F 78 B2
Châteauneuf-d'Ille-et-Vilaine F 57 B4
Châteauneuf-du-Faou F 56 B2
Châteauneuf-du-Pape F 78 B3
Châteauneuf-en-Thymerais F 58 B2
Châteauneuf la-Forêt F 67 C6
Châteauneuf-le-Rouge F 79 C4
Châteauneuf-sur-Charente F 67 C4
Châteauneuf-sur-Cher F 68 B2
Châteauneuf-sur-Loire F 58 C3
Châteauneuf-sur-Sarthe F 57 C5
Châteauponsac F 67 B6
Châteauredon F 79 B5
Châteaurenard, *Bouches du Rhône* F 78 C3
Châteaurenard, *Loiret* F 59 C3
Châteauroux F 68 B1
Châteauroux-les-Alpes F 79 B5
Châteauvillain F 59 B5
Châtel F 70 B1
Châtel-Censoir F 68 A3
Châtel-de-Neuvre F 68 B3
Châtel-Montagne F 68 B3
Châtel-St. Denis CH 70 B1
Châtel-sur-Moselle F 60 B2
Châtelaillon-Plage F 66 B3
Châtelaudren F 56 B3
Châtelet B 49 C5
Châtelguyon F 68 C3
Châtellerault F 67 B5
Châtelus-Malvaleix F 68 B2
Châtenois F 60 B1
Châtenois-les-Forges F 70 A1
Chatham GB 31 C4
Châtillon I 70 C2
Châtillon-Coligny F 59 C3
Châtillon-en-Bazois F 68 A3
Châtillon-en-Diois F 79 B4
Châtillon-sur Chalaronne F 69 B4
Châtillon-sur-Indre F 67 B6
Châtillon-sur-Loire F 58 C3
Châtillon-sur-Marne F 59 A4
Châtillon-sur-Seine F 59 C5
Châtres F 59 B4
Chatteris GB 30 B4
Chatton GB 25 C6
Chauchina E 100 B2
Chaudes-Aigues F 78 B2
Chaudrey F 59 B5
Chauffailles F 69 B4
Chaulnes F 58 A3
Chaument Gistoux B 49 C5
Chaumergy F 69 B5
Chaumont F 59 B6
Chaumont-en-Vexin F 58 A2
Chaumont-Porcien F 59 A5
Chaumont-sur-Aire F 59 B6
Chaumont-sur-Loire F 67 A6
Chaunay F 67 B5
Chauny F 59 A4
Chaussin F 69 B5
Chauvigny F 67 B5
Chavagnes-en-Paillers F 66 B3
Chavanges F 59 B5
Chaves P 87 C3
Chavignon F 59 A4
Chazelles-sur-Lyon F 69 C4
Chazey-Bons F 69 C5
Cheadle, *Greater Manchester* GB 26 B3
Cheadle, *Staffordshire* GB 27 C4
Cheb CZ 52 C2
Chebsara RUS 7 B15
Checa E 95 B5
Chęciny PL 55 C5
Cheddar GB 29 B5
Cheddleton GB 26 B3
Chef-Boutonne F 67 B4
Chekalin RUS 7 D14
Chekhovo RUS 47 A6
Cheles E 93 C3
Chella E 96 B2
Chelles F 58 B3
Chełm PL 11 A7
Chełmno, *Kujawsko-Pomorskie* PL 47 B4
Chełmno, *Wielkopolskie* PL 54 A3
Chelmsford GB 31 C4
Chełmża PL 47 B4
Cheltenham GB 29 B5
Chelva E 96 B1
Chémery F 67 A6
Chemery-sur-Bar F 59 A5
Chemillé F 67 A4
Chemin F 69 B5
Chemnitz D 52 C2
Chénerailles F 68 B2
Cheniménil F 60 B2
Chenonceaux F 67 A6
Chenôve F 69 A4
Chepelare BG 116 A6
Chepstow GB 29 B5
Chera E 96 B2
Cherasco I 80 B1
Cherbonnières F 67 C4
Cherbourg F 57 A4
Cherchiara di Calábria I 106 B3
Cherepovets RUS 7 B14
Cherkasy UA 11 B12
Chernihiv UA 7 F11
Chernivtsi UA 11 B8
Chernobyl = Chornobyl UA 7 F11
Chernyakhovsk RUS 6 D6
Chéroy F 59 B3
Cherven BY 7 E10
Chervonohrad UA 11 A8
Cherykaw BY 7 E11
Chesham GB 31 C3
Cheshunt GB 31 C3
Chessy-lès-Pres F 59 B4
Cheste E 96 B2
Chester GB 26 B3
Chester-le-Street GB 25 D6
Chesterfield GB 27 B4
Chevagnes F 68 B3
Chevanceaux F 67 C4
Chevillon F 59 B6
Chevilly F 58 B2
Chew Magna GB 29 B5
Chézery-Forens F 69 B5
Chialamberto I 70 C2
Chiampo I 71 C6
Chianale I 79 B6
Chianciano Terme I 81 C5
Chiaramonte Gulfi I 109 B3
Chiaramonti I 110 B1
Chiaravalle I 82 C2
Chiaravalle Centrale I 106 C3
Chiaréggio I 71 B4
Chiari I 71 C4
Chiaromonte I 106 A3
Chiasso CH 70 C4
Chiávari I 80 B3
Chiavenna I 71 B4
Chiché F 67 B4
Chichester GB 31 D3
Chiclana de la Frontera E 99 C4
Chiclana de Segura E 100 A2
Chiddingfold GB 31 C3
Chieri I 80 A1
Chiesa in Valmalenco I 71 B4
Chieti I 103 A7
Chieti Scalo I 103 A7
Chiéuti I 103 B8
Chigirin UA 11 B12
Chigwell GB 31 C4
Chiliomodi GR 117 E4
Chillarón de Cuenca E 95 B4
Chillarón del Rey E 95 B4
Chilleurs-aux-Bois F 58 B3
Chillón E 100 A1
Chilluevar E 100 B2
Chiloeches E 95 B3
Chimay B 49 C5
Chimeneas E 100 B2
Chinchilla de Monte Aragón E 96 C1
Chinchón E 95 B3
Chingford GB 31 C4
Chinon F 67 A5
Chióggia I 72 C2
Chiomonte I 79 A5
Chipiona E 99 C4
Chippenham GB 29 B5
Chipping Campden GB 29 A6
Chipping Norton GB 31 C2
Chipping Ongar GB 31 C4
Chipping Sodbury GB 29 B5
Chirac F 78 B2
Chirbury GB 26 C2
Chirens F 69 C5
Chirivel E 101 B3
Chirk GB 26 C2
Chirnside GB 25 C5
Chişinău = Khisinev MD 11 C10
Chişineu Criş RO 10 C6
Chissey-en-Morvan F 69 A4
Chiusa I 71 B6
Chiusa di Pésio I 80 B1
Chiusa Scláfani I 108 B2
Chiusaforte I 72 B3
Chiusi I 81 C5
Chiva E 96 B2
Chivasso I 70 C2
Chlewiska PL 55 B5
Chludowo PL 46 C2
Chlum u Třeboně CZ 63 B5
Chlumec nad Cidlinou CZ 53 C5
Chmielnik PL 55 C5
Chobienia PL 54 B1
Chobienice PL 53 A5
Choceň CZ 53 D6
Choceń PL 47 C5
Chochołow PL 65 A5
Chocianów PL 53 B5
Chociw PL 55 B4
Chociwel PL 46 B1
Choczewo PL 46 A3
Chodaków PL 55 A5
Chodecz PL 47 C5
Chodov CZ 52 C2
Chodzież PL 46 C2
Chojna PL 45 C6
Chojnice PL 46 B3
Chojno, *Kujawsko-Pomorskie* PL 47 C5
Chojno, *Wielkopolskie* PL 46 C2
Chojnów PL 53 B5
Cholet F 66 A4
Chomérac F 78 B3
Chomutov CZ 52 C3
Chop UA 11 B7
Chora GR 117 E3
Chora Sfakion GR 117 G6
Chorges F 79 B5
Chorley GB 26 B3
Chornobyl = Chernobyl UA 7 F11
Chortkiv UA 11 B8
Chorzew PL 54 B3
Chorzów PL 54 C3
Choszczno PL 46 B1
Chotcza-Józefów PL 55 B6
Chotěboř CZ 63 A6
Chouilly F 59 A5
Chouto P 92 B2
Chouzy-sur-Cisse F 67 A6
Chozas de Abajo E 88 B1
Chrast, *Vychodočeský* CZ 64 A1
Chrást, *Západočeský* CZ 63 A4
Chrastava CZ 53 C4
Chřibská CZ 53 C4
Christchurch GB 29 C6
Christiansfeld DK 39 D2
Chroberz PL 55 C5
Chropyně CZ 64 A3
Chrudim CZ 53 D5
Chrzanów PL 55 C4
Chtelnica SK 64 B3
Chudovo RUS 7 B11
Chueca E 94 C3
Chulmleigh GB 28 C4
Chur CH 71 B4
Church Stretton GB 26 C3
Churriana E 100 C1
Churwalden CH 71 B4
Chvalšiny CZ 63 B5
Chwaszczyno PL 47 A4
Chynava CZ 53 C4
Chýnov CZ 63 A5
Ciacova RO 75 C6
Ciadîr-Lunga MD 11 C10
Ciadoncha E 88 B3
Cianciana I 108 B2
Ciano d'Enza I 81 B4
Ciążen PL 54 A2
Cibakhaza H 75 B5
Ciborro P 92 C2
Cicagna I 80 B3
Cicciano I 103 C7
Ćićevac SRB 85 C6
Ciciliano I 102 B5
Cicognolo I 71 C5
Cidadelhe P 87 D3
Cide TR 16 A6
Cidones E 89 C4
Ciechanów, *Dolnośląskie* PL 54 B1
Ciechanów, *Mazowieckie* PL 47 C6
Ciechocinek PL 47 C4
Cielądz PL 55 B5
Ciemnik PL 46 B1
Ciempozuelos E 95 B3
Ciepielów PL 55 B6
Čierny Balog SK 65 B5
Cierp F 77 D3
Cierpice PL 47 C4
Ciervana E 89 A3
Cierznie PL 46 B3
Cieslé PL 47 C6
Cieszyn PL 65 A4
Cieutat F 76 C3
Cieza E 101 A4
Cifer SK 64 B3
Çifteler TR 118 C6
Cifuentes E 95 B4
Cigales E 88 C2
Cigliano I 70 C3
Cihanbeyli TR 16 B6
Čilipi HR 105 A4
Cillas E 95 B5
Cilleros E 93 A4
Cilleruelo de Arriba E 88 C3
Cilleruelo de Bezana E 88 B3
Cimalmotto CH 70 B3
Cimanes del Tejar E 88 B1
Ciminna I 108 B2
Cimişlia MD 11 C10
Cimoláis I 72 B2
Cîmpulung RO 11 D8
Çınarcık TR 118 B4
Cinctorres E 90 C2
Cinderford GB 29 B5
Çine TR 119 E3
Činěves CZ 53 C5
Ciney B 49 C6
Cinfães P 87 C2
Cingia de Botti I 81 A4
Cingoli I 82 C2
Cinigiano I 81 D5
Cinobaňa SK 65 B5
Cinq-Mars-la-Pile F 67 A5
Cinquefrondí I 106 C3
Cintegabelle F 77 C4
Cintruénigo E 89 B5
Ciółkowo PL 47 C5
Ciperez E 87 D4
Cirat E 96 A2
Cirella I 106 B2
Cirencester GB 29 B6
Cirey-sur-Vezouze F 60 B2
Ciria E 89 C5
Ciriè I 70 C2
Cirigliano I 104 C2
Cirò I 107 B4
Cirò Marina I 107 B4
Ciry-le-Noble F 69 B4
Cislău RO 11 D9
Cismon del Grappa I 72 C1
Cisneros E 88 B2
Cissac-Médoc F 66 C4
Čista CZ 52 C3
Cisterna di Latina I 102 B5
Cistérniga E 88 C2
Cisternino I 104 C3
Cistierna E 88 B1
Čitluk BIH 84 C2
Citov CZ 53 C4
Città del Vaticano = Vatican City I 102 B5
Città della Pieve I 81 D6
Città di Castello I 82 C1
Città Sant'Angelo I 103 A7
Cittadella I 72 C1
Cittaducale I 102 A5
Cittanova I 106 C3
Ciudad Real E 94 D3
Ciudad Rodrigo E 93 A4
Ciudadela de Menorca E 97 B3
Cividale del Friuli I 72 B3
Cívita I 102 A6
Cívita Castellana I 102 A5
Civitanova Alta I 82 C2
Civitanova Marche I 82 C2
Civitavécchia I 102 A4
Civitella di Romagna I 81 B5
Civitella di Tronto I 82 D2
Civitella Roveto I 103 B6
Civray F 67 B5
Çivril TR 119 D4
Cízur Mayor E 76 D1
Cjutadilla E 91 B4
Clabhach GB 24 B1
Clachan GB 22 D2
Clachan na Luib GB 22 D1
Clacton-on-Sea GB 31 C5
Cladich GB 24 B2
Claggan GB 24 B2
Clairvaux-les-Lacs F 69 B5
Clamecy F 68 A3
Claonaig GB 24 C2
Clarecastle IRL 20 B3
Claregalway IRL 20 A3
Claremorris IRL 18 C2
Clarinbridge IRL 20 A3
Clashmore GB 23 D4
Clashmore IRL 21 B4
Claudy GB 19 B4
Clausthal-Zellerfeld D 51 B6
Cláut I 72 B2
Clay Cross GB 27 B4
Claye-Souilly F 58 B3
Cléder F 56 B1
Cleethorpes GB 27 B5
Clefmont F 60 B1
Cléguérec F 56 B2
Clelles F 79 B4
Clenze D 44 C2
Cleobury Mortimer GB 29 A5
Cléon-d'Andran F 78 B3
Cléré-les-Pins F 67 A5
Clères F 58 A2
Clermont F 58 A3
Clermont-en-Argonne F 59 A6
Clermont-Ferrand F 68 C3
Clermont-l'Hérault F 78 C2
Clerval F 69 A6
Clervaux L 50 C2
Clèry-St. André F 58 C2
Cles I 71 B6
Clevedon GB 29 B5
Cleveleys GB 26 B2
Cley GB 30 B5
Clifden IRL 18 C1
Clifford GB 29 A4
Clisson F 66 A3
Clitheroe GB 26 B3
Clogh IRL 21 B4
Cloghan, *Donegal* IRL 19 B4
Cloghan, *Offaly* IRL 21 A4
Clogheen IRL 21 B4
Clogher GB 19 B4
Cloghjordan IRL 20 B3

Clohars-Carnoët F 56 C2
Clonakilty IRL 20 C3
Clonaslee IRL 21 A4
Clondalkin IRL 21 A5
Clones IRL 19 B4
Clonmany IRL 19 A4
Clonmel IRL 21 B4
Clonmellon IRL 19 C4
Clonord IRL 21 A4
Clonroche IRL 21 B5
Cloone IRL 19 C4
Cloppenburg D 43 C5
Closeburn GB 25 C4
Clough GB 19 B6
Clova GB 25 B4
Clovelly GB 28 C3
Clowne GB 27 B4
Cloyes-sur-le-Loir F 58 C2
Cloyne IRL 20 C3
Cluis F 68 B1
Cluj-Napoca RO 11 C7
Clun GB 26 C2
Clunes GB 24 B3
Cluny F 69 B4
Cluses F 69 B6
Clusone I 71 C4
Clydach GB 28 B4
Clydebank GB 24 C3
Coachford IRL 20 C3
Coagh GB 19 B5
Coalisland GB 19 B5
Coalville GB 27 C4
Coaña E 86 A4
Çobanlar TR 118 D5
Cobas E 86 A2
Cobertelade E 89 C4
Cobeta E 95 B4
Cóbh IRL 20 C3
Cobreces E 88 A2
Coburg D 51 C6
Coca E 94 A2
Cocentaina E 96 C2
Cochem D 50 C3
Cockburnspath GB 25 C5
Cockermouth GB 26 A2
Codigoro I 82 B1
Codogno I 71 C4
Codos E 89 C5
Codróipo I 72 C2
Codrongianos I 110 B1
Coelhoso P 87 C4
Coesfeld D 50 B3
Coevorden NL 42 C3
Cofrentes E 96 B1
Cogeces del Monte E 88 C2
Coggeshall GB 31 C4
Cognac F 67 C4
Cogne I 70 C2
Cognin F 69 C5
Cogolin F 79 C5
Cogollos de Guadix E 100 B2
Cogollos-Vega E 100 B2
Cogolludo E 95 B3
Coimbra P 92 A2
Coín E 100 C1
Coirós E 86 A2
Čoka SRB 75 C5
Col SLO 73 C4
Colares P 92 C1
Cölbe D 51 C4
Colbitz D 52 A1
Colchester GB 31 C4
Coldingham GB 25 C5
Colditz D 52 B2
Coldstream GB 25 C5
Colebrooke GB 28 C4
Colera E 91 A6
Coleraine GB 19 A5
Colfiorito I 82 C1
Cólico I 71 B4
Coligny F 69 B5
Colindres E 89 A3
Coll de Nargó E 91 A4
Collado-Mediano E 94 B2
Collado Villalba E 94 B3
Collagna I 81 B4
Collanzo E 88 A1
Collat F 68 C3
Colle di Val d'Elsa I 81 C5
Colle Isarco I 71 B6
Colle Sannita I 103 B7
Collécchio I 81 B4
Colledimezzo I 103 B7
Colleferro I 102 B6
Collelongo I 103 B6
Collepasso I 107 A5
Collepepe I 82 D1
Collesalvetti I 81 C4
Collesano I 108 B2
Colli a Volturno I 103 B7
Collin GB 25 C4
Collinée F 56 B3
Collingham, *Nottinghamshire* GB 27 B5
Collingham, *West Yorkshire* GB 27 B4
Collinghorst D 43 B4
Cóllio I 71 C5
Collobrières F 79 C5
Collon IRL 19 C5
Collooney IRL 18 B3
Colmar F 60 B3
Colmars F 79 B5
Colmenar E 100 C1
Colmenar de la Sierra E 95 A3
Colmenar de Oreja E 95 B3
Colmenar Viejo E 94 B3
Colmonel GB 24 C3
Colne GB 26 B3
Colobraro I 106 A3
Cologna Véneta I 71 C6
Cologne = Köln D 50 C2
Cologne F 77 C3
Cologne al Serio I 71 C4
Colombey-les-Belles F 60 B1
Colombey-les-deux-Églises F 59 B5
Colombres E 88 A2
Colomera E 100 B2
Colomers E 91 A5
Colomiers F 77 C4
Colònia de Sant Jordi E 97 B3
Colorno I 81 B4
Colos P 98 B2
Cölpin D 45 B5
Colpy GB 23 D6
Colsterworth GB 30 B3
Coltishall GB 30 B5
Colunga E 88 A1
Colwell GB 25 C5
Colwyn Bay GB 26 B2
Colyford GB 29 C4
Coma-ruga E 91 B4
Comácchio I 82 B1
Combarros E 86 B4
Combeaufontaine F 60 C1
Comber GB 19 B6
Comblain-au-Pont B 49 C6
Combloux F 70 C1
Combourg F 57 B4
Combronde F 68 C3
Comeglians I 72 B2
Comillas E 88 A2
Comines F 49 C4
Cómiso I 109 C3
Comloşu Mare RO 75 C5
Commensacq F 76 B2
Commentry F 68 B2
Commerau D 53 B4
Commercy F 60 B1
Como I 71 C4
Cómpeta E 100 C2
Compiègne F 58 A3
Comporta P 92 C2
Comps-sur-Artuby F 79 C5
Comrat MD 11 C10
Comrie GB 25 B4
Comunanza I 82 D2
Cona, *Emilia Romagna* I 81 B5
Cona, *Veneto* I 72 C2
Concarneau F 56 C2
Conceição P 98 B2
Conches-en-Ouche F 58 B1
Concordia Sagittária I 72 C2
Concordia sulla Sécchia I 81 B4
Concots F 77 B4
Condat F 68 C2
Condé-en-Brie F 59 B4
Condé-sur-l'Escaut F 49 C4
Conde-sur-Marne F 59 A5
Condé-sur-Noireau F 57 B5
Condeixa P 92 A2
Condemios de Abajo E 95 A3
Condemios de Arriba E 95 A3
Condino I 71 C5
Condom F 77 C3
Condove I 70 C2
Condrieu F 69 C4
Conegliano I 72 C2
Conflans-sur-Lanterne F 60 C2
Confolens F 67 B5
Conforto E 86 A3
Cong IRL 18 C2
Congleton GB 26 B3
Congosto E 86 B4
Congosto de Valdavia E 88 B2
Congostrina E 95 A3
Conil de la Frontera E 99 C4
Coningsby GB 27 B5
Coniston GB 26 A2
Conlie F 57 B5
Conliège F 69 B5
Conna IRL 20 B3
Connah's Quay GB 26 B2
Connantre F 59 B4
Connaugh IRL 20 B3
Connaux F 78 B3
Connel GB 24 B2
Connerré F 58 B1
Cononbridge GB 23 D4
Čonoplja SRB 75 C4
Conques F 77 B5
Conques-sur-Orbiel F 77 C5
Conquista E 100 A1
Conquista de la Sierra E 93 B5
Consándolo I 81 B5
Consélice I 81 B5
Conselve I 72 C1
Consenvoye F 59 A6
Consett GB 25 D6
Consolação P 92 B1
Constancia P 92 B2
Constanco E 86 A2
Constanța RO 11 D10
Constanti E 91 B4
Constantina E 99 B5
Consuegra E 95 C3
Consuma I 81 C5
Contarina I 82 A1
Contay F 48 D3
Conthey CH 70 B2
Contigliano I 102 A5
Contis-Plage F 76 B1
Contrada I 103 C7
Contres F 67 A6
Contrexéville F 60 B1
Controne I 103 C8
Contursi Termi I 103 C8
Conty F 58 A3
Conversano I 104 C3
Conwy GB 26 B2
Cookstown GB 19 B5
Coole F 59 B5
Coolgreany IRL 21 B5
Cooneen GB 19 B4
Cootehill IRL 19 B4
Cope E 101 B4
Copenhagen = København DK 41 D2
Copertino I 105 C4
Copparo I 81 B5
Coppenbrugge D 51 A5
Corabia RO 11 E8
Córaci I 106 B3
Coralići BIH 83 B4
Corato I 104 B2
Coray F 56 B2
Corbeil-Essonnes F 58 B3
Corbeny F 59 A4
Corbera E 96 B2
Corbie F 58 A3
Corbigny F 68 A3
Corbion B 59 A5
Corbridge GB 25 D5
Corby GB 30 B3
Corconte E 88 A3
Corcubión E 86 B1
Corcumello I 103 A6
Cordenòns I 72 C2
Cordes-sur-Ciel F 77 B4
Córdoba E 100 B1
Cordobilla de Lácara E 93 B4
Cordovado I 72 C2
Corella E 89 B5
Coreses E 88 C1
Corfe Castle GB 29 C5
Corga de Lobão P 87 D2
Cori I 102 B5
Coria E 93 B4
Coria del Río E 99 B4
Corigliano Cálabro I 106 B3
Corinaldo I 82 C1
Corinth = Korinthos GR 117 E4
Cório I 70 C2
Coripe E 99 C5
Cork IRL 20 C3
Corlay F 56 B2
Corleone I 108 B2
Corleto Monforte I 103 C8
Corleto Perticara I 104 C2
Çorlu TR 118 A2
Cormainville F 58 B2
Cormatin F 69 B4
Cormeilles F 58 A1
Cormery F 67 A5
Cormòns I 72 C3
Cormoz F 69 B5
Cornago E 89 B4
Cornberg D 51 B5
Cornellana E 86 A4
Corneşti MD 11 C10
Corníglio I 81 B4
Cornimont F 60 C2
Corniolo I 81 C5
Cornuda I 72 C2
Cornudella de Montsant E 90 B3
Cornudilla E 89 B3
Cornus F 78 C2
Çorovodë AL 116 B2
Corpach GB 24 B2
Corps F 79 B4
Corps Nuds F 57 C4
Corral de Almaguer E 95 C3
Corral de Ayllon E 89 C3
Corral de Calatrava E 100 A1
Corral-Rubio E 101 A4
Corrales E 88 C1
Corran GB 24 B2
Corredoiras E 86 A2
Corréggio I 81 B4
Corrèze F 68 C1
Corridónia I 82 C2
Corris GB 26 C2
Corrubedo E 86 B1
Córsico I 71 C4
Corsock GB 25 C4
Corte F 102 A2
Corte de Peleas E 93 C4
Corte Pinto P 98 B3
Corteconcepción E 99 B4
Cortegaca P 87 D2
Cortegada E 87 B2
Cortegana E 99 B4
Cortemaggiore I 81 B3
Cortemilia I 80 B2
Cortes E 89 C5
Cortes de Aragón E 90 C2
Cortes de Arenoso E 96 A2
Cortes de Baza E 101 B3
Cortes de la Frontera E 99 C5
Cortes de Pallás E 96 B2
Cortiçadas P 92 C2
Cortico P 87 C3
Cortijo de Arriba E 94 C2
Cortijos Nuevos E 101 A3
Cortina d'Ampezzo I 72 B2
Corton GB 30 B5
Cortona I 81 C5
Coruche P 92 C2
Corullón E 86 B4
Çorum TR 16 A7
Corvara in Badia I 72 B1
Corvera E 101 B4
Corwen GB 26 C2
Cosenza I 106 B3
Cosham GB 31 D2
Coslada E 95 B3
Cosne-Cours-sur-Loire F 68 A2
Cosne d'Allier F 68 B2
Cospeito E 86 A3
Cossato I 70 C3
Cossaye F 68 B3
Cossé-le-Vivien F 57 C5
Cossonay CH 69 B6
Costa da Caparica P 92 C1
Costa de Santo André P 98 A2
Costa Nova P 92 A2
Costalpino I 81 C5
Costaros F 78 B2
Costeşti RO 11 D8
Costigliole d'Asti I 80 B2
Costigliole Saluzzo I 80 B1
Coswig, *Sachsen-Anhalt* D 52 B2
Coswig, *Sachsen* D 52 B3
Cotherstone GB 27 A4
Cotronei I 107 B3
Cottbus D 53 B4
Cottenham GB 30 B4
Cottingham GB 27 B5
Coublanc F 60 C1
Couches F 69 B4
Couço P 92 C2
Coucouron F 78 B2
Coucy-le-Château-Auffrique F 59 A4
Couëron F 66 A3
Couflens F 77 D4
Couhé F 67 B5
Couiza F 77 D5
Coulags GB 22 D3
Coulanges F 68 B3
Coulanges-la-Vineuse F 59 C4
Coulanges-sur-Yonne F 68 A3
Couleuvre F 68 B2
Coulmier-le-Sec F 59 C5
Coulommiers F 59 B4
Coulonges-sur-l'Autize F 67 B4
Coulounieix-Chamiers F 67 C5
Coulport GB 24 B3
Coupar Angus GB 25 B4
Coupéville F 59 B5
Couptrain F 57 B5
Cour-Cheverny F 67 A6
Cour-et-Buis F 69 C4
Coura P 87 C2
Courcelles B 49 C5
Courcelles-Chaussy F 60 A2
Courchevel F 70 C1
Courcôme F 67 C5
Courçon F 66 B4
Courgenay CH 70 A2
Courmayeur I 70 C1
Courniou F 78 C1
Cournon-d'Auvergne F 68 C3
Cournonterral F 78 C2
Courpière F 68 C3
Cours-la-Ville F 69 B4
Coursan F 78 C2
Courseulles-sur-Mer F 57 A5
Courson-les-Carrières F 59 C4
Courtalain F 58 B2
Courtenay F 59 B4
Courtomer F 58 B1
Courville, *Eure-et-Loir* F 58 B2
Courville, *Marne* F 59 A4
Coussac-Bonneval F 67 C6
Coutances F 57 A4
Couterne F 57 B5
Coutras F 76 A2
Couvet CH 70 B1
Couvin B 49 C5
Couzon F 68 B3
Covadonga E 88 A1
Covaleda E 89 C4
Covarrubias E 89 B3
Covas P 87 C2
Cove GB 22 D3
Coventry GB 30 B2
Coverack GB 28 C2
Covigliáio I 81 B5
Covilhã P 92 A3
Cowbridge GB 29 B4
Cowdenbeath GB 25 B4
Cowes GB 31 D2
Cox F 77 C4
Cózar E 100 A2
Cozes F 66 C4
Cozzano F 102 B2
Craco I 104 C2
Craibstone GB 23 D6
Craighouse GB 24 C2
Craignure GB 24 B2
Crail GB 25 B5
Crailsheim D 61 A6
Craiova RO 11 D7
Cramlington GB 25 C6
Cranleigh GB 31 C3
Craon F 57 C5
Craonne F 59 A4
Craponne F 69 C4
Craponne-sur-Arzon F 68 C3
Crathie GB 23 D5
Crato P 92 B3
Craughwell IRL 20 A3
Craven Arms GB 26 C3
Crawford GB 25 C4
Crawinkel D 51 C6
Crawley GB 31 C3
Creag Ghoraidh GB 22 D1
Crecente E 87 B2
Crèches-sur-Saône F 69 B4
Crécy-en-Ponthieu F 48 C2
Crécy-la-Chapelle F 59 B3
Crécy-sur-Serre F 59 A4
Crediton GB 29 C4
Creeslough IRL 19 A4
Creetown GB 24 D3
Creeve GB 19 B5
Creglingen D 61 A6
Creil F 58 A3
Creissels F 78 B2
Crema I 71 C4
Cremeaux F 68 C3
Crémenes E 88 B1
Crémieu F 69 C5
Cremlingen D 51 A6
Cremona I 81 A4
Creney F 59 B5
Črenšovci SLO 73 B6
Créon F 76 B2
Crepaja SRB 85 A5
Crépey F 60 B1
Crépy F 59 A4
Crépy-en-Valois F 59 A3
Cres HR 83 B3
Crescentino I 70 C3
Crespino I 81 B5
Crespos E 94 B2
Cressage GB 26 C3
Cressensac F 77 A4
Cressia F 69 B5
Crest F 79 B4
Cresta CH 71 B4
Créteil F 58 B3
Creully F 57 A5
Creussen D 62 A2
Creutzwald F 60 A2
Creuzburg D 51 B6
Crevalcore I 81 B5
Crèvecœur-le-Grand F 58 A3
Crevillente E 101 A5
Crévola d'Ossola I 70 B3
Crewe GB 26 B3
Crewkerne GB 29 C5
Criales E 89 B3
Crianlarich GB 24 B3
Criccieth GB 26 C1
Crickhowell GB 29 B4
Cricklade GB 29 B6
Crieff GB 25 B4
Criel-sur-Mer F 48 C2
Crikvenica HR 73 C4
Crillon F 58 A2
Crimmitschau D 52 C2
Crimond GB 23 D7
Crinitz D 53 B3
Cripán E 89 B4
Criquetot-l'Esneval F 57 A6
Crispiano I 104 C3
Crissolo I 79 B6
Cristóbal E 93 A5
Crivitz D 44 B3
Črna SLO 73 B4
Crna Bara, *Srbija* SRB 85 B4
Crna Bara, *Vojvodina* SRB 75 C5
Crnac HR 74 C2
Crnča SRB 85 B4
Crni Lug BIH 83 B5
Crni Lug HR 73 C4
Črni Vrh SLO 73 C4
Crnjelovo Donje BIH 85 B4
Črnomelj SLO 73 C5
Crocketford GB 25 C4
Crocq F 68 C2
Crodo I 70 B3
Croglin GB 25 D5
Crolly IRL 18 A3
Cromarty GB 23 D4
Cromer GB 30 B5
Cronat F 68 B3
Crookhaven IRL 20 C2
Crookstown IRL 20 C3
Croom IRL 20 B3
Cropalati I 106 B3
Crópani I 107 C3
Crosbost GB 22 C2
Crosby GB 26 B2
Crosía I 106 B3
Cross-Hands GB 28 B3
Crossakiel IRL 19 C4
Crosshaven IRL 20 C3
Crosshill GB 24 C3
Crossmolina IRL 18 B2
Crotone I 107 B4
Crottendorf D 52 C2
Crouy F 59 A4
Crowborough GB 31 C4
Crowland GB 30 B3
Crowthorne GB 31 C3
Croyde GB 28 B3
Croydon GB 31 C3
Crozon F 56 B1
Cruas F 78 B3
Cruceni RO 75 B6
Crúcoli I 107 B4
Cruden Bay GB 23 D7
Crudgington GB 26 C3
Cruis F 79 B4
Crumlin GB 19 B5
Cruseilles F 69 B6
Crusheen IRL 20 B3
Cruz de Incio E 86 B3
Crvenka SRB 75 C4
Črveny Kamen SK 64 A4
Csabacsüd H 75 B5
Csabrendek H 74 A2
Csákánydoroszló H 74 B1
Csákvár H 74 A3
Csanádapáca H 75 B5
Csanádpalota H 75 B5
Csány H 65 C5
Csanytelek H 75 B5
Csapod H 74 A1
Császár H 74 A3
Császártöltés H 75 B4
Csávoly H 75 B4
Csemö H 75 A4
Csengöd H 75 B4
Csépa H 75 B5
Csepreg H 74 A1
Cserkeszölö H 75 B5
Csernely H 65 B6
Csesztreg H 74 B1
Csökmö H 75 A6
Csököly H 74 B2
Csokonyavisonta H 74 B2
Csólyospálos H 75 B4
Csongrád H 75 B5
Csopak H 74 B2
Csorna H 64 C3
Csorvás H 75 B5
Csurgo H 74 B2
Cuacos de Yuste E 93 A5
Cualedro E 87 C3
Cuanca de Campos E 88 B1
Cuba P 98 A3
Cubel E 95 A5
Cubelles E 91 B4
Cubillos E 89 C4
Cubillos del Sil E 86 B4
Cubjac F 67 C5
Cubo de la Solana E 89 C4
Çubuk TR 16 A6
Cuckfield GB 31 C3
Cucuron F 79 C4
Cudillero E 86 A4
Cuéllar E 88 C2
Cuenca E 95 B4
Cuers F 79 C5
Cuerva E 94 C2
Cueva de Agreda E 89 C5
Cuevas Bajas E 100 B1
Cuevas de San Clemente E 89 B3
Cuevas de San Marcos E 100 B1
Cuevas del Almanzora E 101 B4
Cuevas del Becerro E 99 C5
Cuevas del Campo E 100 B3
Cuevas del Valle E 94 B1
Cuges-les-Pins F 79 C4
Cúglieri I 110 B1
Cugnaux F 77 C4
Cuijk NL 50 B1
Cuinzier F 69 B4
Cuiseaux F 69 B5
Cuisery F 69 B5
Culan F 68 B2
Culemborg NL 49 B6
Cúllar E 101 B3
Cullaville GB 19 B5
Cullera E 96 B2
Cullivoe GB 22 A7
Cullompton GB 29 C4
Cully CH 70 B1
Culoz F 69 C5
Cults GB 23 D6
Cumbernauld GB 25 C4
Cumbres de San Bartolomé E 99 A4
Cumbres Mayores E 99 A4
Cumiana I 80 B1
Čumić SRB 85 B5
Cumnock GB 24 C3
Çumra TR 16 C6
Cúneo I 80 B1
Cunlhat F 68 C3
Čunski HR 83 B3
Cuntis E 86 B2
Cuorgnè I 70 C2
Cupar GB 25 B4
Cupello I 103 A7
Cupra Maríttima I 82 C2
Cupramontana I 82 C2
Čuprija SRB 85 C6
Curinga I 106 C3
Currelos E 86 B3
Currie GB 25 C4
Curtea de Argeş RO 11 D8
Curtici RO 75 B6
Curtis E 86 A2
Curtis Santa Eulalia E 86 A2
Čurug SRB 75 C5
Cusano Mutri I 103 B7
Cushendall GB 19 A5
Cusset F 68 B3
Cussy-les-Forges F 68 A4
Custines F 60 B2
Cutanda E 90 C1
Cutro I 107 B3
Cutrofiano I 107 A5
Cuts F 59 A4
Cuvilly F 58 A3
Cuxhaven D 43 B5
Cvikov CZ 53 C4
Cwmbran GB 29 B4
Cybinka PL 53 A4
Czacz PL 54 A1
Czajków PL 54 B3
Czaplinek PL 46 B2
Czarlin PL 47 A4
Czarna-Dąbrówka PL 46 A3
Czarna Woda PL 47 B4
Czarnca PL 55 C4
Czarne PL 46 B2
Czarnków PL 46 C2
Czarnowo PL 47 B4
Czarnozyly PL 54 B3
Czarny Bór PL 53 C6
Czarny-Dunajec PL 65 A5
Czarny Las PL 54 B2
Czchow PL 65 A6
Czechowice-Dziedzice PL 65 A4
Czempiń PL 54 A1
Czermno PL 55 B5
Czernichow PL 55 D4
Czerniejewo PL 46 C3
Czernikowo PL 47 C4
Czersk PL 46 B3
Czerwieńsk PL 53 A5
Czerwionka-Leszczyny PL 54 C3
Czerwonka PL 47 B6
Częstochowa PL 55 C4
Czeszewo PL 46 C3
Człopa PL 46 B2
Człuchów PL 46 B3
Czołpino PL 46 A3

D

Daaden D 50 C3
Dabas H 75 A4
Dąbie PL 54 A3
Dąbki PL 46 A2
Dabo F 60 B3
Dabrowa PL 46 C3
Dąbrowa Górnicza PL 55 C4
Dąbrowa Tarnowska PL 55 C5
Dąbrowice PL 55 A4
Dabrowno PL 47 B6
Dachau D 62 B2
Dačice CZ 63 A6
Daday TR 16 A6
Dağ TR 119 E5
Dagali N 32 B5
Dägebüll D 39 E1
Dagmersellen CH 70 A2
Dahlen D 52 B2
Dahlenburg D 44 B2
Dahme D 52 B3
Dahn D 60 A3
Dähre D 44 C2
Daikanvik S 115 B13
Dail bho Dheas GB 22 C2
Dailly GB 24 C3
Daimiel E 95 C3
Daingean IRL 21 A4
Đakovica SRB 10 E6
Đakovo HR 74 C3
Dal, *Akershus* N 34 B3
Dal, *Telemark* N 32 C5
Dala-Floda S 36 B1
Dala-Husby S 36 B2
Dala-Järna S 36 B1
Dalaas A 71 A5
Dalabrog GB 22 D1
Dalaman TR 119 F3
Dalarö S 37 C5
Dalbeattie GB 25 D4
Dalby DK 39 D3
Dalby, *Skåne* S 41 D3
Dalby, *Uppsala* S 37 C4
Dalby, *Värmland* S 34 B4
Dale, *Pembrokeshire* GB 28 B2
Dale, *Shetland* GB 22 A7
Dale, *Hordaland* N 32 B2
Dale, *Sogn og Fjordane* N 32 A2
Dalen, *Akershus* N 34 C3
Dalen, *Telemark* N 33 C5
Daleszyce PL 55 C5
Dalhalvaig GB 23 C5
Dalheim L 60 A2
Dalhem S 37 E5
Dalias E 100 C3
Dalj HR 75 C3
Dalkeith GB 25 C4
Dalkey IRL 21 A5
Dalmally GB 24 B3
Dalmellington GB 24 C3
Dalmose DK 39 D4
Daløy N 32 A1
Dalry, *Dumfries & Galloway* GB 24 C3
Dalry, *North Ayrshire* GB 24 C3
Dalrymple GB 24 C3
Dals Långed S 35 D4
Dals Rostock S 35 D4
Dalseter N 32 A6
Dalsjöfors S 40 B3
Dalskog S 35 D4
Dalston GB 25 D5
Dalstorp S 40 B3
Dalton-in-Furness GB 26 A2
Daluis F 79 B5
Dalum D 43 C4
Dalum S 40 B3
Dalvík IS 111 B7
Dalwhinnie GB 24 B3
Dalyan TR 119 F3
Damasi GR 116 C4
Damasławek PL 46 C3
Damazan F 76 B3
Damës AL 105 C5
Dammarie-les-Lys F 58 B3
Dammartin-en-Goële F 58 A3
Damme D 43 C5
Damnica PL 46 A3
Dampierre F 69 A5
Dampierre-sur-Salon F 69 A5
Damüls A 71 A4
Damville F 58 B2
Damvillers F 59 A6
Damwoude NL 42 B2
Danasjö S 115 B13
Danbury GB 31 C4
Dangé-St. Romain F 67 B5
Dångebo S 40 C5
Dangers F 58 B2
Dangeul F 58 B1
Danilovgrad CG 105 A5
Danischenhagen D 44 A2
Daniszyn PL 54 B2
Danjoutin F 60 C2
Dannas S 40 B3
Dannemarie F 60 C3
Dannemora S 36 B4
Dannenberg D 44 B3
Dánszentmiklós H 75 A4
Dány H 75 A4
Daoulas F 56 B1
Darabani RO 11 B9
Darány H 74 C2
Darda HR 74 C3
Dardesheim D 51 B6
Darfeld D 50 A3
Darfo I 71 C5
Dargiń PL 46 A2
Dargun D 45 B4
Darlington GB 27 A4
Darłowo PL 46 A2
Darmstadt D 61 A4
Darney F 60 B2
Daroca E 95 A5
Darque P 87 C2
Darragh IRL 20 B2
Dartford GB 31 C4
Dartington GB 28 C4
Dartmouth GB 29 C4
Darton GB 27 B4
Daruvar HR 74 C2
Darvas H 75 A6
Darvel GB 24 C3
Darwen GB 26 B3
Dassel D 51 B5
Dassow D 44 B2
Datça TR 119 F2
Datteln D 50 B3
Dattenfeld D 50 C3
Daugard DK 39 D2
Daugavpils LV 7 D9
Daumeray F 57 C5
Daun D 50 C2
Daventry GB 30 B2
Davle CZ 63 A5
Davor HR 84 A2
Davos CH 71 B4
Davutlar TR 119 E2
Davyd Haradok BY 7 E9
Dawlish GB 29 C4
Dax F 76 C1
Dazkırı TR 119 E4
De Cocksdorp NL 42 B1
De Haan B 49 B4
De Koog NL 42 B1
De Panne B 48 B3
De Wijk NL 42 C3
Deal GB 31 C5
Deauville F 57 A6
Deba E 89 A4
Debar MK 116 A2
Debe Wielkie PL 55 A6
Dębica PL 55 C6
Dębnica Kaszubska PL 46 A3
Dębno PL 45 C6
Dębołęka PL 54 B3
Dębowa Łaka PL 47 B5
Debrc SRB 85 B4
Debrecen H 10 C6
Debrznica PL 53 A5
Debrzno PL 46 B3
Debstedt D 43 B5
Decazeville F 77 B5

Dechtice SK 64 B3
Decima I 102 B5
Decimomannu I 110 C1
Děčín CZ 53 C4
Decize F 68 B3
Decollatura I 106 B3
Decs H 74 B3
Dedaj AL 105 A5
Deddington GB 31 C2
Dedeler TR 118 B5
Dedelow D 45 B5
Dedemli TR 119 E7
Dedemsvaart NL 42 C3
Dédestapolcsány H 65 B6
Dedovichi RUS 7 C10
Deeping St. Nicholas GB 30 B3
Dég H 74 B3
Degaña E 86 B4
Degeberga S 41 D4
Degerby FIN 36 B7
Degerfors S 37 C1
Degerhamn S 41 C6
Degernes N 35 C3
Deggendorf D 62 B3
Deggingen D 61 B5
Dego I 80 B2
Degolados P 93 B3
Dehesas de Guadix E 100 B2
Dehesas Viejas E 100 B2
Deia E 97 B2
Deining D 62 A2
Deinze B 49 C4
Déiva Marina I 80 B3
Dej RO 11 C7
Deje S 35 C5
Delabole GB 28 C3
Delary S 40 C3
Delbrück D 51 B4
Delden NL 50 A2
Deleitosa E 93 B5
Delekovec HR 74 B1
Delémont CH 70 A2
Delft NL 49 A5
Delfzijl NL 42 B3
Délia I 108 B2
Delianuova I 106 C2
Deliblato SRB 85 B6
Delice TR 16 B6
Deliceto I 103 B8
Delitzsch D 52 B2
Dellach A 72 B3
Delle F 70 A2
Delme F 60 B2
Delmen-horst D 43 B5
Delnice HR 73 C4
Delsbo S 115 F13
Delvin IRL 19 C4
Delvinë AL 116 C2
Demandice SK 65 B4
Demen D 44 B3
Demidov RUS 7 D11
Demigny F 69 B4
Demirci TR 118 C3
Demirköy TR 118 A2
Demirtaş TR 118 B4
Demmin D 45 B5
Demonte I 79 B6
Demyansk RUS 7 C12
Den Burg NL 42 B1
Den Ham NL 42 C3
Den Helder NL 42 C1
Den Oever NL 42 C2
Denain F 49 C4
Denbigh GB 26 B2
Dender-monde B 49 B5
Denekamp NL 42 C3
Denholm GB 25 C5
Denia E 96 C3
Denizli TR 119 E4
Denkendorf D 62 B2
Denklingen D 50 C3
Denny GB 25 B4
Denta RO 75 C6
Déols F 68 B1
Derbent TR 119 D3
Derby GB 27 C4
Dereköy TR 118 A2
Derenberg D 51 B6
Derinkuyu TR 16 B7
Dermbach D 51 C6
Dermulo I 71 B6
Deronje SRB 75 C4
Derrygonnelly GB 19 B4
Derrylin GB 19 B4
Derry/Londonderry GB 19 B4
Dersingham GB 30 B4
Deruta I 82 D1
Dervaig GB 24 B1
Derval F 57 C4
Derveni GR 117 D4
Derventa BIH 84 B2
Dervock GB 19 A5
Desana I 70 C3
Descartes F 67 B5
Desenzano del Garda I 71 C5
Deset N 34 A3
Deševa BIH 84 C3
Desfina GR 116 D4
Desimirovac SRB 85 B5
Désio I 71 C4
Deskati GR 116 C3
Deskle SLO 72 B3
Desná CZ 53 C5
Dešov CZ 63 B6
Despotovac SRB 85 B6
Despotovo SRB 75 C4
Dessau D 52 B2
Deštná CZ 63 A5
Destriana E 87 B4
Désulo I 110 B2
Desvres F 48 C2
Deszk H 75 B5
Deta RO 75 C6
Detmold D 51 B4
Dětřichov CZ 64 A3
Dettelbach D 61 A6
Dettingen, Baden-Württemberg D 61 B5
Dettingen, Baden-Württemberg D 61 C5
Dettwiller F 60 B3
Detva SK 65 B5
Deurne NL 50 B1
Deutsch Wagram A 64 B2
Deutschkreutz A 64 C2
Deutschlandsberg A 73 B5
Deva RO 11 D7
Dévaványa H 75 A5
Devecikonağı TR 118 C3
Devecser H 74 A2
Develi TR 16 B7
Deventer NL 50 A2
Devil's Bridge GB 28 A4
Devin BG 116 A6
Devinska Nova Ves SK 64 B2
Devizes GB 29 B6
Devonport GB 28 C3
Devrek TR 118 A6
Devrekâni TR 16 A6
Ðevrske HR 83 C4
Dewsbury GB 27 B4
Deza E 89 C4
Dežanovac HR 74 C2
Dezzo I 71 C5
Dhali CY 120 A2
Dheftera CY 120 A2
Dherinia CY 120 A2
Dhërmi AL 105 C5
Diamante I 106 B2
Dianalund DK 39 D4
Diano d'Alba I 80 B2
Diano Marina I 80 C2
Dicomano I 81 C5
Didcot GB 31 C2
Didimoticho GR 118 A1
Die F 79 B4
Diebling F 60 A2
Dieburg D 61 A4
Diego del Carpio E 93 A5
Diekirch L 60 A2
Diélette F 57 A4
Diémoz F 69 C5
Dienten am Hochkönig A 72 A2
Diepenbeck B 49 C6
Diepholz D 43 C5
Dieppe F 58 A2
Dierberg D 45 B4
Dierdorf D 50 C3
Dieren NL 50 A2
Dierhagen D 44 A4
Diesdorf D 44 C2
Diessen D 62 C2
Diest B 49 C6
Dietenheim D 61 B6
Dietfurt D 62 A2
Dietikon CH 70 A3
Dietzenbach D 51 C4
Dieue-sur-Meuse F 60 A1
Dieulefit F 79 B4
Dieulouard F 60 B2
Dieuze F 60 B2
Diever NL 42 C3
Diez D 50 C4
Diezma E 100 B2
Differdange L 60 A1
Digermulen N 112 D4
Dignac F 67 C5
Dignano I 72 B2
Digne-les-Bains F 79 B5
Digny F 58 B2
Digoin F 68 B3
Dijon F 69 A5
Dikanäs S 115 B13
Dikili TR 118 C1
Diksmuide B 48 B3
Dilar E 100 B2
Dillenburg D 50 C4
Dillingen, Bayern D 61 B6
Dillingen, Saarland D 60 A2
Dilsen B 50 B1
Dimaro I 71 B5
Dimitrovgrad BG 11 E8
Dimitsana GR 117 E4
Dinami I 106 C3
Dinan F 57 B3
Dinant B 49 C5
Dinar TR 119 D5
Dinard F 57 B3
Dinek TR 118 C6
Dingden D 50 B2
Dingelstädt D 51 B6
Dingle IRL 20 B1
Dingle S 35 D3
Dingolfing D 62 B3
Dingtuna S 37 C3
Dingwall GB 23 D4
Dinkelsbühl D 61 A6
Dinkelscherben D 62 B1
Dinklage D 43 C5
Dinslaken D 50 B2
Dinxperlo NL 50 B2
Diö S 40 C4
Diósgyör H 65 B6
Diósjeno H 65 C5
Diou F 68 B3
Dippen GB 24 C2
Dipperz D 51 C5
Dippoldiswalde D 53 C3
Dirdal N 33 D3
Dirksland NL 49 B5
Dirlewang D 61 C6
Dischingen D 61 B6
Disentis CH 70 B3
Diso I 107 A5
Diss GB 30 B5
Dissen D 50 A4
Distington GB 26 A2
Ditzingen D 61 B5
Ditzum D 43 B4
Divača SLO 72 C3
Dives-sur-Mer F 57 A5
Divín SK 65 B5
Divion F 48 C3
Divišov CZ 63 A5
Divjakë AL 105 C5
Divonne les Bains F 69 B6
Dixmont F 59 B4
Dizy-le-Gros F 59 A5
Djúpivogur IS 111 C11
Djupvasshytta N 114 E4
Djura S 36 B1
Djurås S 36 B2
Djurmo S 36 B2
Djursdala S 40 B5
Dlouhá Loucka CZ 64 A3
Długowola PL 55 B6
Dmitriyev Lgovskiy RUS 7 E13
Dmitrov RUS 7 C14
Dmitrovsk-Orlovskiy RUS 7 E13
Dno RUS 7 C10
Doade E 86 B3
Dobanovci SRB 85 B5
Dobbertin D 44 B4
Dobbiaco I 72 B2
Dobczyce PL 65 A6
Dobele LV 6 C7
Döbeln D 52 B3
Doberlug-Kirchhain D 52 B3
Dobern D 53 B4
Dobersberg A 63 B6
Dobiegniew PL 46 C1
Dobieszyn PL 55 B6
Doboj BIH 84 B3
Dobošnica BIH 84 B3
Doboz H 75 B6
Dobrá CZ 65 A4
Dobra, Wielkopolskie PL 54 B3
Dobra, Zachodnio-Pomorskie PL 45 B6
Dobra, Zachodnio-Pomorskie PL 45 B7
Dobrá Niva SK 65 B5
Dobřany CZ 63 A4
Dobre, Kujawsko-Pomorskie PL 47 C4
Dobre, Mazowieckie PL 55 A6
Dobre Miasto PL 47 B6
Dobreta-Turnu-Severin RO 11 D7
Dobri H 74 B1
Dobri Do SRB 85 D6
Dobrica SRB 75 C5
Dobrich BG 11 E9
Dobříš CZ 63 A5
Dobro E 89 B3
Dobrodzień PL 54 C3
Döbrököz H 74 B3
Dobromierz PL 53 C6
Dobrosołowo PL 47 C4
Dobroszyce PL 54 B2
Dobrota CG 105 A4
Dobrovnik SLO 73 B6
Dobrush BY 7 E11
Dobruška CZ 53 C6
Dobrzany PL 46 B1
Dobrzen Wielki PL 54 C2
Dobrzyca, Wielkopolskie PL 46 B2
Dobrzyca, Wielkopolskie PL 54 B2
Dobrzyca, Zachodnio-Pomorskie PL 46 A1
Dobrzyń nad Wisłą PL 47 C5
Dobšiná SK 65 B6
Dobwalls GB 28 C3
Dochamps B 49 C6
Docking GB 30 B4
Docksta S 115 D15
Doddington GB 25 C5
Doderhult S 40 B6
Doesburg NL 50 A2
Doetinchem NL 50 B2
Doğanhisar TR 119 D6
Dogliani I 80 B1
Dogueno P 98 B3
Dois Portos P 92 B1
Doische B 49 C5
Dojč SK 64 B3
Dokka N 34 B2
Dokkedal DK 38 C3
Dokkum NL 42 B2
Dokležovje SLO 73 B6
Doksy CZ 53 C4
Dokuz TR 119 D7
Dol-de-Bretagne F 57 B4
Dolancourt F 59 B5
Dolceácqua I 80 C1
Dole F 69 A5
Dølemo N 33 D5
Dolenja vas SLO 73 C4
Dolenjske Toplice SLO 73 C5
Dolfor GB 26 C2
Dolgarrog GB 26 B2
Dolgellau GB 26 C2
Doliana GR 116 C2
Dolianova I 110 C2
Dolice PL 45 B7
Doljani HR 83 B5
Döllach im Mölltal A 72 B2
Dolle D 44 C3
Dollnstein D 62 B2
Dollot F 59 B4
Döllstadt D 51 B6
Dolná Strehová SK 65 B5
Dolné Saliby SK 64 B3
Dolni Benešov CZ 64 A4
Dolni Bousov CZ 53 C5
Dolni Kounice CZ 64 A2
Dolni Kralovice CZ 63 A6
Dolni Újezd CZ 64 A2
Dolni Žandov CZ 52 C2
Dolný Kubín SK 65 A5
Dolo I 72 C2
Dolores E 96 C2
Dolovo SRB 85 B5
Dölsach A 72 B2
Dolsk PL 54 B2
Dolwyddelan GB 26 B2
Dolynska UA 11 B12
Domaljevac BIH 84 A3
Domaniç TR 118 C4
Domaniža SK 65 A4
Domanovići BIH 84 C2
Domašov CZ 54 C2
Domaszék H 75 B4
Domaszków PL 54 C1
Domaszowice PL 54 B2
Domat-Ems CH 71 B4
Domažlice CZ 62 A3
Dombås N 114 E6
Dombasle-sur-Meurthe F 60 B2
Dombegyház H 75 B6
Dombóvár H 74 B3
Domène F 69 C5
Domérat F 68 B2
Domfessel F 60 B3
Domfront F 57 B5
Domfront-en-Champagne F 57 B6
Domingão P 92 B2
Domingo Pérez, Granada E 100 B2
Domingo Pérez, Toledo E 94 C2
Dömitz D 44 B3
Dommartin F 59 B5
Dommartin-le-Franc F 59 B5
Domme F 77 B4
Dommitzsch D 52 B2
Domodóssola I 70 B3
Domokos GR 116 C4
Domoszló H 65 C6
Dompaire F 60 B2
Dompierre-du-Chemin F 57 B4
Dompierre-sur-Besbre F 68 B3
Dompierre-sur-Mer F 66 B3
Domrémy-la-Pucelle F 60 B1
Dömsöd H 75 A4
Domsure F 69 B5
Dómus de Maria I 110 D1
Domusnóvas I 110 C1
Domvena GR 117 D4
Domžale SLO 73 B4
Don Alvaro E 93 C4
Don Benito E 93 C5
Doña Mencía E 100 B1
Donado E 87 B4
Donaghadee GB 19 B6
Donaueschingen D 61 C4
Donauwörth D 62 B1
Doncaster GB 27 B4
Donegal IRL 18 B3
Donestebe-Santesteban E 76 C1
Donges F 66 A2
Dongo I 71 B4
Donington GB 30 B3
Doniños E 86 A2
Donja Bebrina HR 84 A3
Donja Brela HR 84 C1
Donja Dubica BIH 84 A3
Donja Dubrava HR 74 B1
Donja Kupčina HR 73 C5
Donja Mutnica SRB 85 C6
Donja Šatornja SRB 85 B5
Donja Stubica HR 73 C5
Donje Brišnik BIH 84 C2
Donje Ljupče SRB 85 D6
Donje Stative HR 73 C5
Donji-Andrijevci HR 74 C3
Donji Kazanci BIH 83 C5
Donji Koričáni BIH 84 B2
Donji Lapac HR 83 B4
Donji Malovan BIH 84 C2
Donji Miholjac HR 74 C3
Donji Mosti HR 74 B1
Donji Poloj HR 73 C5
Donji-Rujani BIH 83 C5
Donji Srb HR 83 B5
Donji Svilaj BIH 84 A3
Donji Tovarnik SRB 85 B4
Donji Vakuf BIH 84 B2
Donnalucata I 109 C3
Donnemarie-Dontilly F 59 B4
Donnersbach A 73 A4
Donnersbachwald A 73 A4
Donnerskirchen A 64 C2
Donorático I 81 C4
Donostia-San Sebastián E 76 C1
Donovaly SK 65 B5
Donzenac F 67 C6
Donzère F 78 B3
Donzy F 68 A3
Doonbeg IRL 20 B2
Doorn NL 49 A6
Dor E 86 A1
Dorchester GB 29 C5
Dørdal N 33 D6
Dordrecht NL 49 B5
Dörenthe D 50 A3
Dores GB 23 D4
Dorf Mecklenburg D 44 B3
Dorfen D 62 B3
Dorfgastein A 72 A3
Dorfmark D 43 C6
Dorgali I 110 B2
Dorking GB 31 C3
Dormagen D 50 B2
Dormánd H 65 C6
Dormans F 59 A4
Dornava SLO 73 B5
Dornbirn A 71 A4
Dornburg D 52 B1
Dorndorf D 51 C6
Dornecy F 68 A3
Dornes F 68 B3
Dornhan D 61 B4
Dornie GB 22 D3
Dornoch GB 23 D4
Dornum D 43 B4
Dorog H 65 C4
Dorogobuzh RUS 7 D12
Dorohoi RO 11 C9
Dorotea S 115 C13
Dorotowo PL 47 B6
Dörpen D 43 C4
Dorsten D 50 B2
Dortan F 69 B5
Dortmund D 50 B3
Doruchów PL 54 B3
Dorum D 43 B5
Dörverden D 43 C6
Dörzbach D 61 A5
Dos Aguas E 96 B2
Dos Hermanas E 99 B5
Dos-Torres E 100 A1
Dosbarrios E 95 C3
Döşemealtı TR 119 F5
Dospat BG 116 A6
Dötlingen D 43 C5
Dottignies B 49 C4
Döttingen CH 70 A3
Douai F 49 C4
Douarnenez F 56 B1
Douchy F 59 C4
Douchy-les-Mines F 49 C4
Doucier F 69 B5
Doudeville F 58 A1
Doué-la-Fontaine F 67 A4
Douglas, Isle of Man GB 26 A1
Douglas, South Lanarkshire GB 25 C4
Doulaincourt F 59 B6
Doulevant-le-Château F 59 B5
Doullens F 48 C3
Dounby GB 23 B5
Doune GB 24 B3
Dounreay GB 23 C5
Dour B 49 C4
Dourdan F 58 B3
Dourgne F 77 C5
Dournazac F 67 C5
Douro Calvo P 87 D3
Douvaine F 69 B6
Douvres-la-Délivrande F 57 A5
Douzy F 59 A6
Dover GB 31 C5
Dovje SLO 72 B3
Dovre N 114 F6
Downham Market GB 30 B4
Downhill GB 19 A5
Downpatrick GB 19 B6
Dowra IRL 18 B3
Doxato GR 116 A6
Doyet F 68 B2
Dozule F 57 A5
Drača SRB 85 B5
Dračevo BIH 84 D3
Drachten NL 42 B3
Draga SLO 73 C4
Drăgăşani RO 11 D8
Dragatuš SLO 73 C5
Dragichyn BY 7 E8
Draginja SRB 85 B4
Dragobi AL 105 A5
Dragocvet SRB 85 C6
Dragolovci BIH 84 B2
Dragoni I 103 B7
Dragør DK 41 D2
Dragotina HR 73 C6
Dragotinja BIH 83 A5
Dragozetići HR 82 A3
Draguignan F 79 C5
Drahnsdorf D 52 B3
Drahonice CZ 63 A5
Drahovce SK 64 B3
Drama GR 116 A6
Drammen N 35 C2
Drangedal N 33 C6
Drangsnes IS 111 B4
Dransfeld D 51 B5
Dranske D 45 A5
Draperstown GB 19 B5
Drassburg A 64 C2
Drávaszabolcs H 74 C3
Dravograd SLO 73 B5
Drawno PL 46 B1
Drawsko Pomorskie PL 46 B1
Drayton GB 30 B5
Draženov CZ 62 A3
Draževac SRB 85 B5
Dražice HR 73 C4
Drebkau D 53 B4
Dreieich D 51 C4
Dreisen D 61 A4
Dren SRB 85 C5
Drenovac SRB 85 B6
Drenovci HR 84 B3
Drensteinfurt D 50 B3
Dresden D 53 B3
Dretyń PL 46 A2
Dreux F 58 B2
Dřevohostice CZ 64 A3
Drevsjø N 114 F9
Drewitz D 52 A2
Drezdenko PL 46 C1
Drežnica HR 83 A4
Drežnik-Grad HR 83 B4
Drietona SK 64 B3
Driffield GB 27 A5
Drimnin GB 24 B2
Drimoleague IRL 20 C2
Dringenberg D 51 B5
Drinić BIH 83 B5
Drinjača BIH 85 B4
Drinovci BIH 84 C2
Driopida GR 117 E6
Drivstua N 114 E6
Drlače SRB 85 B4
Drnholec CZ 64 B2
Drniš HR 83 C5
Drnje HR 74 B1
Drnovice CZ 64 A2
Dro I 71 C5
Drøbak N 35 C2
Drobin PL 47 C6
Drochia MD 11 B9
Drochtersen D 43 B6
Drogheda IRL 19 C5
Drohobych UA 11 B7
Droitwich Spa GB 29 A5
Drołtowice PL 54 B2
Dromahair IRL 18 B3
Dromcolliher IRL 20 B3
Dromore, Down GB 19 B5
Dromore, Tyrone GB 19 B4
Dromore West IRL 18 B3
Dronero I 79 B6
Dronfield GB 27 B4
Drongan GB 24 C3
Dronninglund DK 38 B3
Dronrijp NL 42 B2
Dronten NL 42 C2
Drosendorf A 63 B6
Drösing A 64 B2
Drottningholm S 37 C4
Droué F 58 B2
Drulingen F 60 B3
Drumbeg GB 22 C3
Drumcliff IRL 18 B3
Drumgask GB 23 D4
Drumkeeran IRL 18 B3
Drummore GB 24 D3
Drumnadrochit GB 23 D4
Drumquin GB 19 B4
Drumshanbo IRL 18 B3
Drumsna IRL 19 C4
Drunen NL 49 B6
Druskininkai LT 6 D7
Druten NL 49 B6
Druya BY 7 D9
Družetići SRB 85 B5
Drvar BIH 83 B5
Drvenik HR 84 C2
Drwalew PL 55 B6
Drymen GB 24 B3
Drynoch GB 22 D2
Drzewce PL 54 A2
Drzewiany PL 46 B2
Drzewica PL 55 B5
Dualchi I 110 B1
Duas Igrejas P 87 C4
Dub SRB 85 C4
Dubá CZ 53 C4
Dubăsari MD 11 C10
Duben D 53 B3
Dübendorf CH 70 A3
Dubi CZ 53 C3
Dubica HR 74 C1
Dublin IRL 21 A5
Dubna RUS 7 C14
Dubňany CZ 64 B3
Dubnica nad Váhom SK 64 B4
Dubnik SK 65 C4
Dubno UA 11 A8
Dubodiel SK 64 B4
Dubona SRB 85 B5
Dubovac SRB 85 B6
Dubovic BIH 83 B5
Dubranec HR 73 C5
Dubrava HR 74 C1
Dubrave BIH 84 B3
Dubravica HR 73 C5
Dubravica SRB 85 B6
Dubrovnik HR 84 D3
Dubrovytsya UA 7 F9
Ducey F 57 B4
Duchcov CZ 53 C3
Ducherow D 45 B5
Dučina SRB 85 B5
Duclair F 58 A1
Dudar H 74 A2
Duddington GB 30 B3
Duderstadt D 51 B6
Dudeştii Vechi RO 75 B5
Dudley GB 26 C3
Dueñas E 88 C2
Duesund N 32 B2
Dueville I 72 C1
Duffel B 49 B5
Duffield GB 27 C4
Dufftown GB 23 D5
Duga Poljana SRB 85 C5
Duga Resa HR 73 C5
Dugi Rat HR 83 C5
Dugny-sur-Meuse F 59 A6
Dugo Selo HR 73 C6
Dugopolje HR 83 C5
Duino I 72 C3
Duisburg D 50 B2
Dukat AL 105 C5
Dukhovshchina RUS 7 D12
Dukovany CZ 64 A2
Duleek IRL 19 C5
Dülken D 50 B2
Dülmen D 50 B3
Dulovo BG 11 E9
Dulpetorpet N 34 B4
Dulverton GB 29 B4
Dumbarton GB 24 C3
Dümerek TR 118 C6
Dumfries GB 25 C4
Dumlupınar TR 118 D4
Dümpelfeld D 50 C2
Dun Laoghaire IRL 21 A5
Dun-le-Palestel F 67 B6
Dun-les-Places F 68 A4
Dun-sur-Auron F 68 B2
Dun-sur-Meuse F 59 A6
Dunaalmás H 65 C4
Dunabogdány H 65 C5
Dunafalva H 74 B3
Dunaföldvár H 74 B3
Dunaharaszti H 75 A4
Dunajská Streda SK 64 C3
Dunakeszi H 65 C5
Dunakiliti H 64 C3
Dunakömlöd H 74 B3
Dunapataj H 75 B3
Dunaszekcső H 74 B3
Dunaszentgyorgy H 74 B3
Dunatetétlen H 75 B4
Dunaújváros H 74 B3
Dunavecse H 75 B3
Dunbar GB 25 B5
Dunbeath GB 23 C5
Dunblane GB 25 B4
Dunboyne IRL 21 A5
Dundalk IRL 19 B5
Dundee GB 25 B5
Dundrennan GB 25 D4
Dundrum GB 19 B6
Dunfanaghy IRL 19 A4
Dunfermline GB 25 B4
Dungannon GB 19 B5
Dungarvan IRL 21 B4
Dungiven GB 19 B5
Dunglow IRL 18 B3
Dungourney IRL 20 C3
Duninowo PL 46 A2
Ðunis SRB 85 C6
Dunkeld GB 25 B4
Dunker S 37 C3
Dunkerque = Dunkirk F 48 B3
Dunkineely IRL 18 B3
Dunkirk = Dunkerque F 48 B3
Dunlavin IRL 21 A5
Dunleer IRL 19 C5
Dunlop GB 24 C3
Dunloy GB 19 A5
Dunmanway IRL 20 C2
Dunmore IRL 18 C3
Dunmore East IRL 21 B5
Dunmurry GB 19 B5
Dunnet GB 23 C5
Dunningen D 61 B4
Dunoon GB 24 C3
Duns GB 25 C5
Dunscore GB 25 C4
Dunsford GB 28 C4
Dunshaughlin IRL 21 A5
Dunstable GB 31 C3
Dunster GB 29 B4
Dunvegan GB 22 D2
Duplek SLO 73 B5
Dupnitsa BG 11 E7
Durach D 61 C6
Durağan TR 16 A7
Durak TR 118 C3
Ðurakovac SRB 85 D5
Durana E 89 B4
Durance F 76 B3
Durango E 89 A4
Durankulak BG 11 E10
Duras F 76 B3
Durban-Corbières F 78 D1
Dürbheim D 61 B4
Durbuy B 49 C6
Dúrcal E 100 C2
Ðurdjenovac HR 74 C3
Ðurdjevac HR 74 B2
Ðurdjevik BIH 84 B3
Düren D 50 C2
Durham GB 25 D6
Ðurinci SRB 85 B5
Durlach D 61 B4
Ðurmanec HR 73 B5
Durness GB 22 C4
Dürnkrut A 64 B2
Dürrboden CH 71 B4
Dürrenboden CH 70 B3
Durrës AL 105 B5
Durrow IRL 21 B4
Durrus IRL 20 C2
Dursunbey TR 118 C3
Durtal F 57 C5
Durup DK 38 C1
Durusu TR 118 A3
Dusina BIH 84 C2
Dusnok H 75 B3
Dusocin PL 47 B4
Düsseldorf D 50 B2
Dusslingen D 61 B5
Duszniki PL 46 C2
Duszniki-Zdrój PL 54 C1
Dutovlje SLO 72 C3
Duvebo S 40 A4
Duved S 115 D9
Düzağac TR 118 D5
Düzce TR 118 B6
Dvärsätt S 115 D11
Dvor HR 83 A5
Dvorce CZ 64 A3
Dvorniky SK 64 B3
Dvory nad Žitavou SK 64 C4
Dvůr Králové nad Labem CZ 53 C5
Dyatkovo RUS 7 E13
Dybvad DK 38 B3
Dyce GB 23 D6
Dygowo PL 46 A1
Dykehead GB 25 B4
Dymchurch GB 31 C5
Dymer UA 11 A11
Dyrnes N 114 D4
Dywity PL 47 B6
Džanići BIH 84 C2
Dziadowa Kłoda PL 54 B2
Działdowo PL 47 B6
Działoszyce PL 55 C5
Działoszyn PL 54 B3
Dziemiany PL 46 A3
Dzierząźnia PL 47 C6
Dzierzgoń PL 47 B5
Dzierzgowo PL 47 B6
Dzierżoniów PL 54 C1
Dzisna BY 7 D10
Dziwnów PL 45 A6
Dzyarzhynsk BY 7 E9
Dzyatlava BY 7 E8

E

Ea E 89 A4
Eaglesfield GB 25 C4
Ealing GB 31 C3
Eardisley GB 29 A4
Earl Shilton GB 30 B2
Earls Barton GB 30 B3
Earlston GB 25 C5
Easington GB 27 B6
Easky IRL 18 B3
East Calder GB 25 C4
East Dereham GB 30 B4
East Grinstead GB 31 C4
East Ilsley GB 31 C2
East Kilbride GB 24 C3
East Linton GB 25 C5
East Markham GB 27 B5
East Wittering GB 31 D3
Eastbourne GB 31 D4
Easter Skeld GB 22 A7
Eastleigh GB 31 D2
Easton GB 29 C5
Eaton Socon GB 30 B3
Eaux-Bonnes F 76 D2
Eauze F 76 C3
Ebberup DK 39 D2
Ebbs A 62 C3
Ebbw Vale GB 29 B4
Ebeleben D 51 B6
Ebeltoft DK 39 C3
Eben im Pongau A 72 A3
Ebene Reichenau A 72 B3
Ebensee A 63 C4
Ebensfeld D 51 C6
Eberbach D 61 A4
Ebergötzen D 51 B6
Ebermann-Stadt D 62 A2
Ebern D 51 C6
Eberndorf A 73 B4
Ebersbach D 53 B4
Ebersberg D 62 B2
Ebersdorf, Bayern D 52 C1
Ebersdorf, Niedersachsen D 43 B6
Eberstein A 73 B4
Eberswalde D 45 C5
Ebnat-Kappel CH 71 A4
Éboli I 103 C8
Ebrach D 61 A6
Ebreichsdorf A 64 C2
Ebreuil F 68 B3
Ebstorf D 44 B2
Ecclefechan GB 25 C4
Eccleshall GB 26 C3
Eceabat TR 118 B1
Echallens CH 69 B6
Echauri E 76 D1
Echinos GR 116 A7
Echiré F 67 B4
Echirolles F 69 C5
Echourgnac F 76 A3
Echt NL 50 B1
Echte D 51 B6
Echternach L 60 A2

Ecija E 99 B5
Ečka SRB 75 C5
Eckartsberga D 52 B1
Eckelshausen D 51 C4
Eckental D 62 A2
Eckernförde D 44 A1
Eckerö FIN 36 B6
Eckington GB 27 B4
Éclaron F 59 B5
Écommoy F 58 C1
Écouché F 57 B5
Ecouis F 58 A2
Ecséd H 65 C5
Ecsegfalva H 75 A5
Écueillé F 67 A6
Ed S 35 D3
Eda S 34 C4
Eda glasbruk S 34 C4
Edam NL 42 C2
Edane S 35 C4
Edderton GB 23 D4
Ede NL 49 A6
Edebäck S 34 B5
Edebo S 36 B5
Edelény H 65 B6
Edelschrott A 73 A5
Edemissen D 44 C2
Edenbridge GB 31 C4
Edenderry IRL 21 A4
Edenkoben D 61 A4
Edesheim D 61 A4
Edessa GR 116 B4
Edewecht D 43 B4
Edgeworthstown IRL 19 C4
Edinburgh GB 25 C4
Edineţ MD 11 B9
Edirne TR 118 A1
Edland N 33 C4
Edolo I 71 B5
Edøy N 114 D5
Edremit TR 118 C2
Eds bruk S 40 A6
Edsbro S 36 C5
Edsbyn S 36 A2
Edsele S 115 D13
Edsleskog S 35 C4
Edsvalla S 35 C5
Eekloo B 49 B4
Eemshaven NL 42 B3
Eerbeek NL 50 A2
Eersel NL 49 B6
Eferding A 63 B5
Effiat F 68 B3
Efteløt N 35 C1
Egeln D 52 B1
Eger H 65 C6
Egerbakta H 65 C6
Egernsund DK 39 E2
Egersund N 33 D3
Egerszólát H 65 C6
Egervár H 74 B1
Egg A 71 A4
Egg D 61 B6
Eggby S 35 D5
Eggedal N 32 B6
Eggenburg A 64 B1
Eggenfelden D 62 B3
Eggesin D 45 B6
Eggum N 112 D2
Egham GB 31 C3
Éghezée B 49 C5
Egiertowo PL 47 A4
Egilsstaðir IS 111 B11
Egina GR 117 E5
Eginio GR 116 B4
Egio GR 117 D4
Égletons F 68 C2
Egling D 62 C2
Eglinton GB 19 A4
Eglisau CH 61 C4
Égliseneuve-d'Entraigues F 68 C2
Eglofs D 61 C5
Egmond aan Zee NL 42 C1
Egna I 71 B6
Egosthena GR 117 D5
Egremont GB 26 A2
Eğridir TR 119 E5
Egtved DK 39 D2
Eguilles F 79 C4
Eguilly-sous-Bois F 59 B5
Éguzon-Chantôme F 67 B6
Egyek H 65 C6
Egyházasrádóc H 74 A1
Ehekirchen D 62 B2
Ehingen D 61 B5
Ehra-Lessien D 44 C2
Ehrang D 60 A2
Ehrenfriedersdorf D 52 C2
Ehrenhain D 52 C2
Ehrenhausen A 73 B5
Ehringshausen D 51 C4
Ehrwald A 71 A5
Eibar E 89 A4
Eibelstadt D 61 A6
Eibenstock D 52 C2
Eibergen NL 50 A2
Eibiswald A 73 B5
Eichenbarleben D 52 A1
Eichendorf D 62 B3
Eichstätt D 62 B2
Eickelborn D 50 B4
Eide, *Hordaland* N 32 B3
Eide, *Møre og Romsdal* N 114 E4
Eidet N 112 C7
Eidfjord N 32 B4
Eidsberg N 35 C3
Eidsbugarden N 32 A5
Eidsdal N 114 E4
Eidsfoss N 35 C2
Eidskog N 34 B4
Eidsvåg, *Hordaland* N 32 B2
Eidsvåg, *Møre og Romsdal* N 114 E5
Eidsvoll N 34 B3
Eikefjord N 114 F2
Eikelandsosen N 32 B2
Eiken N 33 D4
Eikesdal N 114 E5
Eikstrand N 35 C1
Eilenburg D 52 B2
Eilsleben D 52 A1
Eina N 34 B2
Einbeck D 51 B5
Eindhoven NL 49 B6
Einsiedeln CH 70 A3
Einville-au-Jard F 60 B2
Eisenach D 51 C6
Eisenberg, *Rheinland-Pfalz* D 61 A4
Eisenberg, *Thüringen* D 52 C1
Eisenerz A 73 A4
Eisenhüttenstadt D 53 A4
Eisenkappel A 73 B4
Eisenstadt A 64 C2
Eisentratten A 72 B3
Eisfeld D 51 C6
Eisleben D 52 B1
Eislingen D 61 B5
Eitensheim D 62 B2
Eiterfeld D 51 C5
Eitorf D 50 C3
Eivindvik N 32 B2
Eivissa = Ibiza E 97 C1
Eixo P 92 A2
Ejby DK 39 D2
Ejea de los Caballeros E 90 A1
Ejstrupholm DK 39 D2
Ejulve E 90 C2
Eke B 49 C4
Ekeby, *Gotland* S 37 E5
Ekeby, *Skåne* S 41 D2
Ekeby, *Uppsala* S 36 B5
Ekeby-Almby S 37 C2
Ekenäs S 35 D5
Ekenässjön S 40 B5
Ekerö S 37 C4
Eket S 41 C3
Eketorp S 41 C6
Ekevik S 40 A6
Ekkerøy N 113 B19
Ekshärad S 34 B5
Eksingedal N 32 B2
Eksjö S 40 B4
Eksta S 37 E5
Ekträsk S 115 C16
El Alamo, *Madrid* E 94 B3
El Alamo, *Sevilla* E 99 B4
El Algar E 101 B5
El Almendro E 98 B3
El Alquián E 101 C3
El Arahal E 99 B5
El Arenal E 94 B1
El Arguellite E 101 A3
El Astillero E 88 A3
El Ballestero E 101 A3
El Barco de Ávila E 93 A5
El Berrón E 88 A1
El Berrueco E 95 B3
El Bodón E 93 A4
El Bonillo E 95 D4
El Bosque E 99 C5
El Bullaque E 94 C2
El Burgo E 100 C1
El Burgo de Ebro E 90 B2
El Burgo de Osma E 89 C3
El Burgo Ranero E 88 B1
El Buste E 89 C5
El Cabaco E 93 A4
El Callejo E 89 A3
El Campillo E 99 B4
El Campillo de la Jara E 94 C1
El Cañavete E 95 C4
El Carpio E 100 B1
El Carpio de Tajo E 94 C2
El Casar E 95 B3
El Casar de Escalona E 94 B2
El Castillo de las Guardas E 99 B4
El Centenillo E 100 A2
El Cerro E 93 A5
El Cerro de Andévalo E 99 B4
El Comenar E 99 C5
El Coronil E 99 B5
El Crucero E 86 A4
El Cubo de Tierra del Vino E 88 C1
El Cuervo E 99 C4
El Ejido E 101 C3
El Escorial E 94 B2
El Espinar E 94 B2
El Frago E 90 A2
El Franco E 86 A4
El Frasno E 89 C5
El Garrobo E 99 B4
El Gastor E 99 C5
El Gordo E 93 B5
El Grado E 90 A3
El Granado E 98 B3
El Grao de Castelló E 96 B3
El Grau E 96 C2
El Higuera E 100 B1
El Hijate E 101 B3
El Hontanar E 96 A1
El Hoyo E 100 A2
El Madroño E 99 B4
El Maillo E 93 A4
El Masnou E 91 B5
El Mirón E 93 A5
El Molar E 95 B3
El Molinillo E 94 C2
El Morell E 91 B4
El Muyo E 89 C3
El Olmo E 88 C3
El Palo E 100 C1
El Pardo E 94 B3
El Payo E 93 A4
El Pedernoso E 95 C4
El Pedroso E 99 B5
El Peral E 95 C5
El Perelló, *Tarragona* E 90 C3
El Perelló, *Valencia* E 96 B2
El Picazo E 95 C4
El Pinell de Bray E 90 B3
El Piñero E 88 C1
El Pla de Santa Maria E 91 B4
El Pobo E 90 C2
El Pobo de Dueñas E 95 B5
El Pont d'Armentera E 91 B4
El Port de la Selva E 91 A6
El Port de Llançà E 91 A6
El Port de Sagunt E 96 B2
El Prat de Llobregat E 91 B5
El Provencio E 95 C4
El Puente E 89 A3
El Puente del Arzobispo E 93 B5
El Puerto E 86 A4
El Puerto de Santa María E 99 C4
El Real de la Jara E 99 B4
El Real de San Vincente E 94 B2
El Robledo E 94 C2
El Rocio E 99 B4
El Rompido E 99 B3
El Ronquillo E 99 B4
El Royo E 89 C4
El Rubio E 100 B1
El Sabinar E 101 A3
El Saler E 96 B2
El Salobral E 101 A4
El Saucejo E 99 B5
El Serrat AND 91 A4
El Temple E 90 B2
El Tiemblo E 94 B2
El Toboso E 95 C4
El Tormillo E 90 B2
El Torno E 93 A5
El Valle de las Casas E 88 B1
El Vellón E 95 B3
El Vendrell E 91 B4
El Villar de Arnedo E 89 B4
El Viso E 100 A1
El Viso del Alcor E 99 B5
Élancourt F 58 B2
Elassona GR 116 C4
Elati GR 116 C3
Elbasan AL 116 A2
Elbeuf F 58 A1
Elbingerode D 51 B6
Elbląg PL 47 A5
Elburg NL 42 C2
Elche E 96 C2
Elche de la Sierra E 101 A3
Elchingen D 61 B6
Elda E 101 A5
Eldena D 44 B3
Eldingen D 44 C2
Elefsina GR 117 D5
Elek H 75 B6
Elemir SRB 75 C5
Eleutheroupoli GR 116 B6
Elgå N 114 E8
Elgin GB 23 D5
Elgoibar E 89 A4
Elgol GB 22 D2
Elgshøa N 34 A4
Elie GB 25 B5
Elizondo E 76 C1
Ełk PL 6 E7
Elkhovo BG 11 E9
Ellenberg D 61 A6
Ellesmere GB 26 C3
Ellesmere Port GB 26 B3
Ellezelles B 49 C4
Ellingen D 62 A1
Ellmau A 72 A2
Ellon GB 23 D6
Ellös S 35 D3
Ellrich D 51 B6
Ellwangen D 61 B6
Elm CH 71 B4
Elm D 43 B6
Elmadağ TR 16 B6
Elmalı TR 119 F4
Elmshorn D 43 B6
Elmstein D 60 A3
Elne F 91 A5
Elnesvågen N 114 E4
Elorrio E 89 A4
Elöszállás H 74 B3
Elouda GR 117 G7
Éloyes F 60 B2
Elphin GB 22 C3
Els Castells E 91 A4
Elsdorf D 50 C2
Elsenfeld D 61 A5
Elsfleth D 43 B5
Elspeet NL 50 A1
Elst NL 50 B1
Elstead GB 31 C3
Elster D 52 B2
Elsterberg D 52 C2
Elsterwerda D 52 B3
Elstra D 53 B4
Eltmann D 51 D6
Eltville D 50 C4
Elvas P 93 C3
Elvebakken N 113 C12
Elven F 56 C3
Elverum N 34 B3
Elvington GB 27 B5
Elxleben D 51 B6
Ely GB 30 B4
Elzach D 61 B4
Elze D 51 A5
Emådalen S 36 A1
Embleton GB 25 C6
Embonas GR 119 F2
Embrun F 79 B5
Embún E 90 A2
Emden D 43 B4
Emecik TR 119 F2
Emet TR 118 C4
Emirdağ TR 118 C6
Emlichheim D 42 C3
Emmaboda S 40 C5
Emmaljunga S 41 C3
Emmeloord NL 42 C2
Emmen CH 70 A3
Emmen NL 42 C3
Emmendingen D 60 B3
Emmer-Compascuum NL 43 C4
Emmerich D 50 B2
Emmern D 51 A5
Emöd H 65 C6
Émpoli I 81 C4
Emsbüren D 43 C4
Emsdetten D 43 C4
Emsfors S 40 B6
Emskirchen D 62 A1
Emstek D 43 C5
Emsworth GB 31 D3
Emyvale IRL 19 B5
Enafors S 115 D9
Enånger S 115 F14
Encamp AND 91 A4
Encarnaçao P 92 C1
Encinas de Abajo E 94 B1
Encinas de Esgueva E 88 C2
Encinas Reales E 100 B1
Encinasola E 99 A4
Encio E 89 B3
Enciso E 89 B4
Enden N 114 F7
Endingen D 60 B3
Endrinal E 93 A5
Endröd H 75 B5
Enebakk N 34 C3
Eneryda S 40 C4
Enese H 64 C3
Enez TR 116 B8
Enfield IRL 21 A5
Eng A 72 A1
Enge-sande D 39 E1
Engelberg CH 70 B3
Engelhartszell A 63 B4
Engelskirchen D 50 C3
Engen D 61 C4
Enger N 34 B2
Engerdal N 114 F8
Engerneset N 34 A4
Engesvang DK 39 C2
Enghien B 49 C5
Engstingen D 61 B5
Engter D 43 C5
Enguera E 96 C2
Enguidanos E 95 C5
Enkenbach D 60 A3
Enkhuizen NL 42 C2
Enklinge FIN 36 B7
Enköping S 37 C4
Enna I 109 B3
Ennezat F 68 C3
Ennigerloh D 50 B4
Enningdal N 35 C3
Ennis IRL 20 B3
Enniscorthy IRL 21 B5
Enniskean IRL 20 C3
Enniskillen GB 19 B4
Ennistimon IRL 20 B2
Enns A 63 B5
Eno FIN 3 E29
Enontekiö FIN 113 D12
Ens NL 42 C2
Enschede NL 50 A2
Ensdorf D 62 A2
Ensisheim F 60 C3
Enstaberga S 37 D3
Enstone GB 31 C2
Entlebuch CH 70 A3
Entrácque I 80 B1
Entradas P 98 B2
Entrains-sur-Nohain F 68 A3
Entrambasaguas E 88 A3
Entrambasmestas E 88 A3
Entraygues-sur-Truyère F 77 B5
Entre-os-Rios P 87 C2
Entrevaux F 79 C5
Entrin Bajo E 93 C4
Entroncamento P 92 B2
Entzheim F 60 B3
Envermeu F 58 A2
Enviken S 36 B2
Enying H 74 B3
Enzingerboden A 72 A2
Enzklösterle D 61 B4
Épagny F 59 A4
Epalinges CH 70 B1
Epannes F 67 B4
Epanomi GR 116 B4
Epe D 50 A3
Epe NL 42 C2
Épernay F 59 A4
Épernon F 58 B2
Epfig F 60 B3
Epierre F 69 C6
Épila E 90 B1
Épinac F 69 B4
Épinal F 60 B2
Episcopia I 106 A3
Episkopi CY 120 B1
Epitalio GR 117 E3
Epoisses F 69 A4
Eppenbrunn D 60 A3
Eppendorf D 52 C3
Epping GB 31 C4
Eppingen D 61 A4
Epsom GB 31 C3
Epworth GB 27 B5
Eraclea I 72 C2
Eraclea Mare I 72 C2
Erba I 71 C4
Erbach, *Baden-Württemberg* D 61 B5
Erbach, *Hessen* D 61 A4
Erbalunga F 102 A2
Erbendorf D 62 A3
Érchie I 105 C3
Ercolano I 103 C7
Ercsi H 74 A3
Érd H 74 A3
Erdek TR 118 B2
Erdemli TR 16 C7
Erdevik SRB 85 A4
Erding D 62 B2
Erdötelek H 65 C6
Erdut HR 75 C4
Erdweg D 62 B2
Ereğli, *Konya* TR 16 C7
Ereğli, *Zonguldak* TR 118 A6
Erenkaya TR 119 E7
Eresfjord N 114 E5
Eresos GR 116 C7
Eretria GR 116 D5
Erfde D 43 A6
Erfjord N 33 C3
Erfstadt D 50 C2
Erfurt D 52 C1
Ērgli LV 7 C8
Ergoldsbach D 62 B3
Eriboll GB 22 C4
Érice I 108 A1
Ericeira P 92 C1
Eriksberg S 115 B12
Eriksmåla S 40 C5
Eringsboda S 40 C5
Eriswil CH 70 A2
Erithres GR 117 D5
Erkelenz D 50 B2
Erkner D 45 C5
Erkrath D 50 B2
Erla E 90 A2
Erlangen D 62 A2
Erli I 80 B2
Erlsbach A 72 B2
Ermelo NL 49 A6
Ermenak TR 16 C6
Ermenonville F 58 A3
Ermezinde P 87 C2
Ermidas P 98 A2
Ermioni GR 117 E5
Ermoupoli GR 117 E6
Ermsleben D 52 B1
Erndtebrück D 50 C4
Ernée F 57 B5
Ernestinovo HR 74 C3
Ernstbrunn A 64 B2
Erolzheim D 61 B6
Erquelinnes B 49 C5
Erquy F 56 B3
Erra P 92 C2
Erratzu E 76 C1
Errindlev DK 44 A3
Erro E 76 D1
Ersa F 102 A2
Érsekcsanád H 75 B3
Ersekë AL 116 B2
Érsekvadkert H 65 C5
Erstein F 60 B3
Erstfeld CH 70 B3
Ertebølle DK 38 C2
Ertingen D 61 B5
Ervedal, *Coimbra* P 92 A2
Ervedal, *Portalegre* P 92 B3
Ervenik HR 83 B4
Ervidel P 98 B2
Ervy-le-Châtel F 59 B4
Erwitte D 51 B4
Erxleben D 52 A1
Erzsébet H 74 B3
Es Caná E 97 B1
Es Castell E 97 B4
Es Mercadal E 97 B4
Es Migjorn Gran E 97 B4
Es Port d'Alcúdia E 97 B3
Es Pujols E 97 C1
Es Soleràs E 90 B3
Esbjerg DK 39 D1
Esbly F 58 B3
Escacena del Campo E 99 B4
Escairón E 86 B3
Escalada E 88 B3
Escalante E 89 A3
Escalaplano I 110 C2
Escalona E 94 B2
Escalona del Prado E 94 A2
Escalonilla E 94 C2
Escalos de Baixo P 92 B3
Escalos de Cima P 92 B3
Escamilla E 95 B4
Escañuela E 100 B1
Escatrón E 90 B2
Esch-sur-Alzette L 60 A1
Esch-sur-Sûre L 60 A1
Eschach D 61 C5
Eschau D 61 A5
Eschede D 44 C2
Eschenau D 62 A2
Eschenbach D 62 A2
Eschenz CH 61 C4
Eschershausen D 51 B5
Eschwege D 51 B6
Eschweiler D 50 C2
Escobasa de Almazán E 89 C4
Escoeuilles F 48 C2
Escombreras E 101 B5
Escos F 76 C1
Escource F 76 B1
Escragnolles F 79 C5
Escrick GB 27 B4
Escurial E 93 B5
Escurial de la Sierra E 93 A5
Esens D 43 B4
Esgos E 87 B3
Esher GB 31 C3
Eskdalemuir GB 25 C4
Eskifjörður IS 111 B12
Eskilhem S 37 E5
Eskilsäter S 35 D5
Eskilstrup DK 39 E4
Eskilstuna S 37 C3
Eskipazar TR 118 B7
Eskişehir TR 118 C5
Eslarn D 62 A3
Eslava E 89 B5
Eslida E 96 B2
Eslohe D 50 B4
Eslöv S 41 D3
Eşme TR 119 D3
Espa N 34 B3
Espalion F 78 B1
Esparragalejo E 93 C4
Esparragosa del Caudillo E 93 C5
Esparragossa de la Serena E 93 C5
Esparreguera E 91 B4
Esparron F 79 C4
Espe N 32 B3
Espedal N 33 D3
Espejo, *Alava* E 89 B3
Espejo, *Córdoba* E 100 B1
Espeland N 32 B2
Espelkamp D 43 C5
Espeluche F 78 B3
Espeluy E 100 A2
Espera E 99 C5
Esperança P 93 B3
Espéraza F 77 D5
Espéria I 103 B6
Espevær N 33 C2
Espiel E 99 A5
Espinama E 88 A2
Espiñaredo E 86 A3
Espinasses F 79 B5
Espinelves E 91 B5
Espinhal P 92 A2
Espinho P 87 C2
Espinilla E 88 A2
Espinosa de Cerrato E 88 C3
Espinosa de los Monteros E 89 A3
Espinoso del Rey E 94 C2
Espirito Santo P 98 B3
Espluga de Francolí E 91 B4
Esplús E 90 B3
Espolla E 91 A5
Espoo FIN 6 A8
Esporles E 97 B2
Esposende P 87 C2
Espot E 91 A4
Esquedas E 90 A2
Esquivias E 94 B3
Essay F 57 B6
Essen B 49 B5
Essen, *Niedersachsen* D 43 C4
Essen, *Nordrhein-Westfalen* D 50 B3
Essenbach D 62 B3
Essertaux F 58 A3
Essingen D 61 B6
Esslingen D 61 B5
Essoyes F 59 B5
Estacas E 87 B2
Estadilla E 90 A3
Estagel F 78 D1
Estaires F 48 C3
Estang F 76 C2
Estarreja P 87 D2
Estartit E 91 A6
Estavayer-le-Lac CH 70 B1
Este I 72 C1
Esteiro E 86 A2
Estela P 87 C2
Estella E 89 B4
Estellencs E 97 B2
Estepa E 100 B1
Estépar E 88 B3
Estepona E 99 C5
Esternay F 59 B4
Esterri d'Aneu E 91 A4
Esterwegen D 43 C4
Estissac F 59 B4
Estivadas E 87 B3
Estivareilles F 68 B2
Estivella E 96 B2
Estói P 98 B3
Estopiñán E 90 B3
Estoril P 92 C1
Estoublon F 79 C5
Estrée-Blanche F 48 C3
Estrées-St. Denis F 58 A3
Estrela P 98 A3
Estremera E 95 B3
Estremoz P 92 C3
Estuna S 36 C5
Esyres F 67 A5
Esztergom H 65 C4
Etables-sur-Mer F 56 B3
Étain F 60 A1
Étalans F 69 A6
Etalle B 60 A1
Étampes F 58 B3
Etang-sur-Arroux F 69 B4
Étaples F 48 C2
Etauliers F 67 C4
Etili TR 118 C1
Etna N 34 B1
Etne N 33 C2
Etoges F 59 B4
Etoliko GR 116 D3
Eton GB 31 C3
Etréaupont F 59 A4
Étréchy F 58 B3
Étrépagny F 58 A2
Étretat F 57 A6
Étrœungt F 49 C4
Étroubles I 70 C2
Ettal D 62 C2
Ettelbruck L 60 A2
Etten NL 49 B5
Ettenheim D 60 B3
Ettington GB 29 A6
Ettlingen D 61 B4
Ettringen D 62 B1
Etuz F 69 A5
Etxarri-Aranatz E 89 B4
Etyek H 74 A3
Eu F 48 C2
Euerdorf D 51 C6
Eulate E 89 B4
Eupen B 50 C2
Europoort NL 49 B5
Euskirchen D 50 C2
Eutin D 44 A2
Evanger N 32 B3
Évaux-les-Bains F 68 B2
Evciler, *Afyon* TR 119 D4
Evciler, *Çanakkale* TR 118 C1
Evenskjær N 112 D5
Evenstad N 34 A3
Evercreech GB 29 B5
Evergem B 49 B4
Everöd S 41 D4
Eversberg D 51 B4
Everswinkel D 50 B3
Evertsberg S 34 A5
Evesham GB 29 A6
Évian-les-Bains F 69 B6
Evisa F 102 A1
Evje N 33 D4
Evolène CH 70 B2
Évora P 92 C3
Evoramonte P 92 C3
Evran F 57 B4
Evrecy F 57 A5
Évreux F 58 A2
Évron F 57 B5
Évry F 58 B3
Ewell GB 31 C3
Ewersbach D 50 C4
Excideuil F 67 C6
Exeter GB 29 C4
Exmes F 57 B6
Exminster GB 29 C4
Exmouth GB 29 C4
Eydehamn N 33 D5
Eye, *Peterborough* GB 30 B3
Eye, *Suffolk* GB 30 B5
Eyemouth GB 25 C5
Eyguians F 79 B4
Eyguières F 79 C4
Eygurande F 68 C2
Eylie F 77 D3
Eymet F 77 B3
Eymoutiers F 68 C1
Eynsham GB 31 C2
Eyrarbakki IS 111 D4
Eystrup D 43 C6
Ezaro E 86 B1
Ezcaray E 89 B4
Ezcároz E 76 D1
Ezine TR 118 C1
Ezmoriz P 87 D2

F

Fabara E 90 B3
Fábbrico I 81 B4
Fåberg N 34 A2
Fabero E 86 B4
Fábiánsebestyén H 75 B5
Fåborg DK 39 D3
Fabrègues F 78 C2
Fabriano I 82 C1
Fabrizia I 106 C3
Facha P 87 C2
Facinas E 99 C5
Fačkov SK 65 A4
Fadagosa P 92 B3
Fadd H 74 B3
Faédis I 72 B3
Faenza I 81 B5
Fafe P 87 C2
Fagagna I 72 B3
Făgăras RO 11 D8
Fågelberget S 115 C11
Fågelfors S 40 B5
Fågelmara S 41 C5
Fågelsta S 37 D2
Fagerås S 35 C5
Fagerheim N 32 B4
Fagerhøy N 34 A1
Fagerhult S 40 B5
Fagerlund N 34 B2
Fagernes, *Oppland* N 32 B6
Fagernes, *Troms* N 112 C8
Fagersanna S 35 D6
Fagersta S 36 B2
Fåglavik S 35 D5
Fagnano Castello I 106 B3
Fagnières F 59 B5
Faido CH 70 B3
Fains F 59 B6
Fairford GB 29 B6
Fairlie GB 24 C3
Fajsz H 74 B3
Fakenham GB 30 B4
Fåker S 115 D11
Fakse DK 39 D5
Fakse Ladeplads DK 41 D2
Falaise F 57 B5
Falcade I 72 B1
Falcarragh IRL 18 A3
Falces E 89 B5
Fălciu RO 11 C10
Falconara I 109 B3
Falconara Marittima I 82 C2
Falcone I 109 A4
Faldingworth GB 27 B5
Falerum S 37 D3
Făleşti MD 11 C9
Falkenberg, *Bayern* D 62 A3
Falkenberg, *Bayern* D 62 B3
Falkenberg, *Brandenburg* D 52 B3
Falkenberg S 40 C2
Falkensee D 45 C5
Falkenstein, *Bayern* D 62 A3
Falkenstein, *Sachsen* D 52 C2
Falkenthal D 45 C5
Falkirk GB 25 B4
Falkland GB 25 B4
Falköping S 35 D5
Fall D 62 C2
Falla S 37 D2
Fallingbostel D 43 C6
Falmouth GB 28 C2
Falset E 90 B3
Fălticeni RO 11 C9
Falun S 36 B2
Famagusta CY 120 A2
Fammestad N 32 B2
Fana N 32 B2
Fanano I 81 B4
Fanari GR 116 C3
Fanjeaux F 77 C5
Fano I 82 C2
Fântânele RO 75 B6
Fara in Sabina I 102 A5
Fara Novarese I 70 C3
Faramontanos de Tábara E 88 C1
Farasdues E 90 A1
Fårbo S 40 B6
Fareham GB 31 D2
Färentuna S 37 C4
Färgelanda S 35 D3
Färila S 115 F12
Faringdon GB 31 C2
Faringe S 36 C5
Farini I 80 B3
Fariza E 87 C4
Färjestaden S 41 C6
Farkadona GR 116 C4
Farkasfa H 73 B6
Farlete E 90 B2
Färlöv S 41 C4
Farmos H 75 A4
Farná SK 65 C4
Färnäs S 36 B1
Farnborough GB 31 C3
Farnese I 102 A4
Farnham GB 31 C3
Farnroda D 51 C6
Faro P 98 B3
Fåro S 37 E6
Fårösund S 37 E6
Farra d'Alpago I 72 B2
Farranfore IRL 20 B2
Farre DK 39 C2
Farsala GR 116 C4
Farsø DK 38 C2
Farsund N 33 D3
Farum DK 41 D2
Fårup DK 38 C2
Fasana I 103 C8
Fasano I 104 C3
Fáskrúðsfjörður IS 111 C11
Fassberg D 44 C2
Fastiv UA 11 A10
Fastnäs S 34 B5
Fatesh RUS 7 E13
Fátima P 92 B2
Fatmomakke S 115 B12
Fättjaur S 115 B12

Faucogney-et-la-Mer F 60 C2
Fauguerolles F 76 B3
Faulenrost D 45 B4
Faulquemont F 60 A2
Fauquembergues F 48 C3
Fauske N 112 E4
Fauville-en-Caux F 58 A1
Fauvillers B 60 A1
Fåvang N 34 A2
Favara E 96 B2
Favara I 108 B2
Faverges F 69 C6
Faverney F 60 C1
Faversham GB 31 C4
Favignana I 108 B1
Fawley GB 31 D2
Fay-aux-Loges F 58 C3
Fayence F 79 C5
Fayet F 78 C1
Fayl-Billot F 60 C1
Fayón E 90 B3
Fearn GB 23 D5
Fécamp F 58 A1
Feda N 33 D3
Fedje N 32 B1
Feeny GB 19 B4
Fegen S 40 B3
Fegyvernek H 75 A5
Fehrbellin D 45 C4
Fehring A 73 B6
Feichten A 71 A5
Feiring N 34 B3
Feistritz im Rosental A 73 B4
Feke TR 16 C7
Feketić SRB 75 C4
Felanitx E 97 B3
Feld am See A 72 B3
Feldbach A 73 B5
Feldberg D 45 B5
Feldkirch A 71 A4
Feldkirchen in Kärnten A 73 B4
Feldkirchen-Westerham D 62 C2
Felgueiras P 87 C2
Felitto I 103 C8
Félix E 101 C3
Felixstowe GB 31 C5
Felizzano I 80 B2
Felletin F 68 C2
Fellingsbro S 37 C2
Felnac RO 75 B6
Felnémet H 65 C6
Felpéc H 74 A2
Fels am Wagram A 64 B1
Felsberg D 51 B5
Felsönyék H 74 B3
Felsöszentiván H 75 B4
Felsöszentmárton H 74 C2
Felsözsolca H 65 B6
Felsted DK 39 E2
Feltre I 72 B1
Femsjö S 40 C3
Fenagh IRL 19 B4
Fene E 86 A2
Fenestrelle I 79 A6
Fénétrange F 60 B3
Feneu F 57 C5
Fengersfors S 35 D4
Fenit IRL 20 B2
Fensmark DK 39 D4
Fenwick GB 24 C3
Feolin Ferry GB 24 C1
Ferbane IRL 21 A4
Ferdinandovac HR 74 B2
Ferdinandshof D 45 B5
Fère-Champenoise F 59 B4
Fère-en-Tardenois F 59 A4
Ferentillo I 102 A5
Ferentino I 103 B6
Feres GR 116 B8
Feria E 93 C4
Feričanci HR 74 C2
Ferizli TR 118 B5
Ferla I 109 B3
Ferlach A 73 B4
Ferleiten A 72 A2
Fermil P 87 C3
Fermo I 82 C2
Fermoselle E 87 C4
Fermoy IRL 20 B3
Fernán Nuñéz E 100 B1
Fernán Peréz E 101 C3
Fernancabellero E 94 C3
Fernão Ferro P 92 C1
Fernay-Voltaire F 69 B6
Ferndown GB 29 C6
Ferness GB 23 D5
Fernhurst GB 31 C3
Ferns IRL 21 B5
Ferpécle CH 70 B2
Ferrals-les-Corbières F 78 C1
Ferrandina I 104 C2
Ferrara I 81 B5
Ferrara di Monte Baldo I 71 C5
Ferreira E 86 A3
Ferreira do Alentejo P 98 A2
Ferreira do Zêzere P 92 B2
Ferreras de Abajo E 87 C4
Ferreras de Arriba E 87 C4
Ferreries E 97 B4
Ferreruela E 90 B1
Ferreruela de Tabara E 87 C4
Ferret CH 70 C2
Ferrette F 70 A2
Ferriere I 80 B3
Ferrière-la-Grande F 49 C4
Ferrières, *Hautes-Pyrénées* F 76 C2
Ferrières, *Loiret* F 58 B3
Ferrières, *Oise* F 58 A3
Ferrières-sur-Sichon F 68 B3
Ferrol E 86 A2
Ferryhill GB 27 A4
Fertörakos H 64 C2
Fertöszentmiklós H 64 C2
Ferwerd NL 42 B2
Festieux F 59 A4
Festøy N 114 E3
Festvåg N 112 E3
Feteşti RO 11 D9
Fethard, *Tipperary* IRL 21 B4
Fethard, *Wexford* IRL 21 B5
Fethiye TR 119 F4
Fetsund N 34 C3
Fettercairn GB 25 B5
Feucht D 62 A2
Feuchtwangen D 61 A6
Feudingen D 50 C4
Feuges F 59 B5
Feuquières F 58 A2
Feurs F 69 C4
Fevik N 33 D5
Ffestiniog GB 26 C2
Fiamignano I 102 A6
Fiano I 70 C2
Ficarazzi I 108 A2
Ficarolo I 81 B5
Fichtelberg D 52 C1
Ficulle I 82 D1
Fidenza I 81 B4
Fidjeland N 33 D3
Fieberbrunn A 72 A2
Fier AL 105 C5
Fiera di Primiero I 72 B1
Fierzë AL 105 A6
Fiesch CH 70 B3
Fiesso Umbertiano I 81 B5
Figari F 102 B2
Figeac F 77 B5
Figeholm S 40 B6
Figgjo N 33 D2
Figline Valdarno I 81 C5
Figols E 90 A3
Figueira da Foz P 92 A2
Figueira de Castelo Rodrigo P 87 D4
Figueira dos Caveleiros P 98 A2
Figueiredo P 92 B3
Figueiredo de Alva P 87 D3
Figueiró dos Vinhos P 92 B2
Figueres E 91 A5
Figueroles E 96 A2
Figueruela de Arriba E 87 C4
Filadélfia I 106 C3
Fil'akovo SK 65 B5
Filderstadt D 61 B5
Filey GB 27 A5
Filiaşi RO 11 D7
Filiates GR 116 C2
Filiatra GR 117 E3
Filipstad S 35 C6
Filisur CH 71 B4
Fillan N 114 D5
Filotio GR 117 E7
Filottrano I 82 C2
Filskov DK 39 D2
Filton GB 29 B5
Filtvet N 35 C2
Filzmoos A 72 A3
Finale Emília I 81 B5
Finale Lígure I 80 B2
Fiñana E 101 B3
Finby FIN 36 B7
Fincham GB 30 B4
Finchingfield GB 31 C4
Findhorn GB 23 D5
Findochty GB 23 D6
Finike TR 119 F5
Finkenberg A 72 A1
Finnea IRL 19 C4
Finneidfjord N 115 A10
Finnerödja S 37 D1
Finnskog N 34 B4
Finnsnes N 112 C7
Finntorp S 35 C4
Finócchio I 102 B5
Finsjö S 40 B6
Finsland N 33 D4
Finspång S 37 D2
Finsterwalde D 53 B3
Finsterwolde NL 43 B4
Finstown GB 23 B5
Fintona GB 19 B4
Fionnphort GB 24 B1
Fiorenzuola d'Arda I 81 B3
Firenze = Florence I 81 C5
Firenzuola I 81 B5
Firmi F 77 B5
Firminy F 69 C4
Firmo I 106 B3
Fischamend Markt A 64 B2
Fischbach A 73 A5
Fischbach D 60 A3
Fischbeck D 44 C4
Fischen D 71 A5
Fishbourne GB 31 D2
Fishguard GB 28 B3
Fiskardo GR 116 D2
Fiskebäckskil S 35 D3
Fiskebøl N 112 D3
Fismes F 59 A4
Fisterra E 86 B1
Fitero E 89 B5
Fitjar N 32 C2
Fiuggi I 102 B6
Fiumata I 102 A6
Fiumefreddo Brúzio I 106 B3
Fiumefreddo di Sicília I 109 B4
Fiumicino I 102 B5
Fivemiletown GB 19 B4
Fivizzano I 81 B4
Fjæra N 32 C3
Fjälkinge S 41 C4
Fjällåsen S 112 E9
Fjällbacka S 35 D3
Fjärdhundra S 36 C3
Fjellerup DK 38 C3
Fjerritslev DK 38 B2
Fjordgard N 112 C6
Fjugesta S 37 C1
Flå N 32 B6
Flåbygd N 33 C5
Flaça E 91 A5
Flace F 69 B4
Fladungen D 51 C6
Flaine F 70 B1
Flaka FIN 36 B7
Flåm N 32 B4
Flamatt CH 70 B2
Flamborough GB 27 A5
Flammersfeld D 50 C3
Flassans-sur-Issole F 79 C5
Flatdal N 33 C5
Flateby N 34 C3
Flateland N 33 C4
Flateyri IS 111 A2
Flatøydegard N 32 B6
Flatråker N 32 C2
Flattach A 72 B3
Flatvarp S 37 E3
Flauenskjold DK 38 B3
Flavigny-sur-Moselle F 60 B2
Flavy-le-Martel F 59 A4
Flawil CH 71 A4
Flayosc F 79 C5
Flechtingen D 44 C3
Fleckeby D 44 A1
Fleet GB 31 C3
Fleetmark D 44 C3
Fleetwood GB 26 B2
Flehingen D 61 A4
Flekke N 32 A2
Flekkefjord N 33 D3
Flen S 37 C3
Flensburg D 39 E2
Fleringe S 37 E5
Flerohopp S 40 C5
Flers F 57 B5
Flesberg N 32 C6
Fleurance F 77 C3
Fleuré F 67 B5
Fleurier CH 69 B6
Fleurus B 49 C5
Fleury, *Hérault* F 78 C2
Fleury, *Yonne* F 59 C4
Fleury-les-Aubrais F 58 C2
Fleury-sur-Andelle F 58 A2
Fleury-sur-Orne F 57 A5
Flieden D 51 C5
Flimby GB 26 A2
Flims CH 71 B4
Flines-lèz-Raches F 49 C4
Flint GB 26 B2
Flirey F 60 B1
Flirsch A 71 A5
Flisa N 34 B4
Flisby S 40 B4
Fliseryd S 40 B6
Flix E 90 B3
Flixecourt F 48 C3
Flize F 59 A5
Flobecq B 49 C4
Floby S 35 D5
Floda S 40 B2
Flodden GB 25 C5
Flogny-la-Chapelle F 59 C4
Flöha D 52 C3
Flonheim D 61 A4
Florac F 78 B2
Floreffe B 49 C5
Florence = Firenze I 81 C5
Florennes B 49 C5
Florensac F 78 C2
Florentin F 77 C5
Florenville B 59 A6
Flores de Avila E 94 B1
Floresta I 109 B3
Floreşti MD 11 C10
Florídia I 109 B4
Florina GR 116 B3
Florø N 114 F2
Flörsheim D 51 C4
Floss D 62 A3
Fluberg N 34 B2
Flúðir IS 111 C5
Flühli CH 70 B3
Flumet F 69 C6
Fluminimaggiore I 110 C1
Flums CH 71 A4
Flyeryd S 41 C5
Flygsfors S 40 C5
Foča BIH 84 C3
Foça TR 118 D1
Fochabers GB 23 D5
Focşani RO 11 D9
Foel GB 26 C2
Foeni RO 75 C5
Fogdö S 37 C3
Fóggia I 104 B1
Foglianise I 103 B7
Föglö FIN 36 B7
Fohnsdorf A 73 A4
Foiano della Chiana I 81 C5
Foix F 77 D4
Fojnica BIH 84 C3
Fojnica BIH 84 C2
Fokino RUS 7 E13
Fokstua N 114 E6
Földeák H 75 B5
Foldereid N 114 C9
Főldes H 75 A6
Folegandros GR 117 F6
Folelli F 102 A2
Folgaria I 71 C6
Folgosinho P 92 A3
Folgoso de la Ribera E 86 B4
Folgoso do Courel E 86 B3
Foligno I 82 D1
Folkärna S 36 B3
Folkestad N 114 E3
Folkestone GB 31 C5
Follafoss N 114 D8
Folldal N 114 E6
Follebu N 34 A2
Follina I 72 C2
Föllinge S 115 D11
Follónica I 81 D4
Fölsbyn S 35 C4
Foncebadón E 86 B4
Foncine-le-Bas F 69 B6
Fondevila E 87 C2
Fondi I 103 B6
Fondo I 71 B6
Fonelas E 100 B2
Fonfría, *Teruel* E 90 C1
Fonfría, *Zamora* E 87 C4
Fonnes N 32 B1
Fonni I 110 B2
Font-Romeu F 91 A5
Fontaine F 59 B5
Fontaine de Vaucluse F 79 C4
Fontaine-Française F 69 A5
Fontaine-le-Dun F 58 A1
Fontainebleau F 58 B3
Fontan F 80 B1
Fontanarejo E 94 C2
Fontane I 80 B1
Fontanélice I 81 B5
Fontanières F 68 B2
Fontanosas E 100 A1
Fonteblanda I 102 A4
Fontenay-le-Comte F 66 B4
Fontenay-Trésigny F 59 B3
Fontevrault-l'Abbaye F 67 A5
Fontiveros E 94 B2
Fontoy F 60 A1
Fontpédrouse F 91 A5
Fontstown IRL 21 A5
Fonyód H 74 B2
Fonz E 90 A3
Fonzaso I 72 B1
Fóppolo I 71 B4
Föra S 41 B6
Forbach D 61 B4
Forbach F 60 A2
Forcall E 90 C2
Forcalquier F 79 C4
Forcarei E 86 B2
Forchheim D 62 A2
Forchtenau A 64 C2
Forchtenberg D 61 A5
Ford GB 24 B2
Førde, *Hordaland* N 33 C2
Førde, *Sogn og Fjordane* N 32 A2
Förderstedt D 52 B1
Førdesfjorden N 33 C2
Fordham GB 30 B4
Fordingbridge GB 29 C6
Fordon PL 47 B4
Fordongiánus I 110 C1
Forenza I 104 C1
Foresta di Búrgos I 110 B1
Forfar GB 25 B5
Forges-les-Eaux F 58 A2
Foria I 106 A2
Forio I 103 C6
Forjães P 87 C2
Førland N 33 D4
Forlì I 81 B6
Forlimpopoli I 82 B1
Formazza I 70 B3
Formby GB 26 B2
Formerie F 58 A2
Fórmia I 103 B6
Formígine I 81 B4
Formigliana I 70 C3
Formiguères F 91 A5
Fornalutx E 97 B2
Fornåsa S 37 D2
Fornelli I 110 B1
Fornells E 97 A4
Fornelos de Montes E 87 B2
Fornes E 100 C2
Forneset N 112 C8
Forni Avoltri I 72 B2
Forni di Sopra I 72 B2
Forni di Sotto I 72 B2
Forno, *Piemonte* I 70 C3
Forno, *Piemonte* I 79 A6
Forno Alpi-Gráie I 70 C2
Forno di Zoldo I 72 B2
Fornos de Algodres P 92 A3
Fornovo di Taro I 81 B4
Foros do Arrão P 92 B2
Forráskút H 75 B4
Forres GB 23 D5
Forriolo E 87 B3
Fors S 36 B3
Forsand N 33 D3
Forsbacka S 36 B3
Forserum S 40 B4
Forshaga S 35 C5
Forsheda S 40 B3
Forsinain GB 23 C5
Førslev DK 39 D4
Forslöv S 41 C2
Forsmark, *Uppsala* S 36 B5
Forsmark, *Västerbotten* S 115 B12
Forsmo S 115 D14
Forsnäs S 115 A15
Forsnes N 114 D5
Forssa FIN 3 F25
Forssjöbruk S 37 D3
Forst D 53 B4
Forsvik S 37 D1
Fort Augustus GB 22 D4
Fort-Mahon-Plage F 48 C2
Fort William GB 24 B2
Fortanete E 90 C2
Forte dei Marmi I 81 C4
Fortezza I 72 B1
Forth GB 25 C4
Fortrie GB 23 D6
Fortrose GB 23 D4
Fortun N 32 A4
Fortuna E 101 A4
Fortuneswell GB 29 C5
Forvik N 115 B9
Fos F 77 D3
Fos-sur-Mer F 78 C3
Fosdinovo I 81 B4
Foss N 32 B6
Fossacésia I 103 A7
Fossano I 80 B1
Fossato di Vico I 82 C1
Fossbakken N 112 D6
Fosse-la-Ville B 49 C5
Fossombrone I 82 C1
Fot H 65 C5
Fouchères F 59 B5
Fouesnant F 56 C1
Foug F 60 B1
Fougères F 57 B4
Fougerolles F 60 C2
Foulain F 59 B6
Fountainhall GB 25 C5
Fouras F 66 C3
Fourchambault F 68 A3
Fourmies F 49 C5
Fourna GR 116 C3
Fournels F 78 B2
Fourni GR 119 E1
Fournols F 68 C3
Fourques F 91 A5
Fourquevaux F 77 C4
Fours F 68 B3
Fowey GB 28 C3
Foxdale GB 26 A1
Foxford IRL 18 C2
Foyers GB 23 D4
Foynes IRL 20 B2
Foz E 86 A3
Foz do Arelho P 92 B1
Foz do Giraldo P 92 B3
Foza I 72 C1
Frabosa Soprana I 80 B1
Frades de la Sierra E 93 A5
Fraga E 90 B3
Fragagnano I 104 C3
Frailes E 100 B2
Fraire B 49 C5
Fraize F 60 B2
Framlingham GB 30 B5
Frammersbach D 51 C5
Framnes N 35 C2
França P 87 C4
Françaltroff F 60 B2
Francavilla al Mare I 103 A7
Francavilla di Sicília I 109 B4
Francavilla Fontana I 104 C3
Francavilla in Sinni I 106 A3
Francescas F 77 B3
Franco P 87 C3
Francofonte I 109 B3
Francos E 89 C3
Frändefors S 35 D4
Franeker NL 42 B2
Frangy F 69 B5
Frankenau D 51 B4
Frankenberg, *Hessen* D 51 B4
Frankenberg, *Sachsen* D 52 C3
Frankenburg A 63 B4
Frankenfels A 63 C6
Frankenmarkt A 63 C4
Frankenthal D 61 A4
Frankfurt, *Brandenburg* D 45 C6
Frankfurt, *Hessen* D 51 C4
Frankowo PL 47 A6
Frankrike S 115 D10
Fränsta S 115 E13
Františkovy Lázně CZ 52 C2
Franzburg D 45 A4
Frascati I 102 B5
Frasdorf D 62 C3
Fraserburgh GB 23 D6
Frashër AL 116 B2
Frasne F 69 B6
Frasnes-lez-Anvaing B 49 C4
Frasseto F 102 B2
Frastanz A 71 A4
Fratel P 92 B3
Fratta Todina I 82 D1
Frauenau D 63 B4
Frauenfeld CH 70 A3
Frauenkirchen A 64 C2
Frauenstein D 52 C3
Frauental A 73 B5
Frayssinet F 77 B4
Frayssinet-le-Gélat F 77 B4
Frechas P 87 C3
Frechen D 50 C2
Frechilla E 88 B2
Freckenhorst D 50 B3
Fredeburg D 50 B4
Fredelsloh D 51 B5
Fredeng N 34 B2
Fredensborg DK 41 D2
Fredericia DK 39 D2
Frederiks DK 39 C2
Frederikshavn DK 38 B3
Frederikssund DK 39 D5
Frederiksværk DK 39 D5
Fredrika S 115 C15
Fredriksberg S 34 B6
Fredriksdal S 40 B4
Fredrikstad N 35 C2
Fregenal de la Sierra E 99 A4
Fregene I 102 B5
Freiberg D 52 C3
Freiburg, *Baden-Württemberg* D 60 C3
Freiburg, *Niedersachsen* D 43 B6
Freienhagen D 51 B5
Freienhufen D 53 B3
Freiensteinau D 51 C5
Freihung D 62 A2
Freilassing D 62 C3
Freisen D 60 A3
Freising D 62 B2
Freistadt A 63 B5
Freital D 52 B3
Freixedas P 93 A3
Freixo de Espada à Cinta P 87 C4
Fréjus F 79 C5
Fremdingen D 61 B6
Frenštát pod Radhoštěm CZ 64 A4
Freren D 43 C4
Freshford IRL 21 B4
Freshwater GB 31 D2
Fresnay-sur-Sarthe F 57 B6
Fresne-St. Mamès F 69 A5
Fresneda de la Sierra E 95 B4
Fresneda de la Sierra Tiron E 89 B3
Fresnedillas E 94 B2
Fresnes-en-Woevre F 60 A1
Fresno Alhandiga E 94 B1
Fresno de la Ribera E 88 C1
Fresno de la Vega E 88 B1
Fresno de Sayago E 87 C5
Fresnoy-Folny F 58 A2
Fresnoy-le-Grand F 59 A4
Fressenville F 48 C2
Fresvik N 32 A3
Fréteval F 58 C2
Fretigney F 69 A5
Freudenberg, *Baden-Württemberg* D 61 A5
Freudenberg, *Nordrhein-Westfalen* D 50 C3
Freudenstadt D 61 B4
Freux B 49 D6
Frévent F 48 C3
Freyburg D 52 B1
Freyenstein D 44 B4
Freyming-Merlebach F 60 A2
Freystadt D 62 A2
Freyung D 63 B4
Frias de Albarracin E 95 B5
Fribourg CH 70 B2
Frick CH 70 A3
Fridafors S 41 C4
Fridaythorpe GB 27 A5
Friedberg A 73 A6
Friedberg, *Bayern* D 62 B1
Friedberg, *Hessen* D 51 C4
Friedeburg D 43 B4
Friedewald D 51 C5
Friedland, *Brandenburg* D 53 A4
Friedland, *Mecklenburg-Vorpommern* D 45 B5
Friedland, *Niedersachsen* D 51 B5
Friedrichroda D 51 C6
Friedrichsdorf D 51 C4
Friedrichshafen D 61 C5
Friedrichskoog D 43 A5
Friedrichstadt D 43 A6
Friedrichswalde D 45 B5
Friesach A 73 B4
Friesack D 45 C4
Friesenheim D 60 B3
Friesoythe D 43 B4
Friggesund S 115 F13
Frigiliana E 100 C2
Frihetsli N 112 D8
Frillesås S 40 B2
Frinnaryd S 40 B4
Frinton-on-Sea GB 31 C5
Friockheim GB 25 B5
Friol E 86 A3
Fristad S 40 B2
Fritsla S 40 B2
Fritzlar D 51 B5
Frizington GB 26 A2
Frödinge S 40 B6
Froges F 69 C5
Frohburg D 52 B2
Frohnhausen D 50 C4
Frohnleiten A 73 A5
Froissy F 58 A3
Frombork PL 47 A5
Frome GB 29 B5
Frómista E 88 B2
Fröndenberg D 50 B3
Fronsac F 76 B2
Front I 70 C2
Fronteira P 92 B3
Frontenay-Rohan-Rohan F 67 B4
Frontenhausen D 62 B3
Frontignan F 78 C2
Fronton F 77 C4
Fröseke S 40 C5
Frosinone I 103 B6
Frosolone I 103 B7
Frosta N 114 D7
Frøstrup DK 38 B1
Frosunda S 37 C5
Frouard F 60 B2
Frövi S 37 C2
Frøyset N 32 B2
Fruges F 48 C3
Frutigen CH 70 B2
Frýdek-Místek CZ 65 A4
Frýdlant CZ 53 C5
Frydlant nad Ostravicí CZ 65 A4
Frygnowo PL 47 B6
Fryšták CZ 64 A3
Fucécchio I 81 C4
Fuencaliente, *Ciudad Real* E 100 A1
Fuencaliente, *Ciudad Real* E 94 C3
Fuencemillán E 95 B3
Fuendejalón E 89 C5
Fuengirola E 100 C1
Fuenlabrada E 94 B3
Fuenlabrada de los Montes E 94 C2
Fuensalida E 94 B2
Fuensanta E 101 B4
Fuensanta de Martos E 100 B2
Fuente al Olmo de Iscar E 88 C2
Fuente-Alamo E 101 A4
Fuente-Álamo de Murcia E 101 B4
Fuente Dé E 88 A2
Fuente de Cantos E 99 A4
Fuente de Santa Cruz E 94 A2
Fuente del Arco E 99 A5
Fuente del Conde E 100 B1
Fuente del Maestre E 93 C4
Fuente el Fresno E 94 C3
Fuente el Saz de Jarama E 95 B3
Fuente el Sol E 94 A2
Fuente Obejuna E 99 A5
Fuente Palmera E 99 B5
Fuente-Tójar E 100 B1
Fuente Vaqueros E 100 B2
Fuentealbilla E 96 B1
Fuentecén E 88 C3
Fuenteguinaldo E 93 A4
Fuentelapeña E 88 C1
Fuentelcésped E 89 C3
Fuentelespino de Haro E 95 C4
Fuentelespino de Moya E 95 C5
Fuentenovilla E 95 B3
Fuentepelayo E 94 A2
Fuentepinilla E 89 C4
Fuenterroble de Salvatierra E 93 A5
Fuenterrobles E 96 B1
Fuentes E 95 C4
Fuentes de Andalucía E 99 B5
Fuentes de Ebro E 90 B2
Fuentes de Jiloca E 89 C5
Fuentes de la Alcarria E 95 B4
Fuentes de León E 99 A4
Fuentes de Nava E 88 B2
Fuentes de Oñoro E 93 A4
Fuentes de Ropel E 88 B1
Fuentesauco, *Segovia* E 88 C2
Fuentesaúco, *Zamora* E 94 A1
Fuentespalda E 90 C3
Fuentespina E 88 C3
Fuentidueña E 88 C3
Fuentidueña de Tajo E 95 B3
Fuerte del Rey E 100 B2
Fügen A 72 A1
Fuglebjerg DK 39 D4
Fuglevik N 35 C2
Fuhrberg D 44 C1
Fulda D 51 C5
Fulgatore I 108 B1
Fully CH 70 B2
Fulnek CZ 64 A3
Fülöpszállás H 75 B4
Fulpmes A 71 A6
Fulunäs S 34 A5
Fumay F 49 D5
Fumel F 77 B3
Funäsdalen S 115 E9
Fundão P 92 A3
Funzie GB 22 A8
Furadouro P 87 D2
Fure N 32 A2
Fürstenau, *Niedersachsen* D 43 C4
Furstenau, *Nordrhein-Westfalen* D 51 B5
Fürstenberg D 45 B5
Fürstenfeld A 73 A6
Fürstenfeldbruck D 62 B2
Fürstenstein D 63 B4
Fürstenwalde D 45 C6
Fürstenwerder D 45 B5
Fürstenzell D 63 B4
Fürth, *Bayern* D 62 A1
Fürth, *Hessen* D 61 A4
Furth im Wald D 62 A3
Furtwangen D 61 B4
Furuby S 40 C5
Furudal S 36 A2
Furuflaten N 112 C9
Furulund S 41 D3
Furusjö S 40 B3
Fusa N 32 B2
Fuscaldo I 106 B3
Fusch an der Grossglocknerstrasse A 72 A2
Fushë Arrëz AL 105 A6
Fushë-Krujë AL 105 B5
Fusina I 72 C2
Fusio CH 70 B3
Füssen D 62 C1
Fustiñana E 89 B5
Futog SRB 75 C4
Futrikelv N 112 C8
Füzesabony H 65 C6
Füzesgyarmat H 75 A6
Fužine HR 73 C4
Fyllinge S 40 C2
Fynshav DK 39 E2
Fyresdal N 33 C5

G

Gaaldorf A 73 A4
Gabaldón E 95 C5
Gabarret F 76 C3
Gabčíkovo SK 64 C3
Gąbin PL 47 C5
Gabriac F 78 B1
Gabrovo BG 11 E8
Gaby I 70 C2
Gacé F 58 B1
Gacko BIH 84 C3
Gäddede S 115 C11
Gadebusch D 44 B3
Gadmen CH 70 B3
Gádor E 101 C3
Gádoros H 75 B5
Gael F 57 B3
Gærum DK 38 B3
Găeşti RO 11 D8
Gaeta I 103 B6
Gafanhoeira P 92 C2
Gaflenz A 63 C5
Gagarin RUS 7 D13
Gaggenau D 61 B4
Gagliano Castelferrato I 109 B3
Gagliano del Capo I 107 B5
Gagnet S 36 B2
Gaibanella I 81 B5

Gaildorf D 61 B5
Gaillac F 77 C4
Gaillefontaine F 58 A2
Gaillon F 58 A2
Gainsborough GB 27 B5
Gairloch GB 22 D3
Gairlochy GB 24 B3
Gáiro I 110 C2
Gaj HR 74 C2
Gaj SRB 85 B6
Gaja-la-Selve F 77 C4
Gajanejos E 95 B4
Gajary SK 64 B2
Gajdobra SRB 75 C4
Galan F 77 C3
Galanta SK 64 B3
Galapagar E 94 B2
Galápagos E 95 B3
Galaroza E 99 B4
Galashiels GB 25 C5
Galatas GR 117 E5
Galaţi RO 11 D10
Galatina I 107 A5
Galatista GR 116 B5
Galátone I 107 A5
Galaxidi GR 117 D4
Galdakao E 89 A4
Galeata I 81 C5
Galende E 87 B4
Galera E 101 B3
Galéria F 102 A1
Galgamácsa H 65 C5
Galgate GB 26 B3
Galgon F 76 B2
Galices P 92 A3
Galinduste E 93 A5
Galinoporni CY 120 A3
Galisteo E 93 B4
Galków PL 55 B4
Gallarate I 70 C3
Gallardon F 58 B2
Gallegos de Argañán E 93 A4
Gallegos del Solmirón E 93 A5
Galleguillos de Campos E 88 B1
Galleno I 81 C4
Galliate I 70 C3
Gallicano I 81 B4
Gállio I 72 C1
Gallípoli I 107 A4
Gallipoli = Gelibolu TR 118 B1
Gällivare S 112 E9
Gallizien A 73 B4
Gallneukirchen A 63 B5
Gällö S 115 E12
Gallocanta E 95 B5
Gällstad S 40 B3
Gallur E 90 B1
Galmisdale GB 24 B1
Galmpton GB 29 C4
Galston GB 24 C3
Galta N 33 C2
Galtelli I 110 B2
Galten DK 39 C2
Galtür A 71 B5
Galve de Sorbe E 95 A3
Galveias P 92 B2
Gálvez E 94 C2
Galway IRL 20 A2
Gamaches F 48 D2
Gámbara I 71 C5
Gambárie I 106 C2
Gambassi Terme I 81 C4
Gambatesa I 103 B7
Gambolò I 70 C3
Gaming A 63 C6
Gamla Uppsala S 36 C4
Gamleby S 40 B6
Gamlingay GB 30 B3
Gammelgarn S 37 E5
Gammelstad S 3 D25
Gammertingen D 61 B5
Gams CH 71 A4
Gamvik, *Finnmark* N 113 A17
Gamvik, *Finnmark* N 113 B11
Gan F 76 C2
Gáname E 87 C4
Ganda di Martello I 71 B5
Gandarela P 87 C2
Ganddal N 33 D2
Ganderkesee D 43 B5
Gandesa E 90 B3
Gandía E 96 C2
Gandino I 71 C4
Gandrup DK 38 B3
Ganges F 78 C2
Gånghester S 40 B3
Gangi I 109 B3
Gangkofen D 62 B3
Gannat F 68 B3
Gannay-sur-Loire F 68 B3
Gänserdorf A 64 B2
Ganzlin D 44 B4
Gap F 79 B5
Gara H 75 B4
Garaballa E 96 B1
Garaguso I 104 C2
Garbayuela E 94 C1
Garbhallt GB 24 B2
Garbsen D 43 C6
Garching D 62 B3
Garciaz E 93 B5
Garcihernández E 94 B1
Garcillán E 94 B2
Garcinarro E 95 B4
Garcisobaco E 99 C5
Garda I 71 C5
Gardanne F 79 C4
Gärdås S 34 B5
Gårdby S 41 C6
Gardeja PL 47 B4
Gardelegen D 44 C3
Gardermoen N 34 B3
Gardiki GR 116 D3
Garding D 43 A5
Gardone Riviera I 71 C5
Gardone Val Trómpia I 71 C5
Gárdony H 74 A3
Gardouch F 77 C4
Gards Köpinge S 41 D4
Gårdsjö S 37 D1
Gårdskär S 36 B4
Garein F 76 B2
Garelochhead GB 24 B3
Garéoult F 79 C5
Garešnica HR 74 C1
Garéssio I 80 B2
Garforth GB 27 B4
Gargaliani GR 117 E3
Gargaligas E 93 B5
Gargallo E 90 C2
Garganta la Olla E 93 A5
Gargantiel E 100 A1
Gargellen A 71 B4
Gargilesse-Dampierre F 67 B6
Gargnano I 71 C5
Gargnäs S 115 B14
Gárgoles de Abajo E 95 B4
Gargrave GB 26 B3
Garitz D 52 B2
Garlasco I 70 C3
Garlieston GB 24 D3
Garlin F 76 C2
Garlitos E 94 D1
Garmisch-Partenkirchen D 71 A6
Garnat-sur-Engièvre F 68 B3
Garpenberg S 36 B3
Garphyttan S 37 C1
Garray E 89 C4
Garrel D 43 C5
Garriguella E 91 A6
Garrison GB 18 B3
Garrovillas E 93 B4
Garrucha E 101 B4
Gars-a-Kamp A 63 B6
Garsås S 36 B1
Garsdale Head GB 26 A3
Gärsnäs S 41 D4
Garstang GB 26 B3
Gartow D 44 B3
Gartz D 45 B6
Garvagh GB 19 B5
Garvão P 98 B2
Garve GB 22 D4
Garwolin PL 55 B6
Garz D 45 A5
Garzyn PL 54 B1
Gąsawa PL 46 C3
Gåsborn S 34 C6
Gaschurn A 71 B5
Gascueña E 95 B4
Gasny F 58 A2
Gąsocin PL 47 C6
Gastes F 76 B1
Gastouni GR 117 E3
Gastouri GR 116 C1
Gata E 93 A4
Gata HR 83 C5
Gata de Gorgos E 96 C3
Gatchina RUS 7 B11
Gatehouse of Fleet GB 24 D3
Gátér H 75 B4
Gateshead GB 25 D6
Gátova E 96 B2
Gattendorf A 64 B2
Gatteo a Mare I 82 B1
Gattinara I 70 C3
Gattorna I 80 B3
Gaucín E 99 C5
Gaulstad N 114 D9
Gaupne N 32 A4
Gautefall N 33 C5
Gauting D 62 B2
Gauto S 115 A13
Gava E 91 B5
Gavardo I 71 C5
Gavarnie F 76 D2
Gavi I 80 B2
Gavião P 92 B3
Gavirate I 70 C3
Gävle S 36 B4
Gavoi I 110 B2
Gavorrano I 81 D4
Gavray F 57 B4
Gavrio GR 117 E6
Gävunda S 34 B6
Gaweinstal A 64 B2
Gaworzyce PL 53 B5
Gawroniec PL 46 B2
Gaydon GB 30 B2
Gayton GB 30 B4
Gazipaşa TR 119 F7
Gazoldo degli Ippoliti I 71 C5
Gazzuolo I 81 A4
Gbelce SK 65 C4
Gdańsk PL 47 A4
Gdinj HR 84 C1
Gdov RUS 7 B9
Gdów PL 65 A6
Gdynia PL 47 A4
Gea de Albarracín E 95 B5
Geary GB 22 D2
Géaudot F 59 B5
Geaune F 76 C2
Gebesee D 51 B6
Gebiz TR 119 E5
Gebze TR 118 B4
Géderlak H 75 B3
Gedern D 51 C5
Gedinne B 49 D5
Gediz TR 118 D4
Gèdre F 76 D3
Gedser DK 44 A3
Gedsted DK 38 C2
Geel B 49 B5
Geesthacht D 44 B2
Geetbets B 49 C6
Gefell D 52 C1
Gehrden D 51 A5
Gehren D 52 C1
Geilenkirchen D 50 C2
Geilo N 32 B5
Geinsheim D 61 A4
Geisa D 51 C5
Geiselhöring D 62 B3
Geiselwind D 61 A6
Geisenfeld D 62 B2
Geisenhausen D 62 B3
Geisenheim D 50 D4
Geising D 53 C3
Geisingen D 61 C4
Geislingen D 61 B5
Geistthal A 73 A5
Geiterygghytta N 32 B4
Geithain D 52 B2
Geithus N 34 C1
Gela I 109 B3
Geldermalsen NL 49 B6
Geldern D 50 B2
Geldrop NL 49 B6
Geleen NL 50 C1
Gelembe TR 118 C2
Gelendost TR 119 D6
Gelibolu = Gallipoli TR 118 B1
Gelida E 91 B4
Gelnhausen D 51 C5
Gelnica SK 65 B6
Gelsa E 90 B2
Gelse H 74 B1
Gelsenkirchen D 50 B3
Gelsted DK 39 D2
Geltendorf D 62 B2
Gelterkinden CH 70 A2
Gelting D 39 E2
Gelu RO 75 B6
Gelves E 99 B4
Gembloux B 49 C5
Gemeaux F 69 A5
Gémenos F 79 C4
Gemerská Poloma SK 65 B6
Gemerská Ves SK 65 B6
Gemert NL 50 B1
Gemla S 40 C4
Gemlik TR 118 B4
Gemmenich B 50 C1
Gemona del Friuli I 72 B3
Gémozac F 67 C4
Gemund D 50 C2
Gemünden, *Bayern* D 51 C5
Gemünden, *Hessen* D 51 C4
Gemünden, *Rheinland-Pfalz* D 60 A3
Genappe B 49 C5
Génave E 101 A3
Genazzano I 102 B5
Gençay F 67 B5
Gencsapáti H 74 A1
Gendringen NL 50 B2
Genelard F 69 B4
Genemuiden NL 42 C3
Generalski Stol HR 73 C5
Geneva = Genève CH 69 B6
Genevad S 40 C3
Genève = Geneva CH 69 B6
Genevriéres F 60 C1
Gengenbach D 61 B4
Genillé F 67 A6
Genk B 49 C6
Genlis F 69 A5
Gennep NL 50 B1
Genner DK 39 D2
Gennes F 67 A4
Genoa = Génova I 80 B2
Genola I 80 B1
Génova = Genoa I 80 B2
Genowefa PL 54 A3
Gensingen D 60 A3
Gent = Ghent B 49 B4
Genthin D 44 C4
Gentioux F 68 C1
Genzano di Lucánia I 104 C2
Genzano di Roma I 102 B5
Georgenthal D 51 C6
Georgsmarienhütte D 50 A4
Gera D 52 C2
Geraards-bergen B 49 C4
Gerace I 106 C3
Geraci Sículo I 109 B3
Geraki GR 117 F4
Gérardmer F 60 B2
Geras A 63 B6
Gerbéviller F 60 B2
Gerbini I 109 B3
Gerbstedt D 52 B1
Gerði IS 111 C9
Gerede TR 118 B7
Gerena E 99 B4
Geretsried D 62 C2
Gérgal E 101 B3
Gergy F 69 B4
Gerindote E 94 C2
Gerjen H 74 B3
Gerlos A 72 A2
Germay F 59 B6
Germencik TR 119 E2
Germering D 62 B2
Germersheim D 61 A4
Gërneç AL 105 C5
Gernika-Lumo E 89 A4
Gernrode D 52 B1
Gernsbach D 61 B4
Gernsheim D 61 A4
Geroda D 51 C5
Gerola Alta I 71 B4
Geroldsgrun D 52 C1
Gerolsbach D 62 B2
Gerolstein D 50 C2
Gerolzhofen D 61 A6
Gerovo HR 73 C4
Gerpinnes B 49 C5
Gerrards Cross GB 31 C3
Gerri de la Sal E 91 A4
Gersfeld D 51 C5
Gerstetten D 61 B6
Gersthofen D 62 B1
Gerstungen D 51 C6
Gerswalde D 45 B5
Gerzat F 68 C3
Gerze TR 16 A7
Gerzen D 62 B3
Gescher D 50 B3
Geseke D 51 B4
Geslau D 61 A6
Gespunsart F 59 A5
Gesté F 66 A3
Gestorf D 51 A5
Gesualda I 103 C8
Gesunda S 36 B1
Geta FIN 36 B6
Getafe E 94 B3
Getinge S 40 C2
Getxo E 89 A4
Geversdorf D 43 B6
Gevgelija MK 116 A4
Gevora del Caudillo E 93 C4
Gevrey-Chambertin F 69 A4
Gex F 69 B6
Gey D 50 C2
Geyikli TR 118 C1
Geysir IS 111 C5
Geyve TR 118 B5
Gföhl A 63 B6
Ghedi I 71 C5
Ghent = Gent B 49 B4
Gheorgheni RO 11 C8
Ghigo I 79 B6
Ghilarza I 110 B1
Ghisonaccia F 102 A2
Ghisoni F 102 A2
Gialtra GR 116 D4
Gianitsa GR 116 B4
Giardinetto Vécchio I 103 B8
Giardini Naxos I 109 B4
Giarratana I 109 B3
Giarre I 109 B4
Giat F 68 C2
Giaveno I 80 A1
Giazza I 71 C6
Giba I 110 C1
Gibellina Nuova I 108 B1
Gibostad N 112 C7
Gibraleón E 99 B4
Gibraltar GBZ 99 C5
Gic H 74 A2
Gideå S 115 D16
Gideåkroken S 115 C14
Gidle PL 55 C4
Giebelstadt D 61 A5
Gieboldehausen D 51 B6
Gielniów PL 55 B5
Gielow D 45 B4
Gien F 58 C3
Giengen D 61 B6
Giens F 79 C5
Giera RO 75 C5
Gieselwerder D 51 B5
Giessen D 51 C4
Gieten NL 42 B3
Giethoorn NL 42 C3
Giffaumont-Champaubert F 59 B5
Gifford GB 25 C5
Gifhorn D 44 C2
Gige H 74 B2
Giglio Porto I 102 A3
Gignac F 78 C2
Gijón E 88 A1
Gilena E 100 B1
Gilford GB 19 B5
Gillberga S 35 C4
Gilleleje DK 41 C2
Gilley F 69 A6
Gilley-sur-Loire F 68 B3
Gillingham, *Dorset* GB 29 B5
Gillingham, *Medway* GB 31 C4
Gilocourt F 59 A3
Gilserberg D 51 C5
Gilsland GB 25 D5
Gilze NL 49 B5
Gimåt S 115 D15
Gimo S 36 B5
Gimont F 77 C3
Ginasservis F 79 C4
Gingelom B 49 C6
Gingst D 45 A5
Ginosa I 104 C2
Ginzling A 72 A1
Giões P 98 B3
Gióia dei Marsi I 103 B6
Gióia del Colle I 104 C2
Gióia Sannitica I 103 B7
Gióia Táuro I 106 C2
Gioiosa Iónica I 106 C3
Gioiosa Marea I 109 A3
Giosla GB 22 C2
Giovinazzo I 104 B2
Girifalco I 106 C3
Giromagny F 60 C2
Girona E 91 B5
Gironcourt-sur-Vraine F 60 B1
Gironella E 91 A4
Gironville-sous-les-Côtes F 60 B1
Girvan GB 24 C3
Gislaved S 40 B3
Gislev DK 39 D3
Gisors F 58 A2
Gissi I 103 A7
Gistad S 37 D2
Gistel B 48 B3
Gistrup DK 38 C3
Giswil CH 70 B3
Githio GR 117 F4
Giugliano in Campania I 103 C7
Giulianova I 82 D2
Giulvăz RO 75 C5
Giurgiu RO 11 E8
Give DK 39 D2
Givet F 49 C5
Givors F 69 C4
Givry B 49 C5
Givry F 69 B4
Givry-en-Argonne F 59 B5
Givskud DK 39 D2
Giżałki PL 54 A2
Gizeux F 67 A5
Giżycko PL 6 D6
Gizzeria I 106 C3
Gizzeria Lido I 106 C3
Gjedved DK 39 D2
Gjegjan AL 105 B6
Gjendesheim N 32 A5
Gjerde N 32 B3
Gjerlev DK 38 C3
Gjermundshamn N 32 B2
Gjerrild DK 38 C3
Gjerstad N 33 D6
Gjesås N 34 B4
Gjesvær N 113 A14
Gjirokastër AL 116 B2
Gjøfjell N 35 C2
Gjøl DK 38 B2
Gjøra N 114 E6
Gjøvik N 34 B2
Gladbeck D 50 B2
Gladenbach D 51 C4
Gladstad N 114 B8
Glamis GB 25 B5
Glamoč BIH 84 B1
Glamsbjerg DK 39 D3
Gland CH 69 B6
Glandorf D 50 A3
Glanegg A 73 B4
Glanshammar S 37 C2
Glarus CH 70 A4
Glasgow GB 24 C3
Glashütte, *Bayern* D 62 C2
Glashütte, *Sachsen* D 53 C3
Glastonbury GB 29 B5
Glatzau A 73 B5
Glauchau D 52 C2
Glava S 35 C4
Glavatičevo BIH 84 C3
Glavičice BIH 85 B4
Glavnik SRB 85 D6
Gledica SRB 85 C5
Glein A 73 A4
Glein N 115 A9
Gleinstätten A 73 B5
Gleisdorf A 73 A5
Glenamoy IRL 18 B2
Glenarm GB 19 B6
Glenavy GB 19 B5
Glenbarr GB 24 C2
Glenbeigh IRL 20 B2
Glenbrittle GB 22 D2
Glencoe GB 24 B2
Glencolumbkille IRL 18 B3
Glendalough IRL 21 A5
Glenealy IRL 21 B5
Glenelg GB 22 D3
Glenfinnan GB 24 B2
Glengarriff IRL 20 C2
Glenluce GB 24 D3
Glennamaddy IRL 18 C3
Glenrothes GB 25 B4
Glenties IRL 18 B3
Glesborg DK 38 C3
Glesien D 52 B2
Gletsch CH 70 B3
Glewitz D 45 A4
Glifada GR 117 E5
Glimåkra S 41 C4
Glin IRL 20 B2
Glina HR 73 C6
Glinde D 44 B2
Glinojeck PL 47 C6
Glinsk IRL 20 A1
Gliwice PL 54 C3
Glödnitz A 73 B4
Gloggnitz A 64 C1
Głogoczów PL 65 A5
Glogonj SRB 85 B5
Glogovac SRB 85 B6
Głogów PL 53 B6
Głogówek PL 54 C2
Glomel F 56 B2
Glomfjord N 112 F2
Glommen S 40 C2
Glommersträsk S 115 B16
Glonn D 62 C2
Glorenza I 71 B5
Gloria P 92 B2
Glosa GR 116 C5
Glossop GB 27 B4
Gloucester GB 29 B5
Głowaczów PL 55 B6
Glówczyce PL 46 A3
Glöwen D 44 C4
Głowno PL 55 B4
Gložan SRB 75 C4
Głubczyce PL 54 C2
Głuchołazy PL 54 C2
Głuchów PL 55 B5
Głuchowo PL 54 A1
Glücksburg D 39 E2
Glückstadt D 43 B6
Glumina BIH 84 B4
Glumsø DK 39 D4
Glušci SRB 85 B4
Glusk BY 7 E10
Głuszyca PL 53 C6
Glyn Neath GB 29 B4
Glyngøre DK 38 C1
Gmünd, *Karnten* A 72 B3
Gmünd, *Nieder Östereich* A 63 B5
Gmund D 62 C2
Gmunden A 63 C4
Gnarp S 115 E14
Gnarrenburg D 43 B6
Gnesau A 72 B3
Gnesta S 37 C4
Gnięchowice PL 54 B1
Gniew PL 47 B4
Gniewkowo PL 47 C4
Gniezno PL 46 C3
Gnoien D 45 B4
Gnojnice BIH 84 C2
Gnojno PL 55 C5
Gnosall GB 26 C3
Gnosjö S 40 B3
Göbel TR 118 B3
Göçbeyli TR 118 C2
Goch D 50 B2
Gochsheim D 51 C6
Göd H 65 C5
Godalming GB 31 C3
Godby FIN 36 B6
Goddelsheim D 51 B4
Gódega di Sant'Urbano I 72 C2
Godegård S 37 D2
Godelheim D 51 B5
Goderville F 58 A1
Goðdalir IS 111 B6
Godiasco I 80 B3
Godič SLO 73 B4
Godkowo PL 47 A5
Godmanchester GB 30 B3
Gödöllö H 65 C5
Gödre H 74 B2
Godshill GB 31 D2
Godzikowice PL 54 C2
Godziszewo PL 47 A4
Goes NL 49 B4
Goetzenbrück F 60 B3
Góglio I 70 B3
Gogolin PL 54 C3
Göhren D 45 A5
Goirle NL 49 B6
Góis P 92 A2
Góito I 71 C5
Goizueta E 76 C1
Gojna Gora SRB 85 C5
Gójsk PL 47 C5
Gökçedağ TR 118 C3
Gökçen TR 119 D2
Gökçeören TR 119 D3
Gökçeyazı TR 118 C2
Göktepe TR 119 E3
Gol N 32 B5
Gola HR 74 B2
Gola N 34 A1
Gołańcz PL 46 C3
Gölbaşı TR 16 B6
Gölby FIN 36 B6
Gölcük, *Kocaeli* TR 118 B4
Gölcük, *Niğde* TR 16 B7
Golčův Jenikov CZ 63 A6
Gołczewo PL 45 B6
Goldach CH 71 A4
Goldbach D 51 C5
Goldbeck D 44 C3
Goldberg D 44 B4
Goldelund D 43 A6
Goldenstedt D 43 C5
Gołębiewo PL 47 A4
Golegã P 92 B2
Goleniów PL 45 B6
Golfo Aranci I 110 B2
Gölhisar TR 119 E4
Golina PL 54 A3
Gölle H 74 B3
Göllersdorf A 64 B2
Golling an der Salzach A 63 C4
Gölmarmara TR 118 D2
Golnice PL 53 B5
Golnik SLO 73 B4
Gölova TR 119 F5
Gölpazarı TR 118 B5
Gols A 64 C2
Golspie GB 23 D5
Golssen D 52 B3
Golub-Dobrzyń PL 47 B5
Golubac SRB 85 B6
Golubinci SRB 85 B5
Golubovci CG 105 A5
Goluchów PL 54 B2
Golzow D 52 A2
Gomagoi I 71 B5
Gómara E 89 C4
Gomaringen D 61 B5
Gömbe TR 119 F4
Gömeç TR 118 C1
Gomel = Homyel BY 7 E11
Gomes Aires P 98 B2
Gómezserracin E 88 C2
Gommern D 52 A1
Gomulin PL 55 B4
Gonäs S 36 B2
Goncelin F 69 C5
Gończyce PL 55 B6
Gondomar E 87 B2
Gondomar P 87 C2
Gondrecourt-le-Château F 60 B1
Gondrin F 76 C3
Gönen, *Balıkesir* TR 118 B2
Gönen, *Isparta* TR 119 E5
Gonfaron F 79 C5
Goñi E 76 D1
Goni GR 116 C4
Goni I 110 C2
Gonnesa I 110 C1
Gonnosfanádiga I 110 C1
Gönyü H 64 C3
Gonzaga I 81 B4
Goodrich GB 29 B5
Goodwick GB 28 A2
Gooik B 49 C5
Goole GB 27 B5
Goor NL 50 A2
Göpfritz an der Wild A 63 B6
Goppenstein CH 70 B2
Göppingen D 61 B5
Gor E 100 B3
Góra, *Dolnośląskie* PL 54 B1
Góra, *Mazowieckie* PL 47 C6
Góra Kalwaria PL 55 B6
Gorafe E 100 B2
Gorawino PL 46 B1
Goražde BIH 84 C3
Gordaliza del Pino E 88 B1
Gördes TR 118 D3
Gørding DK 39 D1
Górdola CH 70 B3
Gordon GB 25 C5
Gordoncillo E 88 B1
Gorebridge GB 25 C4
Gorenja Vas SLO 73 B4
Gorenje Jelenje HR 73 C4
Gorey GB 57 A3
Gorey IRL 21 B5
Gorgonzola I 71 C4
Gorica HR 83 B4
Gorican HR 74 B1
Gorinchem NL 49 B5
Goring GB 31 C2
Goritsy RUS 7 C14
Göritz D 45 B5
Gorízia I 72 C3
Górki PL 47 C5
Gorleben D 44 B3
Gorleston-on-sea GB 30 B5
Gørlev DK 39 D4
Görlitz D 53 B4
Górliz E 89 A4
Görmin D 45 B5
Górna Grupa PL 47 B4
Gorna Oryakhovitsa BG 11 E8
Gornja Gorevnica SRB 85 C5
Gornja Klina SRB 85 D5
Gornja Ploča HR 83 B4
Gornja Radgona SLO 73 B5
Gornja Sabanta SRB 85 C6
Gornja Trešnjevica SRB 85 B5
Gornja Tuzla BIH 84 B3
Gornje Polje CG 84 D3
Gornje Ratkovo BIH 84 B1
Gornji Grad SLO 73 B4
Gornji Humac HR 83 C5
Gornji Jasenjani BIH 84 C2
Gornji Kamengrad BIH 83 B5
Gornji Kneginec HR 73 B6
Gornji Kokoti CG 105 A5
Gornji Kosinj HR 83 B4
Gornji Milanovac SRB 85 B5
Gornji Podgradci BIH 84 A2
Gornji Ravno BIH 84 C2
Gornji Sjenicak HR 73 C5
Gornji Vakuf BIH 84 C2
Górno PL 55 C5
Görömböly H 65 B6
Górowo Iławeckie PL 47 A6
Gorran Haven GB 28 C3
Gorredijk NL 42 B3
Gorron F 57 B5
Gorseinon GB 28 B3
Gort IRL 20 A3
Gortin GB 19 B4
Görzke D 52 A2
Gorzkowice PL 55 B4
Górzno, *Kujawsko-Pomorskie* PL 47 B5
Górzno, *Zachodnio-Pomorskie* PL 46 B1
Gorzów Śląski PL 54 B3
Gorzów Wielkopolski PL 45 C7
Górzyca PL 45 C6
Gorzyce PL 54 D3
Górzyn, *Lubuskie* PL 53 B4
Gorzyń, *Wielkopolskie* PL 46 C1
Gorzyno PL 46 A3
Gosaldo I 72 B1
Gosau A 63 C4
Gosberton GB 30 B3
Gościcino PL 47 A4
Gościęcin PL 54 C3
Gościm PL 46 C1
Gościno PL 46 A1
Gosdorf A 73 B5
Gosforth GB 26 A2
Goslar D 51 B6
Goslice PL 47 C5
Gospič HR 83 B4
Gosport GB 31 D2
Goss Ilsede D 51 A6
Gössäter S 35 D5
Gossau CH 71 A4
Gössnitz D 52 C2
Gössweinstein D 62 A2
Gostimë AL 105 C6
Gostkow PL 55 B4
Göstling an der Ybbs A 63 C5
Gostomia PL 46 B2
Gostycyn PL 46 B3
Gostyń PL 54 B2
Gostynin PL 47 C5
Goszczyn PL 55 B5
Göta S 35 D4
Göteborg = Gothenburg S 38 B4
Götene S 35 D5
Gotha D 51 C6
Gothem S 37 E5
Gothenburg = Göteborg S 38 B4
Gotse Delchev BG 116 A5
Gottersdorf D 62 B3
Göttingen D 51 B5
Gottne S 115 D15
Götzis A 71 A4
Gouarec F 56 B2
Gouda NL 49 A5
Goudhurst GB 31 C4
Goumenissa GR 116 B4
Goura GR 117 E4
Gourdon F 77 B4
Gourgançon F 59 B5
Gourin F 56 B2
Gournay-en-Bray F 58 A2
Gourock GB 24 C3
Gouveia P 92 A3
Gouvy B 50 C1
Gouzeacourt F 49 C4
Gouzon F 68 B2
Govedari HR 84 D2
Govérnolo I 81 A4
Gowarczów PL 55 B5
Gowerton GB 28 B3
Gowidlino PL 46 A3
Gowran IRL 21 B4
Goyatz D 53 A4
Göynük, *Antalya* TR 119 F5
Göynük TR 118 B5
Gozdnica PL 53 B5
Gozdowo PL 47 C5
Gozee B 49 C5
Graal-Müritz D 44 A4
Grab BIH 84 D3
Grabenstätt D 62 C3
Grabhair GB 22 C2
Gråbo S 38 B5
Grabovac HR 84 C1
Grabovac SRB 85 B5
Grabovci SRB 85 B4
Grabow D 44 B3
Grabów PL 55 A4
Grabow nad Pilicą PL 55 B6
Grabów nad Prosną PL 54 B3
Grabowno PL 46 B3
Grabs CH 71 A4
Gračac HR 83 B4
Gračanica BIH 84 B3
Gračanica SRB 85 D6
Graçay F 68 A1
Gracen AL 105 B5
Grad SLO 73 B6
Gradac BIH 84 D3
Gradac CG 85 C4
Gradac HR 84 C2
Gradac SRB 85 C5
Gradačac BIH 84 B3
Gradec HR 74 C1
Gradefes E 88 B1
Grades A 73 B4
Gradil P 92 C1
Gradina CG 85 C4
Gradina HR 74 C2
Gradisca d'Isonzo I 72 C3
Gradište HR 74 C3
Grado E 86 A4
Grado I 72 C3
Grærup Strand DK 39 D1
Græsted DK 41 C2
Gräfenau D 63 B4
Gräfenberg D 62 A2
Gräfenhainichen D 52 B2
Grafenschlag A 63 B6
Grafenstein A 73 B4

Gräfenthal D 52 C1
Grafentonna D 51 B6
Grafenwöhr D 62 A2
Grafing D 62 B2
Grafling D 62 B3
Gräfsnäs S 40 A2
Gragnano I 103 C7
Grahovo CG 84 D3
Grahovo SLO 72 B3
Graiguenamanagh IRL 21 B5
Grain GB 31 C4
Grainau D 71 A6
Graja de Iniesta E 95 C5
Grajera E 89 C3
Gram DK 39 D2
Gramais A 71 A5
Gramat F 77 B4
Gramatneusiedl A 64 B2
Grambow D 45 B6
Grammichele I 109 B3
Gramsh AL 116 B2
Gramzow D 45 B6
Gran N 34 B2
Granada E 100 B2
Granard IRL 19 C4
Grañas E 86 A3
Granátula de Calatrava E 100 A2
Grancey-le-Château F 59 C6
Grand-Champ F 56 C3
Grand Couronne F 58 A2
Grand-Fougeray F 57 C4
Grandas de Salime E 86 A4
Grandcamp-Maisy F 57 A4
Grândola P 98 A2
Grandpré F 59 A5
Grandrieu B 49 C5
Grandrieu F 78 B2
Grandson CH 70 B1
Grandvillars F 70 A1
Grandvilliers F 58 A2
Grañén E 90 B2
Grangärde S 36 B1
Grange IRL 18 B3
Grange-over-Sands GB 26 A3
Grangemouth GB 25 B4
Granges-de Crouhens F 77 D3
Granges-sur-Vologne F 60 B2
Grängesberg S 36 B1
Gräningen D 44 C4
Granitola-Torretta I 108 B1
Granja, *Évora* P 98 A3
Granja, *Porto* P 87 C2
Granja de Moreruela E 88 C1
Granja de Torrehermosa E 93 C5
Gränna S 40 A4
Grannäs, *Västerbotten* S 115 B13
Grannäs, *Västerbotten* S 115 B14
Granö S 115 C16
Granollers E 91 B5
Granowiec PL 54 B2
Granowo PL 54 A1
Gransee D 45 B5
Gransherad N 33 C6
Grantham GB 27 C5
Grantown-on-Spey GB 23 D5
Grantshouse GB 25 C5
Granville F 57 B4
Granvin N 32 B3
Gräsås S 40 C2
Grasbakken N 113 B17
Grasberg D 43 B6
Grasmere GB 26 A2
Gräsmyr S 115 D16
Grasö S 36 B5
Grassano I 104 C2
Grassau D 62 C3
Grasse F 79 C5
Grassington GB 27 A4
Gråsten DK 39 E2
Grästorp S 35 D4
Gratkorn A 73 A5
Gråträsk S 115 B16
Gratwein A 73 A5
Graulhet F 77 C4
Graus E 90 A3
Grávalos E 89 B5
Gravberget N 34 B4
Grave NL 50 B1
Gravedona I 71 B4
Gravelines F 48 B3
Gravellona Toce I 70 C3
Gravendal S 36 B1
's-Gravendeel NL 49 B5
's-Gravenhage = The Hague NL 49 A5
Gravens DK 39 D2
's-Gravenzande NL 49 B5
Gravesend GB 31 C4
Graveson F 78 C3
Gravina in Púglia I 104 C2
Gray F 69 A5
Grayrigg GB 26 A3
Grays GB 31 C4
Grayshott GB 31 C3
Grayvoron RUS 7 F13
Graz A 73 A5
Grazalema E 99 C5
Grążawy PL 47 B5
Grazzano Visconti I 80 B3
Greåker N 35 C3
Great Dunmow GB 31 C4
Great Malvern GB 29 A5
Great Torrington GB 28 C3
Great Waltham GB 31 C4
Great Yarmouth GB 30 B5
Grebbestad S 35 D3
Grebenstein D 51 B5
Grębocice PL 53 B6
Grębocin PL 47 B4
Greding D 62 A2
Gredstedbro DK 39 D1
Greenhead GB 25 D5
Greenisland GB 19 B6
Greenlaw GB 25 C5
Greenock GB 24 C3
Greenway GB 28 B3
Greenwich GB 31 C4
Grefrath D 50 B2
Greifenburg A 72 B3
Greiffenberg D 45 B5
Greifswald D 45 A5
Grein A 63 B5
Greipstad N 33 D4
Greiz D 52 C2
Grenaa DK 39 C3
Grenade F 77 C4
Grenade-sur-l'Adour F 76 C2
Grenchen CH 70 A2
Grendi N 33 D4
Grenivík IS 111 B7
Grenoble F 69 C5
Gréoux-les-Bains F 79 C4
Gresenhorst D 44 A4
Gressoney-la-Trinité I 70 C2
Gressoney-St.-Jean I 70 C2
Gressthal D 51 C6
Gressvik N 35 C2
Gresten A 63 C6
Gretna GB 25 D4
Greussen D 51 B6
Greve in Chianti I 81 C5
Greven, *Mecklenburg-Vorpommern* D 44 B2
Greven, *Nordrhein-Westfalen* D 50 A3
Grevena GR 116 B3
Grevenbroich D 50 B2
Grevenbrück D 50 B4
Grevenmacher L 60 A2
Grevesmühlen D 44 B3
Grevestrand DK 41 D2
Grevie S 41 C2
Greystoke GB 26 A3
Greystones IRL 21 A5
Grez-Doiceau B 49 C5
Grez-en-Bouère F 57 C5
Grèzec F 77 B4
Grezzana I 71 C6
Grgar SLO 72 B3
Grgurevci SRB 85 A4
Gries A 71 A6
Gries in Sellrain A 71 A6
Griesbach D 63 B4
Griesheim D 61 A4
Grieskirchen A 63 B4
Griffen A 73 B4
Grignan F 78 B3
Grignano I 72 C3
Grigno I 72 B1
Grignols F 76 B2
Grignon F 69 C6
Grijota E 88 B2
Grijpskerk NL 42 B3
Gril AL 105 A5
Grillby S 37 C4
Grimaud F 79 C5
Grimbergen B 49 C5
Grimma D 52 B2
Grimmen D 45 A5
Grimmialp CH 70 B2
Grimsås S 40 B3
Grimsby GB 27 B5
Grimslöv S 40 C4
Grímsstaðir IS 111 B9
Grimstad N 33 D5
Grimstorp S 40 B4
Grindavík IS 111 D3
Grindelwald CH 70 B3
Grindheim N 33 D4
Grindsted DK 39 D1
Griñón E 94 B3
Gripenberg S 40 B4
Gripsholm S 37 C4
Grisolles F 77 C4
Grisslehamn S 36 B5
Gritley GB 23 C6
Grizebeck GB 26 A2
Grndina BIH 84 B1
Gröbming A 72 A3
Gröbzig D 52 B1
Grocka SRB 85 B5
Gröditz D 52 B3
Gródki PL 47 B6
Grodków PL 54 C2
Grodziec PL 54 A3
Grodzisk Mazowiecki PL 55 A5
Groenlo NL 50 A2
Groesbeek NL 50 B1
Grohote HR 83 C5
Groitzsch D 52 B2
Groix F 56 C2
Grójec PL 55 B5
Grom PL 47 B6
Gromiljca BIH 84 C3
Grömitz D 44 A2
Gromnik PL 65 A6
Gromo I 71 C4
Gronau, *Niedersachsen* D 51 A5
Gronau, *Nordrhein-Westfalen* D 50 A3
Grønbjerg DK 39 C1
Grönenbach D 61 C6
Grong N 114 C9
Grönhögen S 41 C6
Groningen D 52 B1
Groningen NL 42 B3
Grønnestrand DK 38 B2
Grono CH 71 B4
Grönskåra S 40 B5
Grootegast NL 42 B3
Gropello Cairoli I 70 C3
Grorud N 34 C2
Grósio I 71 B5
Grošnica SRB 85 C5
Gross Beeren D 45 C5
Gross Berkel D 51 A5
Gross-botwar D 61 B5
Gross-Dölln D 45 B5
Gross-Gerau D 61 A4
Gross-hartmansdorf D 52 C3
Gross Kreutz D 45 C4
Gross Lafferde D 51 A6
Gross Leutheb D 53 A4
Gross Muckrow D 53 A4
Gross Oesingen D 44 C2
Gross Reken D 50 B3
Gross Sarau D 44 B2
Gross Särchen D 53 B4
Gross Schönebeck D 45 C5
Gross Umstadt D 61 A4
Gross Warnow D 44 B3
Gross-Weikersdorf A 64 B1
Gross-Welle D 44 B4
Gross Wokern D 44 B4
Grossalmerode D 51 B5
Grossarl A 72 A3
Grossbodungen D 51 B6
Grossburgwedel D 44 C1
Grosschönau D 53 C4
Grossenbrode D 44 A3
Grossengottern D 51 B6
Grossenhain D 52 B3
Grossenkneten D 43 C5
Grossenlüder D 51 C5
Grossensee D 44 B2
Grossenzersdorf A 64 B2
Grosseto I 81 D5
Grossgerungs A 63 B5
Grossglobnitz A 63 B6
Grosshabersdorf D 62 A1
Grossharras A 64 B2
Grosshöchstetten CH 70 B2
Grosskrut A 64 B2
Grosslohra D 51 B6
Grossmehring D 62 B2
Grossostheim D 61 A5
Grosspertholz A 63 B5
Grosspetersdorf A 73 A6
Grosspostwitz D 53 B4
Grossraming A 63 C5
Grossräschen D 53 B4
Grossrinderfeld D 61 A5
Grossröhrsdorf D 53 B4
Grossschirma D 52 C3
Grossschweinbarth A 64 B2
Grosssiegharts A 63 B6
Grosssölk A 72 A3
Grosswarasdorf A 74 A1
Grosswilfersdorf A 73 A5
Grostenquin F 60 B2
Grosuplje SLO 73 C4
Grotli N 114 E4
Grötlingbo S 37 E5
Grottáglie I 104 C3
Grottaminarda I 103 B8
Grottammare I 82 D2
Grotte di Castro I 81 D5
Grotteria I 106 C3
Gróttole I 104 C2
Grouw NL 42 B2
Grov N 112 D6
Grova N 33 C5
Grove E 86 B2
Grua N 34 B2
Grube D 44 A3
Grubišno Polje HR 74 C2
Gruda HR 105 A4
Grude BIH 84 C2
Grudovo BG 11 E9
Grudusk PL 47 B6
Grudziądz PL 47 B4
Grue N 34 B4
Gruissan F 78 C2
Grullos E 86 A4
Grumo Áppula I 104 B2
Grums S 35 C5
Grünau im Almtal A 63 C4
Grünberg D 51 C4
Grünburg A 63 C5
Grundarfjörður IS 111 C2
Gründau D 51 C5
Gründelhardt D 61 A5
Grundforsen S 34 A4
Grundlsee A 63 C4
Grundsund S 35 D3
Grunewald D 53 B3
Grungedal N 33 C4
Grunow D 53 A4
Grünstadt D 61 A4
Gruvberget S 36 A3
Gruyères CH 70 B2
Gruža SRB 85 C5
Grybów PL 65 A6
Grycksbo S 36 B2
Gryfice PL 45 B7
Gryfino PL 45 B6
Gryfów Śląski PL 53 B5
Gryllefjord N 112 C6
Grymyr N 34 B2
Gryt S 37 D3
Grytgöl S 37 D2
Grythyttan S 37 C1
Grytnäs S 37 D4
Grzmiąca PL 46 B2
Grzybno PL 45 B6
Grzywna PL 47 B4
Gschnitz A 71 A6
Gschwend D 61 B5
Gstaad CH 70 B2
Gsteig CH 70 B2
Guadahortuna E 100 B2
Guadalajara E 95 B3
Guadalaviar E 95 B5
Guadalcanal E 99 A5
Guadalcázar E 100 B1
Guadalix de la Sierra E 94 B3
Guadálmez E 100 A1
Guadalupe E 93 B5
Guadamur E 94 C2
Guadarrama E 94 B2
Guadiaro E 99 C5
Guadix E 100 B2
Guagnano I 105 C3
Guagno F 102 A1
Guajar-Faragüit E 100 C2
Gualchos E 100 C2
Gualdo Tadino I 82 C1
Gualtieri I 81 B4
Guarcino I 103 B6
Guarda P 92 A3
Guardamar del Segura E 96 C2
Guardão P 92 A2
Guardavalle I 106 C3
Guardea I 102 A5
Guárdia I 103 C8
Guardia Sanframondi I 103 B7
Guardiagrele I 103 A7
Guardiarégia I 103 B7
Guardias Viejas E 100 C3
Guardiola de Bergueda E 91 A4
Guardo E 88 B2
Guareña E 93 C4
Guaro E 100 C1
Guarromán E 100 A2
Guasila I 110 C2
Guastalla I 81 B4
Gubbhögen S 115 C12
Gúbbio I 82 C1
Guben D 53 B4
Gubin PL 53 B4
Guča SRB 85 C5
Gudå N 114 D8
Gudavac BIH 83 B5
Guddal N 32 A2
Güderup DK 39 E2
Gudhem S 35 D5
Gudhjem DK 41 D4
Gudovac HR 74 C1
Gudow D 44 B2
Güdül TR 118 B7
Gudvangen N 32 B3
Guebwiller F 60 C3
Guéjar-Sierra E 100 B2
Guéméné-Penfao F 57 C4
Guéméné-sur-Scorff F 56 B2
Güeñes E 89 A3
Guer F 57 C3
Guérande F 66 A2
Guéret F 68 B1
Guérigny F 68 A3
Guesa E 76 D1
Gueugnon F 68 B4
Guglionesi I 103 B7
Gühlen Glienicke D 45 B4
Guia P 92 B2
Guichen F 57 C4
Guidizzolo I 71 C5
Guidónia-Montecélio I 102 B5
Guiglia I 81 B4
Guignes F 58 B3
Guijo E 100 A1
Guijo de Coria E 93 A4
Guijo de Santa Bábera E 93 A5
Guijuelo E 93 A5
Guildford GB 31 C3
Guillaumes F 79 B5
Guillena E 99 B4
Guillestre F 79 B5
Guillos F 76 B2
Guilsfield GB 26 C2
Guilvinec F 56 C1
Guimarães P 87 C2
Guincho P 92 C1
Guînes F 48 C2
Guingamp F 56 B2
Guipavas F 56 B1
Guisborough GB 27 A4
Guiscard F 59 A4
Guiscriff F 56 B2
Guise F 59 A4
Guisona E 91 B4
Guitiriz E 86 A3
Guîtres F 76 A2
Gujan-Mestras F 76 B1
Gulbene LV 7 C9
Gulçayır TR 118 C6
Guldborg DK 39 E4
Gullabo S 40 C5
Gullane GB 25 B5
Gullbrå N 32 B3
Gullbrandstorp S 40 C2
Gulleråsen S 36 A2
Gullhaug N 35 C2
Gullringen S 40 B5
Gullspång S 35 D6
Gullstein N 114 D5
Güllük TR 119 E2
Gülnar TR 16 C6
Gülpınar TR 116 C8
Gülşehir TR 16 B7
Gulsvik N 34 B1
Gumiel de Hizán E 88 C3
Gummersbach D 50 B3
Gümüldür TR 119 D2
Gümüşhaciköy TR 16 A7
Gümüşova TR 118 B5
Gundel-fingen D 60 B3
Gundelfingen D 61 B6
Gundelsheim D 61 A5
Gunderschoffen F 60 B3
Gunderts-hausen A 62 B3
Gundinci HR 74 C3
Gündoğmuş TR 119 F7
Güney, *Burdur* TR 119 E4
Güney, *Denizli* TR 119 D3
Gunja HR 84 B3
Günlüce TR 119 F3
Gunnarn S 115 B14
Gunnarskog S 34 C4
Gunnebo S 40 B6
Gunnislake GB 28 C3
Günselsdorf A 64 C2
Guntersblum D 61 A4
Guntersdorf A 64 B2
Guntin E 86 B3
Günyüzü TR 118 C6
Günzburg D 61 B6
Gunzenhausen D 62 A1
Güre, *Balıkesir* TR 118 C1
Güre, *Uşak* TR 118 D4
Gurk A 73 B4
Gurrea de Gállego E 90 A2
Gürsu TR 118 B4
Gušće HR 74 C1
Gusev RUS 6 D7
Gusinje CG 105 A5
Gusmar AL 105 C5
Güspini I 110 C1
Gusselby S 37 C2
Güssing A 73 A6
Gusswerk A 63 C6
Gustav Adolf S 34 B5
Gustavsberg S 37 C5
Gustavsfors S 35 C4
Güstrow D 44 B4
Gusum S 37 D3
Gutcher GB 22 A7
Gutenstein A 64 C1
Gütersloh D 51 B4
Guttannen CH 70 B3
Guttaring A 73 B4
Guttau D 53 B4
Güttingen CH 61 C5
Gützkow D 45 B5
Guzów PL 55 A5
Gvardeysk RUS 6 D6
Gvarv N 33 C6
Gvozd CG 85 D4
Gvozdansko HR 73 C6
Gwda Wielka PL 46 B2
Gwennap GB 28 C2
Gy F 69 A5
Gyál H 75 A4
Gyarmat H 74 A2
Gyé-sur-Seine F 59 B5
Gyékényes H 74 B2
Gylling DK 39 D3
Gyoma H 75 B5
Gyömöre H 74 A2
Gyömrö H 75 A4
Gyón H 75 A4
Gyöngyfa H 74 C2
Gyöngyös H 65 C5
Gyöngyöspata H 65 C5
Gyönk H 74 B3
Györ H 64 C3
Györszemere H 74 A2
Gypsera CH 70 B2
Gysinge S 36 B3
Gyttorp S 37 C1
Gyula H 75 B6
Gyulafirátót H 74 A2
Gyulaj H 74 B3

H

Haacht B 49 C5
Haag, *Nieder Östereich* A 63 B5
Haag, *Ober Östereich* A 63 B4
Haag D 62 B3
Haaksbergen NL 50 A2
Haamstede NL 49 B4
Haan D 50 B3
Haapajärvi FIN 3 E26
Haapsalu EST 6 B7
Haarlem NL 42 C1
Habas F 76 C2
Habay B 60 A1
Habo S 40 B4
Håbol S 35 D4
Habry CZ 63 A6
Habsheim F 60 C3
Hachenburg D 50 C3
Hacıbektaş TR 16 B7
Hacılar TR 16 B7
Hacinas E 89 C3
Hackås S 115 E11
Hacketstown IRL 21 B5
Hackthorpe GB 26 A3
Hadamar D 50 C4
Hädanberg S 115 D15
Haddington GB 25 C5
Hadersdorf am Kamp A 63 B6
Haderslev DK 39 D2
Haderup DK 39 C1
Hadım TR 119 F7
Hadleigh, *Essex* GB 31 C4
Hadleigh, *Suffolk* GB 30 B4
Hadlow GB 31 C4
Hadmersleben D 52 A1
Hadsten DK 39 C3
Hadsund DK 38 C3
Hadyach UA 7 F13
Hadžići BIH 84 C3
Hægebostad N 33 D4
Hægeland N 33 D4
Hafnarfjörður IS 111 C4
Hafnir IS 111 D3
Hafslo N 32 A4
Haganj HR 74 C1
Hagby S 40 C6
Hage D 43 B4
Hagen, *Niedersachsen* D 43 B5
Hagen, *Nordrhein-Westfalen* D 50 B3
Hagenbach D 61 A4
Hagenow D 44 B3
Hagetmau F 76 C2
Hagfors S 34 B5
Häggenås S 115 D11
Hagondange F 60 A2
Hagsta S 36 B4
Haguenau F 60 B3
Hahnbach D 62 A2
Hahnslätten D 50 C4
Hahót H 74 B1
Haiger D 50 C4
Haigerloch D 61 B4
Hailsham GB 31 D4
Hainburg A 64 B2
Hainfeld A 64 B1
Hainichen D 52 C3
Hajdúböszörmény H 10 C6
Hajdučica SRB 75 C5
Hajdúszoboszló H 75 A6
Hajnáčka SK 65 B5
Hajnówka PL 6 E7
Hajós H 75 B4
Håkafot S 115 C11
Hakkas S 113 F10
Håksberg S 36 B2
Halaszi H 64 C3
Halberstadt D 52 B1
Halberton GB 29 C4
Hald Ege DK 39 C2
Haldem D 43 C5
Halden N 35 C3
Haldensleben D 52 A1
Halenbeck D 44 B4
Halesowen GB 26 C3
Halesworth GB 30 B5
Halfing D 62 C3
Halhjem N 32 B2
Håliden S 34 B5
Halifax GB 27 B4
Häljelöt S 37 D3
Halkida GR 116 D5
Halkirk GB 23 C5
Hall S 37 E5
Hall in Tirol A 71 A6
Hälla S 115 D14
Hallabro S 41 C5
Hällabrottet S 37 C2
Halland GB 31 D4
Hällaryd, *Blekinge* S 41 C4
Hallaryd, *Kronoberg* S 40 C3
Hällberga S 37 C3
Hällbybrunn S 37 C3
Halle B 49 C5
Halle, *Nordrhein-Westfalen* D 51 A4
Halle, *Sachsen-Anhalt* D 52 B1
Hålleberga S 40 C5
Hällefors S 36 C1
Hälleforsnäs S 37 C3
Hallein A 62 C4
Hällekis S 35 D5
Hallen, *Jämtland* S 115 D11
Hållen, *Uppsala* S 36 B4
Hallenberg D 51 B4
Hällestad S 37 D2
Hällevadsholm S 35 D3
Hällevik S 41 C4
Hälleviksstrand S 35 D3
Hallingby N 34 B2
Hallingeberg S 40 B6
Hallingen N 32 B6
Hällnäs, *Norrbotten* S 115 A15
Hällnäs, *Uppsala* S 36 B4
Hällnäs, *Västerbotten* S 115 C16
Hallormsstaður IS 111 B11
Hallsberg S 37 C2
Hållsta S 37 C3
Hallstahammar S 37 C3
Hallstatt A 72 A3
Hallstavik S 36 B5
Halltorp S 40 C6
Halluin F 49 C4
Hallviken S 115 D12
Hallworthy GB 28 C3
Halmstad S 40 C2
Hals DK 38 B3
Halsa N 114 D5
Halstead GB 31 C4
Haltdalen N 114 E8
Haltern D 50 B3
Haltwhistle GB 25 D5
Halvarsgårdarna S 36 B2
Halver D 50 B3
Halvrimmen DK 38 B2
Ham F 59 A4
Hamar N 34 B3
Hamarhaug N 32 B2
Hamarøy N 112 D4
Hambach F 60 A3
Hambergen D 43 B5
Hambergsund S 35 D3
Hambledon GB 31 D2
Hambuhren D 44 C1
Hamburg D 44 B2
Hamdibey TR 118 C2
Hamdorf D 43 A6
Hämeenlinna FIN 3 F26
Hameln = Hamlin D 51 A5
Hamersleben D 52 A1
Hamidiye TR 118 C5
Hamilton GB 24 C3
Hamina FIN 7 A9
Hamlagrø N 32 B3
Hamlin = Hameln D 51 A5
Hamm D 50 B3
Hammar S 37 D1
Hammarland FIN 36 B6
Hammarö S 35 C5
Hammarstrand S 115 D13
Hamme B 49 B5
Hammel DK 39 C2
Hammelburg D 51 C5
Hammelspring D 45 B5
Hammenhög S 41 D4
Hammerdal S 115 D12
Hammerfest N 113 B12
Hammershøj DK 38 C2
Hammerum DK 39 C2
Hamminkeln D 50 B2
Hamnavoe GB 22 A7
Hamneda S 40 C3
Hamningberg N 113 B19
Hamoir B 49 C6
Hamont B 49 B6
Hámor H 65 B6
Hamra, *Gävleborg* S 115 F12
Hamra, *Gotland* S 37 F5
Hamrångefjärden S 36 B4
Hamstreet GB 31 C4
Hamsund N 112 D4
Han CG 84 D3
Han TR 118 C5
Han i Hotit AL 105 A5
Han Knežica BIH 83 A5
Han Pijesak BIH 84 B3
Hanaskog S 41 C4
Hanau D 51 C4
Händelöp S 40 B6
Handlová SK 65 B4
Hanerau-Hademarschen D 43 A6
Hånger S 40 B3
Hanhimaa FIN 113 E14
Hanken S 37 D1
Hankensbüttel D 44 C2
Hanko FIN 6 B7
Hannover D 43 C6
Hannut B 49 C6
Hansnes N 112 C8
Hanstedt D 44 B2
Hanstholm DK 38 B1
Hantsavichy BY 7 E9
Hanušovice CZ 54 C1
Haparanda S 3 D26
Haradok BY 7 D10
Harads S 3 C24
Häradsbäck S 40 C4
Häradsbygden S 36 B2
Harbo S 36 B4
Harboør DK 38 C1
Harburg, *Bayern* D 62 B1
Harburg, *Hamburg* D 44 B1
Hårby DK 39 D3
Harc H 74 B3
Hardegarijp NL 42 B2
Hardegsen D 51 B5
Hardelot Plage F 48 C2
Hardenbeck D 45 B5
Hardenberg NL 42 C3
Harderwijk NL 42 C2
Hardheim D 61 A5
Hardt D 61 B4
Hareid N 114 E3
Haren D 43 C4
Haren NL 42 B3
Harestua N 34 B2
Harfleur F 57 A6
Harg S 36 B5
Hargicourt F 49 D4
Hargnies F 49 C5
Hargshamn S 36 B5
Härja S 40 A3
Harkány H 74 C3
Härkeberga S 37 C4
Harkebrügge D 43 B4
Harlech GB 26 C1
Harleston GB 30 B5
Hårlev DK 41 D2
Harlingen NL 42 B2
Harlösa S 41 D3
Harlow GB 31 C4
Harmancık TR 118 C4
Harmånger S 115 F14
Härnevi S 37 C4
Härnösand S 115 E14
Haro E 89 B4
Haroldswick GB 22 A8
Háromfa H 74 B2
Haroué F 60 B2
Harpenden GB 31 C3
Harplinge S 40 C2
Harpstedt D 43 C5
Harrogate GB 27 A4
Harrow GB 31 C3
Härryda S 40 B2
Harsefeld D 43 B6
Harsewinkel D 50 B4
Hârşova RO 11 D9
Harstad N 112 D5
Harsum D 51 A5
Harsvik N 114 C7
Harta H 75 B4
Hartberg A 73 A5
Hartburn GB 25 C6
Hartennes F 59 A4
Hartest GB 30 B4
Hartha D 52 B2
Hartland GB 28 C3
Hartlepool GB 27 A4
Hartmanice CZ 63 A4
Hartmannsdorf A 73 A5
Harvassdal N 115 B11
Harwell GB 31 C2
Harwich GB 31 C5
Harzgerode D 52 B1
Häselgehr A 71 A5
Haselünne D 43 C4
Hasköy TR 118 A1
Haslach D 61 B4
Haslach an der Mühl A 63 B5
Hasle DK 41 D4
Haslemere GB 31 C3
Haslev DK 39 D4
Hasloch D 61 A5
Hasparren F 76 C1
Hassela S 115 E13
Hasselfelde D 51 B6
Hasselfors S 37 C1
Hasselt B 49 C6
Hasselt NL 42 C3
Hassfurt D 51 C6
Hassleben D 45 B5
Hässleholm S 41 C3
Hasslö S 41 C5
Hassloch D 61 A4
Hästbo S 36 B4
Hastersboda FIN 36 B7
Hästholmen S 37 D1
Hastière-Lavaux B 49 C5
Hastigrow GB 23 C5
Hastings GB 31 D4
Hästveda S 41 C3
Hasvik N 113 B11
Hatfield, *Hertfordshire* GB 31 C3
Hatfield, *South Yorkshire* GB 27 B5
Hatherleigh GB 28 C3
Hathersage GB 27 B4
Hatlestrand N 32 B2
Hattem NL 42 C3
Hatten D 43 B5
Hatten F 60 B3
Hattfjelldal N 115 B10
Hatting DK 39 D2
Hattingen D 50 B3
Hattstadt F 60 B3
Hattstedt D 43 A6
Hatvan H 65 C5
Hatvik N 32 B2
Hau D 50 B2
Haudainville F 59 A6
Hauganes IS 111 B7
Haugastøl N 32 B4
Hauge N 33 D3
Haugesund N 33 C2
Haughom N 33 D3
Haugsdal N 32 B2
Haugsdorf A 64 B2
Haukedal N 32 A3
Haukeland N 32 B2
Haukeligrend N 33 C4
Haukeliseter N 32 C4
Haukipudas FIN 3 D26
Haulerwijk NL 42 B3
Haunersdorf D 62 B3
Haus N 32 B2
Hausach D 61 B4
Hausham D 62 C2
Hausmannstätten A 73 B5
Hausvik N 33 D3
Haut-Fays B 49 C6
Hautajärvi FIN 113 F18
Hautefort F 67 C6
Hauterives F 69 C5
Hauteville-Lompnès F 69 C5
Hautmont F 49 C4
Hautrage B 49 C4
Hauzenberg D 63 B4
Havant GB 31 D3
Havdhem S 37 E5
Havdrup DK 39 D5
Havelange B 49 C6
Havelberg D 44 C4
Havelte NL 42 C3
Haverfordwest GB 28 B3
Haverhill GB 30 B4
Havering GB 31 C4
Håverud S 35 D4
Havířov CZ 65 A4
Havixbeck D 50 B3

Havlíčkův Brod CZ 63 A6
Havndal DK 38 C3
Havneby DK 39 D1
Havnebyen DK 39 D4
Havnsø DK 39 D4
Havøysund N 113 A13
Havran TR 118 C2
Havrebjerg DK 39 D4
Havsa TR 118 A1
Havstenssund S 35 D3
Havza TR 16 A7
Hawes GB 26 A3
Hawick GB 25 C5
Hawkhurst GB 31 C4
Hawkinge GB 31 C5
Haxey GB 27 B5
Hay-on-Wye GB 29 A4
Hayange F 60 A2
Haydarlı TR 119 D5
Haydon Bridge GB 25 D5
Hayle GB 28 C2
Haymana TR 118 C7
Hayrabolu TR 118 A2
Haysyn UA 11 B10
Hayvoron UA 11 B10
Haywards Heath GB 31 D3
Hazebrouck F 48 C3
Hazlov CZ 52 C2
Heacham GB 30 B4
Headcorn GB 31 C4
Headford IRL 20 A2
Heanor GB 27 B4
Héas F 76 D3
Heathfield GB 31 D4
Hebden Bridge GB 26 B3
Heberg S 40 C2
Heby S 36 C3
Hechingen D 61 B4
Hechlingen D 62 B1
Hecho E 76 D2
Hechtel B 49 B6
Hechthausen D 43 B6
Heckelberg D 45 C5
Heckington GB 27 C5
Hecklingen D 52 B1
Hed S 37 C2
Hedalen N 34 B1
Hedared S 40 B2
Heddal N 33 C6
Hédé F 57 B4
Hede S 115 E10
Hedekas S 35 D3
Hedemora S 36 B2
Hedensted DK 39 D2
Hedersleben D 52 B1
Hedesunda S 36 B4
Hedge End GB 31 D2
Hedon GB 27 B5
Heede D 43 C4
Heek D 50 A3
Heemstede NL 42 C1
Heerde NL 42 C3
's-Heerenberg NL 50 B2
Heerenveen NL 42 C2
Heerhugowaard NL 42 C1
Heerlen NL 50 C1
Heeze NL 49 B6
Heggenes N 32 A6
Hegra N 114 D8
Hegyeshalom H 64 C3
Hegyközség H 74 A1
Heia N 114 C9
Heide D 43 A6
Heidelberg D 61 A4
Heiden D 50 B2
Heidenau D 53 C3
Heidenheim D 61 B6
Heidenreichstein A 63 B6
Heikendorf D 44 A2
Heilam GB 22 C4
Heiland N 33 D5
Heilbad Heiligenstadt D 51 B6
Heilbronn D 61 A5
Heiligenblut A 72 A2
Heiligendamn D 44 A3
Heiligendorf D 44 C2
Heiligengrabe D 44 B4
Heiligenhafen D 44 A2
Heiligenhaus D 50 B2
Heiligenkreuz A 73 B6
Heiligenstadt D 62 A2
Heiloo NL 42 C1
Heilsbronn D 62 A1
Heim N 114 D6
Heimburg D 51 B6
Heimdal N 114 D7
Heinerscheid L 50 C2
Heinersdorf D 45 C6
Heining D 63 B4
Heiningen D 61 B5
Heinola FIN 3 F27
Heinsberg D 50 B2
Heist-op-den-Berg B 49 B5
Hejde S 37 E5
Hejdeby S 37 E5
Hejls DK 39 D2
Hejnice CZ 53 C5
Hel PL 47 A4
Helchteren B 49 B6
Heldburg D 51 C6
Heldrungen D 52 B1
Helechosa E 94 C2
Helensburgh GB 24 B3
Helfenberg A 63 B5
Helgen N 33 C6
Helgeroa N 35 D1
Hella IS 111 D5
Hella N 32 A3
Helland N 112 D5
Hellas S 35 D4
Helle N 33 D3
Helleland N 33 D3
Hellendoorn NL 42 C3
Hellenthal D 50 C2
Hellesøy N 32 B1
Hellesylt N 114 E3
Hellevoetsluis NL 49 B5
Helligskogen N 112 C9
Hellín E 101 A4
Hellissandur IS 111 C2
Hellnar IS 111 C2
Hellum DK 38 B3
Hellvi S 37 E5
Hellvik N 33 D2
Helm-brechts D 52 C1
Helmond NL 49 B6
Helmsdale GB 23 C5
Helmsley GB 27 A4
Helmstedt D 51 A6
Hel'pa SK 65 B5
Helsa D 51 B5
Helsby GB 26 B3
Helsingborg S 41 C2
Helsinge DK 41 C2
Helsingør DK 41 C2
Helsinki FIN 6 A8
Helston GB 28 C2
Hemau D 62 A2
Hemavan S 115 B12
Hemel Hempstead GB 31 C3
Hemer D 50 B3
Héming F 60 B2
Hemmet DK 39 D1
Hemmingstedt D 43 A6
Hemmoor D 43 B6
Hemnes N 35 C3
Hemnesberget N 115 A10
Hemse S 37 E5
Hemsedal N 32 B5
Hemslingen D 43 B6
Hemsworth GB 27 B4
Hen N 34 B2
Henån S 35 D3
Hendaye F 76 C1
Hendek TR 118 B5
Hendungen D 51 C6
Henfield GB 31 D3
Hengelo, *Gelderland* NL 50 A2
Hengelo, *Overijssel* NL 50 A2
Hengersberg D 62 B4
Hengoed GB 29 B4
Hénin-Beaumont F 48 C3
Henley-on-Thames GB 31 C3
Hennan S 115 E12
Henne Strand DK 39 D1
Henneberg D 51 C6
Hennebont F 56 C2
Hennigsdorf D 45 C5
Hennset N 114 D5
Hennstedt, *Schleswig-Holstein* D 43 A6
Hennstedt, *Schleswig-Holstein* D 43 A6
Henrichemont F 68 A2
Henryków PL 54 C2
Henrykowo PL 47 A6
Hensås N 32 A5
Henstedt-Ulzburg D 44 B1
Heppenheim D 61 A4
Herad, *Buskerud* N 32 B6
Herad, *Vest-Agder* N 33 D3
Heradsbygd N 34 B3
Heraklion = Iraklio GR 117 G7
Herálec CZ 64 A2
Herand N 32 B3
Herbault F 58 C2
Herbern D 50 B3
Herbertstown IRL 20 B3
Herbeumont B 59 A6
Herbignac F 66 A2
Herbisse F 59 B5
Herbitzheim F 60 A3
Herbolzheim D 60 B3
Herborn D 50 C4
Herbrechtingen D 61 B6
Herby PL 54 C3
Herceg-Novi CG 105 A4
Hercegovać HR 74 C2
Hercegovacka Goleša SRB 85 C4
Hercegszántó H 75 C3
Herchen D 50 C3
Heréd H 65 C5
Hereford GB 29 A5
Herefoss N 33 D5
Hereke TR 118 B4
Herencia E 95 C3
Herend H 74 A2
Herent B 49 C5
Herentals B 49 B5
Hérépian F 78 C2
Herfølge DK 41 D2
Herford D 51 A4
Herguijuela E 93 B5
Héric F 66 A3
Héricourt F 60 C2
Héricourt-en-Caux F 58 A1
Hérimoncourt F 70 A1
Heringsdorf D 44 A3
Herisau CH 71 A4
Hérisson F 68 B2
Herk-de-Stad B 49 C6
Herlufmagle DK 39 D4
Hermagor A 72 B3
Hermannsburg D 44 C2
Hermansverk N 32 A3
Heřmanův Městec CZ 53 D5
Herment F 68 C2
Hermeskeil D 60 A2
Hermisende E 87 C4
Hermonville F 59 A4
Hermsdorf D 52 C1
Hernani E 76 C1
Hernansancho E 94 B2
Herne D 50 B3
Herne Bay GB 31 C5
Hernes N 34 B3
Herning DK 39 C1
Herøya N 35 C1
Herramelluri E 89 B3
Herräng S 36 B5
Herre N 33 C6
Herrenberg D 61 B4
Herrera E 100 B1
Herrera de Alcántara E 92 B3
Herrera de los Navarros E 90 B1
Herrera de Pisuerga E 88 B2
Herrera del Duque E 94 C1
Herrerias E 98 B3
Herreros del Suso E 94 B1
Herrestad S 35 D3
Herrhamra S 37 D4
Herritslev DK 44 A3
Herrlisheim F 60 B3
Herrljunga S 40 A3
Herrnhut D 53 B4
Herrsching D 62 B2
Hersbruck D 62 A2
Hersby S 37 C5
Herscheid D 50 B3
Herselt B 49 B5
Herso GR 116 A4
Herstal B 49 C6
Herstmonceux GB 31 D4
Herten D 50 B3
Hertford GB 31 C3
's-Hertogenbosch NL 49 B6
Hervás E 93 A5
Hervik N 33 C2
Herxheim D 61 A4
Herzberg, *Brandenburg* D 45 C4
Herzberg, *Brandenburg* D 52 B3
Herzberg, *Niedersachsen* D 51 B6
Herzebrock D 50 B4
Herzfelde D 45 C5
Herzlake D 43 C4
Herzogen-aurach D 62 A1
Herzogenbuchsee CH 70 A2
Herzogenburg A 63 B6
Herzsprung D 44 B4
Hesby N 33 C2
Hesdin F 48 C3
Hesel D 43 B4
Heskestad N 33 D3
Hessdalen N 114 E8
Hesselager DK 39 D3
Hesseng N 113 C18
Hessisch Lichtenau D 51 B5
Hessisch-Oldendorf D 51 A5
Hestra S 40 B3
Heswall GB 26 B2
Hetlevik N 32 B2
Hettange-Grande F 60 A2
Hetton-le-Hole GB 25 D6
Hettstedt D 52 B1
Heuchin F 48 C3
Heudicourt-sous-les-Côtes F 60 B1
Heunezel F 60 B2
Heuqueville F 57 A6
Heves H 65 C6
Héviz H 74 B2
Hexham GB 25 D5
Heysham GB 26 A3
Heytesbury GB 29 B5
Hidas H 74 B3
Hieflau A 63 C5
Hiendelaencina E 95 A4
Hiersac F 67 C5
High Bentham GB 26 A3
High Hesket GB 25 D5
High Wycombe GB 31 C3
Highclere GB 31 C2
Highley GB 26 C3
Higuera de Arjona E 100 B2
Higuera de Calatrava E 100 B1
Higuera de la Serena E 93 C5
Higuera de la Sierra E 99 B4
Higuera de Vargas E 93 C4
Higuera la Real E 99 A4
Higuera de Llerena E 93 C4
Higueruela E 96 C1
Híjar E 90 B2
Hilchenbach D 50 B4
Hildburghausen D 51 C6
Hilden D 50 B2
Hilders D 51 C5
Hildesheim D 51 A5
Hilgay GB 30 B4
Hillared S 40 B3
Hille D 51 A4
Hillegom NL 49 A5
Hillerød DK 41 D2
Hillerstorp S 40 B3
Hillesheim D 50 C2
Hillestad N 35 C2
Hillmersdorf D 52 B3
Hillsborough GB 19 B5
Hillswick GB 22 A7
Hilpoltstein D 62 A2
Hiltpoltstein D 62 A2
Hilvarenbeek NL 49 B6
Hilversum NL 49 A6
Himarë AL 116 B1
Himbergen D 44 B2
Himesháza H 74 B3
Himmelberg A 73 B4
Himmelpforten D 43 B6
Himód H 74 A2
Hinckley GB 30 B2
Hindås S 40 B2
Hindelang D 71 A5
Hindelbank CH 70 A2
Hinderavåg N 33 C2
Hindhead GB 31 C3
Hinojosa del Valle E 93 C4
Hinnerup DK 39 C3
Hinneryd S 40 C3
Hinojal E 93 B4
Hinojales E 99 B4
Hinojos E 99 B4
Hinojosa del Duque E 93 C5
Hinojosas de Calatrava E 100 A1
Hinterhornbach A 71 A5
Hinterriss A 71 A6
Hintersee A 63 C4
Hintersee D 45 B6
Hinterstoder A 63 C5
Hintertux A 72 A1
Hinterweidenthal D 60 A3
Hinwil CH 70 A3
Hios GR 116 D8
Hippolytushoef NL 42 C1
Hirschaid D 62 A1
Hirschau D 62 A2
Hirschfeld D 53 B3
Hirschhorn D 61 A4
Hirsingue F 60 C3
Hirson F 59 A5
Hirtshals DK 38 B2
Hirzenhain D 51 C5
Hisarcık TR 118 C4
Hishult S 41 C3
Hitchin GB 31 C3
Hitra N 114 D5
Hittarp S 41 C2
Hittisau A 71 A4
Hittun N 32 A1
Hitzacker D 44 B3
Hjallerup DK 38 B3
Hjällstad S 34 B5
Hjältevad S 40 B5
Hjärnarp S 41 C2
Hjartdal N 33 C5
Hjellestad N 32 B2
Hjelmeland N 33 C3
Hjelset N 114 E4
Hjerkinn N 114 E6
Hjerm DK 38 C1
Hjerpsted DK 39 D1
Hjerting DK 39 D1
Hjo S 35 D6
Hjordkær DK 39 D2
Hjørring DK 38 B2
Hjorted S 40 B6
Hjortkvarn S 37 D2
Hjortnäs S 36 B1
Hjortsberga S 40 C4
Hjukse N 33 C6
Hjuksebø N 33 C6
Hjulsjö S 36 C1
Hliník nad Hronom. SK 65 B4
Hlinsko CZ 64 A1
Hlío IS 111 A10
Hlohovec SK 64 B3
Hluboká nad Vltavou CZ 63 A5
Hlučín CZ 64 A4
Hlukhiv UA 7 F12
Hlyboka UA 11 B8
Hlybokaye BY 7 D9
Hniezdne SK 65 A6
Hnilec SK 65 B6
Hnúšťa SK 65 B5
Hobol H 74 B2
Hobro DK 38 C2
Hobscheid L 60 A1
Hocalar TR 119 D4
Hochdonn D 43 A6
Hochdorf CH 70 A3
Hochfelden F 60 B3
Hochspeyer D 60 A3
Höchst im Odenwald D 61 A5
Höchstadt, *Bayern* D 62 A1
Höchstädt, *Bayern* D 61 B6
Hochstenbach D 50 C3
Höckendorf D 52 C3
Hockenheim D 61 A4
Hoddesdon GB 31 C3
Hodejov SK 65 B5
Hodenhagen D 43 C6
Hodkovice CZ 53 C5
Hódmezővásárhely H 75 B5
Hodnet GB 26 C3
Hodonín CZ 64 B3
Hodslavice CZ 64 A4
Hoedekenskerke NL 49 B4
Hoegaarden B 49 C5
Hoek van Holland NL 49 B5
Hoenderlo NL 50 A1
Hof D 52 C1
Hof N 35 C2
Hofbieber D 51 C5
Hoff GB 26 A3
Hofgeismar D 51 B5
Hofheim, *Bayern* D 51 C6
Hofheim, *Hessen* D 51 C4
Hofkirchen im Mühlkreis A 63 B4
Höfn IS 111 C10
Hofors S 36 B3
Hofsós IS 111 B6
Hofstad N 114 C7
Höganäs S 41 C2
Högbo S 36 B3
Hogdal S 35 C3
Høgebru N 32 A4
Högfors S 36 C2
Högklint S 37 E5
Högsäter S 35 D4
Högsby S 40 B6
Högsjö S 37 C2
Hogstad S 37 D2
Hőgyész H 74 B3
Hohen Neuendorf D 45 C5
Hohenau A 64 B2
Hohenberg A 63 C6
Hohenbucko D 52 B3
Hohenburg D 62 A2
Hohendorf D 45 A4
Hohenems A 71 A4
Hohenhameln D 51 A6
Hohenhausen D 51 A4
Hohenkirchen D 43 B4
Hohenlinden D 62 B2
Hohenlockstedt D 43 B6
Hohenmölsen D 52 B2
Hohennauen D 44 C4
Hohenseeden D 52 A2
Hohentauern A 73 A4
Hohentengen D 70 A3
Hohenwepel D 51 B5
Hohenwestedt D 43 A6
Hohenwutzen D 45 C6
Hohenzieritz D 45 B5
Hohn D 43 A6
Hohne D 44 C2
Hohnstorf D 44 B2
Højer DK 39 E1
Højslev Stby DK 38 C2
Hok S 40 B4
Hökerum S 40 B3
Hökhuvud S 36 B5
Hokksund N 34 C1
Hökön S 40 C4
Hol N 32 B5
Hola Pristan UA 11 C12
Hólar IS 111 B6
Holbæk, *Aarhus Amt.* DK 38 C3
Holbæk, *Vestsjællands Amt.* DK 39 D4
Holbeach GB 30 B4
Holdenstedt D 44 C2
Holdhus N 32 B2
Holdorf D 43 C5
Holeby DK 44 A3
Hølen N 35 C2
Hølervasseter N 32 B6
Holešov CZ 64 A3
Holguera E 93 B4
Holíč SK 64 B3
Holice CZ 53 C5
Holice SK 64 C3
Höljes S 34 B4
Hollabrunn A 64 B2
Hollandstoun GB 23 B6
Høllen N 33 D4
Hollfeld D 52 D1
Hollstadt D 51 C6
Hollum NL 42 B2
Höllviksnäs S 41 D2
Holm N 114 B9
Hólmavík IS 111 B4
Holmbukt N 113 B10
Holme-on-Spalding-Moor GB 27 B5
Holmedal S 35 C3
Holmegil N 35 C3
Holmen N 34 B2
Holmes Chapel GB 26 B3
Holmestrand N 35 C2
Holmfirth GB 27 B4
Holmfoss N 113 C19
Holmsbu N 35 C2
Holmsjö S 41 C5
Holmsund S 3 E24
Holmsveden S 36 A3
Holmudden S 37 E6
Hölö S 37 C4
Holøydal N 114 E8
Holsbybrunn S 40 B5
Holseter N 34 A1
Holsljunga S 40 B2
Holstebro DK 39 C1
Holsted DK 39 D1
Holsworthy GB 28 C3
Holt D 39 E2
Holt, *Norfolk* GB 30 B5
Holt, *Wrexham* GB 26 B3
Holt IS 111 D6
Holt N 33 D5
Holten NL 50 A2
Holtwick D 50 A3
Holum N 33 D4
Holwerd NL 42 B2
Holycross IRL 21 B4
Holyhead GB 26 B1
Holýšov CZ 62 A4
Holywell GB 26 B2
Holywood GB 19 B6
Holzdorf D 52 B3
Holzhausen D 51 A4
Holzheim D 61 B6
Holzkirchen D 62 C2
Holzminden D 51 B5
Holzthaleben D 51 B6
Homberg, *Hessen* D 51 B5
Homberg, *Hessen* D 51 C5
Homburg D 60 A3
Hommelstø N 115 B9
Hommersåk N 33 D2
Homokmegy H 75 B4
Homokszentgyörgy H 74 B2
Homrogd H 65 B6
Homyel = Gomel BY 7 E11
Honaz TR 119 E4
Hondarribia E 76 C1
Hondón de los Frailes E 101 A5
Hondschoote F 48 C3
Hönebach D 51 C5
Hønefoss N 34 B2
Honfleur F 57 A6
Høng DK 39 D4
Honiton GB 29 C4
Hönningen D 50 C2
Honningsvåg N 113 B14
Hönö S 38 B4
Honrubia E 95 C4
Hontalbilla E 88 C2
Hontheim D 50 C2
Hontianske-Nemce SK 65 B4
Hontoria de la Cantera E 88 B3
Hontoria de Valdearados E 89 C3
Hontoria del Pinar E 89 C3
Hoofddorp NL 49 A5
Hoogerheide NL 49 B5
Hoogeveen NL 42 C3
Hoogezand-Sappemeer NL 42 B3
Hoogkarspel NL 42 C2
Hoogkerk NL 42 B3
Hoogstede D 42 C3
Hoogstraten B 49 B5
Hook GB 31 C3
Hooksiel D 43 B5
Höör S 41 D3
Hoorn NL 42 C2
Hope GB 26 B2
Hope under Dinmore GB 29 A5
Hopen N 112 E4
Hopfgarten A 72 A2
Hopfgarten in Defereggen A 72 B2
Hopseidet N 113 B16
Hopsten D 43 C4
Hoptrup DK 39 D2
Hora Svatého Sebestiána CZ 52 C3
Horaždóvice CZ 63 A4
Horb am Neckar D 61 B4
Horbelev DK 39 E5
Hørby DK 38 B3
Hörby S 41 D3
Horcajada de la Torre E 95 B4
Horcajo de los Montes E 94 C2
Horcajo de Santiago E 95 C3
Horcajo-Medianero E 93 A5
Horche E 95 B3
Horda S 40 B4
Hordabø N 32 B1
Hordalia N 32 C3
Hordvik N 32 B2
Hořesedly CZ 52 C3
Horezu RO 11 D8
Horgen CH 70 A3
Horgoš SRB 75 B4
Hořice CZ 53 C5
Horjul SLO 73 B4
Horka D 53 B4
Hörken S 36 B1
Horki BY 7 D11
Hörle S 40 B4
Horn A 63 B6
Horn D 51 B4
Horn N 34 B2
Horn S 40 B5
Horna E 101 A4
Horná Mariková SK 64 A4
Horná Streda SK 64 B3
Horná Štrubna SK 65 B4
Horná Súča SK 64 B3
Hornachos E 93 C4
Hornachuelos E 99 B5
Hornanes N 32 C2
Hornbæk, *Aarhus Amt.* DK 38 C2
Hornbæk, *Frederiksværk* DK 41 C2
Hornberg D 61 B4
Hornburg D 51 A6
Horncastle GB 27 B5
Horndal S 36 B3
Horndean GB 31 D2
Horne, *Fyns Amt.* DK 39 D3
Horne, *Ribe Amt.* DK 39 D1
Hörnebo S 35 D6
Horneburg D 43 B6
Hörnefors S 115 D16
Horní Bečva CZ 64 A4
Horni Benešov CZ 64 A3
Horni Cerekev CZ 63 A6
Horní Jiřetín CZ 52 C3
Horní Lomná CZ 65 A4
Horní Maršov CZ 53 C5
Horní Planá CZ 63 B5
Horni Slavkov CZ 52 C2
Horni Vltavice CZ 63 B4
Hornindal N 114 F3
Hørning DK 39 C3
Hörningsholm S 37 C4
Hornnes N 33 D4
Horno D 53 B4
Hornos E 101 A3
Hornoy-le-Bourg F 58 A2
Hornsea GB 27 B5
Hornsjø N 34 A2
Hornslet DK 39 C3
Hornstein A 64 C2
Hörnum D 39 E1
Hornum DK 38 C2
Horný Tisovník SK 65 B5
Horodenka UA 11 B8
Horodnya UA 7 F11
Horodok, *Khmelnytskyy* UA 11 B9
Horodok, *Lviv* UA 11 B7
Horodyshche UA 11 B11
Horokhiv UA 11 A8
Horovice CZ 63 A4
Horred S 40 B2
Hörröd S 41 D4
Hörsching A 63 B5
Horsens DK 39 D2
Horsham GB 31 C3
Hørsholm DK 41 D2
Horslunde DK 39 E4
Horšovský Týn CZ 62 A3
Horst NL 50 B2
Horstel D 50 A3
Horsten D 43 B4
Horstmar D 50 A3
Hort H 65 C5
Horta P 87 C3
Horten N 35 C2
Hortezuela E 89 C4
Hortiguela E 89 B3
Hortobágy H 75 A6
Horton in Ribblesdale GB 26 A3
Hørve DK 39 D4
Hörvik S 41 C4
Horwich GB 26 B3
Hosanger N 32 B2
Hösbach D 51 C5
Hosena D 53 B4
Hosenfeld D 51 C5
Hosingen L 50 C2
Hospental CH 70 B3
Hospital IRL 20 B3
Hossegor F 76 C1
Hosszuhetény H 74 B3
Hostal de Ipiés E 90 A2
Hoštálkova CZ 64 A3
Hostalric E 91 B5
Hostens F 76 B2
Hostěradice CZ 64 B2
Hostinné CZ 53 C5
Hostomice CZ 63 A5
Hostouň CZ 62 A3
Hotagen S 115 D11
Hoting S 115 C13
Hotolicht AL 116 A2
Hotton B 49 C6
Houdain F 48 C3
Houdan F 58 B2
Houdelaincourt F 60 B1
Houeillès F 76 B3
Houffalize B 50 C1
Houghton-le-Spring GB 25 D6
Houlberg DK 39 C2
Houlgate F 57 A5
Hounslow GB 31 C3
Hourtin F 66 C3
Hourtin-Plage F 66 C3
Houthalen B 49 B6
Houyet B 49 C5
Hov DK 39 D3
Hov N 34 B2
Hova S 35 D6
Høvåg N 33 D5
Hovborg DK 39 D1
Hovda N 32 B6
Hovden N 33 C4
Hove GB 31 D3
Hovedgård DK 39 D2
Hovelhof D 51 B4
Hoven DK 39 D1
Hovet N 32 B5
Hovingham GB 27 A5
Hovmantorp S 40 C5
Hovsta S 37 C2
Howden GB 27 B5
Howe D 44 B2
Höxter D 51 B5
Hoya D 43 C6
Hoya de Santa Maria E 99 B4
Hoya-Gonzalo E 95 D5
Høyanger N 32 A3
Hoyerswerda D 53 B4
Høyjord N 35 C2
Hoylake GB 26 B2
Høylandet N 114 C9
Hoym D 52 B1
Høymyr N 32 C6
Hoyo de Manzanares E 94 B3
Hoyo de Pinares E 94 B2
Hoyocasero E 94 B2
Hoyos E 93 A4
Hoyos del Espino E 93 A5
Hrabusiče SK 65 B6
Hradec Králové CZ 53 C5
Hradec nad Moravicí CZ 64 A3
Hrádek CZ 64 B2
Hrádek nad Nisou CZ 53 C4
Hradište SK 65 B4
Hrafnagil IS 111 B7
Hrafnseyri IS 111 B2
Hranice, *Severomoravsky* CZ 64 A3
Hranice, *Západočeský* CZ 52 C2
Hranovnica SK 65 B6
Hrasnica BIH 84 C3
Hrastnik SLO 73 B5
Hrebenka UA 11 A12
Hřensko CZ 53 C4
Hriňová SK 65 B5
Hrisoupoli GR 116 B6
Hrochov CZ 64 A2
Hrochův Tynec CZ 53 D5
Hrodna BY 6 E7
Hrodzyanka BY 7 E10
Hronov CZ 53 C6
Hronský Beňadik SK 65 B4
Hrotovice CZ 64 A2
Hrtkovci SRB 85 B4
Hrun IS 111 A5
Hrušov SK 65 B5
Hrušovany nad Jevišovkou CZ 64 B2
Hřuštin SK 65 A5
Hrvaćani BIH 84 B2
Hrvace HR 83 C5
Hrymayliv UA 11 B9
Huben A 72 B2
Hückel-hoven D 50 B2
Hückeswagen D 50 B3
Hucknall GB 27 B4
Hucqueliers F 48 C2
Huddersfield GB 27 B4
Huddinge S 37 C4
Huddunge S 36 B3
Hude D 43 B5
Hudiksvall S 115 F14
Huélago E 100 B2
Huélamo E 95 B5
Huelgoat F 56 B2
Huelma E 100 B2
Huelva E 99 B4
Huéneja E 100 B3
Huércal de Almeria E 101 B3
Huércal-Overa E 101 B4
Huerta de Abajo E 89 B3
Huerta de Valdecarabanos E 95 C3
Huerta del Rey E 89 C3
Huertahernando E 95 B4
Huesa E 100 B2
Huesca E 90 A2
Huéscar E 101 B3
Huete E 95 B4
Huétor Tájar E 100 B1
Hüfingen D 61 C4
Hufthamar N 32 B2
Hugh Town GB 28 D1
Huglfing D 62 C2
Huissen NL 50 B1
Huittinen FIN 3 F25
Huizen NL 49 A6
Hulín CZ 64 A3
Hüls D 50 B2
Hulsig DK 38 B3
Hulst NL 49 B5
Hult S 40 B5
Hulta S 40 A6
Hulteby S 35 C6
Hulterstad S 41 C6
Hultsfred S 40 B5
Humanes E 95 B3
Humberston GB 27 B5
Humble DK 39 E3
Humenné SK 10 B6
Humilladero E 100 B1
Humlebæk DK 41 D2
Humlum DK 38 C1
Hummelsta S 37 C3
Humpolec CZ 63 A6
Humshaugh GB 25 C5
Hundåla N 115 B9
Hundested DK 39 D4
Hundvåg N 33 C2
Hundvin N 32 B2
Hunedoara RO 11 D7
Hünfeld D 51 C5
Hungen D 51 C4
Hungerford GB 31 C2
Hunndalen N 34 B2
Hunnebostrand S 35 D3
Hunstanton GB 30 B4
Huntingdon GB 30 B3
Huntley GB 29 B5
Huntly GB 23 D6
Hünxe D 50 B2
Hurbanovo SK 64 C4
Hürbel D 61 B5
Hurdal N 34 B3
Hurezani RO 11 D7
Hurlford GB 24 C3

Kamień PL 55 B5
Kamień Krajeński PL 46 B3
Kamień Pomorski PL 45 B6
Kamieniec Zabk PL 54 C1
Kamienka SK 65 A6
Kamienna Góra PL 53 C6
Kamieńsk PL 55 B4
Kaminka UA 11 B12
Kamiros Skala GR 119 F2
Kamnik SLO 73 B4
Kamp-Lintfort D 50 B2
Kampen NL 42 C2
Kampinos PL 55 A5
Kampor HR 83 B3
Kamyanets-Podil's'kyy UA 11 B9
Kamyanka-Buz'ka UA 11 A8
Kamýk n Vltavou CZ 63 A5
Kanal SLO 72 B3
Kanalia GR 116 C4
Kandalaksha RUS 3 C30
Kandanos GR 117 G5
Kandel D 61 A4
Kandern D 60 C3
Kandersteg CH 70 B2
Kandila GR 117 E4
Kandıra TR 118 A5
Kandyty PL 47 A6
Kanfanar HR 82 A2
Kangasala FIN 3 F26
Kangos S 113 E11
Kangosjärvi FIN 113 E12
Kaninë AL 105 C5
Kaniów PL 53 B4
Kanjiža SRB 75 B5
Kankaanpää FIN 3 F25
Kannus FIN 3 E25
Kanturk IRL 20 B3
Kaonik SRB 85 C6
Kapaklı TR 118 A2
Kapellen A 63 C6
Kapellen B 49 B5
Kapellskär S 37 C6
Kapfenberg A 73 A5
Kapfenstein A 73 B5
Kaplice CZ 63 B5
Kapljuh BIH 83 B5
Kápolna H 65 C6
Kápolnásnyék H 74 A3
Kaposfö H 74 B2
Kaposfüred H 74 B2
Kaposszekcsö H 74 B3
Kaposvár H 74 B2
Kapp N 34 B2
Kappel D 60 B3
Kappeln D 44 A1
Kappelshamn S 37 E5
Kappl A 71 A5
Kappstad S 35 C5
Kaprun A 72 A2
Kaptol HR 74 C2
Kapuvár H 64 C3
Karaadilli TR 119 D5
Karabiğa TR 118 B2
Karabük TR 118 A7
Karaburun TR 118 D1
Karacabey TR 118 B3
Karacaköy TR 118 A3
Karacaören TR 119 D5
Karacasu TR 119 E3
Karachev RUS 7 E13
Karácsond H 65 C6
Karád H 74 B2
Karahallı TR 119 D4
Karaisali TR 16 C7
Karaman, *Balıkesir* TR 118 C3
Karaman, *Karaman* TR 16 C6
Karamanlı TR 119 E4
Karamürsel TR 118 B4
Karan SRB 85 C4
Karancslapujto H 65 B5
Karaova TR 119 E2
Karapınar TR 16 C6
Karasjok N 113 C14
Karasu TR 118 A5
Karataş, *Adana* TR 16 C7
Karataş, *Manisa* TR 119 D3
Karatoprak TR 119 E2
Karavostasi CY 120 A1
Kårbenning S 36 B3
Kårberg S 37 D1
Kårböle S 115 F12
Karbunara AL 105 C5
Karby D 44 A1
Karby DK 38 C1
Kårby, *Kalmar* S 40 B6
Karby, *Stockholm* S 37 C5
Karcag H 75 A5
Karczew PL 55 A6
Karczów PL 54 C2
Karczowiska PL 53 B6
Kardamena GR 119 F2
Kardamila GR 116 D8
Kardamili GR 117 F4
Kardašova Rečice CZ 63 A5
Kardis S 113 F12
Karditsa GR 116 C3
Kärdla EST 6 B7
Kardoskút H 75 B5
Karesuando S 113 D11
Kargı TR 16 A7
Kargowa PL 53 A5
Karigasniemi FIN 113 C14
Karise DK 41 D2
Karistos GR 117 D6
Karkkila FIN 6 A8
Karl Liebknecht RUS 7 F13
Karlholmsbruk S 36 B4
Karlino PL 46 A1
Karlobag HR 83 B4
Karlovac HR 73 C5
Karlovasi GR 119 E1
Karlovčic SRB 85 B5
Karlovice CZ 54 C2
Karlovo BG 11 E8
Karlovy Vary CZ 52 C2
Karłowice PL 54 C2
Karlsborg S 37 D1
Karlshamn S 41 C4
Karlshöfen D 43 B6
Karlshus N 35 C2
Karlskoga S 37 C1
Karlskrona S 41 C5
Karlsrud N 32 B5
Karlsruhe D 61 A4
Karlstad S 35 C5
Karlstadt D 51 D5
Karlstetten A 63 B6
Karlstift A 63 B5
Karlstorp S 40 B5
Karmacs H 74 B2
Karmin PL 54 B2
Kärna S 38 B4
Karnobat BG 11 E9
Karojba HR 72 C3
Karow D 44 B4
Karpacz PL 53 C5
Karpathos GR 119 G2
Karpenisi GR 116 D3
Karpuzlu TR 119 E2
Kärrbo S 37 C3
Karrebaeksminde DK 39 D4
Karshult S 40 B3
Karsin PL 46 B3
Kårsta S 37 C5
Karstädt D 44 B3
Kartal TR 118 B4
Kartitsch A 72 B2
Kartuzy PL 47 A4
Karup DK 39 C2
Karviná CZ 65 A4
Kås DK 38 B2
Kaş TR 119 F4
Kasaba TR 119 F4
Kašava CZ 64 A3
Kåseberga S 41 D4
Kasejovice CZ 63 A4
Kasfjord N 112 D5
Kashin RUS 7 C14
Kašina HR 73 C6
Kasina-Wielka PL 65 A6
Kaskinen FIN 3 E24
Kašperské Hory CZ 63 A4
Kassandrino GR 116 B5
Kassel D 51 B5
Kassiopi GR 116 C1
Kastamonu TR 16 A6
Kastav HR 73 C4
Kaštel-Stari HR 83 C5
Kaštel Zegarski HR 83 B4
Kasteli GR 117 G5
Kastellaun D 50 C3
Kastelli GR 117 G7
Kasterlee B 49 B5
Kastl D 62 A2
Kastlösa S 41 C6
Kastorf D 44 B2
Kastoria GR 116 B3
Kastorio GR 117 E4
Kastraki GR 117 F7
Kastrosikia GR 116 C2
Kastsyukovichy BY 7 E12
Kaszaper H 75 B5
Katakolo GR 117 E3
Katapola GR 117 F7
Katastari GR 117 E2
Katerbow D 45 C4
Katerini GR 116 B4
Kathikas CY 120 B1
Kätkesuando S 113 D12
Katlenburg-Lindau D 51 B6
Kato Achaia GR 117 D3
Káto Pyrgos CY 120 A1
Katouna GR 116 D3
Katovice CZ 63 A4
Katowice PL 55 C4
Katrineberg S 36 A3
Katrineholm S 37 D3
Kattarp S 41 C2
Kattavia GR 119 G2
Katthammarsvik S 37 E5
Kattilstorp S 40 A3
Katwijk NL 49 A5
Kąty Wrocławskie PL 54 B1
Katymár H 75 B4
Katzenelnbogen D 50 C3
Katzhütte D 52 C1
Kaub D 50 C3
Kaufbeuren D 62 C1
Kauhajoki FIN 3 E25
Kauhava FIN 3 E25
Kaukonen FIN 113 E13
Kaulsdorf D 52 C1
Kaunas LT 6 D7
Kaunisvaara S 113 E12
Kaupanger N 32 A4
Kautokeino N 113 C12
Kautzen A 63 B6
Kavadarci MK 116 A4
Kavajë AL 105 B5
Kavakköy TR 118 B1
Kavaklı TR 118 A2
Kavaklıdere TR 119 E3
Kavala GR 116 B6
Kavarna BG 11 E10
Kävlinge S 41 D3
Kawcze PL 46 A2
Kaxås S 115 D10
Kaxholmen S 40 B4
Kaymakçı TR 119 D3
Kaymaz TR 118 C6
Kaynarca TR 118 A5
Käyrämö FIN 113 F15
Kayseri TR 16 B7
Kaysersberg F 60 B3
Kazanlŭk BG 11 E8
Kazár H 65 B5
Kazimierza Wielka PL 55 C5
Kazincbarcika H 65 B6
Kaźmierz PL 46 C2
Kcynia PL 46 B3
Kdyně CZ 62 A4
Kea GR 117 E6
Keadow IRL 18 B3
Keady GB 19 B5
Kecel H 75 B4
Keçiborlu TR 119 E5
Kecskemét H 75 B4
Kėdainiai LT 6 D7
Kędzierzyn-Koźle PL 54 C3
Keel IRL 18 C1
Keenagh IRL 19 C4
Keerbergen B 49 B5
Kefalos GR 119 F2
Kefken TR 118 A5
Keflavík IS 111 C3
Kegworth GB 27 C4
Kehl D 60 B3
Kehrigk D 53 A3
Keighley GB 27 B4
Keila EST 6 B8
Keillmore GB 24 C2
Keiss GB 23 C5
Keith GB 23 D6
Kelberg D 50 C2
Kelbra D 51 B7
Kelč CZ 64 A3
Kelchsau A 72 A2
Këlcyrë AL 116 B2
Keld GB 26 A3
Kelebia H 75 B4
Kelekçi TR 119 E4
Kelemér H 65 B6
Keles TR 118 C4
Kelheim D 62 B2
Kell D 60 A2
Kellas GB 23 D5
Kellinghusen D 43 B6
Kelloselkä FIN 113 F17
Kells GB 19 B5
Kells IRL 19 C5
Kelmis B 50 C2
Kelokedhara CY 120 B1
Kelottijärvi FIN 113 D11
Kelsall GB 26 B3
Kelso GB 25 C5
Kelsterbach D 51 C4
Keltneyburn GB 24 B3
Kelujärvi FIN 113 E16
Kemaliye TR 119 D3
Kemalpaşa TR 119 D2
Kematen A 71 A6
Kemberg D 52 B2
Kemer, *Antalya* TR 119 F5
Kemer, *Burdur* TR 119 E5
Kemer, *Muğla* TR 119 F4
Kemerkaya TR 118 D6
Kemeten A 73 A6
Kemi FIN 3 D26
Kemijärvi FIN 113 F16
Kemnath D 62 A2
Kemnay GB 23 D6
Kemnitz, *Brandenburg* D 52 A2
Kemnitz, *Mecklenburg-Vorpommern* D 45 A5
Kempen D 50 B2
Kempsey GB 29 A5
Kempten D 61 C6
Kemptthal CH 70 A3
Kendal GB 26 A3
Kenderes H 75 A5
Kengyel H 75 A5
Kenilworth GB 30 B2
Kenmare IRL 20 C2
Kenmore GB 25 B4
Kennacraig GB 24 C2
Kenyeri H 74 A2
Kenzingen D 60 B3
Kepez TR 118 B1
Kępice PL 46 A2
Kępno PL 54 B3
Kepsut TR 118 C3
Keramoti GR 116 B6
Keräntöjärvi S 113 E12
Keratea GR 117 E5
Kerava FIN 7 A8
Kerecsend H 65 C6
Kerekegyhaza H 75 B4
Kerepestarcsa H 75 A4
Keri GR 117 E2
Kérien F 56 B2
Kerkafalva H 74 B1
Kerken D 50 B2
Kerkrade NL 50 C2
Kerkyra GR 116 C1
Kerlouan F 56 B1
Kernascléden F 56 B2
Kernhof A 63 C6
Kerns CH 70 B3
Kerpen D 50 C2
Kerrysdale GB 22 D3
Kerta H 74 A2
Kerteminde DK 39 D3
Kerzers CH 70 B2
Keşan TR 118 B1
Kesgrave GB 30 B5
Kesh GB 19 B4
Keskin TR 16 B6
Kesselfall A 72 A2
Kestenga RUS 3 D29
Keswick GB 26 A2
Keszthely H 74 B2
Kétegyháza H 75 B6
Kéthely H 74 B2
Kętrzyn PL 6 D6
Kettering GB 30 B3
Kettlewell GB 26 A3
Kęty PL 65 A5
Ketzin D 45 C4
Keula D 51 B6
Keuruu FIN 3 E26
Kevelaer D 50 B2
Kevermes H 75 B6
Kevi SRB 75 C4
Keyingham GB 27 B5
Keynsham GB 29 B5
Kežmarok SK 65 A6
Kharmanli BG 11 F8
Khaskovo BG 11 F8
Kherson UA 11 C12
Khimki RUS 7 D14
Khisinev = Chişinău MD 11 C10
Khmelnik UA 11 B9
Khmelnytskyy UA 11 B9
Khodoriv UA 11 B8
Kholm RUS 7 C11
Khorol UA 11 B12
Khotyn UA 11 B9
Khoyniki BY 7 F10
Khust UA 11 B7
Khvoynaya RUS 7 B13
Kiato GR 117 D4
Kibæk DK 39 C1
Kiberg N 113 B19
Kicasalih TR 118 A1
Kičevo MK 116 A3
Kidderminster GB 26 C3
Kidlington GB 31 C2
Kidsgrove GB 26 B3
Kidwelly GB 28 B3
Kiefersfelden D 62 C3
Kiel D 44 A2
Kielce PL 55 C5
Kiełczygłów PL 54 B4
Kielder GB 25 C5
Kiełpino PL 47 A4
Kielpiny PL 47 B5
Kierinki FIN 113 E14
Kiernozia PL 55 A4
Kierspe D 50 B3
Kietrz PL 54 C3
Kietz D 45 C6
Kiev = Kyyiv UA 11 A11
Kiezmark PL 47 A4
Kiffisia GR 117 D5
Kifino Selo BIH 84 C3
Kihlanki FIN 113 E12
Kihlanki S 113 E12
Kiistala FIN 113 E14
Kije PL 55 C5
Kijevo HR 83 C5
Kikallen N 32 B2
Kikinda SRB 75 C5
Kil N 33 D6
Kil, *Örebro* S 37 C2
Kil, *Värmland* S 35 C5
Kila S 35 C4
Kilafors S 36 A3
Kilb Rabenstein A 63 B6
Kilbaha IRL 20 B2
Kilbeggan IRL 21 A4
Kilberry GB 24 C2
Kilbirnie GB 24 C3
Kilboghamn N 112 F2
Kilbotn N 112 D5
Kilchattan GB 24 C2
Kilchoan GB 24 B1
Kilcock IRL 21 A5
Kilconnell IRL 20 A3
Kilcormac IRL 21 A4
Kilcreggan GB 24 C3
Kilcullen IRL 21 A5
Kilcurry IRL 19 B5
Kildare IRL 21 A5
Kildinstroy RUS 3 B30
Kildonan GB 23 C5
Kildorrery IRL 20 B3
Kilegrend N 33 C5
Kilen N 33 C5
Kilgarvan IRL 20 C2
Kiliya UA 11 D10
Kilkee IRL 20 B2
Kilkeel GB 19 B5
Kilkenny IRL 21 B4
Kilkieran IRL 20 A2
Kilkinlea IRL 20 B2
Kilkis GR 116 A4
Kill IRL 21 B4
Killadysert IRL 20 B2
Killala IRL 18 B2
Killaloe IRL 20 B3
Killarney IRL 20 B2
Killashandra IRL 19 B4
Killashee IRL 19 C4
Killearn GB 24 B3
Killeberg S 40 C4
Killeigh IRL 21 A4
Killenaule IRL 21 B4
Killimor IRL 20 A3
Killin GB 24 B3
Killinaboy IRL 20 B2
Killinge S 112 E9
Killinick IRL 21 B5
Killorglin IRL 20 B2
Killucan IRL 21 A4
Killybegs IRL 18 B3
Killyleagh GB 19 B6
Kilmacrenan IRL 19 A4
Kilmacthomas IRL 21 B4
Kilmaine IRL 18 C2
Kilmallock IRL 20 B3
Kilmarnock GB 24 C3
Kilmartin GB 24 B2
Kilmaurs GB 24 C3
Kilmeadan IRL 21 B4
Kilmeedy IRL 20 B3
Kilmelford GB 24 B2
Kilmore Quay IRL 21 B5
Kilmuir GB 23 D4
Kilnaleck IRL 19 C4
Kilninver GB 24 B2
Kilpisjärvi FIN 112 C9
Kilrea GB 19 B5
Kilrush IRL 20 B2
Kilsmo S 37 C2
Kilsyth GB 24 C3
Kiltoom IRL 20 A3
Kilwinning GB 24 C3
Kimasozero RUS 3 D29
Kimi GR 116 D6
Kimolos GR 117 F6
Kimovsk RUS 7 D14
Kimratshofen D 61 C6
Kimry RUS 7 C14
Kimstad S 37 D2
Kinbrace GB 23 C5
Kincardine GB 25 B4
Kincraig GB 23 D5
Kindberg A 73 A5
Kindelbruck D 52 B1
Kingarrow IRL 18 B3
Kingisepp RUS 7 B10
King's Lynn GB 30 B4
Kingsbridge GB 28 C4
Kingsclere GB 31 C2
Kingscourt IRL 19 C5
Kingsteignton GB 29 C4
Kingston, *Greater London* GB 31 C3
Kingston, *Moray* GB 23 D5
Kingston Bagpuize GB 31 C2
Kingston upon Hull GB 27 B5
Kingswear GB 29 C4
Kingswood GB 29 B5
Kington GB 29 A4
Kingussie GB 23 D4
Kınık, *Antalya* TR 119 F4
Kınık, *İzmir* TR 118 C2
Kinloch, *Highland* GB 22 C4
Kinloch, *Highland* GB 22 D2
Kinloch Rannoch GB 24 B3
Kinlochbervie GB 22 C3
Kinlochewe GB 22 D3
Kinlochleven GB 24 B3
Kinlochmoidart GB 24 B2
Kinloss GB 23 D5
Kinlough IRL 18 B3
Kinn N 34 B2
Kinna S 40 B2
Kinnared S 40 B3
Kinnarp S 40 A3
Kinne-Kleva S 35 D5
Kinnegad IRL 21 A4
Kinnitty IRL 21 A4
Kinrooi B 50 B1
Kinross GB 25 B4
Kinsale IRL 20 C3
Kinsarvik N 32 B3
Kintarvie GB 22 C2
Kintore GB 23 D6
Kinvarra IRL 20 A3
Kioni GR 116 D2
Kiparissia GR 117 E3
Kipfenburg D 62 B2
Kippen GB 24 B3
Kiraz TR 119 D3
Kirazlı TR 118 B1
Kirberg D 50 C4
Kirchbach in Steiermark A 73 B5
Kirchberg CH 70 A2
Kirchberg, *Baden-Württemberg* D 61 A5
Kirchberg, *Rheinland-Pfalz* D 60 A3
Kirchberg am Wechsel A 64 C1
Kirchberg an der Pielach A 63 B6
Kirchberg in Tirol A 72 A2
Kirchbichl A 72 A2
Kirchdorf, *Bayern* D 63 B4
Kirchdorf, *Mecklenburg-Vorpommern* D 44 B3
Kirchdorf, *Niedersachsen* D 43 C5
Kirchdorf an der Krems A 63 C5
Kirchdorf in Tirol A 72 A2
Kirchenlamitz D 52 C1
Kirchenthumbach D 62 A2
Kirchhain D 51 C4
Kirchheim, *Baden-Württemberg* D 61 B5
Kirchheim, *Bayern* D 61 B6
Kirchheim, *Hessen* D 51 C5
Kirchheim-bolanden D 61 A4
Kirchhundem D 50 B4
Kirchlintein D 43 C6
Kirchschlag A 73 A6
Kirchweidach D 62 B3
Kirchzarten D 60 C3
Kircubbin GB 19 B6
Kireç TR 118 C3
Kırıkkale TR 16 B6
Kirillov RUS 7 B15
Kirishi RUS 7 B12
Kirk Michael GB 26 A1
Kırka TR 118 C5
Kırkağaç TR 118 C2
Kirkbean GB 25 D4
Kirkbride GB 25 D4
Kirkby GB 26 B3
Kirkby Lonsdale GB 26 A3
Kirkby Malzeard GB 27 A4
Kirkby Stephen GB 26 A3
Kirkbymoorside GB 27 A5
Kirkcaldy GB 25 B4
Kirkcolm GB 24 D2
Kirkconnel GB 24 C3
Kirkcowan GB 24 D3
Kirkcudbright GB 24 D3
Kirke Hyllinge DK 39 D4
Kirkehamn N 33 D3
Kirkelly IRL 18 C3
Kirkenær N 34 B4
Kirkenes N 113 C19
Kirkham GB 26 B3
Kirkintilloch GB 24 C3
Kirkjubæjarklaustur IS 111 D7
Kirkkonummi FIN 6 A8
Kırklareli TR 118 A2
Kirkmichael GB 25 B4
Kirkoswald GB 24 C3
Kirkpatrick Fleming GB 25 C4
Kirkton of Glenisla GB 25 B4
Kirkwall GB 23 C6
Kirkwhelpington GB 25 C6
Kirn D 60 A3
Kiro AL 105 A5
Kirov RUS 7 D13
Kirovohrad UA 11 B12
Kirovsk RUS 3 C30
Kirriemuir GB 25 B5
Kırşehir TR 16 B7
Kirton GB 30 B3
Kirton in Lindsey GB 27 B5
Kirtorf D 51 C5
Kiruna S 112 E9
Kisa S 40 B5
Kisač SRB 75 C4
Kisbér H 74 A3
Kiseljak BIH 84 C3
Kisielice PL 47 B5
Kisköre H 75 A5
Kiskőrös H 75 B4
Kiskunfélegyháza H 75 B4
Kiskunhalas H 75 B4
Kiskunlacháza H 75 A3
Kiskunmajsa H 75 B4
Kisláng H 74 B3
Kisslegg D 61 C5
Kissolt H 75 B4
Kissónerga CY 120 B1
Kist D 61 A5
Kistanje HR 83 C4
Kistelek H 75 B4
Kisterenye H 65 B5
Kisújszállás H 75 A5
Kisvárda H 11 B7
Kisvejke H 74 B3
Kiszkowo PL 46 C3
Kiszombor H 75 B5
Kitee FIN 3 E29
Kithnos GR 117 E6
Kiti CY 120 B2
Kitkiöjärvi S 113 E12
Kitkiöjoki S 113 E12
Kittelfjäll S 115 B12
Kittendorf D 45 B4
Kittilä FIN 113 E13
Kittlitz D 53 B4
Kittsee A 64 B3
Kitzbühel A 72 A2
Kitzingen D 61 A6
Kiuruvesi FIN 3 E27
Kivertsi UA 11 A8
Kividhes CY 120 B1
Kivik S 41 D4
Kivotos GR 116 B3
Kiwity PL 47 A6
Kıyıköy TR 118 A3
Kızılcabölük TR 119 E4
Kızılcadağ TR 119 E4
Kızılcahamam TR 16 A6
Kızılırmak TR 16 A6
Kızılkaya TR 119 E5
Kızılkuyu TR 118 D6
Kızılören, *Afyon* TR 119 D5
Kızılören, *Konya* TR 119 E7
Kjeldebotn N 112 D5
Kjellerup DK 39 C2
Kjellmyra N 34 B4
Kjøllefjord N 113 B16
Kjopmannskjaer N 35 C2
Kjøpsvik N 112 D5
Kl'ačno SK 65 B4
Kladanj BIH 84 B3
Kläden D 44 C3
Klädesholmen S 38 B4
Kladnica SRB 85 C5
Kladnice HR 83 C5
Kladno CZ 53 C4
Kladruby CZ 62 A3
Klagenfurt A 73 B4
Klågerup S 41 D3
Klagstorp S 41 D3
Klaipėda LT 6 D6
Klaistow D 52 A2
Klaksvík FO 2 E10
Klana HR 73 C4
Klanac HR 83 B4
Klanjec HR 73 B5
Klardorf D 62 A3
Klarup DK 38 B3
Klašnice BIH 84 B2
Klässbol S 35 C4
Klášterec nad Ohří CZ 52 C3
Klášťor pod Znievom SK 65 B4
Klatovy CZ 63 A4
Klaus an der Pyhrnbahn A 63 C5
Klazienaveen NL 42 C3
Kłecko PL 46 C3
Kleczew PL 47 C4
Klein Plasten D 45 B4
Klein Sankt Paul A 73 B4
Kleinsölk A 72 A3
Kleinzell A 64 C1
Klejtrup DK 38 C2
Klek SRB 75 C5
Klemensker DK 41 D4
Klenak SRB 85 B4
Klenci pod Cerchovem CZ 62 A3
Klenica PL 53 B5
Klenje SRB 85 B4
Klenoec MK 116 A2
Klenovec SK 65 B5
Klenovica HR 83 A3
Klenovnik HR 73 B6
Kleppe N 33 D2
Kleppestø N 32 B2
Kleptow D 45 B5
Kletnya RUS 7 E12
Kleve D 50 B2
Klevshult S 40 B4
Klewki PL 47 B6
Kličevac SRB 85 B6
Kliening A 73 B4
Klietz D 44 C4
Klikuszowa PL 65 A5
Klimkovice CZ 64 A4
Klimontów PL 55 C6
Klimovichi BY 7 E11
Klimpfjäll S 115 B11
Klin RUS 7 C14
Klina SRB 85 D5
Klinča Sela HR 73 C5
Klingenbach A 64 C2
Klingenberg D 61 A5
Klingenmunster D 61 A4
Klingenthal D 52 C2
Klinken D 44 B3
Klintehamn S 37 E5
Klintsy RUS 7 E12
Kliny PL 55 B5
Klipley DK 39 E2
Klippan S 41 C3
Klis HR 83 C5
Klitmøller DK 38 B1
Klitten S 34 A6
Klixbüll D 39 E1
Kljajićevo SRB 75 C4
Ključ BIH 83 B5
Klobouky CZ 64 B2
Kłobuck PL 54 C3
Klockestrand S 115 E14
Kłodawa, *Lubuskie* PL 45 C7
Kłodawa, *Wielkopolskie* PL 54 A3
Kłodzko PL 54 C1
Kløfta N 34 B3
Klokkarvik N 32 B2
Klokkerholm DK 38 B3
Klokočov SK 65 A4
Kłomnice PL 55 C4
Klonowa PL 54 B3
Kloosterzande NL 49 B5
Kłopot PL 53 A4
Klos AL 116 A2
Kloštar Ivanić HR 73 C6
Kloster D 45 A5
Kloster DK 39 C1
Klösterle A 71 A5
Klostermansfeld D 52 B1
Klosterneuburg A 64 B2
Klosters CH 71 B4
Kloten CH 70 A3
Klötze D 44 C3
Klövsjö S 115 E11
Kluczbork PL 54 C3
Kluczewo PL 46 B2
Kluisbergen B 49 C4
Klundert NL 49 B5
Klutz D 44 B3
Klwów PL 55 B5
Klyetsk BY 7 E9
Knaben N 33 D3
Knaften S 115 C15
Knapstad N 35 C3
Knäred S 40 C3
Knaresborough GB 27 A4
Knarvik N 32 B2
Knebel DK 39 C3
Knebworth GB 31 C3
Knesebeck D 44 C2
Knesselare B 49 B4
Knežak SLO 73 C4
Kneževi Vinogradi HR 74 C3
Kneževo HR 74 C3
Knić SRB 85 C5
Knighton GB 29 A4
Knin HR 83 B5
Knislinge S 41 C4
Knittelfeld A 73 A4
Knivsta S 37 C4
Knock IRL 18 C3
Knocktopher IRL 21 B4
Knokke-Heist B 49 B4
Knowle GB 30 B2
Knurów PL 54 C3
Knutby S 36 C5
Knutsford GB 26 B3
Kobarid SLO 72 B3
København = Copenhagen DK 41 D2
Kobenz A 73 A4
Kobersdorf A 64 C2
Kobiernice PL 65 A5
Kobierzyce PL 54 C1
Kobilje SLO 73 B6
Kobiór PL 54 C3
Koblenz CH 61 C4
Koblenz D 50 C3
Kobryn BY 6 E8
Kobylanka PL 45 B6
Kobylin PL 54 B2
Kobyłka PL 55 A6
Kobylniki PL 47 C6
Kocaali TR 118 A5
Kocaaliler TR 119 E5
Kocaeli = İzmit TR 118 B4
Kočani MK 11 F7
Koçarlı TR 119 E2
Koceljevo SRB 85 B4
Kočerin BIH 84 C2
Kočevje SLO 73 C4
Kočevska Reka SLO 73 C4
Kochel am see D 62 C2
Kocs H 64 C4
Kocsér H 75 A4
Kocsola H 74 B3
Koczala PL 46 B3
Kodal N 35 C2
Kode S 38 B4
Kodersdorf D 53 B4
Kodrab PL 55 B4
Koekelare B 48 B3
Kofçaz TR 118 A2
Köflach A 73 A5
Køge DK 41 D2
Kohlberg D 62 A3
Kohtla-Järve EST 7 B9
Köinge S 40 B2
Kojetín CZ 64 A3
Kökar FIN 36 C7
Kokava SK 65 B5
Kokkola FIN 3 E25
Kokori BIH 84 B2
Kokoski PL 47 A4
Koksijde B 48 B3
Kola BIH 84 B2
Kola RUS 3 B30
Köla S 34 C4
Kołacin PL 55 B4
Kolari FIN 113 E12
Kolárovo SK 64 C3
Kolašin CG 85 D4
Kolbäck S 37 C3
Kolbacz PL 45 B6
Kolbeinsstaðir IS 111 C3
Kolbermoor D 62 C3
Kołbiel PL 55 A6
Kolbnitz A 72 B3
Kolbotn N 34 C2
Kolbu N 34 B2
Kolby Kås DK 39 D3
Kolczewo PL 45 B6
Kolczyglowy PL 46 A3
Kolding DK 39 D2
Kölesd H 74 B3
Kolgrov N 32 A1
Kolín CZ 53 C5
Kolind DK 39 C3
Kolinec CZ 63 A4
Koljane HR 83 C5
Kølkær DK 39 C2
Kölleda D 52 B1
Kollum NL 42 B3
Köln = Cologne D 50 C2
Koło PL 54 A3
Kołobrzeg PL 46 A1
Kolochau D 52 B3
Kolomyya UA 11 B8
Kolonje AL 105 C5
Kolonowskie PL 54 C3
Koloveč CZ 62 A4
Kolpino RUS 7 B11
Kolpny RUS 7 E14
Kolrep D 44 B4
Kölsillre S 115 E12
Kolsko PL 53 B5
Kolsva S 37 C2
Kolta SK 65 B4
Kolunič BIH 83 B5
Koluszki PL 55 B4
Kolut SRB 75 C3
Kolvereid N 114 C8
Kølvrå DK 39 C2
Komagvær N 113 B19
Koman AL 105 A5
Komarica BIH 84 B2
Komárno SK 64 C4
Komárom H 64 C4
Komatou Yialou CY 120 A3
Komboti GR 116 C3
Komen SLO 72 C3
Komin HR 84 C2
Komiža HR 83 C5
Komjáti H 65 B6
Komjatice SK 64 B4
Komletinci HR 75 C3
Komló, *Baranya* H 74 B3
Kömlo, *Heves* H 65 C6
Komoča SK 64 C4
Komorane SRB 85 D5
Komorniki PL 54 A1
Komorzno PL 54 B3
Komotini GR 116 A7
Konak SRB 75 C5
Konakovo RUS 7 C14
Konary PL 55 B6

Konarzyny	PL	46	B3
Kondias	GR	116	C7
Kondorfa	H	73	B6
Kondoros	H	75	B5
Kondrovo	RUS	7	D13
Køng	DK	39	D4
Konga	S	40	C5
Köngäs	FIN	113	E13
Kongerslev	DK	38	C3
Kongsberg	N	35	C1
Kongshamn	N	33	D5
Kongsmark	DK	39	D1
Kongsmoen	N	115	C9
Kongsvik	N	112	D5
Kongsvinger	N	34	B4
Konice	CZ	64	A2
Konie	PL	55	B5
Koniecpol	PL	55	C4
Königs Wusterhausen	D	52	A3
Königsberg	D	51	C6
Königsbronn	D	61	B6
Königsbrück	D	53	B3
Königsbrunn	D	62	B1
Konigsdorf	D	62	C2
Königsee	D	52	C1
Königshorst	D	45	C4
Königslutter	D	51	A6
Königssee	D	62	C3
Königstein, *Hessen*	D	51	C4
Königstein, *Sachsen*	D	53	C4
Königstetten	A	64	B2
Königswartha	D	53	B4
Konigswiesen	A	63	B5
Königswinter	D	50	C3
Konin	PL	54	A3
Konispol	AL	116	C2
Konitsa	GR	116	B2
Köniz	CH	70	B2
Konjevići	BIH	85	B4
Konjevrate	HR	83	C5
Konjic	BIH	84	C2
Konjščina	HR	73	B6
Könnern	D	52	B1
Konnerud	N	35	C2
Konopiska	PL	54	C3
Konotop	PL	53	B5
Konotop	UA	7	F12
Końskie	PL	55	B5
Konsmo	N	33	D4
Konstancin-Jeziorna	PL	55	A6
Konstantynów Łódźki	PL	55	B4
Konstanz	D	61	C5
Kontich	B	49	B5
Kontiolahti	FIN	3	E28
Konya	TR	119	E7
Konz	D	60	A2
Kópasker	IS	111	A9
Kópavogur	IS	111	C4
Kopčany	SK	64	B3
Koper	SLO	72	C3
Kopervik	N	33	C2
Kópháza	H	64	C2
Kopice	PL	54	C2
Kopidlno	CZ	53	C5
Köping	S	37	C2
Köpingebro	S	41	D3
Köpingsvik	S	41	C6
Koplik	AL	105	A5
Köpmanholmen	S	115	D15
Koppang	N	34	A3
Koppangen	N	112	C9
Kopparberg	S	36	C1
Koppelo	FIN	113	D16
Koppom	S	35	C4
Koprivlen	BG	116	A5
Koprivna	BIH	84	B3
Koprivnica	HR	74	B1
Kopřivnice	CZ	64	A4
Köprübaşı	TR	118	D3
Koprzywnica	PL	55	C6
Kopstal	L	60	A2
Kopychyntsi	UA	11	B8
Kopytkowo	PL	47	B4
Korbach	D	51	B4
Körbecke	D	50	B4
Korçë	AL	116	B2
Korčula	HR	84	D2
Korczyców	PL	53	A4
Korenevo	RUS	7	F13
Korenita	SRB	85	B4
Korets	UA	11	A9
Korfantów	PL	54	C2
Körfez	TR	118	B4
Korgen	N	115	A10
Korinth	DK	39	D3
Korinthos = Corinth	GR	117	E4
Korita	BIH	83	B5
Korita	HR	84	D2
Korithi	GR	117	E2
Korkuteli	TR	119	E5
Körmend	H	74	A1
Korne	PL	46	A3
Korneuburg	A	64	B2
Kornevo	RUS	47	A6
Kórnik	PL	54	A2
Kornsjø	N	35	D3
Környe	H	74	A3
Koromačno	HR	82	B3
Koroni	GR	117	F3
Koronos	GR	117	E7
Koronowo	PL	46	B3
Körösladány	H	75	B6
Köröstarcsa	H	75	B6
Korosten	UA	11	A10
Korostyshev	UA	11	A10
Korpilombolo	S	113	F12
Korsberga, *Jönköping*	S	40	B5
Korsberga, *Skaraborg*	S	35	D6
Korshavn	N	35	C2
Korskrogen	S	115	F12
Korsnäs	S	36	B2
Korsør	DK	39	D4
Korsun Shevchenkovskiy	UA	11	B11
Kortrijk	B	49	C4
Korucu	TR	118	C2
Koryčany	CZ	64	A3
Koryukovka	UA	7	F12
Korzeńsko	PL	54	B1
Korzybie	PL	46	A2
Kos	GR	119	F2
Kosakowo	PL	47	A4
Kosanica	CG	85	C4
Kosaya Gora	RUS	7	D14
Kösching	D	62	B2
Kościan	PL	54	A1
Kościelec	PL	54	A3
Kościerzyna	PL	46	A3
Koserow	D	45	A5
Košetice	CZ	63	A6
Košice	SK	10	B6
Kosjerić	SRB	85	C4
Koška	HR	74	C3
Koskullskulle	S	112	E9
Kosovska Mitrovica	SRB	85	D5
Kosta	S	40	C5
Kostajnica	HR	74	C1
Kostajnik	SRB	85	B4
Kostanica	CG	105	A5
Kostanjevica	SLO	73	C5
Kostelec na Hané	CZ	64	A3
Kostelec nad Černými Lesy	CZ	53	D4
Kostice	CZ	53	C3
Kostkowo	PL	47	A4
Kostojevići	SRB	85	B4
Kostolac	SRB	85	B6
Kostomłoty	PL	54	B1
Kostopil	UA	11	A9
Kostów	PL	54	B3
Kostrzyn, *Lubuskie*	PL	45	C6
Kostrzyn, *Wielkopolskie*	PL	46	C3
Koszalin	PL	46	A2
Koszęcin	PL	54	C3
Kőszeg	H	74	A1
Koszwaly	PL	47	A4
Koszyce	PL	55	C5
Kot	SLO	73	C5
Kotala	FIN	113	E17
Kotë	AL	105	C5
Kótelek	H	75	A5
Köthen	D	52	B1
Kotka	FIN	7	A9
Kotomierz	PL	47	B4
Kotor	CG	105	A4
Kotor Varoš	BIH	84	B2
Kotoriba	HR	74	B1
Kotorsko	BIH	84	B3
Kotovsk	UA	11	C10
Kotraža	SRB	85	C5
Kotronas	GR	117	F4
Kötschach	A	72	B2
Kötzting	D	62	A3
Koudum	NL	42	C2
Kouřim	CZ	53	C4
Kout na Šumave	CZ	62	A4
Kouvola	FIN	3	F27
Kovačevac	SRB	85	B5
Kovačica	SRB	85	A5
Kovdor	RUS	3	C29
Kovel'	UA	11	A8
Kovilj	SRB	75	C5
Kovin	SRB	85	B5
Kovren	CG	85	C4
Kowal	PL	47	C5
Kowalewo Pomorskie	PL	47	B4
Kowalów	PL	45	C6
Kowary	PL	53	C5
Köyceğiz	TR	119	F3
Kozan	TR	16	C7
Kozani	GR	116	B3
Kozarac	BIH	84	B1
Kozarac	HR	73	C5
Kozárovce	SK	65	B4
Kozelets	UA	11	A11
Kozelsk	RUS	7	D13
Kozica	HR	84	C2
Koziegłowy	PL	55	C4
Kozienice	PL	55	B6
Kozina	SLO	72	C3
Kozje	SLO	73	B5
Kozlu	TR	118	A6
Kozluk	BIH	85	B4
Koźmin	PL	54	B2
Koźminek	PL	54	B3
Kozolupy	CZ	63	A4
Kożuchów	PL	53	B5
Kožuhe	BIH	84	B3
Kozyatyn	UA	11	B10
Kozyürük	TR	118	A1
Krackow	D	45	B6
Kraddsele	S	115	B13
Krąg	PL	46	A2
Kragenæs	DK	39	E4
Kragerø	N	33	D6
Krągi	PL	46	B2
Kragujevac	SRB	85	B5
Kraiburg	D	62	B3
Krajenka	PL	46	B2
Krajišnik	SRB	75	C5
Krajková	CZ	52	C2
Krajné	SK	64	B3
Krajnik Dolny	PL	45	B6
Krakača	BIH	83	A4
Kråklingbo	S	37	E5
Kraków	PL	55	C4
Krakow am See	D	44	B4
Králíky	CZ	54	C1
Kraljevica	HR	73	C4
Kraljevo	SRB	85	C5
Kráľ'ov Brod	SK	64	B3
Kral'ovany	SK	65	A5
Kralovice	CZ	52	D3
Kralupy nad Vltavou	CZ	53	C4
Králův Dvůr	CZ	63	A5
Kramfors	S	115	E14
Kramsach	A	72	A1
Kramsk	PL	54	A3
Kråmvik	N	32	C5
Kranenburg	D	50	B2
Krania	GR	116	C3
Krania Elasonas	GR	116	C4
Kranichfeld	D	52	C1
Kranidi	GR	117	E5
Kranj	SLO	73	B4
Kranjska Gora	SLO	72	B3
Krapanj	HR	83	C4
Krapina	HR	73	B5
Krapje	HR	74	C1
Krapkowice	PL	54	C2
Kraselov	CZ	63	A4
Krašić	HR	73	C5
Krāslava	LV	7	D9
Kraslice	CZ	52	C2
Krasna	PL	55	B5
Krasna Lipa	CZ	53	C4
Kraśnik	PL	11	A7
Krašnja	SLO	73	B4
Krásno	SK	65	A4
Krasno Polje	HR	83	B4
Krásnohorské Podhradie	SK	65	B6
Krasnozavodsk	RUS	7	C15
Krasnystaw	PL	11	A7
Krasnyy	RUS	7	D11
Krasnyy Kholm	RUS	7	B14
Krasocin	PL	55	C5
Kraszewice	PL	54	B3
Kraszkowice	PL	54	B3
Kratigos	GR	118	C1
Kraubath	A	73	A4
Krausnick	D	53	A3
Krautheim	D	61	A5
Kravaře, *Severočeský*	CZ	53	C4
Kravaře, *Severomoravsky*	CZ	64	A4
Kravarsko	HR	73	C6
Kraznějov	CZ	63	A4
Krčedin	SRB	75	C5
Krefeld	D	50	B2
Kregme	DK	39	D5
Krembz	D	44	B3
Kremenchuk	UA	11	B12
Kremenets	UA	11	A8
Kremmen	D	45	C5
Kremna	SRB	85	C4
Kremnica	SK	65	B4
Krempe	D	43	B6
Krems	A	63	B6
Kremsbrücke	A	72	B3
Kremsmünster	A	63	B5
Křemže	CZ	63	B5
Křenov	CZ	64	A2
Krepa	PL	54	B3
Krępa Krajeńska	PL	46	B2
Krepsko	PL	46	B2
Kreševo	BIH	84	C3
Kressbronn	D	61	C5
Krestena	GR	117	E3
Kretinga	LT	6	D6
Krettsy	RUS	7	B12
Kreuth	D	62	C2
Kreuzau	D	50	C2
Kreuzlingen	CH	61	C5
Kreuztal	D	50	C3
Krewelin	D	45	C5
Krezluk	BIH	84	B2
Krieglach	A	73	A5
Kriegsfeld	D	60	A3
Kriens	CH	70	A3
Krimml	A	72	A2
Krimpen aan de IJssel	NL	49	B5
Křinec	CZ	53	C5
Kristdala	S	40	B6
Kristiansand	N	33	D5
Kristianstad	S	41	C4
Kristiansund	N	114	D4
Kristiinankaupunki	FIN	3	E24
Kristinefors	S	34	B4
Kristinehamn	S	35	C6
Kriváň	SK	65	B5
Křivokát	CZ	53	C3
Krivoy Rog = Kryvyy Rih	UA	11	C12
Kriź	HR	74	C1
Křižanov	CZ	64	A2
Križevci	HR	74	B1
Krk	HR	83	A3
Krka	SLO	73	C4
Krnjača	SRB	85	B5
Krnjak	HR	73	C5
Krnjeuša	BIH	83	B5
Krnjevo	SRB	85	B6
Krnov	CZ	54	C2
Krobia	PL	54	B1
Kroczyce	PL	55	C4
Krøderen	N	34	B1
Krokees	GR	117	F4
Krokek	S	37	D3
Krokom	S	115	D11
Krokowa	PL	47	A4
Krokstad-elva	N	34	C1
Kroksund	N	35	C3
Krolevets	UA	7	F12
Kroměříž	CZ	64	A3
Krommenie	NL	42	C1
Krompachy	SK	65	B6
Kromy	RUS	7	E13
Kronach	D	52	C1
Kronshagen	D	44	A2
Kronshtadt	RUS	7	B10
Kröpelin	D	44	A3
Kropp	D	43	A6
Kroppenstedt	D	52	B1
Kropstädt	D	52	B2
Krościenko nad Dunajcem	PL	65	A6
Kröslin	D	45	A5
Krośnice	PL	54	B2
Krośniewice	PL	55	A4
Krosno	PL	10	B6
Krosno Odrzańskie	PL	53	A5
Krostitz	D	52	B2
Krotoszyn	PL	54	B2
Krottendorf	A	73	A5
Krouna	CZ	64	A2
Krowiarki	PL	54	C3
Krrabë	AL	105	B5
Kršan	HR	73	C4
Krško	SLO	73	C5
Krstac	CG	84	C3
Krstur	SRB	75	B5
Křtiny	CZ	64	A2
Kruft	D	50	C3
Kruishoutem	B	49	C4
Krujë	AL	105	B5
Krulyewshchyna	BY	7	D9
Krumbach	A	73	A6
Krumbach	D	61	B6
Krumovgrad	BG	116	A7
Krün	D	71	A6
Krupá	CZ	53	C3
Krupa na Vrbasu	BIH	84	B2
Krupanj	SRB	85	B4
Krupina	SK	65	B5
Krupka	CZ	53	C3
Krupki	BY	7	D10
Kruså	DK	39	E2
Kruščica	BIH	84	B2
Kruševac	SRB	85	C6
Kruševo	MK	116	A3
Kruszwica	PL	47	C4
Kruszyn	PL	47	C5
Krute	CG	105	A5
Krychaw	BY	7	E11
Krynica	PL	65	A6
Krynica Morska	PL	47	A5
Kryvyy Rih = Krivoy Rog	UA	11	C12
Krzęcin	PL	46	B1
Krzelów	PL	54	B1
Krzepice	PL	54	C3
Krzepielów	PL	53	B6
Krzeszowice	PL	55	C4
Krzeszyce	PL	45	C7
Krzynowlaga Mała	PL	47	B6
Krzywiń	PL	54	B1
Krzyż Wielkopolski	PL	46	C2
Krzyżanowice	PL	54	D3
Krzyżowa	PL	65	A5
Ksiaz Wielkopolski, *Małopolskie*	PL	55	C5
Książ Wielkopolski, *Wielkopolskie*	PL	54	A2
Ktębowiec	PL	46	B2
Kübekháza	H	75	B5
Küblis	CH	71	B4
Kuç	AL	105	C5
Kuchary	PL	54	B2
Kuchl	A	63	C4
Kucice	PL	47	C6
Kuciste	HR	84	D2
Kućište	SRB	85	D5
Kuçovë	AL	105	C5
Küçükbahçe	TR	118	D1
Küçükköy	TR	118	C1
Küçükkuyu	TR	118	C1
Kucura	SRB	75	C4
Kuczbork-Osada	PL	47	B6
Kuddby	S	37	D3
Kudowa-Zdrój	PL	53	C6
Kufstein	A	62	C3
Kuggeboda	S	41	C5
Kuggörana	S	115	F14
Kühbach	D	62	B2
Kuhmo	FIN	3	D28
Kuhmoinen	FIN	3	F26
Kuhnsdorf	A	73	B4
Kuhstedt	D	43	B5
Kuinre	NL	42	C2
Kuivastu	EST	6	B7
Kukës	AL	10	E6
Kuklin	PL	47	B6
Kukljica	HR	83	B4
Kukujevci	SRB	85	A4
Kula, *Srbija*	SRB	85	B6
Kula, *Vojvodina*	SRB	75	C4
Kula	TR	119	D3
Kuldīga	LV	6	C6
Kulen Vakuf	BIH	83	B5
Kulina	BIH	84	B3
Kullstedt	D	51	B6
Kulmain	D	62	A2
Kulmbach	D	52	C1
Kulu	TR	16	B6
Kumafşarı	TR	119	E4
Kumane	SRB	75	C5
Kumanovo	MK	10	E6
Kumbağ	TR	118	B2
Kumdanlı	TR	119	D5
Kumkale	TR	118	C1
Kumla	S	37	C2
Kumlakyrkby	S	36	C3
Kumlinge	FIN	36	B7
Kumluca	TR	119	F5
Kumrovec	HR	73	B5
Kunadacs	H	75	B4
Kunágota	H	75	B6
Kunbaja	H	75	B4
Kunda	EST	7	B9
Kundl	A	72	A1
Kunes	N	113	B15
Kunfehértó	H	75	B4
Kungälv	S	38	B4
Kungs-Husby	S	37	C4
Kungsängen	S	37	C4
Kungsäter	S	40	B2
Kungsbacka	S	38	B5
Kungsgården	S	36	B3
Kungshamn	S	35	D3
Kungsör	S	37	C3
Kunhegyes	H	75	A5
Kunmadaras	H	75	A5
Kunovice	CZ	64	A3
Kunów	PL	55	C6
Kunowo, *Wielkopolskie*	PL	54	B2
Kunowo, *Zachodnio-Pomorskie*	PL	45	B6
Kunštát	CZ	64	A2
Kunszállás	H	75	B4
Kunszentmárton	H	75	B5
Kunszentmiklós	H	75	A4
Kunžak	CZ	63	A6
Künzelsau	D	61	A5
Kuolayarvi	RUS	113	F18
Kuopio	FIN	3	E27
Kuosku	FIN	113	E17
Kup	H	74	A2
Kup	PL	54	C2
Kupa	H	65	B6
Kupari	HR	84	D3
Kupci	SRB	85	C6
Kupferzell	D	61	A5
Kupinec	HR	73	C5
Kupinečki Kraljevac	HR	73	C5
Kupinovo	SRB	85	B5
Kupirovo	HR	83	B5
Kupjak	HR	73	C4
Kuppenheim	D	61	B4
Kupres	BIH	84	C2
Küps	D	52	C1
Kurbnesh	AL	105	B6
Kurd	H	74	B3
Kurdzhali	BG	116	A7
Küre	TR	16	A6
Kuressaare	EST	6	B7
Kurikka	FIN	3	E25
Kuřim	CZ	64	A2
Kuřivody	CZ	53	C4
Kurki	PL	47	B6
Kurort Oberwiesenthal	D	52	C2
Kurort Schmalkalden	D	51	C6
Kurort Stolberg	D	51	B6
Kurort Wippra	D	52	B1
Kurów	PL	11	A7
Kurowice	PL	55	B4
Kurravaara	S	112	E9
Kursk	RUS	7	F14
Kursu	FIN	113	F17
Kuršumlija	SRB	85	C6
Kuršumlijska Banja	SRB	85	C6
Kurşunlu, *Bursa*	TR	118	B4
Kurşunlu, *Çankırı*	TR	16	A6
Kurtakko	FIN	113	E13
Kürten	D	50	B3
Kurucaşile	TR	16	A6
Kurzelów	PL	55	C4
Kusadak	SRB	85	B5
Kuşadası	TR	119	E2
Kusel	D	60	A3
Kusey	D	44	C3
Küsnacht	CH	70	A3
Kütahya	TR	118	C4
Kutenholz	D	43	B6
Kutina	HR	74	C1
Kutjevo	HR	74	C2
Kutná Hora	CZ	53	D5
Kutno	PL	55	A4
Kuttara	FIN	113	D15
Küttingen	CH	70	A3
Kúty	SK	64	B3
Kuusamo	FIN	3	D28
Kuusankoski	FIN	3	F27
Kuvshinovo	RUS	7	C13
Kuyucak	TR	119	E3
Kuzmin	SRB	85	A4
Kuźnia Raciborska	PL	54	C3
Kuźnica Czarnkowska	PL	46	C2
Kuźnica Żelichowska	PL	46	C2
Kvænangsbotn	N	113	C11
Kværndrup	DK	39	D3
Kvaløysletta	N	112	C7
Kvalsund	N	113	B12
Kvam, *Nord-Trøndelag*	N	114	C8
Kvam, *Oppland*	N	114	F6
Kvamsøy	N	32	A3
Kvanndal	N	32	B3
Kvänum	S	35	D5
Kvås	N	33	D4
Kvasice	CZ	64	A3
Kvelde	N	35	C1
Kvenna	N	114	E5
Kvernaland	N	33	D2
Kvibille	S	40	C2
Kvicksund	S	37	C3
Kvidinge	S	41	C3
Kvikkjokk	S	112	F6
Kvikne	N	114	E7
Kvilda	CZ	63	A4
Kville	S	35	D3
Kvillsfors	S	40	B5
Kvinesdal	N	33	D3
Kvinlog	N	33	D3
Kvinnherad	N	32	C3
Kvissel	DK	38	B3
Kvissleby	S	115	E14
Kviteseid	N	33	C5
Kvitsøy	N	33	C2
Kwakowo	PL	46	A3
Kwidzyn	PL	47	B4
Kwilcz	PL	46	C2
Kyjov	CZ	64	B3
Kyle of Lochalsh	GB	22	D3
Kyleakin	GB	22	D3
Kylerhea	GB	22	D3
Kylestrome	GB	22	C3
Kyllburg	D	50	C2
Kyllini	GR	117	E3
Kynšperk nad Ohří	CZ	52	C2
Kyperounda	CY	120	B1
Kyrenia	CY	120	A2
Kyritz	D	44	C4
Kyrkesund	S	38	A4
Kyrkhult	S	41	C4
Kyrksæterøra	N	114	D6
Kysucké Nové Mesto	SK	65	A4
Kythira	GR	117	F4
Kythréa	CY	120	A2
Kyustendil	BG	11	E7
Kyyiv = Kiev	UA	11	A11
Kyyjärvi	FIN	3	E26

L

La Adrada	E	94	B2
La Alameda	E	100	A2
La Alberca	E	93	A4
La Alberca de Záncara	E	95	C4
La Albergueria de Argañán	E	93	A4
La Albuera	E	93	C4
La Aldea del Portillo del Busto	E	89	B3
La Algaba	E	99	B4
La Aliseda de Tormes	E	93	A5
La Almarcha	E	95	C4
La Almolda	E	90	B2
La Almunia de Doña Godina	E	89	C5
La Antillas	E	98	B3
La Arena	E	86	A4
La Aulaga	E	99	B4
La Balme-de-Sillingy	F	69	C6
La Bañeza	E	88	B1
La Barca de la Florida	E	99	C5
La Barre-de-Monts	F	66	B2
La Barre-en-Ouche	F	58	B1
La Barrosa	E	99	C4
La Barthe-de-Neste	F	77	C3
La Bassée	F	48	C3
La Bastide-de-Sèrou	F	77	C4
La Bastide-des-Jourdans	F	79	C4
La Bastide-Puylaurent	F	78	B2
La Bathie	F	69	C6
La Baule-Escoublac	F	66	A2
La Bazoche-Gouet	F	58	B1
La Bégude-de-Mazenc	F	78	B3
La Bernerie-en-Retz	F	66	A2
La Bisbal d'Empordà	E	91	B6
La Boissière	F	57	A6
La Bourboule	F	68	C2
La Bóveda de Toro	E	88	C1
La Brède	F	76	B2
La Bresse	F	60	B2
La Bridoire	F	69	C5
La Brillanne	F	79	C4
La Bruffière	F	66	A3
La Bussière	F	58	C3
La Caillère	F	66	B4
La Caletta, *Cágliari*	I	110	C1
La Caletta, *Núoro*	I	110	B2
La Calmette	F	78	C3
La Calzada de Oropesa	E	93	B5
La Campana	E	99	B5
La Cañada	E	94	B2
La Canourgue	F	78	B2
La Capelle	F	49	D4
La Cardanchosa	E	99	A5
La Caridad	E	86	A4
La Carlota	E	100	B1
La Carolina	E	100	A2
La Cava	E	90	C3
La Cavalerie	F	78	B2
La Celle-en-Moravan	F	69	A4
La Celle-St. Avant	F	67	A5
La Cerca	E	89	B3
La Chaise-Dieu	F	68	C3
La Chaize-Giraud	F	66	B3
La Chaize-le-Vicomte	F	66	B3
La Chambre	F	69	C6
La Chapelaude	F	68	B2
La Chapelle-d'Angillon	F	68	A2
La Chapelle-en-Aalgaudémar	F	79	B5
La Chapelle-en-Vercors	F	79	B4
La Chapelle-Glain	F	57	C4
La Chapelle-la-Reine	F	58	B3
La Chapelle-Laurent	F	68	C3
La Chapelle-St. Luc	F	59	B5
La Chapelle-sur-Erdre	F	66	A3
La Chapelle-Vicomtesse	F	58	C2
La Charce	F	79	B4
La Charité-sur-Loire	F	68	A3
La Chartre-sur-le-Loir	F	58	C1
La Châtaigneraie	F	67	B4
La Châtre	F	68	B1
La Chaussée-sur-Marne	F	59	B5
La Chaux-de-Fonds	CH	70	A1
La Cheppe	F	59	A5
La Chèze	F	56	B3
La Ciotat	F	79	C4
La Clayette	F	69	B4
La Clusaz	F	69	C6
La Codosera	E	93	B3
La Concha	E	88	A3
La Condamine-Châtelard	F	79	B5
La Contienda	E	99	A4
La Coquille	F	67	C5
La Coronada	E	93	C5
La Côte-St. André	F	69	C5
La Cotinière	F	66	C3
La Courtine	F	68	C2
La Crau	F	79	C5
La Crèche	F	67	B4
La Croix	F	67	A5
La Croix-Valmer	F	79	C5
La Cumbre	E	93	B5
La Douze	F	77	A3
La Espina	E	86	A4
La Estrella	E	94	C1
La Farga de Moles	E	91	A4
La Fatarella	E	90	B3
La Felipa	E	95	C5
La Fère	F	59	A4
La Ferrière, *Indre-et-Loire*	F	58	C1
La Ferrière, *Vendée*	F	66	B3
La Ferrière-en-Parthenay	F	67	B4
La-Ferté-Alais	F	58	B3
La Ferté-Bernard	F	58	B1
La Ferté-Frênel	F	58	B1
La Ferté-Gaucher	F	59	B4
La Ferté-Imbault	F	68	A1
La Ferté-Macé	F	57	B5
La Ferté-Milon	F	59	A4
La Ferté-St. Aubin	F	58	C2
La Ferté-St.Cyr	F	58	C2
La Ferté-sous-Jouarre	F	59	B4
La Ferté-Vidame	F	58	B1
La Ferté Villeneuil	F	58	C2
La Feuillie	F	58	A2
La Flèche	F	57	C5
La Flotte	F	66	B3
La Font de la Figuera	E	101	A5
La Fouillade	F	77	B5
La Fregeneda	E	87	D4
La Fresneda	E	90	C3
La Fuencubierta	E	99	B6
La Fuente de San Esteban	E	87	D4
La Fulioala	E	91	B4
La Gacilly	F	57	C3
La Galera	E	90	C3
La Garde-Freinet	F	79	C5
La Garnache	F	66	B3
La Garriga	E	91	B5
La Garrovilla	E	93	C4
La Gaubretière	F	66	B3
La Gineta	E	95	C4
La Granadella, *Alicante*	E	96	C3
La Granadella, *Lleida*	E	90	B3
La Grand-Combe	F	78	B3
La Grande-Croix	F	69	C4
La Grande-Motte	F	78	C3
La Granja d'Escarp	E	90	B3
La Granjuela	E	93	C5
La Grave	F	79	A5
La Gravelle	F	57	B4
La Guardia	E	95	C3
La Guardia de Jaén	E	100	B2
La Guerche-de-Bretagne	F	57	C4
La Guerche-sur-l'Aubois	F	68	B2
La Guérinière	F	66	B2
La Haba	E	93	C5
La Haye-du-Puits	F	57	A4
La Haye-Pesnel	F	57	B4
La Herlière	F	48	C3
La Hermida	E	88	A2
La Herrera	E	95	D4
La Higuera	E	101	A4
La Hiniesta	E	88	C1
La Horcajada	E	93	A5
La Horra	E	88	C3
La Hulpe	B	49	C5
La Hutte	F	57	B6
La Iglesuela	E	94	B2
La Iglesuela del Cid	E	90	C2
La Iruela	E	100	B3
La Javie	F	79	B5
La Jonchère-St. Maurice	F	67	B6
La Jonquera	E	91	A5
La Lantejuela	E	99	B5
La Línea de la Concepción	E	99	C5
La Llacuna	E	91	B4
La Londe-les-Maures	F	79	C5
La Loupe	F	58	B2
La Louvière	B	49	C5
La Luisiana	E	99	B5
La Machine	F	68	B3
la Maddalena	I	110	A2
La Mailleraye-sur-Seine	F	58	A1
La Malène	F	78	B2
La Mamola	E	100	C2
La Manresana dels Prats	E	91	B4
La Masadera	E	90	B2
La Mata	E	94	C2
La Mata de Ledesma	E	94	A1
La Mata de Monteagudo	E	88	B1
La Meilleraye-de-Bretagne	F	66	A3
La Ménitré	F	67	A4
La Mojonera	E	101	C3
La Mole	F	79	C5
La Molina	E	91	A4
La Monnerie-le-Montel	F	68	C3
La Morera	E	93	C4
La Mothe-Achard	F	66	B3
La Mothe-St. Héray	F	67	B4
La Motte-Chalançon	F	79	B4
La Motte-du-Caire	F	79	B5
La Motte-Servolex	F	69	C5
La Mudarra	E	88	C2
La Muela	E	90	B1
La Mure	F	79	B4
La Nava	E	99	B4
La Nava de Ricomalillo	E	94	C2
La Nava de Santiago	E	93	B4
La Neuve-Lyre	F	58	B1
La Neuveville	CH	70	A2
La Nocle-Maulaix	F	68	B3
La Nuez de Arriba	E	88	B3
La Paca	E	101	B4
La Pacaudière	F	68	B3
La Palma d'Ebre	E	90	B3
La Palma del Condado	E	99	B4
La Palme	F	78	D2
La Palmyre	F	66	C3
La Parra	E	93	C4
La Pedraja de Portillo	E	88	C2
La Peraleja	E	95	B4
La Petit-Pierre	F	60	B3
La Pinilla	E	101	B4
La Plagne	F	70	C1
La Plaza	E	86	A4
La Pobla de Lillet	E	91	A4
La Pobla de Vallbona	E	96	B2
La Pobla Llarga	E	96	B2
La Pola de Gordón	E	88	B1
la Porta	F	102	A2
La Pouëze	F	66	A4
La Póveda de Soria	E	89	B4
La Preste	F	91	A5
La Primaube	F	77	B5
La Puebla de Almoradie	E	95	C3
La Puebla de Cazalla	E	99	B5
La Puebla de los Infantes	E	99	B5

Lopar HR 83 B3
Lopare BIH 84 B3
Lopera E 100 B1
Lopigna F 102 A1
Loppersum NL 42 B3
Łopuszna PL 65 A6
Łopuszno PL 55 C5
Lor F 59 A5
Lora N 114 E5
Lora de Estepa E 100 B1
Lora del Río E 99 B5
Loranca del Campo E 95 B4
Lörby S 41 C4
Lorca E 101 B4
Lorch D 50 C3
Lørenfallet N 34 B3
Lørenskog N 34 C2
Loreo I 82 A1
Loreto I 82 C2
Lorgues F 79 C5
Lorica I 106 B3
Lorient F 56 C2
Lorignac F 67 C4
Lörinci H 65 C5
Loriol-sur-Drôme F 78 B3
Lormes F 68 A3
Loro Ciuffenna I 81 C5
Lorqui E 101 A4
Lörrach D 60 C3
Lorrez-le-Bocage F 59 B3
Lorris F 58 C3
Lorup D 43 C4
Łoś PL 55 B5
Los S 115 F12
Los Alcázares E 101 B5
Los Arcos E 89 B4
Los Barios de Luna E 88 B1
Los Barrios E 99 C5
Los Caños de Meca E 99 C4
Los Cerricos E 101 B3
Los Corrales E 100 B1
Los Corrales de Buelna E 88 A2
Los Dolores E 101 B4
Los Gallardos E 101 B4
Los Hinojosos E 95 C4
Los Isidros E 96 B1
Los Molinos E 94 B2
Los Morales E 99 B5
Los Navalmorales E 94 C2
Los Navalucillos E 94 C2
Los Nietos E 101 B5
Los Palacios y Villafranca E 99 B5
Los Pozuelos de Calatrava E 100 A1
Los Rábanos E 89 C4
Los Santos E 93 A5
Los Santos de la Humosa E 95 B3
Los Santos de Maimona E 93 C4
Los Tijos E 88 A2
Los Villares E 100 B2
Los Yébenes E 94 C3
Losacino E 87 C4
Losar de la Vera E 93 A5
Losenstein A 63 C5
Losheim, *Nordrhein-Westfalen* D 50 C2
Losheim, *Saarland* D 60 A2
Losne F 69 A5
Løsning DK 39 D2
Lossburg D 61 B4
Losse F 76 B2
Losser NL 50 A3
Lossiemouth GB 23 D5
Lössnitz D 52 C2
Loštice CZ 64 A2
Lostwithiel GB 28 C3
Løten N 34 B3
Lotorp S 37 D2
Lottefors S 36 A3
Löttorp S 41 B7
Lotyń PL 46 B2
Lotzorai I 110 C2
Louargat F 56 B2
Loudéac F 56 B3
Loudun F 67 A5
Loué F 57 C5
Loughborough GB 27 C4
Loughbrickland GB 19 B5
Loughrea IRL 20 A3
Louhans F 69 B5
Louisburgh IRL 18 C2
Loukhi RUS 3 C30
Loulay F 67 B4
Loulé P 98 B2
Louny CZ 53 C3
Lourdes F 76 C2
Lourenzá E 86 A3
Loures P 92 C1
Loures-Barousse F 77 C3
Louriçal P 92 A2
Lourinhã P 92 B1
Lourmarin F 79 C4
Loury F 58 C3
Lousa, *Bragança* P 87 C3
Lousa, *Castelo Branco* P 92 B3
Lousã, *Coimbra* P 92 A2
Lousa, *Lisboa* P 92 C1
Lousada E 86 B3
Lousada P 87 C2
Louth GB 27 B5
Loutra Edipsou GR 116 D5
Loutraki GR 117 E4
Loutropoli Thermis GR 118 C1
Louverné F 57 B5
Louvie-Juzon F 76 C2
Louviers F 58 A2
Louvigné-du-Désert F 57 B4
Louvois F 59 A5
Lova I 72 C2
Lovasberény H 74 A3
Lövåsen S 34 C5
Lovászpatona H 74 A2
Lövberga S 115 D12
Lovech BG 11 E8
Lövenich D 50 B2
Lóvere I 71 C5
Lövestad S 41 D3
Loviisa FIN 7 A9
Lovikka S 113 E11
Lovinobaňa SK 65 B5
Loviste HR 84 C2
Lovke HR 73 C4
Lovnäs S 34 A5
Lövö H 74 A1
Lovosice CZ 53 C4
Lovozero RUS 3 C31
Lovran HR 73 C4
Lovreć HR 84 C1
Lovrenc na Pohorju SLO 73 B5
Lovrin RO 75 C5
Lövstabruk S 36 B4
Löwenberg D 45 C5
Löwenstein D 61 A5
Lowestoft GB 30 B5
Lowick GB 25 C6
Łowicz PL 55 A4
Loxstedt D 43 B5
Loyew BY 7 F11
Lož SLO 73 C4
Loza CZ 63 A4
Łozina PL 54 B2
Loznica SRB 85 B4
Lozničko Polje SRB 85 B4
Lozorno SK 64 B3
Lozovik SRB 85 B6
Lozoya E 94 B3
Lozoyuela E 94 B3
Lozzo di Cadore I 72 B2
Luanco E 88 A1
Luarca E 86 A4
Lubaczów PL 11 A7
Lubań PL 53 B5
Lubanie PL 47 C4
Lubanów PL 55 B4
Lubars D 52 A2
Lubasz PL 46 C2
Lubawa PL 47 B5
Lubawka PL 53 C6
Lübbecke D 51 A4
Lübben D 53 B3
Lübbenau D 53 B3
Lubczyna PL 45 B6
Lübeck D 44 B2
Lubenec CZ 52 C3
Lubersac F 67 C6
Lübesse D 44 B3
Lubia E 89 C4
Lubian E 87 B4
Lubiatowo PL 45 B7
Lubichowo PL 47 B4
Lubicz Dolny PL 47 B4
Lubień PL 65 A5
Lubień Kujawski PL 47 C5
Lubienia PL 55 B6
Lubieszewo PL 46 B1
Lubin, *Dolnośląskie* PL 53 B6
Lubin, *Zachodnio-Pomorskie* PL 45 B6
Lublin, *Lubelskie* PL 11 A7
Lubliniec PL 54 C3
Lubmin D 45 A5
Lubniewice PL 45 C7
Lubny UA 11 A12
Lubochnia PL 55 B5
Lubomierz, *Dolnośląskie* PL 53 B5
Lubomierz, *Małopolskie* PL 65 A6
Lubomino PL 47 A6
Luboń PL 54 A1
L'ubotín SK 65 A6
Lubowidz PL 47 B5
Łubowo, *Wielkopolskie* PL 46 C3
Łubowo, *Zachodnio-Pomorskie* PL 46 B2
Lubraniec PL 47 C4
Lubrin E 101 B3
Lubrza PL 54 C2
Lubsko PL 53 B4
Lübtheen D 44 B3
Lubuczewo PL 46 A3
Luby CZ 52 C2
Lübz D 44 B4
Luc F 78 B2
Luc-en-Diois F 79 B4
Luc-sur-Mer F 57 A5
Lucainena de las Torres E 101 B3
Lucan IRL 21 A5
Lučani SRB 85 C5
Lúcar E 101 B3
Luçay-le-Mâle F 67 A6
Lucca I 81 C4
Lucciana F 102 A2
Lucé F 58 B2
Luče SLO 73 B4
Lucena, *Córdoba* E 100 B1
Lucena, *Huelva* E 99 B4
Lucenay-les-Aix F 68 B3
Lucenay-l'Evêque F 69 A4
Lučenec SK 65 B5
Luceni E 90 B1
Lucens CH 70 B1
Lucera I 103 B8
Luceram F 80 C1
Lüchow D 44 C3
Luciana E 94 D2
Lucignano I 81 C5
Lucija SLO 72 C3
Lucka D 52 B2
Luckau D 53 B3
Luckenwalde D 52 A3
Lückstedt D 44 C3
Luco dei Marsi I 103 B6
Luçon F 66 B3
Ludanice SK 64 B4
Ludbreg HR 74 B1
Lüdenscheid D 50 B3
Lüderitz D 44 C3
Lüdersdorf D 44 B2
Ludgershall GB 31 C2
Ludgo S 37 D4
Lüdinghausen D 50 B3
Ludlow GB 29 A5
Ludomy PL 46 C2
Ludvika S 36 B2
Ludweiler Warndt D 60 A2
Ludwigsburg D 61 B5
Ludwigsfelde D 52 A3
Ludwigshafen D 61 A4
Ludwigslust D 44 B3
Ludwigsstadt D 52 C1
Ludza LV 7 C9
Luesia E 90 A1
Luftkurort Arendsee D 44 C3
Lug BIH 84 D3
Lug HR 74 C3
Luga RUS 7 B10
Lugagnano Val d'Arda I 81 B3
Lugano CH 70 B3
Lugau D 52 C2
Lugnas S 35 D5
Lúgnola I 102 A5
Lugny F 69 B4
Lugo E 86 A3
Lugo I 81 B5
Lugoj RO 10 D6
Lugones E 88 A1
Lugros E 100 B2
Luhačovice CZ 64 A3
Luhe D 62 A3
Luino I 70 C3
Luintra E 87 B3
Lújar E 100 C2
Luka nad Jihlavou CZ 63 A6
Lukavac BIH 84 B3
Lukavika BIH 84 B3
Lukovë AL 116 C1
Lukovica SLO 73 B4
Lukovit BG 11 E8
Lukovo HR 83 B3
Lukovo SRB 85 C6
Lukovo Šugorje HR 83 B4
Łuków PL 6 F7
Łukowice Brzeskie PL 54 C2
Luksefjell N 33 C6
Łukta PL 47 B6
Lula I 110 B2
Luleå S 3 D25
Lüleburgaz TR 118 A2
Lumbarda HR 84 D2
Lumbier E 90 A1
Lumbrales E 87 D4
Lumbreras E 89 B4
Lumbres F 48 C3
Lummelunda S 37 E5
Lummen B 49 C6
Lumparland FIN 36 B7
Lumpiaque E 90 B1
Lumsås DK 39 D4
Lumsden GB 23 D6
Lumsheden S 36 B3
Lun HR 83 B3
Luna E 90 A2
Lunamatrona I 110 C1
Lunano I 82 C1
Lunas F 78 C2
Lund N 114 C8
Lund, *Skåne* S 41 D3
Lund, *Västra Götaland* S 35 C4
Lundamo N 114 D7
Lunde DK 39 D1
Lunde, *Sogn og Fjordane* N 32 A3
Lunde, *Sogn og Fjordane* N 32 A3
Lunde, *Telemark* N 33 C6
Lunde S 115 E14
Lundebyvollen N 34 B4
Lunden D 43 A6
Lunderseter N 34 B4
Lunderskov DK 39 D2
Lundsberg S 35 C6
Lüneburg D 44 B2
Lunel F 78 C3
Lünen D 50 B3
Lunéville F 60 B2
Lungern CH 70 B3
Lungro I 106 B3
Luninyets BY 7 E9
Lünne D 43 C4
Lunner N 34 B2
Lunteren NL 49 A6
Lunz am See A 63 C6
Luogosanto I 110 A2
Łupawa PL 46 A3
Lupión E 100 A2
Lupoglav HR 73 C4
Luppa D 52 B2
Luque E 100 B1
Lurago d'Erba I 71 C4
Lúras I 110 B2
Lurcy-Lévis F 68 B2
Lure F 60 C2
Lurgan GB 19 B5
Luri F 102 A2
Lury-sur-Arnon F 68 A2
Lušci Palanka BIH 83 B5
Lusévera I 72 B3
Lushnjë AL 105 C5
Lusignan F 67 B5
Lusigny-sur-Barse F 59 B5
Lusnić BIH 84 C1
Luso P 92 A2
Lusówko PL 46 C2
Luspebryggan S 112 E8
Luss GB 24 B3
Lussac F 76 B2
Lussac-les-Châteaux F 67 B5
Lussac-les-Eglises F 67 B6
Lussan F 78 B3
Lüssow D 44 B4
Lustenau A 71 A4
Luštěnice CZ 53 C4
Luster N 32 A4
Lutago I 72 B1
Lutherstadt Wittenberg D 52 B2
Lütjenburg D 44 A2
Lutnes N 34 A4
Lutocin PL 47 C5
Lutomiersk PL 55 B4
Luton GB 31 C3
Lutry CH 70 B1
Lutry PL 47 A6
Lutsk UA 11 A8
Lutter am Barenberge D 51 B6
Lutterworth GB 30 B2
Lututów PL 54 B3
Lützen D 52 B2
Lutzow D 44 B3
Luusua FIN 113 F16
Luvos S 112 F7
Luxembourg L 60 A2
Luxeuil-les-Bains F 60 C2
Luxey F 76 B2
Luz, *Évora* P 92 C3
Luz, *Faro* P 98 B2
Luz, *Faro* P 98 B3
Luz-St. Sauveur F 76 D2
Luzarches F 58 A3
Luže CZ 64 A2
Luzech F 77 B4
Luzern CH 70 A3
Luzino PL 47 A4
Luzy F 68 B3
Luzzi I 106 B3
L'viv UA 11 B8
Lwówek PL 46 C2
Lwówek Śląski PL 53 B5
Lyakhavichy BY 7 E9
Lybster GB 23 C5
Lychen D 45 B5
Lychkova RUS 7 C12
Lyckeby S 41 C5
Lycksele S 115 C15
Lydd GB 31 D4
Lydford GB 28 C3
Lydney GB 29 B5
Lyepyel BY 7 D10
Lygna N 34 B2
Lykkja N 32 B5
Lykling N 33 C2
Lyme Regis GB 29 C5
Lymington GB 31 D2
Lympne GB 31 C5
Lyndhurst GB 31 D2
Lyneham GB 29 B6
Lyness GB 23 C5
Lyngdal, *Buskerud* N 32 C6
Lyngdal, *Vest-Agder* N 33 D4
Lyngør N 33 D6
Lyngsa DK 38 B3
Lyngseidet N 112 C9
Lyngsnes N 114 C8
Lynmouth GB 28 B4
Lynton GB 28 B4
Lyntupy BY 7 D9
Lyon F 69 C4
Lyons-la-Forêt F 58 A2
Lyozna BY 7 D11
Lyrestad S 35 D6
Lysá nad Labem CZ 53 C4
Lysá pod Makytou SK 64 A4
Lysebotn N 33 C3
Lysekil S 35 D3
Lysice CZ 64 A2
Lysomice PL 47 B4
Lysøysund N 114 D6
Lyss CH 70 A2
Lystrup DK 39 C3
Lysvik S 34 B5
Łyszkowice PL 55 B4
Lytham St. Anne's GB 26 B2
Lyuban RUS 7 B11
Lyubertsy RUS 7 D14
Lyuboml' UA 11 A8
Lyubytino RUS 7 B12
Lyudinovo RUS 7 E13

M

Maaninkavaara FIN 113 F17
Maarheeze NL 49 B6
Maaseik B 50 B1
Maastricht NL 50 C1
Mablethorpe GB 27 B6
Mably F 68 B4
Macael E 101 B3
Maçanet de Cabrenys E 91 A5
Mação P 92 B2
Macau F 76 A2
Maccagno-Agra I 70 B3
Maccarese I 102 B5
Macchiagódena I 103 B7
Macclesfield GB 26 B3
Macduff GB 23 D6
Maceda E 87 B3
Macedo de Cavaleiros P 87 C4
Maceira, *Guarda* P 92 A3
Maceira, *Leiria* P 92 B2
Macelj HR 73 B5
Macerata I 82 C2
Macerata Féltria I 82 C1
Machault F 59 A5
Machecoul F 66 B3
Machrihanish GB 24 C2
Machynlleth GB 26 C2
Macieira P 87 C2
Maciejowice PL 55 B6
Macinaggio F 102 A2
Mackenrode D 51 B6
Mačkovci SLO 73 B6
Macomer I 110 B1
Macon B 49 C5
Mâcon F 69 B4
Macotera E 94 B1
Macroom IRL 20 C3
Macugnaga I 70 C2
Madan BG 116 A6
Madängsholm S 35 D5
Madaras H 75 B4
Maddaloni I 103 B7
Made NL 49 B5
Madeley GB 26 C3
Maderuelo E 89 C3
Madetkoski FIN 113 E15
Madley GB 29 A5
Madocsa H 75 B3
Madona LV 7 C9
Madonna di Campíglio I 71 B5
Madrid E 94 B3
Madridejos E 95 C3
Madrigal de la Vera E 93 A5
Madrigal de las Altas Torres E 94 A1
Madrigalejo E 93 B5
Madrigalejo de Monte E 88 B3
Madriguera E 89 C3
Madrigueras E 95 C5
Madroñera E 93 B5
Maël-Carhaix F 56 B2
Maella E 90 B3
Maello E 94 B2
Maesteg GB 29 B4
Mafra P 92 C1
Magacela E 93 C5
Magallon E 89 C5
Magaluf E 97 B2
Magán E 94 C3
Magaña E 89 C4
Magasa I 71 C5
Magaz E 88 C2
Magdeburg D 52 A1
Magenta I 70 C3
Magescq F 76 C1
Maghera GB 19 B5
Magherafelt GB 19 B5
Maghull GB 26 B3
Magione I 82 C1
Maglaj BIH 84 B3
Maglehem S 41 D4
Magliano de'Marsi I 103 A6
Magliano in Toscana I 102 A4
Magliano Sabina I 102 A5
Maglić SRB 75 C4
Máglie I 107 A5
Maglód H 75 A4
Magnac-Bourg F 67 C6
Magnac-Laval F 67 B6
Magnieres F 60 B2
Magnor N 34 C4
Magnuszew PL 55 B6
Magny-Cours F 68 B3
Magny-en-Vexin F 58 A2
Mágocs H 74 B3
Magoute P 92 C1
Maguilla E 93 C5
Maguiresbridge GB 19 B4
Magyarbóly H 74 C3
Magyarkeszi H 74 B3
Magyarszék H 74 B3
Mahala CG 105 A5
Mahide E 87 C4
Mahilyow BY 7 E11
Mahmudiye TR 118 C5
Mahora E 95 C5
Mahovo HR 73 C6
Mähring D 62 A3
Maia E 76 C1
Maia P 87 C2
Maiaelrayo E 95 A3
Maials E 90 B3
Maîche F 70 A1
Máida I 106 C3
Maiden Bradley GB 29 B5
Maiden Newton GB 29 C5
Maidenhead GB 31 C3
Maidstone GB 31 C4
Maienfeld CH 71 A4
Maignelay Montigny F 58 A3
Maijanen FIN 113 E14
Maillezais F 66 B4
Mailly-le-Camp F 59 B5
Mailly-le-Château F 59 C4
Mainar E 89 C5
Mainbernheim D 61 A6
Mainburg D 62 B2
Mainhardt D 61 A5
Maintal D 51 C4
Maintenon F 58 B2
Mainvilliers F 58 B2
Mainz D 50 C4
Maiorca P 92 A2
Mairena de Aljarafe E 99 B4
Mairena del Alcor E 99 B5
Maisach D 62 B2
Maishofen A 72 A2
Maison-Rouge F 59 B4
Maissau A 64 B1
Maisse F 58 B3
Maizières-lès-Vic F 60 B2
Maja HR 73 C6
Majadahonda E 94 B3
Majadas E 93 B5
Majavatn N 115 B10
Majs H 74 C3
Majšperk SLO 73 B5
Makarska HR 84 C2
Makkum NL 42 B2
Maklár H 65 C6
Makó H 75 B5
Makoszyce PL 54 C2
Makov SK 65 A4
Makovac SRB 85 D6
Maków Podhalański PL 65 A5
Mąkowarsko PL 46 B3
Makrakomi GR 116 D4
Malå S 115 B15
Mala Bosna SRB 75 B4
Mala Kladuša BIH 73 C5
Mala Krsna SRB 85 B6
Malá Lehota SK 65 B4
Mala Pijace SRB 75 B4
Mala Plana SRB 85 C6
Mala Subotica HR 74 B1
Mala Vyska UA 11 B11
Malacky SK 64 B3
Maladzyechna BY 7 D9
Málaga E 100 C1
Malagón E 94 C3
Malaguilla E 95 B3
Malahide IRL 21 A5
Malalbergo I 81 B5
Malanów PL 54 B3
Malaucène F 79 B4
Malaunay F 58 A2
Malaya Vishera RUS 7 B12
Malborghetto I 72 B3
Malbork PL 47 A5
Malborn D 60 A2
Malbuisson F 69 B6
Malcésine I 71 C5
Malchin D 45 B4
Malching D 63 B4
Malchow D 44 B4
Malcocinado E 99 A5
Malczyce PL 54 B1
Maldegem B 49 B4
Maldon GB 31 C4
Małdyty PL 47 B5
Malè I 71 B5
Malemort F 67 C6
Malente D 44 A2
Målerås S 40 C5
Males GR 117 G7
Malesherbes F 58 B3
Malesina GR 116 D5
Malestroit F 56 C3
Maletto I 109 B3
Malexander S 40 A5
Malfa I 106 C1
Malgrat de Mar E 91 B5
Malhadas P 87 C4
Mali Lošinj HR 83 B3
Malia CY 120 B1
Malia GR 117 G7
Malicorne-sur-Sarthe F 57 C5
Malijai F 79 B5
Malildjoš SRB 75 C4
Målilla S 40 B5
Malin IRL 19 A4
Málinec SK 65 B5
Målingsbo S 36 C2
Maliniec PL 54 A3
Malinska HR 83 A3
Maliq AL 116 B2
Maljevac HR 73 C5
Malkara TR 118 B1
Małki PL 47 B5
Malko Tŭrnovo BG 11 E9
Mallaig GB 22 D3
Mallaranny IRL 18 C2
Mallemort F 79 C4
Mallén E 89 C5
Malléon F 77 C4
Mallersdorf-Pfaffenberg D 62 B3
Málles Venosta I 71 B5
Malling DK 39 C3
Mallnitz A 72 B3
Mallow IRL 20 B3
Mallwyd GB 26 C2
Malm N 114 C8
Malmbäck S 40 B4
Malmberget S 112 E9
Malmby S 37 C4
Malmédy B 50 C2
Malmesbury GB 29 B5
Malmköping S 37 C3
Malmö S 41 D3
Malmon S 35 D3
Malmslätt S 37 D2
Malnate I 70 C3
Malo I 71 C6
Maloarkhangelsk RUS 7 E14
Małogoszcz PL 55 C5
Maloja CH 71 B4
Małomice PL 53 B5
Måløy N 114 F2
Maloyaroslovets RUS 7 D14
Malpartida E 93 B4
Malpartida de la Serena E 93 C5
Malpartida de Plasencia E 93 B4
Malpas E 90 A3
Malpas GB 26 B3
Malpica P 92 B3
Malpica de Bergantiños E 86 A2
Malpica de Tajo E 94 C2
Malsch D 61 B4
Malšice CZ 63 A5
Malta A 72 B3
Maltat F 68 B3
Maltby GB 27 B4
Malung S 34 B5
Malungsfors S 34 B5
Maluszów PL 45 C7
Maluszyn PL 55 C4
Malva E 88 C1
Malvaglia CH 70 B3
Malveira P 92 C1
Malvik N 114 D7
Malyn UA 11 A10
Mamarrosa P 92 A2
Mamer L 60 A2
Mamers F 58 B1
Mamirolle F 69 A6
Mammendorf D 62 B2
Mámmola I 106 C3
Mamoiada I 110 B2
Mamonovo RUS 47 A5
Mamurras AL 105 B5
Maňa SK 64 B4
Manacor E 97 B3
Manavgat TR 119 F6
Mancera de Abajo E 94 B1
Mancha Real E 100 B2
Manchester GB 26 B3
Manching D 62 B2
Manchita E 93 C4
Manciano I 102 A4
Manciet F 76 C3
Mandal N 33 D4
Mandanici I 109 A4
Mándas I 110 C2
Mandatoríccio I 107 B3
Mandayona E 95 B4
Mandelieu-la-Napoule F 79 C5
Mandello del Lário I 71 C4
Mandelsloh D 43 C6
Manderfeld B 50 C2
Manderscheid D 50 C2
Mandino Selo BIH 84 C2
Mandoudi GR 116 D5
Mandra GR 117 D5
Mandraki GR 119 F2
Mandúria I 104 C3
Mane, *Alpes-de-Haute-Provence* F 79 C4
Mane, *Haute-Garonne* F 77 C3
Manérbio I 71 C5
Mañeru E 89 B5
Manetin CZ 52 D3
Manfredónia I 104 B1
Mangalia RO 11 E10
Manganeses de la Lampreana E 88 C1
Manganeses de la Polvorosa E 88 B1
Mangen N 34 C3
Manger N 32 B2
Mangiennes F 60 A1
Mangotsfield GB 29 B5
Mångsbodarna S 34 A5
Mangualde P 92 A3
Maniago I 72 B2
Manilva E 99 C5
Manisa TR 118 D2
Manises E 96 B2
Mank A 63 B6
Månkarbo S 36 B4
Manlleu E 91 B5
Manna DK 38 B2
Männedorf CH 70 A3
Mannersdorf am Leithagebirge A 64 C2
Mannheim D 61 A4
Manningtree GB 31 C5
Manoppello I 103 A7
Manorbier GB 28 B3
Manorhamilton IRL 18 B3
Manosque F 79 C4
Manowo PL 46 A2
Manresa E 91 B4
Månsarp S 40 B4
Månsåsen S 115 D11
Manschnow D 45 C6
Mansfeld D 52 B1
Mansfield GB 27 B4
Mansilla de Burgos E 88 B3
Mansilla de las Mulas E 88 B1
Manskog S 35 C4
Mansle F 67 C5
Manso F 102 A1
Manteigas P 92 A3
Mantel D 62 A3
Mantes-la-Jolie F 58 B2
Mantes-la-Ville F 58 B2
Manthelan F 67 A5
Mantorp S 37 D2
Mántova I 71 C5
Mänttä FIN 3 E26
Manuel E 96 B2
Manyas TR 118 B2
Manzanal de Arriba E 87 B4
Manzanares E 95 C3
Manzanares el Real E 94 B3
Manzaneda, *León* E 87 B4
Manzaneda, *Orense* E 87 B3
Manzanedo E 88 B3
Manzaneque E 94 C3
Manzanera E 96 A2
Manzanilla E 99 B4
Manzat F 68 C2
Manziana I 102 A5
Manziat F 69 B4
Maó E 97 B4
Maoča BIH 84 B3
Maqueda E 94 B2
Mara E 89 C5
Maramaraereğlisi TR 118 B2
Maraña E 88 A1
Maranchón E 95 A4
Maranello I 81 B4
Marano I 103 C7
Marano Lagunare I 72 C3
Marans F 66 B3
Maratea I 106 B2
Marateca P 92 C2
Marathokambos GR 119 E1
Marathonas GR 117 D5
Marathóvouno CY 120 A2
Marazion GB 28 C2
Marbach, *Baden-Württemberg* D 61 B5
Marbach, *Hessen* D 51 C5
Marbach F 60 B2
Marbäck S 40 B3
Mårbacka S 34 C5
Marbella E 100 C1
Marboz F 69 B5
Marburg D 51 C4
Marcali H 74 B2
Marčana HR 82 B2
Marcaria I 81 A4
Marcelová SK 64 C4
Marcenat F 68 C2
March GB 30 B4
Marchamalo E 95 B3
Marchaux F 69 A6
Marche-en-Famenne B 49 C6
Marchegg A 64 B2
Marchena E 99 B5
Marchenoir F 58 C2
Marcheprime F 76 B2
Marciac F 76 C3
Marciana Marina I 81 D4
Marcianise I 103 B7
Marcigny F 68 B4
Marcilla E 89 B5
Marcillac-la-Croisille F 68 C2
Marcillac-Vallon F 77 B5
Marcillat-en-Combraille F 68 B2
Marcille-sur-Seine F 59 B4
Marcilloles F 69 C5
Marcilly-le-Hayer F 59 B4
Marcinkowice PL 46 B2
Marciszów PL 53 C6
Marck F 48 C2
Marckolsheim F 60 B3
Marco de Canevezes P 87 C2
Mårdsele S 115 C16
Mårdsjö S 115 D12
Mareham le Fen GB 27 B5
Marek S 40 B5
Marennes F 66 C3
Maresquel F 48 C2
Mareuil F 67 C5
Mareuil-en-Brie F 59 B4
Mareuil-sur-Arnon F 68 B2
Mareuil-sur-Lay F 66 B3
Mareuil-sur-Ourcq F 59 A4
Margam GB 28 B4
Margariti GR 116 C2
Margate GB 31 C5
Margaux F 76 A2
Margerie-Hancourt F 59 B5
Margès F 69 C5
Margherita di Savóia I 104 B2
Margita SRB 75 C6
Margone I 70 C2
Margonin PL 46 C3

Marguerittes F 78 C3
Margut F 59 A6
Maria E 101 B3
Maria Neustift A 63 C5
Maria Saal A 73 B4
Mariager DK 38 C2
Mariana E 95 B4
Mariannelund S 40 B5
Marianópoli I 108 B2
Mariánské Lázně CZ 52 D2
Mariapfarr A 72 A3
Mariazell A 63 C6
Maribo DK 39 E4
Maribor SLO 73 B5
Marieberg S 37 C2
Mariefred S 37 C4
Mariehamn FIN 36 B6
Marieholm S 41 D3
Mariembourg B 49 C5
Marienbaum D 50 B2
Marienberg D 52 C3
Marienheide D 50 B3
Mariental D 51 B4
Mariestad S 35 D5
Marieux F 48 C3
Marigliano I 103 C7
Marignane F 79 C4
Marigny, *Jura* F 69 B5
Marigny, *Manche* F 57 A4
Marigny-le-Châtel F 59 B4
Marija Bistrica HR 73 B6
Marijampolė LT 6 D7
Marin E 87 B2
Marina HR 83 C5
Marina del Cantone I 103 C7
Marina di Acquappesa I 106 B2
Marina di Alberese I 81 D5
Marina di Amendolara I 106 B3
Marina di Árbus I 110 C1
Marina di Campo I 81 D4
Marina di Carrara I 81 B4
Marina di Castagneto-Donorático I 81 C4
Marina di Cécina I 81 C4
Marina di Gáiro I 110 C2
Marina di Ginosa I 104 C2
Marina di Gioiosa Iónica I 106 C3
Marina di Grosseto I 81 D4
Marina di Léuca I 107 B5
Marina di Massa I 81 B4
Marina di Novàglie I 107 B5
Marina di Pisa I 81 C4
Marina di Ragusa I 109 C3
Marina di Ravenna I 82 B1
Marina di Torre Grande I 110 C1
Marina Romea I 82 B1
Marinaleda E 100 B1
Marine de Sisco F 102 A2
Marinella I 108 B1
Marinella di Sarzana I 81 B4
Marineo I 108 B2
Marines F 58 A2
Maringues F 68 C3
Marinha das Ondas P 92 A2
Marinha Grande P 92 B2
Marinhas P 87 C2
Marino I 102 B5
Marjaliza E 94 C3
Markabygd N 114 D8
Markaryd S 40 C3
Markdorf D 61 C5
Markelo NL 50 A2
Market Deeping GB 30 B3
Market Drayton GB 26 C3
Market Harborough GB 30 B3
Market Rasen GB 27 B5
Market Warsop GB 27 B4
Market Weighton GB 27 B5
Markethill GB 19 B5
Markgröningen D 61 B5
Markhausen D 43 C4
Marki PL 55 A6
Markina-Xemein E 89 A4
Markinch GB 25 B4
Märkische Buchholz D 53 A3
Markitta S 113 E10
Markkleeberg D 52 B2
Marklohe D 43 C6
Marknesse NL 42 C2
Markneukirchen D 52 C2
Markopoulo GR 117 E5
Markovac SRB 85 B6
Markowice PL 54 C3
Markranstädt D 52 B2
Marksuhl D 51 C6
Markt Allhau A 73 A6
Markt Bibart D 61 A6
Markt Erlbach D 62 A1
Markt-heidenfeld D 61 A5
Markt Indersdorf D 62 B2
Markt Rettenbach D 61 C6
Markt Schwaben D 62 B2
Markt-Übelbach A 73 A5
Marktbreit D 61 A6
Marktl D 62 B3
Marktleuthen D 52 C1
Marktoberdorf D 62 C1
Marktredwitz D 52 C2
Markusica HR 74 C3
Markušovce SK 65 B6
Marl D 50 B3
Marlborough, *Devon* GB 28 C4
Marlborough, *Wiltshire* GB 29 B6
Marle F 59 A4
Marlieux F 69 B5
Marlow D 45 A4
Marlow GB 31 C3
Marma S 36 B4
Marmagne F 69 B4
Marmande F 76 B3
Marmara TR 118 B2
Marmaris TR 119 F3
Marmelete P 98 B2
Marmolejo E 100 A1
Marmoutier F 60 B3
Marnay F 69 A5
Marne D 43 B6
Marnheim D 61 A4
Marnitz D 44 B3
Maroldsweisach D 51 C6
Marolles-les-Braults F 58 B1
Maromme F 58 A2
Marone I 71 C5
Maronia GR 116 B7
Maroslele H 75 B5
Maróstica I 72 C1
Marotta I 82 C2
Marpisa GR 117 E7
Marquion F 49 C4
Marquise F 48 C2
Marradi I 81 B5
Marrasjärvi FIN 113 F14
Marraskoski FIN 113 F14
Marratxi E 97 B2
Marrúbiu I 110 C1
Marrum NL 42 B2
Marrupe E 94 B2
Mars-la-Tours F 60 A1
Marsac F 77 C5
Marsac-en-Livradois F 68 C3
Marságlia I 80 B3
Marsala I 108 B1
Marsberg D 51 B4
Marsciano I 82 D1
Marseillan F 78 C2
Marseille = Marseilles F 79 C4
Marseille en Beauvaisis F 58 A2
Marseilles = Marseille F 79 C4
Mársico Nuovo I 104 C1
Marske-by-the-Sea GB 27 A4
Marsliden S 115 B12
Marson F 59 B5
Märsta S 37 C4
Marstal DK 39 E3
Marstrand S 38 B4
Marta I 102 A4
Martano I 107 A5
Martel F 77 B4
Martelange B 60 A1
Martfeld D 43 C6
Martfű H 75 A5
Martham GB 30 B5
Marthon F 67 C5
Martiago E 93 A4
Martigné-Briand F 67 A4
Martigné-Ferchaud F 57 C4
Martigne-sur-Mayenne F 57 B5
Martigny CH 70 B2
Martigny-les-Bains F 60 B1
Martigues F 79 C4
Martim-Longo P 98 B3
Martin SK 65 A4
Martin de la Jara E 100 B1
Martin Muñoz de las Posadas E 94 A2
Martina CH 71 B5
Martina Franca I 104 C3
Martinamor E 94 B1
Martinengo I 71 C4
Martinsberg A 63 B6
Martinšćica HR 82 B3
Martinshöhe D 60 A3
Martinsicuro I 82 D2
Martinszell D 61 C6
Mártis I 110 B1
Martofte DK 39 D3
Martonvásár H 74 A3
Martorell E 91 B4
Martos E 100 B2
Martres Tolosane F 77 C3
Martti FIN 113 E17
Marugán E 94 B2
Marúggio I 104 C3
Marvão P 92 B3
Marvejols F 78 B2
Marville F 60 A1
Marwałd PL 47 B5
Marykirk GB 25 B5
Marypark GB 23 D5
Maryport GB 26 A2
Marytavy GB 28 C3
Marzabotto I 81 B5
Marzahna D 52 B2
Marzahne D 45 C4
Marzamemi I 109 C4
Marzocca I 82 C2
Mas-Cabardès F 77 C5
Mas de Barberáns E 90 C3
Mas de las Matas E 90 C2
Masa E 88 B3
Máscali I 109 B4
Mascaraque E 94 C3
Mascarenhas P 87 C3
Mascioni I 103 A6
Masegoso E 101 A3
Masegoso de Tajuña E 95 B4
Masera I 70 B3
Masevaux F 60 C2
Masfjorden N 32 B2
Masham GB 27 A4
Masi N 113 C12
Maside E 87 B2
Maslacq F 76 C2
Maslinica HR 83 C5
Maslovare BIH 84 B2
Masone I 80 B2
Massa I 81 B4
Massa Fiscáglia I 81 B6
Massa Lombarda I 81 B5
Massa Lubrense I 103 C7
Massa Maríttima I 81 C4
Massa Martana I 82 D1
Massafra I 104 C3
Massamagrell E 96 B2
Massanassa E 96 B2
Massarosa I 81 C4
Massat F 77 D4
Massay F 68 A1
Massbach D 51 C6
Masseret F 67 C6
Masseube F 77 C3
Massiac F 68 C3
Massignac F 67 C5
Massing D 62 B3
Massmechelen B 50 C1
Masterud N 34 B4
Mästocka S 40 C3
Masty BY 6 E8
Masúa I 110 C1
Masueco E 87 C4
Masugnsbyn S 113 E11
Mašun SLO 73 C4
Maszewo, *Lubuskie* PL 53 A4
Maszewo, *Zachodnio-Pomorskie* PL 45 B7
Mata de Alcántara E 93 B4
Matala GR 117 H6
Matalebreras E 89 C4
Matallana de Torio E 88 B1
Matamala E 89 C4
Mataporquera E 88 B2
Matapozuelos E 88 C2
Mataró E 91 B5
Matarocco I 108 B1
Mataruge CG 85 C4
Mataruška Banja SRB 85 C5
Matélica I 82 C2
Matera I 104 C2
Mateševo CG 85 D4
Mátészalka H 11 C7
Matet E 96 B2
Matfors S 115 E14
Matha F 67 C4
Mathay F 70 A1
Matignon F 57 B3
Matilla de los Caños del Rio E 94 B1
Matlock GB 27 B4
Matosinhos P 87 C2
Matour F 69 B4
Mátrafüred H 65 C5
Mátraterenye H 65 B5
Matre, *Hordaland* N 32 B2
Matre, *Hordaland* N 32 C2
Matrei am Brenner A 71 A6
Matrei in Osttirol A 72 A2
Matrice I 103 B7
Matsdal S 115 B12
Mattarello I 71 B6
Mattersburg A 64 C2
Mattighofen A 62 B4
Mattinata I 104 B2
Mattos P 92 B2
Mattsee A 62 C4
Mattsmyra S 36 A2
Matulji HR 73 C4
Maubert-Fontaine F 59 A5
Maubeuge F 49 C4
Maubourguet F 76 C3
Mauchline GB 24 C3
Maud GB 23 D6
Mauer-kirchen A 62 B4
Mauern D 62 B2
Mauguio F 78 C3
Maulbronn D 61 B4
Maule F 58 B2
Mauléon F 67 B4
Mauléon-Barousse F 77 D3
Mauléon-Licharre F 76 C2
Maulévrier F 67 A4
Maum IRL 18 C2
Maurach A 72 A1
Maure-de-Bretagne F 57 C4
Maureilhan F 78 C2
Mauriac F 68 C2
Mauron F 57 B3
Maurs F 77 B5
Maury F 77 D5
Maussane-les-Alpilles F 78 C3
Mautern A 63 B6
Mautern im Steiermark A 73 A4
Mauterndorf A 72 A3
Mauthausen A 63 B5
Mauthen A 72 B2
Mauvezin F 77 C3
Mauzé-sur-le-Mignon F 67 B4
Maxent F 57 C3
Maxey-sur-Vaise F 60 B1
Maxial P 92 B1
Maxieira P 92 B2
Maxwellheugh GB 25 C5
Mayalde E 88 C1
Maybole GB 24 C3
Mayen D 50 C3
Mayenne F 57 B5
Mayet F 58 C1
Maylough IRL 18 C3
Mayorga E 88 B1
Mayres F 78 B3
Mayrhofen A 72 A1
Mazagón E 99 B4
Mazaleón E 90 B3
Mazamet F 77 C5
Mazan F 79 B4
Mazara del Vallo I 108 B1
Mazarambroz E 94 C2
Mazarete E 95 B4
Mazaricos E 86 B2
Mazarrón E 101 B4
Mažeikiai LT 6 C7
Mazères F 77 C4
Mazères-sur-Salat F 77 C3
Mazières-en-Gâtine F 67 B4
Mazin HR 83 B4
Mazuelo E 88 B3
Mazyr BY 7 E10
Mazzarino I 109 B3
Mazzarrà Sant'Andrea I 109 A4
Mazzo di Valtellina I 71 B5
Mchowo PL 47 B6
Mdzewo PL 47 C6
Mealabost GB 22 C2
Mealhada P 92 A2
Méan B 49 C6
Meana Sardo I 110 C2
Meaulne F 68 B2
Meaux F 59 B3
Mebonden N 114 D8
Mecerreyes E 89 B3
Mechelen B 49 B5
Mechernich D 50 C2
Mechnica PL 54 C3
Mechowo PL 45 B7
Mechterstädt D 51 C6
Mecidiye TR 118 B1
Mecikal PL 46 B3
Mecina-Bombarón E 100 C2
Mecitözü TR 16 A7
Meckenbeuren D 61 C5
Meckenheim, *Rheinland-Pfalz* D 50 C3
Meckenheim, *Rheinland-Pfalz* D 61 A4
Meckesheim D 61 A4
Mecseknádasd H 74 B3
Meda I 71 C4
Meda P 87 D3
Medak HR 83 B4
Mede I 80 A2
Medebach D 51 B4
Medelim P 93 A3
Medemblik NL 42 C2
Medena Selista BIH 84 B1
Medesano I 81 B4
Medevi S 37 D1
Medgidia RO 11 D10
Medgyesháza H 75 B6
Medhamn S 35 C5
Mediaş RO 11 C8
Medicina I 81 B5
Medina de las Torres E 93 C4
Medina de Pomar E 89 B3
Medina de Rioseco E 88 C1
Medina del Campo E 88 C2
Medina Sidonia E 99 C5
Medinaceli E 95 A4
Medinilla E 93 A5
Medja SRB 75 C5
Medjedja BIH 85 C4
Medulin HR 82 B2
Meduno I 72 B2
Medveda SRB 85 B6
Medvedja SRB 85 C6
Medvedov SK 64 C3
Medvide HR 83 B4
Medvode SLO 73 B4
Medzev SK 65 B6
Medžitlija MK 116 B3
Meerane D 52 C2
Meerle B 49 B5
Meersburg D 61 C5
Meeuwen B 49 B6
Megalo Horio GR 119 F2
Megalopoli GR 117 E4
Megara GR 117 D5
Megève F 69 C6
Meggenhofen A 63 B4
Megra RUS 7 A14
Mehamn N 113 A16
Mehedeby S 36 B4
Méhkerék H 75 B6
Mehun-sur-Yèvre F 68 A2
Meigle GB 25 B4
Meijel NL 50 B1
Meilen CH 70 A3
Meilhan F 76 C2
Meimôa P 93 A3
Meina I 70 C3
Meine D 44 C2
Meinersen D 44 C2
Meinerzhagen D 50 B3
Meiningen D 51 C6
Meira E 86 A3
Meiringen CH 70 B3
Meisenheim D 60 A3
Meissen D 52 B3
Meitingen D 62 B1
Meix-devant-Virton B 60 A1
Męka PL 54 B3
Meka Gruda BIH 84 C3
Mel I 72 B2
Melbu N 112 D3
Melč CZ 64 A3
Meldal N 114 D6
Méldola I 82 B1
Meldorf D 43 A6
Melegnano I 71 C4
Melenci SRB 75 C5
Melendugno I 105 C4
Melfi I 104 C1
Melfjordbotn N 112 F2
Melgaço P 87 B2
Melgar de Arriba E 88 B1
Melgar de Fernamental E 88 B2
Melgar de Yuso E 88 B2
Melhus N 114 D7
Meliana E 96 B2
Melide CH 70 C3
Melide E 86 B2
Melides P 98 A2
Meligales GR 117 E3
Melilli I 109 B4
Melinovac HR 83 B4
Melisenda I 110 C2
Melisey F 60 C2
Mélito di Porto Salvo I 109 B4
Melk A 63 B6
Melksham GB 29 B5
Mellanström S 115 B15
Mellbystrand S 40 C2
Melle B 49 B4
Melle D 50 A4
Melle F 67 B4
Mellendorf D 43 C6
Mellerud S 35 D4
Mellieha M 107 C5
Mellösa S 37 C3
Mellrichstadt D 51 C6
Mělnické Vtelno CZ 53 C4
Mělník CZ 53 C4
Melón E 87 B2
Melrose GB 25 C5
Mels CH 71 A4
Melsungen D 51 B5
Meltaus FIN 113 F14
Meltham GB 27 B4
Melton Mowbray GB 30 B3
Meltosjärvi FIN 113 F13
Melun F 58 B3
Melvaig GB 22 D3
Melvich GB 23 C5
Mélykút H 75 B4
Melzo I 71 C4
Memaliaj AL 116 B1
Membrilla E 95 D3
Membrio E 93 B3
Memer F 77 B4
Memmelsdorf D 51 D6
Memmingen D 61 C6
Memoria P 92 B2
Mena UA 7 F12
Menàggio I 71 B4
Menai Bridge GB 26 B1
Menasalbas E 94 C2
Menat F 68 B2
Mendavia E 89 B4
Mendaza E 89 B4
Mende F 78 B2
Menden D 50 B3
Menderes TR 119 D2
Mendig D 50 C3
Mendiga P 92 B2
Mendrisio CH 70 C3
Ménéac F 56 B3
Menemen TR 118 D2
Menen B 49 C4
Menesjärvi FIN 113 D15
Menetou-Salon F 68 A2
Menfi I 108 B1
Ménfőcsanak H 64 C3
Mengamuñoz E 94 B2
Mengen D 61 B5
Mengen TR 118 B7
Mengeš SLO 73 B4
Mengíbar E 100 B2
Mengkofen D 62 B3
Menou F 68 A3
Mens F 79 B4
Menslage D 43 C4
Mensträsk S 115 B16
Mentana I 102 A5
Menton F 80 C1
Méntrida E 94 B2
Méobecq F 67 B6
Méounes-les-Montrieux F 79 C4
Meppel NL 42 C3
Meppen D 43 C4
Mequinenza E 90 B3
Mer F 58 C2
Mera, *Coruña* E 86 A2
Mera, *Coruña* E 86 A3
Meråker N 114 D8
Merano I 71 B6
Merate I 71 C4
Mercadillo E 89 A3
Mercatale I 82 C1
Mercatino Conca I 82 C1
Mercato San Severino I 103 C7
Mercato Saraceno I 82 C1
Merching D 62 B1
Merchtem B 49 C5
Merdrignac F 56 B3
Merdžanići BIH 84 C2
Meré E 88 A2
Mere GB 29 B5
Meréville F 58 B3
Merfeld D 50 B3
Méribel F 69 C6
Méribel Motraret F 69 C6
Meriç TR 118 A1
Mérida E 93 C4
Mérignac F 76 B2
Měřín CZ 64 A1
Mering D 62 B1
Merkendorf D 62 A1
Merklin CZ 63 A4
Merksplas B 49 B5
Merlånna S 37 C3
Merlimont Plage F 48 C2
Mern DK 39 D5
Mernye H 74 B2
Mers-les-Bains F 48 C2
Mersch L 60 A2
Merseburg D 52 B1
Merthyr Tydfil GB 29 B4
Mertingen D 62 B1
Mértola P 98 B3
Méru F 58 A3
Merufe P 87 B2
Mervans F 69 B5
Merville F 48 C3
Méry-sur-Seine F 59 B4
Merzen D 43 C4
Merzifon TR 16 A7
Merzig D 60 A2
Mesagne I 105 C3
Mesão Frio P 87 C3
Mesas de Ibor E 93 B5
Meschede D 50 B4
Meschers-sur-Gironde F 66 C4
Meshchovsk RUS 7 D13
Meslay-du-Maine F 57 C5
Mesna N 34 A2
Mesnalien N 34 A2
Mesocco CH 71 B4
Mésola I 82 B1
Mesologi GR 116 D3
Mesopotamo GR 116 C2
Mesoraca I 107 B3
Messac F 57 C4
Messancy B 60 A1
Messdorf D 44 C3
Messei F 57 B5
Messejana P 98 B2
Messelt N 34 A3
Messina I 109 A4
Messingen D 43 C4
Messini GR 117 E4
Messkirch D 61 C5
Messlingen S 115 E9
Messtetten D 61 B4
Mesta GR 117 D7
Mestanza E 100 A1
Městec Králové CZ 53 C5
Mestlin D 44 B3
Město Albrechtice CZ 54 C2
Město Libavá CZ 64 A3
Město Touškov CZ 63 A4
Mestre I 72 C2
Mesvres F 69 B4
Mesztegnyő H 74 B2
Meta I 103 C7
Metajna HR 83 B4
Metelen D 50 A3
Methana GR 117 E5
Methlick GB 23 D6
Methven GB 25 B4
Methwold GB 30 B4
Metković HR 84 C2
Metlika SLO 73 C5
Metnitz A 73 B4
Metslawier NL 42 B3
Metsovo GR 116 C3
Metten D 62 B3
Mettendorf D 50 D2
Mettet B 49 C5
Mettingen D 50 A3
Mettlach D 60 A2
Mettlen CH 70 B2
Mettmann D 50 B2
Metz F 60 A2
Metzervisse F 60 A2
Metzingen D 61 B5
Meulan F 58 A2
Meung-sur-Loire F 58 C2
Meuselwitz D 52 B2
Meuzac F 67 C6
Mevagissey GB 28 C3
Mexborough GB 27 B4
Meximieux F 69 C5
Mey GB 23 C5
Meyenburg D 44 B4
Meyerhöfen D 43 C5
Meylan F 69 C5
Meymac F 68 C2
Meyrargues F 79 C4
Meyrueis F 78 B2
Meyssac F 77 A4
Meysse F 78 B3
Meyzieu F 69 C4
Mèze F 78 C2
Mézériat F 69 B5
Mežica SLO 73 B4
Mézidon-Canon F 57 A5
Mézières-en-Brenne F 67 B6
Mézières-sur-Issoire F 67 B5
Mézilhac F 78 B3
Mézilles F 59 C4
Mézin F 76 B3
Mezőberény H 75 B6
Mezőcsát H 65 C6
Mezőfalva H 74 B3
Mezőhegyes H 75 B5
Mezőkeresztes H 65 C6
Mezőkomárom H 74 B3
Mezőkövácsháza H 75 B5
Mezőkövesd H 65 C6
Mezőörs H 74 A2
Mézos F 76 B1
Mezőszilas H 74 B3
Mezőtúr H 75 A5
Mezquita de Jarque E 90 C2
Mezzano, *Emilia Romagna* I 81 B6
Mezzano, *Trentino Alto Adige* I 72 B1
Mezzojuso I 108 B2
Mezzoldo I 71 B4
Mezzolombardo I 71 B6
Mgarr M 107 C5
Mglin RUS 7 E12
Miajadas E 93 B5
Miały PL 46 C2
Mianowice PL 46 A3
Miasteczko Krajeńskie PL 46 B3
Miasteczko Śl. PL 54 C3
Miastko PL 46 A2
Michalovce SK 10 B6
Michałowice PL 55 C4
Michelau D 61 A6
Michelbach D 61 A6
Micheldorf A 63 C5
Michelhausen A 64 B1
Michelsneukirchen D 62 A3
Michelstadt D 61 A5
Michendorf D 52 A3
Michurin BG 11 E9
Mickleover GB 27 C4
Mid Yell GB 22 A7
Midbea GB 23 B6
Middelburg NL 49 B4
Middelfart DK 39 D2
Middelharnis NL 49 B5
Middelkerke B 48 B3
Middelstum NL 42 B3
Middlesbrough GB 27 A4
Middleton GB 24 B1
Middleton Cheney GB 30 B2
Middleton-in-Teesdale GB 26 A3
Middletown GB 19 B5
Middlewich GB 26 B3
Middlezoy GB 29 B5
Midhurst GB 31 D3
Midleton IRL 20 C3
Midlum D 43 B5
Midsomer Norton GB 29 B5
Midtgulen N 114 F2
Midtskogberget N 34 A4
Midwolda NL 43 B4
Miechów PL 55 C5
Miedes de Aragón E 89 C5
Miedes de Atienza E 95 A3
Międzybodzie Bielskie PL 65 A5
Międzybórz PL 54 B2
Międzychód PL 46 C1
Międzylesie PL 54 C1
Międzyrzec Podlaski PL 6 F7
Międzyrzecz PL 46 C1
Międzywodzie PL 45 A6
Międzyzdroje PL 45 B6
Miejska Górka PL 54 B1
Miélan F 76 C3
Mielec PL 55 C6
Mielęcin PL 45 B6
Mielno, *Warmińsko-Mazurskie* PL 47 B6
Mielno, *Zachodnio-Pomorskie* PL 46 A2
Miengo E 88 A3
Mieraslompolo FIN 113 C16
Miercurea Ciuc RO 11 C8
Mieres, *Asturias* E 88 A1
Mieres, *Girona* E 91 A5
Mieroszów PL 53 C6
Mierzyn PL 55 B4
Miesau D 60 A3
Miesbach D 62 C2
Mieścisko PL 46 C3
Mieste D 44 C3
Miesterhorst D 44 C3
Mieszków PL 54 A2
Mieszkowice PL 45 C6
Mietków PL 54 C1
Migennes F 59 C4
Miggiano I 107 B5
Migliánico I 103 A7
Migliarino I 81 B5
Migliónico I 104 C2
Mignano Monte Lungo I 103 B6
Migné F 67 B6
Miguel Esteban E 95 C3
Miguelturra E 94 D3
Mihajlovac SRB 85 B5
Miháld H 74 B2
Mihalgazi TR 118 B5
Mihalıççık TR 118 C6
Mihályi H 74 A2
Mihla D 51 B6
Mihohnić HR 83 A3
Miholjsko HR 73 C5
Mihovljan HR 73 B5
Mijares E 94 B2
Mijas E 100 C1
Mijoska CG 85 D4
Mike H 74 B2
Mikhnevo RUS 7 D14
Mikines GR 117 E4
Mikkeli FIN 3 F27
Mikkelvik N 112 B8
Mikleuš HR 74 C2
Mikołajki Pomorskie PL 47 B5
Mikołów PL 54 C3
Mikonos GR 117 E7
Mikorzyn PL 54 B3
Mikro Derio GR 116 A8
Mikstat PL 54 B2
Mikulášovice CZ 53 C4
Mikulov CZ 64 B2
Mikulovice CZ 54 C2
Milagro E 89 B5
Miłakowo PL 47 A6
Milan = Milano I 71 C4
Miland N 32 C5
Milano = Milan I 71 C4
Milano Marittima I 82 B1
Milas TR 119 E2
Milazzo I 109 A4
Mildenhall GB 30 B4
Milejewo PL 47 A5
Milelín CZ 53 C5
Miletić SRB 75 C4
Miletićevo SRB 75 C6
Mileto I 106 C3
Milevsko CZ 63 A5
Milford IRL 19 A4
Milford Haven GB 28 B2
Milford on Sea GB 31 D2
Milhão P 87 C4
Milići BIH 84 B4
Miličín CZ 63 A5
Milicz PL 54 B2
Milín CZ 63 A5
Militello in Val di Catánia I 109 B3
Miljevina BIH 84 C3
Milkowice PL 53 B6
Millançay F 68 A1
Millares E 96 B2
Millas F 91 A5
Millau F 78 B2
Millesimo I 80 B2
Millevaches F 68 C2
Millom GB 26 A2
Millport GB 24 C3
Millstatt A 72 B3
Millstreet, *Cork* IRL 20 B2
Millstreet, *Waterford* IRL 21 B4
Milltown, *Galway* IRL 18 C3
Milltown, *Kerry* IRL 20 B1
Milltown Malbay IRL 20 B2
Milly-la-Forêt F 58 B3
Milmarcos E 95 A5
Milmersdorf D 45 B5
Milna HR 83 C5
Milnthorpe GB 26 A3
Miločaj SRB 85 C5
Milogórze PL 47 A6
Miłomłyn PL 47 B5
Milos GR 117 F6
Miloševo SRB 85 B6
Miłosław PL 54 A2
Milot AL 105 B5
Milówka PL 65 A5
Miltach D 62 A3
Miltenberg D 61 A5
Milton Keynes GB 31 B3
Miltzow D 45 A5
Milutovac SRB 85 C6
Milverton GB 29 B4
Milzyn PL 47 C4
Mimice HR 84 C1
Mimizan F 76 B1
Mimizan-Plage F 76 B1
Mimoň CZ 53 C4
Mina de Juliana P 98 B2
Mina de São Domingos P 98 B3
Minas de Riotinto E 99 B4
Minateda E 101 A4
Minaya E 95 C4
Minde P 92 B2
Mindelheim D 61 B6
Mindelstetten D 62 B2
Minden D 51 A4
Mindszent H 75 B5
Minehead GB 29 B4
Mineo I 109 B3
Minerbe I 71 C6
Minérbio I 81 B5
Minervino Murge I 104 B2
Minglanilla E 95 C5
Mingorria E 94 B2

Minnesund N 34 B3
Miño E 86 A2
Miño de San Esteban E 89 C3
Minsen D 43 B4
Minsk BY 7 E9
Mińsk Mazowiecki PL 55 A6
Minsterley GB 26 C3
Mintlaw GB 23 D6
Minturno I 103 B6
Mionica BIH 84 B3
Mionica SRB 85 B5
Mios F 76 B2
Mira E 96 B1
Mira I 72 C2
Mira P 92 A2
Mirabel E 93 B4
Mirabel-aux-Baronnies F 79 B4
Mirabella Eclano I 103 B8
Mirabella Imbáccari I 109 B3
Mirabello I 81 B5
Miradoux F 77 B3
Miraflores de la Sierra E 94 B3
Miralrio E 95 B4
Miramar P 87 C2
Miramare I 82 B1
Miramas F 78 C3
Mirambeau F 67 C4
Miramont-de-Guyenne F 77 B3
Miranda de Arga E 89 B5
Miranda de Ebro E 89 B4
Miranda do Corvo P 92 A2
Miranda do Douro P 87 C4
Mirande F 77 C3
Mirandela P 87 C3
Mirandilla E 93 C4
Mirándola I 81 B5
Miranje HR 83 B4
Mirano I 72 C2
Miras AL 116 B2
Miravet E 90 B3
Miré F 57 C5
Mirebeau F 67 B5
Mirebeau-sur-Bèze F 69 A5
Mirecourt F 60 B2
Mirepoix F 77 C4
Mires GR 117 G6
Miribel F 69 C4
Miričina BIH 84 B3
Mirina GR 116 C7
Mirna SLO 73 C5
Miroslav CZ 64 B2
Mirosławice PL 54 C1
Mirosławiec PL 46 B2
Mirošov CZ 63 A4
Mirotice CZ 63 A5
Mirovice CZ 63 A5
Mirow D 45 B4
Mirsk PL 53 C5
Mirzec PL 55 B6
Misi FIN 113 F15
Misilmeri I 108 A2
Miske H 75 B4
Miskolc H 65 B6
Mislinja SLO 73 B5
Missanello I 104 C2
Missillac F 66 A2
Mistelbach A 64 B2
Mistelbach D 62 A2
Misten N 112 E3
Misterbianco I 109 B4
Misterhult S 40 B6
Mistretta I 109 B3
Misurina I 72 B2
Mitchelstown IRL 20 B3
Mithimna GR 116 C8
Mithoni GR 117 F3
Mitilini GR 118 C1
Mitilinii GR 119 E1
Mittelberg, *Tirol* A 71 B5
Mittelberg, *Vorarlberg* A 71 A5
Mittenwald D 71 A6
Mittenwalde D 52 A3
Mitter-Kleinarl A 72 A3
Mitterback A 63 C6
Mitterdorf im Mürztal A 73 A5
Mittersheim F 60 B2
Mittersill A 72 A2
Mitterskirchen D 62 B3
Mitterteich D 62 A3
Mitton F 76 B2
Mittweida D 52 C2
Mitwitz D 52 C1
Mizhhir'ya UA 11 B7
Mjällby S 41 C4
Mjåvatn N 33 D5
Mjöbäck S 40 B2
Mjölby S 37 D2
Mjølfjell N 32 B3
Mjøndalen N 35 C2
Mjørlund N 34 B2
Mladá Boleslav CZ 53 C4
Mladá Vožice CZ 63 A5
Mladé Buky CZ 53 C5
Mladenovac SRB 85 B5
Mladenovo SRB 75 C4
Mladikovine BIH 84 B2
Mława PL 47 B6
Mlinište BIH 84 B1
Młodzieszyn PL 55 A5
Mlogoszyn PL 55 A4
Młynary PL 47 A5
Mnichóvice CZ 63 A5
Mnichovo Hradiště CZ 53 C4
Mniów PL 55 B5
Mnisek nad Hnilcom SK 65 B6
Mníšek pod Brdy CZ 63 A5
Mniszek PL 55 B5
Mniszków PL 55 B5
Mo, *Hedmark* N 34 B3
Mo, *Hordaland* N 32 B2
Mo, *Møre og Romsdal* N 114 E5
Mo, *Telemark* N 33 C4
Mo, *Gävleborg* S 36 A3
Mo, *Västra Götaland* S 35 D3
Mo i Rana N 115 A11
Moaña E 87 B2
Moate IRL 21 A4
Mocejón E 94 C3
Močenok SK 64 B3
Mochales E 95 A4
Mochowo PL 47 C5
Mochy PL 53 A6
Mockern D 52 A1
Mockfjärd S 36 B1
Möckmühl D 61 A5
Mockrehna D 52 B2
Moclin E 100 B2
Mocsa H 64 C4
Mőcsény H 74 B3
Modane F 70 C1
Modbury GB 28 C4
Módena I 81 B4
Möðrudalur IS 111 B10
Módica I 109 C3
Modigliana I 81 B5
Modlin PL 47 C6
Mödling A 64 B2
Modliszewice PL 55 B5
Modliszewko PL 46 C3
Modogno I 104 B2
Modra SK 64 B3
Modran BIH 84 B2
Modriča BIH 84 B3
Modrý Kamen SK 65 B5
Moëlan-sur-Mer F 56 C2
Moelfre GB 26 B1
Moelv N 34 B2
Moen N 112 C7
Moena I 72 B1
Moerbeke B 49 B4
Moers D 50 B2
Móes P 87 D3
Moffat GB 25 C4
Mogadouro P 87 C4
Mogata S 37 D3
Móggio Udinese I 72 B3
Mogielnica PL 55 B5
Mogilany PL 65 A5
Mogilno PL 46 C3
Mogliano I 82 C2
Mogliano Véneto I 72 C2
Mogor E 87 B2
Mógoro I 110 C1
Moguer E 99 B4
Mohács H 74 C3
Moheda S 40 B4
Mohedas E 93 A4
Mohedas de la Jara E 93 B5
Mohelnice CZ 64 A2
Mohill IRL 19 C4
Möhlin CH 70 A2
Moholm S 35 D6
Mohorn D 52 B3
Mohyliv-Podil's'kyy UA 11 B9
Moi N 33 D3
Moià E 91 B5
Móie I 82 C2
Moimenta da Beira P 87 D3
Moirans F 69 C5
Moirans-en-Montagne F 69 B5
Moisaküla EST 7 B8
Moisdon-la-Rivière F 57 C4
Moissac F 77 B4
Moita, *Coimbra* P 92 A2
Moita, *Guarda* P 93 A3
Moita, *Santarém* P 92 B2
Moita, *Setúbal* P 92 C1
Moita dos Ferreiros P 92 B1
Moixent E 101 A5
Mojacar E 101 B4
Mojados E 88 C2
Mojkovac CG 85 D4
Mojmírovce SK 64 B4
Mojtin SK 65 B4
Möklinta S 36 B3
Mokošica HR 84 D3
Mokra Gora SRB 85 C4
Mokro Polje HR 83 B5
Mokronog SLO 73 C5
Mokrzyska PL 55 C5
Møkster N 32 B2
Mol B 49 B6
Mol SRB 75 C5
Mola di Bari I 104 B3
Molai GR 117 F4
Molare I 80 B2
Molaretto I 70 C2
Molas F 77 C3
Molassano I 80 B2
Molbergen D 43 C4
Mold GB 26 B2
Molde N 114 E4
Møldrup DK 38 C2
Moledo do Minho P 87 C2
Molfetta I 104 B2
Molfsee D 44 A2
Moliden S 115 D15
Molières F 77 B4
Molina de Aragón E 95 B5
Molina de Segura E 101 A4
Molinar E 89 A3
Molinaseca E 86 B4
Molinella I 81 B5
Molinet F 68 B3
Molini di Tures I 72 B1
Molinicos E 101 A3
Molinos de Duero E 89 C4
Molins de Rei E 91 B5
Moliterno I 104 C1
Molkom S 35 C5
Mollas AL 105 C6
Möllbrücke A 72 B3
Mölle S 41 C2
Molledo E 88 A2
Möllenbeck D 45 B5
Mollerussa E 90 B3
Mollet de Perelada E 91 A5
Mollina E 100 B1
Mölln D 44 B2
Mölló E 91 A5
Mollösund S 35 D3
Mölltorp S 37 D1
Mölnbo S 37 C4
Mölndal S 38 B5
Mölnlycke S 38 B5
Molompize F 68 C3
Moloy F 69 A4
Molsheim F 60 B3
Moltzow D 45 B4
Molve HR 74 B2
Molveno I 71 B5
Molvizar E 100 C2
Molzbichl A 72 B3
Mombaróccio I 82 C1
Mombeltrán E 94 B1
Mombris D 51 C5
Mombuey E 87 B4
Momchilgrad BG 116 A7
Mommark DK 39 E3
Momo I 70 C3
Monaghan IRL 19 B5
Monar Lodge GB 22 D4
Monasterace Marina I 106 C3
Monasterevin IRL 21 A4
Monasterio de Rodilla E 89 B3
Monastir I 110 C2
Monbahus F 77 B3
Monbazillac F 77 B3
Moncada E 96 B2
Moncalieri I 80 A1
Moncalvo I 80 A2
Monção P 87 B2
Moncarapacho P 98 B3
Moncel-sur-Seille F 60 B2
Monchegorsk RUS 3 C30
Mönchengladbach = Munchen-Gladbach D 50 B2
Mónchio della Corti I 81 B4
Monchique P 98 B2
Monclar-de-Quercy F 77 C4
Moncofa E 96 B2
Moncontour F 56 B3
Moncoutant F 67 B4
Monda E 100 C1
Mondariz E 87 B2
Mondavio I 82 C1
Mondéjar E 95 B3
Mondello I 108 A2
Mondim de Basto P 87 C3
Mondolfo I 82 C2
Mondoñedo E 86 A3
Mondorf-les-Bains L 60 A2
Mondoubleau F 58 C1
Mondovì I 80 B1
Mondragon F 78 B3
Mondragone I 103 B6
Mondsee A 63 C4
Monéglia I 80 B3
Monegrillo E 90 B2
Monein F 76 C2
Monemvasia GR 117 F5
Mónesi I 80 B1
Monesiglio I 80 B2
Monesterio E 99 A4
Monestier-de-Clermont F 79 B4
Monestiés F 77 B5
Monéteau F 59 C4
Moneygall IRL 21 B4
Moneymore GB 19 B5
Monfalcone I 72 C3
Monfero E 86 A2
Monflanquin F 77 B3
Monflorite E 90 A2
Monforte P 92 B3
Monforte da Beira E 92 B3
Monforte da Beira P 92 B3
Monforte d'Alba I 80 B1
Monforte de Lemos E 86 B3
Monforte de Moyuela E 90 B1
Monforte del Cid E 96 C2
Monghidoro I 81 B5
Mongiana I 106 C3
Monguelfo I 72 B2
Monheim D 62 B1
Moniaive GB 25 C4
Monifieth GB 25 B5
Monikie GB 25 B5
Monistrol-d'Allier F 78 B2
Monistrol de Montserrat E 91 B4
Monistrol-sur-Loire F 68 C4
Mönkebude D 45 B5
Monkton GB 24 C3
Monmouth GB 29 B5
Monnaie F 67 A5
Monnerville F 58 B3
Monnickendam NL 42 C2
Monolithos GR 119 F2
Monópoli I 104 C3
Monor H 75 A4
Monóvar E 101 A5
Monpazier F 77 B3
Monreal D 50 C3
Monreal E 76 D1
Monreal del Campo E 95 B5
Monreale I 108 A2
Monroy E 93 B4
Monroyo E 90 C2
Mons B 49 C4
Monsaraz P 92 C3
Monschau D 50 C2
Monségur F 76 B3
Monsélice I 72 C1
Mønshaug N 32 B3
Monster NL 49 A5
Mönsterås S 40 B6
Monsummano Terme I 81 C4
Mont-de-Marsan F 76 C2
Mont-Louis F 91 A5
Mont-roig del Camp E 90 B3
Mont-St. Aignan F 58 A2
Mont-St. Vincent F 69 B4
Mont-sous-Vaudrey F 69 B5
Montabaur D 50 C3
Montafia I 80 B2
Montagnac F 78 C2
Montagnana I 71 C6
Montaigu F 66 B3
Montaigu-de-Quercy F 77 B4
Montaiguët-en-Forez F 68 B3
Montaigut F 68 B2
Montaigut-sur-Save F 77 C4
Montainville F 58 B2
Montalbán E 90 C2
Montalbán de Córdoba E 100 B1
Montalbano Elicona I 109 A4
Montalbano Iónico I 104 C2
Montalbo E 95 C4
Montalcino I 81 C5
Montaldo di Cósola I 80 B3
Montalegre P 87 C3
Montalieu-Vercieu F 69 C5
Montalivet-les-Bains F 66 C3
Montallegro I 108 B2
Montalto delle Marche I 82 D2
Montalto di Castro I 102 A4
Montalto Pavese I 80 B3
Montalto Uffugo I 106 B3
Montalvão P 92 B3
Montamarta E 88 C1
Montana BG 11 E7
Montana-Vermala CH 70 B2
Montánchez E 93 B4
Montanejos E 96 A2
Montano Antilia I 106 A2
Montans F 77 C4
Montargil P 92 B2
Montargis F 58 C3
Montastruc-la-Conseillère F 77 C4
Montauban F 77 B4
Montauban-de-Bretagne F 57 B3
Montbard F 59 C5
Montbarrey F 69 A5
Montbazens F 77 B5
Montbazon F 67 A5
Montbéliard F 70 A1
Montbenoit F 69 B6
Montbeugny F 68 B3
Montblanc E 91 B4
Montbozon F 69 A6
Montbrison F 68 C4
Montbron F 67 C5
Montbrun-les-Bains F 79 B4
Montceau-les-Mines F 69 B4
Montcenis F 69 B4
Montchanin F 69 B4
Montcornet F 59 A5
Montcuq F 77 B4
Montdardier F 78 C2
Montdidier F 58 A3
Monte-Carlo MC 80 C1
Monte Clara P 92 B3
Monte Clérigo P 98 B2
Monte da Pedra P 92 B3
Monte de Goula P 92 B3
Monte do Trigo P 92 C3
Monte Gordo P 98 B3
Monte Juntos P 92 C3
Monte Porzio I 82 C2
Monte Real P 92 B2
Monte Redondo P 92 B2
Monte Romano I 102 A4
Monte San Giovanni Campano I 103 B6
Monte San Savino I 81 C5
Monte Sant'Ángelo I 104 B1
Monte Vilar P 92 B1
Monteagudo E 101 A4
Monteagudo de las Vicarias E 89 C4
Montealegre E 88 C2
Montealegre del Castillo E 101 A4
Montebello Iónico I 109 B4
Montebello Vicentino I 71 C6
Montebelluna I 72 C2
Montebourg F 57 A4
Montebruno I 80 B3
Montecarotto I 82 C2
Montecassiano I 82 C2
Montecastrilli I 102 A5
Montecatini Terme I 81 C4
Montécchio I 82 C1
Montécchio Emilia I 81 B4
Montécchio Maggiore I 71 C6
Montech F 77 C4
Montechiaro d'Asti I 80 A2
Montecórice I 103 C7
Montecorvino Rovella I 103 C7
Montederramo E 87 B3
Montedoro I 108 B2
Montefalco I 82 D1
Montefalcone di Val Fortore I 103 B8
Montefalcone nel Sánnio I 103 B7
Montefano I 82 C2
Montefiascone I 102 A5
Montefiorino I 81 B4
Montefortino I 82 D2
Montefranco I 102 A5
Montefrio E 100 B2
Montegiordano Marina I 106 A3
Montegiórgio I 82 C2
Montegranaro I 82 C2
Montehermoso E 93 A4
Montejicar E 100 B2
Montejo de la Sierra E 95 A3
Montejo de Tiermes E 89 C3
Montel-de-Gelat F 68 C2
Monteleone di Púglia I 103 B8
Monteleone di Spoleto I 102 A5
Monteleone d'Orvieto I 81 D6
Montelepre I 108 A2
Montelibretti I 102 A5
Montelier F 79 B4
Montélimar F 78 B3
Montella E 91 A4
Montella I 103 C8
Montellano E 99 B5
Montelupo Fiorentino I 81 C5
Montemaggiore Belsito I 108 B2
Montemagno I 80 B2
Montemayor E 100 B1
Montemayor de Pinilla E 88 C2
Montemésola I 104 C3
Montemilleto I 103 B7
Montemilone I 104 B1
Montemolin E 99 A4
Montemónaco I 82 D2
Montemor-o-Novo P 92 C2
Montemor-o-Velho P 92 A2
Montemurro I 104 C1
Montendre F 67 C4
Montenegro de Cameros E 89 B4
Montenero di Bisáccia I 103 B7
Monteneuf F 57 C3
Monteparano I 104 C3
Montepescali I 81 D5
Montepiano I 81 B5
Montepulciano I 81 C5
Montereale I 103 A6
Montereale Valcellina I 72 B2
Montereau-Faut-Yonne F 59 B3
Monterénzio I 81 B5
Monteroni d'Arbia I 81 C5
Monteroni di Lecce I 105 C4
Monterosso al Mare I 80 B3
Monterosso Almo I 109 B3
Monterosso Grana I 79 B6
Monterotondo I 102 A5
Monterotondo Maríttimo I 81 C4
Monterrey E 87 C3
Monterroso E 86 B3
Monterrubio de la Serena E 93 C5
Monterubbiano I 82 C2
Montes Velhos P 98 B2
Montesa E 96 C2
Montesalgueiro E 86 A2
Montesano sulla Marcellana I 104 C1
Montesárchio I 103 B7
Montescaglioso I 104 C2
Montesclaros E 94 B2
Montesilvano I 103 A7
Montespértoli I 81 C5
Montesquieu-Volvestre F 77 C4
Montesquiou F 77 C3
Montestruc-sur-Gers F 77 C3
Montevarchi I 81 C5
Montéveglio I 81 B5
Montfaucon F 66 A3
Montfaucon-d'Argonne F 59 A6
Montfaucon-en-Velay F 69 C4
Montferrat, *Isère* F 69 C5
Montferrat, *Var* F 79 C5
Montfort-en-Chalosse F 76 C2
Montfort-l'Amaury F 58 B2
Montfort-le-Gesnois F 58 B1
Montfort-sur-Meu F 57 B4
Montfort-sur-Risle F 58 A1
Montgai E 90 B3
Montgaillard F 76 C3
Montgenèvre F 79 B5
Montgiscard F 77 C4
Montgomery GB 26 C2
Montguyon F 67 C4
Monthermé F 59 A5
Monthey CH 70 B1
Monthois F 59 A5
Monthureux-sur-Saône F 60 B1
Monti I 110 B2
Monticelli d'Ongina I 81 A3
Montichiari I 71 C5
Monticiano I 81 C5
Montiel E 100 A3
Montier-en-Der F 59 B5
Montieri I 81 C5
Montiglio I 80 A2
Montignac F 77 A4
Montigny-le-Roi F 60 C1
Montigny-lès-Metz F 60 A2
Montigny-sur-Aube F 59 C5
Montijo E 93 C4
Montijo P 92 C2
Montilla E 100 B1
Montillana E 100 B2
Montilly F 68 B3
Montivilliers F 57 A6
Montjaux F 78 B1
Montjean-sur-Loire F 66 A4
Montlhéry F 58 B3
Montlieu-la-Garde F 67 C4
Montlouis-sur-Loire F 67 A5
Montluçon F 68 B2
Montluel F 69 C5
Montmarault F 68 B2
Montmartin-sur-Mer F 57 B4
Montmédy F 59 A6
Montmélian F 69 C6
Montmeyan F 79 C5
Montmeyran F 78 B3
Montmirail, *Marne* F 59 B4
Montmirail, *Sarthe* F 58 B1
Montmiral F 69 C5
Montmirat F 78 C3
Montmirey-le-Château F 69 A5
Montmoreau-St. Cybard F 67 C5
Montmorency F 58 B3
Montmorillon F 67 B5
Montmort-Lucy F 59 B4
Montoir-de-Bretagne F 66 A2
Montoire-sur-le-Loir F 58 C1
Montoito P 92 C3
Montolieu F 77 C5
Montório al Vomano I 103 A6
Montoro E 100 A1
Montpellier F 78 C2
Montpezat-de-Quercy F 77 B4
Montpezat-sous-Bouzon F 78 B3
Montpon-Ménestérol F 76 A3
Montpont-en-Bresse F 69 B5
Montréal, *Aude* F 77 C5
Montréal, *Gers* F 76 C3
Montredon-Labessonnié F 77 C5
Montréjeau F 77 C3
Montrésor F 67 A6
Montresta I 110 B1
Montret F 69 B5
Montreuil, *Pas de Calais* F 48 C2
Montreuil, *Seine St. Denis* F 58 B3
Montreuil-aux-Lions F 59 A4
Montreuil-Bellay F 67 A4
Montreux CH 70 B1
Montrevault F 66 A3
Montrevel-en-Bresse F 69 B5
Montrichard F 67 A6
Montricoux F 77 B4
Montrond-les-Bains F 69 C4
Montrose GB 25 B5
Montroy E 96 B2
Monts-sur-Guesnes F 67 B5
Montsalvy F 77 B5
Montsauche-les-Settons F 68 A4
Montseny E 91 B5
Montsoreau F 67 A5
Montsûrs F 57 B5
Montuenga E 94 A2
Montuïri E 97 B3
Monturque E 100 B1
Monza I 71 C4
Monzón E 90 B3
Monzón de Campos E 88 B2
Moorbad Lobenstein D 52 C1
Moordorf D 43 B4
Moorslede B 49 C4
Moos D 61 C4
Moosburg D 62 B2
Moosburg im Kärnten A 73 B4
Mór H 74 A3
Mora E 94 C3
Móra P 92 C2
Mora S 36 A1
Mora de Rubielos E 96 A2
Móra d'Ebre E 90 B3
Móra la Nova E 90 B3
Moraby S 36 B2
Moradillo de Roa E 88 C3
Morag PL 47 B5
Mórahalom H 75 B4
Moraime E 86 A1
Morais P 87 C4
Moral de Calatrava E 100 A2
Moraleda de Zafayona E 100 B2
Moraleja E 93 A4
Moraleja del Vino E 88 C1
Morales de Toro E 88 C1
Morales de Valverde E 88 C1
Morales del Vino E 88 C1
Moralina E 87 C4
Morano Cálabro I 106 B3
Mörarp S 41 C2
Morasverdes E 93 A4
Morata de Jalón E 89 C5
Morata de Jiloca E 89 C5
Morata de Tajuña E 95 B3
Moratalla E 101 A4
Moravče SLO 73 B4
Moravec CZ 64 A2
Moraviţa RO 75 C6
Morávka CZ 65 A4
Moravská Třebová CZ 64 A2
Moravské Budějovice CZ 64 A1
Moravské Lieskové SK 64 B3
Moravske Toplice SLO 73 B6
Moravský-Beroun CZ 64 A3
Moravský Krumlov CZ 64 A2
Moravský Svätý Ján SK 64 B3
Morawica PL 55 C5
Morawin PL 54 B3
Morbach D 60 A3
Morbegno I 71 B4
Morbier F 69 B6
Mörbisch am See A 64 C2
Mörbylånga S 41 C6
Morcenx F 76 B2
Morciano di Romagna I 82 C1
Morcone I 103 B7
Morcuera E 89 C3
Mordelles F 57 B4
Mordoğan TR 119 D1
Moréac F 56 C3
Morebattle GB 25 C5
Morecambe GB 26 A3
Moreda, *Granada* E 100 B2
Moreda, *Oviedo* E 88 A1
Morée F 58 C2
Moreles de Rey E 88 B1
Morella E 90 C2
Moreruela de los Infanzones E 88 C1
Morés E 89 C5
Móres I 110 B1
Morestel F 69 C5
Moret-sur-Loing F 58 B3
Moreton-in-Marsh GB 29 B6
Moretonhampstead GB 28 C4
Moretta I 80 B1
Moreuil F 58 A3
Morez F 69 B6
Mörfelden D 51 D4
Morgat F 56 B1
Morges CH 69 B6
Morgex I 70 C2
Morgongåva S 36 C3
Morhange F 60 B2
Morhet B 49 D6
Mori I 71 C5
Morialmé B 49 C5
Morianes P 98 B3
Moriani Plage F 102 A2
Mórichida H 74 A2
Moriles E 100 B1
Morille E 94 B1
Moringen D 51 B5
Morjärv S 3 C25
Morkarla S 36 B4
Mørke DK 39 C3
Mørkøv DK 39 D4
Morkovice-Slížany CZ 64 A3
Morlaàs F 76 C2
Morlaix F 56 B2
Morley F 59 B6
Mörlunda S 40 B5
Mormanno I 106 B2
Mormant F 59 B3
Mornant F 69 C4
Mornay-Berry F 68 A2
Morokovo CG 85 D4
Morón de Almazán E 89 C4
Morón de la Frontera E 99 B5
Morović SRB 85 A4
Morozzo I 80 B1
Morpeth GB 25 C6
Morphou CY 120 A1
Mörrum S 41 C4
Morsbach D 50 C3
Mörsch D 61 B4
Mörsil S 115 D10
Morsum D 39 E1
Mørsvikbotn N 112 E4
Mortagne-au-Perche F 58 B1
Mortagne-sur-Gironde F 66 C4
Mortagne-sur-Sèvre F 66 B4
Mortágua P 92 A2
Mortain F 57 B5
Mortara I 70 C3
Morteau F 69 A6
Mortegliano I 72 C3
Mortelle I 109 A4
Mortemart F 67 B5
Mortimer's Cross GB 29 A5
Mortrée F 57 B6
Mörtschach A 72 B2
Mortsel B 49 B5
Morud DK 39 D3
Morwenstow GB 28 C3
Moryń PL 45 C6
Morzeszczyn PL 47 B4
Morzewo PL 47 B5
Morzine F 70 B1
Mosalsk RUS 7 D13
Mosbach D 61 A5
Mosbjerg DK 38 B3
Mosby N 33 D4
Mosca P 87 C4
Moscavide P 92 C1
Moščenica HR 73 C6
Mošćenice HR 73 C4
Moščenicka Draga HR 73 C4
Mosciano Sant'Ángelo I 82 D2
Mościsko PL 54 C1
Moscow = Moskva RUS 7 D14
Mosina PL 54 A1
Mosjøen N 115 B10
Moskog N 32 A3
Moskorzew PL 55 C4
Moskosel S 115 B16
Moskuvarra FIN 113 E15
Moskva = Moscow RUS 7 D14
Moslavina Podravska HR 74 C2
Moşniţa Nouă RO 75 C6
Moso in Passiria I 71 B6
Mosonmagyaróvár H 64 C3
Mošorin SRB 75 C5
Mošovce SK 65 B4
Mosqueruela E 90 C2
Moss N 35 C2
Mossfellsbær IS 111 C4
Mössingen D 61 B5
Mosstrand N 32 C5
Most CZ 52 C3
Most na Soči SLO 72 B3
Mosta M 107 C5
Mostar BIH 84 C2
Mosterhamn N 33 C2
Mostki PL 53 A5

Móstoles E 94 B3
Mostová SK 64 B3
Mostowo PL 46 A2
Mostuéjouls F 78 B2
Mosty PL 45 B6
Mostys'ka UA 11 B7
Mosvik N 114 D7
Mota del Cuervo E 95 C4
Mota del Marqués E 88 C1
Motala S 37 D2
Motherwell GB 25 C4
Möthlow D 45 C4
Motilla del Palancar E 95 C5
Motnik SLO 73 B4
Motovun HR 72 C3
Motril E 100 C2
Motta I 71 C6
Motta di Livenza I 72 C2
Motta Montecorvino I 103 B8
Motta Visconti I 70 C3
Mottisfont GB 31 C2
Móttola I 104 C3
Mou DK 38 C3
Mouchard F 69 B5
Moudon CH 70 B1
Moudros GR 116 C7
Mougins F 79 C5
Mouilleron en-Pareds F 66 B4
Mouliherne F 67 A5
Moulinet F 80 C1
Moulins F 68 B3
Moulins-Engilbert F 68 B3
Moulins-la-Marche F 58 B1
Moulismes F 67 B5
Moult F 57 A5
Mount Bellew Bridge IRL 20 A3
Mountain Ash GB 29 B4
Mountfield GB 19 B4
Mountmellick IRL 21 A4
Mountrath IRL 21 A4
Mountsorrel GB 30 B2
Moura P 98 A3
Mourão P 92 C3
Mourenx F 76 C2
Mouriés F 78 C3
Mourmelon-le-Grand F 59 A5
Mouronho P 92 A2
Mouscron B 49 C4
Mousehole GB 28 C2
Moussac F 78 C3
Moussey F 60 B2
Mousteru F 56 B2
Moustey F 76 B2
Moustiers-Ste. Marie F 79 C5
Mouthe F 69 B6
Mouthier-Haute-Pierre F 69 A6
Mouthoumet F 77 D5
Moutier CH 70 A2
Moûtiers F 69 C6
Moutiers-les-Mauxfaits F 66 B3
Mouy F 58 A3
Mouzaki GR 116 C3
Mouzon F 59 A6
Møvik N 32 B2
Moville IRL 19 A4
Moy, *Highland* GB 23 D4
Moy, *Tyrone* GB 19 B5
Moycullen IRL 20 A2
Moyenmoutier F 60 B2
Moyenvic F 60 B2
Mózar E 88 C1
Mozhaysk RUS 7 D14
Mozirje SLO 73 B4
Mözs H 74 B3
Mozzanica I 71 C4
Mramorak SRB 85 B5
Mrčajevci SRB 85 C5
Mrkonjić Grad BIH 84 B2
Mrkopalj HR 73 C4
Mrmoš SRB 85 C6
Mrocza PL 46 B3
Mroczeń PL 54 B2
Mroczno PL 47 B5
Mrozy PL 55 A6
Mrzezyno PL 45 A7
Mšec CZ 53 C3
Mšeno CZ 53 C4
Mstów PL 55 C4
Mstsislaw BY 7 D11
Mszana Dolna PL 65 A6
Mszczonów PL 55 B5
Mtsensk RUS 7 E14
Muć HR 83 C5
Múccia I 82 C2
Much D 50 C3
Much Marcle GB 29 B5
Much Wenlock GB 26 C3
Mücheln D 52 B1
Muchów PL 53 B6
Mucientes E 88 C2
Muckross IRL 20 B2
Mucur TR 16 B7
Muda P 98 B2
Mudanya TR 118 B3
Mudau D 61 A5
Müden D 44 C2
Mudersbach D 50 C3
Mudurnu TR 118 B6
Muel E 90 B1
Muelas del Pan E 88 C1
Muess D 44 B3
Muff IRL 19 A4
Mugardos E 86 A2
Muge P 92 B2
Mügeln, *Sachsen-Anhalt* D 52 B3
Mügeln, *Sachsen* D 52 B3
Múggia I 72 C3
Muğla TR 119 E3
Mugnano I 82 C1
Mugron F 76 C2
Mugueimes E 87 C3
Muhi H 65 C6
Mühlacker D 61 B4
Mühlbach am Hochkönig A 72 A3
Mühlberg, *Brandenburg* D 52 B3
Mühlberg, *Thüringen* D 51 C6
Mühldorf A 72 B3
Mühldorf D 62 B3
Muhleberg CH 70 B2
Mühleim D 61 B4
Muhlen-Eichsen D 44 B3
Mühlhausen, *Bayern* D 62 A1
Mühlhausen, *Thüringen* D 51 B6
Mühltroff D 52 C1
Muhos FIN 3 D27
Muhr A 72 A3
Muine Bheag IRL 21 B5
Muir of Ord GB 23 D4
Muirkirk GB 24 C3
Muirteira P 92 B1
Mukacheve UA 11 B7
Muker GB 26 A3
Mula E 101 A4
Mulben GB 23 D5
Mulegns CH 71 B4
Mules I 71 B6
Mülheim D 50 B2
Mulhouse F 60 C3
Muljava SLO 73 C4
Mullanys Cross IRL 18 B3
Müllheim D 60 C3
Mullhyttan S 37 C1
Mullinavat IRL 21 B4
Mullingar IRL 21 A4
Mullion GB 28 C2
Müllrose D 53 A4
Mullsjö S 40 B3
Mulseryd S 40 B3
Munaðarnes IS 111 A4
Munana E 94 B1
Muñás E 86 A4
Münchberg D 52 C1
Müncheberg D 45 C6
München = Munich D 62 B2
Munchen-Gladbach = Mönchen-gladbach D 50 B2
Münchhausen D 51 C4
Mundaka E 89 A4
Münden D 51 B5
Munderfing A 63 B4
Munderkingen D 61 B5
Mundesley GB 30 B5
Munera E 95 C4
Mungia E 89 A4
Munich = München D 62 B2
Muñico E 94 B1
Muniesa E 90 B2
Munka-Ljungby S 41 C2
Munkebo DK 39 D3
Munkedal S 35 D3
Munkflohögen S 115 D11
Munkfors S 34 C5
Munktorp S 37 C3
Münnerstadt D 51 C6
Muñopepe E 94 B2
Muñotello E 94 B1
Münsingen CH 70 B2
Münsingen D 61 B5
Munsö S 37 C4
Münster CH 70 B3
Münster, *Hessen* D 61 A4
Münster, *Niedersachsen* D 44 C2
Münster, *Nordrhein-Westfalen* D 50 B3
Munster F 60 B3
Muntibar E 89 A4
Münzkirchen A 63 B4
Muodoslompolo S 113 E12
Muonio FIN 113 E12
Muotathal CH 70 B3
Mur-de-Barrez F 77 B5
Mur-de-Bretagne F 56 B2
Mur-de-Sologne F 67 A6
Muradiye TR 118 D2
Murakeresztúr H 74 B1
Murán SK 65 B6
Murano I 72 C2
Muras E 86 A3
Murat F 78 A1
Murat-sur-Vèbre F 78 C1
Muratlı TR 118 A2
Murato F 102 A2
Murau A 73 A4
Muravera I 110 C2
Murazzano I 80 B2
Murça P 87 C3
Murchante E 89 B5
Murchin D 45 B5
Murcia E 101 B4
Murczyn PL 46 C3
Mureck A 73 B5
Mürefte TR 118 B2
Muret F 77 C4
Murg CH 71 A4
Murguia E 89 B4
Muri CH 70 A3
Murias de Paredes E 86 B4
Muriedas E 88 A3
Muriel Viejo E 89 C4
Murillo de Rio Leza E 89 B4
Murillo el Fruto E 89 B5
Murino CG 85 D4
Muriqan AL 105 A5
Murlaggan GB 22 E3
Murmansk RUS 3 B30
Murmashi RUS 3 B30
Murnau D 62 C2
Muro E 97 B3
Muro F 102 A1
Muro de Alcoy E 96 C2
Muro Lucano I 103 C8
Murol F 68 C2
Muron F 66 B4
Muros E 86 B1
Muros de Nalón E 86 A4
Murowana Goślina PL 46 C3
Mürren CH 70 B2
Murrhardt D 61 B5
Murska Sobota SLO 73 B6
Mursko Središce HR 73 B6
Murtas E 100 C2
Murten CH 70 B2
Murter HR 83 C4
Murtiçi TR 119 F6
Murtosa P 87 D2
Murvica HR 83 B4
Murviel-lès-Béziers F 78 C2
Mürzsteg A 63 C6
Murzynowo PL 46 C1
Mürzzuschlag A 63 C6
Musculdy F 76 C2
Mushqeta AL 105 B5
Muskö S 37 C5
Mušov CZ 64 B2
Musselburgh GB 25 C4
Musselkanaal NL 43 C4
Mussidan F 77 A3
Mussomeli I 108 B2
Musson B 60 A1
Mussy-sur-Seine F 59 C5
Mustafakemalpaşa TR 118 B3
Muszaki PL 47 B6
Muszyna PL 65 A6
Mut TR 16 C6
Muta SLO 73 B5
Muthill GB 25 B4
Mutné SK 65 A5
Mutriku E 89 A4
Muttalip TR 118 C5
Mutterbergalm A 71 A6
Muxía E 86 A1
Muxilka-Ugarte E 89 A4
Muzillac F 66 A2
Mužla SK 65 C4
Muzzano del Turgnano I 72 C3
Mybster GB 23 C5
Myckelgensjö S 115 D14
Myennes F 68 A2
Myjava SK 64 B3
Myking N 32 B2
Mykland N 33 D5
Mykolayiv = Nikolayev UA 11 C12
Myra N 33 D6
Myrdal N 32 B4
Myre, *Nordland* N 112 C4
Myre, *Nordland* N 112 D4
Myresjö S 40 B4
Myrhorod UA 11 B12
Mýri IS 111 B8
Myrtou CY 120 A2
Mysen N 35 C3
Mysłakowice PL 53 C5
Myślenice PL 65 A5
Myślibórz PL 45 C6
Mysłowice PL 55 C4
Myszków PL 55 C4
Mytishchi RUS 7 D14
Mýtna SK 65 B5
Mýtne Ludany SK 65 B4
Mýto CZ 63 A4

N

N Unnaryd S 40 B3
Nå N 32 B3
Naaldwijk NL 49 B5
Naantali FIN 6 A6
Naas IRL 21 A5
Nabais P 92 A3
Nabbelund S 41 B7
Nabburg D 62 A3
Načeradec CZ 63 A5
Náchod CZ 53 C6
Nacław PL 46 A2
Nadarzyce PL 46 B2
Nadarzyn PL 55 A5
Nádasd H 74 B1
Nădlac RO 75 B5
Nádudvar H 75 A6
Nadvirna UA 11 B8
Nærbø N 33 D2
Næsbjerg DK 39 D1
Næstved DK 39 D4
Näfels CH 70 A4
Nafpaktos GR 116 D3
Nafplio GR 117 E4
Nagel D 52 D1
Nagele NL 42 C2
Naggen S 115 E13
Nagłowice PL 55 C5
Nagold D 61 B4
Nagore E 76 D1
Nagyatád H 74 B2
Nagybajom H 74 B2
Nagybaracska H 74 B3
Nagybátony H 65 C5
Nagyberény H 74 B3
Nagybörzsöny H 65 C4
Nagycenk H 64 C2
Nagydorog H 74 B3
Nagyfüged H 65 C6
Nagyhersány H 74 C3
Nagyigmánd H 64 C4
Nagyiván H 75 A5
Nagykanizsa H 74 B1
Nagykáta H 75 A4
Nagykonyi H 74 B3
Nagykörös H 75 A4
Nagykörü H 75 A5
Nagylóc H 65 B5
Nagymágocs H 75 B5
Nagymányok H 74 B3
Nagymaros H 65 C4
Nagyoroszi H 65 B5
Nagyrábé H 75 A6
Nagyréde H 65 C5
Nagyszékely H 74 B3
Nagyszénás H 75 B5
Nagyszokoly H 74 B3
Nagytöke H 75 B5
Nagyvázsony H 74 B2
Nagyvenyim H 74 B3
Naharros E 95 B4
Nahe D 44 B2
Naidăş RO 85 B6
Naila D 52 C1
Nailloux F 77 C4
Nailsworth GB 29 B5
Naintré F 67 B5
Nairn GB 23 D5
Najac F 77 B4
Nájera E 89 B4
Nak H 74 B3
Nakksjø N 33 C6
Nakło nad Notecią PL 46 B3
Nakskov DK 39 E4
Nalda E 89 B4
Nälden S 115 D11
Nálepkovo SK 65 B6
Nalliers F 66 B3
Nallıhan TR 118 B6
Nalzen F 77 D4
Nalžouské Hory CZ 63 A4
Namdalseid N 114 C8
Náměšť nad Oslavou CZ 64 A2
Námestovo SK 65 A5
Namnå N 34 B4
Namsos N 114 C8
Namsskogan N 115 C10
Namur B 49 C5
Namysłów PL 54 B2
Nançay F 68 A2
Nanclares de la Oca E 89 B4
Nancy F 60 B2
Nangis F 59 B4
Nannestad N 34 B3
Nant F 78 B2
Nanterre F 58 B3
Nantes F 66 A3
Nanteuil-le-Haudouin F 58 A3
Nantiat F 67 B6
Nantua F 69 B5
Nantwich GB 26 B3
Naoussa, *Imathia* GR 116 B4
Naoussa, *Cyclades* GR 117 E7
Napajedla CZ 64 A3
Napiwoda PL 47 B6
Naples = Nápoli I 103 C7
Nápoli = Naples I 103 C7
Nar S 37 E5
Nara N 32 A1
Naraval E 86 A4
Narberth GB 28 B3
Narbonne F 78 C1
Narbonne-Plage F 78 C2
Narbuvollen N 114 E8
Narcao I 110 C1
Nardò I 107 A5
Narken S 113 F11
Narmo N 34 B3
Narni I 102 A5
Naro I 108 B2
Naro Fominsk RUS 7 D14
Narón E 86 A2
Narros del Castillo E 94 B1
Narta HR 74 C1
Naruszewo PL 47 C6
Narva EST 7 B10
Narvik N 112 D6
Narzole I 80 B1
Näs FIN 36 B7
Nås, *Dalarnas* S 36 B1
Nås, *Gotland* S 37 E5
Näsåker S 115 D13
Năsăud RO 11 C8
Nasavrky CZ 64 A1
Nasbinals F 78 B2
Näshull S 40 B5
Našice HR 74 C3
Nasielsk PL 47 C6
Naso I 109 A3
Nassau D 50 C3
Nassenfels D 62 B2
Nassenheide D 45 C5
Nassereith A 71 A5
Nässjö S 40 B4
Nastätten D 50 C3
Näsum S 41 C4
Näsviken S 115 D12
Natalinci SRB 85 B5
Nater-Stetten D 62 B2
Naters CH 70 B3
Nattavaara S 112 F9
Natters A 71 A6
Nattheim D 61 B6
Nättraby S 41 C5
Naturno I 71 B5
Naucelle F 77 B5
Nauders A 71 B5
Nauen D 45 C4
Naul IRL 19 C5
Naumburg D 52 B1
Naundorf D 52 C3
Naunhof D 52 B2
Naustdal N 32 A2
Nautijaur S 112 F8
Nautsi RUS 113 D18
Nava E 88 A1
Nava de Arévalo E 94 B2
Nava de la Asunción E 94 A2
Nava del Rey E 88 C1
Navacerrada E 94 B2
Navaconcejo E 93 A5
Navafriá E 94 A3
Navahermosa E 94 C2
Navahrudak BY 7 E8
Naval E 90 A3
Navalacruz E 94 B2
Navalcán E 94 B1
Navalcarnero E 94 B2
Navaleno E 89 C3
Navalmanzano E 94 A2
Navalmoral E 94 B2
Navalmoral de la Mata E 93 B5
Naválón E 96 C2
Navalonguilla E 93 A5
Navalperal de Pinares E 94 B2
Navalpino E 94 C2
Navaltalgordo E 94 B2
Navaltoril E 94 C2
Navaluenga E 94 B2
Navalvillar de Pela E 93 B5
Navan IRL 19 C5
Navaperal de Tormes E 93 A5
Navapolatsk BY 7 D10
Navarclés E 91 B4
Navarredonda de Gredos E 93 A5
Navarrenx F 76 C2
Navarrés E 96 B2
Navarrete E 89 B4
Navarrevisca E 94 B2
Navás E 91 B4
Navas de Oro E 94 A2
Navas de San Juan E 100 A2
Navas del Madroño E 93 B4
Navas del Rey E 94 B2
Navas del Sepillar E 100 B1
Navascués E 76 D1
Navasfrias E 93 A4
Nave I 71 C5
Nave de Haver P 93 A4
Nävekvarn S 37 D3
Navelli I 103 A6
Navenby GB 27 B5
Näverkärret S 37 C2
Naverstad S 35 D3
Navés E 91 B4
Navezuelas E 93 B5
Navia E 86 A4
Navia de Suarna E 86 B4
Navilly F 69 B5
Navlya RUS 7 E13
Năvodari RO 11 D10
Naxos GR 117 E7
Nay F 76 C2
Nazaré P 92 B1
Nazarje SLO 73 B4
Nazilli TR 119 E3
Nazza D 51 B6
Ndroq AL 105 B5
Nea Anchialos GR 116 C4
Nea Epidavros GR 117 E5
Nea Flippias GR 116 C2
Nea Kalikratia GR 116 B5
Nea Makri GR 117 D5
Nea Moudania GR 116 B5
Nea Peramos GR 116 B6
Nea Stira GR 117 D6
Nea Visa GR 118 A1
Nea Zichni GR 116 A5
Neap GB 22 A7
Neapoli, *Kozani* GR 116 B3
Neapoli, *Kriti* GR 117 G7
Neapoli, *Lakonia* GR 117 F5
Neath GB 28 B4
Nebljusi HR 83 B4
Neblo SLO 72 B3
Nebolchy RUS 7 B12
Nebra D 52 B1
Nebreda E 88 C3
Nechanice CZ 53 C5
Neckargemünd D 61 A4
Neckarsulm D 61 A5
Neda E 86 A2
Neded SK 64 B3
Nedelišće HR 73 B6
Nederweert NL 50 B1
Nedre Gärdsjö S 36 B2
Nedre Soppero S 113 D10
Nedreberg N 34 B3
Nedstrand N 33 C2
Nedvědice CZ 64 A2
Nędza PL 54 C3
Neede NL 50 A2
Needham Market GB 30 B5
Needingworth GB 30 B3
Neermoor D 43 B4
Neeroeteren B 50 B1
Neerpelt B 49 B6
Neesen D 51 A4
Neetze D 44 B2
Nefyn GB 26 C1
Negbina SRB 85 C4
Negotin SRB 11 D7
Negotino MK 116 A4
Negrar I 71 C5
Negredo E 95 A4
Negreira E 86 B2
Nègrepelisse F 77 B4
Negru Vodă RO 11 E10
Negueira de Muñiz E 86 A4
Neheim D 50 B3
Neila E 89 B4
Néive I 80 B2
Nejdek CZ 52 C2
Nekla PL 46 C3
Neksø DK 41 D5
Nelas P 92 A3
Nelaug N 33 D5
Nelidovo RUS 7 C12
Nelim FIN 113 D17
Nellingen D 61 B5
Nelson GB 26 B3
Neman RUS 6 D7
Nemea GR 117 E4
Nemesgörzsöny H 74 A2
Nemeskér H 74 A1
Nemesnádudvar H 75 B4
Nemesszalók H 74 A2
Németkér H 74 B3
Nemours F 58 B3
Nemška Loka SLO 73 C5
Nemšová SK 64 B4
Nenagh IRL 20 B3
Nenince SK 65 B5
Nenita GR 117 D8
Nenzing A 71 A4
Neo Chori GR 116 D3
Neochori GR 116 C3
Neon Petritsi GR 116 A5
Nepi I 102 A5
Nepomuk CZ 63 A4
Nérac F 77 B3
Neratovice CZ 53 C4
Nerchau D 52 B2
Néré F 67 C4
Neresheim D 61 B6
Nereto I 82 D2
Nerezine HR 82 B3
Nerežišća HR 83 C5
Neringa LT 6 D6
Néris-les Bains F 68 B2
Nerito I 103 A6
Nerja E 100 C2
Néronde F 69 C4
Nérondes F 68 B2
Nerpio E 101 A3
Nersingen D 61 B6
Nerva E 99 B4
Nervesa della Battáglia I 72 C2
Nervi I 80 B3
Nes, *Buskerud* N 34 B1
Nes, *Hedmark* N 34 B2
Nes, *Sør-Trøndelag* N 114 D6
Nes NL 42 B2
Nesbyen N 32 B6
Neset N 114 F7
Nesflaten N 33 C3
Nesjahverfi IS 111 C10
Neskaupstaður IS 111 B12
Nesland N 33 C4
Neslandsvatn N 33 D6
Nesle F 59 A3
Nesna N 115 A10
Nesoddtangen N 34 C2
Nesovice CZ 64 A3
Nesselwang D 61 C6
Nesslau CH 71 A4
Nessmersiel D 43 B4
Nesso I 71 C4
Nesterov UA 11 A7
Nestorio GR 116 B3
Nesttun N 32 B2
Nesvady SK 64 C4
Nesvatnstemmen N 33 D5
Nether Stowey GB 29 B4
Netland N 33 D3
Netolice CZ 63 A5
Netphen D 50 C4
Netstal CH 70 A4
Nettancourt F 59 B5
Nettetal D 50 B2
Nettlingen D 51 A6
Nettuno I 102 B5
Neu Darchau D 44 B2
Neu-Isenburg D 51 C4
Neu Kaliss D 44 B3
Neu Lübbenau D 53 A3
Neu-markt am Wallersee A 63 C4
Neu-petershain D 53 B4
Neu-Ravensburg D 61 C5
Neu-Ulm D 61 B6
Neualbenreuth D 52 D2
Neubeckum D 50 B4
Neubrandenburg D 45 B5
Neubruch-hausen D 43 C5
Neubukow D 44 A3
Neuburg D 62 B2
Neuchâtel CH 70 B1
Neudau A 73 A6
Neudietendorf D 51 C6
Neudorf D 61 A4
Neuenbürg, *Baden-Württemberg* D 61 B4
Neuenburg, *Niedersachsen* D 43 B4
Neuendorf D 45 A5
Neuenhagen D 45 C5
Neuenhaus D 42 C3
Neuenkirchen, *Niedersachsen* D 43 B6
Neuenkirchen, *Niedersachsen* D 43 C5
Neuenkirchen, *Nordrhein-Westfalen* D 50 A3
Neuenkirchen, *Nordrhein-Westfalen* D 50 C3
Neuenrade D 50 B3
Neuenwalde D 43 B5
Neuerburg D 50 C2
Neuf-Brisach F 60 B3
Neufahrn, *Bayern* D 62 B2
Neufahrn, *Bayern* D 62 B3
Neufchâteau B 60 A1
Neufchâteau F 60 B1
Neufchâtel-en-Bray F 58 A2
Neufchâtel-sur-Aisne F 59 A5
Neuflize F 59 A5
Neugersdorf D 53 C4
Neuhardenberg D 45 C6
Neuharlingersiel D 43 B4
Neuhaus, *Bayern* D 62 A2
Neuhaus, *Bayern* D 63 B4
Neuhaus, *Niedersachsen* D 43 B6
Neuhaus, *Niedersachsen* D 44 B2
Neuhaus, *Niedersachsen* D 51 B5
Neuhaus a Rennweg D 52 C1
Neuhausen CH 61 C4
Neuhausen ob Eck D 61 C4
Neuhof, *Bayern* D 62 A1
Neuhof, *Hessen* D 51 C5
Neuhofen an der Krems A 63 B5
Neuillé-Pont-Pierre F 67 A5
Neuilly-en-Thelle F 58 A3
Neuilly-le-Réal F 68 B3
Neuilly-l'Évêque F 60 C1
Neuilly-St. Front F 59 A4
Neukalen D 45 B4
Neukirch D 53 B4
Neukirchen A 62 B4
Neukirchen, *Hessen* D 51 C5
Neukirchen, *Schleswig-Holstein* D 39 E1
Neukirchen-am Grossvenediger A 72 A2
Neukirchen bei Heiligen Blut D 62 A3
Neukloster D 44 B3
Neulengbach A 64 B1
Neulise F 68 C4
Neum BIH 84 D2
Neumagen D 60 A2
Neumarkt D 62 A2
Neumarkt im Hausruckkreis A 63 B4
Neumarkt im Mühlkreis A 63 B5
Neumarkt im Steiermark A 73 A4
Neumarkt Sankt Veit D 62 B3
Neumünster D 44 A1
Neunburg vorm Wald D 62 A3
Neung-sur-Beuvron F 68 A1
Neunkirch, *Luzern* CH 70 A3
Neunkirch, *Schaffhausen* CH 61 C4
Neunkirchen A 64 C2
Neunkirchen, *Nordrhein-Westfalen* D 50 C3
Neunkirchen, *Saarland* D 60 A3
Neunkirchen am Brand D 62 A2
Neuötting D 62 B3
Neureut D 61 A4
Neuruppin D 45 C4
Neusäss D 62 B1
Neusiedl A 64 C2
Neuss D 50 B2
Neussargues-Moissac F 68 C2
Neustadt, *Bayern* D 62 A1
Neustadt, *Bayern* D 62 A3
Neustadt, *Bayern* D 62 B2
Neustadt, *Brandenburg* D 44 C4
Neustadt, *Hessen* D 51 C5
Neustadt, *Niedersachsen* D 43 C6
Neustadt, *Rheinland-Pfalz* D 61 A4
Neustadt, *Sachsen* D 53 B4
Neustadt, *Schleswig-Holstein* D 44 A2
Neustadt, *Thüringen* D 52 C1
Neustadt, *Thüringen* D 52 C1
Neustadt-Glewe D 44 B3
Neustift im Stubaital A 71 A6
Neustrelitz D 45 B5
Neutal A 73 A6
Neutrebbin D 45 C6
Neuves-Maisons F 60 B2
Neuvic, *Corrèze* F 68 C2
Neuvic, *Dordogne* F 77 A3
Neuville-aux-Bois F 58 B3
Neuville-de-Poitou F 67 B5
Neuville-les-Dames F 69 B5
Neuville-sur-Saône F 69 C4
Neuvy-le-Roi F 58 C1
Neuvy-St. Sépulchre F 68 B1
Neuvy-Santour F 59 B4
Neuvy-sur-Barangeon F 68 A2
Neuwied D 50 C3
Neuzelle D 53 A4
Névache F 79 A5
Neveklov CZ 63 A5
Nevel RUS 7 D10
Neverfjord N 113 B12
Nevers F 68 B3
Nevesinje BIH 84 C3
Névez F 56 C2
Nevlunghavn N 35 D1
Nevşehir TR 16 B7
New Abbey GB 25 D4
New Aberdour GB 23 D6
New Alresford GB 31 C2
New Costessey GB 30 B5
New Cumnock GB 24 C3
New Galloway GB 24 C3
New Mills GB 27 B4
New Milton GB 31 D2
New Pitsligo GB 23 D6
New Quay GB 28 A3
New Radnor GB 29 A4
New Romney GB 31 D4
New Ross IRL 21 B5
New Scone GB 25 B4
Newark-on-Trent GB 27 B5
Newbiggin-by-the-Sea GB 25 C6
Newbliss IRL 19 B4
Newborough GB 26 B1
Newbridge IRL 21 A5
Newbridge on Wye GB 29 A4
Newburgh, *Aberdeenshire* GB 23 D6
Newburgh, *Fife* GB 25 B4
Newbury GB 31 C2
Newby Bridge GB 26 A3
Newcastle GB 19 B6
Newcastle Emlyn GB 28 A3
Newcastle-under-Lyme GB 26 B3
Newcastle-upon-Tyne GB 25 D6
Newcastle West IRL 20 B2
Newcastleton GB 25 C5
Newchurch GB 29 A4
Newent GB 29 B5
Newham GB 31 C4
Newhaven GB 31 D4
Newington GB 31 C5
Newinn IRL 21 B4
Newlyn GB 28 C2
Newmachar GB 23 D6
Newmarket, *Suffolk* GB 30 B4
Newmarket, *Western Isles* GB 22 C2
Newmarket IRL 20 B3
Newmarket-on-Fergus IRL 20 B3
Newport, *Isle of Wight* GB 31 D2
Newport, *Newport* GB 29 B5
Newport, *Pembrokeshire* GB 28 A3
Newport, *Telford & Wrekin* GB 26 C3
Newport, *Mayo* IRL 18 C2
Newport, *Tipperary* IRL 20 B3
Newport-on-Tay GB 25 B5
Newport Pagnell GB 30 B3
Newquay GB 28 C2
Newry GB 19 B5
Newton Abbot GB 29 C4
Newton Arlosh GB 25 D4
Newton Aycliffe GB 27 A4
Newton Ferrers GB 28 C3
Newton Stewart GB 24 D3
Newtonhill GB 23 D6
Newtonmore GB 23 D4
Newtown, *Herefordshire* GB 29 A5
Newtown, *Powys* GB 26 C2

Newtown Cunningham IRL 19 B4
Newtown Hamilton GB 19 B5
Newtown St. Boswells GB 25 C5
Newtown Sands IRL 20 B2
Newtownabbey GB 19 B6
Newtownards GB 19 B6
Newtownbutler GB 19 B4
Newtownmountkennedy IRL 21 A5
Newtownshandrum IRL 20 B3
Newtownstewart GB 19 B4
Nexon F 67 C6
Neyland GB 28 B3
Nibbiano I 80 B3
Nibe DK 38 C2
Nicaj-Shalë AL 105 A5
Nicastro I 106 C3
Niccone I 82 C1
Nice F 80 C1
Nickelsdorf A 64 C3
Nicolosi I 109 B4
Nicosia CY 120 A2
Nicosia I 109 B3
Nicótera I 106 C2
Nidda D 51 C5
Nidzica PL 47 B6
Niebla E 99 B4
Nieborów PL 55 A5
Niebüll D 39 E1
Niechanowo PL 46 C3
Niechorze PL 45 A7
Niedalino PL 46 A2
Nieder-Olm D 61 A4
Niederaula D 51 C5
Niederbipp CH 70 A2
Niederbronn-les-Bains F 60 B3
Niederfischbach D 50 C3
Niedergörsdorf D 52 B2
Niederkrüchten D 50 B2
Niederndorf A 62 C3
Niedersachswerfen D 51 B6
Niederstetten D 61 A5
Niederurnen CH 70 A4
Niederwölz A 73 A4
Niedoradz PL 53 B5
Niedzica PL 65 A6
Niegosławice PL 53 B5
Nieheim D 51 B5
Niemcza PL 54 C1
Niemegk D 52 A2
Niemodlin PL 54 C2
Nienburg, *Niedersachsen* D 43 C6
Nienburg, *Sachsen-Anhalt* D 52 B1
Niepołomice PL 55 C5
Nierstein D 61 A4
Niesky D 53 B4
Niestronno PL 46 C3
Nieświń PL 55 B5
Nieszawa PL 47 C4
Nieul-le-Dolent F 66 B3
Nieul-sur-Mer F 66 B3
Nieuw-Amsterdam NL 42 C3
Nieuw-Buinen NL 42 C3
Nieuw-Weerdinge NL 42 C3
Nieuwe Niedorp NL 42 C1
Nieuwe-Pekela NL 42 B3
Nieuwe-schans NL 43 B4
Nieuwegein NL 49 A6
Nieuwerkerken B 49 C6
Nieuwolda NL 42 B3
Nieuwpoort B 48 B3
Niğde TR 16 C7
Nigrita GR 116 B5
Nigüelas E 100 C2
Nijar E 101 C3
Nijemci HR 75 C4
Nijkerk NL 49 A6
Nijlen B 49 B5
Nijmegen NL 50 B1
Nijverdal NL 42 C3
Nikel RUS 113 C19
Nikinci SRB 85 B4
Nikiti GR 116 B5
Nikitsch A 74 A1
Nikkaluokta S 112 E8
Nikla H 74 B2
Niklasdorf A 73 A5
Nikolayev = Mykolayiv UA 11 C12
Nikšić CG 84 D3
Nilivaara S 113 E10
Nîmes F 78 C3
Nimis I 72 B3
Nimtofte DK 39 C3
Nin HR 83 B4
Nindorf D 43 A6
Ninemilehouse IRL 21 B4
Ninove B 49 C5
Niort F 67 B4
Niš SRB 10 E6
Nisa P 92 B3
Niscemi I 109 B3
Nissafors S 40 B3
Nissan-lez-Ensérune F 78 C2
Nissedal N 33 C5
Nissumby DK 38 C1
Nisterud N 33 C6
Niton GB 31 D2
Nitra SK 64 B4
Nitrianske-Pravno SK 65 B4
Nitrianske Rudno SK 65 B4
Nitry F 59 C4
Nittedal N 34 B2
Nittenau D 62 A3
Nittendorf D 62 A2
Nivala FIN 3 E26
Nivelles B 49 C5
Nivenskoye RUS 47 A6
Nivnice CZ 64 B3
Nizhyn UA 11 A11
Nižná SK 65 A5
Nižná Boca SK 65 B5
Niżne Repaše SK 65 A6
Nizza Monferrato I 80 B2
Njarðvík IS 111 D3
Njegŭsevo SRB 75 C4
Njivice HR 73 C4
Njurundabommen S 115 E14
Njutånger S 115 F14
Noailles F 58 A3
Noain E 76 D1
Noale I 72 C2
Noalejo E 100 B2
Noblejas E 95 C3
Noceda E 86 B4
Nocera Inferiore I 103 C7
Nocera Terinese I 106 B3
Nocera Umbra I 82 C1
Noceto I 81 B4
Noci I 104 C3
Nocìglia I 107 A5
Nodeland N 33 D4
Nödinge S 38 B5
Nods F 69 A6
Noé F 77 C4
Noépoli I 106 A3
Noeux-les-Mines F 48 C3
Noez E 94 C2
Nogales E 93 C4
Nogara I 71 C6
Nogarejas E 87 B4
Nogaro F 76 C2
Nogent F 59 B6
Nogent l'Artaud F 59 B4
Nogent-le-Roi F 58 B2
Nogent-le-Rotrou F 58 B1
Nogent-sur-Seine F 59 B4
Nogent-sur-Vernisson F 58 C3
Nogersund S 41 C4
Noguera E 95 B5
Noguerones E 100 B1
Nohfelden D 60 A3
Nohn D 50 C2
Noia E 86 B2
Noicáttaro I 104 B2
Noirétable F 68 C3
Noirmoutier-en-l'Île F 66 A2
Noja E 89 A3
Nojewo PL 46 C2
Nokia FIN 3 F25
Nol S 38 B5
Nola I 103 C7
Nolay F 69 B4
Noli I 80 B2
Nolnyra S 36 B4
Nombela E 94 B2
Nomeny F 60 B2
Nomexy F 60 B2
Nonancourt F 58 B2
Nonant-le-Pin F 57 B6
Nonántola I 81 B5
Nonaspe E 90 B3
None I 80 B1
Nontron F 67 C5
Nonza F 102 A2
Noordhorn NL 42 B3
Noordwijk NL 49 A5
Noordwijkerhout NL 49 A5
Noordwolde NL 42 C3
Noppikoski S 36 A1
Nora S 37 C2
Nørager DK 38 C2
Norberg S 36 B2
Norboda S 36 B5
Nórcia I 82 D2
Nord-Odal N 34 B3
Nordagutu N 33 C6
Nordanås S 115 C15
Nordausques F 48 C3
Nordborg DK 39 D2
Nordby, *Aarhus Amt.* DK 39 D3
Nordby, *Ribe Amt.* DK 39 D1
Norddeich D 43 B4
Norddorf D 43 A5
Norden D 43 B4
Nordenham D 43 B5
Norderhov N 34 B2
Norderney D 43 B4
Norderstapel D 43 A6
Norderstedt D 44 B2
Nordfjord N 113 B19
Nordfjordeid N 114 F3
Nordfold N 112 E4
Nordhalben D 52 C1
Nordhausen D 51 B6
Nordheim vor der Rhön D 51 C6
Nordholz D 43 B5
Nordhorn D 43 C4
Nordingrå S 115 E15
Nordkjosbotn N 112 C8
Nordli N 115 C10
Nördlingen D 61 B6
Nordmaling S 115 D16
Nordmark S 34 C6
Nordmela N 112 C4
Nordre Osen N 34 A3
Nordsinni N 34 B1
Nørdstedalsseter N 114 F4
Nordstemmen D 51 A5
Nordvågen N 113 B15
Nordwalde D 50 A3
Noreña E 88 A1
Noresund N 34 B1
Norg NL 42 B3
Norheimsund N 32 B3
Norie S 41 C4
Norma I 102 B5
Nornäs S 34 A5
Norra Vi S 40 B5
Norrahammar S 40 B4
Norråker S 115 C12
Norrala S 36 A3
Nørre Åby DK 39 D2
Nørre Alslev DK 39 E4
Nørre Lyndelse DK 39 D3
Nørre Nebel DK 39 D1
Nørre Snede DK 39 D2
Nørre Vorupør DK 38 C1
Norrent-Fontes F 48 C3
Nørresundby DK 38 B2
Norrhult Klavreström S 40 B5
Norrköping S 37 D3
Norrskedika S 36 B5
Norrsundet S 36 B4
Norrtälje S 36 C5
Nors DK 38 B1
Norsbron S 35 C5
Norsholm S 37 D2
Norsjö S 115 C16
Nort-sur-Erdre F 66 A3
Nörten-Hardenberg D 51 B5
North Berwick GB 25 B5
North Charlton GB 25 C6
North Frodingham GB 27 B5
North Kessock GB 23 D4
North Molton GB 28 B4
North Petherton GB 29 B4
North Somercotes GB 27 B6
North Tawton GB 28 C4
North Thoresby GB 27 B5
North Walsham GB 30 B5
Northallerton GB 27 A4
Northampton GB 30 B3
Northeim D 51 B6
Northfleet GB 31 C4
Northleach GB 29 B6
Northpunds GB 22 B7
Northwich GB 26 B3
Norton GB 27 A5
Nortorf D 44 A1
Nörvenich D 50 C2
Norwich GB 30 B5
Norwick GB 22 A8
Nøsen N 32 B5
Nosivka UA 11 A11
Nossa Senhora do Cabo P 92 C1
Nossebro S 35 D4
Nössemark S 35 C3
Nossen D 52 B3
Notaresco I 103 A6
Noto I 109 C4
Notodden N 33 C6
Nottingham GB 27 C4
Nottuln D 50 B3
Nouan-le-Fuzelier F 68 A2
Nouans-les-Fontaines F 67 A6
Nougaroulet F 77 C3
Nouvion F 48 C2
Nouzonville F 59 A5
Nova H 74 B1
Nová Baňa SK 65 B4
Nová Bystrica SK 65 A5
Nová Bystřice CZ 63 A6
Nova Crnja SRB 75 C5
Nova Gorica SLO 72 C3
Nova Gradiška HR 74 C2
Nova Levante I 71 B6
Nova Odesa UA 11 C11
Nová Paka CZ 53 C5
Nova Pazova SRB 85 B5
Nová Pec CZ 63 B4
Nova Siri I 106 A3
Nova Topola BIH 84 A2
Nova Varoš SRB 85 C4
Nova Zagora BG 11 E8
Novafeltria I 82 C1
Nováky SK 65 B4
Novalaise F 69 C5
Novales E 90 A2
Novalja HR 83 B3
Novara I 70 C3
Novara di Sicilia I 109 A4
Novate Mezzola I 71 B4
Novaya Ladoga RUS 7 A12
Nové Hrady CZ 63 B5
Nové Město SK 64 B3
Nové Město na Moravě CZ 64 A2
Nové Město nad Metují CZ 53 C6
Nové Město pod Smrkem CZ 53 C5
Nové Mitrovice CZ 63 A4
Nové Sady SK 64 B3
Nové Strašeci CZ 53 C3
Nové Zámky SK 64 C4
Novelda E 101 A5
Novellara I 81 B4
Noventa di Piave I 72 C2
Noventa Vicentina I 71 C6
Novés E 94 B2
Noves F 78 C3
Novés de Segre E 91 A4
Novgorod RUS 7 B11
Novhorod-Siverskyy UA 7 F12
Novi Bečej SRB 75 C5
Novi di Módena I 81 B4
Novi Kneževac SRB 75 B5
Novi Lígure I 80 B2
Novi Marof HR 73 B6
Novi Pazar BG 11 E9
Novi Pazar SRB 85 C5
Novi Sad SRB 75 C4
Novi Slankamen SRB 75 C5
Novi Travnik BIH 84 B2
Novi Vinodolski HR 83 A3
Novigrad, *Istarska* HR 72 C3
Novigrad, *Zadarsko-Kninska* HR 83 B4
Novigrad Podravski HR 74 B1
Noville B 50 C1
Novion-Porcien F 59 A5
Novo Brdo SRB 85 D6
Novo Mesto SLO 73 C5
Novo Miloševo SRB 75 C5
Novo Selo BIH 84 A2
Novo Selo, *Kosovo* SRB 85 D5
Novo Selo, *Srbija* SRB 85 C5
Novohrad-Volynskyy UA 11 A9
Novomirgorod UA 11 B11
Novorzhev RUS 7 C10
Novoselë AL 105 C5
Novoselytsya UA 11 B9
Novosil RUS 7 E14
Novosokolniki RUS 7 C10
Novoukrayinka UA 11 B11
Novovolynsk UA 11 A8
Novozybkov RUS 7 E11
Novska HR 74 C1
Nový Bor CZ 53 C4
Nový Bydžov CZ 53 C5
Novy-Chevrières F 59 A5
Novy Dwór Mazowiecki PL 47 C6
Nový-Hrozenkov CZ 64 A4
Nový Jičín CZ 64 A4
Novy Knin CZ 63 A5
Novyy Buh UA 11 C12
Nowa Cerekwia PL 54 C2
Nowa Karczma PL 47 A4
Nowa Kościoł PL 53 B5
Nowa Ruda PL 54 C1
Nowa Słupia PL 55 C6
Nowa Sól PL 53 B5
Nowa Wieś PL 47 B5
Nowa-Wieś Wielka PL 47 C4
Nowe PL 47 B4
Nowe Brzesko PL 55 C5
Nowe Grudze PL 55 A4
Nowe Miasteczko PL 53 B5
Nowe Miasto, *Mazowieckie* PL 47 C6
Nowe Miasto, *Mazowieckie* PL 55 B5
Nowe Miasto Lubawskie PL 47 B5
Nowe Miasto nad Wartą PL 54 A2
Nowe Skalmierzyce PL 54 B3
Nowe Warpno PL 45 B6
Nowica PL 47 A5
Nowogard PL 45 B7
Nowogród Bobrzanski PL 53 B5
Nowogrodziec PL 53 B5
Nowosolna PL 55 B4
Nowy Dwór Gdański PL 47 A5
Nowy Korczyn PL 55 C5
Nowy Sącz PL 65 A6
Nowy Staw PL 47 A5
Nowy Targ PL 65 A6
Nowy Tomyśl PL 46 C2
Nowy Wiśnicz PL 65 A6
Noyal-Pontivy F 56 B3
Noyalo F 56 C3
Noyant F 67 A5
Noyelles-sur-Mer F 48 C2
Noyen-sur-Sarthe F 57 C5
Noyers F 59 C4
Noyers-sur-Cher F 67 A6
Noyers-sur-Jabron F 79 B4
Noyon F 59 A3
Nozay F 66 A3
Nuaillé F 66 A4
Nuaillé-d'Aunis F 66 B4
Nuars F 68 A3
Nubledo E 88 A1
Nuéno E 90 A2
Nuestra Señora Sa Verge des Pilar E 97 C1
Nueva E 88 A2
Nueva Carteya E 100 B1
Nuevalos E 95 A5
Nuits F 59 C5
Nuits-St. Georges F 69 A4
Nule I 110 B2
Nules E 96 B2
Nulvi I 110 B1
Numana I 82 C2
Numansdorp NL 49 B5
Nümbrecht D 50 C3
Nunchritz D 52 B3
Nuneaton GB 30 B2
Nunnanen FIN 113 D13
Nuñomoral E 93 A4
Nunspeet NL 42 C2
Nuorgam FIN 113 B16
Núoro I 110 B2
Nurallao I 110 C2
Nuremberg = Nürnberg D 62 A2
Nurmes FIN 3 E28
Nürnberg = Nuremberg D 62 A2
Nurri I 110 C2
Nürtingen D 61 B5
Nus I 70 C2
Nusnäs S 36 B1
Nusplingen D 61 B4
Nuštar HR 74 C3
Nyåker S 115 D16
Nyáregyháza H 75 A4
Nyarlörinc H 75 B4
Nyasvizh BY 7 E9
Nybble S 35 C6
Nybergsund N 34 A4
Nybøl DK 39 E2
Nyborg DK 39 D3
Nybro S 40 C5
Nybster GB 23 C5
Nyby DK 39 E5
Nye S 40 B5
Nyékládháza H 65 C6
Nyergesujfalu H 65 C4
Nyhammar S 36 B1
Nyhyttan S 37 C1
Nyirád H 74 A2
Nyirbátor H 11 C7
Nyíregyháza H 10 C6
Nyker DK 41 D4
Nykil S 37 D2
Nykirke N 34 B2
Nykøbing, *Falster* DK 39 E4
Nykøbing, *Vestsjællands Amt.* DK 39 D4
Nykøbing M DK 38 C1
Nyköping S 37 D4
Nykroppa S 35 C6
Nykvarn S 37 C4
Nykyrke S 37 D1
Nyland S 115 D14
Nylars DK 41 D4
Nymburk CZ 53 C5
Nynäshamn S 37 D4
Nyon CH 69 B6
Nyons F 79 B4
Nýřany CZ 63 A4
Nýrsko CZ 62 A4
Nyrud N 113 C18
Nysa PL 54 C2
Nysäter S 35 C4
Nyseter N 114 E5
Nyskoga S 34 B4
Nysted DK 44 A3
Nystrand N 35 C1
Nyúl H 64 C3
Nyvoll N 113 B12

O

O Barco E 86 B4
O Bolo E 87 B3
O Carballiño E 86 B2
O Corgo E 86 B3
Ö Lagnö S 37 C5
O Näsberg S 34 B5
O Páramo E 86 B3
O Pedrouzo E 86 B2
O Pino E 86 B2
O Porriño E 87 B2
O Rosal E 87 C2
Oadby GB 30 B2
Oakengates GB 26 C3
Oakham GB 30 B3
Oanes N 33 D3
Obalj BIH 84 C3
Oban GB 24 B2
Obdach A 73 A4
Obejo E 100 A1
Ober Grafendorf A 63 B6
Ober-Morlen D 51 C4
Oberammergau D 62 C2
Oberasbach D 62 A1
Oberau D 62 C2
Oberaudorf D 62 C3
Oberbruck F 60 C2
Oberdiessbach CH 70 B2
Oberdorf CH 70 A2
Oberdrauburg A 72 B2
Obere Stanz A 73 A5
Oberelsbach D 51 C6
Obergünzburg D 61 C6
Obergurgl A 71 B6
Oberhausen D 50 B2
Oberhof D 51 C6
Oberkirch D 61 B4
Oberkirchen D 51 B4
Oberkochen D 61 B6
Obermassfeld-Grimmenthal D 51 C6
Obermünchen D 62 B2
Obernai F 60 B3
Obernberg A 63 B4
Obernburg D 61 A5
Oberndorf D 61 B4
Oberndorf bei Salzburg A 62 C3
Obernkirchen D 51 A5
Oberort A 73 A5
Oberpullendorf A 74 A1
Oberriet CH 71 A4
Oberröblingen D 52 B1
Oberrot D 61 A5
Oberstaufen D 61 C6
Oberstdorf D 71 A5
Obertauern A 72 A3
Obertilliach A 72 B2
Obertraubling D 62 B3
Obertraun A 72 A3
Obertrubach D 62 A2
Obertrum A 62 C4
Oberursel D 51 C4
Obervellach A 72 B3
Oberviechtach D 62 A3
Oberwart A 73 A6
Oberwesel D 50 C3
Oberwinter D 50 C3
Oberwölzstadt A 73 A4
Oberzell D 63 B4
Obice PL 55 C5
Óbidos P 92 B1
Obilić SRB 85 D6
Obing D 62 C3
Objat F 67 C6
Objazda PL 46 A3
Öblarn A 73 A4
Obninsk RUS 7 D14
Oborniki PL 46 C2
Oborniki Śląskie PL 54 B1
Obornjača SRB 75 C4
Oboyan RUS 7 F14
Obrenovac SRB 85 B5
Obrež, *Srbija* SRB 85 C6
Obrež, *Vojvodina* SRB 85 B4
Obrigheim D 61 A5
Obrov SLO 73 C4
Obrovac HR 83 B4
Obrovac SRB 75 C4
Obrovac Sinjski HR 83 C5
Obruk TR 16 B6
Obrzycko PL 46 C2
Obudovac BIH 84 B3
Ocaña E 95 C3
Occhiobello I 81 B5
Occimiano I 80 A2
Očevlja BIH 84 B3
Ochagavía E 76 D1
Ochakiv UA 11 C11
Ochiltree GB 24 C3
Ochla PL 53 B5
Ochotnica-Dolna PL 65 A6
Ochotnica-Górna PL 65 A6
Ochsenfurt D 61 A6
Ochsenhausen D 61 B5
Ochtendung D 50 C3
Ochtrup D 50 A3
Ocieka PL 55 C6
Ockelbo S 36 B3
Öckerö S 38 B4
Ocniţa MD 11 B9
Očová SK 65 B5
Ócsa H 75 A4
Öcseny H 74 B3
Öcsöd H 75 B5
Octeville F 57 A4
Ocypel PL 47 B4
Ödåkra S 41 C2
Odby DK 38 C1
Odda N 32 B3
Odder DK 39 D3
Ödeborg S 35 D3
Odeceixe P 98 B2
Odechów PL 55 B6
Odeleite P 98 B3
Odemira P 98 B2
Ödemiş TR 119 D2
Ödensbacken S 37 C2
Odense DK 39 D3
Odensjö, *Jönköping* S 40 B4
Odensjö, *Kronoberg* S 40 C3
Oderberg D 45 C6
Oderzo I 72 C2
Odesa = Odessa UA 11 C11
Ödeshög S 37 D1
Odessa = Odesa UA 11 C11
Odiáxere P 98 B2
Odie GB 23 B6
Odiham GB 31 C3
Odintsovo RUS 7 D14
Odivelas P 98 A2
Odolanów PL 54 B2
Odón E 95 B5
Odorheiu Secuiesc RO 11 C8
Odoyevo RUS 7 E14
Odrowaz PL 55 B5
Odry CZ 64 A3
Odrzywół PL 55 B5
Ødsted DK 39 D2
Odžaci SRB 75 C4
Odžak BIH 84 A3
Oebisfelde D 44 C2
Oederan D 52 C3
Oeding D 50 B2
Oegstgeest NL 49 A5
Oelde D 50 B4
Oelsnitz D 52 C2
Oer-Erkenschwick D 50 B3
Oerlinghausen D 51 B4
Oettingen D 62 B1
Oetz A 71 A5
Oeventrop D 50 B4
Offanengo I 71 C4
Offenbach D 51 C4
Offenburg D 60 B3
Offida I 82 D2
Offingen D 61 B6
Offranville F 58 A2
Ofir P 87 C2
Ofte N 33 C5
Ofterschwang D 71 A5
Oggiono I 71 C4
Ogihares E 100 B2
Ogliastro Cilento I 103 C8
Ogliastro Marina I 103 C7
Ogmore-by-Sea GB 29 B4
Ogna N 33 D2
Ogre LV 6 C8
Ogrodzieniec PL 55 C4
Ogulin HR 73 C5
Ögur IS 111 A3
Ohanes E 101 B3
Ohey B 49 C6
Ohlstadt D 62 C2
Ohrdorf D 44 C2
Ohrdruf D 51 C6
Ohrid MK 116 A2
Öhringen D 61 A5
Oia E 87 B2
Oiã P 92 A2
Oiartzun E 76 C1
Oilgate IRL 21 B5
Oimbra E 87 C3
Oiselay-et-Grachaux F 69 A5
Oisemont F 48 D2
Oisterwijk NL 49 B6
Öja S 37 E5
Öje S 34 B5
Ojén E 100 C1
Ojrzeń PL 47 C6
Ojuelos Altos E 99 A5
Okalewo PL 47 B5
Okány H 75 B6
Okehampton GB 28 C3
Okhtyrka UA 7 F13
Oklaj HR 83 C5
Økneshamn N 112 D4
Okoč SK 64 C3
Okoličné SK 65 A5
Okonek PL 46 B2
Okonin PL 47 B4
Okřisky CZ 64 A1
Oksa PL 55 C5
Oksbøl DK 39 D1
Oksby DK 39 D1
Øksfjord N 113 B11
Øksna N 34 B3
Okučani HR 74 C2
Okulovka RUS 7 B12
Ólafsfjörður IS 111 A7
Ólafsvík IS 111 C2
Olagüe E 76 D1
Oland N 33 D5
Olargues F 78 C1
Oława PL 54 C2
Olazagutia E 89 B4
Olbernhau D 52 C3
Ólbia I 110 B2
Olching D 62 B2
Old Deer GB 23 D6
Oldbury GB 29 B5
Oldcastle IRL 19 C4
Oldeberkoop NL 42 C3
Oldeboorn NL 42 B2
Olden N 114 F3
Oldenbrok D 43 B5
Oldenburg, *Niedersachsen* D 43 B5
Oldenburg, *Schleswig-Holstein* D 44 A2
Oldenzaal NL 50 A2
Olderdalen N 112 C9
Olderfjord N 113 B14
Oldersum D 43 B4
Oldervik N 112 C7
Oldham GB 26 B3
Oldisleben D 52 B1
Oldmeldrum GB 23 D6
Olea E 88 B2
Oleby S 34 B5
Olechów PL 55 B6
Oledo P 92 B3
Oléggio I 70 C3
Oleiros, *Coruña* E 86 A2
Oleiros, *Coruña* E 86 B1
Oleiros P 92 B3
Oleksandriya, *Kirovohrad* UA 11 B12
Oleksandriya, *Rivne* UA 11 A9
Oleksandrovka UA 11 B12
Olen B 49 B5
Ølen N 33 C2
Olenegorsk RUS 3 B30
Olenino RUS 7 C12
Olesa de Montserrat E 91 B4
Oleśnica PL 54 B2
Olešnice CZ 64 A2
Olesno PL 54 C3
Oletta F 102 A2
Olette F 91 A5
Olevsk UA 11 A9
Olfen D 50 B3
Olgiate Comasco I 70 C3
Olginate I 71 C4
Ølgod DK 39 D1
Olgrinmore GB 23 C5
Olhão P 98 B3
Olhavo P 92 B1
Oliana E 91 A4
Olias del Rey E 94 C3
Oliena I 110 B2
Oliete E 90 C2
Olimbos GR 119 G2
Olite E 89 B5
Oliva E 96 C2
Oliva de la Frontera E 99 A4
Oliva de Mérida E 93 C4
Oliva de Plasencia E 93 A4
Olivadi I 106 C3
Olival P 92 B2
Olivar E 100 C2
Olivares E 99 B4
Olivares de Duero E 88 C2
Olivares de Júcar E 95 C4
Oliveira de Azeméis P 87 D2
Oliveira de Frades P 87 D2
Oliveira do Conde P 92 A3
Oliveira do Douro P 87 C2
Oliveira do Hospital P 92 A3
Olivenza E 93 C3
Olivet F 58 C2
Olivone CH 70 B3
Öljehult S 41 C5
Olkusz PL 55 C4
Ollerton GB 27 B4
Ollerup DK 39 D3
Olliergues F 68 C3
Ölmbrotorp S 37 C2
Ölme S 35 C5
Olmedilla de Alarcón E 95 C4
Olmedillo de Roa E 88 C3
Olmedo E 88 C2
Olmedo I 110 B1
Olmeto F 102 B1
Olmillos de Castro E 87 C4
Olmos de Ojeda E 88 B2
Olney GB 30 B3
Ołobok PL 54 B3
Olocau del Rey E 90 C2
Olofström S 41 C4
Olomouc CZ 64 A3
Olonets RUS 3 F30
Olonne-sur-Mer F 66 B3
Olonzac F 78 C1
Oloron-Ste. Marie F 76 C2
Olost E 91 B5
Olot E 91 A5
Olovo BIH 84 B3
Olpe D 50 B3
Olsberg D 51 B4
Olsene B 49 C4
Olserud S 35 C5
Olshammar S 37 D1
Olshanka UA 11 B11
Olszanica PL 53 B5
Olsztyn, *Śląskie* PL 55 C4
Olsztyn, *Warmińsko-Mazurskie* PL 47 B6
Olsztynek PL 47 B6
Olszyna PL 53 B5
Oltedal N 33 D3
Olten CH 70 A2
Olteniţa RO 11 D9
Olula del Rio E 101 B3
Ølve N 32 B2
Olvega E 89 C5
Olvera E 99 C5
Olympia GR 117 E3
Olzai I 110 B2
Omagh GB 19 B4
Omalos GR 117 G5
Omegna I 70 C3
Omiš HR 83 C5
Omišalj HR 73 C4
Ommen NL 42 C3
Omodhos CY 120 B1
Omoljica SRB 85 B5
On B 49 C6
Oña E 89 B3
Onano I 81 D5
Oñati E 89 A4
Onda E 96 B2
Ondara E 96 C3
Ondarroa E 89 A4
Onesse-et-Laharie F 76 B1
Oneşti RO 11 C9
Onhaye B 49 C5
Onich GB 24 B2
Onil E 96 C2
Onis E 88 A2
Önnestad S 41 C4
Onsala S 38 B5
Ontinyent E 96 C2
Ontur E 101 A4
Onzain F 67 A6
Onzonilla E 88 B1
Oost-Vlieland NL 42 B2
Oostburg NL 49 B4
Oostende B 48 B3
Oosterend NL 42 B2
Oosterhout NL 49 B5
Oosterwolde NL 42 C3
Oosterzele B 49 C4
Oosthuizen NL 42 C2
Oostkamp B 49 B4
Oostmalle B 49 B5
Oostvoorne NL 49 B5
Ootmarsum NL 42 C3
Opalenica PL 54 A1
Opařany CZ 63 A5
Oparić SRB 85 C6
Opatija HR 73 C4
Opatów, *Śląskie* PL 54 C3
Opatów, *Świętokrzyskie* PL 55 C6
Opatów, *Wielkopolskie* PL 54 B3

Pedreguer E 96 C3
Pedrera E 100 B1
Pedro Abad E 100 B1
Pedro Bernardo E 94 B2
Pedro-Martinez E 100 B2
Pedro Muñoz E 95 C4
Pedroche E 100 A1
Pedrógão, *Beja* P 98 A3
Pedrogao, *Castelo Branco* P 92 A3
Pedrógão, *Leiria* P 92 B2
Pedrógão Grande P 92 B2
Pedrola E 90 B1
Pedrosa de Tobalina E 89 B3
Pedrosa del Rey E 88 C1
Pedrosa del Rio Urbel E 88 B3
Pedrosillo de los Aires E 94 B1
Pedrosillo el Ralo E 94 A1
Pędzewo PL 47 B4
Peebles GB 25 C4
Peel GB 26 A1
Peenemünde D 45 A5
Peer B 49 B6
Pega P 93 A3
Pegalajar E 100 B2
Pegau D 52 B2
Peggau A 73 A5
Pegli I 80 B2
Pegnitz D 62 A2
Pego E 96 C2
Pegões-Estação P 92 C2
Pegões Velhos P 92 C2
Pęgów PL 54 B1
Pegswood GB 25 C6
Peguera E 97 B2
Pehlıvanköy TR 118 A1
Peine D 51 A6
Peisey-Nancroix F 70 C1
Peissenberg D 62 C2
Peiting D 62 C1
Peitz D 53 B4
Péjo I 71 B5
Pelagićevo BIH 84 B3
Pelahustán E 94 B2
Pełczyce PL 46 B1
Pelhřimov CZ 63 A6
Pélissanne F 79 C4
Pelkosenniemi FIN 113 E16
Pellegrino Parmense I 81 B3
Pellegrue F 76 B3
Pellérd H 74 B3
Pellestrina I 72 C2
Pellevoisin F 67 B6
Pellizzano I 71 B5
Pello FIN 113 F13
Pello S 113 F12
Peloche E 93 B5
Pelplin PL 47 B4
Pelussin F 69 C4
Pély H 75 A5
Pembroke GB 28 B3
Pembroke Dock GB 28 B3
Peña de Cabra E 94 B1
Peñacerrada E 89 B4
Penacova P 92 A2
Peñafiel E 88 C2
Penafiel P 87 C2
Peñaflor E 99 B5
Peñalba de Santiago E 86 B4
Peñalsordo E 93 C5
Penalva do Castelo P 92 A3
Penamacôr P 93 A3
Peñaparda E 93 A4
Peñaranda de Bracamonte E 94 B1
Peñaranda de Duero E 89 C3
Peñarroya de Tastavins E 90 C3
Peñarroya-Pueblonuevo E 93 C5
Peñarrubla E 86 B3
Penarth GB 29 B4
Peñas de San Pedro E 101 A4
Peñascosa E 101 A3
Peñausende E 88 C1
Penc H 65 C5
Pencoed GB 29 B4
Pendalofos GR 116 B3
Pendeen GB 28 C2
Pendine GB 28 B3
Pendueles E 88 A2
Penedono P 87 D3
Penela P 92 A2
Penhas Juntas P 87 C3
Peniche P 92 B1
Penicuik GB 25 C4
Penig D 52 C2
Penilhos P 98 B3
Peñíscola E 90 C3
Penistone GB 27 B4
Penkridge GB 26 C3
Penkun D 45 B6
Penmarch F 56 C1
Pennabilli I 82 C1
Penne I 103 A6
Penne-d'Agenais F 77 B3
Pennes I 71 B5
Pennyghael GB 24 B1
Peno RUS 7 C12
Penpont GB 25 C4
Penrhyndeudraeth GB 26 C1
Penrith GB 26 A3
Penryn GB 28 C2
Pentraeth GB 26 B1
Penybontfawr GB 26 C2
Penygroes, *Carmarthenshire* GB 28 B3
Penygroes, *Gwynedd* GB 26 B1
Penzance GB 28 C2
Penzberg D 62 C2
Penzlin D 45 B5
Pepeljevac SRB 85 C6
Pepinster B 50 C1
Peqin AL 105 B5
Pér H 64 C3
Pera Boa P 93 A3
Perachora GR 117 D4
Perafita P 87 C2
Peraleda de la Mata E 93 B5
Peraleda de San Román E 93 B5
Peraleda del Zaucejo E 93 C5
Perales de Alfambra E 90 C1
Perales de Tajuña E 95 B3
Perales del Puerto E 93 A4
Peralta E 89 B5
Peralta de la Sal E 90 B3
Peralva P 98 B3
Peralveche E 95 B4
Perama GR 117 G6
Perast CG 105 A4
Perbál H 65 C4
Perchtoldsdorf A 64 B2
Percy F 57 B4
Perdasdefogu I 110 C2
Perdiguera E 90 B2
Peredo P 87 C4
Peregu Mare RO 75 B5
Pereiro, *Faro* P 98 B3
Pereiro, *Guarda* P 87 D3
Pereiro, *Santarém* P 92 B2
Pereiro de Aguiar E 87 B3
Perelada E 91 A6
Perelejos de las Truchas E 95 B5
Pereña E 87 C4
Pereruela E 88 C1
Pereyaslav-Khmelnytskyy UA 11 A11
Pérfugas I 110 B1
Perg A 63 B5
Pérgine Valsugana I 71 B6
Pérgola I 82 C1
Pergusa I 109 B3
Periam RO 75 B5
Periana E 100 C1
Périers F 57 A4
Périgueux F 67 C5
Perino I 80 B3
Perjasica HR 73 C5
Perkáta H 74 A3
Perković HR 83 C5
Perleberg D 44 B3
Perlez SRB 75 C5
Përmet AL 116 B2
Pernarec CZ 62 A4
Pernek SK 64 B3
Pernes P 92 B2
Pernes-les-Fontaines F 79 B4
Pernik BG 11 E7
Pernink CZ 52 C2
Pernitz A 64 C1
Pero Pinheiro P 92 C1
Peroguarda P 98 A2
Pérols F 78 C2
Péronne F 59 A3
Péronnes B 49 C5
Perorrubio E 94 A3
Perosa Argentina I 79 B6
Perozinho P 87 C2
Perpignan F 91 A5
Perranporth GB 28 C2
Perranzabuloe GB 28 C2
Perrecy-les-Forges F 69 B4
Perrero I 79 B6
Perrignier F 69 B6
Perros-Guirec F 56 B2
Persan F 58 A3
Persberg S 34 C6
Persenbeug A 63 B6
Pershore GB 29 A5
Perstorp S 41 C3
Perth GB 25 B4
Pertisau A 72 A1
Pertoča SLO 73 B6
Pertuis F 79 C4
Perućac SRB 85 C4
Perúgia I 82 C1
Perušić HR 83 B4
Péruwelz B 49 C4
Pervomaysk UA 11 B11
Perwez B 49 C5
Pesadas de Burgos E 89 B3
Pesaguero E 88 A2
Pésaro I 82 C1
Pescantina I 71 C5
Pescara I 103 A7
Pescasséroli I 103 B6
Peschici I 104 B2
Peschiera del Garda I 71 C5
Péscia I 81 C4
Pescina I 103 A6
Pesco Sannita I 103 B7
Pescocostanzo I 103 B7
Pescopagano I 103 C8
Peshkopi AL 116 A2
Pesmes F 69 A5
Pesnica SLO 73 B5
Peso da Régua P 87 C3
Pesquera de Duero E 88 C2
Pessac F 76 B2
Pestovo RUS 7 B13
Petalidi GR 117 F3
Pétange L 60 A1
Petas GR 116 C3
Peteranec HR 74 B1
Peterborough GB 30 B3
Peterculter GB 23 D6
Peterhead GB 23 D7
Peterlee GB 25 D6
Petersfield GB 31 C3
Petershagen, *Brandenburg* D 45 C5
Petershagen, *Brandenburg* D 45 C6
Petershagen, *Nordrhein-Westfalen* D 43 C5
Petershausen D 62 B2
Peterswell IRL 20 A3
Pétervására H 65 B6
Petília Policastro I 107 B3
Petín E 87 B3
Pětipsy CZ 52 C3
Petkus D 52 B3
Petlovac HR 74 C3
Petlovača SRB 85 B4
Petöfiszallás H 75 B4
Petra E 97 B3
Petralia Sottana I 109 B3
Petrčane HR 83 B4
Petrelë AL 105 B5
Petrella Tifernina I 103 B7
Petrer E 101 A5
Petreto-Bicchisano F 102 B1
Petrich BG 116 A5
Petrijevci HR 74 C3
Petrinja HR 73 C6
Petrodvorets RUS 7 B10
Pétrola E 101 A4
Petronà I 107 B3
Petronell A 64 B2
Petroşani RO 11 D7
Petrovac CG 105 A4
Petrovac SRB 85 B6
Petrovaradin SRB 75 C4
Petrovice BIH 84 B3
Petrovice CZ 53 C3
Pettenbach A 63 C5
Pettigo IRL 19 B4
Petworth GB 31 D3
Peuerbach A 63 B4
Peuntenansa E 88 A2
Peurasuvanto FIN 113 E15
Pevensey Bay GB 31 D4
Peveragno I 80 B1
Pewsey GB 29 B6
Pewsum D 43 B4
Peyrat-le-Château F 68 C1
Peyrehorade F 76 C1
Peyriac-Minervois F 77 C5
Peyrins F 79 A4
Peyrissac F 67 C6
Peyrolles-en-Provence F 79 C4
Peyruis F 79 B4
Pézarches F 59 B3
Pézenas F 78 C2
Pezinok SK 64 B3
Pezuls F 77 B3
Pfaffenhausen D 61 B6
Pfaffenhofen, *Bayern* D 61 B6
Pfaffenhofen, *Bayern* D 62 B2
Pfaffenhoffen F 60 B3
Pfäffikon CH 70 A3
Pfarrkirchen D 62 B3
Pfeffenhausen D 62 B2
Pfetterhouse F 70 A2
Pforzheim D 61 B4
Pfreimd D 62 A3
Pfronten D 61 C6
Pfullendorf D 61 C5
Pfullingen D 61 B5
Pfunds A 71 B5
Pfungstadt D 61 A4
Pfyn CH 61 C4
Phalsbourg F 60 B3
Philippeville B 49 C5
Philippsreut D 63 B4
Philippsthal D 51 C5
Piacenza I 81 A3
Piacenza d'Adige I 72 C1
Piádena I 71 C5
Piana F 102 A1
Piana Crixia I 80 B2
Piana degli Albanesi I 108 B2
Piana di Monte Verna I 103 B7
Piancastagnáio I 81 D5
Piandelagotti I 81 B4
Pianella, *Abruzzi* I 103 A7
Pianella, *Toscana* I 81 C5
Pianello Val Tidone I 80 B3
Piano I 80 B2
Pianoro I 81 B5
Pians A 71 A5
Pías E 87 B4
Pias P 98 A3
Piaseczno PL 55 A6
Piasek PL 45 C6
Piaski PL 47 A5
Piastów PL 55 A5
Piaszcyna PL 46 A3
Piątek PL 55 A4
Piatra Neamţ RO 11 C9
Piazza al Sérchio I 81 B4
Piazza Armerina I 109 B3
Piazza Brembana I 71 C4
Piazze I 81 D5
Piazzola sul Brenta I 72 C1
Picassent E 96 B2
Piccione I 82 C1
Picerno I 104 C1
Picher D 44 B3
Pickering GB 27 A5
Pico I 103 B6
Picón E 94 C2
Picquigny F 58 A3
Piechowice PL 53 C5
Piecnik PL 46 B2
Piedicavallo I 70 C2
Piedicroce F 102 A2
Piedimonte Etneo I 109 B4
Piedimonte Matese I 103 B7
Piedimulera I 70 B3
Piedipaterno I 82 D1
Piedrabuena E 94 C2
Piedraescrita E 94 C2
Piedrafita E 88 A1
Piedrahita E 93 A5
Piedralaves E 94 B2
Piedras Albas E 93 B4
Piedras Blancas E 88 A1
Piegaro I 82 D1
Piekary Śl. PL 54 C3
Piekoszów PL 55 C5
Pieksämäki FIN 3 E27
Pielenhofen D 62 A2
Pielgrzymka PL 53 B5
Pieniężno PL 47 A6
Pieńsk PL 53 B5
Pienza I 81 C5
Piera E 91 B4
Pieranie PL 47 C4
Pierowall GB 23 B6
Pierre-Buffière F 67 C6
Pierre-de-Bresse F 69 B5
Pierrecourt F 60 C1
Pierrefeu-du-Var F 79 C5
Pierrefitte-Nestalas F 76 D2
Pierrefitte-sur-Aire F 59 B6
Pierrefonds F 59 A3
Pierrefontaine-les-Varans F 69 A6
Pierrefort F 78 B1
Pierrelatte F 78 B3
Pierrepont, *Aisne* F 59 A4
Pierrepont, *Meurthe-et-Moselle* F 60 A1
Piesendorf A 72 A2
Piešťany SK 64 B3
Pieszkowo PL 47 A6
Pieszyce PL 54 C1
Pietarsaari FIN 3 E25
Pietra Ligure I 80 B2
Pietragalla I 104 C1
Pietralunga I 82 C1
Pietramelara I 103 B7
Pietraperzía I 109 B3
Pietrasanta I 81 C4
Pietravairano I 103 B7
Pieve del Cáiro I 80 A2
Pieve di Bono I 71 C5
Pieve di Cadore I 72 B2
Pieve di Cento I 81 B5
Pieve di Soligo I 72 C2
Pieve di Teco I 80 B1
Pieve Santo Stefano I 82 C1
Pieve Torina I 82 C2
Pievepélago I 81 B4
Piges GR 116 C3
Píglio I 102 B6
Pigna I 80 C1
Pignan F 78 C2
Pignataro Maggiore I 103 B7
Pijnacker NL 49 A5
Pikalevo RUS 7 B13
Piła PL 46 B2
Pilar de la Horadada E 101 B5
Pilas E 99 B4
Pilastri I 81 B5
Piława PL 55 B6
Piława Górna PL 54 C1
Piławki PL 47 B5
Pilchowice PL 54 C3
Pilea GR 116 B5
Pilgrimstad S 115 E12
Pili, *Dodekanisa* GR 119 F2
Pili, *Trikala* GR 116 C3
Pilica PL 55 C4
Pilis H 75 A4
Piliscaba H 65 C4
Pilisszántó H 65 C4
Pilisvörösvár H 65 C4
Pilos GR 117 F3
Pilsting D 62 B3
Pilszcz PL 54 C2
Pilterud N 34 C2
Pilu RO 75 B6
Pilzno PL 55 D6
Pina de Ebro E 90 B2
Piñar E 100 B2
Pınarbaşı TR 118 C1
Pınarhisar TR 118 A2
Pinas F 77 C3
Pincehely H 74 B3
Pinchbeck GB 30 B3
Pińczów PL 55 C5
Pineda de la Sierra E 89 B3
Pineda de Mar E 91 B5
Pinerella I 82 B1
Pinerolo I 79 B6
Pineta Grande I 103 C6
Pineto I 103 A7
Piney F 59 B5
Pinggau A 73 A6
Pinhal Novo P 92 C2
Pinhão P 87 C3
Pinheiro, *Aveiro* P 87 C2
Pinheiro, *Aveiro* P 87 D2
Pinheiro Grande P 92 B2
Pinhel P 87 D3
Pinhoe GB 29 C4
Pinilla E 101 A4
Pinilla de Toro E 88 C1
Pinkafeld A 73 A6
Pinneberg D 43 B6
Pinnow D 53 B4
Pino F 102 A2
Pino de Val E 86 B2
Pino del Rio E 88 B2
Pinofranqueado E 93 A4
Pinols F 78 A2
Piñor E 86 B2
Pinos del Valle E 100 C2
Pinos Puente E 100 B2
Pinoso E 101 A4
Pinsk BY 7 E9
Pinto E 94 B3
Pinzano al Tagliamento I 72 B2
Pinzio P 93 A3
Pinzolo I 71 B5
Pióbbico I 82 C1
Piombino I 81 D4
Pionki PL 55 B6
Pionsat F 68 B2
Pióraco I 82 C1
Piornal E 93 A5
Piotrków-Kujawski PL 47 C4
Piotrków Trybunalski PL 55 B4
Piotrkowice PL 55 C5
Piotrowice PL 55 A6
Piotrowo PL 46 C2
Piove di Sacco I 72 C2
Piovene I 71 C6
Piperskärr S 40 B6
Pipriac F 57 C4
Piraeus = Pireas GR 117 E5
Piran SLO 72 C3
Piré-sur-Seiche F 57 B4
Pireas = Piraeus GR 117 E5
Pirgi GR 117 D7
Pirgos, *Ilia* GR 117 E3
Pirgos, *Kriti* GR 117 G7
Piriac-sur-Mer F 66 A2
Piringsdorf A 73 A6
Pirmasens D 60 A3
Pirna D 53 C3
Pirnmill GB 24 C2
Pirot SRB 11 E7
Pirovac HR 83 C4
Pirttivuopio S 112 E8
Pisa I 81 C4
Pisany F 66 C4
Pisarovina HR 73 C5
Pischelsdorf in der Steiermark A 73 A5
Pişchia RO 75 C6
Pisciotta I 106 A2
Písek CZ 63 A5
Pisogne I 71 C5
Pissos F 76 B2
Pissouri CY 120 B1
Pisticci I 104 C2
Pistóia I 81 C4
Piteå S 3 D24
Pitești RO 11 D8
Pithiviers F 58 B3
Pitigliano I 102 A4
Pitkyaranta RUS 3 F29
Pitlochry GB 25 B4
Pitomača HR 74 C2
Pitres E 100 C2
Pittentrail GB 23 D4
Pitvaros H 75 B5
Pivka SLO 73 C4
Pivnice SRB 75 C4
Piwniczna PL 65 A6
Pizarra E 100 C1
Pizzano I 71 B5
Pizzighettone I 71 C4
Pizzo I 106 C3
Pízzoli I 103 A6
Pizzolungo I 108 A1
Pjätteryd S 40 C4
Plabennec F 56 B1
Placencia E 89 A4
Plaffeien CH 70 B2
Plaisance, *Gers* F 76 C3
Plaisance, *Haute-Garonne* F 77 C4
Plaisance, *Tarn* F 77 C5
Plaka GR 116 C7
Plan E 90 A3
Plan-de-Baix F 79 B4
Plan-d'Orgon F 78 C3
Planá CZ 62 A3
Planá nad Lužnici CZ 63 A5
Plaňany CZ 53 C5
Planchez F 68 A4
Plancoët F 57 B3
Plancy-l'Abbaye F 59 B4
Plandište SRB 75 C6
Plánice CZ 63 A4
Planina SLO 73 B5
Planina SLO 73 C4
Plankenfels D 62 A2
Plasencia E 93 A4
Plasenzuela E 93 B4
Plaški HR 83 A4
Plassen, *Buskerud* N 32 B4
Plassen, *Hedmark* N 34 A4
Plášt'ovce SK 65 B5
Plasy CZ 63 A4
Plat HR 84 D3
Platamona Lido I 110 B1
Platania I 106 B3
Platanos GR 117 G5
Platí I 106 C3
Platičevo SRB 85 B4
Platja d'Aro E 91 B6
Plattling D 62 B3
Plau D 44 B4
Plaue, *Brandenburg* D 44 C4
Plaue, *Thüringen* D 51 C6
Plauen D 52 C2
Plav CG 85 D4
Plavecký Mikuláš SK 64 B3
Plavinas LV 7 C8
Plavna SRB 75 C4
Plavnica SK 65 A6
Plavno HR 83 B5
Plavsk RUS 7 E14
Playben F 56 B2
Pléaux F 68 C2
Pleine-Fougères F 57 B4
Pleinfeld D 62 A1
Pleinting D 62 B4
Plélan-le-Grand F 57 C3
Plémet F 56 B3
Pléneuf-Val-André F 56 B3
Plentzia E 89 A4
Plérin F 56 B3
Plešivec SK 65 B6
Plessa D 52 B3
Plessé F 66 A3
Plestin-les-Grèves F 56 B2
Pleszew PL 54 B2
Pleternica HR 74 C2
Plettenberg D 50 B3
Pleubian F 56 B2
Pleumartin F 67 B5
Pleumeur-Bodou F 56 B2
Pleurs F 59 B4
Pleven BG 11 E8
Plevlja CG 85 C4
Plevnik-Drienové SK 65 A4
Pleyber-Christ F 56 B2
Pliego E 101 B4
Pliešovce SK 65 B5
Plitvička Jezera HR 83 B4
Plitvički Ljeskovac HR 83 B4
Ploaghe I 110 B1
Ploče HR 84 C2
Plochingen D 61 B5
Płock PL 47 C5
Ploemeur F 56 C2
Ploërmel F 56 C3
Plœuc-sur-Lie F 56 B3
Plogastel St. Germain F 56 C1
Plogoff F 56 B1
Ploiești RO 11 D9
Plomari GR 118 D1
Plombières-les-Bains F 60 C2
Plomin HR 82 A3
Plön D 44 A2
Plonéour-Lanvern F 56 C1
Płonia PL 45 B6
Płońsk PL 47 C6
Płoskinia PL 47 A5
Plössberg D 62 A3
Płoty PL 45 B7
Plouagat F 56 B2
Plouaret F 56 B2
Plouarzel F 56 B1
Plouay F 56 C2
Ploubalay F 57 B3
Ploubazlanec F 56 B2
Ploudalmézeau F 56 B1
Ploudiry F 56 B1
Plouescat F 56 B1
Plouézec F 56 B3
Plougasnou F 56 B2
Plougastel-Daoulas F 56 B1
Plougonven F 56 B2
Plougonver F 56 B2
Plougrescant F 56 B2
Ploguenast F 56 B3
Plouguerneau F 56 B1
Plouha F 56 B3
Plouhinec F 56 B1
Plouigneau F 56 B2
Ploumanach F 56 B2
Plounévez-Quintin F 56 B2
Plouray F 56 B2
Plouzévédé F 56 B1
Plovdiv BG 11 E8
Plozévet F 56 C1
Plumbridge GB 19 B4
Pluméliau F 56 C3
Plumlov CZ 64 A3
Plungė LT 6 D6
Pluty PL 47 A6
Pluvigner F 56 C3
Plužine BIH 84 C3
Plužine CG 84 C3
Płużnica PL 47 B4
Plymouth GB 28 C3
Plymstock GB 28 C3
Płytnica PL 46 B2
Plyusa RUS 7 B10
Plzeň CZ 63 A4
Pniewy PL 46 C2
Pobes E 89 B4
Poběžovice CZ 62 A3
Pobiedziska PL 46 C3
Pobierowo PL 45 A6
Pobla de Segur E 90 A3
Pobla-Tornesa E 96 A3
Pobladura del Valle E 88 B1
Pobra de Trives E 87 B3
Pobra do Brollón E 86 B3
Pobra do Caramiñal E 86 B2
Pobudje BIH 85 B4
Počátky CZ 63 A6
Poceirão P 92 C2
Pochep RUS 7 E12
Pochinok RUS 7 D12
Pöchlarn A 63 B6
Pociecha PL 55 B5
Pockau D 52 C3
Pocking D 63 B4
Pocklington GB 27 B5
Poda CG 85 D4
Podbořany CZ 52 C3
Podbrdo SLO 72 B3
Podbrezová SK 65 B5
Podčetrtek SLO 73 B5
Poddębice PL 54 B3
Poděbrady CZ 53 C5
Podence P 87 C4
Podensac F 76 B2
Podenzano I 80 B3
Podersdorf am See A 64 C2
Podgaje PL 46 B2
Podgora HR 84 C2
Podgóra PL 55 B6
Podgorač HR 74 C3
Podgorica CG 105 A5
Podgorie AL 116 B2
Podgrad SLO 73 C4
Podhájska SK 65 B4
Podkova BG 116 A7
Podlapača HR 83 B4
Podlejki PL 47 B6
Podlužany SK 65 B4
Podnovlje BIH 84 B3
Podolie SK 64 B3
Podolínec SK 65 A6
Podolsk RUS 7 D14
Podporozhy RUS 7 A13
Podromanija BIH 84 C3
Podturen HR 74 B1
Podujevo SRB 85 D6
Podvín CZ 64 B2
Podwilk PL 65 A5
Poetto I 110 C2
Poggendorf D 45 A5
Poggiardo I 107 A5
Poggibonsi I 81 C5
Póggio a Caiano I 81 C5
Poggio Imperiale I 103 B8
Póggio Mirteto I 102 A5
Póggio Moiano I 102 A5
Póggio Renatico I 81 B5
Póggio Rusco I 81 B5
Pöggstall A 63 B6
Pogny F 59 B5
Pogorzela PL 54 B2
Pogorzelice PL 46 A3
Pogradec AL 116 B2
Pogrodzie PL 47 A5
Pohorelá SK 65 B6
Pohořelice CZ 64 B2
Pohronská Polhora SK 65 B5
Poiares P 92 A2
Poio E 86 B2
Poirino I 80 B1
Poisson F 68 B4
Poissons F 59 B6
Poissy F 58 B3
Poitiers F 67 B5
Poix-de-Picardie F 58 A2
Poix-Terron F 59 A5
Pokka FIN 113 D14
Pokój PL 54 C2
Pokupsko HR 73 C5
Pol E 86 A3
Pol a Charra GB 22 D1
Pola RUS 7 C11
Pola de Allande E 86 A4
Pola de Laviana E 88 A1
Pola de Lena E 88 A1
Pola de Siero E 88 A1
Pola de Somiedo E 86 A4
Polaincourt-et-Clairefontaine F 60 C2
Połajewo PL 46 C2
Polán E 94 C2
Polanica-Zdrój PL 54 C1
Połaniec PL 55 C6
Polanów PL 46 A2
Polatlı TR 118 C7
Polatsk BY 7 D10
Polch D 50 C3
Pólczno PL 46 A3
Połczyn-Zdrój PL 46 B2
Polegate GB 31 D4
Poleñino E 90 B2
Polesella I 81 B5
Polessk RUS 6 D6
Polgárdi H 74 A3
Polhov Gradec SLO 73 B4
Police PL 45 B6
Police nad Metují CZ 53 C6
Polichnitos GR 116 C8
Polička CZ 64 A2
Poličnik HR 83 B4
Policoro I 106 A3
Policzna PL 55 B6
Poligiros GR 116 B5
Polignano a Mare I 104 C3
Poligny F 69 B5
Polis CY 120 A1
Polistena I 106 C3
Polizzi Generosa I 109 B3
Poljana SRB 85 B6
Poljanák HR 83 B4
Poljčane SLO 73 B5
Polje BIH 84 B2
Poljice BIH 83 B5
Poljice BIH 84 B3
Poljna SRB 85 C6
Polkowice PL 53 B6
Polla I 104 C1
Pollas E 88 C1
Pöllau A 73 A5
Polleben D 52 B1
Pollença E 97 B3
Pollenfeld D 62 B2
Pollfoss N 114 F4
Póllica I 106 A2
Polminhac F 77 B5
Polná CZ 63 A6
Polna RUS 7 B10
Polne PL 46 B2
Polomka SK 65 B5
Polonne UA 11 A9
Polperro GB 28 C3
Polruan GB 28 C3
Pöls A 73 A4
Polska Cerekiew PL 54 C3
Poltár SK 65 B5
Põltsamaa EST 7 B8
Polyarny RUS 3 B30
Polyarnyye Zori RUS 3 C30
Polzela SLO 73 B5
Pomarance I 81 C4
Pomarez F 76 C2
Pomárico I 104 C2
Pomáz H 65 C5
Pombal P 92 B2
Pomeroy GB 19 B5
Pomézia I 102 B5
Pomichna UA 11 B11
Pommard F 69 A4
Pommelsbrunn D 62 A2
Pomonte I 81 D4
Pomorie BG 11 E9
Pomos CY 120 A1
Pompei I 103 C7
Pompey F 60 B2
Pomposa I 82 B1
Poncin F 69 B5
Pondorf D 62 B2
Ponferrada E 86 B4
Pongoma RUS 3 D31
Poniec PL 54 B1
Ponikva SLO 73 B5
Poniky SK 65 B5
Pons F 67 C4
Ponsacco I 81 C4
Pont I 70 C2
Pont-a-Celles B 49 C5
Pont-a-Marcq F 49 C4
Pont-à-Mousson F 60 B2
Pont-Audemer F 58 A1
Pont-Aven F 56 C2
Pont Canavese I 70 C2
Pont-Croix F 56 B1
Pont-d'Ain F 69 B5
Pont-de-Beauvoisin F 69 C5
Pont-de-Buis-lès-Quimerch F 56 B1
Pont-de-Chéruy F 69 C5
Pont de Dore F 68 C3
Pont-de-Labeaume F 78 B3
Pont-de-l'Arche F 58 A2
Pont de Molins E 91 A5
Pont-de-Roide F 70 A1
Pont-de-Salars F 78 B1
Pont de Suert E 90 A3
Pont-de-Vaux F 69 B4
Pont-de-Veyle F 69 B4
Pont-d'Espagne F 76 D2
Pont-d'Ouilly F 57 B5
Pont-du-Château F 68 C3
Pont-du-Navoy F 69 B5
Pont-en-Royans F 79 A4
Pont Farcy F 57 B4
Pont-l'Abbé F 56 C1
Pont-l'Évêque F 57 A6
Pont-Remy F 48 C2
Pont-St. Esprit F 78 B3
Pont-St. Mamet F 77 B3
Pont-St. Martin F 66 A3
Pont-St. Martin I 70 C2
Pont-St. Vincent F 60 B2
Pont-Ste. Maxence F 58 A3
Pont Scorff F 56 C2
Pont-sur-Yonne F 59 B4
Pontacq F 76 C2
Pontailler-sur-Saône F 69 A5
Pontão P 92 B2
Pontardawe GB 28 B4
Pontarddulais GB 28 B3

Radom PL 55 B6
Radomice PL 47 C5
Radomin PL 47 B5
Radomsko PL 55 B4
Radomyshl UA 11 A10
Radomyśl Wielki PL 55 C6
Radošina SK 64 B3
Radošovce SK 64 B3
Radostowo PL 47 B6
Radoszewice PL 54 B3
Radoszyce PL 55 B5
Radotin CZ 53 D4
Radoviš MK 116 A4
Radovljica SLO 73 B4
Radowo Wielkie PL 46 B1
Radstadt A 72 A3
Radstock GB 29 B5
Raduc HR 83 B4
Radviliškis LT 6 D7
Radzanów, *Mazowieckie* PL 47 C6
Radzanów, *Mazowieckie* PL 55 B5
Radziejów PL 47 C4
Radziejowice PL 55 A5
Radzovce SK 65 B5
Radzymin PL 55 A6
Radzyń Chełmiński PL 47 B4
Raeren B 50 C2
Raesfeld D 50 B2
Raffadali I 108 B2
Rafina GR 117 D5
Rafsbotn N 113 B12
Ragachow BY 7 E11
Ragály H 65 B6
Rågeleje DK 41 C2
Raglan GB 29 B5
Ragnitz A 73 B5
Ragusa I 109 C3
Rahden D 43 C5
Råholt N 34 B3
Raiano I 103 A6
Raigada E 87 B3
Rain D 62 B1
Rainbach im Mühlkreis A 63 B5
Rainham GB 31 C4
Rairiz de Veiga E 87 B3
Raisdorf D 44 A2
Raisio FIN 6 A7
Raiva, *Aveiro* P 87 C2
Raiva, *Coimbra* P 92 A2
Raja-Jooseppi FIN 113 D17
Rajala FIN 113 E15
Rajcza PL 65 A5
Rajec SK 65 A4
Rájec-Jestřebi CZ 64 A2
Rajecké Teplice SK 65 A4
Rajevo Selo HR 84 B3
Rajhrad CZ 64 A2
Rajić HR 74 C2
Rajka H 64 C3
Rakaca H 65 B6
Rakek SLO 73 C4
Rakhiv UA 11 B8
Rakitna SLO 73 C4
Rakkestad N 35 C3
Rákóczifalva H 75 A5
Rakoniewice PL 53 A6
Rakoszyce PL 54 B1
Raková SK 65 A4
Rakovac BIH 84 A2
Rakovica HR 83 B4
Rakovník CZ 53 C3
Rakow D 45 A5
Raków PL 55 C6
Rakvere EST 7 B9
Ralja SRB 85 B5
Rälla S 41 C6
Ramacastañas E 94 B1
Ramacca I 109 B3
Ramales de la Victoria E 89 A3
Ramberg N 112 D2
Rambervillers F 60 B2
Rambouillet F 58 B2
Rambucourt F 60 B1
Ramdala S 41 C5
Ramerupt F 59 B5
Ramingstein A 72 A3
Ramirás E 87 B2
Ramiswil CH 70 A2
Ramkvilla S 40 B4
Ramme DK 38 C1
Rämmen S 34 B6
Ramnäs S 36 C3
Ramnes N 35 C2
Râmnicu Vâlcea RO 11 D8
Ramonville-St. Agne F 77 C4
Rampside GB 26 A2
Ramsau D 62 C3
Ramsbeck D 51 B4
Ramsberg S 36 C2
Ramsele S 115 D13
Ramsey, *Cambridgeshire* GB 30 B3
Ramsey, *Isle of Man* GB 26 A1
Ramseycleuch GB 25 C4
Ramsgate GB 31 C5
Ramsjö S 115 E12
Ramstein-Meisenbach D 60 A3
Ramsund N 112 D5
Ramundberget S 114 E9
Ramvik S 115 E14
Ranalt A 71 A6
Rånäs S 36 C5
Rånåsfoss N 34 B3
Rance B 49 C5
Ránchio I 82 C1
Randaberg N 33 D2
Randalstown GB 19 B5
Randan F 68 B3
Randazzo I 109 B3
Rånddalen S 115 E10
Randegg A 63 B5
Randers DK 38 C3
Randijaur S 112 F8
Randin E 87 C3
Randsverk N 114 F6
Rånes F 57 B5
Rångedala S 40 B3
Ranis D 52 C1
Rankweil A 71 A4
Rånnaväg S 40 B3
Ränneslöv S 40 C3
Rannoch Station GB 24 B3
Ranovac SRB 85 B6
Ransäter S 34 C5
Ransbach-Baumbach D 50 C3
Ransta S 36 C3
Ranttila FIN 113 C14
Ranua FIN 3 D27
Ranum DK 38 C2
Ranvalhal P 92 B1
Raon-l'Étape F 60 B2
Ráossi I 71 C6
Rapallo I 80 B3
Rapla EST 6 B8
Rapness GB 23 B6
Rapolano Terme I 81 C5
Rapolla I 104 C1
Raposa P 92 B2
Rapperswil CH 70 A3
Raša HR 82 A3
Rasal E 90 A2
Rascafria E 94 B3
Rasdorf D 51 C5
Raseiniai LT 6 D7
Rašica SLO 73 C4
Rasines E 89 A3
Raška SRB 85 C5
Rasquera E 90 B3
Rássina I 81 C5
Rastatt D 61 B4
Rastede D 43 B5
Rastenberg D 52 B1
Rastošnica BIH 84 B3
Rastovac CG 84 D3
Rasueros E 94 A1
Rasy PL 55 B4
Raszków PL 54 B2
Rataje SRB 85 C6
Rätan S 115 E11
Rateče SLO 72 B3
Ratekau D 44 B2
Ratež SLO 73 C5
Rathangan IRL 21 A5
Rathcoole IRL 21 A5
Rathcormack IRL 20 B3
Rathdrum IRL 21 B5
Rathebur D 45 B5
Rathenow D 44 C4
Rathfriland GB 19 B5
Rathkeale IRL 20 B3
Rathmelton IRL 19 A4
Rathmolyon IRL 21 A5
Rathmore IRL 20 B2
Rathmullan IRL 19 A4
Rathnew IRL 21 B5
Rathvilly IRL 21 B5
Ratibořské Hory CZ 63 A5
Ratingen D 50 B2
Ratková SK 65 B6
Ratkovo SRB 75 C4
Ratne UA 6 F8
Ratoath IRL 21 A5
Rattelsdorf D 51 C6
Ratten A 73 A5
Rattosjärvi FIN 113 F13
Rattray GB 25 B4
Rättvik S 36 B2
Ratvika N 114 D7
Ratzeburg D 44 B2
Rätzlingen D 44 C3
Raucourt-et-Flaba F 59 A5
Raudeberg N 114 F2
Raufarhöfn IS 111 A10
Raufoss N 34 B2
Rauhala FIN 113 E13
Rauland N 33 C5
Raulhac F 77 B5
Raulia N 115 B11
Rauma FIN 3 F24
Raundal N 32 B3
Raunds GB 30 B3
Rauris A 72 A3
Rautas S 112 E8
Rautavaara FIN 3 E28
Rauville-la-Bigot F 57 A4
Rauzan F 76 B2
Rava-Rus'ka UA 11 A7
Ravanusa I 108 B2
Ravča HR 84 C2
Ravels B 49 B5
Rävemåla S 40 C5
Ravenglass GB 26 A2
Ravenna I 82 B1
Ravensburg D 61 C5
Rävlanda S 40 B2
Ravna Gora HR 73 C4
Ravne na Koroškem SLO 73 B4
Ravnište SRB 85 C6
Ravnje SRB 85 B4
Ravno BIH 84 D2
Ravno Selo SRB 75 C4
Rawa Mazowiecka PL 55 B5
Rawicz PL 54 B1
Rawtenstall GB 26 B3
Rayleigh GB 31 C4
Ražana SRB 85 B4
Ražanac HR 83 B4
Razboj BIH 84 A2
Razbojna SRB 85 C6
Razes F 67 B6
Razgrad BG 11 E9
Razkrižie SLO 73 B6
Razo E 86 A2
Reading GB 31 C3
Réalmont F 77 C5
Rebais F 59 B4
Reboly RUS 3 E29
Rebordelo P 87 C3
Recanati I 82 C2
Recas E 94 B3
Recaş RO 10 D6
Recco I 80 B3
Recess IRL 18 C2
Recey-sur-Ource F 59 C5
Recezinhos P 87 C2
Rechnitz A 73 A6
Rechytsa BY 7 E11
Recke D 43 C4
Recklinghausen D 50 B3
Recoaro Terme I 71 C6
Recogne B 59 A6
Recoules-Prévinquières F 78 B1
Recsk H 65 C6
Recz PL 46 B1
Red Point GB 22 D3
Reda PL 47 A4
Redalen N 34 B2
Redange L 60 A1
Redcar GB 27 A4
Redditch GB 29 A6
Redefin D 44 B3
Redhill GB 31 C3
Redics H 74 B1
Redkino RUS 7 C14
Redland GB 23 B5
Redlin D 44 B4
Redon F 57 C3
Redondela E 87 B2
Redondo P 92 C3
Redruth GB 28 C2
Redzikowo PL 46 A3
Reepham GB 30 B5
Rees D 50 B2
Reeth GB 27 A4
Reetz D 44 B3
Reftele S 40 B3
Regalbuto I 109 B3
Regen D 62 B4
Regensburg D 62 A3
Regenstauf D 62 A3
Reggello I 81 C5
Réggio di Calábria I 109 A4
Réggio nell'Emília I 81 B4
Reggiolo I 81 B4
Reghin RO 11 C8
Régil E 89 A4
Regna S 37 D2
Regniéville F 60 B1
Regny F 69 C4
Rego da Leirosa P 92 A2
Regöly H 74 B3
Regueiro E 86 B2
Reguengo, *Portalegre* P 92 B3
Reguengo, *Santarém* P 92 B2
Reguengos de Monsaraz P 92 C3
Rehau D 52 C2
Rehburg D 43 C6
Rehden D 43 C5
Rehna D 44 B3
Reichelsheim D 61 A4
Reichelshofen D 61 A6
Reichenau A 64 C1
Reichenbach, *Sachsen* D 52 C2
Reichenbach, *Sachsen* D 53 B4
Reichenfels A 73 A4
Reichensachsen D 51 B6
Reichertshofen D 62 B2
Reichshoffen F 60 B3
Reiden CH 70 A2
Reigada E 86 A4
Reigada P 87 D4
Reigate GB 31 C3
Reillanne F 79 C4
Reillo E 95 C5
Reims F 59 A5
Reinach CH 70 A3
Reinbek D 44 B2
Reinberg D 45 A5
Reine N 112 E2
Reinfeld D 44 B2
Reinheim D 61 A4
Reinli N 32 B6
Reinosa E 88 A2
Reinstorf D 44 B3
Reinsvoll N 34 B2
Reisach A 72 B3
Reiss GB 23 C5
Reit im Winkl D 62 C3
Reitan N 114 E8
Rejmyre S 37 D2
Rekavice BIH 84 B2
Rekovac SRB 85 C6
Relleu E 96 C2
Rém H 75 B4
Remagen D 50 C3
Rémalard F 58 B1
Rembercourt-aux-Pots F 59 B6
Remedios P 92 B1
Remels D 43 B4
Remetea Mare RO 75 C6
Remich L 60 A2
Rémilly F 60 A2
Remiremont F 60 C2
Remolinos E 90 B1
Remoulins F 78 C3
Remscheid D 50 B3
Rémuzat F 79 B4
Rena N 34 A3
Renaison F 68 B3
Renazé F 57 C4
Renchen D 61 B4
Rencurel F 79 A4
Rende I 106 B3
Rendina GR 116 C5
Rendsburg D 43 A6
Renedo E 88 C2
Renens CH 69 B6
Renfrew GB 24 C3
Rengsjö S 36 A3
Reni UA 11 D10
Rennebu N 114 E6
Rennerod D 50 C4
Rennertshofen D 62 B2
Rennes F 57 B4
Rennes-les-Bains F 77 D5
Rennweg A 72 A3
Rens DK 39 E2
Rensjön S 112 D8
Rentería E 76 C1
Rentjärn S 115 B15
Répcelak H 74 A2
Repojoki FIN 113 D14
Repvåg N 113 B14
Requena E 96 B1
Réquista F 77 B5
Rerik D 44 A3
Resana I 72 C1
Resarö S 37 C5
Reschen = Résia I 71 B5
Resen MK 116 A3
Resende P 87 C3
Résia = Reschen I 71 B5
Reşiţa RO 10 D6
Resko PL 46 B1
Resnik SRB 85 B5
Ressons-sur-Matz F 58 A3
Restábal E 100 C2
Resuttano I 109 B3
Retamal E 93 C4
Retford GB 27 B5
Rethel F 59 A5
Rethem D 43 C6
Rethimno GR 117 G6
Retie B 49 B6
Retiers F 57 C4
Retortillo E 87 D4
Retortillo de Soria E 89 C3
Retournac F 68 C4
Rétság H 65 C5
Rettenegg A 73 A5
Retuerta del Bullaque E 94 C2
Retz A 64 B1
Retzbach D 61 A5
Reuden D 52 A2
Reuilly F 68 A2
Reus E 91 B4
Reusel NL 49 B6
Reuterstadt Stavenhagen D 45 B4
Reuth D 62 A3
Reutlingen D 61 B5
Reutte A 71 A5
Reuver NL 50 B2
Revel F 77 C4
Revello I 80 B1
Revenga E 94 B2
Revest-du-Bion F 79 B4
Révfülöp H 74 B2
Revigny-sur-Ornain F 59 B5
Revin F 59 A5
Řevnice CZ 63 A5
Řevničov CZ 53 C3
Revo I 71 B6
Revsnes N 32 A4
Revúca SK 65 B6
Rewa PL 47 A4
Rewal PL 45 A7
Rexbo S 36 B2
Reyðarfjörður IS 111 B11
Reyero E 88 B1
Reykhólar IS 111 B3
Reykholt, *Árnessýsla* IS 111 C5
Reykholt, *Borgarfjarðarsýsla* IS 111 C4
Reykjahlið IS 111 B9
Reykjavík IS 111 C4
Rezé F 66 A3
Rēzekne LV 7 C9
Rezovo BG 11 F10
Rezzato I 71 C5
Rezzoáglio I 80 B3
Rhade D 43 B6
Rhaunen D 60 A3
Rhayader GB 29 A4
Rheda-Wiedenbrück D 50 B4
Rhede, *Niedersachsen* D 43 B4
Rhede, *Nordrhein-Westfalen* D 50 B2
Rheinau D 60 B3
Rheinbach D 50 C2
Rheinberg D 50 B2
Rheine D 50 A3
Rheinfelden D 70 A2
Rheinsberg D 45 B4
Rhêmes-Notre-Dame I 70 C2
Rhenen NL 49 B6
Rhens D 50 C3
Rheydt D 50 B2
Rhiconich GB 22 C4
Rhinow D 44 C4
Rhiw GB 26 C1
Rho I 70 C4
Rhoden D 51 B5
Rhodes GR 119 F3
Rhondda GB 29 B4
Rhosllanerchrugog GB 26 B2
Rhosneigr GB 26 B1
Rhossili GB 28 B3
Rhubodach GB 24 C2
Rhuddlan GB 26 B2
Rhyl GB 26 B2
Rhynie GB 23 D6
Riala S 37 C5
Riallé F 66 A3
Riaño E 88 B1
Riano I 102 A5
Rians F 79 C4
Rianxo E 86 B2
Riaza E 89 C3
Riba E 89 A3
Riba de Saelices E 95 B4
Riba-Roja de Turia E 96 B2
Riba-roja d'Ebre E 90 B3
Ribadavia E 87 B2
Ribadeo E 86 A3
Ribadesella E 88 A1
Ribaflecha E 89 B4
Ribaforada E 89 C5
Ribare SRB 85 B6
Ribariće SRB 85 D5
Ribe DK 39 D1
Ribeauvillé F 60 B3
Ribécourt-Dreslincourt F 59 A3
Ribeira da Pena P 87 C3
Ribeira de Piquín E 86 A3
Ribemont F 59 A4
Ribera I 108 B2
Ribera de Cardós E 91 A4
Ribera del Fresno E 93 C4
Ribérac F 67 C5
Ribes de Freser E 91 A5
Ribesalbes E 96 A2
Ribiers F 79 B4
Ribnica BIH 84 B3
Ribnica SLO 73 C4
Ribnica SRB 85 C5
Ribnica na Potorju SLO 73 B5
Ribnik HR 73 C5
Rîbniţa MD 11 C10
Ribnitz-Damgarten D 44 A4
Ribolla I 81 D5
Řicany, *Jihomoravský* CZ 64 A2
Řicany, *Středočeský* CZ 53 D4
Riccia I 103 B7
Riccione I 82 B1
Ricco Del Golfo I 81 B3
Richebourg F 59 B6
Richelieu F 67 A5
Richisau CH 70 A3
Richmond, *Greater London* GB 31 C3
Richmond, *North Yorkshire* GB 27 A4
Richtenberg D 45 A4
Richterswil CH 70 A3
Rickling D 44 A2
Rickmansworth GB 31 C3
Ricla E 89 C5
Riddarhyttan S 36 C2
Ridderkerk NL 49 B5
Riddes CH 70 B2
Ridjica SRB 75 C4
Riec-sur-Bélon F 56 C2
Ried A 63 B4
Ried im Oberinntal A 71 A5
Riedenburg D 62 B2
Riedlingen D 61 B5
Riedstadt D 61 A4
Riegersburg A 73 B5
Riego de la Vega E 88 B1
Riego del Camino E 88 C1
Riello E 88 B1
Riemst B 49 C6
Rienne B 49 D5
Riénsena E 88 A2
Riesa D 52 B3
Riese Pio X I 72 C1
Riesi I 109 B3
Riestedt D 52 B1
Rietberg D 51 B4
Rieti I 102 A5
Rietschen D 53 B4
Rieumes F 77 C4
Rieupeyroux F 77 B5
Rieux F 77 C4
Riez F 79 C5
Rīga LV 6 C8
Riggisberg CH 70 B2
Rignac F 77 B5
Rignano Gargánico I 104 B1
Rigolato I 72 B2
Rigside GB 25 C4
Rigutino I 81 C5
Riihimäki FIN 3 F26
Rijeka HR 73 C4
Rijeka Crnojevića CG 105 A5
Rijen NL 49 B5
Rijkevorsel B 49 B5
Rijssen NL 50 A2
Rilić BIH 84 C2
Rilievo I 108 B1
Rillé F 67 A5
Rillo de Gallo E 95 B5
Rimavská Baňa SK 65 B5
Rimavská Seč SK 65 B6
Rimavská Sobota SK 65 B6
Rimbo S 36 C5
Rimforsa S 37 D2
Rímini I 82 B1
Rîmnicu Sărat RO 11 D9
Rimogne F 59 A5
Rimpar D 61 A5
Rimske Toplice SLO 73 B5
Rincón de la Victoria E 100 C1
Rincón de Soto E 89 B5
Rindal N 114 D6
Rinde N 32 A3
Ringarum S 37 D3
Ringaskiddy IRL 20 C3
Ringe DK 39 D3
Ringebu N 34 A2
Ringkøbing DK 39 C1
Ringsaker N 34 B2
Ringsted DK 39 D4
Ringwood GB 29 C6
Rinkaby S 41 D4
Rinkabyholm S 40 C6
Rinlo E 86 A3
Rinn A 71 A6
Rinteln D 51 A5
Rio E 86 B3
Rio do Coures P 92 B2
Rio Douro P 87 C3
Rio Frio P 92 C2
Rio frio de Riaza E 95 A3
Rio Maior P 92 B2
Rio Marina I 81 D4
Rio Tinto P 87 C2
Riobo E 86 B2
Riodeva E 96 A1
Riofrio E 94 B2
Riofrio de Aliste E 87 C4
Riogordo E 100 C1
Rioja E 101 C3
Riola I 81 B5
Riola Sardo I 110 C1
Riolobos E 93 B4
Riom F 68 C3
Riom-ès-Montagnes F 68 C2
Riomaggiore I 81 B3
Rion-des-Landes F 76 C2
Rionegro del Puente E 87 B4
Rionero in Vúlture I 104 C1
Riopar E 101 A3
Riós E 87 C3
Rioseco E 88 A1
Rioseco de Tapia E 88 B1
Riotord F 69 C4
Riotorto E 86 A3
Rioz F 69 A6
Ripač BIH 83 B4
Ripacándida I 104 C1
Ripanj SRB 85 B5
Ripatransone I 82 D2
Ripley GB 27 B4
Ripoll E 91 A5
Ripon GB 27 A4
Riposto I 109 B4
Ripsa S 37 D3
Risan CG 105 A4
Risbäck S 115 C12
Risca GB 29 B4
Rischenau D 51 B5
Riscle F 76 C2
Risebo S 40 A6
Risnes N 32 A2
Rišňovce SK 64 B3
Risør N 33 D6
Risøyhamn N 112 D4
Rissna S 115 D12
Ritsem S 112 E6
Ritterhude D 43 B5
Riutula FIN 113 D15
Riva del Garda I 71 C5
Riva Lígure I 80 C1
Rivanazzano I 80 B3
Rivarolo Canavese I 70 C2
Rivarolo Mantovano I 81 A4
Rive-de-Gier F 69 C4
Rivedoux-Plage F 66 B3
Rivello I 106 A2
Rivergaro I 80 B3
Rives F 69 C5
Rivesaltes F 78 D1
Rivignano I 72 C3
Rivne UA 11 A9
Rívoli I 80 A1
Rivolta d'Adda I 71 C4
Rixheim F 60 C3
Rixo S 35 D3
Riza GR 116 B5
Rizokarpaso CY 120 A3
Rjukan N 32 C5
Rø DK 41 D4
Rö S 37 C5
Roa E 88 C3
Roa N 34 B2
Roade GB 30 B3
Roager DK 39 D1
Roaldkvam N 33 C3
Roanne F 68 B4
Robakowo PL 47 B4
Róbbio I 70 C3
Röbel D 45 B4
Roberton GB 25 C5
Robertville B 50 C2
Robin Hood's Bay GB 27 A5
Robleda E 93 A4
Robledillo de Trujillo E 93 B5
Robledo, *Albacete* E 101 A3
Robledo, *Orense* E 86 B4
Robledo de Chavela E 94 B2
Robledo del Buey E 94 C2
Robledo del Mazo E 94 C2
Robledollano E 93 B5
Robles de la Valcueva E 88 B1
Robliza de Cojos E 87 D5
Robres E 90 B2
Robres del Castillo E 89 B4
Rocafort de Queralt E 91 B4
Rocamadour F 77 B4
Rocca di Mezzo I 103 A6
Rocca di Papa I 102 B5
Rocca Imperiale I 106 A3
Rocca Priora I 82 C2
Rocca San Casciano I 81 B5
Rocca Sinibalda I 102 A5
Roccabernarda I 107 B3
Roccabianca I 81 A4
Roccadáspide I 103 C8
Roccagorga I 102 B6
Roccalbegna I 81 D5
Roccalumera I 109 B4
Roccamena I 108 B2
Roccamonfina I 103 B6
Roccanova I 106 A3
Roccapalumba I 108 B2
Roccapassa I 103 A6
Roccaraso I 103 B7
Roccasecca I 103 B6
Roccastrada I 81 C5
Roccatederighi I 81 C5
Roccella Iónica I 106 C3
Rocchetta Sant'António I 103 B8
Rocester GB 27 C4
Rochdale GB 26 B3
Roche-lez-Beaupré F 69 A6
Rochechouart F 67 C5
Rochefort B 49 C6
Rochefort F 66 C4
Rochefort-en-Terre F 56 C3
Rochefort-Montagne F 68 C2
Rochefort-sur-Nenon F 69 A5
Rochemaure F 78 B3
Rocheservière F 66 B3
Rochester, *Medway* GB 31 C4
Rochester, *Northumberland* GB 25 C5
Rochlitz D 52 B2
Rociana del Condado E 99 B4
Rockenhausen D 60 A3
Rockhammar S 37 C2
Rockneby S 40 C6
Ročko Polje HR 73 C4
Ročov CZ 53 C3
Rocroi F 59 A5
Roda de Bara E 91 B4
Roda de Ter E 91 B5
Rodach D 51 C6
Rodalben D 60 A3
Rødberg N 32 B5
Rødby DK 44 A3
Rødbyhavn DK 44 A3
Rødding, *Sønderjyllands Amt.* DK 39 D2
Rødding, *Viborg Amt.* DK 38 C1
Rödeby S 41 C5
Rodeiro E 86 B3
Rødekro DK 39 D2
Roden NL 42 B3
Ródenas E 95 B5
Rodenkirchen D 43 B5
Rödental D 52 C1
Rödermark D 51 D4
Rodewisch D 52 C2
Rodez F 77 B5
Rodi Gargánico I 104 B1
Roding D 62 A3
Rödjebro S 36 B4
Rødkærsbro DK 39 C2
Rodolivas GR 116 B5
Rodoñá E 91 B4
Rødvig DK 41 D2
Roermond NL 50 B1
Roesbrugge B 48 C3
Roeschwoog F 61 B4
Roeselare B 49 C4
Roetgen D 50 C2
Roffiac F 78 A2
Röfors S 37 D1
Rofrano I 106 A2
Rogač HR 83 C5
Rogačica SRB 85 B4
Rogalinek PL 54 A1
Rogaška Slatina SLO 73 B5
Rogatec SLO 73 B5
Rogatica BIH 84 C4
Rogatyn UA 11 B8
Rogätz D 52 A1
Roggendorf D 44 B3
Roggiano Gravina I 106 B3
Roghadal GB 22 D2
Rogliano F 102 A2
Rogliano I 106 B3
Rognan N 112 E4
Rogne N 32 A6
Rognes F 79 C4
Rogny-les-7-Ecluses F 59 C3
Rogowo PL 46 C3
Rogóz PL 47 A6
Rogoznica HR 83 C4
Rogoźnica PL 53 B6
Rogoźno PL 46 C2
Rohan F 56 B3
Röhlingen D 61 B6
Rohožnik SK 64 B3
Rohr D 51 C6
Rohr im Gebirge A 63 C6
Rohrbach A 63 B4
Rohrbach-lès-Bitche F 60 A3
Rohrberg D 44 C3
Röhrnbach D 63 B4
Roisel F 59 A4
Roja LV 6 C7
Rojales E 96 C2
Röjeråsen S 36 B1
Rojewo PL 47 C4
Rokiciny PL 55 B4
Rokietnica PL 46 C2
Rokiškis LT 7 D8
Rokitki PL 53 B5
Rokitno RUS 7 F13
Rokycany CZ 63 A4
Rolampont F 59 C6
Rold DK 38 C2
Røldal N 32 C3
Rolde NL 42 C3
Rollag N 32 B6
Rollán E 94 B1
Rolle CH 69 B6
Roma = Rome I 102 B5
Roma S 37 E5
Romagnano Sésia I 70 C3
Romagné F 57 B4
Romakloster S 37 E5
Roman RO 11 C9
Romana I 110 B1
Romanèche-Thorins F 69 B4
Romano di Lombardia I 71 C4
Romans-sur-Isère F 79 A4
Romanshorn CH 71 A4
Rombas F 60 A2
Rome = Roma I 102 B5
Romeán E 86 B3
Romenay F 69 B5
Romeral E 95 C3
Römerstein D 61 B5
Rometta I 109 A4
Romford GB 31 C4
Romhány H 65 C5
Römhild D 51 C6
Romilly-sur-Seine F 59 B4
Romny UA 11 A12
Romodan UA 11 B12
Romont CH 70 B1
Romorantin-Lanthenay F 68 A1
Romrod D 51 C5
Romsey GB 31 D2
Rømskog N 35 C3
Rønbjerg DK 38 C1
Roncal E 76 D2
Ronce-les-Bains F 66 C3
Ronchamp F 60 C2
Ronchi dei Legionari I 72 C3
Ronciglione I 102 A5
Ronco Canavese I 70 C2
Ronco Scrivia I 80 B2
Ronda E 99 C5
Rønde DK 39 C3
Rone S 37 E5
Ronehamn S 37 E5
Rong N 32 B1
Rönnäng S 38 B4
Rønne DK 41 D4
Ronneburg D 52 C2
Ronneby S 41 C5
Rönneshytta S 37 D2
Rönninge S 37 C4
Rönnöfors S 115 D10
Rönö S 37 D3
Ronov nad Doubravou CZ 63 A6
Ronse B 49 C4
Roosendaal NL 49 B5
Roosky IRL 19 C4
Ropczyce PL 55 C6
Ropeid N 33 C3
Ropinsalmi FIN 113 D10
Ropuerelos del Páramo E 88 B1

Sanchonuño E 88 C2
Sancoins F 68 B2
Sancti-Petri E 99 C4
Sancti-Spiritus E 87 D4
Sand, *Hedmark* N 34 B3
Sand, *Rogaland* N 33 C3
Sanda S 37 E5
Sandane N 114 F3
Sandanski BG 116 A5
Sandared S 40 B2
Sandarne S 36 A4
Sandau D 44 C4
Sandbach D 63 B4
Sandbach GB 26 B3
Sandbank GB 24 C3
Sandbanks GB 29 C6
Sandbukt N 112 C10
Sandby DK 39 E4
Sande D 43 B5
Sande, *Sogn og Fjordane* N 32 A2
Sande, *Vestfold* N 35 C2
Sandefjord N 35 C2
Sandeid N 33 C2
Sandersleben D 52 B1
Sanderstølen N 32 B6
Sandes N 33 D4
Sandesneben D 44 B2
Sandhead GB 24 D3
Sandhem S 40 B3
Sandhorst D 43 B4
Sandhurst GB 31 C3
Sandıklı TR 119 D5
Sandillon F 58 C3
Sandl A 63 B5
Sandnes N 33 D2
Sandness GB 22 A7
Sandnessjøen N 115 A9
Sando E 87 D4
Sandomierz PL 55 C6
Sándorfalva H 75 B5
Sandown GB 31 D2
Sandøysund N 35 C2
Sandrigo I 72 C1
Sandsele S 115 B14
Sandset N 112 D3
Sandsjöfors S 40 B4
Sandstad N 114 D6
Sandvatn N 33 D3
Sandvig-Allinge DK 41 D4
Sandvika, *Akershus* N 34 C2
Sandvika, *Hedmark* N 34 B3
Sandvika, *Nord-Trøndelag* N 114 D9
Sandviken S 36 B3
Sandvikvåy N 32 C2
Sandwich GB 31 C5
Sandy GB 30 B3
Sangatte F 48 C2
Sangerhausen D 52 B1
Sangineto Lido I 106 B2
Sangonera la Verde E 101 B4
Sangüesa E 90 A1
Sanguinet F 76 B1
Sanica BIH 83 B5
Sanitz D 44 A4
Sankt Aegyd am Neuwalde A 63 C6
Sankt Andrä A 73 B4
Sankt Andreasberg D 51 B6
Sankt Anna S 37 D3
Sankt Anna am Aigen A 73 B5
Sankt Anton am Arlberg A 71 A5
Sankt Anton an der Jessnitz A 63 C6
Sankt Augustin D 50 C3
Sankt Blasien D 61 C4
Sankt Englmar D 62 A3
Sankt Gallen A 63 C5
Sankt Gallen CH 71 A4
Sankt Gallenkirch A 71 A4
Sankt Georgen A 63 B5
Sankt Georgen D 61 B4
Sankt Georgen am Reith A 63 C5
Sankt Georgen ob Judenburg A 73 A4
Sankt Georgen ob Murau A 73 A4
Sankt Gilgen A 63 C4
Sankt Goar D 50 C3
Sankt Goarshausen D 50 C3
Sankt Ingbert D 60 A3
Sankt Jacob A 73 B4
Sankt Jakob in Defereggen A 72 B2
Sankt Johann am Tauern A 73 A4
Sankt Johann am Wesen A 63 B4
Sankt Johann im Pongau A 72 A3
Sankt Johann in Tirol A 72 A2
Sankt Katharein an der Laming A 73 A5
Sankt Kathrein am Hauenstein A 73 A5
Sankt Lambrecht A 73 A4
Sankt Leonhard am Forst A 63 B6
Sankt Leonhard im Pitztal A 71 A5
Sankt Lorenzen A 72 B2
Sankt Marein, *Steiermark* A 73 A5
Sankt Marein, *Steiermark* A 73 A5
Sankt Margarethen im Lavanttal A 73 B4
Sankt Margrethen CH 71 A4
Sankt Michael A 73 A5
Sankt Michael im Burgenland A 73 A6
Sankt Michael im Lungau A 72 A3
Sankt Michaelisdonn D 43 B6
Sankt Niklaus CH 70 B2
Sankt Nikolai im Sölktal A 73 A4
Sankt Olof S 41 D4
Sankt Oswald D 63 B4
Sankt Paul A 73 B4
Sankt Paul F 79 B5
Sankt Peter D 61 B4
Sankt Peter am Kammersberg A 73 A4
Sankt Peter-Ording D 43 A5
Sankt-Peterburg = St. Petersburg RUS 7 B11
Sankt Pölten A 63 B6
Sankt Radegund A 73 A5
Sankt Ruprecht an der Raab A 73 A5
Sankt Salvator A 73 B4
Sankt Stefan A 73 B4
Sankt Stefan an der Gail A 72 B3
Sankt Stefan im Rosental A 73 B5
Sankt Valentin A 63 B5
Sankt Veit an der Glan A 73 B4
Sankt Veit an der Gölsen A 63 B6
Sankt Veit in Defereggen A 72 B2
Sankt Wendel D 60 A3
Sankt Wolfgang A 63 C4
Sankt Wolfgang D 62 B3
Sanlúcar de Barrameda E 99 C4
Sanlúcar de Guadiana E 98 B3
Sanlúcar la Mayor E 99 B4
Sanluri I 110 C1
Sânmihaiu Roman RO 75 C6
Sänna S 37 D1
Sannazzaro de'Burgondi I 80 A2
Sanne D 44 C3
Sannicandro di Bari I 104 B2
Sannicandro Gargánico I 104 B1
Sânnicolau Mare RO 75 B5
Sannidal N 33 D6
Sanniki PL 47 C5
Sanok PL 11 B7
Sanquhar GB 25 C4
Sansepolcro I 82 C1
Sanski Most BIH 83 B5
Sant Agustí de Lluçanès E 91 A5
Sant Antoni Abat E 97 C1
Sant Antoni de Calonge E 91 B6
Sant Boi de Llobregat E 91 B5
Sant Carles de la Ràpita E 90 C3
Sant Carlos E 97 B1
Sant Celoni E 91 B5
Sant Climent E 97 B4
Sant Feliu E 91 B5
Sant Feliu de Codines E 91 B5
Sant Feliu de Guíxols E 91 B6
Sant Feliu Sasserra E 91 B5
Sant Ferran E 97 C1
Sant Francesc de Formentera E 97 C1
Sant Francesc de ses Salines E 97 C1
Sant Hilari Sacalm E 91 B5
Sant Hipòlit de Voltregà E 91 A5
Sant Jaume dels Domenys E 91 B4
Sant Joan Baptista E 97 B1
Sant Joan de les Abadesses E 91 A5
Sant Jordi E 90 C3
Sant Josep E 97 C1
Sant Julià de Loria AND 91 A4
Sant Llorenç de Morunys E 91 A4
Sant Llorenç des Carctassar E 97 B3
Sant Llorenç Savall E 91 B5
Sant Luis E 97 B4
Sant Martí de Llemaná E 91 A5
Sant Marti de Maldá E 91 B4
Sant Marti Sarroca E 91 B4
Sant Mateu E 90 C3
Sant Miquel E 97 B1
Sant Pau de Seguries E 91 A5
Sant Pere de Riudebitlles E 91 B4
Sant Pere Pescador E 91 A6
Sant Pere Sallavinera E 91 B4
Sant Quirze de Besora E 91 A5
Sant Rafel E 97 C1
Sant Ramon E 91 B4
Sant Vincenç de Castellet E 91 B4
Santa Agnès E 97 B1
Santa Amalia E 93 B4
Santa Ana, *Cáceres* E 93 B5
Santa Ana, *Jaén* E 100 B2
Santa Ana de Pusa E 94 C2
Santa Barbara E 90 C3
Santa Bárbara P 98 B2
Santa Barbara de Casa E 98 B3
Santa Bárbara de Padrões P 98 B3
Santa Catarina P 98 B3
Santa Caterina di Pittinuri I 110 B1
Santa Caterina Villarmosa I 109 B3
Santa Cesárea Terme I 107 A5
Santa Clara-a-Nova P 98 B2
Santa Clara-a-Velha P 98 B2
Santa Clara de Louredo P 98 B3
Santa Coloma de Farners E 91 B5
Santa Coloma de Gramenet E 91 B5
Santa Coloma de Queralt E 91 B4
Santa Colomba de Curueño E 88 B1
Santa Colomba de Somoza E 86 B4
Santa Comba E 86 A2
Santa Comba Dáo P 92 A2
Santa Comba de Rossas P 87 C4
Santa Cristina I 71 C4
Santa Cristina de la Polvorosa E 88 B1
Santa Croce Camerina I 109 C3
Santa Croce di Magliano I 103 B7
Santa Cruz E 86 A2
Santa Cruz P 92 B1
Santa Cruz de Alhama E 100 B2
Santa Cruz de Campezo E 89 B4
Santa Cruz de Grio E 89 C5
Santa Cruz de la Salceda E 89 C3
Santa Cruz de la Sierra E 93 B5
Santa Cruz de la Zarza E 95 C3
Santa Cruz de Moya E 96 B1
Santa Cruz de Mudela E 100 A2
Santa Cruz de Paniagua E 93 A4
Santa Cruz del Retamar E 94 B2
Santa Cruz del Valle E 94 B1
Santa Doménica Talao I 106 B2
Santa Doménica Vittória I 109 B3
Santa Elena E 100 A2
Santa Elena de Jamuz E 88 B1
Santa Eufemia E 100 A1
Santa Eufémia d'Aspromonte I 106 C2
Santa Eulalia E 95 B5
Santa Eulália P 92 C3
Santa Eulalia de Oscos E 86 A3
Santa Eulàlia des Riu E 97 C1
Santa Fe E 100 B2
Santa Fiora I 81 D5
Santa Gertrude I 71 B5
Santa Giustina I 72 B2
Santa Iria P 98 B3
Santa Leocadia P 87 C2
Santa Lucia-de-Porto-Vecchio F 102 B2
Santa Lucia del Mela I 109 A4
Santa Luzia P 98 B2
Santa Maddalena Vallalta I 72 B2
Santa Magdalena de Polpis E 90 C3
Santa Margalida E 97 B3
Santa Margarida P 92 B2
Santa Margarida do Sado P 98 A2
Santa Margaridao de Montbui E 91 B4
Santa Margherita I 110 D1
Santa Margherita di Belice I 108 B2
Santa Margherita Ligure I 80 B3
Santa Maria CH 71 B5
Santa Maria E 90 A2
Santa Maria al Bagno I 107 A4
Santa Maria Cápua Vétere I 103 B7
Santa Maria da Feira P 87 D2
Santa Maria de Cayón E 88 A3
Santa Maria de Corco E 91 A5
Santa Maria de Huerta E 95 A4
Santa Maria de la Alameda E 94 B2
Santa Maria de las Hoyas E 89 C3
Santa Maria de Mercadillo E 89 C3
Santa Maria de Nieva E 101 B4
Santa Maria de Trassierra E 100 B1
Santa Maria del Camí E 97 B2
Santa Maria del Campo E 88 B3
Santa Maria del Campo Rus E 95 C4
Santa Maria del Páramo E 88 B1
Santa Maria del Taro I 80 B3
Santa Maria della Versa I 80 B2
Santa Maria di Licodia I 109 B3
Santa Maria-di-Rispéscia I 81 D5
Santa Maria la Palma I 110 B1
Santa María la Real de Nieva E 94 A2
Santa Maria Maggiore I 70 B3
Santa Maria Ribarredonda E 89 B3
Santa Marina del Rey E 88 B1
Santa Marinella I 102 A4
Santa Marta, *Albacete* E 95 C4
Santa Marta, *Badajoz* E 93 C4
Santa Marta de Magasca E 93 B4
Santa Marta de Penaguião P 87 C3
Santa Marta de Tormes E 94 B1
Santa Ninfa I 108 B1
Santa Olalla, *Huelva* E 99 B4
Santa Olalla, *Toledo* E 94 B2
Santa Pau E 91 A5
Santa Pola E 96 C2
Santa Ponça E 97 B2
Santa Severa F 102 A2
Santa Severa I 102 A4
Santa Severina I 107 B3
Santa Sofia I 81 C5
Santa Suzana, *Évora* P 92 C3
Santa Suzana, *Setúbal* P 92 C2
Santa Teresa di Riva I 109 B4
Santa Teresa Gallura I 110 A2
Santa Uxía E 86 B2
Santa Valburga I 71 B5
Santa Vittória in Matenano I 82 C2
Santacara E 89 B5
Santadi I 110 C1
Santaella E 100 B1
Sant'Ágata dei Goti I 103 B7
Sant'Ágata di Ésaro I 106 B2
Sant'Ágata di Puglia I 103 B8
Sant'Agata Feltria I 82 C1
Sant'Ágata Militello I 109 A3
Santana, *Évora* P 92 C2
Santana, *Setúbal* P 92 C1
Santana da Serra P 98 B2
Sant'Ana de Cambas P 98 B3
Santana do Mato P 92 C2
Sant'Anastasia I 103 C7
Santander E 88 A3
Sant'Andrea Frius I 110 C2
Sant'Ángelo dei Lombardi I 103 C8
Sant'Angelo in Vado I 82 C1
Sant'Angelo Lodigiano I 71 C4
Sant'Antíoco I 110 C1
Sant'Antonio-di-Gallura I 110 B2
Santanyí E 97 B3
Santarcángelo di Romagna I 82 B1
Santarém P 92 B2
Santas Martas E 88 B1
Sant'Caterina I 81 D5
Santed E 95 A5
Sant'Egidio alla Vibrata I 82 D2
Sant'Elia a Pianisi I 103 B7
Sant'Elia Fiumerapido I 103 B6
Santelices E 88 A3
Sant'Elpídio a Mare I 82 C2
Santéramo in Colle I 104 C2
Santervas de la Vega E 88 B2
Santhià I 70 C3
Santiago de Alcántara E 92 B3
Santiago de Calatrava E 100 B1
Santiago de Compostela E 86 B2
Santiago de la Espade E 101 A3
Santiago de la Puebla E 94 B1
Santiago de la Ribera E 101 B5
Santiago de Litem P 92 B2
Santiago del Campo E 93 B4
Santiago do Cacém P 98 B2
Santiago do Escoural P 92 C2
Santiago Maior P 92 C3
Santibáñez de Béjar E 93 A5
Santibáñez de la Peña E 88 B2
Santibáñez de Murias E 88 A1
Santibáñez de Vidriales E 87 B4
Santibáñez el Alto E 93 A4
Santibáñez el Bajo E 93 A4
Santillana E 88 A2
Santiponce E 99 B4
Santisteban del Puerto E 100 A2
Santiuste de San Juan Bautiste E 94 A2
Santiz E 94 A1
Sant'Ilario d'Enza I 81 B4
Santo Aleixo P 98 A3
Santo Amado P 98 A3
Santo Amaro P 92 C3
Santo André P 98 A2
Santo Domingo E 93 C3
Santo Domingo de la Calzada E 89 B4
Santo Domingo de Silos E 89 C3
Santo Estêvão, *Faro* P 98 B3
Santo Estêvão, *Santarém* P 92 C2
Santo-Pietro-di Tenda F 102 A2
Santo Spirito I 104 B2
Santo Stefano d'Aveto I 80 B3
Santo Stéfano di Camastra I 109 B3
Santo Stefano di Magra I 81 B3
Santo Stéfano Quisquina I 108 B2
Santo Tirso P 87 C2
Santo Tomé E 100 A2
Santok PL 46 C1
Santomera E 101 A4
Santoña E 89 A3
Sant'Oreste I 102 A5
Santotis E 88 A2
Santovenia, *Burgos* E 89 B3
Santovenia, *Zamora* E 88 C1
Santpedor E 91 B4
Santu Lussurgiu I 110 B1
Santutzi E 89 A3
Sanxenxo E 86 B2
Sanza I 104 C1
São Aleixo P 92 C3
São Barnabé P 98 B2
São Bartolomé da Serra P 98 A2
São Bartolomeu de Messines P 98 B2
São Bento P 87 C2
São Brás P 98 B3
São Brás de Alportel P 98 B3
São Braz do Reguedoura P 92 C2
São Cristóvão P 92 C2
São Domingos P 98 B2
São Geraldo P 92 C2
São Jacinto P 92 A2
São João da Madeira P 87 D2
São João da Pesqueira P 87 C3
São João da Ribeira P 92 B2
São João da Serra P 87 D2
São João da Venda P 98 B3
São João dos Caldeireiros P 98 B3
São Julião P 92 B3
São Leonardo P 92 C3
São Luis P 98 B2
São Manços P 92 C3
São Marcos da Ataboeira P 98 B3
Saõ Marcos da Serra P 98 B2
São Marcos de Campo P 92 C3
São Martinho da Cortiça P 92 A2
São Martinho das Amoreiras P 98 B2
São Martinho do Porto P 92 B1
São Matias, *Beja* P 98 A3
São Matias, *Évora* P 92 C2
São Miguel d'Acha P 92 A3
São Miguel de Machede P 92 C3
São Pedro da Torre P 87 C2
São Pedro de Muel P 92 B1
São Pedro de Solis P 98 B3
São Pedro do Sul P 87 D2
São Romão P 92 C2
São Sebastião dos Carros P 98 B3
São Teotónio P 98 B2
São Torcato P 87 C2
Saorge F 80 C1
Sapataria P 92 C1
Sapes GR 116 A7
Sapiãos P 87 C3
Sappada I 72 B2
Sappen N 112 C10
Sapri I 106 A2
Sarajevo BIH 84 C3
Saramon F 77 C3
Sarandë AL 116 C2
Saranovo SRB 85 B5
Saraorci SRB 85 B6
Saray TR 118 A2
Saraycık TR 118 C4
Sarayköy TR 119 E3
Saraylar TR 118 B2
Sarayönü TR 119 D7
Sarbia PL 46 C2
Sarbinowo, *Zachodnio-Pomorskie* PL 45 C6
Sarbinowo, *Zachodnio-Pomorskie* PL 46 A1
Sárbogárd H 74 B3
Sarcelles F 58 A3
Sarche I 71 B5
Sardara I 110 C1
Sardoal P 92 B2
Sardón de Duero E 88 C2
Sare F 76 C1
S'Arenal E 97 B2
Šarengrad HR 75 C4
Sarentino I 71 B6
Sarezzo I 71 C5
Sargans CH 71 A4
Sári H 75 A4
Sari-d'Orcino F 102 A1
Sarıbeyler TR 118 C2
Sarıcakaya TR 118 B5
Sarıgöl TR 119 D3
Sarıkaya TR 16 B7
Sarıköy TR 118 B2
Sarilhos Grandes P 92 C2
Sariñena E 90 B2
Sarıoba TR 118 C7
Sárisáp H 65 C4
Sariyer TR 118 A4
Sarkad H 75 B6
Sárkeresztes H 74 A3
Sárkeresztúr H 74 A3
Särkijärvi FIN 113 E12
Şarkikaraağaç TR 119 D6
Şarköy TR 118 B2
Sarlat-la-Canéda F 77 B4
Sarliac-sur-l'Isle F 67 C5
Sármellék H 74 B2
Särna S 115 F10
Sarnadas P 92 B3
Sarnano I 82 C2
Sarnen CH 70 B3
Sarnesfield GB 29 A5
Sárnico I 71 C4
Sarno I 103 C7
Sarnonico I 71 B6
Sarnow D 45 B5
Sarny UA 11 A9
Särö S 38 B4
Saronno I 70 C4
Sárosd H 74 A3
Šarovce SK 65 B4
Sarpoil F 68 C3
Sarpsborg N 35 C3
Sarracín E 88 B3
Sarral E 91 B4
Sarralbe F 60 A3
Sarrancolin F 77 D3
Sarras F 69 C4
Sarre I 70 C2
Sarre-Union F 60 B3
Sarreaus E 87 B3
Sarrebourg F 60 B3
Sarreguemines F 60 A3
Sárrétudvari H 75 A6
Sarria E 86 B3
Sarrià de Ter E 91 A5
Sarrión E 96 A2
Sarroca de Lleida E 90 B3
Sarroch I 110 C2
Sarron F 76 C2
Särsina I 82 C1
Sarstedt D 51 A5
Sárszentlőrinc H 74 B3
Sárszentmihaly H 74 A3
Sárszentmiklós H 74 B3
Sarteano I 81 D5
Sartène F 102 B1
Sartilly F 57 B4
Sartirana Lomellina I 80 A2
Saruhanlı TR 118 D2
Sárvár H 74 A1
Sarvisvaara S 113 F10
Sarzana I 81 B3
Sarzeau F 66 A2
Sarzedas P 92 B3
Sas van Gent NL 49 B4
Sasalli TR 119 D1
Sasamón E 88 B2
Sásd H 74 B3
Sasino PL 46 A3
Sássari I 110 B1
Sassello I 80 B2
Sassenberg D 50 B4
Sassetta I 81 C4
Sassnitz D 45 A5
Sasso d'Ombrone I 81 D5
Sasso Marconi I 81 B5
Sassocorvaro I 82 C1
Sassoferrato I 82 C1
Sassoleone I 81 B5
Sassuolo I 81 B4
Sástago E 90 B2
Šaštinske Stráže SK 64 B3
Såtåhaugen N 114 E7
Satão P 87 D3
Såtenäs S 35 D4
Säter S 36 B2
Sätila S 40 B2
Satillieu F 69 C4
Satnica Đakovačka HR 74 C3
Sátoraljaújhely H 10 B6
Satow D 44 B3
Sätra-brunn S 36 C3
Satrup D 43 A6
Satteins A 71 A4
Satu Mare RO 11 C7
Saturnia I 102 A4
Saucats F 76 B2
Saucelle E 87 C4
Sauda N 33 C3
Saudasjøen N 33 C3
Sauðárkrókur IS 111 B6
Sauerlach D 62 C2
Saugues F 78 B2
Sauherad N 33 C6
Saujon F 66 C4
Sauland N 33 C5
Saulces Monclin F 59 A5
Saulgau D 61 B5
Saulgrub D 62 C2
Saulieu F 69 A4
Saulnot F 60 C2
Sault F 79 B4
Sault-Brénaz F 69 C5
Sault-de-Navailles F 76 C2
Saulx F 60 C2
Saulxures-sur-Moselotte F 60 C2
Saulzais-le-Potier F 68 B2
Saumos F 76 B1
Saumur F 67 A4
Saunavaara FIN 113 E16
Saundersfoot GB 28 B3
Saurat F 77 D4
Saurbær, *Borgarfjarðarsýsla* IS 111 C4
Saurbær, *Dalasýsla* IS 111 B4
Saurbær, *Eyjafjarðarsýsla* IS 111 B7
Sáuris I 72 B2
Sausset-les-Pins F 79 C4
Sauteyrargues F 78 C2
Sauvagnat F 68 C2
Sauve F 78 C2
Sauveterre-de-Béarn F 76 C2
Sauveterre-de-Guyenne F 76 B2
Sauviat-sur-Vige F 67 C6
Sauxillanges F 68 C3
Sauzé-Vaussais F 67 B5
Sauzet, *Drôme* F 78 B3
Sauzet, *Lot* F 77 B4
Sauzon F 66 A1
Sava I 104 C3
Savarsin RO 11 C7
Savaştepe TR 118 C2
Savci SLO 73 B6
Säve S 38 B4
Savelletri I 104 C3
Savelli I 107 B3
Savenay F 66 A3
Saverdun F 77 C4
Saverne F 60 B3
Savières F 59 B4
Savigliano I 80 B1
Savignac-les-Eglises F 67 C5
Savignano Irpino I 103 B8
Savignano sul Rubicone I 82 B1
Savigny-sur-Braye F 58 C1
Saviñán E 89 C5
Savines-le-lac F 79 B5
Savino Selo SRB 75 C4
Savio I 82 B1
Sävja S 36 C4
Šavnik CG 85 D4
Savognin CH 71 B4
Savona I 80 B2
Savonlinna FIN 3 F28
Savournon F 79 B4
Sävsjö S 40 B4
Savsjön S 36 C1
Sävsjöström S 40 B5
Savudrija HR 72 C3
Savukoski FIN 113 E17
Sawbridgeworth GB 31 C4
Sawtry GB 30 B3
Sax E 101 A5
Saxdalen S 36 B1
Saxilby GB 27 B5
Saxmundham GB 30 B5
Saxnäs S 115 C12
Saxthorpe GB 30 B5
Sayalonga E 100 C1
Sayatón E 95 B4
Sayda D 52 C3
Säytsjärvi FIN 113 C16
Šazava, *Jihomoravský* CZ 64 A1
Sázava, *Středočeský* CZ 63 A5
Scaër F 56 B2
Scafa I 103 A7
Scalasaig GB 24 B1
Scalby GB 27 A5
Scalea I 106 B2
Scaletta Zanclea I 109 A4
Scalloway GB 22 A7
Scamblesby GB 27 B5
Scandale I 107 B3
Scandiano I 81 B4
Scandicci I 81 C5
Scandolara Ravara I 81 A4
Scanno I 103 B6
Scansano I 81 D5
Scanzano Jónico I 104 C2
Scarborough GB 27 A5
Scardovari I 82 B1
Scardoy GB 22 D4
Scarinish GB 24 B1
Scarperia I 81 C5
Scarriff IRL 20 B3
Scey-sur-Saône et St. Albin F 60 C1
Sch-en-feld D 62 A3
Schachendorf A 73 A6
Schaffhausen CH 61 C4
Schafstädt D 52 B1
Schafstedt D 43 A6
Schäftlarn D 62 C2
Schagen NL 42 C1
Schalkau D 51 C7
Schangnau CH 70 B2
Schapbach D 61 B4
Scharbeutz D 44 A2
Schärding A 63 B4
Scharnitz A 71 A6
Scharrel D 43 B4
Schattendorf A 64 C2
Scheemda NL 42 B3
Scheessel D 43 B6
Schéggia I 82 C1
Scheibbs A 63 B6
Scheibenberg D 52 C2
Scheidegg D 61 C5
Scheifling A 73 A4
Scheinfeld D 61 A6
Schelklingen D 61 B5
Schenefeld, *Schleswig-Holstein* D 43 A6
Schenefeld, *Schleswig-Holstein* D 44 B1
Schenkengsfeld D 51 C5
Scherfede D 51 B5
Schermbeck D 50 B2
Scherpenzeel NL 49 A6
Schesslitz D 52 D1
Scheveningen NL 49 A5
Schiedam NL 49 B5
Schieder-Schwalenberg D 51 B5
Schierling D 62 B3
Schiers CH 71 B4
Schildau D 52 B2
Schillingen D 60 A2
Schillingsfürst D 61 A6
Schilpário I 71 B5
Schiltach D 61 B4
Schiltigheim F 60 B3
Schio I 71 C6
Schirmeck F 60 B3
Schirnding D 52 C2
Schkeuditz D 52 B2
Schkölen D 52 B1

Schlabendorf D 53 B3
Schladen D 51 A6
Schladming A 72 A3
Schlangen D 51 B4
Schleiden D 50 C2
Schleiz D 52 C1
Schleswig D 43 A6
Schleusingen D 51 C6
Schlieben D 52 B3
Schliengen D 60 C3
Schliersee D 62 C2
Schlitz D 51 C5
Schloss Neuhans D 51 B4
Schlossvippach D 52 B1
Schlotheim D 51 B6
Schluchsee D 61 C4
Schlüchtern D 51 C5
Schmallenberg D 50 B4
Schmelz D 60 A2
Schmidmühlen D 62 A2
Schmiedeberg D 53 C3
Schmiedefeld D 51 C6
Schmirn A 72 A1
Schmölln, *Brandenburg* D 45 B6
Schmölln, *Sachsen* D 52 C2
Schnaittach D 62 A2
Schneeberg D 52 C2
Schneizlreuth D 62 C3
Schneverdingen D 44 B1
Schöder A 73 A4
Schoenburg B 50 C2
Schollene D 44 C4
Schöllkrippen D 51 C5
Schomberg D 61 B4
Schönach D 62 B3
Schönau, *Baden-Württemberg* D 60 C3
Schönau, *Bayern* D 62 B3
Schönbeck D 45 B5
Schönberg, *Bayern* D 63 B4
Schönberg, *Mecklenburg-Vorpommern* D 44 B2
Schönberg, *Schleswig-Holstein* D 44 A2
Schönebeck D 52 A1
Schöneck D 52 C2
Schönecken- D 50 C2
Schönermark D 45 B5
Schönewalde D 52 B3
Schongau D 62 C1
Schöngrabern A 64 B2
Schönhagen D 51 B5
Schönhausen D 44 C4
Schöningen D 51 A6
Schönkirchen D 44 A2
Schönsee D 62 A3
Schöntal D 61 A5
Schönthal D 62 A3
Schonungen D 51 C6
Schönwalde D 44 A2
Schoondijke NL 49 B4
Schoonebeek NL 42 C3
Schoonhoven NL 49 B5
Schopfheim D 60 C3
Schöppenstedt D 51 A6
Schörfling A 63 C4
Schorndorf D 61 B5
Schortens D 43 B4
Schotten D 51 C5
Schramberg D 61 B4
Schraplau D 52 B1
Schrattenberg A 64 B2
Schrecksbach D 51 C5
Schrems A 63 B6
Schrobenhausen D 62 B2
Schröcken A 71 A5
Schrozberg D 61 A5
Schruns A 71 A4
Schüpfheim CH 70 B3
Schüttorf D 50 A3
Schwaan D 44 B4
Schwabach D 62 A2
Schwäbisch Gmünd D 61 B5
Schwäbisch Hall D 61 A5
Schwabmünchen D 62 B1
Schwadorf A 64 B2
Schwagstorf D 43 C4
Schwaigern D 61 A5
Schwalmstadt D 51 C5
Schwanberg A 73 B5
Schwanden CH 70 B4
Schwandorf D 62 A3
Schwanebeck D 52 B1
Schwanenstadt A 63 B4
Schwanewede D 43 B5
Schwanfeld D 61 A6
Schwangau D 62 C1
Schwarmstedt D 43 C6
Schwarz-heide D 53 B3
Schwarza D 51 C6
Schwarzach im Pongau A 72 A3
Schwarzau im Gebirge A 63 C6
Schwarzenau A 63 B6
Schwarzenbach D 52 C1
Schwarzenbach am Wald D 52 C1
Schwarzenbek D 44 B2
Schwarzenberg D 52 C2
Schwarzenburg CH 70 B2
Schwaz A 72 A1
Schwechat A 64 B2
Schwedt D 45 B6
Schwei D 43 B5
Schweich D 60 A2
Schweighausen D 60 B3
Schweinfurt D 51 C6
Schweinitz D 52 B3
Schweinrich D 45 B4
Schwelm D 50 B3
Schwemsal D 52 B2
Schwendt A 62 C3
Schwenningen D 61 B4
Schwepnitz D 53 B3
Schwerin D 44 B3
Schwerte D 50 B3
Schweskau D 44 C3
Schwetzingen D 61 A4
Schwyz CH 70 A3
Sciacca I 108 B2
Scicli I 109 C3
Ściechów PL 45 C6
Scigliano I 106 B3
Scilla I 109 A4
Ścinawa PL 54 B1
Scionzier F 69 B6
Scoglitti I 109 C3
Scole GB 30 B5
Sconser GB 22 D2
Scopello, *Piemonte* I 70 C3
Scopello, *Sicilia* I 108 A1
Scordia I 109 B3
Scorzè I 72 C2
Scotch Corner GB 27 A4
Scotter GB 27 B5
Scourie GB 22 C3
Scousburgh GB 22 B7
Scrabster GB 23 C5
Screeb IRL 20 A2
Scremerston GB 25 C6
Scritto I 82 C1
Scunthorpe GB 27 B5
Scuol CH 71 B5
Scúrcola Marsicana I 103 A6
Seaford GB 31 D4
Seaham GB 25 D6
Seahouses GB 25 C6
Seascale GB 26 A2
Seaton GB 29 C4
Sebazac-Concourès F 77 B5
Sebečevo SRB 85 C5
Seben TR 118 B6
Sebersdorf A 73 A5
Sebezh RUS 7 C10
Sebnitz D 53 C4
Seborga I 80 C1
Seby S 41 C6
Seč, *Vychodočeský* CZ 63 A6
Seč, *Západočeský* CZ 63 A4
Sečanj SRB 75 C5
Secemin PL 55 C4
Séchault F 59 A5
Seckau A 73 A4
Seclin F 49 C4
Secondigny F 67 B4
Seda P 92 B3
Sedan F 59 A5
Sedano E 88 B3
Sedbergh GB 26 A3
Sedella E 100 C1
Séderon F 79 B4
Sedgefield GB 27 A4
Sedico I 72 B2
Sédilo I 110 B1
Sédini I 110 B1
Sedlarica HR 74 C2
Sedlčany CZ 63 A5
Sedlec-Prčice CZ 63 A5
Sedlice CZ 63 A4
Sędziejowice PL 55 B4
Sędziszów PL 55 C5
Sędziszów Małapolski PL 55 C6
Seebach F 60 B3
Seeboden A 72 B3
Seefeld, *Brandenburg* D 45 C5
Seefeld, *Niedersachsen* D 43 B5
Seefeld in Tirol A 71 A6
Seeg D 62 C1
Seehausen, *Sachsen-Anhalt* D 44 C3
Seehausen, *Sachsen-Anhalt* D 52 A1
Seeheim-Jugenheim D 61 A4
Seelbach D 60 B3
Seelow D 45 C6
Seelze D 43 C6
Seerhausen D 52 B3
Sées F 57 B6
Seesen D 51 B6
Seeshaupt D 62 C2
Seewalchen A 63 C4
Seferihisar TR 119 D1
Sefkerin SRB 85 A5
Segård N 34 B2
Segerstad S 35 C5
Segesd H 74 B2
Seglinge FIN 36 B7
Segmon S 35 C5
Segonzac F 67 C4
Segorbe E 96 B2
Segovia E 94 B2
Segré F 57 C5
Ségur-les-Villas F 68 C2
Segura E 89 B4
Segura P 93 B3
Segura de León E 99 A4
Segura de los Baños E 90 C2
Segurrilla E 94 B2
Sehnde D 51 A5
Seia P 92 A3
Seiches-sur-le-Loir F 67 A4
Seifhennersdorf D 53 C4
Seignelay F 59 C4
Seijo E 87 C2
Seilhac F 68 C1
Seilles B 49 C6
Seim N 32 B2
Seinäjoki FIN 3 E25
Seissan F 77 C3
Seitenstetten Markt A 63 B5
Seixal P 92 C1
Seiz A 73 A4
Seizthal A 73 A4
Sejerslev DK 38 C1
Seksna RUS 7 B15
Selárdalur IS 111 B1
Selárgius I 110 C2
Selb D 52 C2
Selby GB 27 B4
Selca HR 84 C1
Selcë AL 105 A5
Selce HR 73 C4
Selçuk TR 119 E2
Selde DK 38 C2
Selenča SRB 75 C4
Selendi, *Manisa* TR 118 D2
Selendi, *Manisa* TR 118 D3
Selenicë AL 105 C5
Sélestat F 60 B3
Seleuš SRB 75 C5
Selevac SRB 85 B5
Selfoss IS 111 D5
Selgua E 90 B3
Selice SK 64 B3
Seligenstadt D 51 C4
Seligenthal D 51 C6
Selimiye TR 119 E2
Selizharovo RUS 7 C12
Selja S 36 A1
Selje N 114 E2
Seljelvnes N 112 C8
Seljord N 33 C5
Selkirk GB 25 C5
Sellano I 82 D1
Selles-St. Denis F 68 A1
Selles-sur-Cher F 67 A6
Sellières F 69 B5
Sellin D 45 A5
Sellye H 74 C2
Selm D 50 B3
Selnica ob Dravi SLO 73 B5
Selongey F 59 C6
Selonnet F 79 B5
Selow D 44 B3
Selsey GB 31 D3
Selsingen D 43 B6
Selters D 50 C3
Seltso RUS 7 E13
Seltz F 61 B4
Selva E 97 B2
Selva di Cadore I 72 B2
Selva di Val Gardena I 72 B1
Selvik, *Sogn og Fjordane* N 32 A2
Selvik, *Vestfold* N 35 C2
Selvino I 71 C4
Selyatyn UA 11 C8
Sem N 35 C2
Semeljci HR 74 C3
Semenovka, *Chernihiv* UA 7 E12
Semenovka, *Kremenchuk* UA 11 B12
Semič SLO 73 C5
Semide F 59 A5
Semide P 92 A2
Semily CZ 53 C5
Seminara I 106 C2
Semlac RO 75 B5
Semmen-stedt D 51 A6
Šempeter SLO 73 B5
Semriach A 73 A5
Semur-en-Auxois F 69 A4
Sena E 90 B2
Sena de Luna E 88 B1
Senarpont F 58 A2
Sénas F 79 C4
Senćanski Trešnjevac SRB 75 C4
Sencelles E 97 B2
Senčur SLO 73 B4
Senden, *Bayern* D 61 B6
Senden, *Nordrhein-Westfalen* D 50 B3
Sendenhorst D 50 B3
Sendim P 87 C4
Senec SK 64 B3
Seneffe B 49 C5
Séneghe I 110 B1
Senés E 101 B3
Senez F 79 C5
Senftenberg D 53 B3
Sengouagnet F 77 D3
Sengwarden D 43 B5
Senica SK 64 B3
Senice na Hané CZ 64 A3
Senigállia I 82 C2
Senirkent TR 119 D5
Sénis I 110 C1
Senise I 106 A3
Senj HR 83 B3
Senje SRB 85 C6
Senjehopen N 112 C6
Senjski Rudnik SRB 85 C6
Senlis F 58 A3
Sennan S 40 C2
Sennecey-le-Grand F 69 B4
Sennen GB 28 C2
Senno BY 7 D10
Sénnori I 110 B1
Sennwald CH 71 A4
Sennybridge GB 29 B4
Senohrad SK 65 B5
Senonches F 58 B2
Senones F 60 B2
Senorbì I 110 C2
Senovo SLO 73 B5
Senožeče SLO 73 C4
Senožeti SLO 73 B4
Sens F 59 B4
Sens-de-Bretagne F 57 B4
Senta SRB 75 C5
Senterada E 90 A3
Sentilj SLO 73 B5
Šentjernej SLO 73 C5
Šentjur SLO 73 B5
Senumstad N 33 D5
Seoane E 86 B3
Seon CH 70 A3
Sépeaux F 59 C4
Sépey CH 70 B2
Sepino I 103 B7
Sępólno Krajeńskie PL 46 B3
Seppenrade D 50 B3
Seppois F 70 A2
Septeuil F 58 B2
Sepúlveda E 88 C3
Sequals I 72 B2
Sequeros E 93 A4
Seraincourt F 59 A5
Seraing B 49 C6
Seravezza I 81 C4
Sered' SK 64 B3
Seredka RUS 7 B10
Şereflikoçhisar TR 16 B6
Seregélyes H 74 A3
Seregno I 71 C4
Sérent F 56 C3
Serfaus A 71 A5
Sergiyev Posad RUS 7 C15
Seriate I 71 C4
Sérifontaine F 58 A2
Serifos GR 117 E6
Sérignan F 78 C2
Serik TR 119 F6
Serina I 71 C4
Serinhisar TR 119 E4
Sermaises F 58 B3
Sermaize-les-Bains F 59 B5
Sérmide I 81 B5
Sermoneta I 102 B5
Sernache de Bonjardim P 92 B2
Sernancelhe P 87 D3
Serón E 101 B3
Serón de Najima E 89 C4
Serooskerke NL 49 B4
Seròs E 90 B3
Serpa P 98 B3
Serpukhov RUS 7 D14
Serra de Outes E 86 B2
Serra San Bruno I 106 C3
Serra San Quirico I 82 C2
Serracapriola I 103 B8
Serrada E 88 C2
Serradifalco I 108 B2
Serradilla E 93 B4
Serradilla del Arroyo E 93 A4
Serradilla del Llano E 93 A4
Serramanna I 110 C1
Serramazzoni I 81 B4
Serranillos E 94 B2
Serrapetrona I 82 C2
Serrastretta I 106 B3
Serravalle, *Piemonte* I 70 C3
Serravalle, *Umbria* I 82 D2
Serravalle di Chienti I 82 C1
Serravalle Scrívia I 80 B2
Serre I 103 C8
Serrejón E 93 B5
Serres F 79 B4
Serres GR 116 A5
Serrières F 69 C4
Serrières-de-Briord F 69 C5
Sersale I 106 B3
Sertã P 92 B2
Sertig Dörfli CH 71 B4
Servance F 60 C2
Serverette F 78 B2
Servia GR 116 B4
Servian F 78 C2
Serviers F 78 B3
Servigliano I 82 C2
Serzedelo P 87 C2
Ses Salines E 97 B3
Seseña Nuevo E 95 B3
Sesimbra P 92 C1
Seskinore GB 19 B4
Sesma E 89 B4
Sessa Aurunca I 103 B6
Sesta Godano I 80 B3
Šestanovac HR 84 C1
Sestao E 89 A4
Sestino I 82 C1
Sesto I 72 B2
Sesto Calende I 70 C3
Sesto Fiorentino I 81 C5
Sesto San Giovanni I 71 C4
Séstola I 81 B4
Sestri Levante I 80 B3
Sestriere I 79 B5
Sestroretsk RUS 7 A11
Sestu I 110 C2
Sesvete HR 73 C6
Setcases E 91 A5
Sète F 78 C2
Setenil E 99 C5
Setermoen N 112 D7
Šetonje SRB 85 B6
Setskog N 34 C3
Settalsjølia N 114 E7
Séttimo Torinese I 70 C2
Settimo Vittone I 70 C2
Settle GB 26 A3
Setúbal P 92 C2
Seubersdort D 62 A2
Seùi I 110 C2
Seùlo I 110 C2
Seurre F 69 B5
Sevaster AL 105 C5
Sevel DK 38 C1
Sevenoaks GB 31 C4
Sever do Vouga P 87 D2
Sévérac-le-Château F 78 B2
Severin HR 73 C5
Severomorsk RUS 3 B30
Séveso I 71 C4
Ševětin CZ 63 A5
Sevettijärvi FIN 113 C17
Sévigny F 59 A5
Sevilla = Seville E 99 B5
Sevilla la Nueva E 94 B2
Seville = Sevilla E 99 B5
Sevilleja de la Jara E 94 C2
Sevlievo BG 11 E8
Sevnica SLO 73 B5
Sevojno SRB 85 C4
Sevrier F 69 C6
Sevsk RUS 7 E13
Sexdrega S 40 B3
Seyches F 76 B3
Seyda D 52 B2
Seyðisfjörður IS 111 B12
Seydişehir TR 119 E6
Seyitgazi TR 118 C5
Seyitömer TR 118 C4
Seymen TR 118 A2
Seyne F 79 B5
Seynes F 78 B3
Seyssel F 69 C5
Sežana SLO 72 C3
Sézanne F 59 B4
Sezulfe P 87 C3
Sezze I 102 B6
Sfântu Gheorghe RO 11 D8
Sforzacosta I 82 C2
Sgarasta Mhor GB 22 D1
Shaftesbury GB 29 B5
Shaldon GB 29 C4
Shanagolden IRL 20 B2
Shanklin GB 31 D2
Shap GB 26 A3
Sharpness GB 29 B5
Shawbury GB 26 C3
Shchekino RUS 7 D14
Shchigry RUS 7 F14
Shchors UA 7 F11
Sheerness GB 31 C4
Sheffield GB 27 B4
Shefford GB 31 B3
Shenfield GB 31 C4
Shëngjergj AL 116 A2
Shëngjin AL 105 B5
Shepetivka UA 11 A9
Shepshed GB 27 C4
Shepton Mallet GB 29 B5
Sherborne GB 29 C5
Shercock IRL 19 C5
Sheringham GB 30 B5
Shiel Bridge GB 22 D3
Shieldaig GB 22 D3
Shijak AL 105 B5
Shillelagh IRL 21 B5
Shimsk RUS 7 B11
Shipston-on-Stour GB 29 A6
Shirgjan AL 105 B6
Shklow BY 7 D11
Shkodër AL 105 A5
Shoeburyness GB 31 C4
Shoreham-by-Sea GB 31 D3
Shostka UA 7 F12
Shotley Gate GB 31 C5
Shpola UA 11 B11
Shrewsbury GB 26 C3
Shugozero RUS 7 B13
Shumen BG 11 E9
Siabost GB 22 C2
Siamanna I 110 C1
Sianów PL 46 A2
Siatista GR 116 B3
Siauges-St. Romain F 78 A2
Šiauliai LT 6 D7
Sibari I 106 B3
Sibbhult S 41 C4
Šibenik HR 83 C4
Sibinj HR 74 C2
Sibiu RO 11 D8
Sibnica SRB 85 B5
Sibsey GB 27 B6
Siculiana I 108 B2
Šid SRB 85 A4
Sidari GR 116 C1
Siddeburen NL 42 B3
Sidensjö S 115 D15
Siderno I 106 C3
Sidirokastro GR 116 A5
Sidmouth GB 29 C4
Sidzina PL 65 A5
Siebe N 113 D12
Siebenlehn D 52 B3
Siedlce PL 6 E7
Siedlice PL 46 B1
Siedlinghausen D 51 B4
Siedlisko PL 46 C2
Siegburg D 50 C3
Siegen D 50 C4
Siegenburg D 62 B2
Sieghartskirchen A 64 B2
Siegsdorf D 62 C3
Siekierki PL 45 C6
Sielpia PL 55 B5
Siemiany PL 47 B5
Siena I 81 C5
Sieniawka PL 53 C4
Siennica PL 55 A6
Sienno PL 55 B6
Sieppijärvi FIN 113 E13
Sieradz PL 54 B3
Sieraków, *Śląskie* PL 54 C3
Sieraków, *Wielkopolskie* PL 46 C2
Sierakowice PL 46 A3
Sierck-les-Bains F 60 A2
Sierentz F 60 C3
Sierning A 63 B5
Sierpc PL 47 C5
Sierra de Fuentes E 93 B4
Sierra de Luna E 90 A2
Sierra de Yeguas E 100 B1
Sierre CH 70 B2
Siestrzeń PL 55 A5
Sietamo E 90 A2
Siewierz PL 55 C4
Sigdal N 34 B1
Sigean F 78 C1
Sigerfjord N 112 D4
Sighetu-Marmatiei RO 11 C7
Sighişoara RO 11 C8
Sigillo I 82 C1
Siglufjörður IS 111 A7
Sigmaringen D 61 B5
Signa I 81 C5
Signes F 79 C4
Signy-l'Abbaye F 59 A5
Signy-le-Petit F 59 A5
Sigogne F 67 C4
Sigri GR 116 C7
Sigtuna S 37 C4
Sigueiro E 86 B2
Sigüenza E 95 A4
Sigües E 90 A1
Sigulda LV 6 C8
Siilinjärvi FIN 3 E27
Sikenica SK 65 B4
Sikia GR 116 B5
Sikinos GR 117 F7
Sikkilsdalseter N 32 A6
Siklós H 74 C3
Sikórz PL 47 C5
Sikselet S 115 A14
Silandro I 71 B5
Silánus I 110 B1
Silbaš SRB 75 C4
Silbersted D 43 A6
Şile TR 118 A4
Siles E 101 A3
Silgueiros P 92 A3
Silifke TR 16 C6
Siliqua I 110 C1
Silistra BG 11 D9
Silivri TR 118 A3
Siljan N 35 C1
Siljansnäs S 36 B1
Silkeborg DK 39 C2
Silla E 96 B2
Sillamäe EST 7 B9
Sillé-le-Guillaume F 57 B5
Silleda E 86 B2
Sillenstede D 43 B4
Sillerud S 35 C4
Sillian A 72 B2
Silloth GB 25 D4
Silno PL 46 B3
Silnowo PL 46 B2
Silo HR 73 C4
Sils E 91 B5
Silsand N 112 C6
Silte S 37 E5
Šilute LT 6 D6
Silvalen N 114 B9
Silvaplana CH 71 B4
Silvares P 92 A3
Silvberg S 36 B2
Silverdalen S 40 B5
Silvermines IRL 20 B3
Silverstone GB 30 B2
Silverton GB 29 C4
Silves P 98 B2
Silvi Marina I 103 A7
Simandre F 69 B4
Šimanovci SRB 85 B5
Simard F 69 B5
Simat de Valldigna E 96 B2
Simav TR 118 C3
Simbach, *Bayern* D 62 B3
Simbach, *Bayern* D 62 B4
Simbário I 106 C3
Simeria RO 11 D7
Simi GR 119 F2
Simićevo SRB 85 B6
Simlångsdalen S 40 C3
Simmerath D 50 C2
Simmerberg D 61 C5
Simmern D 50 D3
Simo FIN 3 D26
Šimonovce SK 65 B6
Simonsbath GB 28 B4
Simonstorp S 37 D3
Simontornya H 74 B3
Simplon CH 70 B3
Simrishamn S 41 D4
Sinaia RO 11 D8
Sinalunga I 81 C5
Sinanaj AL 105 C5
Sinarcas E 96 B1
Sincan TR 118 C7
Sincanlı TR 118 D5
Sindal DK 38 B3
Sindelfingen D 61 B5
Sindia I 110 B1
Sındırgı TR 118 C3
Sinekli TR 118 A3
Sines P 98 B2
Sinetta FIN 113 F14
Sineu E 97 B3
Singen D 61 C4
Singleton GB 31 D3
Singsås N 114 E7
Siniscóla I 110 B2
Sinj HR 83 C5
Sinlabajos E 94 A2
Sinn D 50 C4
Sinnai I 110 C2
Sinnes N 33 D3
Sinop TR 16 A7
Sins CH 70 A3
Sinsheim D 61 A4
Sint Annaland NL 49 B5
Sint Annaparochie NL 42 B2
Sint Athonis NL 50 B1
Sint Nicolaasga NL 42 C2
Sint Oedenrode NL 49 B6
Sintra P 92 C1
Sinzheim D 61 B4
Sinzig D 50 C3
Siófok H 74 B3
Sion CH 70 B2
Sion Mills GB 19 B4
Siorac-en-Périgord F 77 B3
Šipanska Luka HR 84 D2
Šipovo BIH 84 B2
Sira N 33 D3
Siracusa I 109 B4
Siret RO 11 C9
Sirevåg N 33 D2
Sirig SRB 75 C4
Sirkka FIN 113 E13
Sirmione I 71 C5
Sirok H 65 C6
Široké SK 65 B6
Široki Brijeg BIH 84 C2
Sirolo I 82 C2
Siruela E 94 D1
Sisak HR 73 C6
Sisante E 95 C4
Šišljavić HR 73 C5
Sissach CH 70 A2
Sissonne F 59 A4
Sistelo P 87 C2
Sisteron F 79 B4
Sistiana I 72 C3
Sistranda N 114 D5
Sitasjaurestugorna S 112 E6
Sitges E 91 B4
Sitia GR 117 G8
Sittard NL 50 B1
Sittensen D 43 B6
Sittingbourne GB 31 C4
Sitzenroda D 52 B2
Sivac SRB 75 C4
Sivaslı TR 119 D4
Siverić HR 83 C5
Sivrihisar TR 118 C6
Sixt-Fer-á-Cheval F 70 B1
Siziano I 71 C4
Sizun F 56 B1
Sjenica SRB 85 C5
Sjoa N 114 F6
Sjøåsen N 114 C8
Sjöbo S 41 D3
Sjøenden, *Hedmark* N 34 A3
Sjøenden, *Hedmark* N 34 B3
Sjøholt N 114 E3
Sjøli N 34 A3
Sjølstad N 114 C9
Sjölunda S 37 C2
Sjømarken S 40 B2
Sjørring DK 38 C1
Sjötofta S 40 B3
Sjötorp S 35 D5
Sjoutnäset S 115 C11
Sjøvegan N 112 D6
Sjuntorp S 35 D4
Skåbu N 32 A6
Skadovsk UA 11 C12
Skælskør DK 39 D4
Skærbæk DK 39 D1
Skafså N 33 C5
Skaftafell IS 111 D9
Skagaströnd IS 111 B5
Skagen DK 38 B3
Skagersvik S 35 D6
Skaiå N 33 D4
Skaidi N 113 B13
Skala GR 117 D2
Skała PL 55 C4
Skala Oropou GR 117 D5
Skala-Podilska UA 11 B9
Skaland N 112 C6
Skalat UA 11 B8
Skalbmierz PL 55 C5
Skålevik N 33 D5
Skalica SK 64 B3
Skalité SK 65 A4
Skällinge S 40 B2
Skalná CZ 52 C2
Skals DK 38 C2
Skalstugan S 114 D9
Skanderborg DK 39 C2
Skåne-Tranås S 41 D3
Skånes-Fagerhult S 41 C3
Skånevik N 33 C2
Skänninge S 37 D2
Skanör med Falsterbo S 41 D2
Skåpafors S 35 C4
Skąpe PL 53 A5
Skara S 35 D5
Skarberget N 112 D5
Skärblacka S 37 D2
Skarda S 115 C15
Skarð IS 111 B3
Skare N 32 C3
Skåre S 35 C5
Skärhamn S 38 B4
Skarnes N 34 B3
Skarp Salling DK 38 C2
Skärplinge S 36 B4
Skarpnatö FIN 36 B6
Skarrild DK 39 D1
Skarstad N 112 D5
Skärstad S 40 B4
Skarsvåg N 113 A14
Skarszewy PL 47 A4
Skårup DK 39 D3
Skärvången S 115 D11
Skarvsjöby S 115 C14
Skaryszew PL 55 B6
Skarżysko-Kamienna PL 55 B5
Skarzysko Ksiazece PL 55 B5
Skatøy N 33 D6
Skattkärr S 35 C5
Skattungbyn S 36 A1
Skatval N 114 D7
Skaulo S 112 E10
Skave DK 39 C1
Skawina PL 55 D4
Skebobruk S 36 C5
Skebokvarn S 37 C3
Skedala S 40 C2
Skedevi S 37 D2
Skedsmokorset N 34 B3
Skee S 35 D3
Skegness GB 27 B6
Skela SRB 85 B5
Skelani BIH 85 C4
Skellefteå S 3 D24
Skelleftehamn S 3 D24
Skelmersdale GB 26 B3
Skelmorlie GB 24 C3
Skelund DK 38 C3
Skender Vakuf BIH 84 B2
Skene S 40 B2
Skępe PL 47 C5
Skepplanda S 40 B2
Skeppshult S 40 B3
Skerries IRL 19 C5
Ski N 35 C2
Skiathos GR 116 C5
Skibbereen IRL 20 C2
Skibotn N 112 C9
Skidra GR 116 B4
Skien N 35 C1
Skierniewice PL 55 B5
Skillingaryd S 40 B4
Skillinge S 41 D4
Skillingmark S 34 C4
Skilloura CY 120 A2
Skinnardai S 37 C5
Skinnskatteberg S 36 C2
Skipmannvik N 112 E4
Skipness GB 24 C2
Skipsea GB 27 B5
Skipton GB 26 B3
Skiptvet N 35 C3
Skiros GR 116 D6
Skivarp S 41 D3
Skive DK 38 C2
Skjærhalden N 35 C3
Skjånes N 113 B17
Skjeberg N 35 C3
Skjeggedal N 32 B3
Skjeljanger N 32 B1
Skjeljavik N 32 C2
Skjern DK 39 D1
Skjervøy N 112 B9
Skjold, *Rogaland* N 33 C2
Skjold, *Troms* N 112 C8
Skjoldastraumen N 33 C2
Skjolden N 32 A4
Skjønhaug N 35 C3
Skjøtningsberg N 113 A16
Škocjan SLO 73 C5
Skoczów PL 65 A4
Skodborg DK 39 D2
Škofja Loka SLO 73 B4
Škofljica SLO 73 C4
Skog S 36 A3
Skoganvarre N 113 C14
Skogen S 35 C4
Skogfoss N 113 C18
Skoghall S 35 C5
Skogly N 113 C18
Skogn N 114 D8

Skognes N 112 C8
Skogstorp, *Halland* S 40 C2
Skogstorp, *Södermanland* S 37 C3
Skoki PL 46 C3
Skokloster S 37 C4
Sköldinge S 37 C3
Skole UA 11 B7
Skollenborg N 35 C1
Sköllersta S 37 C2
Skomlin PL 54 B3
Skonseng N 115 A11
Skopelos GR 116 C5
Skopje MK 10 E6
Skoppum N 35 C2
Skórcz PL 47 B4
Skorogoszcz PL 54 C2
Skoroszów PL 54 B2
Skorovatn N 115 C10
Skorped S 115 D14
Skørping DK 38 C2
Skotfoss N 33 C6
Skotniki PL 55 B4
Skotselv N 34 C1
Skotterud N 34 C4
Skottorp S 40 C2
Skovby DK 39 E2
Skövde S 35 D5
Skovsgård DK 38 B2
Skrad HR 73 C4
Skradin HR 83 C4
Skradnik HR 73 C5
Skråmestø N 32 B1
Škrdlovice CZ 64 A1
Skrea S 40 C2
Skreia N 34 B2
Skrolsvik N 112 C5
Skruv S 40 C5
Skrwilno PL 47 B5
Skrydstrup DK 39 D2
Skucani BIH 84 C1
Skudeneshavn N 33 C2
Skui N 34 C2
Skulsk PL 47 C4
Skultorp S 35 D5
Skultuna S 37 C3
Skuodas LT 6 C6
Skurup S 41 D3
Skute N 34 B2
Skuteč CZ 64 A1
Skutskär S 36 B4
Skutvik N 112 D4
Skvyra UA 11 B10
Skwierzyna PL 46 C1
Skýcov SK 65 B4
Skyllberg S 37 D1
Skyttmon S 115 D12
Skyttorp S 36 B4
Sládkovičovo SK 64 B3
Slagelse DK 39 D4
Slagharen NL 42 C3
Slagnäs S 115 B15
Slaidburn GB 26 B3
Slane IRL 19 C5
Slangerup DK 41 D2
Slano HR 84 D2
Slantsy RUS 7 B10
Slaný CZ 53 C4
Slap SLO 72 B3
Šlapanice CZ 64 A2
Slåstad N 34 B3
Slatina BIH 84 C2
Slatina HR 74 C2
Slatina RO 11 D8
Slatina SRB 85 C5
Slatiňany CZ 64 A1
Slatinice CZ 64 A3
Slättberg S 36 A1
Slattum N 34 C2
Slavičin CZ 64 A3
Slavkov CZ 64 B3
Slavkov u Brna CZ 64 A2
Slavkovica SRB 85 B5
Slavonice CZ 63 B6
Slavonski Brod HR 74 C3
Slavonski Kobas HR 84 A2
Slavŏsovce SK 65 B6
Slavskoye RUS 47 A6
Slavuta UA 11 A9
Sława, *Lubuskie* PL 53 B6
Sława, *Zachodnio-Pomorskie* PL 46 B1
Slawharad BY 7 E11
Sławków PL 55 C4
Sławno, *Wielkopolskie* PL 46 C3
Sławno, *Zachodnio-Pomorskie* PL 46 A2
Sławoborze PL 46 B1
Sl'ažany SK 64 B4
Sleaford GB 27 C5
Sleðbrjótur IS 111 B11
Sledmere GB 27 A5
Sleights GB 27 A5
Slemmestad N 34 C2
Ślesin PL 47 C4
Sliač SK 65 B5
Sliema M 107 C5
Sligo IRL 18 B3
Slite S 37 E5
Slitu N 35 C3
Sliven BG 11 E9
Śliwice PL 47 B4
Slobozia RO 11 D9
Slochteren NL 42 B3
Slöinge S 40 C2
Słomniki PL 55 C5
Slonim BY 7 E8
Słońsk PL 45 C6
Slootdorp NL 42 C1
Slottsbron S 35 C5
Slough GB 31 C3
Slövag N 32 B2
Slovenj Gradec SLO 73 B5
Slovenska Bistrica SLO 73 B5
Slovenská L'upča SK 65 B5
Slovenská-Ves SK 65 A6
Slovenské Darmoty SK 65 B5
Slovenske Konjice SLO 73 B5
Słubice PL 45 C6
Sluderno I 71 B5
Sluis NL 49 B4
Šluknov CZ 53 B4
Slunj HR 83 A4
Słupca PL 54 A2
Słupia PL 55 B4
Słupiec PL 54 C1
Słupsk PL 46 A3
Slutsk BY 7 E9
Smålandsstenar S 40 B3
Smalåsen N 115 B10
Smardzewo PL 53 A5
Smarhon BY 7 D9
Smarje SLO 73 B5
Šmarjeta SLO 73 C5
Šmartno SLO 73 B4
Smečno CZ 53 C4
Smedby S 40 C6
Smědec CZ 63 B5
Smederevo SRB 85 B5
Smederevska Palanka SRB 85 B5
Smedjebacken S 36 B2
Smęgorzów PL 55 C6
Smeland N 33 D5
Smidary CZ 53 C5
Śmigiel PL 54 A1
Smila UA 11 B11
Smilde NL 42 C3
Smiřice CZ 53 C5
Smithfield GB 25 D5
Śmitowo PL 46 B2
Smögen S 35 D3
Smogulec PL 46 B3
Smołdzino PL 46 A3
Smolenice SK 64 B3
Smolensk RUS 7 D12
Smolnik SK 65 B6
Smolyan BG 116 A6
Smuka SLO 73 C4
Smygehamn S 41 D3
Smykow PL 55 B5
Snainton GB 27 A5
Snaith GB 27 B4
Snaptun DK 39 D3
Snarby N 112 C8
Snarum N 34 B1
Snåsa N 115 C9
Snedsted DK 38 C1
Sneek NL 42 B2
Sneem IRL 20 C2
Snejbjerg DK 39 C1
Snihurivka UA 11 C12
Snillfjord N 114 D6
Šnjegotina BIH 84 B2
Snøde DK 39 D3
Snøfjord N 113 B13
Snogebaek DK 41 D5
Snyatyn UA 11 B8
Soave I 71 C6
Sober E 86 B3
Sobernheim D 60 A3
Soběslav CZ 63 A5
Sobienie Jeziory PL 55 B6
Sobota, *Dolnośląskie* PL 53 B5
Sobota, *Łódzkie* PL 55 A4
Sobotište SK 64 B3
Sobotka CZ 53 C5
Sobótka, *Dolnośląskie* PL 54 C1
Sobótka, *Wielkopolskie* PL 54 B2
Sobra HR 84 D2
Sobrado, *Coruña* E 86 A2
Sobrado, *Lugo* E 86 B3
Sobral da Adica P 98 A3
Sobral de Monte Argraço P 92 C1
Sobreira Formosa P 92 B3
Søby DK 39 E3
Soca SLO 72 B3
Sočanica SRB 85 C5
Sochaczew PL 55 A5
Sochos GR 116 B5
Socodor RO 75 B6
Socol RO 85 B6
Socovos E 101 A4
Socuéllamos E 95 C4
Sodankylä FIN 113 E15
Soderåkra S 40 C6
Söderala S 36 A3
Söderås S 36 B2
Söderbärke S 36 B2
Söderby-Karl S 36 C5
Söderfors S 36 B4
Söderhamn S 36 A4
Söderköping S 37 D3
Söderö S 40 B5
Södertälje S 37 C4
Södingberg A 73 A5
Södra Finnö S 37 D3
Södra Ny S 35 C5
Södra Råda S 35 C6
Södra Sandby S 41 D3
Södra Vi S 40 B5
Sodražica SLO 73 C4
Sodupe E 89 A3
Soengas P 87 C2
Soest D 50 B4
Soest NL 49 A6
Sofades GR 116 C4
Sofia = Sofiya BG 11 E7
Sofikon GR 117 E5
Sofiya = Sofia BG 11 E7
Şofronea RO 75 B6
Sögel D 43 C4
Sogliano al Rubicone I 82 B1
Sogndalsfjøra N 32 A4
Søgne N 33 D4
Söğüt, *Bilecik* TR 118 B5
Söğüt, *Burdur* TR 119 E4
Söğütköy TR 119 F3
Söğütlu TR 118 B5
Soham GB 30 B4
Sohland D 53 B4
Sohren D 60 A3
Soignies B 49 C5
Soissons F 59 A4
Söjtör H 74 B1
Sokal' UA 11 A8
Söke TR 119 E2
Sokna N 34 B1
Sokndal N 33 D3
Soknedal N 114 E7
Soko BIH 84 B3
Sokolac BIH 84 C3
Sokółka PL 6 E7
Sokolov CZ 52 C2
Sokołów Podlaski PL 6 E7
Sokołowo PL 54 A3
Sola N 33 D2
Solana de los Barros E 93 C4
Solana del Pino E 100 A1
Solánas I 110 C2
Solares E 88 A3
Solarino I 109 B4
Solarussa I 110 C1
Solas GB 22 D1
Solber-gelva N 34 C2
Solberg S 115 D14
Solberga S 40 B4
Solbjørg N 32 B2
Solčany SK 64 B4
Solčava SLO 73 B4
Solda I 71 B5
Sölden A 71 B6
Solec Kujawski PL 47 B4
Solec nad Wisłą PL 55 B6
Soleils F 79 C5
Solenzara F 102 B2
Solera E 100 B2
Solesmes F 49 C4
Soleto I 107 A5
Solgne F 60 B2
Solheim N 32 B2
Solheimsvik N 33 C3
Solignac F 67 C6
Solihull GB 27 C4
Solin HR 83 C5
Solingen D 50 B3
Solivella E 91 B4
Solkan SLO 72 C3
Söll A 72 A2
Sollana E 96 B2
Sollebrunn S 35 D4
Sollefteå S 115 D14
Sollen-tuna S 37 C4
Sollenau A 64 C2
Sóller E 97 B2
Sollerön S 36 B1
Søllested DK 39 E4
Solliès-Pont F 79 C5
Sollihøgda N 34 C2
Solnechnogorsk RUS 7 C14
Solnice CZ 53 C6
Solofra I 103 C7
Solomiac F 77 C3
Solopaca I 103 B7
Solórzano E 89 A3
Solothurn CH 70 A2
Solre-le-Château F 49 C5
Solsona E 91 B4
Solsvik N 32 B1
Solt H 75 B4
Soltau D 44 C1
Soltsy RUS 7 B11
Soltszentimre H 75 B4
Soltvadkert H 75 B4
Solumsmoen N 34 C1
Solund N 32 A1
Solva GB 28 B2
Sölvesborg S 41 C4
Solymár H 65 C4
Soma TR 118 C2
Somain F 49 C4
Somberek H 74 B3
Sombernon F 69 A4
Sombor SRB 75 C4
Sombreffe B 49 C5
Someren NL 50 B1
Somero FIN 6 A7
Somersham GB 30 B3
Somerton GB 29 B5
Sominy PL 46 A3
Somma Lombardo I 70 C3
Sommariva del Bosco I 80 B1
Sommarøy N 112 C7
Sommarset N 112 E4
Sommatino I 109 B3
Somme-Tourbe F 59 A5
Sommeilles F 59 B5
Sommen S 37 D1
Sommepy-Tahure F 59 A5
Sömmerda D 52 B1
Sommerfeld D 45 C5
Sommersted DK 39 D2
Sommesous F 59 B5
Sommières F 78 C3
Sommières-du-Clain F 67 B5
Somo E 88 A3
Somogyfajsz H 74 B2
Somogyjád H 74 B2
Somogysámson H 74 B2
Somogysárd H 74 B2
Somogyszil H 74 B3
Somogyszob H 74 B2
Somogyvár H 74 B2
Somontin E 101 B3
Somosiero E 95 A3
Somosköújfalu H 65 B5
Sompolno PL 47 C4
Sompuis F 59 B5
Son N 35 C2
Son Bou E 97 B4
Son en Breugel NL 49 B6
Son Servera E 97 B3
Sonceboz CH 70 A2
Soncillo E 88 B3
Soncino I 71 C4
Sondalo I 71 B5
Søndeled N 33 D6
Sønder Bjert DK 39 D2
Sønder Felding DK 39 D1
Sønder Hygum DK 39 D1
Sønder Omme DK 39 D1
Sønderborg DK 39 E2
Sønderby DK 39 E2
Sønderho DK 39 D1
Sondershausen D 51 B6
Søndersø DK 39 D3
Søndervig DK 39 C1
Søndre Enningdal Kappel N 35 D3
Sondrio I 71 B4
Soneja E 96 B2
Songe N 33 D6
Songeons F 58 A2
Sonkamuotka FIN 113 D12
Sonkovo RUS 7 C14
Sönnarslöv S 41 D4
Sonneberg D 52 C1
Sonnefeld D 52 C1
Sonnewalde D 52 B3
Sonnino I 102 B6
Sonogno CH 70 B3
Sonsbeck D 50 B2
Sonseca E 94 C3
Sønsterud N 34 B4
Sonstorp S 37 D2
Sonta SRB 75 C4
Sontheim D 61 B6
Sonthofen D 71 A5
Sontra D 51 B5
Sopelana E 89 A4
Sopje HR 74 C2
Šoporňa SK 64 B3
Sopot PL 47 A4
Sopot SRB 85 B5
Sopotnica MK 116 A3
Sopron H 64 C2
Šor SRB 85 B4
Sora I 103 B6
Soragna I 81 B4
Söråker S 115 E14
Sorano I 81 D5
Sorbara I 81 B5
Sorbas E 101 B3
Sórbolo I 81 B4
Sörbygden S 115 E13
Sordal N 33 D4
Sordale GB 23 C5
Sore F 76 B2
Sörenberg CH 70 B3
Soresina I 71 C4
Sorèze F 77 C5
Sörforsa S 115 F14
Sorges F 67 C5
Sórgono I 110 B2
Sorgues F 78 B3
Sorgun TR 16 B7
Soria E 89 C4
Soriano Cálabro I 106 C3
Soriano nel Cimino I 102 A5
Sorihuela del Guadalimar E 100 A2
Sorisdale GB 24 B1
Sørkjosen N 112 C9
Sørli N 115 C10
Sormás H 74 B1
Sörmjöle S 115 D17
Sørmo N 112 D7
Sornac F 68 C2
Sorø DK 39 D4
Soroca MD 11 B10
Sørreisa N 112 C7
Sorrento I 103 C7
Sorsele S 115 B14
Sörsjön S 34 A5
Sorso I 110 B1
Sort E 91 A4
Sortavala RUS 3 F29
Sortino I 109 B4
Sortland N 112 D4
Sørum N 34 B2
Sørumsand N 34 C3
Sorunda S 37 C4
Sörup D 44 A1
Sørvær N 113 B11
Sørvågen N 112 E1
Sorvik S 36 B2
Sørvika N 114 E8
Sos F 76 B3
Sos del Rey Católico E 90 A1
Sösdala S 41 C3
Sošice HR 73 C5
Sośnica PL 46 B2
Sośnicowice PL 54 C3
Sośno PL 46 B3
Sosnovyy Bor RUS 7 B10
Sosnowiec PL 55 C4
Sospel F 80 C1
Šoštanj SLO 73 B5
Sotaseter N 114 F4
Sotillo de Adrada E 94 B2
Sotillo de la Ribera E 88 C3
Sotin HR 75 C4
Sotkamo FIN 3 D28
Soto de la Marina E 88 A3
Soto de los Infantes E 86 A4
Soto de Real E 94 B3
Soto de Ribera E 88 A1
Soto del Barco E 86 A4
Soto y Amío E 88 B1
Sotobañado y Priorato E 88 B2
Sotoserrano E 93 A4
Sotresgudo E 88 B2
Sotrondio E 88 A1
Sotta F 102 B2
Sottomarina I 72 C2
Sottrum D 43 B6
Sottunga FIN 36 B7
Sotuelamos E 95 C4
Souain F 59 A5
Soual F 77 C5
Soucy F 59 B4
Souda GR 117 G6
Soudron F 59 B5
Souesmes F 68 A2
Soufflenheim F 60 B3
Soufli GR 116 A8
Souillac F 77 B4
Souilly F 59 A6
Soulac-sur-Mer F 66 C3
Soulaines-Dhuys F 59 B5
Soulatgé F 77 D5
Soultz-Haut-Rhin F 60 C3
Soultz-sous-Forêts F 60 B3
Soumagne B 50 C1
Soumoulou F 76 C2
Souppes-sur-Loing F 58 B3
Souprosse F 76 C2
Sourdeval F 57 B5
Soure P 92 A2
Sournia F 77 D5
Souro Pires P 87 D3
Sourpi GR 116 C4
Sours F 58 B2
Sousceyrac F 77 B5
Sousel P 92 C3
Soustons F 76 C1
Soutelo de Montes E 86 B2
South Brent GB 28 C4
South Cave GB 27 B5
South Hayling GB 31 D3
South Molton GB 28 B4
South Ockendon GB 31 C4
South Petherton GB 29 C5
South Shields GB 25 D6
South Tawton GB 28 C4
South Woodham Ferrers GB 31 C4
Southam GB 30 B2
Southampton GB 31 D2
Southborough GB 31 C4
Southend GB 24 C2
Southend-on-Sea GB 31 C4
Southport GB 26 B2
Southwell GB 27 B5
Southwold GB 30 B5
Souto P 92 A3
Souto da Carpalhosa P 92 B2
Soutochao E 87 C3
Souvigny F 68 B3
Souzay-Champigny F 67 A4
Soverato I 106 C3
Soveria Mannelli I 106 B3
Sövestad S 41 D3
Sovetsk RUS 6 D6
Sovići BIH 84 C2
Sovicille I 81 C5
Søvik N 114 E3
Sowerby GB 27 A4
Soyaux F 67 C5
Søyland N 33 D2
Spa B 50 C1
Spadafora I 109 A4
Spaichingen D 61 B4
Spakenburg NL 49 A6
Spalding GB 30 B3
Spálené Poříčí CZ 63 A4
Spalt D 62 A1
Spangenberg D 51 B5
Spangereid N 33 D4
Spantekow D 45 B5
Sparanise I 103 B7
Sparbu N 114 D8
Sparkær DK 38 C2
Sparkford GB 29 B5
Sparreholm S 37 C3
Sparta = Sparti GR 117 F4
Spartà I 109 A4
Sparti = Sparta GR 117 E4
Spas-Demensk RUS 7 D13
Spean Bridge GB 24 B3
Speicher D 60 A2
Speichersdorf D 62 A2
Speke GB 26 B3
Spello I 82 D1
Spenge D 51 A4
Spennymoor GB 25 D6
Spentrup DK 38 C3
Sperenberg D 52 A3
Sperlinga I 109 B3
Sperlonga I 103 B6
Spetalen N 35 C2
Spetses GR 117 E5
Speyer D 61 A4
Spézet F 56 B2
Spezzano Albanese I 106 B3
Spezzano della Sila I 106 B3
Spiddle IRL 20 A2
Spiegelau D 63 B4
Spiekeroog D 43 B4
Spiez CH 70 B2
Spigno Monferrato I 80 B2
Spijk NL 42 B3
Spijkenisse NL 49 B5
Spilamberto I 81 B5
Spili GR 117 G6
Spilimbergo I 72 B2
Spilsby GB 27 B6
Spinazzola I 104 C2
Spincourt F 60 A1
Spind N 33 D3
Spindleruv-Mlyn CZ 53 C5
Spinoso I 104 C1
Špišjć Bukovica HR 74 C2
Spišská Belá SK 65 A6
Spišská Nová Ves SK 65 B6
Spisská Stará Ves SK 65 A6
Spišské-Hanušovce SK 65 A6
Spišské Podhradie SK 65 B6
Spišské Vlachy SK 65 B6
Spišský-Štvrtok SK 65 B6
Spital A 63 C5
Spital am Semmering A 63 C6
Spittal an der Drau A 72 B3
Spittle of Glenshee GB 25 B4
Spitz A 63 B6
Spjærøy N 35 C2
Spjald DK 39 C1
Spjelkavik N 114 E3
Spjutsbygd S 41 C5
Split HR 83 C5
Splügen CH 71 B4
Spodsbjerg DK 39 E3
Spofforth GB 27 B4
Spohle D 43 B5
Spoleto I 82 D1
Spoltore I 103 A7
Spondigna I 71 B5
Sponvika N 35 C3
Spornitz D 44 B3
Spotorno I 80 B2
Spraitbach D 61 B5
Sprakensehl D 44 C2
Spręcowo PL 47 B6
Spremberg D 53 B4
Spresiano I 72 C2
Sprimont B 49 C6
Springe D 51 A5
Sproatley GB 27 B5
Spuž CG 105 A5
Spydeberg N 35 C3
Spytkowice PL 55 D4
Squillace I 106 C3
Squinzano I 105 C4
Sračinec HR 73 B6
Srbac BIH 84 A2
Srbica SRB 85 D5
Srbobran SRB 75 C4
Srebrenica BIH 85 B4
Srebrenik BIH 84 B3
Središče SLO 73 B6
Śrem PL 54 A2
Sremska Mitrovica SRB 85 B4
Sremski Karlovci SRB 75 C4
Srní CZ 63 A4
Srnice Gornje BIH 84 B3
Srock PL 55 B4
Środa Śląska PL 54 B1
Środa Wielkopolski PL 54 A2
Srpska Crnja SRB 75 C5
Srpski Itebej SRB 75 C5
Srpski Miletić SRB 75 C4
Staatz A 64 B2
Stabbursnes N 113 B13
Staberdorf D 44 A3
Stabroek B 49 B5
Stachy CZ 63 A4
Stade D 43 B6
Staden B 49 C4
Staðarfell IS 111 B3
Stadl an der Mur A 72 A3
Stadskanaal NL 42 C3
Stadtallendorf D 51 C5
Stadthagen D 51 A5
Stadtilm D 52 C1
Stadtkyll D 50 C2
Stadtlauringen D 51 C6
Stadtlengsfeld D 51 C6
Stadtlohn D 50 B2
Stadtoldendorf D 51 B5
Stadtroda D 52 C1
Stadtsteinach D 52 C1
Stäfa CH 70 A3
Staffanstorp S 41 D3
Staffelstein D 51 C6
Staffin GB 22 D2
Stafford GB 26 C3
Stainach A 73 A4
Staindrop GB 27 A4
Staines GB 31 C3
Stainville F 59 B6
Stainz A 73 B5
Staithes GB 27 A5
Staïti I 106 D3
Stäket S 37 C4
Stakroge DK 39 D1
Štalać SRB 85 C6
Štalcerji SLO 73 C4
Stalden CH 70 B2
Stalham GB 30 B5
Stalheim N 32 B3
Stallarholmen S 37 C4
Ställberg S 36 C1
Ställdalen S 36 C1
Stallhofen A 73 A5
Stalon S 115 C12
Stalowa Wola PL 11 A7
Stamford GB 30 B3
Stamford Bridge GB 27 B5
Stamnes N 32 B2
Stams A 71 A5
Stamsried D 62 A3
Stamsund N 112 D2
Stanford le Hope GB 31 C4
Stånga S 37 E5
Stange N 34 B3
Stanghella I 72 C1
Stanhope GB 25 D5
Stanišić SRB 75 C4
Stanisławów PL 55 A6
Staňkov CZ 62 A4
Stankovci HR 83 C4
Stanley GB 25 D6
Stans CH 70 B3
Stansted Mountfitchet GB 31 C4
Stanzach A 71 A5
Stapar SRB 75 C4
Staphorst NL 42 C3
Staplehurst GB 31 C4
Stąporków PL 55 B5
Stara Baška HR 83 B3
Stara Fužina SLO 72 B3
Stara Kamienica PL 53 C5
Stara Kiszewa PL 47 B4
Stará L'ubovňa SK 65 A6
Stara Moravica SRB 75 C4
Stara Novalja HR 83 B3
Stara Pazova SRB 85 B5
Stará Turá SK 64 B3
Stara Zagora BG 11 E8
Starachowice PL 55 B6
Staraya Russa RUS 7 C11
Stårbsnäs S 36 C6
Starčevo SRB 85 B5
Stare Dlutowo PL 47 B5
Staré Hamry CZ 65 A4
Stare Jablonki PL 47 B6
Staré Město CZ 64 A3
Stare Pole PL 47 A5
Stare Sedlo CZ 63 A5
Stare Strącze PL 53 B6
Stargard Szczeciński PL 45 B7
Stårheim N 114 F2
Stari Banovci SRB 85 B5
Stari Bar CG 105 A5
Stari Gradac HR 74 C2
Stari Jankovci HR 75 C3
Stari Majdan BIH 83 B5
Stari-Mikanovci HR 74 C3
Stari Raušić SRB 85 D5
Starigrad, *Ličko-Senjska* HR 83 B3
Starigrad, *Splitsko-Dalmatinska* HR 83 C5
Starigrad-Paklenica HR 83 B4
Staritsa RUS 7 C13
Starkenbach A 71 A5
Starnberg D 62 C2
Staro Petrovo Selo HR 74 C2
Staro Selo HR 73 C6
Staro Selo SRB 85 B6
Starodub RUS 7 E12
Starogard PL 46 B1
Starogard Gdański PL 47 B4
Starokonstyantyniv UA 11 B9
Stary Brzozów PL 55 A5
Stary Dzierzgoń PL 47 B5
Starý Hrozenkov CZ 64 B3
Stary Jaroslaw PL 46 A2
Stary Plzenec CZ 63 A4
Stary Sącz PL 65 A6
Starý Smokovec SK 65 A6
Staryy Chartoriysk UA 11 A8
Staškov SK 65 A4
Stassfurt D 52 B1
Staszów PL 55 C6
Stathelle N 35 C1
Staufen D 60 C3
Staunton GB 29 B5
Štavalj SRB 85 C5
Stavang N 32 A2
Stavanger N 33 D2
Stavåsnäs S 34 B4
Stavby S 36 B5
Staveley GB 27 B4
Stavelot B 50 C1
Stavenisse NL 49 B5
Stavern N 35 D2
Stavnäs S 35 C4
Stavoren NL 42 C2
Stavros CY 120 A1
Stavros GR 116 B5
Stavroupoli GR 116 A6
Stavseng N 32 A6
Stavsiø N 34 B2
Stavsnäs S 37 C5
Stawiszyn PL 54 B3
Steane N 33 C5
Steblevë AL 116 A2
Stechelberg CH 70 B2
Štěchovice CZ 63 A5
Stechow D 44 C4
Steckborn CH 61 C4
Stede Broek NL 42 C2
Steeg A 71 A5
Steenbergen NL 49 B5
Steenvoorde F 48 C3
Steenwijk NL 42 C3
Štefanje HR 74 C1
Steffisburg CH 70 B2
Stegaurach D 62 A1
Stege DK 41 E2
Stegelitz D 45 B5
Stegersbach A 73 A6
Stegna PL 47 A5
Steimbke D 43 C6
Stein GB 22 D2
Stein an Rhein CH 61 C4
Steinach A 71 A6
Steinach, *Baden-Württemberg* D 61 B4
Steinach, *Bayern* D 51 C6
Steinach, *Thüringen* D 52 C1
Steinau, *Bayern* D 51 C5
Steinau, *Niedersachsen* D 43 B5
Steinbeck D 45 C5
Steinberg am Rofan A 72 A1
Steindorf A 73 B4
Steine N 32 B2
Steinen D 60 C3
Steinfeld A 72 B3
Steinfeld D 43 C5
Steinfurt D 50 A3
Steingaden D 62 C1
Steinhagen D 51 A4
Steinheid D 52 C1
Steinheim, *Bayern* D 61 B6
Steinheim, *Nordrhein-Westfalen* D 51 B5
Steinhöfel D 45 C6
Steinhorst D 44 C2
Steinigtwolmsdorf D 53 B4
Steinkjer N 114 C8
Steinsholt N 35 C1
Stekene B 49 B5
Stelle D 44 B2
Stellendam NL 49 B5
Stenåsa S 41 C6
Stenay F 59 A6
Stenberga S 40 B5
Stendal D 44 C3
Stenhammar S 35 D5
Stenhamra S 37 C4
Stenhousemuir GB 25 B4
Stenlose DK 41 D2
Stensätra S 36 B3
Stensele S 115 B14
Stenstorp S 35 D5
Stenstrup DK 39 D3
Stenudden S 112 F6
Stenungsund S 38 A4
Štěpánov CZ 64 A3
Stephanskirchen D 62 C3
Stepnica PL 45 B6
Stepojevac SRB 85 B5
Stepping DK 39 D2
Sterbfritz D 51 C5
Sternberg D 44 B3
Šternberk CZ 64 A3
Sterup D 44 A1
Stęszew PL 54 A1
Štěti CZ 53 C4
Stevenage GB 31 C3
Stewarton GB 24 C3
Steyerburg D 43 C6
Steyning GB 31 D3
Steyr A 63 B5
Stężyca PL 46 A3
Stezzano I 71 C4
Stia I 81 C5
Stibb Cross GB 28 C3
Sticciano Scalo I 81 D5
Stidsvig S 41 C3
Stiens NL 42 B2
Stige DK 39 D3
Stigen S 35 D4
Stigliano I 104 C2
Stigtomta S 37 D3
Stilida GR 116 D4
Stilla N 113 C12
Stillington GB 27 A4
Stilo I 106 C3
Stintino I 110 B1
Stio I 103 C8
Štip MK 116 A4
Stira GR 117 D6
Stirling GB 25 B4
Štítnik SK 65 B6
Štíty CZ 54 D1
Stjärnhov S 37 C4
Stjärnsund S 36 B3
Stjørdalshalsen N 114 D7

Stobnica PL 55 B4
Stobno PL 46 B2
Stobreč HR 83 C5
Stochov CZ 53 C3
Stockach D 61 C5
Stöckalp CH 70 B3
Stockaryd S 40 B4
Stockbridge GB 31 C2
Stockerau A 64 B2
Stockheim D 52 C1
Stockholm S 37 C5
Stockport GB 26 B3
Stocksbridge GB 27 B4
Stockton-on-Tees GB 27 A4
Stod CZ 62 A4
Stöde S 115 E13
Stöðvarfjörður IS 111 C12
Stødi N 112 F4
Stoer GB 22 C3
Stoholm DK 38 C2
Stoke Ferry GB 30 B4
Stoke Fleming GB 29 C4
Stoke Mandeville GB 31 C3
Stoke-on-Trent GB 26 B3
Stokesley GB 27 A4
Stokke N 35 C2
Stokkemarke DK 39 E4
Stokken N 33 D5
Stokkseyri IS 111 D4
Stokkvågen N 115 A10
Stokmarknes N 112 D3
Štoky CZ 63 A6
Stolac BIH 84 C2
Stølaholmen N 32 A3
Stolberg D 50 C2
Stolin BY 7 F9
Stollberg D 52 C2
Stöllet S 34 B5
Stollhamm D 43 B5
Stolno PL 47 B4
Stolpen D 53 B4
Stolzenau D 43 C6
Stompetoren NL 42 C1
Ston HR 84 D2
Stonařov CZ 63 A6
Stone GB 26 C3
Stonehaven GB 25 B5
Stonehouse GB 25 C4
Stongfjorden N 32 A2
Stonndalen N 32 B4
Stony Stratford GB 30 B3
Stopanja SRB 85 C6
Stopnica PL 55 C5
Storå S 37 C2
Storås N 114 D6
Storby FIN 36 B6
Stordal, *Møre og Romsdal* N 114 E4
Stordal, *Nord-Trøndelag* N 114 D8
Store GB 23 B6
Store Damme DK 41 E2
Store Heddinge DK 41 D2
Store Herrestad S 41 D3
Store Levene S 35 D4
Store Molvik N 113 B17
Store Skedvi S 36 B2
Store Vika S 37 D4
Storebø N 32 B2
Storebro S 40 B5
Storelv N 113 B11
Støren N 114 D7
Storfjellseter N 114 F7
Storfjord N 112 C8
Storfjorden N 114 E3
Storfors S 35 C6
Storforshei N 112 F3
Storhøliseter N 32 A6
Storjord N 112 F4
Storkow, *Brandenburg* D 53 A3
Storkow, *Mecklenburg-Vorpommern* D 45 B6
Storli N 114 E6
Storlien S 114 D9
Stornara I 104 B1
Stornoway GB 22 C2
Storo I 71 C5
Storozhynets UA 11 B8
Storrington GB 31 D3
Storseleby S 115 C13
Storsjön S 36 A3
Storslett N 112 C10
Storsteinnes N 112 C8
Storuman S 115 B14
Störvattnet S 115 E9
Storvik N 112 F2
Storvik S 36 B3
Storvreta S 36 C4
Štós SK 65 B6
Stössen D 52 B1
Stotel D 43 B5
Stötten D 62 C1
Stotternheim D 52 B1
Stouby DK 39 D2
Stourbridge GB 26 C3
Stourport-on-Severn GB 29 A5
Støvring DK 38 C2
Stow GB 25 C5
Stow-on-the-Wold GB 29 B6
Stowbtsy BY 7 E9
Stowmarket GB 30 B5
Straach D 52 B2
Strabane GB 19 B4
Strachan GB 23 D6
Strachur GB 24 B2
Strackholt D 43 B4
Stradbally IRL 20 B1
Stradella I 80 A3
Straelen D 50 B2
Stragari SRB 85 B5
Strakonice CZ 63 A4
Strålsnäs S 37 D2
Stralsund D 45 A5
Strand N 34 A3
Stranda, *Møre og Romsdal* N 114 E3
Strandby DK 38 B3
Strandebarm N 32 B3
Strandhill IRL 18 B3
Strandlykkja N 34 B3
Strandvik N 32 B2
Strangford GB 19 B6
Strängnäs S 37 C4
Strångsjö S 37 D3
Stráni CZ 64 B3
Stranice SLO 73 B5
Stranorlar IRL 19 B4
Stranraer GB 24 D2
Strasatti I 108 B1
Strasbourg F 60 B3
Strasburg D 45 B5
Strašice CZ 63 A4
Strass im Steiermark A 73 B5
Stråssa S 37 C2
Strassburg A 73 B4
Strasskirchen D 62 B3
Strasswalchen A 63 C4
Stratford-upon-Avon GB 29 A6
Strathaven GB 24 C3
Strathdon GB 23 D5
Strathkanaird GB 22 D3
Strathpeffer GB 23 D4
Strathy GB 23 C5
Strathyre GB 24 B3
Stratinska BIH 84 B1
Stratton GB 28 C3
Straubing D 62 B3
Straulas I 110 B2
Straume N 33 C6
Straumen, *Nord-Trøndelag* N 114 D8
Straumen, *Nordland* N 112 E4
Straumsjøen N 112 D3
Straumsnes N 112 E4
Straupitz D 53 B4
Strausberg D 45 C5
Straussfurt D 51 B7
Strawczyn PL 55 C5
Straž nad Nezárkou CZ 63 A5
Stráž Pod Ralskem CZ 53 C4
Straža SLO 73 C5
Straža SRB 85 B6
Strážnice CZ 64 B3
Strážný CZ 63 B4
Štrbské Pleso SK 65 A6
Strečno SK 65 A4
Street GB 29 B5
Strehla D 52 B3
Strekov SK 65 C4
Strem A 73 A6
Stremska-Rača SRB 85 B4
Strengberg A 63 B5
Strengelvåg N 112 D4
Streoci SRB 85 D5
Stresa I 70 C3
Streufdorf D 51 C6
Strib DK 39 D2
Striberg S 37 C1
Střibro CZ 62 A3
Strichen GB 23 D6
Strigno I 71 B6
Štrigova HR 73 B6
Strijen NL 49 B5
Strizivojna HR 74 C3
Strmica HR 83 B5
Strmilov CZ 63 A6
Ströhen D 43 C5
Strokestown IRL 18 C3
Stromberg, *Nordrhein-Westfalen* D 50 B4
Stromberg, *Rheinland-Pfalz* D 60 A3
Stromeferry GB 22 D3
Strömnäs S 115 C13
Stromness GB 23 C5
Strömsberg S 36 B4
Strömsbruk S 115 F14
Strömsfors S 37 D3
Strömsnäsbruk S 40 C3
Strömstad S 35 D3
Strömsund, *Jämtland* S 115 D12
Strömsund, *Västerbotten* S 115 B13
Stronachlachar GB 24 B3
Stróngoli I 107 B4
Stronie Śląskie PL 54 C1
Strontian GB 24 B2
Stroppiana I 70 C3
Stroud GB 29 B5
Stroumbi CY 120 B1
Stróża PL 65 A5
Strücklingen D 43 B4
Struer DK 38 C1
Struga MK 116 A2
Strugi Krasnyye RUS 7 B10
Strumica MK 116 A4
Strumien PL 65 A4
Struy GB 22 D4
Stružec HR 74 C1
Stryków PL 55 B4
Stryn N 114 F3
Stryy UA 11 B7
Strzałkowo PL 54 A2
Strzegocin PL 47 C6
Strzegom PL 54 C1
Strzegowo PL 47 C6
Strzelce PL 55 A4
Strzelce Krajeńskie PL 46 C1
Strzelce Kurowo PL 46 C1
Strzelce Opolskie PL 54 C3
Strzelin PL 54 C2
Strzelno PL 47 C4
Strzepcz PL 47 A4
Strzybnica PL 54 C3
Strzygi PL 47 B5
Stubal SRB 85 C5
Stubbekøbing DK 39 E5
Stuben A 71 A5
Stubenberg A 73 A5
Stubline SRB 85 B5
Studená CZ 63 A6
Studenci HR 84 C2
Studenica SRB 85 C5
Studenka CZ 64 A4
Studenzen A 73 A5
Studienka SK 64 B3
Studland GB 29 C6
Studley GB 29 A6
Studzienice PL 46 A3
Stuer D 44 B4
Stugudal N 114 E8
Stugun S 115 D12
Stuhr D 43 B5
Stukenbrock D 51 B4
Stülpe D 52 A3
Stupava SK 64 B3
Stupnik HR 73 C5
Stupsk PL 47 B6
Sturkö S 41 C5
Sturminster Newton GB 29 C5
Štúrovo SK 65 C4
Sturton GB 27 B5
Stuttgart D 61 B5
Stvolny CZ 52 C3
Stykkishólmur IS 111 B3
Styri N 34 B3
Stysö S 38 B4
Suances E 88 A2
Subbiano I 81 C5
Subiaco I 102 B6
Subotica SRB 75 B4
Subotište SRB 85 B4
Sučany SK 65 A4
Suceava RO 11 C9
Sucha-Beskidzka PL 65 A5
Suchacz PL 47 A5
Suchań PL 46 B1
Suchdol nad Lužnice CZ 63 B5
Suchedniów PL 55 B5
Suchorze PL 46 A3
Suchteln D 50 B2
Sucina E 101 B5
Suckow D 44 B3
Sućuraj HR 84 C2
Sudbury GB 30 B4
Suddesjaur S 115 B16
Suden D 43 A5
Süderbrarup D 44 A1
Süderlügum D 39 E1
Súðavík IS 111 A3
Suðureyri IS 111 A2
Sudoměřice u Bechyně CZ 63 A5
Sudovec HR 73 B6
Sudzha RUS 7 F13
Sueca E 96 B2
Suelli I 110 C2
Sugenheim D 61 A6
Sugères F 68 C3
Sugny B 59 A5
Suhl D 51 C6
Suhlendorf D 44 C2
Suho Polje BIH 85 B4
Suhopolje HR 74 C2
Şuhut TR 119 D5
Šuica BIH 84 C2
Suippes F 59 A5
Sukhinichi RUS 7 D13
Sukobin CG 105 A5
Sukošan HR 83 B4
Sükösd H 75 B3
Suków PL 55 C5
Šul'a SK 65 B5
Suldalsosen N 33 C3
Suldrup DK 38 C2
Sulechów PL 53 A5
Sulęcin PL 45 C7
Sulęczyno PL 46 A3
Sulejów PL 55 B4
Sulejówek PL 55 A6
Süleymanlı TR 118 D2
Sulgen CH 71 A4
Sulibórz PL 46 B1
Sulina RO 11 D10
Sulingen D 43 C5
Suliszewo PL 46 B1
Sulitjelma N 112 E5
Sułkowice PL 65 A5
Süller TR 119 D4
Sully-sur-Loire F 58 C3
Sulmierzyce, *Łódzkie* PL 55 B4
Sulmierzyce, *Wielkopolskie* PL 54 B2
Sulmona I 103 A6
Süloğlu TR 118 A1
Sułoszowa PL 55 C4
Sulów PL 54 B2
Sulsdorf D 44 A3
Sultandağı TR 119 D6
Sülüklü TR 118 D7
Suluova TR 16 A7
Sulvik S 35 C4
Sülysáp H 75 A4
Sülz D 61 B4
Sulzbach, *Baden-Württemberg* D 61 A5
Sulzbach, *Baden-Württemberg* D 61 B5
Sulzbach, *Bayern* D 61 A5
Sulzbach, *Saarland* D 60 A3
Sulzbach-Rosenberg D 62 A2
Sülze D 44 C2
Sulzfeld D 51 C6
Sumartin HR 84 C1
Sumburgh GB 22 B7
Sümeg H 74 B2
Sumiswald CH 70 A2
Šumná CZ 64 B1
Šumperk CZ 54 D1
Šumvald CZ 64 A3
Sumy UA 7 F13
Sunbilla E 76 C1
Sünching D 62 B3
Sund FIN 36 B7
Sund S 35 C3
Sundborn S 36 B2
Sundby DK 38 C1
Sunde N 32 C2
Sunde bru N 33 D6
Sunderland GB 25 D6
Sundern D 50 B4
Sundhultsbrunn S 40 B4
Sundnäs S 115 A14
Sunds DK 39 C2
Sundsfjord N 112 F3
Sundsvall S 115 E14
Sungurlu TR 16 A7
Suni I 110 B1
Sunja HR 74 C1
Sunnansjö S 36 B1
Sunnaryd S 40 B3
Sunndalsøra N 114 E5
Sunne S 34 C5
Sunnemo S 34 C5
Sunnersberg S 35 D5
Suolovuopmio N 113 C12
Suomussalmi FIN 3 D28
Suoyarvi RUS 3 E30
Super Sauze F 79 B5
Supetar HR 83 C5
Supetarska Draga HR 83 B3
Supino I 102 B6
Šuplja Stijena CG 84 C4
Surahammar S 37 C3
Šurany SK 64 B4
Surazh BY 7 D11
Surazh RUS 7 E12
Surbo I 105 C4
Surčin SRB 85 B5
Surgères F 66 B4
Surhuisterveen NL 42 B3
Súria E 91 B4
Surin F 67 B5
Surka N 34 B2
Surnadalsøra N 114 E5
Sursee CH 70 A3
Surte S 38 B5
Surwold D 43 C4
Sury-le-Comtal F 69 C4
Susa I 70 C2
Šušara SRB 85 B6
Susch CH 71 B5
Susegana I 72 C2
Süsel D 44 A2
Sušice CZ 63 A4
Šušnjevica HR 73 C4
Sussen D 61 B5
Susurluk TR 118 C3
Susz PL 47 B5
Sütçüler TR 119 E5
Sutivan HR 83 C5
Sutjeska SRB 75 C5
Sutomore CG 105 A5
Sutri I 102 A5
Sutton GB 31 C3
Sutton Coldfield GB 27 C4
Sutton-in-Ashfield GB 27 B4
Sutton-on-Sea GB 27 B6
Sutton-on-Trent GB 27 B5
Sutton Scotney GB 31 C2
Sutton Valence GB 31 C4
Suvaja BIH 83 B5
Suvereto I 81 C4
Suvorov RUS 7 D14
Suwałki PL 6 D7
Suze-la-Rousse F 78 B3
Suzzara I 81 B4
Svabensverk S 36 A2
Svalbarð IS 111 A10
Svalöv S 41 D3
Svanabyn S 115 C13
Svanberga S 36 C5
Svaneke DK 41 D5
Svanesund S 35 D3
Svängsta S 41 C4
Svannäs S 115 A15
Svanskog S 35 C4
Svanstein S 113 F12
Svappavaara S 112 E10
Svärdsjö S 36 B2
Svarstad N 35 C1
Svartå, *Örebro* S 37 C1
Svärta, *Södermanland* S 37 D4
Svartå, *Värmland* S 34 C5
Svärtinge S 37 D3
Svartnäs S 36 B3
Svartnes N 112 E3
Svarttjärn S 115 B13
Svatsum N 34 A1
Svätý Jur SK 64 B3
Svätý Peter SK 64 C4
Svedala S 41 D3
Sveg S 115 E11
Sveindal N 33 D4
Sveio N 33 C2
Svejbæk DK 39 C2
Svelgen N 114 F2
Svelvik N 35 C2
Svendborg DK 39 D3
Svene N 32 C6
Svenljunga S 40 B3
Svennevad S 37 C2
Svenstavik S 115 E11
Svenstrup DK 38 C2
Švermov CZ 53 C4
Sveti Ivan Zabno HR 74 C1
Sveti Ivan Zelina HR 73 C6
Sveti Nikola CG 105 B5
Sveti Rok HR 83 B4
Sveti Stefan CG 105 A4
Světla nad Sázavou CZ 63 A6
Svetlyy RUS 47 A6
Svetvinčenat HR 82 A2
Švica HR 83 B4
Svidník SK 10 B6
Švihov CZ 63 A4
Svilajnac SRB 85 B6
Svilengrad BG 11 F9
Svindal N 35 C3
Svinhult S 40 B5
Svinna SK 64 B4
Svinninge DK 39 D4
Svinninge S 37 C5
Sviritsa RUS 7 A12
Svishtov BG 11 E8
Svislach BY 6 E8
Svit SK 65 A6
Svitavy CZ 64 A2
Svitlovodsk UA 11 B12
Svodin SK 65 C4
Svolvær N 112 D3
Svortemyr N 32 A2
Svortland N 32 C2
Svratka CZ 64 A2
Svrčinovec SK 65 A4
Svullrya N 34 B4
Svyetlahorsk BY 7 E10
Swadlincote GB 27 C4
Swaffham GB 30 B4
Swanage GB 29 C6
Swanley GB 31 C4
Swanlinbar IRL 19 B4
Swansea GB 28 B4
Swarzędz PL 46 C3
Swatragh GB 19 B5
Świątki PL 47 B6
Świdnica, *Dolnośląskie* PL 54 C1
Świdnica, *Lubuskie* PL 53 B5
Świdnik PL 11 A7
Świdwin PL 46 B1
Świebodzice PL 53 C6
Świebodzin PL 53 A5
Świecie PL 47 B4
Świedziebnia PL 47 B5
Świeradów Zdrój PL 53 C5
Świerki PL 54 C1
Swierzawa PL 53 B5
Swierzno PL 45 B6
Swięta PL 45 B6
Swieta Anna PL 55 C4
Świętno PL 53 A6
Swifterbant NL 42 C2
Swindon GB 29 B6
Swineshead GB 30 B3
Swinford IRL 18 C3
Świnoujście PL 45 B6
Swinton GB 25 C5
Swobnica PL 45 B6
Swords IRL 21 A5
Swornegacie PL 46 B3
Sya S 37 D2
Syasstroy RUS 7 A12
Sycewice PL 46 A2
Sychevka RUS 7 D13
Syców PL 54 B2
Sycowice PL 53 A5
Sydnes N 33 C2
Syfteland N 32 B2
Syke D 43 C5
Sykkylven N 114 E3
Sylling N 34 C2
Sylte N 114 E4
Symbister GB 22 A7
Symington GB 25 C4
Symonds Yat GB 29 B5
Sypniewo, *Kujawsko-Pomorskie* PL 46 B3
Sypniewo, *Wielkopolskie* PL 46 B2
Syserum S 40 B6
Sysslebäck S 34 B4
Syväjärvi FIN 113 E14
Szabadbattyán H 74 A3
Szabadegyháza H 74 A3
Szabadszállás H 75 B4
Szadek PL 54 B3
Szajol H 75 A5
Szakály H 74 B3
Szakcs H 74 B3
Szakmár H 75 B4
Szalánta H 74 C3
Szałas PL 55 B5
Szalkszentmárton H 75 B4
Szalonna H 65 B6
Szamocin PL 46 B3
Szamotuły PL 46 C2
Szany H 74 A2
Szarvas H 75 B5
Szarvaskő H 65 C6
Szászvár H 74 B3
Százhalombatta H 74 A3
Szczawa PL 65 A6
Szczawnica PL 65 A6
Szczecin PL 45 B6
Szczecinek PL 46 B2
Szczekociny PL 55 C4
Szczerców PL 55 B4
Szczucin PL 55 C6
Szczuczarz PL 46 B2
Szczurkowo PL 47 A6
Szczurowa PL 55 C5
Szczyrk PL 65 A5
Szczytna PL 54 C1
Szczytno PL 6 E6
Szczyty PL 54 B3
Szécsény H 65 B5
Szederkény H 74 C3
Szedres H 74 B3
Szeged H 75 B5
Szeghalom H 75 A6
Szegvár H 75 B5
Székesfehérvár H 74 A3
Székkutas H 75 B5
Szekszárd H 74 B3
Szemplino Czarne PL 47 B6
Szemud PL 47 A4
Szendehely H 65 C5
Szendrő H 65 B6
Szentendre H 65 C5
Szentes H 75 B5
Szentgotthárd H 73 B6
Szentlászló H 74 B2
Szentlőrinc H 74 B2
Szentmártonkáta H 75 A4
Szenyér H 74 B2
Szeremle H 74 B3
Szerep H 75 A6
Szigetszentmiklós H 75 A4
Szigetvár H 74 B2
Szikáncs H 75 B5
Szikszó H 65 B6
Szil H 74 A2
Szilvásvárad H 65 B6
Szklarska Poreba PL 53 C5
Szlichtyngowa PL 53 B6
Szob H 65 C4
Szolnok H 75 A5
Szombathely H 74 A1
Szorosad H 74 B3
Szpetal Graniczny PL 47 C5
Szprotawa PL 53 B5
Szreńsk PL 47 B6
Sztum PL 47 B5
Sztutowo PL 47 A5
Szubin PL 46 B3
Szücsi H 65 C5
Szulmierz PL 47 C6
Szulok H 74 B2
Szumanie PL 47 C5
Szwecja PL 46 B2
Szydłów, *Łódzkie* PL 55 B4
Szydłów, *Świętokrzyskie* PL 55 C6
Szydłowiec PL 55 B5
Szydlowo, *Mazowieckie* PL 47 B6
Szydłowo, *Wielkopolskie* PL 46 B2
Szymanów PL 55 A5
Szynkielów PL 54 B3
Szynwald PL 55 D6

T

Tab H 74 B3
Tabanera la Luenga E 94 A2
Tabaqueros E 96 B1
Tábara E 88 C1
Tabenera de Cerrato E 88 B2
Taberg S 40 B4
Tabernas E 101 B3
Tabiano Bagni I 81 B4
Taboada E 86 B3
Taboadela E 87 B3
Tábor CZ 63 A5
Táborfalva H 75 A4
Taborište HR 73 C6
Tábua P 92 A2
Tabuaco P 87 C3
Tabuenca E 89 C5
Tabuyo del Monte E 87 B4
Täby S 37 C5
Tác H 74 A3
Tachov CZ 62 A3
Tadcaster GB 27 B4
Tadley GB 31 C2
Tafalla E 89 B5
Tafjord N 114 E4
Taganheira P 98 B2
Tågarp S 41 D2
Tággia I 80 C1
Tagliacozzo I 102 A6
Táglio di Po I 82 A1
Tagnon F 59 A5
Tahal E 101 B3
Tahitótfalu H 65 C5
Tahtaköprü TR 118 C4
Tailfingen D 61 B5
Taillis F 57 B4
Tain GB 23 D4
Tain-l'Hermitage F 78 A3
Taipadas P 92 C2
Taivalkoski FIN 3 D28
Takene S 35 C5
Takovo SRB 85 B5
Taksony H 75 A4
Tal E 86 B2
Tal-Y-Llyn GB 26 C2
Talachyn BY 7 D10
Talamello I 82 C1
Talamone I 102 A4
Talant F 69 A4
Talarrubias E 93 B5
Talas TR 16 B7
Talaván E 93 B4
Talavera de la Reina E 94 C2
Talavera la Real E 93 C4
Talayuela E 93 B5
Talayuelas E 96 B1
Talgarth GB 29 B4
Talgje N 33 C2
Talhadas P 92 A2
Táliga E 93 C3
Talizat F 78 A2
Tálknafjörður IS 111 B2
Talla I 81 C5
Talladale GB 22 D3
Tallaght IRL 21 A5
Tallard F 79 B5
Tällberg S 36 B1
Tallinn EST 6 B8
Talloires F 69 C6
Tallow IRL 21 B4
Tallsjö S 115 C15
Talmay F 69 A5
Talmont-St. Hilaire F 66 B3
Talmont-sur-Gironde F 66 C4
Talne UA 11 B11
Talsano I 104 C3
Talsi LV 6 C7
Talvik N 113 B11
Talybont GB 26 C2
Tamajón E 95 B3
Tamame E 88 C1
Tamames E 93 A4
Tamarit de Mar E 91 B4
Tamarite de Litera E 90 B3
Tamariu E 91 B6
Tamási H 74 B3
Tambach-Dietharz D 51 C6
Tameza E 86 A4
Tammisaari FIN 6 A7
Tampere FIN 3 F25
Tamsweg A 72 A3
Tamurejo E 94 D2
Tamworth GB 27 C4
Tana bru N 113 B17
Tañabueyes E 89 B3
Tanakajd H 74 A1
Tananger N 33 D2
Tanaunella I 110 B2
Tancarville F 58 A1
Tandsjöborg S 115 F11
Tånga S 41 C2
Tangelic H 74 B3
Tangen N 34 B3
Tangerhütte D 44 C3
Tangermünde D 44 C3
Tanhua FIN 113 E16
Taninges F 69 B6
Tankavaara FIN 113 D16
Tann D 51 C6
Tanna D 52 C1
Tannadice GB 25 B5
Tannåker S 40 C3
Tännäs S 115 E9
Tannay, *Ardennes* F 59 A5
Tannay, *Nièvre* F 68 A3
Tannenbergsthal D 52 C2
Tännesberg D 62 A3
Tannheim A 71 A5
Tanowo PL 45 B6
Tanum S 35 D3
Tanumshede S 35 D3
Tanus F 77 B5
Tanvald CZ 53 C5
Taormina I 109 B4
Tapa EST 7 B8
Tapfheim D 62 B1
Tapia de Casariego E 86 A4
Tapio F 77 C4
Tápióbicske H 75 A4
Tápiógyörgye H 75 A4
Tápióság H 75 A4
Tápiószecső H 75 A4
Tápiószele H 75 A4
Tápiószentmárton H 75 A4
Tapolca H 74 B2
Tapolcafö H 74 A2
Tar HR 72 C3
Tarabo S 40 B2
Taradell E 91 B5
Taraklı TR 118 B5
Taramundi E 86 A3
Tarancón E 95 B3
Táranto I 104 C3
Tarare F 69 C4
Tarascon F 78 C3
Tarascon-sur-Ariège F 77 D4
Tarashcha UA 11 B11
Tarazona E 89 C5
Tarazona de la Mancha E 95 C5
Tarbena E 96 C2
Tarbert GB 24 C2
Tarbert IRL 20 B2
Tarbes F 76 C3
Tarbet GB 24 B3
Tarbolton GB 24 C3
Tarcento I 72 B3
Tarčin BIH 84 C3
Tarczyn PL 55 B5
Tardajos E 88 B3
Tardelcuende E 89 C4
Tardets-Sorholus F 76 C2
Tardienta E 90 B2
Tärendö S 113 E11
Targon F 76 B2
Târgovişte RO 11 D8
Târgu-Jiu RO 11 D7
Târgu Mureş RO 11 C8
Târgu Ocna RO 11 C9
Târgu Secuiesc RO 11 D9
Tarifa E 99 C5
Tariquejas E 98 B3
Tarján H 65 C4
Tárkany H 64 C4
Tarland GB 23 D6
Tarłów PL 55 B6
Tarm DK 39 D1
Tarmstedt D 43 B6
Tärnaby S 115 B12
Tarnalelesz H 65 B6
Tarnaörs H 65 C6
Târnăveni RO 11 C8
Tårnet N 113 C19
Tarnobrzeg PL 55 C6
Tarnos F 76 C1
Tarnów, *Lubuskie* PL 45 C6
Tarnów, *Małopolskie* PL 55 C5
Tarnowo Podgórne PL 46 C2
Tarnowskie Góry PL 54 C3
Tärnsjö S 36 B3
Tårnvik N 112 E4
Tarouca P 87 C3
Tarp D 43 A6
Tarquínia I 102 A4
Tarquínia Lido I 102 A4
Tarragona E 91 B4
Tárrega E 91 B4
Tarrenz A 71 A5
Tårs, *Nordjyllands* DK 38 B3
Tårs, *Storstrøms* DK 39 E4
Tarsia I 106 B3
Tarsus TR 16 C7
Tartas F 76 C2
Tartu EST 7 B9
Tarussa RUS 7 D14
Tarves GB 23 D6
Tarvísio I 72 B3
Taşağıl TR 119 F6
Täsch CH 70 B2
Taşköprü TR 16 A7
Tasov CZ 64 A2
Tasovčići BIH 84 C2
Tåstrup DK 41 D2
Taşucu TR 16 C6
Tát H 65 C4
Tata H 65 C4
Tatabánya H 74 A3
Tatahása H 75 B4
Tatarbunary UA 11 D10
Tatárszentgyörgy H 75 A4
Tatranská-Lomnica SK 65 A6
Tau N 33 C2
Tauber-bischofsheim D 61 A5
Taucha D 52 B2
Taufkirchen D 62 B3
Taufkirchen an der Pram A 63 B4
Taulé F 56 B2
Taulignan F 78 B3
Taulov DK 39 D2
Taunton GB 29 B4
Taunusstein D 50 C4
Tauragė LT 6 D7
Taurianova I 106 C3
Taurisano I 107 B5
Tauste E 90 B1
Tauves F 68 C2
Tavankut SRB 75 B4
Tavannes CH 70 A2
Tavarnelle val di Pesa I 81 C5
Tavas TR 119 E4
Tavaux F 69 A5
Tävelsås S 40 C4
Taverna I 106 B3
Taverne CH 70 B3
Tavernelle I 82 C1
Tavernes de la Valldigna E 96 B2
Tavérnola Bergamasca I 71 C5
Taverny F 58 A3
Tavescan E 91 A4
Taviano I 107 B5
Tavira P 98 B3
Tavistock GB 28 C3
Tavnik SRB 85 C5
Tavşanlı TR 118 C4
Tayinloan GB 24 C2
Taynuilt GB 24 B2

Tayport GB 25 B5
Tázlár H 75 B4
Tazones E 88 A1
Tczew PL 47 A4
Tczów PL 55 B6
Teangue GB 22 D3
Teano I 103 B7
Teba E 100 C1
Tebay GB 26 A3
Techendorf A 72 B3
Tecklenburg D 50 A3
Tecko-matorp S 41 D3
Tecuci RO 11 D9
Tefenni TR 119 E4
Tegelsmora S 36 B4
Tegernsee D 62 C2
Teggiano I 104 C1
Tegoleto I 81 C5
Teichel D 52 C1
Teignmouth GB 29 C4
Teillay F 57 C4
Teillet F 77 C5
Teisendorf D 62 C3
Teistungen D 51 B6
Teixeiro E 86 A2
Tejada de Tiétar E 93 A5
Tejado E 89 C4
Tejares E 94 B1
Tejn DK 41 D4
Teke TR 118 A4
Tekirdağ TR 118 B2
Tekovské-Lužany SK 65 B4
Telavåg N 32 B1
Telč CZ 63 A6
Telese Terme I 103 B7
Telford GB 26 C3
Telfs A 71 A6
Telgárt SK 65 B6
Telgte D 50 B3
Tellingstedt D 43 A6
Telšiai LT 6 D7
Telti I 110 B2
Teltow D 45 C5
Tembleque E 95 C3
Temelin CZ 63 A5
Temerin SRB 75 C4
Temiño E 89 B3
Témpio Pausánia I 110 B2
Temple Sowerby GB 26 A3
Templederry IRL 20 B3
Templemore IRL 21 B4
Templin D 45 B5
Temse B 49 B5
Ten Boer NL 42 B3
Tenay F 69 C5
Tenbury Wells GB 29 A5
Tenby GB 28 B3
Tence F 78 A3
Tende F 80 B1
Tenhult S 40 B4
Tenja HR 74 C3
Tenneville B 49 C6
Tennevoll N 112 D6
Tensta S 36 B4
Tenterden GB 31 C4
Teo E 86 B2
Teora I 103 C8
Tepasto FIN 113 E13
Tepelenë AL 116 B2
Teplá CZ 52 D2
Teplice CZ 53 C3
Teplička nad Váhom SK 65 A4
Tepsa FIN 113 E14
Ter Apel NL 43 C4
Tera E 89 C4
Téramo I 103 A6
Terborg NL 50 B2
Terchová SK 65 A5
Terebovlya UA 11 B8
Teremia Mare RO 75 C5
Terena P 92 C3
Teresa de Cofrentes E 96 B1
Terešov CZ 63 A4
Terezín CZ 53 C4
Terezino Polje HR 74 C2
Tergnier F 59 A4
Teriberka RUS 3 B31
Terlizzi I 104 B2
Termas de Monfortinho P 93 A4
Terme di Súio I 103 B6
Terme di Valdieri I 79 B6
Termens E 90 B3
Termes F 78 B2
Términi Imerese I 108 B2
Terminillo I 102 A5
Térmoli I 103 B8
Termonfeckin IRL 19 C5
Ternberg A 63 C5
Terndrup DK 38 C3
Terneuzen NL 49 B4
Terni I 102 A5
Ternitz A 64 C2
Ternopil UA 11 B8
Terpan AL 105 C6
Terpni GR 116 B5
Terracina I 102 B6
Terråk N 115 B9
Terralba I 110 C1
Terranova di Pollino I 106 B3
Terranova di Sibari I 106 B3
Terras do Bouro P 87 C2
Terrasini I 108 A2
Terrassa E 91 B5
Terrasson-la-Villedieu F 77 A4
Terrazos E 89 B3
Terriente E 95 B5
Terrugem P 92 C3
Tertenía I 110 C2
Teruel E 90 C1
Tervola FIN 3 C26
Tervuren B 49 C5
Terzaga E 95 B5
Tešanj BIH 84 B2
Tesáske-Mlyňany SK 65 B4
Teslić BIH 84 B2
Tessin D 44 A4
Tessy-sur-Vire F 57 B4
Tét H 74 A2
Tetbury GB 29 B5
Teterchen F 60 A2
Teterow D 45 B4
Teteven BG 11 E8
Tetiyev UA 11 B10
Tetovo MK 10 E6
Tettau D 52 C1
Tettnang D 61 C5
Teublitz D 62 A3
Teuchern D 52 B2
Teulada E 96 C3
Teulada I 110 D1
Teupitz D 52 A3
Teurajärvi S 113 F11
Teutschenthal D 52 B1
Tevel H 74 B3
Teviothead GB 25 C5
Tewkesbury GB 29 B5
Thale D 52 B1
Thalfang D 60 A2
Thalgau A 63 C4
Thalkirch CH 71 B4
Thalmässing D 62 A2
Thalwil CH 70 A3
Thame GB 31 C3
Thann F 60 C3
Thannhausen D 61 B6
Thaon-les-Vosges F 60 B2
Tharandt D 52 C3
Tharsis E 99 B3
Thasos GR 116 B6
Thatcham GB 31 C2
Thaxted GB 31 C4
Thayngen CH 61 C4
The Barony GB 23 B5
The Hague = 's-Gravenhage NL 49 A5
The Mumbles GB 28 B4
Theale GB 31 C2
Thebes = Thiva GR 117 D5
Theding-hausen D 43 C6
Theessen D 52 A2
Themar D 51 C6
Thénezay F 67 B4
Thenon F 67 C6
Therouanne F 48 C3
Thessaloniki = Salonica GR 116 B4
Thetford GB 30 B4
Theth AL 105 A5
Theux B 50 C1
Thézar-les-Corbières F 78 C1
Thèze F 76 C2
Thiberville F 58 A1
Thibie F 59 B5
Thiéblemont-Farémont F 59 B5
Thiendorf D 53 B3
Thiene I 71 C6
Thierrens CH 70 B1
Thiers F 68 C3
Thiesi I 110 B1
Thiessow D 45 A5
Thiezac F 77 A5
Þingeyri IS 111 B2
Þingvellir IS 111 C4
Thionville F 60 A2
Thira GR 117 F7
Thiron-Gardais F 58 B1
Thirsk GB 27 A4
Thisted DK 38 C1
Thiva = Thebes GR 117 D5
Thivars F 58 B2
Thiviers F 67 C5
Thizy F 69 B4
Tholen NL 49 B5
Tholey D 60 A3
Thomas Street IRL 20 A3
Thomastown IRL 21 B4
Thônes F 69 C6
Thonnance-les-Joinville F 59 B6
Thonon-les-Bains F 69 B6
Thorame-Basse F 79 B5
Thorame-Haute F 79 B5
Thorens-Glières F 69 C6
Thorigny-sur-Oreuse F 59 B4
Thörl A 73 A5
Þorlákshöfn IS 111 D4
Thornaby on Tees GB 27 A4
Thornbury GB 29 B5
Thorne GB 27 B5
Thornhill, *Dumfries & Galloway* GB 25 C4
Thornhill, *Stirling* GB 24 B3
Thornthwaite GB 26 A2
Thornton-le-Dale GB 27 A5
Þórshöfn IS 111 A10
Thouarcé F 67 A4
Thouars F 67 B4
Thrapston GB 30 B3
Threlkeld GB 26 A2
Thrumster GB 23 C5
Thueyts F 78 B3
Thuin B 49 C5
Thuir F 91 A5
Thumau D 52 C1
Thun CH 70 B2
Thuret F 68 C3
Thurey F 69 B5
Thüringen A 71 A4
Thurins F 69 C4
Thürkow D 45 B4
Thurles IRL 21 B4
Thurmaston GB 30 B2
Thurø By DK 39 D3
Thursby GB 25 D4
Thurso GB 23 C5
Thury-Harcourt F 57 B5
Thusis CH 71 B4
Thyborøn DK 38 C1
Þykkvibær IS 111 D5
Thyregod DK 39 D2
Tibi E 96 C2
Tibro S 35 D6
Tidaholm S 35 D5
Tidan S 35 D6
Tidersrum S 40 B5
Tiedra E 88 C1
Tiefenbach D 62 A3
Tiefencastel CH 71 B4
Tiefenort D 51 C6
Tiefensee D 45 C5
Tiel NL 49 B6
Tielmes E 95 B3
Tielt B 49 B4
Tienen B 49 C6
Tiengen D 61 C4
Tiercé F 57 C5
Tierga E 89 C5
Tiermas E 90 A1
Tierp S 36 B4
Tierrantona E 90 A3
Tighina MD 11 C10
Tighnabruaich GB 24 C2
Tignes F 70 C1
Tigy F 58 C3
Tihany H 74 B2
Tijnje NL 42 B2
Tijola E 101 B3
Tikhvin RUS 7 B12
Til Châtel F 69 A5
Tilburg NL 49 B6
Tilh F 76 C2
Tillac F 76 C3
Tillberga S 37 C3
Tille F 58 A3
Tillicoultry GB 25 B4
Tilloy Bellay F 59 A5
Tilly F 67 B6
Tilly-sur-Seulles F 57 A5
Tim DK 39 C1
Timau I 72 B3
Timbaki GR 117 G6
Timi CY 120 B1
Timişoara RO 75 C6
Timmele S 40 B3
Timmendorfer Strand D 44 B2
Timmernabben S 40 C6
Timmersdala S 35 D5
Timoleague IRL 20 C3
Timolin IRL 21 B5
Timrå S 115 E14
Timsfors S 40 C3
Timsgearraidh GB 22 C1
Tinajas E 95 B4
Tinalhas P 92 B3
Tinchebray F 57 B5
Tincques F 48 C3
Tineo E 86 A4
Tinglev DK 39 E2
Tingsryd S 40 C4
Tingstäde S 37 E5
Tingvoll N 114 E5
Tinlot B 49 C6
Tinnoset N 33 C6
Tinos GR 117 E7
Tintagel GB 28 C3
Tinténiac F 57 B4
Tintern GB 29 B5
Tintigny B 60 A1
Tione di Trento I 71 B5
Tipperary IRL 20 B3
Tiptree GB 31 C4
Tirana = Tiranë AL 105 B5
Tiranë = Tirana AL 105 B5
Tirano I 71 B5
Tiraspol MD 11 C10
Tire TR 119 D2
Tires I 71 B6
Tiriez E 95 D4
Tirig E 90 C3
Tiriolo I 106 C3
Tirnavos GR 116 C4
Tirrénia I 81 C4
Tirschenreuth D 62 A3
Tirstrup DK 39 C3
Tirteafuera E 100 A1
Tishono RUS 47 A6
Tišnov CZ 64 A2
Tisovec SK 65 B5
Tisselskog S 35 D4
Tistedal N 35 C3
Tistrup DK 39 D1
Tisvildeleje DK 39 C5
Tiszaalpár H 75 B4
Tiszabö H 75 A5
Tiszadorogma H 65 C6
Tiszaföldvár H 75 B5
Tiszafüred H 65 C6
Tiszajenö H 75 A5
Tiszakécske H 75 B5
Tiszakürt H 75 B5
Tiszanána H 75 A5
Tiszaörs H 75 A5
Tiszaroff H 75 A5
Tiszasüly H 75 A5
Tiszasziget H 75 B5
Tiszaszőlős H 75 A5
Titaguas E 96 B1
Titel SRB 75 C5
Titisee-Neustadt D 61 C4
Tito I 104 C1
Titova Korenica HR 83 B4
Titran N 114 D5
Tittling D 63 B4
Tittmoning D 62 B3
Titz D 50 B2
Tiurajärvi FIN 113 E13
Tivat CG 105 A4
Tived S 37 D1
Tiverton GB 29 C4
Tivisa E 90 B3
Tívoli I 102 B5
Tjæreborg DK 39 D1
Tjällmo S 37 D2
Tjåmotis S 112 F7
Tjautjas S 112 E9
Tjøme N 35 C2
Tjong N 112 F2
Tjonnefoss N 33 D5
Tjörn IS 111 B5
Tjörnarp S 41 D3
Tjøtta N 115 B9
Tkon HR 83 C4
Tleń PL 47 B4
Tlmače SK 65 B4
Tłuchowo PL 47 C5
Tlumačov CZ 64 A3
Tóalmas H 75 A4
Toano I 81 B4
Toba D 51 B6
Tobarra E 101 A4
Tobercurry IRL 18 B3
Tobermore GB 19 B5
Tobermory GB 24 B1
Toberonochy GB 24 B2
Tobha Mor GB 22 D1
Tobo S 36 B4
Tocane-St. Apre F 67 C5
Tocha P 92 A2
Tocina E 99 B5
Töcksfors S 35 C3
Tocón E 100 B2
Todal N 114 E5
Todi I 82 D1
Todmorden GB 26 B3
Todorici BIH 84 B2
Todtmoos D 61 C4
Todtnau D 60 C3
Toén E 87 B3
Tofta, *Gotland* S 37 E5
Tofta, *Skaraborg* S 35 D5
Toftbyn S 36 B2
Tofte N 35 C2
Töftedal S 35 D3
Tofterup DK 39 D1
Toftlund DK 39 D2
Tófü H 74 B3
Tohmo FIN 113 F16
Tokarnia PL 55 C5
Tokary PL 54 B3
Tokod H 65 C4
Tököl H 75 A3
Tolastadh bho Thuath GB 22 C2
Toledo E 94 C2
Tolentino I 82 C2
Tolfa I 102 A4
Tolg S 40 B4
Tolga N 114 E8
Tolkmicko PL 47 A5
Tolko PL 47 A6
Tollarp S 41 D3
Tollered S 40 B2
Tølløse DK 39 D4
Tolmachevo RUS 7 B10
Tolmezzo I 72 B3
Tolmin SLO 72 B3
Tolna H 74 B3
Tolnanémedi H 74 B3
Tolob GB 22 B7
Tolosa E 89 A4
Tolosa P 92 B3
Tolox E 100 C1
Tolpuddle GB 29 C5
Tolva E 90 A3
Tolve I 104 C2
Tomar P 92 B2
Tomarza TR 16 B7
Tomaševac SRB 75 C5
Tomašica BIH 83 B5
Tomášikovo SK 64 B3
Tomašouka BY 6 F7
Tomášovce SK 65 B5
Tomaszów Mazowiecki PL 55 B5
Tomatin GB 23 D5
Tombeboeuf F 77 B3
Tomdoun GB 22 D3
Tomelilla S 41 D3
Tomellosa E 95 B4
Tomelloso E 95 C3
Tomiño E 87 C2
Tomintoul GB 23 D5
Tomislavgrad BIH 84 C2
Tomisław PL 53 B5
Tomisławice PL 47 C4
Tomnavoulin GB 23 D5
Tompa H 75 B4
Tompaládony H 74 A1
Tomra N 114 E3
Tomter N 35 C2
Tona E 91 B5
Tonara I 110 B2
Tonbridge GB 31 C4
Tondela P 92 A2
Tønder DK 39 E1
Tongeren B 49 C6
Tongue GB 23 C4
Tönisvorst D 50 B2
Tønjum N 32 A4
Tonkopuro FIN 113 F17
Tonnay-Boutonne F 67 C4
Tonnay-Charente F 66 C4
Tonneins F 77 B3
Tonnerre F 59 C4
Tonnes N 115 A10
Tönning D 43 A5
Tonsåsen N 32 B6
Tønsberg N 35 C2
Tonstad N 33 D3
Toomyvara IRL 20 B3
Toormore IRL 20 C2
Topares E 101 B3
Topas E 94 A1
Toplița RO 11 C8
Topola SRB 85 B5
Topolčani MK 116 A3
Topoľčany SK 64 B4
Topoľčianky SK 65 B4
Topolje HR 73 C6
Topólka PL 47 C4
Topoľ'niky SK 64 C3
Toponár H 74 B2
Toporów PL 53 A5
Topsham GB 29 C4
Topusko HR 73 C5
Toques E 86 B3
Tor Vaiánica I 102 B5
Torà E 91 B4
Toral de los Guzmanes E 88 B1
Toral de los Vados E 86 B4
Torbalı TR 119 D2
Torbjörntorp S 35 D5
Torbole I 71 C5
Torchiarolo I 105 C4
Torcross GB 29 C4
Torcy-le-Petit F 58 A2
Torda SRB 75 C5
Tørdal N 33 C5
Tordehumos E 88 C1
Tordera E 91 B5
Tordesillas E 88 C1
Tordesilos E 95 B5
Töre S 3 D25
Töreboda S 35 D6
Toreby DK 39 E4
Torekov S 41 C2
Torella dei Lombardi I 103 C8
Torellò E 91 A5
Toreno E 86 B4
Torfou F 66 A3
Torgau D 52 B3
Torgelow D 45 B6
Torgueda P 87 C3
Torhamn S 41 C5
Torhop N 113 B16
Torhout B 49 B4
Torigni-sur-Vire F 57 A5
Torija E 95 B3
Toril E 95 B5
Torino = Turin I 80 A1
Toritto I 104 C2
Torkovichi RUS 7 B11
Torla E 90 A2
Tormänen FIN 113 D16
Tormestorp S 41 C3
Tórmini I 71 C5
Tornada P 92 B1
Tornal'a SK 65 B6
Tornavacas E 93 A5
Tornby DK 38 B2
Tornesch D 43 B6
Torness GB 23 D4
Torniella I 81 C5
Tornimparte I 103 A6
Torning DK 39 C2
Tornio FIN 3 D26
Tornjoš SRB 75 C4
Tornos E 95 B5
Toro E 88 C1
Törökszentmiklós H 75 A5
Toropets RUS 7 C11
Torpa S 40 C3
Torpè I 110 B2
Torphins GB 23 D6
Torpo N 32 B5
Torpoint GB 28 C3
Torpsbruk S 40 B4
Torquay GB 29 C4
Torquemada E 88 B2
Torralba de Burgo E 89 C4
Torralba de Calatrava E 94 C3
Torrão P 98 A2
Torre Annunziata I 103 C7
Torre Canne I 104 C3
Torre Cardela E 100 B2
Torre das Vargens P 92 B3
Torre de Coelheiros P 92 C3
Torre de Dom Chama P 87 C3
Torre de Juan Abad E 100 A2
Torre de la Higuera E 99 B4
Torre de Miguel Sesmero E 93 C4
Torre de Moncorvo P 87 C3
Torre de Santa Maria E 93 B4
Torre del Bierzo E 86 B4
Torre del Burgo E 95 B3
Torre del Campo E 100 B2
Torre del Greco I 103 C7
Torre del Lago Puccini I 81 C4
Torre del Mar E 100 C1
Torre dell'Orso I 105 C4
Torre do Terranho P 87 D3
Torre Faro I 109 A4
Torre la Ribera E 90 A3
Torre los Negros E 90 C1
Torre Orsáia I 106 A2
Torre-Pacheco E 101 B5
Torre Péllice I 79 B6
Torre Santa Susanna I 105 C3
Torreblacos E 89 C4
Torreblanca E 96 A3
Torreblascopedro E 100 A2
Torrecaballeros E 94 A2
Torrecampo E 100 A1
Torrecilla E 95 B4
Torrecilla de la Jara E 94 C2
Torrecilla de la Orden E 94 A1
Torrecilla del Pinar E 88 C2
Torrecilla en Cameros E 89 B4
Torrecillas de la Tiesa E 93 B5
Torredembarra E 91 B4
Torredonjimeno E 100 B2
Torregrosa E 90 B3
Torreira P 87 D2
Torrejón de Ardoz E 95 B3
Torrejón de la Calzada E 94 B3
Torrejón del Rey E 95 B3
Torrejon el Rubio E 93 B4
Torrejoncillo E 93 B4
Torrelaguna E 95 B3
Torrelapaja E 89 C5
Torrelavega E 88 A2
Torrelobatón E 88 C1
Torrelodones E 94 B3
Torremaggiore I 103 B8
Torremanzanas E 96 C2
Torremayor E 93 C4
Torremezzo di Falconara I 106 B3
Torremocha E 93 B4
Torremolinos E 100 C1
Torrenieri I 81 C5
Torrenostra E 96 A3
Torrenova I 102 B5
Torrent E 96 B2
Torrente de Cinca E 90 B3
Torrenueva, *Ciudad Real* E 100 A2
Torrenueva, *Granada* E 100 C2
Torreorgaz E 93 B4
Torreperogil E 100 A2
Torres E 100 B2
Torres-Cabrera E 100 B1
Torres de la Alameda E 95 B3
Torres Novas P 92 B2
Torres Vedras P 92 B1
Torresandino E 88 C3
Torrevieja E 96 D2
Torri del Benaco I 71 C5
Torricella I 104 C3
Torridon GB 22 D3
Torriglia I 80 B3
Torrijos E 94 C2
Tørring DK 39 D2
Torrita di Siena I 81 C5
Torroal P 92 C2
Torroella de Montgrí E 91 A6
Torrox E 100 C2
Torrskog S 35 C4
Torsåker S 36 B3
Torsang S 36 B2
Torsås S 41 C6
Torsby S 34 B4
Torsetra N 34 B2
Torshälla S 37 C3
Tórshavn FO 2 E10
Torslanda S 38 B4
Torsminde DK 39 C1
Törtel H 75 A4
Tórtoles E 93 A5
Tórtoles de Esgueva E 88 C2
Tortoli I 110 C2
Tortona I 80 B2
Tórtora I 106 B2
Tortoreto Lido I 82 D2
Tortorici I 109 A3
Tortosa E 90 C3
Tortosendo P 92 A3
Tortuera E 95 B5
Tortuero E 95 B3
Toruń PL 47 B4
Torup S 40 C3
Torver GB 26 A2
Tørvikbygde N 32 B3
Torviscón E 100 C2
Torzhok RUS 7 C13
Torzym PL 53 A5
Tosbotn N 115 B9
Toscelanor-Maderno I 71 C5
Tosno RUS 7 B11
Tossa de Mar E 91 B5
Tossåsen S 115 E10
Tosse F 76 C1
Tösse S 35 D4
Tossicía I 103 A6
Tostedt D 43 B6
Tosya TR 16 A7
Tószeg H 75 A5
Toszek PL 54 C3
Totana E 101 B4
Totebo S 40 B6
Tôtes F 58 A2
Tótkomlós H 75 B5
Totland N 114 F2
Tøtlandsvik N 33 C3
Totnes GB 28 C4
Tótszerdahely H 74 B1
Tøttdal N 114 C8
Totton GB 31 D2
Touça P 87 C3
Toucy F 59 C4
Toul F 60 B1
Toulon F 79 C4
Toulon-sur-Allier F 68 B3
Toulon-sur-Arroux F 68 B4
Toulouse F 77 C4
Tour de la Parata F 102 B1
Tourcoing F 49 C4
Tourlaville F 57 A4
Tournai B 49 C4
Tournan-en-Brie F 58 B3
Tournay F 76 C3
Tournon-d'Agenais F 77 B3
Tournon-St. Martin F 67 B5
Tournon-sur-Rhône F 78 A3
Tournus F 69 B4
Touro E 86 B2
Touro P 87 D3
Tourouvre F 58 B1
Tourriers F 67 C5
Tours F 67 A5
Tourteron F 59 A5
Tourves F 79 C4
Toury F 58 B2
Touvedo P 87 C2
Touvois F 66 B3
Toužim CZ 52 C2
Tovačov CZ 64 A3
Tovariševo SRB 75 C4
Tovarnik HR 75 C4
Tovdal N 33 D5
Tovrljane SRB 85 C6
Towcester GB 30 B3
Town Yetholm GB 25 C5
Tråastølen N 32 B4
Trabada E 86 A3
Trabadelo E 86 B4
Trabanca E 87 C4
Trabazos E 87 C4
Traben-Trarbach D 50 D3
Trabia I 108 B2
Tradate I 70 C3
Trädet S 40 B3
Trafaria P 92 C1
Tragacete E 95 B5
Tragwein A 63 B5
Traiguera E 90 C3
Trainel F 59 B4
Traisen A 63 B6
Traismauer A 64 B1
Traitsching D 62 A3
Trákhonas CY 120 A2
Tralee IRL 20 B2
Tramacastilla de Tena E 76 D2
Tramagal P 92 B2
Tramariglio I 110 B1
Tramatza I 110 B1
Tramelan CH 70 A2
Tramonti di Sopra I 72 B2
Tramore IRL 21 B4
Trampot F 60 B1
Trana I 80 A1
Tranås S 40 A4
Tranbjerg DK 39 C3
Tranby N 34 C2
Trancoso P 87 D3
Tranebjerg DK 39 D3
Tranekær DK 39 E3
Tranemo S 40 B3
Tranent GB 25 C5
Tranevåg N 33 D3
Trängslet S 34 A5
Tranhult S 40 B3
Trani I 104 B2
Trans-en-Provence F 79 C5
Transtrand S 34 A5
Tranum DK 38 B2
Tranvik S 37 C5
Trápani I 108 A1
Trappes F 58 B3
Traryd S 40 C3
Trasacco I 103 B6
Trasierra E 99 A4
Träslövsläge S 40 B2
Trasmiras E 87 B3
Traspinedo E 88 C2
Trate SLO 73 B5
Trauchgau D 62 C1
Traun A 63 B5
Traunreut D 62 C3
Traunstein D 62 C3
Traunwalchen D 62 C3
Tråvad S 35 D5
Travemünde D 44 B2
Traversétolo I 81 B4
Travnik BIH 84 B2
Travnik SLO 73 C4
Travo F 102 B2
Travo I 80 B3
Trawsfynydd GB 26 C2
Trbovlje SLO 73 B5
Trbušani SRB 85 C5
Treban F 68 B3
Třebařov CZ 64 A2
Trebatsch D 53 A4
Trebbin D 52 A3
Trebechovice pod Orebem CZ 53 C5
Trebel D 44 C3
Třebenice CZ 53 C3
Trébeurden F 56 B2
Třebíč CZ 64 A1
Trebinje BIH 84 D3
Trebisacce I 106 B3
Trebitz D 52 B2
Trebnje SLO 73 C5
Třeboň CZ 63 A5
Třebovice CZ 64 A2
Trebsen D 52 B2
Trebujena E 99 C4
Trecastagni I 109 B4
Trecate I 70 C3
Trecenta I 81 A5
Tredegar GB 29 B4
Tredózio I 81 B5
Treffen A 72 B3
Treffort F 69 B5
Treffurt D 51 B6
Trefnant GB 26 B2
Tregaron GB 28 A4
Trégastel-Plage F 56 B2
Tregnago I 71 C6
Tregony GB 28 C3
Tréguier F 56 B2
Trégunc F 56 C2
Treharris GB 29 B4
Trehörningsjö S 115 D15
Tréia I 82 C2
Treignac F 68 C1
Treignat F 68 B2
Treignes B 49 C5
Treis-Karden D 50 C3
Trekanten S 40 C6
Trélazé F 67 A4
Trelech GB 28 B3
Trélissac F 67 C5
Trelleborg S 41 D3
Trélon F 49 C5
Trélou-sur-Marne F 59 A4
Tremblay-le-Vicomte F 58 B2
Tremés P 92 B2
Tremezzo I 71 C4
Třemošná CZ 63 A4
Tremp E 90 A3
Trenčianska Stankovce SK 64 B3
Trenčianska Turná SK 64 B4
Trenčianske Teplá SK 64 B4
Trenčianske Teplice SK 64 B4
Trenčín SK 64 B4
Trendelburg D 51 B5
Trengereid N 32 B2
Trensacq F 76 B2
Trent D 45 A5
Trento I 71 B6
Treorchy GB 29 B4
Trepča SRB 85 D5
Trept F 69 C5
Trepuzzi I 105 C4
Trescore Balneário I 71 C4
Tresenda I 71 B5
Tresfjord N 114 E4
Tresigallo I 81 B5
Trešnjevica SRB 85 C6
Tresnurághes I 110 B1
Trespaderne E 89 B3
Třešť CZ 63 A6
Trestina I 82 C1
Tretower GB 29 B4
Trets F 79 C4
Tretten N 34 A2
Treuchtlingen D 62 B1
Treuen D 52 C2
Treuenbrietzen D 52 A2
Treungen N 33 C5
Trevelez E 100 C2
Trevi I 82 D1
Trevi nel Lázio I 102 B6
Treviana E 89 B3
Treviglio I 71 C4
Trevignano Romano I 102 A5
Treviso I 72 C2
Trévoux F 69 C4
Treysa D 51 C5
Trézelles F 68 B3
Trezzo sull'Adda I 71 C4
Trhová Kamenice CZ 64 A1
Trhové Sviny CZ 63 B5
Triacastela E 86 B3
Triaize F 66 B3
Trianda GR 119 F3
Triaucourt-en-Argonne F 59 B6
Tribanj Kruščica HR 83 B4
Triberg D 61 B4
Tribsees D 45 A4
Tribuče SLO 73 C5

Villar Perosa I 79 B6
Villaralto E 100 A1
Villarcayo E 89 B3
Villard-de-Lans F 79 A4
Villardeciervos E 87 C4
Villardefrades E 88 C1
Villarejo E 95 A3
Villarejo de Fuentes E 95 C4
Villarejo de Orbigo E 88 B1
Villarejo de Salvanes E 95 B3
Villarejo-Periesteban E 95 C4
Villares del Saz E 95 C4
Villaretto I 79 A6
Villargordo del Cabriel E 96 B1
Villarino E 87 C4
Villarino de Conso E 87 B3
Villarluengo E 90 C2
Villarobe E 89 B3
Villarosa I 109 B3
Villarramiel E 88 B2
Villarrasa E 99 B4
Villarreal de San Carlos E 93 B4
Villarrin de Campos E 88 C1
Villarrobledo E 95 C4
Villarroya de la Sierra E 89 C5
Villarroya de los Pinares E 90 C2
Villarrubia de los Ojos E 95 C3
Villarrubia de Santiago E 95 C3
Villarrubio E 95 C4
Villars-les-Dombes F 69 B5
Villarta E 95 C5
Villarta de los Montes E 94 C2
Villarta de San Juan E 95 C3
Villasana de Mena E 89 A3
Villasandino E 88 B2
Villasante E 89 A3
Villasarracino E 88 B2
Villasayas E 89 C4
Villasdardo E 87 C4
Villaseca de Henares E 95 B4
Villaseca de la Sagra E 94 C3
Villaseca de Laciana E 86 B4
Villaseco de los Gamitos E 87 C4
Villaseco de los Reyes E 87 C4
Villasequilla de Yepes E 94 C3
Villasimíus I 110 C2
Villasmundo I 109 B4
Villasor I 110 C1
Villastar E 90 C1
Villastellone I 80 B1
Villatobas E 95 C3
Villatorp E 93 A5
Villatoya E 96 B1
Villavaliente E 96 B1
Villavelayo E 89 B4
Villavella E 87 B3
Villaver de de Guadalimar E 101 A3
Villaverde del Rio E 99 B5
Villaviciosa E 88 A1
Villaviciosa de Córdoba E 99 A6
Villaviciosa de Odón E 94 B3
Villavieja de Yeltes E 87 D4
Villayón E 86 A4
Villé F 60 B3
Ville-di-Pietrabugno F 102 A2
Ville-sous-la-Ferté F 59 B5
Ville-sur-Illon F 60 B2
Ville-sur-Tourbe F 59 A5
Villebois-Lavalette F 67 C5
Villecerf F 59 B3
Villecomtal F 77 B5
Villedieu-les-Poêles F 57 B4
Villedieu-sur-Indre F 67 B6
Villedômain F 67 A6
Villefagnan F 67 B5
Villefontaine F 69 C5
Villefort F 78 B2
Villefranche-d'Albigeois F 77 C5
Villefranche-d'Allier F 68 B2
Villefranche-de-Lauragais F 77 C4
Villefranche-de-Lonchat F 76 B3
Villefranche-de-Panat F 78 B1
Villefranche-de-Rouergue F 77 B5
Villefranche-du-Périgord F 77 B4
Villefranche-sur-Cher F 68 A1
Villefranche-sur-Mer F 80 C1
Villefranche-sur-Saône F 69 B4
Villegenon F 68 A2
Villel E 96 A1
Villemaur-sur-Vanne F 59 B4
Villemur-sur-Tarn F 77 C4
Villena E 101 A5
Villenauxe-la-Grande F 59 B4
Villenave-d'Ornon F 76 B2
Villeneuve CH 70 B1
Villeneuve F 77 B5
Villeneuve-d'Ascq F 49 C4
Villeneuve-de-Berg F 78 B3
Villeneuve-de-Marsan F 76 C2
Villeneuve-de-Rivière F 77 C3
Villeneuve-la-Guyard F 59 B4
Villeneuve-l'Archevêque F 59 B4
Villeneuve-le-Comte F 58 B3
Villeneuve-lès-Avignon F 78 C3
Villeneuve-les-Corbières F 78 D1
Villeneuve-St. Georges F 58 B3
Villeneuve-sur-Allier F 68 B3
Villeneuve-sur-Lot F 77 B3
Villeneuve-sur-Yonne F 59 B4
Villeréal F 77 B3
Villerias E 88 C2
Villeromain F 58 C2
Villers-Bocage, *Calvados* F 57 A5
Villers-Bocage, *Somme* F 48 D3
Villers-Bretonneux F 58 A3
Villers-Carbonnel F 59 A3
Villers-Cotterêts F 59 A4
Villers-Farlay F 69 B5
Villers-le-Gambon B 49 C5
Villers-le-Lac F 70 A1
Villers-sur-Mer F 57 A6
Villersexel F 60 C2
Villerupt F 60 A1
Villerville F 57 A6
Villeseneux F 59 B5
Villetrun F 58 C2
Villetta Barrea I 103 B6
Villeurbanne F 69 C4
Villeveyrac F 78 C2
Villevocance F 69 C4
Villiers-St. Benoit F 59 C4
Villiers-St. Georges F 59 B4
Villingen D 61 B4
Villmar D 50 C4
Villoldo E 88 B2
Villon F 59 C5
Villoria E 94 B1
Vilnes N 32 A1
Vilnius LT 7 D8
Vils A 62 C1
Vils DK 38 C1
Vilsbiburg D 62 B3
Vilseck D 62 A2
Vilshofen D 63 B4
Vilshult S 41 C4
Vilusi CG 84 D3
Vilvestre E 87 C4
Vilvoorde B 49 C5
Vimeiro P 92 B1
Vimercate I 71 C4
Vimianzo E 86 A1
Vimieiro P 92 C3
Vimioso P 87 C4
Vimmerby S 40 B5
Vimoutiers F 57 B6
Vimperk CZ 63 A4
Vimy F 48 C3
Vinadi CH 71 B5
Vinadio I 79 B6
Vinaixa E 90 B3
Vinarós E 90 C3
Vinäs S 36 B1
Vinay F 69 C5
Vinberg S 40 C2
Vinca F 91 A5
Vinča SRB 85 B5
Vinchiaturo I 103 B7
Vinci I 81 C4
Vindeby DK 39 D3
Vindelgransele S 115 B15
Vindeln S 115 C16
Vinderup DK 38 C1
Vindsvik N 33 C3
Vinets F 59 B5
Vineuil F 58 C2
Vinga RO 75 B6
Vingåker S 37 C2
Vingnes N 34 A2
Vingrau F 78 D1
Vingrom N 34 A2
Vinhais P 87 C4
Vinica HR 73 B6
Vinica SK 65 B5
Vinica SLO 73 C5
Vinicka CG 85 D4
Viniegra de Arriba E 89 B4
Vinje, *Hordaland* N 32 B3
Vinje, *Sør-Trøndelag* N 114 D6
Vinje, *Telemark* N 33 C4
Vinkovci HR 74 C3
Vinliden S 115 C14
Vinninga S 35 D5
Vinnytsya UA 11 B10
Vinon F 68 A2
Vinon-sur-Verdon F 79 C4
Vinslöv S 41 C3
Vintjärn S 36 B3
Vintrosa S 37 C1
Viñuela de Sayago E 87 C5
Viñuelas E 95 B3
Vinuesa E 89 C4
Vinzelberg D 44 C3
Viöl D 43 A6
Viola I 80 B1
Violay F 69 C4
Vipava SLO 72 C3
Vipiteno I 71 B6
Vipperow D 45 B4
Vir BIH 84 C2
Vir HR 83 B4
Vira CH 70 B3
Vire F 57 B5
Vireda S 40 B4
Vireux F 49 C5
Virgen A 72 A2
Virgen de la Cabeza E 100 A1
Virginia IRL 19 C4
Virieu F 69 C5
Virieu-le-Grand F 69 C5
Virje HR 74 B1
Virklund DK 39 C2
Virovitica HR 74 C2
Virpazar CG 105 A5
Virsbo S 36 C3
Virserum S 40 B5
Virtaniemi FIN 113 D17
Virton B 60 A1
Virtsu EST 6 B7
Viry F 69 B6
Vis HR 83 C5
Visbek D 43 C5
Visby DK 39 D1
Visby S 37 E5
Visé B 50 C1
Višegrad BIH 85 C4
Viserba I 82 B1
Viseu P 92 A3
Visiedo E 90 C1
Viskafors S 40 B2
Visland N 33 D3
Vislanda S 40 C4
Visnes N 33 C2
Višnja Gora SLO 73 C4
Višnjan HR 72 C3
Višnové CZ 64 B2
Visnums-Kil S 35 C6
Viso del Marqués E 100 A2
Visoko BIH 84 C3
Visoko SLO 73 B4
Visone I 80 B2
Visp CH 70 B2
Vissefjärda S 40 C5
Visselhövede D 43 C6
Vissenbjerg DK 39 D3
Visso I 82 D2
Vistabella del Maestrat E 96 A2
Vita I 108 B1
Vitanje SLO 73 B5
Vitanovac SRB 85 C5
Vitebsk = Vitsyebsk BY 7 D11
Viterbo I 102 A5
Vitez BIH 84 B2
Vithkuq AL 116 B2
Vitigudino E 87 C4
Vitina BIH 84 C2
Vitina GR 117 E4
Vitis A 63 B6
Vitkov CZ 64 A3
Vitkovac SRB 85 C5
Vitomirica SRB 85 D5
Vitoria-Gasteiz E 89 B4
Vitré F 57 B4
Vitrey-sur-Mance F 60 C1
Vitry-en-Artois F 48 C3
Vitry-le-François F 59 B5
Vitry-sur-Seine F 58 B3
Vitsand S 34 B4
Vitsyebsk = Vitebsk BY 7 D11
Vittangi S 113 E10
Vittaryd S 40 C3
Vitteaux F 69 A4
Vittel F 60 B1
Vittinge S 36 C4
Vittória I 109 C3
Vittório Véneto I 72 C2
Vittsjö S 41 C3
Viù I 70 C2
Viul N 34 B2
Vivario F 102 A2
Viveiro E 86 A3
Vivel del Rio Martin E 90 C2
Viver E 96 B2
Viverols F 68 C3
Viveros E 101 A3
Viviers F 78 B3
Vivonne F 67 B5
Vivy F 67 A4
Vize TR 118 A2
Vizille F 79 A4
Viziñada HR 72 C3
Viziru RO 11 D9
Vizovice CZ 64 A3
Vizvár H 74 B2
Vizzavona F 102 A2
Vizzini I 109 B3
Vlachiotis GR 117 F4
Vlachovice CZ 64 A3
Vlachovo SK 65 B6
Vláchovo Březi CZ 63 A4
Vladimirci SRB 85 B4
Vladimirovac SRB 85 A5
Vladislav CZ 64 A1
Vlagtwedde NL 43 B4
Vlajkovac SRB 85 A6
Vlasenica BIH 84 B3
Vlašim CZ 63 A5
Vlatkovići BIH 84 B2
Vledder NL 42 C3
Vlissingen NL 49 B4
Vlorë AL 105 C5
Vlotho D 51 A4
Vnanje Gorice SLO 73 C4
Vobarno I 71 C5
Voćin HR 74 C2
Vöcklabruck A 63 B4
Vöcklamarkt A 63 C4
Vodanj SRB 85 B5
Voderady SK 64 B3
Vodice, *Istarska* HR 73 C4
Vodice, *Šibenska* HR 83 C4
Vodice SLO 73 B4
Vodňany CZ 63 A5
Vodnjan HR 82 B2
Vodskov DK 38 B3
Voe GB 22 A7
Voerså DK 38 B3
Voghera I 80 B3
Vogogna I 70 B3
Vogošća BIH 84 C3
Vogué F 78 B3
Vohburg D 62 B2
Vohenstrauss D 62 A3
Vöhl D 51 B4
Vöhrenbach D 61 B4
Vöhringen D 61 B6
Void-Vacon F 60 B1
Voiron F 69 C5
Voise F 58 B2
Voisey F 60 C1
Voiteg RO 75 C6
Voiteur F 69 B5
Voitsberg A 73 A5
Vojens DK 39 D2
Vojka SRB 85 B5
Vojlovica SRB 85 B5
Vojnić HR 73 C5
Vojnice SK 65 C4
Vojnik SLO 73 B5
Vojvoda Stepa SRB 75 C5
Volada GR 119 G2
Volargne I 71 C5
Volary CZ 63 B4
Volče SLO 72 B3
Volda N 114 E3
Volendam NL 42 C2
Volga RUS 7 B15
Volimes GR 117 E2
Volissos GR 116 D7
Volkach D 61 A6
Völkermarkt A 73 B4
Volkhov RUS 7 B12
Völklingen D 60 A2
Volkmarsen D 51 B5
Voll N 114 E4
Vollenhove NL 42 C2
Vollore-Montagne F 68 C3
Vollsjö S 41 D3
Volodymyr-Volyns'kyy UA 11 A8
Volokolamsk RUS 7 C13
Volos GR 116 C4
Volosovo RUS 7 B10
Volovets UA 11 B7
Volta Mantovana I 71 C5
Voltággio I 80 B2
Volterra I 81 C4
Voltri I 80 B2
Voltúrara Áppula I 103 B8
Volturara Irpina I 103 C7
Volvic F 68 C3
Volx F 79 C4
Volyně CZ 63 A4
Vonitsa GR 116 D2
Vönöck H 74 A2
Vonsild DK 39 D2
Voorschoten NL 49 A5
Vopnafjörður IS 111 B11
Vorau A 73 A5
Vorbasse DK 39 D2
Vorchdorf A 63 C4
Vorden D 43 C5
Vorden NL 50 A2
Vordernberg A 73 A4
Vordingborg DK 39 D4
Vorë AL 105 B5
Voreppe F 69 C5
Vorey F 68 C3
Vorgod DK 39 C1
Vormsund N 34 B3
Voronezh UA 7 F12
Võru EST 7 C9
Voskopojë AL 116 B2
Voss N 32 B3
Votice CZ 63 A5
Voué F 59 B5
Vouillé F 67 B5
Voulx F 59 B3
Voussac F 68 B3
Vouvray F 67 A5
Vouvry CH 70 B1
Vouzela P 87 D2
Vouziers F 59 A5
Voves F 58 B2
Voxna S 36 A2
Voy GB 23 B5
Voynitsa RUS 3 D29
Voznesensk UA 11 C11
Voznesenye RUS 7 A13
Vrå DK 38 B2
Vrå S 40 C3
Vráble SK 64 B4
Vračenovići CG 84 D3
Vračev Gaj SRB 85 B6
Vraćevsnica SRB 85 B5
Vrådal N 33 C5
Vrakneika GR 117 D3
Vrana HR 83 B3
Vranduk BIH 84 B2
Vrångö S 38 B4
Vrani RO 85 A6
Vranić SRB 85 B5
Vranići BIH 84 C3
Vranja HR 73 C4
Vranjak BIH 84 B3
Vranje SRB 10 E6
Vranov nad Dyje CZ 64 B1
Vranovice CZ 64 B2
Vransko SLO 73 B4
Vrapčići BIH 84 C2
Vratimov CZ 64 A4
Vratsa BG 11 E7
Vrbanja HR 84 B3
Vrbanjci BIH 84 B2
Vrbas SRB 75 C4
Vrbaška BIH 84 A2
Vrbnik, *Primorsko-Goranska* HR 83 A3
Vrbnik, *Zadarsko-Kninska* HR 83 B5
Vrbno p. Pradědem CZ 54 C2
Vrboska HR 83 C5
Vrbov SK 65 A6
Vrbovce SK 64 B3
Vrbové SK 64 B3
Vrbovec HR 73 C6
Vrbovski SRB 85 B5
Vrbovsko HR 73 C5
Vrchlabí CZ 53 C5
Vrčin SRB 85 B5
Vrdy CZ 63 A6
Vrebac HR 83 B4
Vreden D 50 A2
Vrela SRB 85 D5
Vreoci SRB 85 B5
Vretstorp S 37 C1
Vrginmost HR 73 C5
Vrgorac HR 84 C2
Vrhnika SLO 73 C4
Vrhovine HR 83 B4
Vrhpolie SRB 85 B4
Vriezenveen NL 42 C3
Vrigne-aux-Bois F 59 A5
Vrigstad S 40 B4
Vrlika HR 83 C5
Vrmbaje SRB 85 C5
Vrnjačka Banja SRB 85 C5
Vrnograč BIH 73 C5
Vron F 48 C2
Vroomshoop NL 42 C3
Vroutek CZ 52 C3
Vrpolje HR 74 C3
Vršac SRB 85 A6
Vrsar HR 82 A2
Vrsi HR 83 B4
Vrtoče BIH 83 B5
Vrútky SK 65 A4
Všeruby CZ 62 A3
Všestary CZ 53 C5
Vsetín CZ 64 A3
Vuča CG 85 D5
Vučitrn SRB 85 D5
Vučkovica SRB 85 C5
Vught NL 49 B6
Vuillafans F 69 A6
Vukovar HR 75 C4
Vuku N 114 D8
Vulcan RO 11 D7
Vulcanești MD 11 D10
Vuoggatjålme S 112 F5
Vuojärvi FIN 113 E15
Vuolijoki FIN 3 D27
Vuotso FIN 113 D16
Vuzenica SLO 73 B5
Vy-lès Lure F 60 C2
Vyartsilya RUS 3 E29
Vyazma RUS 7 D13
Vyborg RUS 3 F28
Výčapy CZ 64 A1
Výčapy-Opatovce SK 64 B4
Východna SK 65 A5
Vydrany SK 64 B3
Vyerkhnyadzvinsk BY 7 D9
Vyhne SK 65 B4
Vylkove UA 11 D10
Vynohradiv UA 11 B7
Vyshniy Volochek RUS 7 C13
Vyškov CZ 64 A3
Vysoká nad Kysucou SK 65 A4
Vysoké Mýto CZ 53 D6
Vysokovsk RUS 7 C14
Vyšší Brod CZ 63 B5
Vytegra RUS 7 A14

W

Waabs D 44 A1
Waalwijk NL 49 B6
Waarschoot B 49 B4
Wabern D 51 B5
Wąbrzeźno PL 47 B4
Wąchock PL 55 B6
Wachow D 45 C4
Wachów PL 54 C3
Wächtersbach D 51 C5
Wackersdorf D 62 A3
Waddington GB 27 B5
Wadebridge GB 28 C3
Wadelsdorf D 53 B4
Wädenswil CH 70 A3
Wadern D 60 A2
Wadersloh D 50 B4
Wadlew PL 55 B4
Wadowice PL 65 A5
Wagenfeld D 43 C5
Wageningen NL 49 B6
Waghäusel D 61 A4
Waging D 62 C3
Wagrain A 72 A3
Wągrowiec PL 46 C3
Wahlsdorf D 52 B3
Wahlstedt D 44 B2
Wahrenholz D 44 C2
Waiblingen D 61 B5
Waidhaus D 62 A3
Waidhofen an der Thaya A 63 B6
Waidhofen an der Ybbs A 63 C5
Waimes B 50 C2
Wainfleet All Saints GB 27 B6
Waizenkirchen A 63 B4
Wakefield GB 27 B4
Wałbrzych PL 53 C6
Walchensee D 62 C2
Walchsee A 62 C3
Wałcz PL 46 B2
Wald CH 70 A3
Wald-Michelbach D 61 A4
Waldaschaff D 51 D5
Waldbach A 73 A5
Waldböckelheim D 60 A3
Waldbröl D 50 C3
Waldeck D 51 B5
Waldenburg D 52 C2
Waldfischbach-Burgalben D 60 A3
Waldheim D 52 B3
Waldkappel D 51 B5
Waldkirch D 60 B3
Waldkirchen D 63 B4
Waldkirchen am Wesen A 63 B4
Waldkraiburg D 62 B3
Waldmohr D 60 A3
Waldmünchen D 62 A3
Waldring A 62 C3
Waldsassen D 52 C2
Waldshut D 61 C4
Waldstatt CH 71 A4
Waldwisse F 60 A2
Walenstadt CH 71 A4
Walentynowo PL 55 B6
Walichnowy PL 54 B3
Walincourt F 49 C4
Walkenried D 51 B6
Walkeringham GB 27 B5
Wallasey GB 26 B2
Walldürn D 61 A5
Wallenfells D 52 C1
Wallenhorst D 43 C5
Wallers F 49 C4
Wallersdorf D 62 B3
Wallerstein D 61 B6
Wallingford GB 31 C2
Wallitz D 45 B4
Walls GB 22 A7
Wallsbüll D 39 E2
Walmer GB 31 C5
Walsall GB 27 C4
Walshoutem B 49 C6
Walsrode D 43 C6
Waltenhofen D 61 C6
Waltershausen D 51 C6
Waltham Abbey GB 31 C4
Waltham on the Wolds GB 30 B3
Walton-on-Thames GB 31 C3
Walton-on-the-Naze GB 31 C5
Wamba E 88 C2
Wanderup D 43 A6
Wandlitz D 45 C5
Wanfried D 51 B6
Wangen im Allgäu D 61 C5
Wangerooge D 43 B4
Wangersen D 43 B6
Wängi CH 70 A3
Wanna D 43 B5
Wansford GB 30 B3
Wantage GB 31 C2
Wanzleben D 52 A1
Waplewo PL 47 B6
Wapnica PL 46 B1
Wapno PL 46 C3
Warburg D 51 B5
Wardenburg D 43 B5
Ware GB 31 C3
Waregem B 49 C4
Wareham GB 29 C5
Waremme B 49 C6
Waren D 45 B4
Warendorf D 50 B3
Warga NL 42 B2
Warin D 44 B3
Wark GB 25 C5
Warka PL 55 B6
Warkworth GB 25 C6
Warlubie PL 47 B4
Warminster GB 29 B5
Warnemünde D 44 A4
Warnow D 44 B3
Warnsveld NL 50 A2
Warrenpoint GB 19 B5
Warrington GB 26 B3
Warsaw = Warszawa PL 55 A6
Warsingsfehn D 43 B4
Warsow D 44 B3
Warstein D 51 B4
Warszawa = Warsaw PL 55 A6
Warta PL 54 B3
Wartberg A 63 C5
Warth A 71 A5
Warwick GB 30 B2
Warza D 51 C6
Wasbister GB 23 B5
Washington GB 25 D6
Wąsosz PL 54 B1
Wasselonne F 60 B3
Wassen CH 70 B3
Wassenaar NL 49 A5
Wasserauen CH 71 A4
Wasserburg D 62 B3
Wassertrüdingen D 62 A1
Wassy F 59 B5
Wasungen D 51 C6
Watchet GB 29 B4
Waterford IRL 21 B4
Watergrasshill IRL 20 B3
Waterloo B 49 C5
Waterville IRL 20 C1
Watford GB 31 C3
Wathlingen D 44 C2
Watten F 48 C3
Watten GB 23 C5
Wattens A 72 A1
Watton GB 30 B4
Wattwil CH 71 A4
Waunfawr GB 26 B1
Wavignies F 58 A3
Wavre B 49 C5
Wearhead GB 25 D5
Węchadlow PL 55 C5
Wedel D 43 B6
Wedemark D 43 C6
Weedon Bec GB 30 B2
Weener D 43 B4
Weert NL 50 B1
Weesp NL 49 A6
Weeze D 50 B2
Weferlingen D 52 A1
Wegeleben D 52 B1
Weggis CH 70 A3
Węgierska-Górka PL 65 A5
Węgliniec PL 53 B5
Węgorzyno PL 46 B1
Węgrzynice PL 53 A5
Wegscheid D 63 B4
Wehdel D 43 B5
Wehr D 60 C3
Weibersbrunn D 61 A5
Weichering D 62 B2
Weida D 52 C2
Weiden D 62 A3
Weidenberg D 52 D1
Weidenhain D 52 B2
Weidenstetten D 61 B5
Weierbach D 60 A3
Weikersheim D 61 A5
Weil D 62 B1
Weil am Rhein D 60 C3
Weil der Stadt D 61 B4
Weilburg D 50 C4
Weilerswist D 50 C2
Weilheim, *Baden-Württemberg* D 61 B5
Weilheim, *Bayern* D 62 C2
Weilmünster D 51 C4
Weiltensfeld A 73 B4
Weimar D 52 C1
Weinberg D 61 A6
Weinfelden CH 71 A4
Weingarten, *Baden-Württemberg* D 61 A4
Weingarten, *Baden-Württemberg* D 61 C5
Weinheim D 61 A4
Weinstadt D 61 B5
Weismain D 52 C1
Weissbriach A 72 B3
Weissenbach A 71 A5
Weissenberg D 53 B4
Weissenbrunn D 52 C1
Weissenburg D 62 A1
Weissenfels D 52 B1
Weissenhorn D 61 B6
Weissenkirchen A 63 B6
Weissensee D 52 B1
Weissenstadt D 52 C1
Weisskirchen im Steiermark A 73 A4
Weisstannen CH 71 B4
Weisswasser D 53 B4
Weitendorf D 44 B4
Weitersfeld A 64 B1
Weitersfelden A 63 B5
Weitnau D 61 C6
Wéitra A 63 B5
Weiz A 73 A5
Wejherowo PL 47 A4
Welkenraedt B 50 C1
Wellaune D 52 B2
Wellin B 49 C6
Wellingborough GB 30 B3
Wellington, *Somerset* GB 29 C4
Wellington, *Telford & Wrekin* GB 26 C3
Wellingtonbridge IRL 21 B5
Wells GB 29 B5
Wells-next-the-Sea GB 30 B4
Wels A 63 B5
Welschenrohr CH 70 A2
Welshpool GB 26 C2
Welver D 50 B3
Welwyn Garden City GB 31 C3
Welzheim D 61 B5
Welzow D 53 B4
Wem GB 26 C3
Wembury GB 28 C3
Wemding D 62 B1
Wenden D 50 C3
Wendisch Rietz D 53 A4
Wendlingen D 61 B5
Weng A 63 B4
Weng bei Admont A 63 C5
Wengen CH 70 B2
Wenigzell A 73 A5
Wennigsen D 51 A5
Wenns A 71 A5
Wenzenbach D 62 A3
Weppersdorf A 64 C2
Werben D 44 C3
Werbig D 52 B3
Werdau D 52 C2
Werder D 45 C4
Werdohl D 50 B3
Werfen A 72 A3
Werkendam NL 49 B5
Werl D 50 B3
Werlte D 43 C4
Wermelskirchen D 50 B3
Wermsdorf D 52 B2
Wernberg Köblitz D 62 A3
Werne D 50 B3
Werneck D 51 D6
Werneuchen D 45 C5
Wernigerode D 51 B6
Wertach D 61 C6
Wertheim D 61 A5
Wertingen D 62 B1
Weseke D 50 B2
Wesel D 50 B2
Wesenberg D 45 B4
Wesendorf D 44 C2
Wesołowo PL 47 B6
Wesselburen D 43 A5
Wesseling D 50 C2
West Bridgford GB 27 C4
West Bromwich GB 27 C4
West Haddon GB 30 B2
West Kilbride GB 24 C3
West Linton GB 25 C4
West Lulworth GB 29 C5
West Mersea GB 31 C4
West-Terschelling NL 42 B2
West Woodburn GB 25 C5
Westbury, *Shropshire* GB 26 C3
Westbury, *Wiltshire* GB 29 B5
Westbury-on-Severn GB 29 B5
Westendorf A 72 A2
Westensee D 44 A1
Westerbork NL 42 C3
Westerburg D 50 C3
Westerhaar NL 42 C3
Westerholt D 43 B4
Westerkappeln D 50 A3
Westerland D 39 E1
Westerlo B 49 B5
Westerstede D 43 B4
Westheim D 62 A1
Westhill GB 23 D6
Westkapelle B 49 B4
Westkapelle NL 49 B4
Westminster GB 31 C3
Weston GB 26 C3
Weston-super-Mare GB 29 B5
Westport IRL 18 C2
Westruther GB 25 C5
Westward Ho! GB 28 B3
Wetheral GB 25 D5
Wetherby GB 27 B4
Wetter, *Hessen* D 51 C4
Wetter, *Nordrhein-Westfalen* D 50 B3
Wetteren B 49 B4
Wettin D 52 B1
Wettringen D 50 A3
Wetzikon CH 70 A3
Wetzlar D 51 C4
Wewelsfleth D 43 B6
Wexford IRL 21 B5
Weybridge GB 31 C3
Weyer Markt A 63 C5
Weyerbusch D 50 C3
Weyersheim F 60 B3
Weyhe D 43 C5
Weyhill GB 31 C2
Weymouth GB 29 C5
Weyregg A 63 C4
Węzyska PL 53 A4
Whalton GB 25 C6
Whauphill GB 24 D3